6 —

D1122034

/23

WINNER OF THE JULES AND FRANCES LANDRY AWARD FOR 1994

THE BATTLE OF THE WILDERNESS
MAY 5–6, 1864

THE BATTLE OF THE WILDERNESS
MAY 5–6, 1864

Gordon C. Rhea

LOUISIANA STATE UNIVERSITY PRESS *Baton Rouge and London*

Copyright © 1994 by Louisiana State University Press
All rights reserved
Manufactured in the United States of America
First printing
03 02 01 00 99 98 97 96 95 94   5 4 3 2 1

Designer: Glynnis Phoebe
Typeface: Body text Sabon, display Cochin
Typesetter: G & S Typesetters, Inc.
Printer and binder: Thomson-Shore, Inc.

LIBRARY OF CONGRESS CATALOGING-IN-PUBLICATION DATA

Rhea, Gordon C.
    The Battle of the Wilderness, May 5–6, 1864 / Gordon C. Rhea.
        p.   cm.
    Includes bibliographical references and index.
    ISBN 0-8071-1873-7
    1. Wilderness, Battle of the, Va., 1864.   I. Title.
E476.52.R47   1994
973.7'36—dc20   93-42110
                                                          CIP

The paper in this book meets the guidelines for permanence and durability of the Committee on Production Guidelines for Book Longevity of the Council on Library Resources. ∞

Contents

Acknowledgments xiii

Abbreviations xv

INTRODUCTION 1

I
MAY 2–3, 1864   *Lee and Grant Make Their Plans*   8

II
MAY 4   *The Armies Maneuver for Position*   60

III
MAY 5, MORNING   *Lee and Grant Find Surprise and Opportunity*   94

IV
MAY 5, AFTERNOON   *The Grand Offensive Breaks Down*   145

V
MAY 5, EVENING   *Grant Strives for a Coordinated Assault*   222

VI
MAY 6, MORNING   *The Tide Shifts*   283

VII
MAY 6, MIDDAY   *Lee Struggles to Retain the Initiative*   351

VIII
MAY 6, EVENING   *The Armies Reach Stalemate*   404

Appendix: *The Order of Battle*   453

Bibliography   471

Index   491

Illustrations

PICTURES

following page 208

Federal signal officers on Pony Mountain

Federal 6th Corps wagons crossing
the Rapidan at Germanna Ford

Federal 9th Corps trains crossing at Germanna Ford

Saunders' Field

Ewell's earthworks along Saunders' Field

Federal 6th Corps units bushwhacking
above the Orange Turnpike

Grant whittling and thinking

Federal 2nd Corps troops on Brock Road

Todd's Tavern

The Wilderness battlefield

Soldiers rescuing wounded comrades from the flames

Skeletons on the battlefield

MAPS

The eastern theater on May 2   2

The Rapidan front on May 2   23

Humphreys' plan of attack   50

Federal and Confederate movements on May 4   62

The situation during the morning of May 5   96

The situation on May 5 at noon   137

The turnpike front on May 5, 1 P.M.–3 P.M.   146

Saunders' Field on May 5 at 1 P.M.   148

Higgerson's Field on May 5 at 1 P.M.   158

Sedgwick's assault on May 5, 3 P.M.–5 P.M.   177

The Orange Plank Road front on May 5 at 4:30 P.M.   192

The Orange Plank Road front
on May 5, 4:30 P.M.–9:00 P.M.   224

Cavalry maneuvers on the afternoon of May 5   254

The Orange Plank Road front on May 6 at 5:00 A.M.   284

Longstreet's counterattack on May 6, 6 A.M.–10 A.M.   296

Burnside's advance on the morning of May 6   327

Longstreet's flank attack on May 6 at 11 A.M.   352

Burnside's assault on the afternoon of May 6   381

The Brock Road front on May 6 at 5 P.M.   391

Gordon's attack on the evening of May 6   406

Acknowledgments

I WISH ESPECIALLY to thank the historian William Craig, who offered early inspiration and encouragement; Karl E. Sundstrom, who reviewed my draft and offered valuable insight; William D. Matter and Donald Pfanz, who found time in their busy schedules to read and comment on the manuscript; and Robert K. Krick, Chief Historian of the Fredericksburg and Spotsylvania National Military Park, whose ready assistance in all things asked of him, and in much more, made this book possible.

My debts extend to R. Monroe Waugh, recently deceased, who walked with me the overgrown remains of the Rapidan earthworks that he knew since childhood; Patricia J. Hurst, who helped identify numerous Orange County landmarks; and Anne B. Miller, who made available the resources of the Orange County Historical Society. I extend thanks also to librarians and research assistants at the numerous libraries and collections that I visited. Special gratitude must go to Richard J. Sommers and David Keough, who gave me a warm and gracious reception at the United States Army Military History Institute.

I am also indebted to George Skoch, whose wonderful maps constitute an important part of this work, and to Noel Harrison, of the Fredericksburg and Spotsylvania National Military Park, who aided in preparing those maps and afforded me access to parts of the battlefield inaccessible to the general public. Numerous friends read the manuscript and offered their views, including John Fisher, David Nissman, and Bernard Patty. Brian A. Bennett shared with me material about the 140th New York that I had overlooked. Barry L. Blose, of the LSU Press editorial staff, deftly applied his talents to the manuscript. My law partner, Thomas Alkon, deserves special thanks for his thoughtful comments and for putting up with this project during the past several years. And so also do Catherine and Campbell Rhea, who understood when, respectively, their husband and father sought time to investigate and record the deeds of his long-dead friends.

Abbreviations

ADAH   Alabama Department of Archives and History, Montgomery

AU   Special Collections, Auburn University Libraries

B&L   Buel, Clarence C., and Robert U. Johnson, eds. *Battles and Leaders of the Civil War*. 4 vols. New York, 1884–88.

BL   Bentley Historical Library, University of Michigan

BU   Mugar Library, Boston University

CL   William Clements Library, University of Michigan

DU   William R. Perkins Library, Duke University

ECU   Manuscript Department, East Carolina University Libraries

EU   Robert W. Woodruff Library, Emory University

FSMP   Fredericksburg and Spotsylvania National Military Park Library

GDAH   Georgia Department of Archives and History, Atlanta

HSP   Historical Society of Pennsylvania, Philadelphia

HU   Houghton Library, Harvard University

LC   Manuscript Division, Library of Congress

MC   Eleanor S. Brockenbrough Library, Museum of the
            Confederacy, Richmond

MHS   Massachusetts Historical Society, Boston

MDAH   Mississippi Department of Archives and History, Jackson

MOLLUS   Military Order of the Loyal Legions of the United States

NCDAH   North Carolina Department of Archives and History,
            Raleigh

NYHS   New York Historical Society, New York

NYSA   New York State Archives, Albany

OR   *The War of the Rebellion: A Compilation of the Official
            Records of the Union and Confederate Armies.* 130 vols.
            Washington, D.C., 1880–1901. Unless otherwise stated,
            references are to Series I.

PMHSM   *Papers of the Military Historical Society of Massachusetts.*
            14 vols. Boston, 1881–1918.

RL   Rundel Library, Rochester, N.Y.

RU   Special Collections and Archives, Rutgers University
            Libraries

SHC   Southern Historical Collection, University of North
            Carolina

SHSP   *Southern Historical Society Papers.* 49 vols. Richmond,
            1876–1944.

TSL   Tennessee State Library and Archives, Nashville

UG   University of Georgia Libraries

USMHI   United States Army Military History Institute, Carlisle, Pa.

UV   Alderman Library, University of Virginia

VHS   Virginia Historical Society, Richmond

VSL   Virginia State Library, Richmond

THE BATTLE OF THE WILDERNESS
MAY 5–6, 1864

INTRODUCTION

NEAR THE EASTERN end of General Robert E. Lee's Confederate defensive line was a shallow spot in the Rapidan known as Morton's Ford. There the river bent in a lazy loop to create a broad floodplain along its southern bank. Ringed by hills, the place formed a natural amphitheater in which the rebels had front row seats. From heights above, the Richmond Howitzers, an elite Southern artillery unit, commanded the ford and its approaches. Gray-clad pickets patrolled the flat land along the river itself.

An ill-advised skirmish at Morton's Ford confirmed for the northerners that Lee's Rapidan works were as tough as they looked. The business all started in February, 1864, when Major General Benjamin F. Butler, a Union commander known more for his political influence among radical Republicans than for military prowess, decided to chance a surprise attack against Richmond. According to Butler's calculations, a series of Confederate operations along the North Carolina coast must have stripped Richmond's defenses bare. The general proposed that he advance with six thousand troops up the swampy peninsula between the York and James rivers and swoop unannounced into the Confederate capital.

On February 3, Butler aired his plan with Secretary of War Edwin M. Stanton and the Union general-in-chief, Major General Henry W. Halleck. Key to Butler's plan was his recommendation that the Army of the Potomac move against Lee to prevent him from reinforcing Richmond. Major General John Sedgwick, who was temporarily commanding the Army of the Potomac, objected strongly. The roads were soft, he wired Butler, and the Rapidan was "so strongly intrenched that a demonstration upon it would not disturb Lee's army." Nonetheless, on February 5, Halleck ordered Sedgwick

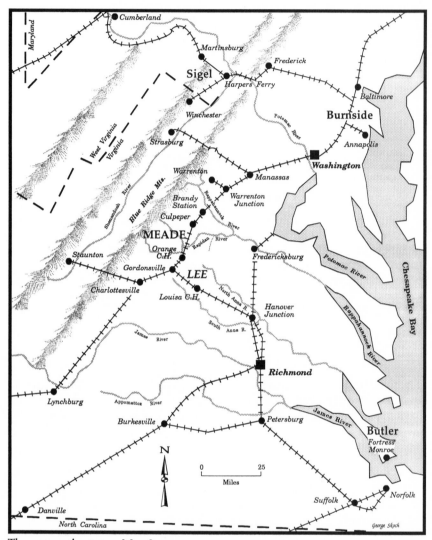

The eastern theater on May 2

to cooperate with Butler. Again warning that a demonstration would only "spoil the chances for the future," Sedgwick sullenly assented. Privately he denounced the affair as "childish."[1]

Scrambling to organize an attack, Sedgwick ordered Federal cavalry to feel out each end of Lee's line and arranged for a corps of infantry to advance at daylight. The rest of the Union army was held in readiness to exploit a possible breakthrough.

Charged with the main effort, the Federal 2nd Corps sloshed knee-deep in mud along rain-soaked roads to Morton's Ford. Pelted by a freezing drizzle, the Union skirmishers leading the assault column slid down the Rapidan's muddy banks into the ice-choked river, holding their cartridge boxes overhead to keep the ammunition dry. The shorter men had to be carried across.

Initially, luck was with the Federals. Shivering Confederate pickets were just finishing their shift and were anxious to return to quarters. Their relief had not yet arrived, but it was deep winter and an enemy attack was the last thing on anyone's mind. The rebel pickets marched off, leaving the crossing untended except for a handful of guards.

Unaware of the Federal buildup at the ford, the Richmond Howitzers remained snugly ensconced at their hillside camp. Sergeant Van McCreery, a self-styled "tonsorial artist" with the outfit's only pair of scissors, occupied himself and his comrades by giving haircuts. Suddenly a wide-eyed picket darted into the Howitzers' camp. "The Yankees are across the river and making for the guns," he shouted. "They will capture them before you get there if you don't hurry up!" The Howitzers bolted for the hill, Sergeant McCreery brandishing his scissors. McCreery's latest customer, Bob McIntosh, ran hatless. His head was half-shaved and a towel flapped around his neck.[2]

By the time the alarm had been sounded, one Union brigade was across the river, another was splashing over at the ford, and a third was forming on the opposite bank. Things looked bad for the

1. Benjamin F. Butler to Henry W. Halleck, February 3, 1864, in OR, XXXIII, 506–507; John Sedgwick to Benjamin F. Butler, February 4, 1864, *ibid.*, 512–13; John Sedgwick to Henry W. Halleck, February 5, 1864, *ibid.*, 514; Theodore Lyman to family, February 5, 1864, in *Meade's Headquarters, 1863–1865: Letters of Colonel Theodore Lyman from the Wilderness to Appomattox*, ed. George R. Agassiz (Boston, 1922), 68.

2. William M. Dame, *From the Rapidan to Richmond and the Spottsylvania Campaign* (Baltimore, 1920), 40.

Confederates. As shells whistled into the Howitzers' position, the men jumped to their pieces and aimed for the advancing Federals. McIntosh's half-bald head evoked peals of laughter from his companions. In short order Lieutenant General Richard S. Ewell, commanding the Confederate 2nd Corps, dashed up from his nearby headquarters at Morton Hall. Reining in his horse, Ewell piped in his distinctive high-pitched voice, "What on earth is the matter here?" A look over the crest answered his question. "Boys, keep them back ten minutes," bellowed the excited, bug-eyed rebel commander, "and I'll have enough men to eat them—without salt." Whirling his mount, Ewell tore down the road. Shortly afterward, two Confederate brigades—the soldiers who had left and their relief, Brigadier General George H. ("Maryland") Steuart's unit—came up at a trot and filed to each side of the smoking battery. With a "whoop and a yell," they pitched into the enemy.[3]

The plain below became a slaughter pen. Lunging forward, the first wave of Yankees hunkered down to avoid the raking fire from above. More Federals poured across but found themselves wedged inside a semicircle of Confederate entrenchments that touched the river on both sides of the ford. Bullets came from all directions but behind. The Yankees managed to secure a toehold in a brick house on an eminence near the rebel works, but pressing farther was manifestly impossible. The trick had become how to get out alive.

Major General Gouverneur K. Warren, temporarily in charge of the Union 2nd Corps, rode with a handful of officers to the house for a better view. Inspired by the sight of Union brass, a Confederate sharpshooter whizzed a bullet over Warren's head. Rebel cannon joined in, and the Federals were lost from view in the smoke from exploding shells. Miraculously, they emerged shortly afterward behind a sheltered dip in the road and slipped back across the river.[4]

Near sunset, a body of Confederates rushed the house and captured it, along with the white-haired black woman inside. Frightened nearly to death, she had hidden when the fighting started. The Federals held on to a wooden outbuilding nearby, and the two sides

---

3. *Ibid.*, 42.

4. Thomas F. Galwey, *The Valiant Hours: An Irishman in the Civil War* (Harrisburg, Pa., 1961), 189.

charged back and forth under cover of darkness. "Scarcely a charge was made but prisoners were obtained on both sides," recalled a New Yorker. "They would run up to each other, grab, and by main force pull them into their own houses." After a half hour or so, the Union soldiers escaped by climbing out a rear window.[5]

During the foggy night that followed, the northerners pulled back over a makeshift bridge. The flash of muskets reminded a Pennsylvania man of "lightning in a pleasant summer evening at home." Brigadier General Alexander Hays, whose Federal division had borne the brunt of the fighting, put on a curious display. A Connecticut soldier wrote home describing how Hays spent the evening "hooting, yelling, and riding right in the rebs faces." Tiring of the sport, the general amused himself "laughing to see the boys get into the mud up to their knees." Rumor had it that he was drunk.[6]

Confederate pickets occupied their old posts by noon the next day. Glum northerners watched from their side as rebel burying parties picked across the battlefield. "Our boys in their blue overcoats," wrote a Union onlooker, "lay scattered about over there with the earth-colored uniforms of the dead Confederates."[7]

Having generated over two hundred Union casualties, the affair was viewed dimly in the Federal ranks, particularly when it was learned that Butler, who had insisted on the diversion in the first place, had abandoned his foray against Richmond on hearing that a deserter had disclosed his plans to the rebels. "So I sacrificed 200 men to aid that fool," Warren bitterly wrote his wife the next day. "I have such a contempt for his military abilities, that I could not express it in decent words." Hays thought he could have taken Lee's works if the whole Union 2nd Corps had been thrown in. Warren soberly concluded that more soldiers would only have lengthened the casualty lists, with no appreciable effect on the outcome. Sedgwick

5. William P. Oberlin to Annie, February 9, 1864, in Civil War Miscellaneous Collection, USMHI; Charles Hamlin to sister, February 9, 1864, in Charles Hamlin Papers, NYSA; George W. Nichols, *A Soldier's Story of His Regiment and Incidentally of the Lawton, Gordon, Evans Brigade* (Jesup, Ga., 1898), 132–39.

6. Charles E. Pollard to mother, February 9, 1864, in Lewis Leigh Collection, USMHI; Charles D. Page, *History of the Fourteenth Regiment, Connecticut Volunteer Infantry* (Meriden, Conn., 1906), 228–29.

7. Galwey, *The Valiant Hours,* 190.

self-righteously reported to Halleck that the venture, hastily launched with insufficient support, had "spoiled the best chance we had for a successful attack on the Rapidan."[8]

Congratulations, tempered by the embarrassment of being caught unprepared, circulated on the Confederate side. A private who had joined the spirited fighting later boasted, "I never took better aim at a bird or a squirrel in my life than I took at those Yankee soldiers. And I never enjoyed a party in my younger days any better." Another wrote to his wife, "I am very sore today. The Yankees came on our side of the river Sunday and we had to run them all day to put them back." Ewell credited himself for the repulse. "Had I not been there," he preened to his brother, "there might have been a disaster the other day at Morton's Ford, but being on the spot, as it were, I was able to give the necessary directions before the enemy got a foothold." Sergeant McCreery lost his scissors in the fray, and McIntosh's half-shaved head continued a source of amusement, especially when a soldier tried to even out the haircut with a hatchet.[9]

The affair at Morton's Ford scarcely qualified as a battle. Measured against the massive casualties of 1863, or against the even more appalling slaughter to come, the fight was little more than a skirmish. But the incident's importance went far beyond the number of men killed or wounded. Alerted to potential weaknesses and the danger of surprise attacks, Lee tightened his defensive works into an impregnable bastion. The Federals were fully aware of Lee's renewed vigilance. Union lookouts in the months following the skirmish invariably described new Confederate gun placements sprouting like fresh crops across the river. Any thought of a frontal assault against Lee's Rapidan fortress was definitively abandoned. When spring arrived and baked the Virginia mud dry, another way would have to be found to pry the rebels from their fortifications and force them to battle on a more promising field.

The need that springtime was to find a better way to bring Lee to

---

8. Gouverneur K. Warren to wife, February 9, 1864, in Gouverneur Kemble Warren Collection, NYSA; John Sedgwick to Henry W. Halleck, February 12, 1864, in OR, XXXIII, 553–54.

9. John B. Crawford to father, February 9, 1864, in John B. Crawford Collection, ADAH; Nichols, *A Soldier's Story of His Regiment*, 135; Richard S. Ewell to brother, February 18, 1864, in *The Making of a Soldier: Letters of R. S. Ewell*, ed. Percy G. Hamlin (Richmond, 1935), 126.

bay. The Battle of the Wilderness, fought on May 5 and 6, 1864, was the first match between Lee and the new Federal general-in-chief, Ulysses S. Grant, fresh from a series of impressive victories in the western theater. Lee's challenge was to come up with a means to defeat a skilled adversary commanding an army double the size of his own. Grant's was to come up with a means to maneuver his wily opponent into battle on terms favorable to the northerners. The tale is one of the most thrilling in American military history.

I

May 2–3, 1864
Lee and Grant Make Their Plans

*"I fear the army cannot
be kept effective."*

EIGHTEEN SIXTY-FOUR opened a season of desperation for the Confederacy and of hope for the Union cause. During the previous year, Federal armies had gained control of the Mississippi River and had consolidated their grip on Tennessee. Not only was the Confederacy now severed from its main river artery but it had lost a substantial portion of its heartland as well. Only two significant Confederate military forces remained. In northern Georgia, General Joseph E. Johnston's rebel army was locked in a standoff against Major General William T. Sherman's tough Union veterans. And in the war's eastern theater, Lee's Army of Northern Virginia was opposed by the largest concentration of Federal military might yet assembled.

Coursing down from the nearby Blue Ridge Mountains, the Rapidan River drew an unofficial boundary between Union-held northern Virginia and the southern part of the state still under Confederate control. Lee's troops waited securely behind an imposing set of earthworks lining the river's southern bank, just above the rustic farming village of Orange Court House. On the river's far side stood Major General George G. Meade's Federal Army of the Potomac.

Meade's objective was the Confederate capital, Richmond, seventy or so miles to the south by road. The Union army, however, had been stymied along the Rapidan since the previous fall. What prevented the Federals from advancing was not the river itself. The problem was the strength of the Confederate works. Lee had taken his stand at a natural fortress. High hills on the southern bank, cleverly lined with interlocking rifle pits and artillery positions, made a Union crossing impossible.

As the campaign season of 1864 approached, Lee faced one of the gravest crises of his military career. Crippling shortages in food, fodder, and men had locked him into a defensive posture strikingly out of character with his usual aggressiveness. "My hands are tied," the rebel commander complained to Richmond.[1]

Once well tended, parts of central Virginia had been stripped bare. To one Confederate the countryside "seemed almost uninhabited and not even the bark of a dog or sound of a bird broke the dreary silence." With Tennessee and northern Virginia in enemy hands, Lee had to draw sustenance from Georgia and the Carolinas. The most direct railway from the Deep South had been irreparably severed, and the remaining lines were agonizingly slow. Lee's fragile umbilical cord, the Orange and Alexandria Railroad, was a single-track affair that when operating at full capacity barely accommodated sufficient trains to feed the army. "Short rations are having a bad effect upon the men, both morally and physically," the Confederate commander reported. An Alabama soldier complained that "a part of the time rations consisted of what appeared to be wheat bran and beef, so poor that on cooking it smelled like glue." As the days began to warm, one southern general published a list of edible wild plants. Years later, the winter's gnawing hunger remained vivid to a Confederate private. "We had more appetite than anything else," he recalled, "and never got enough to satisfy it—even for a time."[2]

Substantial portions of Lee's army had been detached and sent to other endangered regions of the South. Of concern also was the fact that new troops were no longer available. In February, 1864, Richmond tacitly conceded that the Confederacy had been bled dry. Decisions there broadened compulsory military service to include all white males from seventeen to fifty years of age. They also extended terms of enlistment for the war's duration, abolished the hiring of substitutes, and tightened exemptions from military service to include only essential civilian workers. Draconian measures bore little fruit. On April 30, the Confederate Bureau of Conscription reported disturbing news. "Fresh material for the armies can no longer be estimated as an element of future calculation for their increase" was

1. Robert E. Lee to Braxton Bragg, April 16, 1864, in OR, XXXIII, 1285.

2. McHenry Howard, Recollections of a Maryland Confederate Soldier and Staff Officer Under Johnston, Jackson, and Lee (Baltimore, 1914), 253n7, 267; Robert E. Lee to James A. Seddon, January 21, 1864, in OR, XXXIII, 1114; J. Q. Burton, "Forty Seven Regiment Alabama Volunteers, C.S.A.," in Regimental Collection, ADAH; Dame, From the Rapidan to Richmond, 26–30.

its tortuously framed conclusion. In other words, Lee would have to do his best with the soldiers he already had.[3]

Shortfalls in horses and forage exacerbated the Army of Northern Virginia's plight. Dependent on animals to haul heavy guns, Lee's artillery was dispersed along with its horses to pastures on the Virginia Central Railroad near Charlottesville. "Unless there is a change," Lee warned the Confederacy's president, Jefferson Davis, "I fear the army cannot be kept effective, and probably cannot be kept together."[4]

In this season of scarcity, Lee was unquestionably the South's prime asset. "We looked forward to victory under him as confidently as to successive sunrises," recalled a Confederate officer. Lee openly reciprocated his soldiers' admiration. "Never were such men in an army before," the general boasted.[5]

At first blush, Lee's record appeared to justify his reputation. He had burst into national prominence in June, 1862, by rescuing the Confederate capital in a hard-fought series of battles collectively called the Seven Days. Then, through judicious combinations of maneuvering and hard hammering, he had driven the enemy back to Washington. Pressing across the Potomac into Maryland, he had boldly divided his army, captured a Federal garrison, and then managed at the last moment to assemble his command at Antietam Creek and deadlock a Federal force nearly three times the size of his. That winter, Lee had soundly defeated the Federals when they attempted to cross the Rappahannock at Fredericksburg, and the following spring he had achieved a dazzling victory at Chancellorsville by again dividing his army and rolling up a vulnerable Federal flank.

3. Bureau of Conscription Report, April 30, 1864, in OR, Ser. IV, Vol. III, pp. 354–64. A soldier in the 1st Delaware wrote home that "rebs are a coming over very fast some times as many as a hundred a time on the picket line" (Justin Turner to mother, April 25, 1864, in Justin Turner Collection, USMHI).

4. William Pendleton's Report, in OR, Vol. XXXVI, Pt. 1, pp. 1036–40; Lee to Seddon, January 21, 1864, ibid., XXXIII, 1114.

5. Gary W. Gallagher, ed., Fighting for the Confederacy: The Personal Recollections of General Edward Porter Alexander (Chapel Hill, N.C., 1989), 222; Robert E. Lee to John B. Hood, May 21, 1863, in Advance and Retreat: Personal Experiences in the United States and Confederate States Armies, by John B. Hood (New Orleans, 1880), 53.

The prominent feature of Lee's generalship was his unabashed aggressiveness, combined with an irrepressible penchant for taking risks—his "phenomenal audacity," to use Confederate Brigadier General E. Porter Alexander's phrase. Lee's approach maximized the striking power of his smaller army. Thus far, northern commanders had been perfect foils for his brand of warfare.[6]

But the price of waging combat Lee's way was becoming prohibitive. No matter how severe a drubbing he administered, the Federals always returned, stronger than before. Lee's successes had also significantly depleted the South's supply of fighting men. In most of his battles, Lee had lost proportionately as many soldiers as the enemy, and in some cases more. In the long run—setting aside the possibility that the North might simply weary and negotiate a peace—Lee's formula for victory held the seeds of the South's destruction. Unless Lee administered a killing blow, simple mathematics dictated that the North had to win. In this inexorable game of numbers, 1864 stood as Lee's last chance, if indeed it was not already too late.

The war's psychological balance was also beginning to shift. In July, 1863, Lee had advanced into Pennsylvania and waged a grinding three-day battle at Gettysburg. The fight was a watershed for the Army of Northern Virginia and tempered its boast of invincibility. "The army did all it could," was Lee's explanation for the failure. "I fear I required of it impossibilities."[7]

The remainder of 1863 had been a disappointment for him. On Thanksgiving, the Federals had tried to dislodge him by circling east of his Rapidan entrenchments. Spirited resistance bought the Confederates time to dig in above Mine Run, a small stream on Lee's right flank. The northerners retreated, leaving an exasperated Lee to fume, "I am too old to command this army; we should never have permitted these people to get away."[8]

The armies spent the winter of 1863–1864 in close embrace, separated only by the narrow ribbon of water. Following the half-hearted attack at Morton's Ford, Lee tightened his works into an unassailable bastion, symbolic of the defensive posture that circum-

6. Edward P. Alexander, *Military Memoirs of a Confederate* (New York, 1907), 111.

7. Robert E. Lee to Margaret Stuart, July 26, 1863, in *The Wartime Papers of R. E. Lee*, ed. Clifford Dowdey and Louis H. Manarin (New York, 1961), 561.

8. Charles S. Venable, "General Lee in the Wilderness Campaign," in *B&L*, IV, 240.

stances had forced on his army. But the year's disappointments had failed to dull the irrepressible aggressiveness that accounted for his success and, as his critics pointed out, for his failures as well. During the Mine Run campaign a cavalryman, William W. Blackford, received emphatic proof of the general's undaunted military spirit. Arriving at headquarters long before daylight, Blackford found Lee already up, pacing back and forth in shirt sleeves before a fire. Brushing his hair and beard, Lee questioned Blackford sharply about his assessment of the enemy's plan. Suddenly Lee slapped the back of his hairbrush against his left palm and exclaimed, "Captain, if they don't attack us today, we must attack them!" Again he whipped the brush against his palm and stomped for emphasis, eyes brimming with excitement. "We must attack them, sir," he repeated. The brush slammed down for a third time. "And you young men must exert yourselves!" he snapped, as though sheer will could win the day. "You must exert yourselves, sir!" Blackford never forgot Lee's "handsome face all aglow, and his eyes fairly flashing fire as he brandished his brush."[9]

As Lee explained his style of command to a foreign visitor, "I do everything in my power to make my plans as perfect as possible, and to bring the troops upon the field of battle; the rest must be done by my generals and their troops, trusting to Providence for the victory." By 1864, many of the South's best generals had become battlefield casualties. In many instances, second-raters filled their places.

The dearth of proven, dependable leadership was acutely evident at the corps level, where the army's major decisions were made. Just as the Army of Northern Virginia had acquired a distinctive personality—as a lean, ragged, and hungry lot that bore hardship with humor and challenged long odds with daredevil belligerence and a flair for the unexpected—so had each corps developed its own identity reflecting its commander's traits. Heading Lee's three corps this spring were Lieutenant Generals James Longstreet, Richard S. Ewell, and Ambrose P. Hill. They were a feisty, strong-willed, and quarrelsome crew. Each had his quirks, and each had flaws in military judg-

9. William W. Blackford, *War Years with Jeb Stuart* (New York, 1945), 245–46.

ment that precluded Lee's full trust. Lee's task was to harmonize them despite their differences and to find a way to make his top team, already tested at Gettysburg and found wanting, responsive to him and to one another.

Lee's premier fighting unit was Longstreet's 1st Corps, which hailed primarily from the Deep South. Longstreet was a full-bearded, six-foot bear of a man, blue eyed and firm mouthed. Some—particularly Virginians, for whom he developed an intense dislike that was warmly reciprocated—considered him an overrated bore. An aide on the staff of Lee's cavalry commander, Major General James E. B. ("Jeb") Stuart, pronounced Longstreet a "man of limited capacity who acquired reputation for wisdom for never saying anything—the old story of the owl. I do not remember him saying over half a dozen words, beyond 'yes' and 'no' in a consecutive sentence." Even Longstreet's friends conceded that the general's military temperament was occasionally marred by inflexibility, unbending self-confidence, and ambition.[10]

Lee liked and respected his burly general, then the army's most experienced corps commander, and habitually sought his advice. As Lee's adjutant put it, there was "never any doubt about the security of a position" that Longstreet held. But Lee's "War Horse," as Longstreet was called, could also be excessively meticulous, even ponderous, in arranging troops for action. "Longstreet is a very good fighter when he gets into position and gets everything ready," Lee reportedly commented, "but he is slow."[11]

While Lee sought victory through desperate offensive gambles, Longstreet favored defensive tactics that husbanded the army's resources. Openly peeved when Lee rejected his recommendations at Gettysburg, Longstreet displayed a rebellious streak. Even his loyal aide, Lieutenant Colonel G. Moxley Sorrel, admitted that Longstreet "failed to conceal some anger," moved apathetically, and "lacked the

10. Heros von Borcke, *Memoirs of the Confederate War for Independence* (Philadelphia, 1867), 22–23; Blackford, *War Years,* 47; G. Moxley Sorrel, *Recollections of a Confederate Staff Officer* (New York, 1917), 37–38.

11. Walter H. Taylor, *General Lee: His Campaign in Virginia, 1861–1865, with Personal Reminiscences* (Norfolk, Va., 1906), 223; Sorrel, *Recollections,* 116; Jubal A. Early, "Leading Confederates on the Battle of Gettysburg," in *SHSP,* IV, 274. For an Englishman's independent assessment, see Francis W. Dawson, *Reminiscences of Confederate Service,* ed. Bell Wiley (Baton Rouge, 1980), xi.

fire and point of his usual bearing on the battlefield." The fall of 1863 brought more disquieting revelations about Lee's senior corps head. In early September, Longstreet took two divisions to reinforce General Braxton Bragg's Confederate army in northern Georgia. At first, the bracing Georgia air seemed to dispel the lethargy brought on by Gettysburg. Massing troops in column at Chickamauga, Longstreet split the Union army and drove the Yankees in disarray. Soon, however, he was quarreling with Bragg and venting his displeasure in a sluggishness reminiscent of his performance at Gettysburg. Lee's touted War Horse was "greatly overrated," Bragg concluded, ordering him into east Tennessee to "get rid of him and see what he could do on his own resources." The War Horse's stab at independent command ended in an embarrassing Confederate defeat. As a Richmond diarist expressed it, "Detached from General Lee, what a horrible failure is Longstreet!" [12]

Longstreet cursed Bragg, court-martialed one of his division chiefs, and then joined in a bitter feud over who would head his other division. His vindictiveness provoked a reprimand from President Davis. Longstreet's division heads—Brigadier General Joseph B. Kershaw, a tough and seasoned fighter promoted from the brigade level, and jovial Major General Charles W. Field, just returned from convalescence and missing a limb—had never held elevated command or worked in tandem. But by far, the 1st Corps' biggest question mark was Longstreet himself. Chickamauga had confirmed that the general still had his old touch, but adversity had brought out a petty, ugly side.

Even bigger questions swirled around Richard Ewell, the head of Lee's 2nd Corps. Something about the Virginian's appearance and personal habits invited caricature. His bald dome, beaked nose, and bulging eyes reminded some fellow officers of a bird, particularly when he tilted his head and spoke in his distinctive shrill, lisping voice. Ewell was a "compound of anomalies," concluded a friend, the "oddest, most eccentric genius in the Confederate Army." [13]

Ewell had been selected to head Lee's 2nd Corps after Thomas J. ("Stonewall") Jackson's death in May, 1863. He had just recovered

12. Sorrel, *Recollections*, 167; Nathaniel Hughes, ed., *Liddell's Record* (Dayton, 1985), 157; Mary B. Chesnut, *A Diary from Dixie* (New York, 1905), 265.

13. John B. Gordon, *Reminiscences of the Civil War* (New York, 1903), 38.

from the amputation of a leg and had married a widowed cousin, Lizinka Brown. An officer of the 2nd Corps confided in his diary that "from a military point of view the addition of the wife did not compensate for the loss of the leg. We were of the opinion that Ewell was not the same soldier he had been when he was a whole man—and a single one."[14]

Whatever the reason, Ewell was experiencing evident difficulty in adapting to Lee's freewheeling style of command. A subordinate later noted that the general "was never content with his own plan until he had secured the approval of another's judgment." His close friend and division commander, Major General Jubal A. Early, remarked that Ewell was frequently "at a loss as to what opinion to form." In a postwar conversation, Lee confided that he had been aware of Ewell's "faults as a military leader—his quick alternation from elation to despondency, want of decision, etc.," and had discussed these deficiencies "long and earnestly" with him. In the opinion of many, Ewell had failed to rise to his new responsibilities. "Though he has quick military perception and is a splendid executive officer," Ewell's aide, Lieutenant Colonel Alexander S. ("Sandie") Pendleton, wrote home, the general was "too irresolute for so large and independent command." Delicately pronouncing the army's verdict, Porter Alexander concluded that Ewell was "always loved and admired, but he was not always equal to the opportunity."[15]

For the winter of 1863–1864, Ewell set up quarters in Jeremiah Morton's high-ceilinged mansion near the 2nd Corps' encampments. The place was an easy ride to the Rapidan fords, and its columned porch overlooked little Mountain Run, teeming with Ewell's soldiers. Moving in for the winter, the assertive Mrs. Ewell and her daughter quickly ended the boredom. "She manages everything," wrote Colonel James Conner of the headstrong woman, "from the General's affairs down to the courier's, who carries his dispatches." It was a "petticoat government," with Ewell "worse in love than any eighteen year old that you ever saw." Ewell's staff was offended by the wom-

14. Randolph H. McKim, *A Soldier's Recollections* (New York, 1910), 134.

15. Richard Taylor, *Destruction and Reconstruction: Personal Experiences of the Late War* (New York, 1879), 36–37; Early, "Leading Confederates on the Battle of Gettysburg," in *SHSP*, IV, 256; William Allen, Notes of a Postwar Conversation with Lee, March 3, 1868, in William Allen Papers, SHC; William G. Bean, *Stonewall's Man: Sandie Pendleton* (Chapel Hill, N.C., 1959), 151; Alexander, *Military Memoirs*, 360.

en's machinations to secure promotion for Major Campbell Brown, the widow's son and one of Ewell's aides. Conner laughed over the staff's "trepidation about the maneuvering of two women, and one fond, foolish old man." Pendleton wrote his mother disparagingly about his "superannuated chieftain" worn out "by the prostration incident, in a man of his age, upon the amputation [of his leg] and doting so foolishly upon his unattractive spouse."[16]

A sigh of relief is almost audible in the journal entry of Ewell's mapmaker, Major Jedediah Hotchkiss, for April 22, 1864: "Mrs. Ewell went away today."[17]

Entering the spring campaign with three strong division heads—Jubal Early, Major General Edward ("Allegheny") Johnson, and Major General Robert E. Rodes—the Confederate 2nd Corps had a reputation for hard marching and fighting earned during Stonewall's days. The weak link was Ewell. Nothing since Gettysburg suggested that he had mastered the business of command, at least as Lee practiced it, and his declining health made it questionable whether he could still endure active combat.

As for Lee's final corps head, something had gone terribly wrong with Powell Hill—Little Powell, the men called him—since his appointment a year before to command the new Confederate 3rd Corps.

Slender and frail with a prickly sensitivity matching his auburn hair and red battle shirt, Hill had won his reputation leading the self-styled Light Division, a unit renowned for aggressiveness in an army where the trait was commonplace. "As a division commander he had few equals," concluded a former Jackson aide. "He was quick, bold, skillful, and tenacious when the battle had begun." But the qualities that had earned Hill promotion were seldom evident after he assumed corps leadership. Responsibilities of high command, it seemed, had sapped his spontaneity and flair.[18]

Of growing concern also was Hill's health. Illness had forced him

16. James Conner to mother, February 19, 1864, in *Letters of General James Conner, C.S.A.*, ed. Mary C. Moffett (Columbia, S.C., 1933), 115; Sandie Pendleton to mother, November 25, 1863, in *Stonewall's Man*, by Bean, 151.

17. Archie P. McDonald, ed., *Make Me a Map of the Valley: The Civil War Journal of Stonewall Jackson's Topographer* (Dallas, 1973), 153.

18. Henry K. Douglas, *I Rode with Stonewall* (Chapel Hill, N.C., 1940), 148.

to repeat a year at West Point and had left him intermittently bedridden. The general's strength had held while he headed a division, but elevation to corps command brought a rapid deterioration. The coincidence of Hill's physical decline and his unsuccessful struggle to master his new position suggested a psychological component to his malaise. Whatever the cause—recurring organic illness, the unwitting escape mechanism of a proud man swamped in responsibility, or both—Little Powell's sunken eyes and hollow cheeks chronicled the malady's quickening advance.[19]

Hill's division commanders—Major Generals Cadmus M. Wilcox, Henry Heth, and Richard H. Anderson—also drew mixed reviews. Unlike Ewell's 2nd Corps, which in Early, Johnson, and Rodes had strong division heads, Hill's 3rd Corps had no ready replacement for its ailing chief.

Nothing after Gettysburg gave hope that the army's leadership crisis had abated. On the contrary, Longstreet's disastrous independent campaign had decimated his corps and embroiled it in bitter feuds, Ewell was in deteriorating health and feared by some to be in his dotage, and Hill was racked with sickness and haunted by his consistently poor showing. At Gettysburg, where the armies were evenly matched and had ample space to maneuver, Confederate blunders had been costly and almost fatal. In the spring of 1864, outnumbered two to one, the Army of Northern Virginia had no room for mistakes. Deep in its own territory with its back to Richmond, it would not escape defeat if there was another disaster such as in Pennsylvania.

As relieved as Lee was at Longstreet's return, his discussions with the exuberant corps head must have revived disturbing memories. At the "earliest opportunity," Longstreet later recounted, he urged Lee to confine the spring campaign ."to strategic maneuvers until we could show better generalship" than the Federals. Once outgeneraled, thought Longstreet, the enemy would lose confidence. Only then should aggressive tactics be used. Here again was the split in thinking that had divided Lee and his War Horse at Gettysburg. While Lee restlessly stewed over how to pitch into Meade, his chief

19. Hill's health problems were explored by James I. Robertson in *General A. P. Hill: The Story of a Confederate Warrior* (New York, 1987), 11–12.

lieutenant busily plotted how to wage defensive warfare. The evil spirit of Gettysburg still stalked the Army of Northern Virginia.[20]

"Everything indicates a concentrated attack on this front."

Confined to inactivity against his temperament and better judgment, Lee spent the winter of 1863–1864 helping formulate the South's grand strategy. His army in Virginia, Johnston's in Georgia, and Longstreet's detached force in east Tennessee constituted the Confederacy's chief military elements. In early February, Lee recommended taking the offensive to "derange" the enemy's plans. Recognizing that the Confederacy lacked resources to gain permanent advantage from a foray into northern territory, Lee aimed to "alarm and embarrass" the enemy and "prevent his undertaking anything of magnitude against us."[21]

In mid-March, Lee learned that Lieutenant General Ulysses S. Grant had assumed command of all Union armies. Toward the month's end, northern newspapers reported that the new Federal commander in chief intended to make his headquarters with Meade. This suggested that Virginia would be the main theater. Lee at first discounted these stories, which he thought had been planted "to mislead us as to the enemy's intentions." He reasoned that it was unlikely that Grant would concern himself with Richmond until he had secured a western victory.[22]

Three days later, rebel scouts confirmed that Grant had joined Meade at Culpeper Court House, a small town immediately above the Rapidan. Lee changed his mind and predicted a "concentration of troops in this region."[23]

Lee monitored Meade's buildup with concern. "Every train brings in recruits," he informed Davis on March 30, "and it is stated

---

20. James Longstreet, *From Manassas to Appomattox: Memoirs of the Civil War in America* (Philadelphia, 1896), 551.

21. Robert E. Lee to Jefferson Davis, February 3, 1864, in *OR,* XXXIII, 1144.

22. Robert E. Lee to Jefferson Davis, March 25, 1864, in *Lee's Dispatches to Jefferson Davis,* ed. Douglas S. Freeman (New York, 1957), 142, 144.

23. Robert E. Lee to Jefferson Davis, March 30, 1864, in *OR,* XXXIII, 1244–45.

that every available regiment at the North" was joining Meade. It was also rumored—falsely, it later developed—that two additional Federal corps were on their way from the West. Clearly Meade was responsible for the main thrust toward Richmond.[24]

By mid-April, Lee had arrived at a working hypothesis about Grant's plans. As he saw it, Grant was concentrating two major armies, one on the Rapidan under Meade and another at Annapolis under Major General Ambrose E. Burnside. Together they planned to execute a pincer movement against the Confederate capital. Meade's army, Lee wrote Davis, "is intended to move directly on Richmond." Burnside meanwhile was slated to maneuver against the city "in flank or rear," combining with another Federal force and advancing up the James River or coming at Richmond from farther south. Federal units then besieging Charleston, predicted Lee, would probably transfer to the James in Burnside's support. And not to be forgotten were Union troops apparently massing to raid the Shenandoah Valley, Virginia's breadbasket, and threatening Richmond from the west. "Every preparation must be made to meet the approaching storm which will burst in Virginia," was Lee's advice. Securing Richmond was the priority. To that end, Lee suggested advancing part of the Confederate force guarding Charleston into North Carolina. Thus repositioned, it could fend off Burnside whether he came from the Carolina coast or up the James River. If necessary, a small southern contingent could protect Richmond from behind the capital's strong earthworks. The handful of Confederate infantry and cavalry already in the Shenandoah Valley, thought Lee, should suffice to retard the Federals in that quarter until assistance became available from elsewhere. Once the Confederate capital was secure against secondary threats, he could roll up his sleeves and undertake what he viewed as the real work. "I would propose," he petitioned Davis on April 15, "that I draw Longstreet to me and move right against the enemy" across the Rapidan. "Should God give us a crowning victory there," he predicted, "all their plans would be dissipated, and their troops now collecting on the waters of the Chesapeake would be recalled to the defense of Washington." There was just one hitch. "To make this move I must have provisions and forage," explained Lee.

24. Lee to Davis, March 30, 1864, in OR, XXXIII, 1244, April 9, 1864, *ibid.*, 1268–69.

"I am not yet able to call to me the cavalry and artillery. If I am obliged to retire from this line, either by flank movement of the enemy or a want of supplies, great injury will befall us."[25]

Usually in the guise of bungling by Union generals, fortune had rescued the Army of Northern Virginia from tight scrapes in the past. Fortune again intervened. Since early April, Lee had daily expected Meade to advance. Unseasonably heavy rains, however, had kept Virginia's roads impassable. By month's end, even though the mud had firmed, Meade still held his hand. He was waiting, Lee concluded, for his supporting armies. "The delay of the enemy I hope will give us grass sufficient to get our troops together," Lee wrote, referring to the need for forage for horses.[26]

His wish was granted. Longstreet's two divisions returned from their assignment in the western theater and reached Charlottesville on April 20—"loaded up on the cars like all other stock for transportation, or freight of consequence," recalled a soldier from Georgia. From Charlottesville, the men trudged beside the rail line to avoid disrupting supply trains. They continued to Cobham's Depot, six miles below Gordonsville, and bivouacked at the nearby hamlet of Mechanicsville. The barren Rapidan pastures were erupting in verdant green. Lee's cavalry and artillery could begin rejoining his infantry. By the end of April, Lee was able to draw artillery from the Virginia Central Railroad to Liberty Mills, on the left of his Rapidan line.[27]

Although Meade remained stationary, signs of his impending advance multiplied. On April 24, Confederate scouts reported a brigade of Yankee cavalry near Germanna Ford, just past Lee's downriver flank. That night, enemy were spotted at Ely's Ford, the next major crossing east of Germanna Ford. On the twenty-ninth, two brigades of Union cavalry were discovered exploring Lee's other flank. But the big news concerned Burnside. Also on April 29, Lee received word that the stylishly whiskered general had marched from Annapolis to Alexandria with 23,000 men. That meant Burnside was combining with Meade, pushing Federal numbers on the far bank to over

---

25. Robert E. Lee to Jefferson Davis, April 15, 1864, in OR, XXXIII, 1282–83.

26. Robert E. Lee to Jefferson Davis, April 25, 1864, in Lee's Dispatches, ed. Freeman, 166.

27. Francis Marion Howard to mother, April 19, 1864, in Lewis Leigh Collection, USMHI; Robert E. Lee to Jefferson Davis, April 28, 1864, in OR, XXXIII, 1320–21.

120,000. "Everything indicates a concentrated attack on this front," Lee grimly informed Davis. Confederate signal stations were ordered to post sentinels at night to watch for signs of Meade's movement.[28]

According to Lee's returns for April 20, the Army of Northern Virginia had 63,984 soldiers. Additional troops straggled in daily. By May 2, Lee had managed to assemble a fighting force of about 65,000 soldiers. This was considerably more than he had wielded at Antietam, about the number with which he had won his victory at Chancellorsville, and ten to fifteen thousand fewer than he had with him at Gettysburg. But the vexatious problem of how to provision his army continued to stay his hand.[29]

On April 29, Lee journeyed to Gordonsville to review Longstreet's 1st Corps. This was Lee's first opportunity to welcome his War Horse's soldiers back. In a cleared valley with broad pastures, Longstreet's corps formed double columns, flanked by artillery. Lee rode between two gateposts onto the field. Colonel John Bratton, of the 6th South Carolina, described in a letter home how "the troops greeted the old leader with great enthusiasm, really felt." Another soldier remarked that "you never saw such cheering in your life." A bugle sounded, thirteen cannon roared, caps flew high, flags dipped and waved, and drums and fifes struck up "Hail to the Chief." Forty years later, Longstreet's artillery chief remembered that a wave of sentiment "seemed to sweep over the field. All felt the bond which held them together. There was no speaking, but the effect was of a military sacrament." Lee's horse, Traveller, trotted to the center of the veterans. For two hours, the 1st Corps' soldiers paraded by, saluting as they passed. After the grand review, the men again formed two lines. Lee and Longstreet rode with their staffs on inspection around the threadbare troops. A soldier later recalled crowds pressing around Lee to touch his horse, his stirrup, his bridle, and even the general's leg. "Anything that Lee had was sacred to us fellows

28. Lee to Davis, April 25, 1864, in *Lee's Dispatches*, ed. Freeman, 166, April 30, 1864, in *OR*, XXXIII, 1331–32.

29. The returns for April 20 are in *OR*, XXXIII, 1297–1301. Ewell reported 20,710 aggregate present; Hill, 25,391; Stuart, 9,700; and Lee's artillery chief, William Pendleton, 5,547. Longstreet's figures were not included in the returns, but Longstreet and his artillery chief later estimated the size of Longstreet's two available divisions at 10,000 men. See Longstreet, *From Manassas to Appomattox*, 553–54; and Alexander, *Military Memoirs*, 497. For Jubal Early's exhaustive, if characteristically partisan, analysis of the sizes of the opposing armies, see *SHSP*, II, 6–21.

who had just come back," he recounted. Tears were seen tracing down Lee's cheeks. "Does it not make the general proud to see how these men love him?" a chaplain riding with the staff asked one of Lee's aides. "Not proud," answered the aide. "It awes him."[30]

As April faded into May, Lee continued to ponder his alternatives. They boiled down to defending the Rapidan or retiring behind another strong natural position farther south, such as the North Anna River.

Several considerations favored remaining on the Rapidan. These included the strength of the existing earthworks and the fact that battle there would afford Lee room to maneuver. If the Confederates failed to hold the Rapidan, they would still have the option of taking up a new line to the south. But falling back to the North Anna also had advantages. The position there would be every bit as strong as on the Rapidan, with the added benefit that Lee's supply lines would be shortened and the enemy's correspondingly lengthened. Lee also would be able to coordinate closely with Confederate forces coming up from the Carolinas, helping to fend off the expected Union attack up the James River.

After balancing these considerations, Lee elected to join battle on the Rapidan. Retaining freedom to maneuver seems to have been his prime consideration.

Not knowing where the blow would fall, Lee positioned troops to cover the obvious possibilities. Hill and Ewell continued to police the river directly across from Meade. Longstreet remained farther back at Gordonsville, from where he could support the main Confederate line or shuttle reinforcements to Richmond and to the Shenandoah Valley. Cavalry patrolled the countryside on each side of the rebel defenses. Particular attention was paid to the river east of the main Confederate works. Major General Fitzhugh Lee's Con-

---

30. John Bratton to wife, May 3, 1864, in John Bratton Collection, EU; Isaac Cooper to father, April 30, 1864, in FSMP; "Our Army Correspondence," *Daily South Carolinian,* May 11, 1864; Alexander, *Military Memoirs,* 553–54; Frank M. Mixson, *Reminiscences of a Private* (Columbia, S.C., 1910), 63; D. Augustus Dickert, *History of Kershaw's Brigade* (Newberry, S.C., 1899), 340–41.

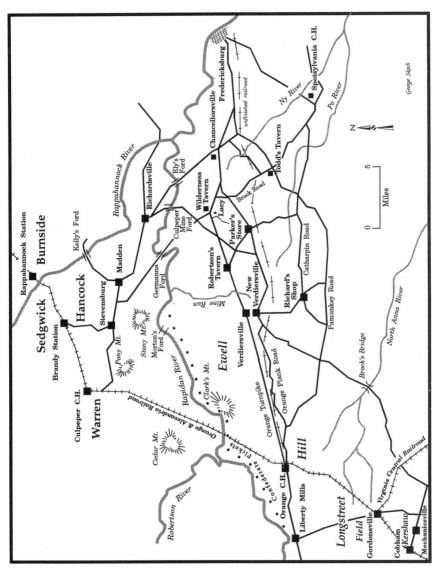

The Rapidan front on May 2

federate cavalry division kept careful watch from Mine Run to Fredericksburg.

The Army of Northern Virginia's usual optimism was tempered by a sense of foreboding. Henry Kyd Douglas, who had served with the army from the start, remarked that a grim, determined mood had replaced the jauntiness of former years. Another Confederate noticed "the conviction that the struggle ahead of us was of a different character from any we had experienced in the past— a sort of premonition of the definite mathematical calculation, in whose hard, unyielding grip it was intended our future should be held and crushed." Convinced that the army had never been in better form—Lee's adjutant, Lieutenant Colonel Walter H. Taylor, discerned a "calm, firm, and positive determination to be victorious, with God's help." Another southerner wrote of the men's "indomitable spirit," their "absolute confidence in General Lee, and their quiet, matter of course, certainty of victory, under him." He later conceded, "As for myself, the thought of being whipped never crossed my mind." [31]

"Great events may transpire in a few days," a North Carolina soldier wrote home. "Lee is in fighting trim." And an Alabama man informed his family: "The whole command is in fine health and excellent spirits and ready for the coming struggle confident of whipping Grant, and that badly. We all believe that this is the last year of the war." [32]

Confederates were disappointed by some of Grant's tactics. All winter they had reminisced about capturing wagons of Yankee sutlers, those independent food purveyors with the Union army who could always be counted on for delicacies. To their dismay, the rebels learned from northern papers that Grant had ordered sutlers to clear out before the campaign opened. "You would have been amused to hear our men's indignation," a Confederate officer wrote home. "They swore it was the meanest, cheapest trick that ever was done. They had looked with so many fond anticipations to plundering the

---

31. Douglas, *I Rode with Stonewall*, 263; Robert Stiles, *Four Years Under Marse Robert* (New York, 1903), 241; Walter H. Taylor, *General Lee*, 230–31; Samuel D. Buck, *With the Old Confeds: Actual Experiences of a Captain in the Line* (Baltimore, 1925), 102.

32. James Linebarger to family, May 3, 1864, in Anne Linebarger Papers, SHC; John L. Runzer to family, May 1, 1864, in Leigh Collection, USMHI.

sutler wagons, that Grant's order was regarded as cheating them of their just dues."[33]

On May 2, Lee ordered his corps and division commanders to Clark's Mountain, a high ridge that dominated the surrounding countryside and afforded a bird's-eye view of Meade's camps. Longstreet, back less than two weeks, was up from Gordonsville with his new division heads, Field and Kershaw. A bachelor again for over a week, Ewell trotted from nearby Morton Hall with Early, Johnson, and Rodes. Hill's division chiefs, Wilcox, Heth, and Anderson, along with their frail commander, were there as well. This was the last time these men would meet.

From the summit, Lee and his generals assessed Grant's possible moves. Six hundred feet below, a shimmering line marked where the Rapidan meandered in a gentle arc from left to right. Earthworks scarred the banks, and Union pickets clustered just across the river. Farther back, at Culpeper, Stevensburg, and Brandy Station, all plainly visible from the mountain, spread cities of huts and white conical tents housing the Army of the Potomac. A ribbon of steel, the Orange and Alexandria Railroad threaded into Culpeper from the distant horizon and then south across the Rapidan to the left of Clark's Mountain, where it rolled through Orange Court House and off toward Gordonsville and its junction with the Virginia Central Railroad.

Raising field glasses as so often during the winter, Lee studied Meade's camps. The bustle confirmed what he already knew. Meade was preparing to move. But what route would he take? It was unlikely that Meade would batter head-on against the rebel defenses. Slicing around Lee's left offered open country for maneuver but posed serious supply problems for the massive Union army. To Lee's right and east, the country was already familiar to Meade, and the invaders could bring in provisions from Fredericksburg and points along the coast as they advanced south. Logic favored a Federal strike downriver, and Lee said so, pointing east and stating that in his opinion the Army of the Potomac would cross at Germanna Ford or Ely's Ford.

33. James Conner to mother, April 3, 1864, in *Letters of General James Conner,* ed. Moffett, 122.

Lee directed his generals to prepare three days' rations and make ready to march. They were not to start, however, until they received word from him. "Notwithstanding the demonstrations made against our front and left at the opening of the campaign of 1864," Lee later confided, "I believed that General Grant would cross the Rapidan on our right, and resolved to attack him whenever he presented himself."[34]

Despite Lee's prophetic language on Clark's Mountain, he felt uncomfortable acting on his estimate of Meade's plans. A Confederate misstep would pose dire consequences. Although Lee considered a downriver route Meade's most likely move, it was also possible that the enemy contemplated striking around his left, or around both his flanks at once, or even hurling some forces directly across the river to pin him in place while maneuvering the remainder around one side of his line or the other.

Forced to relinquish the first move to the Federals, Lee struggled with how best to seize the advantage once the Union army began to march. First, there was the troublesome question of where to place Longstreet's hard-hitting 1st Corps. The War Horse's two divisions were stationed near Gordonsville on the Orange and Alexandria Railroad. Lee saw no choice but to leave them in their camps. For one thing, if a secondary Federal attack up the James River materialized, the 1st Corps might be called upon to make a beeline for the Confederate capital. Immediate access to the railroad was imperative.

Unfortunately, Gordonsville was poorly situated for defending the Rapidan line. The 1st Corps could quickly reach the left end of the Confederate defenses, over by Liberty Mills. But getting to the Confederate right flank, in the direction of Mine Run, would require a full day's march, if not longer. If Meade came the way Lee expected—across the Rapidan at Germanna Ford and Ely's Ford—Longstreet would be unavailable to help forestall the Union advance. The problem did not admit of an easy solution. Shifting Longstreet more to the right would only serve to remove him from the railroad and diminish his ability to protect Richmond.

---

34. Richard S. Ewell's Report, in *OR*, XXXVI, Pt. 1, p. 1070; Jedediah Hotchkiss, "Virginia," in *Confederate Military History*, ed. Clement Evans (Atlanta, 1899), 431–32; Robert E. Lee to William Smith, July 17, 1868, copy in FSMP.

Weighing the possible competing uses of Longstreet's troops—to rush to the aid of Richmond or to shore up the Rapidan line, whichever turned out to be more important—Lee came down in favor of preserving the 1st Corps' rail link with the capital. Kershaw's division was ordered to remain bivouacked at Mechanicsville, below Gordonsville, and Field's division was shifted a few miles above Gordonsville out the road toward Liberty Mills.[35]

Reconciled to countering Meade in the short run with only Ewell's and Hill's corps, the southern commander was doubtless confident that he could hold the existing fortifications along the river. The problem was that Ewell's and Hill's soldiers were doing their job almost too well. The Rapidan earthworks were so strong that Meade was bound to try to sweep around them, in the process interposing his troops between Lee and Richmond. Extending the existing Confederate line to cover all the Rapidan fords was manifestly impossible. There were simply too few gray-clad troops to do that effectively.

Yielding to the reality of the situation, Lee made the difficult decision against trying to fortify all possible river crossings. Instead, he chose to saturate the country beyond each end of his earthworks with cavalry. That mounted trip wire was charged with sounding the alarm as soon as the Federals started their advance. At the first hint of a hostile move, Lee hoped to concentrate his army rapidly in the direction of the enemy. The objective was to catch them crossing the river, or shortly afterward.

On the face of it, Lee's plan had an appealing logic. The possibilities became even more exciting upon a close look at the map. A few miles below the Rapidan fords on Lee's right sprawled a densely wooded tract known as the Wilderness of Spotsylvania. From the rebel perspective, the Wilderness offered an ideal battlefield. Meade's imposing artillery and cavalry would be hobbled, and the Federals would have difficulty bringing their numbers to bear. Accosting Meade in the Wilderness made eminent sense as a southern objective.

For Lee to snag Meade in the toils of the Wilderness, he would have to take steps to retard the Union advance. Otherwise, the Federals might march through the Wilderness before Lee had sufficient

35. Bratton to wife, May 3, 1864, in Bratton Collection, EU; James Longstreet to Charles S. Venable, May 1, 1864, in OR, Vol. XXXVI, Pt. 2, p. 940.

opportunity to maneuver into place. Even Ewell's corps, which held the downriver portion of the Rapidan defensive line, would need nearly a day to swing across the roads radiating from the fords. And if the Confederates failed to win the race against Meade, the consequence would be catastrophic. A massive Union host would stand between the Army of Northern Virginia and the capital it was charged to defend.

Lee had earlier described the first precept of his military philosophy: to do "everything in my power to make my plan as perfect as possible, and to bring the troops upon the field of battle." The Wilderness was clearly the Confederates' most advantageous field of battle. To better the chances of fighting there, one possibility was to fortify Germanna Ford and Ely's Ford. A few well-placed brigades at the crossings might buy the Army of Northern Virginia time to move across Meade's path. A second option involved edging substantial contingents from Ewell, Hill, and perhaps even Longstreet toward the Wilderness. With their marching time reduced, these units would be able to ambush the enemy in the woodland and hold them there until the rest of the Confederate army came up. As Alexander later put it, "In view of the great probabilities that Grant would move upon our right flank very early in May, it does not seem that there would have been any serious difficulty in having both Hill and Ewell out of their winter camps and extended a few miles in that direction and Longstreet's corps even as far down as Todd's Tavern [below the Wilderness]."[36]

The impossibility of removing Longstreet from the rail line prevented Lee from advancing the entire 1st Corps, but there was no compelling reason against sidling substantial elements from Longstreet, Ewell, and Hill toward the Wilderness. Doing so would sharply increase the odds of pinning Grant in the thickets with little weakening of the Confederate defensive works.

Inexplicably, Lee neglected to take any steps calculated to influence Meade's advance or to ensure that the Confederates would reach the Wilderness ahead of him. Fitzhugh Lee's cavalry patrols

---

36. Gallagher, ed., *Fighting for the Confederacy*, 349. A South Carolina soldier also expressed puzzlement over the encampment at Mechanicsville: "I cannot see whence it derives its name. I have seen no machinery about here, in fact nothing of the kind except an old blacksmith shop and that is in pretty dilapidated state" (David Crawford to mother, May 3, 1864, in Book 162, FSMP).

were instructed to sound the alarm on Meade's approach, but they were not expected to offer any serious obstacle to the Union army's progress. No attempt was made to fortify the Rapidan crossings or to hold rebel infantry in readiness to offer resistance. And not a single Confederate unit was ordered toward the Wilderness to get a jump on the northerners.

Leaving the pace of the Federal movement to chance, Lee chose to rely solely on his second precept: "The rest must be done by my generals and their troops, trusting to Providence for the victory."

The gamble exposed the Army of Northern Virginia to fearsome risks. Lee's troops were dangerously outnumbered, and the capacity of his generals remained a matter of genuine concern. By failing to take steps to ensure that his army would meet the enemy on advantageous ground, Lee was courting disaster.

Having neglected to lay plans with his accustomed degree of care, Lee had nothing to fall back on but Providence, the final ingredient in the gray-haired general's formula for victory. Fortunately for the rebels, Providence had not abandoned them. At that very moment, its hand could be seen in decisions being made across the Rapidan by the Union top command.

"Probably no army on earth ever before was in better condition in every respect."

A slender dyspeptic figure paced the Army of the Potomac's sprawling white headquarters tent near Brandy Station, six miles up the Orange and Alexandria Railroad from Culpeper Court House. Hook-nosed George Meade, blustery as a Yankee winter, ran his cold blue eyes over the order his chief of staff, Major General Andrew A. Humphreys, had drafted the day before, perhaps even as Lee and his generals had looked across from Clark's Mountain. The Yankees planned to strike in the way Lee had predicted, swooping downriver around the Confederate right flank and crossing at Germanna Ford and Ely's Ford.

Meade's three infantry corps and his cavalry were tightly tucked into the V of land between the Rappahannock and Rapidan rivers. Gouverneur Warren's 5th Corps was headquartered at Culpeper, with divisions above and below town. Six miles east, Major General Winfield S. Hancock's 2nd Corps blanketed Cole's Hill, a low, round elevation extending from Stevensburg north toward Brandy Station. Acting as Meade's rear, John Sedgwick's 6th Corps spread from Brandy Station back to the Rappahannock. Burnside's 9th Corps, recently arrived from Annapolis, was stationed along the Orange and Alexandria Railroad to Bull Run to protect Meade's vital rail link with the North. Operating independently of the Army of the Potomac, Burnside reported, as did Meade, to Grant.

North of the Rapidan, tin pots, bones, and shell fragments littered a wasteland of stumps and brambles. "Not a house nor a fence, not a tree was to be seen for miles, where once all had been cultivated farm-land, or richly wooded country," recalled one of Grant's aides. "Here and there, a stack of chimneys or a broken cistern marked the site of a former homestead, but every other landmark had been destroyed." So complete was the devastation that "a man could hardly recognize the haunts familiar to him from his childhood." Headstones hacked from boards and hastily scrawled with the names of dead soldiers were the only visible planting. "The houses that have not actually been burnt," an officer wrote home to Massachusetts, "usually look almost worse than those that have; so dreary are they without sashes, and their open doors, and their walls half stripped of boards." Another Federal pondered the formerly proud and prosperous region's wreckage. "I cannot help admiring the constancy of the 'Old Dominion,'" he mused, "in the midst of such suffering and desolation as has been totally unknown to any part of the country."[37]

It was time to move on, and the Yankees were glad of it. "Culpeper is as nasty a hole as I ever beheld," complained a Union veteran. It was the "usual specimen of tumble-down Virginia," thought another, "rather dilapidated and shabby." Most of the town's menfolk were dead, wounded, or across the Rapidan with Lee, and the remaining population of invalids, women, children, and decrepit old men survived on handouts from Meade's commissary. "They were all 'Secesh,'" concluded a Yankee soldier, using a popular term for diehard secessionists, "and the 'Bonnie Blue Flag' was sung with spirit

---

37. Theodore Lyman to family, November 15, 1863, in *Meade's Headquarters*, ed. Agassiz, 48; Adam Badeau, *Military History of Ulysses S. Grant from April, 1861, to April, 1865* (3 vols.; New York, 1881), II, 40–41; Allan Nevins, ed., *Diary of Battle: The Personal Journals of Colonel Charles S. Wainwright* (New York, 1962), 330.

by the lassies who had a hatred of all Yankeedom." Culpeper's women habitually dressed in mourning. "Not a smile was on their faces," remarked a Connecticut veteran, "but instead a scowl or frown met our gaze. Even the little boys and girls looked the same and as for the men they were saucy and ugly."[38]

The war had acquired a decidedly nasty edge as it rolled into its fourth year. The exuberance and sense of gamesmanship of earlier days had died, and chivalry had crumbled in the face of harsh realities. The harassment of civilians and the destruction of private property by Meade's occupying army provoked strong reactions in the Confederates. Ewell's normally even-tempered cartographer fervently prayed that "there might never be born another Yankee and that not one of the race be left on the face of the earth by the first day of June." Ill feelings abounded after a Federal officer was purportedly discovered with orders authorizing him to burn Richmond and assassinate President Davis. When Lee wrote Meade demanding an explanation, the Union commander in chief denied knowledge of the plot.[39]

Brandy Station was a whistle-stop with a handful of houses, a tavern that gave the settlement its name, and an unpainted single-story freight building. This was Meade's nerve center. In this land of scarcity, what the invading army required had to be brought down the Orange and Alexandria Railroad from massive Federal supply warehouses in Alexandria, just across the Potomac River from Washington. Mountains of forage and supplies, stacked three stories high and draped with tarpaulins, lined Brandy Station's sidings. Temporary shelters housed Meade's ordnance, hospital, and clothing departments. Mule-drawn wagons jammed neighboring roads day and night, dispensing goods to the scattered Union camps.

Meade's headquarters occupied a piny knoll near the station. The compound was surrounded by a wall of bushes. In its center, flanked by a telegraph office and chief of staff Humphreys' tent, were Meade's living quarters, an imposing canvas structure. Lesser staff tents clustered in a semicircle around the army commander's, and roughhewn

38. O. B. Curtis, *History of the Twenty-Fourth Michigan of the Iron Brigade* (Detroit, 1891), 217–18; Charles D. Page, *History of the Fourteenth Regiment, Connecticut,* 182; Culpeper Historical Society, *Historic Culpeper* (Culpeper, Va., 1974), 4–5.

39. Bean, *Stonewall's Man,* 155; George E. Pond, "Kilpatrick's and Dahlgren's Raid to Richmond," *B&L,* IV, 95–96.

plank walks tied the little city together. Here were the offices that breathed life into the army. Two infantry regiments stood guard over the compound, and a squadron of cavalry hovered in readiness to escort Meade and his staff on their rounds.[40]

The journalist Sylvanus Cadwallader pulled into Brandy Station on May 2 and awoke the following morning to what he later described as "probably the busiest period I witnessed during the war." Clerks scrambled as the country's largest and most extravagantly provisioned army made ready to move: "Cartridge boxes, haversacks and caissons were all filled, fires were burning day and night for many miles in all directions, troops and trains were taking their assigned positions, staff officers and orderlies were galloping in hot haste carrying orders, whilst the rumble of artillery wheels, the rattling and clanking of mule teams, the shouting, song, and laughter of thousands of men" merged in a deafening din. One soldier likened the frenzy to the docks of New York jammed with ships trying to unload at once. Locomotives chugged in, belching smoke and steam, disgorged supplies and new troops, then puffed back to Alexandria crammed with everything not essential for the march. Whips cracked and oaths flew as mule drivers impatiently jockeyed their teams by the tracks. "An army is as bad as a woman starting on a journey," was Colonel Charles S. Wainwright's explanation for the pandemonium, "so much to be done at the last moment."[41]

The bustle at Brandy Station was a consequence of Grant's decision to flank Lee, which required cutting loose from the railroad on the way around the Rapidan entrenchments. "Flying depots," probably at Fredericksburg and along the coast, were to parallel the army on its journey southward. But until the pace of Meade's advance was known and new supply lines could be established, his nearly hundred thousand men and over sixty thousand horses and mules—to be joined shortly by Burnside's twenty thousand men and their animals—had to survive on what they could carry. The challenge was to make this stupendous host self-sufficient until new supply routes were arranged, at the same time keeping it light on its feet for maneuvering against the agile Confederate army.

40. Alexander Gardner, *Gardner's Photographic Sketchbook of the Civil War* (2 vols.; Washington, D.C., 1866), II, Plate 60; Morris Schaff, *The Battle of the Wilderness* (Boston, 1910), 32–38.
41. Sylvanus Cadwallader, *Three Years with Grant* (New York, 1961), 171–74; Nevins, ed., *Diary of Battle*, 347.

Brigadier General Rufus Ingalls, Meade's quartermaster general and Grant's longtime friend, rose to the occasion. A "chunky, oracular-looking man," Ingalls was not only the "best quartermaster the war produced" but also one of the "best poker players in the army or Congress, and in those days there were some very good ones." Having handsomely provisioned Meade deep in enemy territory all ·winter, Ingalls could boast that no barefoot scarecrows scratched the hard earth for sprouts to ward off starvation on his side of the Rapidan. "Probably no army on earth ever before," Ingalls asserted that spring, "was in better condition in every respect than was the Army of the Potomac." The men agreed. "We now get excellent rations, soft bread, beans, beef, pork, dried apples, coffee, sugar, tea, soap, vinegar, molasses, and potatoes," a northerner noted in his diary. "The soldiers of the Potomac cannot complain of not having good food." [42]

For the foray south, each Federal soldier was given fifty rounds of ammunition, full rations for three days, and partial rations for three more. A supply train of 4,300 wagons, resplendent with embossed scarlet insignia identifying their corps affiliations, hauled an additional ten days' worth of food, forage, and ammunition. Completing Ingalls' grand procession were 835 ambulances and a herd of cattle for slaughter as needed. Lined up end to end, estimated Cadwallader, Meade's supply train would reach from the Rapidan to below Richmond. [43]

Meade had also enlisted the latest technology against the rebels. During the winter, engineers collected old surveys and reports from cavalry reconnaissances, spies, and deserters. The information was incorporated into maps scaled one inch to the mile and printed in bulk. The maps were notoriously unreliable and left more than one bewildered officer "trying to understand the incomprehensible." According to a Federal aide, their "wretched, spongy paper" wore out after a few days in the pocket. To remedy these shortcomings, a squad of engineers was assigned to accompany Meade's front units to gauge distances by paces, horses' gaits, and angles. Findings were

42. Rufus Ingalls' Report, in OR, Vol. XXXVI, Pt. 1, pp. 276–78; Schaff, *The Battle of the Wilderness*, 45; Luther C. Furst Diary, April 17, 1864, in Civil War Miscellaneous Collection, USMHI.

43. Rufus Ingalls to Montgomery C. Meigs, May 3, 1864, in OR, Vol. XXXVI, Pt. 2, pp. 353–54; George G. Meade to Ulysses S. Grant, April 17, 1864, *ibid.*, XXXIII, 889–90; "Inclosure," *ibid.*, 853–55; Cadwallader, *Three Years with Grant*, 175.

to be consolidated on master drawings, photographed, and distributed routinely to Meade's generals. Federal engineers also stockpiled wheeled pontoons to bridge Virginia's rivers and tools for digging roads and trenches. Since signal flags were useless in the relatively flat wooded country below the Rapidan, Meade was to communicate with his generals by telegraph wires temporarily strung from trees and makeshift poles.[44]

The Army of the Potomac's consolidated morning report for April 30, 1864, listed 99,438 soldiers "present for duty equipped," including 73,390 infantry, 12,444 cavalry, 10,230 artillery, and an assortment of engineers and provost guards. The 9th Corps' returns showed 19,331 men ready for battle. All told, Grant was preparing to move against Lee's 65,000 veterans with a combined force of nearly 120,000 combatants.[45]

Raw numbers, however, did not tell the whole story. Compared with the South, the North's manpower pool was nearly inexhaustible, but trained veterans were a precious commodity. Unlike the rebels, Meade's men were soldiers not for the war's duration but for three years only, and many of them had volunteered in 1861. As the spring of 1864 began, Meade faced the prospect of setting out against Lee with an army that was disintegrating from under him. The replacement conscripts by and large had little aptitude or desire for soldiering. Meade's army of volunteer veterans was losing not only its accumulated experience but also the noble motivation that had helped it survive adversity and make success a realistic prospect.

The important question was how deeply the Union army's shift in composition had weakened its fighting capacity. Some units were more affected than others. The 9th Corps' roll listed as "present equipped" over nineteen thousand men, for example, but of those only six thousand were seasoned troops. Excluding "worthless bounty jumpers and such trash," one commentator figured Meade had no more than sixty-five thousand veteran infantry, which taken with Burnside's "good soldiers" gave Grant something like seventy thousand dependable men to throw against Lee. Assigning green re-

44. Theodore Lyman, "Uselessness of the Maps Furnished to Staff of the Army of the Potomac Previous to the Campaign of May, 1864," in *PMHSM*, IV, 79–80; Benjamin Fisher's Report, in *OR*, Vol. XXXVI, Pt. 1, pp. 281–84; Nathaniel Michler's Report, in *OR*, Vol. XXXVI, Pt. 1, pp. 291–96.

45. Army of the Potomac's Report, April 30, 1864, in *OR*, XXXIII, 1036.

cruits—"pigeons for Lee's veterans to shoot at," one soldier later called them—to newly formed regiments rather than to experienced units magnified conscription's deleterious consequences. After factoring in some elusive but important variables—the spirit of Lee's army and the Confederate practice of placing new troops in experienced regiments, to name but a few—Grant's touted edge in numbers began to appear less imposing.[46]

But the Federals were optimistic. "Every soldier is in high spirits," a Yankee wrote home, "and I never saw such confidence in success manifested." Another remarked in his diary, "Troops are drilled almost every day; target practice, artillery practice, and are better disciplined now than they ever were. We have a fine army. I think the best war marshalled." Wainwright, writing his family on the campaign's eve, thought that although probably a third of the troops were inexperienced, "the army was never in better condition, take it altogether." It contained "quite as many [men] as Grant and Meade together can take care of, and properly used ought to be sure to use up Lee."[47]

Using up Lee, however, was going to take a lot more than simple numbers. The Virginian was accustomed to fighting at a disadvantage. Maneuver was his strong point, a card he had ruthlessly exploited over the previous three years. The eastern theater had been a disaster for the North. Richmond remained unconquered, and the rival armies occupied lines that spring not that very different from where they had stood when the war began.

Meade had brought a glimmer of hope by securing at Gettysburg the Union's first real victory in the east. But the administration's brief honeymoon with Meade had been spoiled by the general's cautious

46. Report of Provost Marshal General's Bureau, in OR, Series III, Vol. V, pp. 599–687; Martin McMahon, "From Gettysburg to the Coming of Grant," in B&L, IV, 91–93; Report of the Medical Director, in OR, Vol. XXXVI, Pt. 1, p. 213; Frank Wilkeson, Recollections of a Private Soldier in the Army of the Potomac (New York, 1887), 30–32.

47. Robert G. Carter, Four Brothers in Blue; or, Sunshine and Shadows of War of the Rebellion: A Story of the Great Civil War from Bull Run to Appomattox (Washington, D.C., 1913), 390; Furst Diary, April 18, 1864, in Civil War Miscellaneous Collection, USMHI; Nevins, ed., Diary of Battle, 345.

pursuit of the rebels and Lee's success in maneuvering him to stalemate in central Virginia. Lee's was a "deep game," Meade wrote his wife, "and I am free to admit that in the playing of it he has got the advantage of me."[48]

Emboldened by reports confirming his two-to-one edge over the Army of Northern Virginia, Meade in November, 1863, decided to surprise Lee with a maneuver taken from the crafty rebel's own book. The result was the Mine Run campaign, which was profoundly to influence Federal plans for the 1864 spring offensive.

Meade's strategy was simple. Rather than bucking against the Confederate entrenchments, he planned to cross the Rapidan a few miles downriver and roll up Lee's unprotected right flank. Union delays, however, afforded Lee time to swing around and take up a near-impregnable position behind Mine Run. Retreat being the only sound choice, Meade withdrew to winter quarters around Culpeper.

Washington's reaction was predictable. "Meade is on the back track again, without a fight," fumed Stanton, the secretary of war. Talk of Meade's removal spread, and the criticism stung him. Barely a week after returning, Meade wrote to his friend Winfield Hancock, who was prominently mentioned as his possible successor. "As this army is at present organized, and as its commander is now regarded and treated at Washington," Meade confided, "its command is not to be desired by any reasonable man, nor can it be exercised with any justice or satisfaction to yourself. While, therefore, I should be glad to see you promoted to a high command, as a friend and well-wisher, with my experience I cannot say I could congratulate you if you succeed me."[49]

Union soldiers viewed Meade's performance at Mine Run far differently from the way Meade's superiors did. The soldiers' lives, after all, had been on the line, and they applauded the general's "extraordinary moral courage," as Meade's aide Lieutenant Colonel Theodore Lyman termed it, in canceling a futile assault. "The men and guns stood ready," Lyman wrote home in explaining the magnitude of Meade's decision. "He had only to snap his fingers, and that night

48. George Meade, ed., *The Life and Letters of George Gordon Meade, Major General, United States Army* (2 vols.; New York, 1913), II, 154.
49. Edwin Stanton to Benjamin Butler, December 2, 1863, in *OR,* Vol. XXIX, Pt. 2, p. 537; Almira R. Hancock, *Reminiscences of Winfield Scott Hancock* (New York, 1887), 292.

would probably have seen ten thousand wretched, mangled creatures, lying on those long slopes, exposed to the bitter cold, and out of reach of all help!" Meade put it more bluntly. "I cannot be a party to the wanton slaughter of my troops," he asserted in his report, "for a mere personal end." He was referring, of course, to his political fortunes in Washington.[50]

Looking at the previous year from Meade's perspective, he had thwarted Lee at Gettysburg and checked him during the quick-footed maneuvers that followed. The Mine Run campaign had been brilliantly conceived, almost catching the old Confederate off guard. Meade had come closer than any of his predecessors to matching Lee at his own game. But viewed from the administration's perspective, Meade had been a disappointment. His primary objective, Lee's army, remained intact. And he had also stumbled in his secondary assignment, which was to keep Lee too busy to reinforce the western theater. Gettysburg, which was the cornerstone of Meade's reputation, had come to seem a hollow victory.

While debates raged over Meade's capacity to command the Army of the Potomac, there was well-founded optimism about his subordinates, who had been announced after a long-overdue reorganization. A highly placed officer explained that Meade "believed that he could find three first-class commanders for the army assembled around Brandy Station; he did not feel sure of a fourth, much less of a fifth." The War Department acted upon Meade's judgment, abolishing two corps and expanding the remaining three.[51]

Some questioned the wisdom of enlarging the corps, arguing that they would prove unwieldy. But none contested Meade's choice of generals. The 2nd Corps continued under Winfield Hancock; the 6th Corps retained its old general, John Sedgwick; and the 5th Corps received a new head, Gouverneur K. Warren. A more promising set of commanders had never before assembled under the Union flag.

50. Theodore Lyman to family, November 30, 1863, in *Meade's Headquarters*, ed. Agassiz, 57–58; Nevins, ed., *Diary of Battle*, 308–309.
51. Francis A. Walker, *General Hancock* (New York, 1895), 152–54; Charles Porter, "Opening of the Campaign of 1864," in *PMHSM*, IV, 6.

Hancock's 2nd Corps was the army's elite fighting unit, and Hancock the Superb, as the handsome, striking general had been tagged, was Meade's premier commander. "He was a splendid fellow," concluded Assistant War Secretary Charles Dana after watching Hancock in action, "a brilliant man, as brave as Julius Caesar, and always ready to obey orders, especially if they were fighting orders. He had more of the aggressive spirit than almost anybody else in the army." Hancock's "massive features and heavy folds round the eye" confirmed even to the critical Lyman that the general was a "man of ability." Having starred in the eastern army's major battles and been largely responsible for the few bright spots in its dismal past, Hancock figured prominently when talk turned, as frequently happened during the winter's long months, to Meade's possible successor.[52]

Hancock's was Meade's largest corps, as a consequence of its commander's recognized ability, and three of Hancock's four division commanders—Brigadier Generals Francis C. Barlow and John Gibbon and Major General David B. Birney—were unquestionably among the army's best. Brigadier General Gershom Mott, who had been elevated to division command against Meade's advice, was an uncertain quantity, but the strong trio of Barlow, Gibbon, and Birney was fully expected to compensate for his deficiencies.

The 6th Corps was also in steady and experienced hands. Sedgwick, an affable, scrubby-bearded bachelor obsessed with solitaire, had commanded the corps for over a year. He was methodical and resolute. His life was the army, and his scrupulous attention to his soldiers' needs had earned him the nickname Uncle John. He had served during Meade's absences as the army's temporary head.[53]

Two of Sedgwick's three division heads were of proven quality. Brigadier General Horatio G. Wright had served under Sedgwick since Chancellorsville, and Brigadier General George W. Getty, who had recently resigned as inspector general, was Sedgwick's longtime friend and a soldier of impeccable reputation. Sedgwick's wild card at the division level was Brigadier General James B. Ricketts, who had been away from field service since Antietam. Brigadier General

52. Charles A. Dana, *Recollections of the Civil War* (New York, 1899), 190; Theodore Lyman to family, April 13, 1864, in *Meade's Headquarters*, ed. Agassiz, 82.

53. Schaff, *The Battle of the Wilderness*, 43; Richard Elliott Winslow III, *General John Sedgwick: The Story of a Union Corps Commander* (Novato, Calif., 1982), 144–45.

Truman Seymour's unreliable brigade made up half of Ricketts' division. Nicknamed "Milroy's weary boys," the brigade was still smarting from two demoralizing defeats at the hands of Stonewall Jackson and Ewell and was going to have to be closely watched.

At the reconstituted 5th Corps' helm was Warren, Meade's only new corps commander. He was an odd duck. Something about this intense, scholarly man rubbed people the wrong way. He could be rude and curt, critical to a fault, and often insensitive and boorish, particularly when reciting limericks to his own laughter, oblivious to vacant looks around him. Warren's eyes—two tiny, piercing, jet black coals, one slightly smaller than the other—were the general's prominent feature and put his artillery chief in mind of an Indian. With a weak chin, sallow face, and straight hair plastered across his forehead, Warren appeared more at home behind drafting desks and lecterns than on battlefields. A tunic buttoned askew and pants riding up too short completed the image of an absent-minded professor.

But Warren's unlikely aspect concealed an impressive military mind. Second in his West Point class, Warren had taught mathematics at the academy and after an enviable combat record had found his natural niche as the Army of the Potomac's chief engineer. He had a sharp eye for terrain. His maps were models of clarity, and it was Warren who fathomed Little Round Top's importance at Gettysburg, saving the day for Meade. He had won accolades for his stinging repulse of Hill at Bristoe Station and for his courage in declining to assault Lee's Mine Run works. Warren's faults, which so far had attracted little notice, included a penchant for nitpicking and a tendency to meddle in military matters that were none of his legitimate concern.[54]

Like Meade's other corps commanders, Warren was backed by strong division heads. Three of his subordinates—Brigadier Generals Charles Griffin, John C. Robinson, and Samuel W. Crawford—were hard-nosed professionals, experienced in combat. His fourth, Brigadier General James S. Wadsworth, was at fifty-nine the army's oldest

54. Theodore Lyman to family, October 1, 1863, in *Meade's Headquarters*, ed. Agassiz, 26–27; Schaff, *The Battle of the Wilderness*, 29–31; Nevins, ed., *Diary of Battle*, 338–39. The only published biography on Warren, Emerson Taylor's *Gouverneur Kemble Warren: Life and Letters of an American Soldier* (New York, 1932), is disappointingly shallow. Better is Vincent Flanagan's "The Life of General Gouverneur Kemble Warren" (Ph.D. dissertation, City University of New York, 1969).

division chief and also its wealthiest. Wadsworth had taken time off earlier in the war to wage an unsuccessful campaign for the governorship of New York. He lacked formal military training and insisted on serving without pay. Because of his advanced years and his personal sacrifice, Wadsworth was one of the army's heroes.

The Union army's most profound change this spring involved its cavalry. During 1861 and 1862, Jeb Stuart's rebel troopers had dominated the Federal mounted arm. But the painful lessons in cavalry tactics taught by Stuart were being absorbed. By mid-1863, the Yankees began successfully emulating his style. Hoping to instill even more aggressive spirit into Meade's horsemen, Grant placed an associate from the western theater, Major General Philip H. Sheridan, over the Army of the Potomac's cavalry. "Who this Sheridan was no one seemed to know, only that he came from the West," remarked a Maine cavalryman on inquiring about his new boss's background. Many Northern newspapers assumed that *Sheridan* was a misspelling of *Sherman,* a well-known name in the west.[55]

The cavalry reorganization affected two of Sheridan's three mounted divisions. Grant's former aide Brigadier General James H. Wilson, and Brigadier General Alfred T. A. Torbert, an infantry brigadier who, like Wilson, had never before led cavalry, were given divisions. Brigadier General David McM. Gregg, a holdover from earlier days, was the only experienced general remaining in the corps' top command.

Sheridan and his subordinates were shocked by the condition of the Union army's horseflesh. Stables were so disorganized that Wilson initiated his first inspection by arresting a colonel and threatening the rest with like treatment.[56]

As Sheridan saw it, Meade's practice of having cavalry actively patrol the Federal picket line was the reason for his horses' sorry condition. Meade insisted that the cavalry was "fit for little more than guard and picket duty," while Sheridan countered with the revolutionary notion that Federal riders should serve as an independent striking arm. The upstart cavalry head later recalled that the older

55. Edward P. Tobie, *History of the First Maine Cavalry* (Boston, 1887), 248.

56. James H. Wilson, *Under the Old Flag* (2 vols.; New York, 1912), I, 373–74. Torbert and Gregg reported similar conditions in their commands. See Frederick C. Newhall to Charles Kingsbury, Jr., April 17, 1864, in *OR*, XXXIII, 891–93; and Philip H. Sheridan to Seth Williams, April 19, 1864, in *OR*, XXXIII, 909.

man was "staggered" at his suggestion. Despite reservations, Meade acquiesced in Sheridan's idea. On April 20, he withdrew the jaded horsemen from picket duty and substituted instead small infantry detachments at the fords. Sheridan's men would have their much-needed rest.[57]

On balance, Meade's spring changes brought vigorous and dependable leadership to the Army of the Potomac. The Union infantry had been tightened into three corps and placed under experienced commanders. Excepting Hancock, Meade's generals lacked the flair of Longstreet, Ewell, and Hill, but by the same token they exhibited little of the strong-willed individualism that was proving the bane of Lee's high command. As a team, they held more promise than Lee's temperamental corps heads. Particularly refreshing was Sheridan's attempt to impart a sense of mission to Meade's cavalry.

Possibilities this spring were limited only by Meade's imagination. That, however, was precisely what concerned the nation's president, Abraham Lincoln. As the war's third year opened in Virginia, it was painfully clear that simply doing as well as Lee would not be enough. The result had been stalemate, and if 1864 brought more of the same, the war-weary North might lose its resolve. Victories, not textbook marches and drawn battles, were imperative. A new catalyst was needed, someone who played by different rules that capitalized on the Federal advantage in numbers, someone Lincoln could trust. Grant was the president's answer to the impasse in Virginia.

"That man will fight us
every day and every hour."

Grant had grown up on the western frontier. He was tight-lipped and impenetrable. Although he occasionally loosened up with friends, he never totally relaxed his guard, and attention flustered him. Meade, recording his impressions shortly after their first meeting in March, 1864, wrote that Grant was "not a striking man, is very reticent, has never mixed with the world, indeed is somewhat ill at ease in the

57. Philip H. Sheridan's Report, in *OR*, Vol. XXXVI, Pt. 1, p. 787; Sheridan to Williams, April 19, 1864, *ibid.*, XXXIII, 909; Philip H. Sheridan, *Personal Memoirs of P. H. Sheridan* (2 vols.; New York, 1888), I, 353.

presence of strangers; hence a first impression is never favorable."[58]

The Civil War had rescued Grant from a relentless cycle of misfortune, and he had quickly demonstrated a flair for winning battles. Eighteen sixty-three had been Grant's year. His capture of Vicksburg eclipsed Meade's incomplete victory at Gettysburg. Grant's encore was the dramatic rescue in November, 1863, of a Union army pinned in Chattanooga, which inspired his mentor, Congressman Elihu B. Washburne, to introduce a bill reviving the rank of lieutenant general. Grant was Lincoln's choice for the position.

Grant had a commonsense approach to fighting, laced with a bulldog's tenacity. "I can't spare this man," Lincoln once said of the general. "He fights." Concluding that *U. S. Grant* stood for Up the Spout Grant, Lee's men doubted whether the new Federal commander in chief's reputation would survive an encounter with warfare Virginia style. But Longstreet, Grant's friend at the United States Military Academy and best man at his wedding, had a keener appreciation of the stone-faced Yankee. It would be a serious mistake to underestimate Grant's determination, thought Longstreet, since the new commander had in full measure the dogged persistence lacking in Meade. "That man," Longstreet warned, "will fight us every day and every hour till the end of the war."[59]

In early March, 1864, Grant was summoned to Washington to receive his lieutenant general's commission. After an impromptu reception, Lincoln and Stanton met with him in a small drawing room. Informing Grant that his commission would be presented the next day, Lincoln gave him a copy of the appointment speech he proposed to make and asked the general to prepare appropriate words of acceptance. "First," stressed the president, "say something which shall prevent or obviate any jealousy of you from any of the other generals in the service; and second, something which shall put you on as good terms as possible with the Army of the Potomac."

The cabinet assembled the following afternoon. Accompanying Grant was his son, as well as Brigadier General John A. Rawlins, a kindred sole from Galena, Illinois, and the general's conscience and adviser. After a short speech, Lincoln presented Grant's commission,

58. Meade, *Life and Letters,* II, 191.
59. Conner to mother, April 3, 1864, in *Letters of General James Conner,* ed. Moffett, 122; Horace Porter, *Campaigning with Grant* (New York, 1897), 46–47.

and Grant haltingly read a brief address from nearly illegible notes penciled on a scrap of paper. He mentioned none of the topics suggested by the president the night before. Perhaps his omission was a nervous oversight. Perhaps, as Lincoln's secretary later surmised, "with his deep distrust of Washington politicians, he thought it wise to begin by disregarding all their suggestions." Most likely, it was Grant's way of telling the president that he planned to fight the war as he saw fit.[60]

When the two men had a chance to be alone, Lincoln explained the facts of life to his new commander. Although procrastination by his generals and political pressure had forced Lincoln to intervene in military affairs, he hoped those days were over, particularly now that he had "someone who would take the responsibility and act, and call on him for all the assistance needed; he would pledge himself to use all the powers of the Government in rendering such assistance." Lincoln did not want to know Grant's plans. Everyone "was trying to find out from him something about the contemplated movements," Grant later recalled Lincoln to have said, "and there was always a temptation to 'leak.'" Grant could not have hoped for more. He had secured the president's trust and his commitment not to interfere in the management of the war.[61]

On March 10, Grant caught a train to Brandy Station to chat with Meade. As usual, Meade was having a hard time of it, having spent March 4 and 5 before the Joint Congressional Committee on the Conduct of the War, defending his actions at Gettysburg. His enemies, he wrote his wife, were "conspiring to have me relieved," and Grant's elevation seemed the culmination of those plots. The likelihood of the two generals hitting it off seemed remote. The patrician Meade hobnobbed with worldly men the likes of Lyman; Grant's chief advisers were his brother-in-law and Rawlins, small-town midwesterners of undistinguished background. "I understand," Meade wrote home, "he is indoctrinated in the notion of the superiority of the Western armies, and that the failure of the Army of the Potomac to accomplish anything is due to their commander." Grant,

60. John G. Nicolay and John Hay, *Abraham Lincoln: A History* (10 vols.; New York, 1890), VIII, 340–42.

61. Ulysses S. Grant, *The Personal Memoirs of U.S. Grant* (2 vols.; New York, 1885), II, 473; Horace Porter, *Campaigning with Grant*, 26.

Meade thought, would certainly want to make a fresh try with his own people.[62]

Brass bands greeted the new commander in chief under a drenching downpour at Brandy Station. Foul weather ruled out reviewing the army, so Grant and Meade sat down for a heart-to-heart talk. At forty-eight, Meade was seven years older than his superior, whom he had met briefly during the Mexican War. Meade broached the topic that concerned him most, suggesting, as Grant later recalled, "that I might want an officer who had served with me in the west, mentioning Sherman especially, to take his place; if so, he begged me not to hesitate about making the change." So important was the work ahead, urged Meade, that "no one man should stand in the way of selecting the right men for all positions," and he selflessly promised to serve "to the best of his ability wherever placed." This humble speech, Grant wrote, "gave me a more favorable opinion of Meade than did his great victory at Gettysburg the July before." He assured Meade that he had "no thought of substituting anyone for him," least of all Sherman, who could not be spared from the west.[63]

Surprisingly adept in understanding the political intricacies of his new position, Grant had managed to win over the president and the Army of the Potomac's commander in just three days. Meade gushed to his wife that he was "very much pleased with General Grant," who showed "much more capacity and character than I had expected." But there was still one rub. Grant had changed his mind about remaining in the west and now thought he should make the Army of the Potomac his home. "It was plain that here was the point for the commanding general to be," Grant later wrote, to "resist the pressure that would be brought to bear" on the army's commander "to desist from his own plans and pursue others." Explaining to his wife that Grant planned to travel with the Army of the Potomac "to avoid Washington and its entourage," Meade grumbled that the "ignorant public" would attribute Grant's inevitable success to his "superior merit." Mrs. Meade would see "the Army of the Potomac putting laurels on the brow of another rather than your husband." Nonetheless, Meade promised to give Grant his "heartiest cooperation."[64]

---

62. George Meade, ed., *The Life and Letters*, II, 176.
63. Grant, *The Personal Memoirs*, II, 470; Horace Porter, *Campaigning with Grant*, 29.
64. George Meade, ed., *The Life and Letters*, II, 178, 182; Grant, *The Personal Memoirs*, II, 470.

Grant set up headquarters in a plain brick house near the railway station in Culpeper. Meade rode every day from Brandy Station to visit him. Sensitive to the embarrassment that the proximity was likely to cause Meade, Grant tried, he later explained, "to make General Meade's position as nearly as possible what it would have been had I been in Washington or any other place away from his command." Grant succeeded in allaying the prickly Meade's fears. "He appears very friendly," Meade wrote home, "and at once adopts all my suggestions." As May drew near, Meade happily informed his wife that "Grant has not given an order, nor in the slightest degree interfered with the administration of this army since he arrived, and I doubt if he knows much more about it now than he did before coming here." Meade was miffed, however, by biased press accounts favoring Grant, particularly stories declaring that Grant's headquarters at Culpeper were closer to the enemy than were Meade's Brandy Station tents. "Not content with puffing him," Meade pouted to his wife, "they must have a fling at me." [65]

Meade's staff was also favorably impressed. Lyman thought Grant had a "good deal of rough dignity" and was rather taciturn but quick and decided in his speech. "He habitually wears an expression as if he had determined to drive his head through a brick wall, and was about to do it," the staffer wrote home, closing with what was fast becoming the army's assessment of Grant: "I have much confidence in him." [66]

With Grant exercising a free hand in managing the war, the feuding between Meade and his superiors was finished. Most important, Meade could now confer immediately with Grant on close judgment calls. But though Grant hoped to treat Meade exactly as he treated his other commanders—setting broad objectives but staying away from the minutiae of command—it was hard to imagine him sitting idly by once the fighting started. Ostensibly joining the Army of the Potomac to protect it from political interference, Grant was acutely aware of Lincoln's concern about Meade's cautious streak. Although unstated, part of Grant's mission was to stiffen the eastern army with some of his western tenacity and daring, precisely the qualities Lincoln believed Meade lacked. In Grant and Meade there was a

65. Grant, *The Personal Memoirs*, II, 471; Meade, ed., *The Life and Letters*, II, 183, 185, 187.

66. Theodore Lyman to family, April 12, 1864, in *Meade's Headquarters*, ed. Agassiz, 81.

military marriage between men of disparate philosophies. The time would inevitably arrive when Meade's instincts counseled restraint while Grant's called for more aggressive fighting. The tension inherent in their relationship would necessarily be an important undercurrent in the impending campaign.

*"The first misfortune
of the campaign."*

Grant aimed, he later explained, at a "simultaneous movement all along the line," from one end of the Confederacy to the other, bringing the entire Federal strength to bear. While Union armies east of the Alleghenies were crushing Lee, those west of the mountains were to mete out similar treatment to Johnston, who was commanding the Confederate Army of Tennessee that Grant had already so roughly handled at Chattanooga. Convinced that the rebellion would collapse only when its military power was broken, Grant aimed "first, to use the greatest number of troops practicable against the armed force of the enemy," and second, "to hammer continuously against the armed force of the enemy and his resources, until by mere attrition, if in no other way, there should be nothing left to him" but surrender. "It was a cruel and hardhearted policy," a Confederate later complained, but the logic of Grant's approach was unimpeachable. "With no exchange of prisoners, and the South without any means of recruiting her shattered ranks, while the armies of the North were being constantly augmented from her ample resources both at home and abroad, it was only a matter of time as to who should succeed." [67]

A linchpin of Grant's strategy involved concentrating forces toward common objectives of the Union armies. "The armies in the East and West," Grant later explained, had "acted independently and without concert, like a balky team, no two ever pulling together." This permitted the enemy "to use to great advantage his interior lines of communication for transporting troops from east to west, rein-

---

67. Ulysses S. Grant's Report, in *OR*, Vol. XXXVI, Pt. 1, pp. 12–13; William Frierson Fulton II, *The War Reminiscences of William Frierson Fulton II* (Gaithersburg, Md., 1986), 98.

forcing the army most vigorously pressed, and to furlough large numbers, during seasons of inactivity on our part, to go to their homes and do the work of producing for the support of their armies." On occasion, even Union generals within each theater had pursued unrelated goals. "I determined to stop this," Grant wrote. If he had his way, the war's tempo was also going to accelerate dramatically. The old pattern, as Meade's aide Lyman described it, had been to "lie still and lie still, then up and maneuver and march hard; then a big battle; and then a lot more lie still." Grant promised to undertake "active and continuous operations of all the troops that could be brought into the field, regardless of season and weather." He would offer no quarter until the Confederacy collapsed, from sheer exhaustion if from nothing else.[68]

Lincoln's new general was emphatic about another point. No longer would he waste time trying to capture and occupy southern countryside, which only tied up Federal soldiers. Henceforth, Grant intended to "concentrate all the force possible against the Confederate armies in the field." For the most part, the South's queen cities were secondary goals, important only insofar as their capture helped undermine rebel armies dependent on them.

Grant intended to go at Lee from all sides. Assigned the primary role, the Army of the Potomac would be raised to maximum strength and hurled across the Rapidan. Simultaneously, Benjamin Butler's Army of the James was to advance up the James River's south bank toward Richmond. His job was to sever Lee's supply lines, threaten the Confederate capital, and perhaps combine with Meade, depending on how things fared on the Rapidan. The third attack would come by way of the Shenandoah Valley, where Major General Franz Sigel was slated to threaten Lee's left flank. Hemmed in and isolated from his supplies and reinforcements, Lee would finally be cornered and destroyed.[69]

Grant held Lincoln to his promise to furnish the men and supplies needed to do the job. Thousands of officers and soldiers on furlough were ordered back to their commands, and governors were

68. Grant's Report, in OR, Vol. XXXVI, Pt. 1, p. 12; Theodore Lyman to family, November 1, 1863, in Meade's Headquarters, ed. Agassiz, 41.

69. Grant's Report, in OR, Vol. XXXVI, Pt. 1, p. 14; Ulysses S. Grant to George G. Meade, April 9, 1864, ibid., XXXIII, 827-28.

notified to "strip their departments to the lowest number of men necessary." Meade, under instructions from Grant to reduce his army's possessions "to the very lowest possible standard," ordered excess baggage sent to Alexandria and gave sutlers and civilians ten days to leave. Vast supplies were collected at Alexandria for delivery down the railway once the fighting started, with a duplicate set for shipment down the Virginia coast and then inland on the rivers. Rations for one million feedings, forage for the army's animals, medical supplies for twelve thousand wounded men, and one hundred rounds for each soldier and each cannon were packed for transport.[70]

In mid-March, Burnside's 9th Corps was ordered to Annapolis. The purpose of the move was kept secret, but Grant planned to bring Burnside's forces up to strength and then to fuse them with Meade's army. Burnside's relationship with the Army of the Potomac, however, was touchy. He had once commanded the army and now outranked Meade. Placing Burnside under Meade would constitute a serious breach of military protocol and would inevitably cause friction. Grant's answer was to treat Burnside's corps as a separate army, free from Meade's control, and to coordinate the two forces himself. This awkward solution threatened to inject even more confusion into the already ill defined division of responsibilities between Meade and Grant.

As the weather cleared and the preparations neared completion, Grant scheduled the general advance for early May. On April 25—a delightful spring day freshened by an early morning shower that settled the dust—the 9th Corps swung through Washington. Congress recessed to see the show. An enthusiastic crowd lined the route, and Burnside and his staff joined Lincoln to review the troops as they rolled down Fourteenth Street past the Willard Hotel. It was a grand spectacle. A correspondent reported "banners flying, music swelling on the air, horses prancing, the steady, measured tramp of marching feet, the rolling of the drum, and the harsher music of thundering artillery." Brigadier General Edward Ferrero's black division cheered as it passed the president's reviewing stand. Decked out in Prussian hussar uniforms adorned with buttons, braid, and gold lace, a new cavalry regiment sported "gay short cloaks of orange and blue fluttering in the wind." A company of Delaware Indians was especially

---

70. General Order No. 17, in OR, XXXIII, 816–17.

popular with the onlookers. After dazzling Washington, Burnside's troops disappeared southward across Long Bridge to Alexandria, then followed the Orange and Alexandria Railroad into Virginia. By May 1, the 9th Corps was camped along the tracks between Bull Run and the Rappahannock River.[71]

The day after Burnside left Annapolis, Grant notified Sigel that on May 2 he was to begin his advance into the Shenandoah Valley. A few days later, Butler received his instructions. "If no unforeseen accident prevents," Grant told the Massachusetts general, "I will move from here on Wednesday, the 4th of May. Start your forces on the night of the 4th, so as to be as far up the James River as you can get by daylight the morning of the 5th, and push from that time with all your might for the accomplishment of the object before you."[72]

Grant had saved an important decision for last. Lee was his objective, but it was not immediately apparent how best to get at the Confederate. One school of thought favored advancing against Richmond from the east. Such thinking, however, no longer fit Grant's primary objective. As Grant now perceived it, Richmond was a bad place to fight. The rebels would have the advantage of well-prepared earthworks and would be near supplies and reinforcements. Moreover, shifting Meade to the James River would give the Confederates freedom to maneuver. All things considered, Grant decided that the Rapidan was the best place to wage his war of attrition.

Everyone agreed that a frontal assault would be madness, particularly after the Morton's Ford debacle in February had alerted Lee to his weak points. The previous fall, Lincoln had cautioned Meade against battling Lee "slowly back into his entrenchments at Richmond" and trying to capture him there. "If our army cannot fall upon the enemy and hurt him where he is," the president had emphasized, "it is plain to me it can gain nothing by attempting to fol-

71. Grant, *The Personal Memoirs*, II, 477; Ulysses S. Grant to Ambrose E. Burnside, April 23, 1864, in *OR*, XXXIII, 955; Noah Brooks, *Mr. Lincoln's Washington* (New York, 1896), 313–14; Massachusetts Historical Society, *War Diary and Letters of Stephen Minot Weld* (Boston, 1979), 280, 283.

72. Ulysses S. Grant to Franz Sigel, April 24, 1864, in *OR*, XXXIII, 964; Ulysses S. Grant to Benjamin F. Butler, April 28, 1864, *ibid.*, 1009.

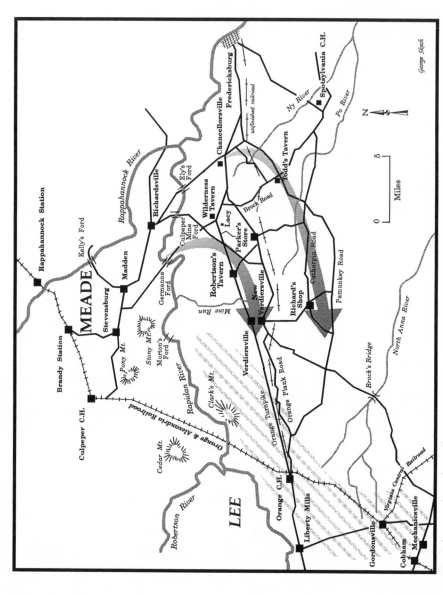

Humphreys' plan of attack

low him over a succession of intrenched lines into a fortified city." The advice was still sound.[73]

Maneuvering Lee from behind his earthworks onto open ground where Grant's impressive edge in infantry, cavalry, and artillery would make a difference seemed the best tack. "The only point upon which I am now in doubt," Grant informed Meade, "is whether it will be better to cross the Rapidan above or below him."[74]

By crossing upriver of Lee, Meade would shield the Union capital against rebel raids. In addition, the country was predominantly farmland and well suited for maneuvering. But there were drawbacks to an upriver campaign. Not only would Lee lie between Meade and Butler, but Meade would be dangerously dependent upon the Orange and Alexandria Railroad for supplies, forcing him to detail troops to capture, guard, and repair the rail line as he advanced. If he failed to seize the railroad below the Rapidan, the campaign would collapse. And as Meade's chief of staff, Humphreys, pointed out, the Federals would have to march forty miles fully exposed to view. A low set of hills called Southwest Mountain ran along the rail line. Under the skillful shovels of Lee's men, the range would quickly become a formidable barrier.

Swinging around the Confederate downriver flank avoided those difficulties but incurred others. On the positive side, Meade would remain in communication with Butler and could be readily supplied by shipments up the navigable rivers from Chesapeake Bay. The chief problem involved the terrain. Once across the Rapidan, the Yankees would become enmeshed in the Wilderness, a broad stretch of impenetrable thickets and dense second growth that had replaced forests cut down to fuel local iron and gold furnaces. The Wilderness was familiar to Meade's veterans and held no fond memories for them. Nearly a year before, Stonewall Jackson's men had torn through the underbrush and rolled up the Federal army at Chancellorsville. Moreover, the tangled vegetation nullified the very advantages that Grant sought to exploit. The place had few negotiable roads, clearings were scarce, and visibility rarely exceeded a few hundred feet. The cavalry was next to useless, cannoneers had no

73. Abraham Lincoln to Henry W. Halleck, September 19, 1863, in OR, Vol. XXIX, Pt. 2, pp. 207–208.
74. Grant to Meade, April 9, 1864, in OR, XXXIII, 828.

fields of fire, and complex infantry maneuvers were impossible. "The region beyond was bad enough, like most of Virginia," wrote one of Hancock's aides. "This, viewed as a battle-ground, was simply infernal."[75]

Once beyond the Wilderness, however, the Army of the Potomac would enter open country suitable for fighting. The key to maneuvering past Lee's downriver flank was getting through the Wilderness as quickly as possible.

Meade's experience in the Mine Run campaign in November was viewed as providing guidance. On that occasion, Lee had learned of Meade's advance at daybreak but still had required nearly thirty hours to reach the Mine Run line. Because this spring the armies were camped in roughly the same positions they had occupied before the Mine Run campaign, Meade assumed that he would have ample time to clear the Wilderness provided he kept moving—and also provided, of course, that Lee took as long as he did the previous November. The latter assumption was critical, but the Federal high command apparently felt comfortable in making it.[76]

Grant picked the downriver route through the Wilderness. What decided the matter for him was the importance of supplying Meade's army. The Army of the Potomac could carry only a "limited quantity," Grant later wrote, which he feared might be insufficient for completing a maneuver around Lee's left. The massive job of arranging the advance was left to Humphreys, Meade's humorless chief of staff. Everyone agreed that this bowlegged, profane little man was a military genius. He was also a loyal supporter of Meade. "Grant will reap all the glory, all the reputation of success," he predicted, "and share none of the obloquy of disaster if such should befall us."[77]

75. *Ibid.*; Andrew A. Humphreys, *The Virginia Campaign of '64 and '65* (New York, 1883), 9–12; Francis A. Walker, *General Hancock,* 160. Details concerning Grant's reasoning are also found in Grant's *The Personal Memoirs,* II, 477–79; Badeau's *Military History,* II, 93–99; William Swinton's *Campaigns of the Army of the Potomac* (New York, 1866), 402–14; and James H. Wilson's *A Life of John A. Rawlins* (New York, 1916), 204–10.

76. Andrew A. Humphreys, *The Virginia Campaign,* 11.

77. Grant, *The Personal Memoirs,* II, 483; Theodore Lyman to family, February 22, 1864, in *Meade's Headquarters,* ed. Agassiz, 73; Dana, *Recollections of the Civil War,* 192; Henry H. Humphreys, *Andrew Atkinson Humphreys: A Biography* (Philadelphia, 1924), 219. Meade reportedly later told a friend, "I wanted to move by the right flank, while General Grant wished to move by the left." According to the story, Grant replied, "General Meade, I wish you to

In selecting the army's route, Humphreys had to anticipate a multitude of contingencies. Once the Federals began sidling downriver around Lee, it was fairly certain that the Confederates would be forced to quit the Rapidan. It was impossible, however, to predict what they would do next. The more obvious responses open to Lee included ignoring Meade and dashing toward Washington along either the Orange and Alexandria Railroad or the Shenandoah Valley; withdrawing behind another fortified line farther south, thereby keeping the Army of Northern Virginia between the Yankees and Richmond; or facing east and engaging Meade. Humphreys had to guard against all three possibilities.

As for Lee's first option, it was not like the Virginian to raid north without first administering a hiding to the Federals. In any event, a Confederate attack on Washington would leave Richmond unprotected, a risk hardly worth the long shot of capturing the Union capital—trading queens, in popular military parlance. And even if Lee were desperate enough to try the gambit, he would have to plow through Burnside's 9th Corps and overcome Washington's formidable circle of forts, easily allowing time for Grant to overtake and destroy him.

It was more likely that Lee would either retreat or try to bring on a fight as the blue throngs began to cross around his defensive line. Retreat for Lee would probably mean withdrawing twenty-five miles to the south behind the next strongest position, the North Anna River. Battle would probably involve the Army of Northern Virginia's occupation of its old Mine Run works.

Humphreys naturally wanted to avoid the impasse of the previous November. Accordingly, he aimed to slip the Army of the Potomac along Lee's right flank to turn the Confederates out of their Rapidan defenses, then scoop the Union forces below Mine Run to force the Confederates from behind that line as well. If the army executed Humphreys' plan properly—a rapid drive to the south and then a turn to the west—it should flush Lee into open country, ensuring Grant the fight he was seeking.

Speed, of course, was crucial. Lee had to be given neither an op-

---

understand that this army is not to maneuver for position." (Henry Carey Baird Papers, in E. C. Gardiner Collection, HSP).

portunity to escape nor a chance to fortify a new defensive position. The Army of the Potomac would do best by fording the Rapidan as near as possible to Lee's downriver flank. Two major crossings—Germanna Ford and Ely's Ford—were suitable. Meade's engineers were acquainted with Germanna Ford from November's Mine Run maneuvers, and Ely's Ford had served as the main Federal bridgehead during the Chancellorsville campaign. The crossings had manageable banks and could be readily spanned with temporary bridges laid across pontoons.

In order to catch Lee napping, Humphreys decided to cross the Federal force in two columns at the two fords. Close to five miles below the Rapidan, Humphreys' prospective routes struck a major east-west thoroughfare called the Orange Turnpike. The road would serve as the army's convenient rallying point. The route from Germanna intersected the turnpike at a weedy clearing dominated by Wilderness Tavern, a ramshackle two-story stagehouse of stones and hewn logs. The road from Ely's Ford emerged at Chancellorsville, the ill-fated site of the Federal headquarters the year before. Wilderness Tavern and Chancellorsville were about five miles apart, but the two wings could readily communicate along the turnpike.

From the Orange Turnpike, Meade would have ready access to several routes pointing like extended fingers toward Lee's position to the west. Northernmost and nearest the Rapidan was the turnpike itself; below the turnpike and parallel to it was Orange Plank Road; and farther south, brushing the Wilderness' lower fringe, were the Catharpin and Pamunkey roads. The latter pair of routes passed below Lee's Mine Run defenses and then hooked north behind the Confederate works. They were exactly the convenient paths for circumventing Lee's earthworks and bringing the rebels to battle on open ground that Humphreys required.

As an alternative, Meade's studious chief of staff considered dropping the Federal army farther south to Spotsylvania Court House. For either the Catharpin-Pamunkey corridor or the Spotsylvania route, the ground to be covered was identical for the first day's march and for part of the second day's. And either was, in Humphreys' words, "subject to material modification or entire abandonment, dependent on the movements of Lee."[78]

78. Andrew A. Humphreys, *The Virginia Campaign*, 12.

After reasoning through the tactical problems posed by the Wilderness and its narrow brush-choked roads, Humphreys settled on crossing Meade's right wing at Germanna Ford and advancing it directly to Catharpin Road just short of Mine Run's headwaters. Simultaneously, the army's left wing was to pursue a longer and more circuitous route, swinging through Ely's Ford and Chancellorsville to the Catharpin-Pamunkey corridor. From there it would continue west until it pulled up next to the other Federal column. Once united, Meade's entire army would be oriented toward Lee. If the rebels fled south, Meade could readily follow and pitch into them at the first opportunity. If they tried to occupy their old Mine Run works, they would be flanked by a powerful Federal force tearing around the lower end of their trenches. Assuming that it was properly executed, Humphreys' plan was designed to pull the teeth from Lee's Rapidan and Mine Run defenses and to precipitate Grant's "speedy battle" on terms favorable to the Union army.

By Humphreys' calculations, if the Union army started at midnight on May 3–4, hard marching could bring it through the Wilderness and nearly to Mine Run before sunset on May 4. That was the optimal timetable for the maneuver. It would get the army out of the heavily wooded terrain and catch Lee by surprise.[79]

Headquarters, however, decided to stop the troops in the Wilderness during the afternoon of May 4. Providence, it seemed, was restoring to Lee the opportunity that he had neglected to achieve by his own planning.

The rejection of Humphreys' optimal timetable—the "first misfortune of the campaign," as Hancock's aide Lieutenant Colonel Francis A. Walker later termed it—was part of an effort to accommodate the slow pace of Ingalls' massive wagon train. Once the Army of the Potomac began its advance, it would depend for several days on the supplies that it carried. It was decided that the infantry should halt early on May 4 to allow the wagons to catch up.

Halting the Army of Potomac in the Wilderness was particularly injudicious because there was no rational basis for believing that Lee

79. Francis A. Walker, *History of the Second Army Corps in the Army of the Potomac* (New York, 1887), 109; Andrew A. Humphreys, *The Virginia Campaign*, 20. Early drafts of the order governing troop movements are in Andrew A. Humphreys Papers, HSP. For the final version, see *OR*, Vol. XXXVI, Pt. 2, pp. 331–34.

would stick to his previous November's pace. This time he was expecting Meade to march, and he was poised to respond at a moment's notice. If Lee learned of Meade's start at sunrise on May 4, Ewell and Hill were manifestly capable of reaching Mine Run by midafternoon. By nightfall, gray-clad soldiers could easily penetrate the Wilderness' western edge. There would be nothing to stop them from advancing up the turnpike and Orange Plank Road into Grant's flank early on the fifth and engaging the Army of the Potomac in the dense wasteland.

Humphreys' plan is liable to another criticism. Based upon events of the fall, the Federal high command reckoned that Lee would leave the Army of the Potomac alone to maneuver. Consequently, the plan failed to include measures to help ensure Lee's quiescence on May 4 and 5. As a British historian later observed, "The alternatives would have been simple, either to finish the maneuver in one day, the period in which Lee had to busy himself with his own preparations, or to provide against the certainty of Lee's interference on the second by telling off a force for the special duty of keeping him occupied during the time necessary for the completion of the maneuver." Preoccupied with safeguarding the army's supplies, headquarters rejected the option of speedily completing the flanking action. The second course—assigning a detachment to keep Lee busy on the Rapidan while the rest of the Federals finished maneuvering in a more leisurely fashion—seems never to have been seriously considered. Feigning an attack past Lee's left with Burnside, or simply advancing Burnside to the major fords along Lee's line, would have forced Lee to detain a sizable portion of his army at the Rapidan. Lee's decision on May 2 to hold Longstreet near Gordonsville suggests that the rebel chief feared precisely that eventuality.[80]

Grant, however, assigned Burnside to guard the rail line passively until Meade's crossing was "perfectly assured." Only after receiving Grant's signal was Burnside to advance. And speed was apparently not a priority. On May 3, Ingalls wrote that he did not expect Burnside to vacate Brandy Station entirely before late on the fifth. The general from Galena had correctly preached concentration and had amassed an impressive force. Yet now that battle was imminent, he

---

80. C. F. Atkinson, *Grant's Campaigns of 1864 and 1865: The Wilderness and Cold Harbor* (London, 1908), 103.

was violating his cardinal rule and relegating the 9th Corps—a force of twenty thousand men, more than in any of Lee's corps—to picket duty. In narrowly defining Burnside's role, Grant lost a handy means of immobilizing Lee.

The Union command's awkward division of responsibility probably accounts in part for the deficiencies in the final plan. Strong-willed Meade and his staff had firm ideas, grounded in long experience, about how to campaign against Lee. Grant seems to have acquiesced in Meade's plan of campaign because deference was the easier course. Burnside's force was accordingly to tag along as an inactive reserve.

Grant may also have become complacent. His earlier victories had been impressive, but they had been won against lesser commanders, with an ease that fostered carelessness. Some of Grant's staff, Lyman noted with dismay, "talked and laughed flippantly about Lee and his army." The lesson of Shiloh, where Grant had dropped his guard and suffered a bloody surprise, was apparently far from the general's mind. Shortly Grant was to learn another lesson, one with which Meade and his predecessors were familiar. It was dangerous to underestimate Lee's capacity to do the unexpected.[81]

But despite the deficiencies in some of the details of the Federal plan, its chances for success appeared good. In less than two months, Grant had brought long-overdue direction to the Federal war effort. For the first time, Union armies would move on a common timetable toward common objectives. Grant's master plan for Virginia—to bring Lee to immediate battle against a force twice the size of his own while two coordinating armies nipped at his flank and rear and wrecked his supply lines—held more promise than anything that had been tried. Later, when the butcher's bill was tallied, critics took issue with Grant's strategy and allocation of troops. William Swinton, a newsman traveling with the Army of the Potomac, thought Grant should have tried a shorter approach from Chesapeake Bay. Others took an opposing view and contended that Grant should have abandoned his subsidiary movements and reinforced Meade with Butler's troops, thereby adding weight to Meade's attacks. Grant, however,

---

81. Ulysses S. Grant to Ambrose E. Burnside, May 2, 1864, in OR, Vol. XXXVI, Pt. 2, p. 337; Ingalls to Meigs, May 3, 1864, *ibid.*, 353; Theodore Lyman to family, April 18, 1864, in *Meade's Headquarters*, ed. Agassiz, 87.

never presumed that Butler and Sigel would accomplish much more than diverting soldiers from Lee. In light of Grant's objectives and the information available to him, his campaign against Lee, at least in its grand sweep, represented the best overall use yet made of Federal troops in the east.

Grant's staff spent the evening of May 3 in pensive anxiety. Now powerless to affect events, several of the general's aides—John Rawlins, Lieutenant Colonel Horace Porter, Colonel Orville E. Babcock, and Adam Badeau—rode to Stevensburg to visit Wilson, whose cavalry was slated to lead the Federal advance across the Rapidan. Only a few months before, Wilson and his visitors had served together in the west. After passing a pleasant hour discussing old times and adventures ahead, the men exchanged a hearty round of handshakes and wishes of good luck.[82]

Returning to Culpeper, the staffers sat around the small, bare front room that served as Grant's headquarters. The general was busy drafting last-minute instructions. At long last, pushing away from his writing table, he fired up a fresh cigar and reviewed the grand campaign with his intimate circle. He was satisfied with his decision to cross below Lee, particularly because it facilitated cooperation with Butler. Once Meade beat Lee, Grant mused, the Confederates would fall back on Richmond to take advantage of its strong defenses. The campaign's decisive battle would be fought around the Confederate capital. To underscore his point, the quiet man from Galena rose, stepped through a cloud of cigar smoke to a map hanging on the wall, and with a sweep of his forefinger drew a line around Richmond and Petersburg. "When my troops are there," he told his aides, "Richmond is mine. Lee must retreat or surrender."[83]

While Grant and his staff discussed the momentous events ahead, hardened veterans shared their knowledge with new recruits. Private Frank Wilkeson, freshly assigned to an artillery company, was advised to reduce his kit to a change of underwear, three pairs of socks, a spare pair of shoes, three plugs of tobacco, a rubber blanket, and

82. Wilson, *Under the Old Flag*, I, 378.
83. Horace Porter, *Campaigning with Grant*, 35–38; Badeau, *Military History*, II, 90–91.

two woolen blankets. Survival on the march, his mentor explained, required sticking to a few simple rules. "Get hold of all the food you can" was a leading principle. "Cut haversacks from dead men. Steal them from infantrymen if you can. Let your aim be to secure food and food and still more food, and keep your eyes open for tobacco." The advice covered other points as well: "Fill your canteen at every stream we cross and wherever you get a chance elsewhere. Never wash your feet until the day's march is over. If you do, they will surely blister." But one goal remained primary. "Get hold of food," a veteran solemnly repeated, shaking his index finger for emphasis, "and hang on to it; you will need it."

The old soldiers also dissuaded Wilkeson from burning his winter camp. "Leave things as they are," they told him with a knowing look. "We may want them before snow flies."[84]

84. Wilkeson, *Recollections*, 39–41.

II

MAY 4
The Armies
Maneuver for Position

*"The movement so far has been as
satisfactory as could be desired."*

ACCORDING TO MEADE'S general orders, Gregg's cavalry division
was to serve as the spearhead of the Federal left wing, crossing Ely's
Ford just ahead of Hancock's infantry corps. Meanwhile Wilson's
cavalry division was to prepare the way for the Union right wing's
movement across Germanna Ford, which was to be conducted by
Warren's and Sedgwick's corps.

Although the Federal infantry advance was not scheduled to start
until almost midnight on May 3–4, important preparatory steps
were initiated earlier in the day. Most critical were the efforts to ensure that routes from Culpeper to the Rapidan fords were secure.

Shortly after dawn on May 3, a Federal force under Gregg began
shifting toward Ely's Ford. The bearded, sharp-eyed Pennsylvanian
led a column that included his cavalry division, twelve canvas boats,
and fourteen wooden French pontoons. The procession jostled south
from an encampment near the Rappahannock until it struck the main
pike from Culpeper to Fredericksburg. Nearby stood an old farmhouse memorable for its "corn cribs, log-stables, and huddled fruit
trees where chickens and turkeys roost, all overlooking a flat field to
the west that is dotted with blackened stumps of primeval oaks."
Willis Madden and his family, free Negroes, ran a tavern there.

Filing left, Gregg's dust-covered column trotted east onto a
sparsely settled finger of land between the Rappahannock and the
Rapidan. The riders stopped at Richardsville, a rustic hamlet two and
a half miles short of Ely's Ford. It could not have been later than
noon. Gregg's main body of cavalry, along with the engineers, bivouacked while detachments of blue riders fanned out country roads
and byways toward the river, picketing houses along the route to

prevent word of Meade's impending movement from leaking to Lee. More engineers arrived from Brandy Station and set about repairing a short wagon track to Culpeper Mine Ford, upstream from Ely's Ford, where most of the wagons were to cross.[1]

A few of the army's wagons—ambulances and "fighting trains," jammed with ammunition and entrenching tools—were to remain with their assigned infantry units. But the majority of the conveyances were Ingalls' responsibility. The trains, packed with surplus ammunition and food and forage for ten days, formed a seemingly endless parade. Years later, one of Meade's officers remembered them rumbling past his tent at Brandy Station all night on their way to Richardsville.[2]

Humphreys' idea was to start secretly at midnight to get a six-hour jump on Lee. Sunrise on the fourth would unavoidably reveal Meade's movement to rebel lookouts on Clark's Mountain, but by then Humphreys expected the fords to be secure and the Federal infantry to be well on its way across the river. To preserve secrecy, division heads were not told their routes of march until after noon on May 3. Foot soldiers were left in ignorance until a few hours before midnight. "Corps and other independent commanders," Meade instructed, "will adopt the most vigorous measures to prevent any bonfires being made on the breaking up of camps, and they will impress on their subordinates the necessity of a strict compliance with this order, in view of the importance of concealing our movement from the enemy." Infractions were treated harshly. The army's provost marshal administered a "hiding on the spot" to a soldier who succumbed to temptation and burned his camp.[3]

Soon after dark, Hancock began bringing together his 2nd Corps. Artillery units were massed in fields around Willis Madden's tavern under a clear, starry sky. An otherwise pleasant bivouac was marred

1. General Order, in *OR,* Vol. XXXVI, Pt. 2, pp. 331–32; Ira Spaulding's Report, *ibid.,* Pt. 1, pp. 304–307; Charles Forsyth to David McM. Gregg, May 2, 1864, *ibid.,* Pt. 2, pp. 342–43; Charles Forsyth to David McM. Gregg, May 3, 1864, *ibid.,* 365–66; Philip H. Sheridan's Report, *ibid.,* Pt. 1, p. 787; Schaff, *The Battle of the Wilderness,* 79.

2. Rufus Ingalls to George G. Meade, May 3, 1864, in *OR,* Vol. XXXVI, Pt. 2, pp. 354–55; Schaff, *The Battle of the Wilderness,* 82–83.

3. Special Order No. 134, in *OR,* Vol. XXXVI, Pt. 2, p. 355; David S. Sparks, ed., *Inside Lincoln's Army: The Diary of Marsena Rudolph Patrick, Provost Marshal General, Army of the Potomac* (New York, 1964), 367.

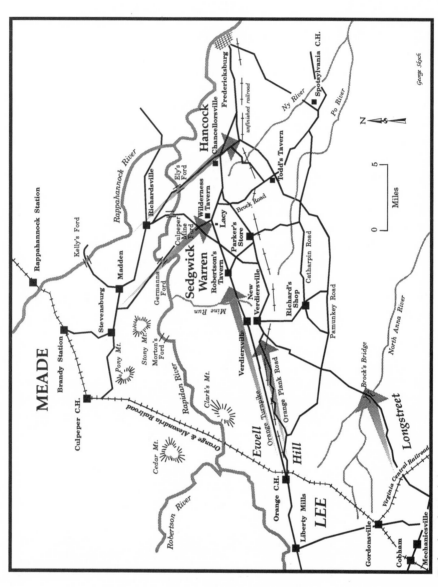

Federal and Confederate movements on May 4

when a runaway wagon stampeded a battery's horses. Several soldiers were crushed under gun carriages.[4]

Between 11 P.M. and midnight, Hancock's infantry began striding from Stevensburg toward Ely's Ford in two columns. Barlow's and Gibbon's divisions advanced out the Culpeper-Fredericksburg Pike, keeping to the woods and fields so as to leave the road free for other troops. Birney's and Mott's divisions followed a more northerly route originating near Brandy Station. As Barlow's column swung past Madden's tavern, troops coming from the north slipped in behind. Gun batteries fell into line with their respective divisions. By sunrise on the fourth, Hancock's corps was united and clearing Richardsville for its rendezvous with Gregg's cavalry at Ely's Ford.[5]

Preparations were also moving apace to secure Germanna Ford for Meade's other wing. At nightfall on May 3, another line of wooden and canvas pontoons began wending its way down Germanna Plank Road. At about 10 P.M., the pontoon trains pulled up half a mile short of Germanna Ford. Word of their arrival promptly went to Wilson, who was waiting in readiness at Stevensburg with his cavalry division. Shortly after midnight, Wilson broke camp and rode south into blackness toward the ford.

While Hancock's 2nd Corps pressed toward Ely's Ford, Warren's 5th Corps, which was to lead Meade's right wing, began its advance to Germanna Ford. Bugles roused the soldiers shortly after midnight. "We boiled our coffee hurriedly," recalled a New Yorker, "rolled our blankets and stumbled at a snail's pace through the almost pitch darkness of the night for some two hours and a half before we had light enough to enable us to distinguish our surroundings." Like Hancock, Warren split his command for the initial stages of the march and then brought it back together. Griffin's division took the lead, followed by the divisions of Crawford, Robinson, and Wadsworth. The 5th Corps continued to a place designated on the campaign map as "ruins." There, under the starry spring sky, an officer directed the soldiers out a dirt road lined with men to prevent them

---

4. John Tidball's Report, in OR, Vol. XXXVI, Pt. 1, p. 507; Frederick M. Edgell's Report, *ibid.*, 518–19.

5. Second Corps General Orders, in OR, Vol. XXXVI, Pt. 2, pp. 356–57; Second Corps Daily Memoranda, *ibid.*, Pt. 1, p. 350.

from going astray in the dark. Near sunup, the 5th Corps broke onto Germanna Plank Road. The Rapidan lay only a short march away. Glancing back, one of Warren's men saw the night sky in the direction of Stevensburg lit by flames. Stragglers, he concluded, were burning deserted buildings in the village.[6]

Meade's third and last infantry corps, Sedgwick's, was scheduled to leave at 4:00 A.M. and to fall in behind Warren. The 6th Corps troops were roused at 2:30 A.M. At the first glow in the east—sunrise was at 4:49—Getty's division started toward the Rapidan, with Wright's and Ricketts' following. Years later, a staffer recalled the agony of that early morning wakening. A few canteens of water poured over his head, a brisk rub, and a dipper of black coffee got him on the road, "albeit in a savage mood." There was a halt for breakfast around 7:00 A.M. and a chance to savor the scents of spring.[7]

Daylight revealed the entire road network north of the Rapidan overflowing with blue-clad troops. The largest army ever assembled in the country was advancing toward the Rapidan fords. Confidence filled the air.

Grant's concern that Lee might disrupt his crossing quickly proved groundless. On the army's right wing, Wilson's lead troopers—Major William Patton's 3rd Indiana Cavalry—which were deployed across the heights overlooking Germanna Ford, prepared to force their way over the river if necessary. At "early dawn"—Wilson place the time in his report at 3 A.M.—Indiana horsemen splashed across to Lee's side of the river. Rebel pickets from the 1st North Carolina cavalry briefly skirmished with the intruders but offered no serious resistance. By 4 A.M., Federal engineers were hauling canvas and wooden pontoons down the steep river bluffs. An hour and a half later, two bridges, forty or fifty feet apart and 220 feet long, spanned the Rapidan. Warren's foot soldiers puffed into sight at 6 A.M. Within an hour, they were thundering over the pontoons,

6. Spaulding's Report, in *OR*, Vol. XXXVI, Pt. 1, p. 306; James H. Wilson's Report, *ibid.*, 875–76; Wilson, *Under the Old Flag*, I, 379; Fifth Corps General Orders, in *OR*, Vol. XXXVI, Pt. 2, pp. 358–59; Porter Farley, "Reminiscences of the 140th Regiment New York Volunteer Infantry," *Rochester Historical Society Publication*, XXII, 236.

7. Sixth Corps General Orders, in *OR*, Vol. XXXVI, Pt. 2, pp. 361–62; Henry Keiser Diary, May 4, 1864, in Harrisburg Civil War Round Table Collection, USMHI; Thomas W. Hyde, *Following the Greek Cross; or, Memories of the Sixth Army Corps* (Boston, 1894), 182.

up three temporary roads chopped into the steep bank, and into the Wilderness. Artillery batteries were assigned to their respective divisions as the infantry units marched past. Warren's artillery chief, although reluctant to disperse his guns, felt it appropriate to do so, because "an unbroken string of artillery over a mile long was certainly somewhat risky through these dense woods."[8]

The left wing at Ely's Ford was also progressing handsomely. Gregg's cavalrymen had broken camp at Richardsville at midnight as scheduled. Two hours later, they reached the Rapidan. "The night was dark, and the air in the hollow near the river was very cold and chilly," recorded a chaplain in Lieutenant Colonel John W. Kester's 1st New Jersey Cavalry. Guided by a scout, a Union company waded across and stealthily began circling behind rebel pickets on the far shore. A Confederate discovered the Federal party and fired a shot to alert his companions. A half dozen southerners were captured. The rest escaped toward Chancellorsville. Work started immediately on a canvas pontoon bridge, and just before 5:30 A.M., Barlow came into sight leading Hancock's infantry. The canvas span was soon completed, and Barlow's men began to cross, some by the bridge and others by wading in water up to their waists. A Pennsylvania soldier recalled "jumping down three feet in the water and holding up our cartridge boxes to keep the ammunition dry." A wooden bridge was in place by 9:15 A.M.[9]

Anxious with anticipation, Meade began this momentous fourth day of May early. He and his staff rose well before dawn, ate, and were on their way from Brandy Station as the sun was clearing the treetops. The roads were hard and excellent, noted Meade's aide Lyman, "full of wagons and black with troops." Meade's entourage passed through Stevensburg and continued toward the river. The day

8. Washington A. Roebling's Report, in Gouverneur Kemble Warren Collection, NYSA; Wilson's Report, in OR, Vol. XXXVI, Pt. 1, p. 875; Spaulding's Report, in OR, Vol. XXXVI, Pt. 1, p. 306; Nevins, ed., Diary of Battle, 348–49.

9. Henry R. Pyne, The History of the First New Jersey Cavalry (Trenton, 1871), 222–23; N. D. Preston, History of the Tenth Regiment of Cavalry, New York State Volunteers (New York, 1892), 170; Isaac H. Ressler Diary, May 4, 1864, in Civil War Times Illustrated Collection, USMHI; Henry C. Campbell Memoir, May 4, 1864, in Civil War Miscellaneous Collection, USMHI. A soldier in the 1st Massachusetts Cavalry noted that the Rapidan was particularly high and swift and that several soldiers were swept a considerable distance downstream. See Stanton P. Allen, Down in Dixie: Life in a Cavalry Regiment in the War Days, from the Wilderness to Appomattox, (Boston, 1888), 210–11.

warmed, and the wayside vibrated with purple violets. Discarded blankets and overcoats marked where soldiers had stopped to rest. Beyond Stevensburg, Meade's headquarters staff crested a small ridge. The army spread grandly before them. "As far as you could see in every direction," one of the riders later recalled, "corps, divisions, brigades, trains, batteries,and squadrons, were moving on in a waving sea of blue; headquarters and regimental flags were fluttering, the morning sun kissing them all, and shimmering gayly from gunbarrels." To a soldier in the 15th New Jersey, the lines of blue-clad troops resembled "fences dividing up the country, but the glitter of many thousand musket barrels showed them to be masses of men moving in column. A thousand battle flags were fluttering in the air. To bugle note and beat of drum marched horsemen, artillery, and foot, to the dark woods and dreadful fields where death should hold high carnival."[10]

There could be no doubt that Confederates were closely monitoring the army's progress. "Our column of troops was plainly seen by daylight from the enemy's signal station at Clark's Mountain," noted Warren's aide Major Washington A. Roebling, "and they had a large signal fire burning."[11]

Around 8:00 A.M., Meade reached Germanna Ford, his headquarters the previous Thanksgiving during the Mine Run events. Memories of the affair were not altogether pleasant for the Federals, but things seemed to be proceeding much better this time. Griffin's division was already over the Rapidan, and the rest of Warren's corps was waiting its turn. At 9:30 A.M., Meade and his staff crossed to the southern bank. Their horses' hoofs beat hollow cadences on the pontoons. Sitting on a bluff seventy feet above the water, Lyman watched as Warren's and then Sedgwick's soldiers filed across the twin bridges at Germanna Ford. How strange it would be, he mused, if each man destined to fall in the coming campaign wore a large badge announcing his fate.[12]

Headquarters was established near the river where Meade could keep a close eye on the army's progress. He was in intimate contact

10. Theodore Lyman to family, May 15, 1864, in *Meade's Headquarters*, ed. Agassiz, 87; Schaff, *The Battle of the Wilderness*, 85; Alanson A. Haines, *History of the Fifteenth Regiment New Jersey Volunteers* (New York, 1883), 140–41.
11. Roebling's Report, in Warren Collection, NYSA.
12. Theodore Lyman to family, June 25, 1864, in *Meade's Headquarters*, ed. Agassiz, 180.

with his right column, which was closest to the enemy, and he also maintained close communication by courier with Hancock, out of sight five miles over on the left. At 6:30 A.M., Hancock reported successfully breaching the Rapidan at Ely's Ford. Meade acknowledged receipt of Hancock's message at 8:35 A.M. and informed him of the status at Germanna Ford, noting that "the crossing here is slow." All day, messages passed between the two generals.[13]

Eager to witness the army's progress, Grant started from Culpeper at 8 A.M. on his bay horse, Cincinnati. He sat on the same weather-beaten saddle he had been using since Fort Donelson. His uniform coat hung unbuttoned, and his overcoat—that of a private soldier—lay strapped behind an orderly's saddle. Usually a plain dresser, Grant had donned a pair of yellowish brown thread gloves and a black slouch felt hat encircled by a gold cord in honor of the occasion. Riding with the commander in chief was a civilian dressed in black. Soldiers buzzed with curiosity to learn whether this funereal figure was Grant's "private undertaker," or perhaps a "parson who had joined headquarters so as to be on hand to read the funeral service over the Southern Confederacy when the boys succeeded in getting it into the 'last ditch.'" The man was none other than Elihu Washburne, Grant's congressional mentor from Illinois, who had been visiting headquarters and decided to stick around and watch his protégé at work.[14]

Cheers rang in Grant's ears as he advanced toward the Rapidan. The newspaperman Sylvanus Cadwallader was mesmerized by "dense columns of troops on the march, with the shimmer of their bright bayonets resembling the glitter of frost on hedgerows in winter." The "soft and balmy" morning, he thought, contributed to a buoyant mood. "Never since its organization had the Army of the Potomac been in better spirits, or more eager to meet the enemy," wrote the journalist, "and never did an army seem to be in better condition for marching or fighting." Another war correspondent, Charles Page, remarked that he had "never seen the army move with more exact order, with a less number of stragglers, and with so little apparent fatigue to the men." Grant's troops, he predicted, would

13. Winfield S. Hancock to George G. Meade, June 25, 1864, in *OR*, Vol. XXXVI, Pt. 2, p. 374; Seth Williams to Winfield S. Hancock, May 4, 1864, *ibid.*

14. Horace Porter, *Campaigning with Grant*, 41–43.

fight "with more than the elan of the French, with more than the pluck of the British. They feel it in their bones—that something allied to these, but better than either or both."[15]

Shortly before noon, Grant crossed Germanna Ford and set up headquarters in an old farmhouse near Meade's tents. The dilapidated structure held only a table and two chairs, and appeared long abandoned. The general-in-chief sat on the steps of a gabled porch and lit one of his ever-present cigars. Across the way, Meade's new headquarters flag—a golden eagle in a silver wreath on a lavender backdrop—fluttered in the breeze. "What's this!—Is Imperial Caesar anywhere about here?" Grant good-naturedly queried his staff.[16]

Thus far, the advance was going surprisingly well, and news from the field continued to be reassuring. Riding ahead of the infantry, Wilson's cavalry division had moved down Germanna Plank Road as far as Wilderness Tavern. Warren's entire infantry corps had disappeared into the leafy expanse, and Sedgwick's troops were filing across in twin lines. At 8:30 A.M., Wilson reported that he had still encountered no rebels. This was important news. It meant that the route was clear to Wilderness Tavern, the first day's objective for Meade's right wing.[17]

Developments on the Federal left flank, over by Richardsville and Ely's Ford, were hidden from Meade's and Grant's view. Hancock's steady stream of dispatches, however, indicated that things were going without a hitch on that front as well. The night march from Stevensburg had been uneventful for the 2nd Corps. At first, the men passed the time singing and making jokes. A bottleneck developed as they neared the approaches to the ford. Laden with up to fifty pounds, the soldiers waited impatiently to cross. Soon sweltering heat put an end to marching songs. Veterans greedily filled their canteens from the river when their turn came to pass. With the Rapidan behind them, the troops wound across a narrow valley and up a steep bluff onto a plateau of dense, scrubby timber. One of the lead men saw Hancock and Gregg together on a little knoll earnestly talking

---

15. Cadwallader, *Three Years with Grant,* 175; Charles A. Page, *Letters of a War Correspondent* (Boston, 1899), 48.

16. Ulysses S. Grant, "Preparing for the Campaigns of '64," in *B&L,* IV, 97n.

17. Williams to Hancock, May 4, 1864, in *OR,* Vol. XXXVI, Pt. 2, p. 374.

over a map. Here less robust soldiers, faces flushed and shirts opened to the neck, gasped to keep up with their units. "We started out with an equipment consisting of a blanket, overcoat, one-half shelter tent, carbine, saber, revolver, forty rounds of ammunition, canteen, haversack, and change of clothing," recalled a Maine soldier. "At first the load was not so bad, but after two hours it began to feel heavy and after four or five hours, heavier, and along toward night it weighed a ton." [18]

The route became paved with discarded overcoats and blankets, torn into shreds to render them useless to the rebels. Artillerymen coming behind scooped up abandoned haversacks and hung them on their limbers and caissons and guns. "The mine was rich," a gunner later recalled with satisfaction, "and we worked it thoroughly." At 9:50 A.M., Hancock reported that his forward units were beginning to pitch camp just beyond Chancellorsville, their first day's goal. In addition, Gregg's cavalry had probed west out Catharpin Road without incident. A little over an hour later, headquarters was informed that two of Hancock's four divisions were in camp and that the remaining troops were "well up." Assurances arrived from Hancock at 1:40 P.M. that "everything is across." [19]

Grant pensively watched Sedgwick's men tramp over the bridges and file away in Warren's direction. Finally he broke the silence. "Well, the movement so far has been as satisfactory as could be desired," he remarked to his aide Porter. "We have succeeded in seizing the fords and crossing the river without loss or delay. Lee must by this time know upon what roads we are advancing, but he may not yet realize the full extent of the movement. We shall probably soon get some indications as to what he intends to do." A newspaperman—probably Cadwallader—posed a question that was on everyone's mind. "General Grant, about how long will it take you to get to Richmond?" he asked. Grant had a ready answer. "I will agree to

18. Timothy Bateman Diary, May 4, 1864, in Civil War Miscellaneous Collection, USMHI; Nathan B. Webb Diary, May 4, 1864, in Nathan B. Webb Papers, CL; Charles Gardner, "My Experience in the First Maine Cavalry," in Civil War Times Illustrated Collection, USMHI.

19. Charles D. Page, *History of the Fourteenth Regiment, Connecticut*, 233–34; Wilkeson, *Recollections*, 42–48; Winfield S. Hancock to George G. Meade, May 4, 1864, in *OR*, Vol. XXXVI, Pt. 2, p. 374; Winfield S. Hancock to Seth Williams, May 4, 1864, *ibid.*, 375.

be there in about four days—that is, if General Lee becomes a party to the agreement; but if he objects, the trip will undoubtedly be prolonged."[20]

No one believed that Lee would not object to Grant's advance. How the rebel chief intended to express his opposition, however, remained a matter for speculation. So far there had been no definite signs that he meant to do anything very quickly.

To keep apprised of developments in the Confederate camps, Meade had left his observation posts on Pony and Stony mountains occupied when the Federal army moved off. Located southeast of Culpeper, these hills overlooked the Rapidan and Lee's defensive line.

During the first few hours of daylight, Federal lookouts perceived no unusual rebel activity. As late as 7:30 A.M., with the Germanna Ford and Ely's Ford bridgeheads firmly in Union hands and Meade's infantry well across at both points, the Stony Mountain lookout reported, "Enemy's camps unchanged. Party in work in rear of Raccoon Ford. Two parties of 100 men have just come down near Dr. Morton's house." There was no way to tell, of course, what was happening behind Clark's Mountain and its subsidiary ranges, but nothing showed Lee to be reacting to Grant's movement. Sometime before 9:30 A.M., however, Stony Mountain decoded a rebel message flashed from Clark's Mountain to Ewell. "From present indications everything seems to be moving to the right, on Germanna and Ely's Ford roads, leaving cavalry in our front," read the intercepted Confederate cipher. There was no question now that Lee was aware of Grant's game. But there was still no evidence that the Confederates had begun to move. "No change as yet," reported the Federal captain at Stony Mountain. Finally, at 11:00 A.M., Meade received his first concrete intelligence suggesting that Lee was responding to the Federal army swarming around his flank. Union observers had adjusted their glasses to decipher signal flags waving on Clark's Mountain and had intercepted another message to Ewell. "We are moving," read the rebel flags. "Had I better not move D. and D. toward New Verdiersville?" The question referred to a small collection of houses on the Orange Turnpike west of Mine Run.[21]

---

20. Horace Porter, *Campaigning with Grant*, 44.
21. Stony Mountain Reports, May 4, 1864, in *OR*, Vol. XXXVI, Pt. 2, pp. 371–72.

To Meade, the import of this was clear. Rather than retreating, the rebels were apparently planning to swing some of their troops around to occupy their position the previous fall at Mine Run. But it also appeared that Lee intended to leave a sizable force to guard the Rapidan. According to Federal lookouts across from Lee's river defenses, the Confederates were still busy digging. "No change yet observed," they reported. Most likely this meant that Lee was still uncertain whether Grant had shifted his entire army or had left a portion of it behind. It appeared too that if Lee intended to shift his entire army to Mine Run, he was going to take his time about it.

But at least now Lee's direction was known. Putting together the signal station's intelligence and dispatches dribbling in from Wilson's scouting parties, Humphreys at 1 P.M. summed up headquarters' view. "Some few shots have been fired toward Robertson's Tavern [on the Orange Turnpike]," he wrote to Hancock. "Enemy moving; some force coming out toward New Verdiersville."

According to the aide Porter—whose memoirs were published thirty-three years later from memorandums jotted down at the time—Meade passed the latest report from Stony Mountain to Grant at about 1 P.M. As Porter remembered it, Grant was elated and remarked, "That gives just the information I wanted. It shows Lee is drawing out from his position, and is pushing across to meet us." Grant viewed the implications as threefold. First, Lee was advancing toward Mine Run, a move he had anticipated and was prepared to meet. Second, nothing about Lee's timing upset Humphreys' schedule. The Union advance could safely continue as planned, including overnighting in the Wilderness. And finally, there was no longer a risk that Lee would turn north toward Washington. Accordingly, at 1:15 P.M., Grant sent a telegram to his 9th Corps commander to make "forced marches until you reach this place. Start your troops now in the rear, the moment they can be got off, and require them to make a night march." [22]

With his entire force mobilized and his first obstacle behind him, Grant drew a deep breath and took a moment to share his relief with Washington. "The crossing of the Rapidan effected," he

---

22. Andrew A. Humphreys to Winfield S. Hancock, May 4, 1864, in *OR*, Vol. XXXVI, Pt. 2, p. 375; Ulysses S. Grant to Ambrose E. Burnside, May 4, 1864, *ibid.*, 380.

wired shortly before 2 P.M. "Forty-eight hours now will demonstrate whether the enemy intends giving battle this side of Richmond. Telegraph Butler that we have crossed the Rapidan."[23]

While Union infantry clattered over pontoon bridges all afternoon without a hitch, Wilson's troopers gingerly felt westward in Lee's direction, keeping a close eye on roads leading toward Mine Run. One Federal party threaded out a trail just below the Rapidan. Working up to Mine Run, the blue-clad horsemen encountered only a few rebel pickets. There was no sign of enemy activity east of the stream.

Around noon, the head of Warren's infantry column trudged into Wilderness Tavern. Exhausted from the long march, the soldiers began erecting tents in the clearing.

With Wilderness Tavern in Warren's hands, Wilson was free to execute the remainder of his assignment for the day. According to Humphreys' plan, Warren's corps was to proceed early the next morning to the little settlement of Parker's Store, on Orange Plank Road. The route followed a remote farm track that meandered southwest for about five miles through extremely dense woods. During the afternoon of the fourth, Wilson was to make sure that the way was cleared of rebels.

Shortly after noon, the main body of Wilson's cavalry began winding out the trail to Parker's Store, while a small force of scouts explored west along the Orange Turnpike. Their objective was Robertson's Tavern, just short of Mine Run. They had instructions to drive away any rebels they encountered and then to rejoin the division.

At about 2 P.M., Wilson's lead brigade reached Parker's Store. Its advance from Wilderness Tavern had been unremarkable. The tired troopers had captured a single Confederate soldier and had caught fleeting sightings of only a "few light parties scattered through the by-roads." Their most interesting discovery was an Englishman— Sime by name—whom they had encountered on one of the Wilderness' narrow, twisting trails. Sime claimed to have left Orange Court

---

23. Ulysses S. Grant to Henry W. Halleck, May 4, 1864, in *OR*, Vol. XXXVI, Pt. 2, p. 370.

House at two the previous afternoon. Ewell and Hill were there, he reported, Longstreet was near Gordonsville, and rebels were "well down" toward Mine Run on all the roads except Orange Plank Road. "He seems well disposed," Warren reported of Sime, "and if properly rewarded may give other valuable information." Assuming that Sime was trustworthy—the motivations of anyone traveling these remote byways deserved particularly close scrutiny—his narrative further confirmed information provided by the Federal observation posts. Lee was mobilizing, but he was not doing so very quickly.[24]

At 3 P.M., the Stony Mountain observation post forwarded the first firm evidence that Lee was abandoning his Rapidan line. "Enemy moving infantry and trains toward Verdiersville," came the message. "Two brigades gone from this front. Camps on Clark's Mountain breaking up." Although the Federal commanders thus knew for certain that Lee's Confederates were swinging around to the east, it was not clear how fast Lee was moving, or how far he intended to go. It still seemed that the Confederates meant to venture no farther than Mine Run.[25]

Wilson's continuing probes supported that impression. As his dust-caked horsemen boiled their evening coffee, Wilson dispatched his last courier of the day. Union patrols, reported the young cavalry chief, had ranged south to Catharpin Road and west to Mine Run but had seen few rebels. Lieutenant Colonel John Hammond's 5th New York had skirmished with enemy scouts on Orange Plank Road about a mile east of Mine Run but had encountered no significant body of enemy infantry. Rodes's division of Ewell's corps was said to be stretched out along the turnpike some twelve miles east of Orange Court House, which would place that unit a good distance short of Mine Run. Headquarters, Wilson declared, could rest assured that there were "patrols and advanced parties well out the Spotsylvania and Orange roads."[26]

Wilson's certainty on the point was mistaken. This was his first experience commanding cavalry, and he had neglected to take pre-

24. Philip H. Sheridan to Andrew A. Humphreys, May 4, 1864, in *OR*, Vol. XXXVI, Pt. 2, pp. 388–89; James H. Wilson to Charles Forsyth, May 4, 1864, *ibid.*, 390.

25. Stony Mountain Reports, May 4, 1864, in *OR*, Vol. XXXVI, Pt. 2, p. 372.

26. Wilson to Forsyth, May 4, 1864, in *OR*, Vol. XXXVI, Pt. 2, p. 390; James H. Wilson to Gouverneur K. Warren, May 4, 1864, *ibid.*, 378.

cautions that would have been second nature to a more seasoned commander. In contrast to his careful reconnaissance of Orange Plank Road, Wilson had carelessly left the Orange Turnpike unattended. His scouts had passed through Robertson's Tavern before dark, observed nothing of interest, then returned cross-country to the division at Parker's Store. Not a single bluecoated horseman remained posted on the turnpike after dark to alert Grant's sleeping army in the event that Lee tried to slip troops through that way.

As Wilson's troopers explored the leafy paths and wagon trails in Meade's advance and off his right flank, the Army of the Potomac's two infantry columns completed their long day's march. At 3:05 P.M., Warren notified Meade that the right wing's lead divisions had settled into "good positions" on the roads that radiated like spokes from Wilderness Tavern. "The men are almost all in camp washing their feet," Warren wrote his commander, "and with a good night's rest will feel fine."[27]

Wilderness Tavern occupied a weed-choked elevation above the intersection of Germanna Plank Road and the Orange Turnpike. Most of the 5th Corps encampments were within easy reach of the crossroads. East of Wilderness Run spread Wadsworth's division, with pickets extended toward Chancellorsville and Hancock. West of the run were Crawford's men. Their lead brigades were posted out the dirt track toward Parker's Store that Wilson had taken earlier that day. Nearby stood Crawford's staff tents, and on a neighboring knoll fluttered Warren's headquarters flag. The tents of Robinson's division dotted Germanna Plank Road half way back to the Rapidan. Poised above Wilderness Run's eastern slope was a fine old dwelling, Ellwood, home of the Lacy family. Four Federal batteries dominated high ground immediately around the house, and additional guns were parked three-quarters of a mile north.

Warren's lead division under Charles Griffin covered the Orange Turnpike toward Lee. Bivouacking a mile or so west of Wilderness Tavern, Griffin's men formed the Army of the Potomac's extreme right flank. Pickets were thrown out the turnpike, but as an officer later conceded, "not with such care as should be exercised in the

---

27. Gouverneur K. Warren to Andrew A. Humphreys, May 4, 1864, in *OR*, Vol. XXXVI, Pt. 2, p. 378.

presence of the enemy." It was erroneously supposed that Wilson's cavalry was patrolling the highway between Griffin's men and Mine Run. No purpose would be served, reasoned Griffin's officers, by disturbing their tired soldiers to correct gaps in the picket line. "It is the most beautiful weather," one of Griffin's men recorded in his diary, "and the troops enjoy the lovely spring day, which pleasure is not spoiled by sight of a single rebel."[28]

Just before nightfall, a Michigan soldier noticed puffs of smoke on the horizon. They seemed to come from distant campfires. Reporting his observation, he was advised that the smoke probably marked camps of Federal cavalrymen picketing the turnpike. The horsemen might want to pass through during the night, he was cautioned, and he should not fire on them.[29]

By evening, Sedgwick's corps, thoroughly blown after a long, hot trek, had also reached its day's objective and was bedding down. Uncle John's troops occupied Germanna Plank Road back to Germanna Ford. Sedgwick's lead division, Getty's, pitched its tents next to Warren's corps. Wright's men spread their blankets behind Getty's, and Ricketts' division covered the remaining stretch to the river.

A soldier of the 6th Corps wrote home that warm weather and unaccustomed exertion "told on us considerably." Some troops found welcome diversion at a secessionist's sawmill located on nearby Flat Run. They appropriated lumber for cooking fires, then dismantled the building itself. The mill's steam engine afforded great fun. After filling the boiler with water from their coffee pots, the soldiers experimented with seeing how fast the old machine could be made to go. One of Sedgwick's brigadiers stayed at a house whose occupants included two attractive girls. His evening's pleasures were marred by the way the ladies were "awfully down on all Union officers." The 6th Corps encampment quieted at an early hour. "Here and there a group might be seen after the majority had gone to rest holding earnest conference as men might well do over whom the shadow of death rested," recalled a soldier in the 37th Massachusetts. "Others,

---

28. Swan, "Battle of the Wilderness," in *PMHSM,* IV, 124; William A. Throop's Report, in *OR,* Vol. XXXVI, Pt. 1, pp. 579–80; Charles Seiser, ed., "August Seiser's Civil War Diary," *Rochester Historical Society Publication,* XXII, 189.

29. George Hopper, "Reminiscences," in MOLLUS Collection, BL.

without thought save of the present moment, were engaged in games or enjoying the luxury which some fortunate foraging enterprise had provided." All told, recorded one of Sedgwick's brigadiers, the evening was "quiet and peaceful, as if there was not a reb within a hundred miles, or ever had been." A soldier from Maryland discussed the song of a distant whippoorwill with an officer. "Our Colonel," he later noted, "remarked it was a good omen."[30]

At Chancellorsville, Hancock's troops were also recovering from their grueling day's march. Some of the 2nd Corps' soldiers had trudged more than twenty-five miles. "More dreaded than battle" is how one veteran described the march, which had been particularly difficult because the troops were in "wretched condition" after the winter's inactivity. "Gone into camp nearly exhausted," a New Jersey soldier summoned the strength to scribble in his diary. Hancock's soldiers pitched camp where many of them had fought the previous year. White with dust from the day's exertions, old-timers picked curiously through debris for mementos. One soldier stumbled on the remains of a horse that had been shot from under him. Another found a comrade's skull pierced through the forehead. "It was a very easy matter to discover just where pools of blood had been," an officer later recorded, "for those particular spots were marked by the greenest tufts of grass and brightest flowers to be found upon the field." A brigadier wrote his wife, "Inclosed you will find two or three pretty violets that I picked upon the very ground where my regiment stood and fought so splendidly." He went on, "The ground was made rich by the blood of our brave soldiers. I thought the flowers would be a relic prised by you."[31]

At 5 P.M., a 160-foot wooden pontoon span was completed at Culpeper Mine Ford. Shortly afterward, Federal supply trains began to roll across the river. From there they were directed to Chancellorsville. Gregg—whose mounted division was busy picketing nearby

30. Alexander Shaler Diary, May 4, 1864, in NYHS; Alanson A. Haines, *History of the Fifteenth Regiment New Jersey*, 141; James L. Bowen, *History of the Thirty-Seventh Regiment Massachusetts Volunteers in the Civil War of 1861–1865* (Holyoke, Mass., 1884), 271–72; Grayson Eichelberer Memoir, May 4, 1864, in Civil War Miscellaneous Collection, USMHI.

31. Bateman Diary, May 4, 1864, in Civil War Miscellaneous Collection, USMHI; Edwin B. Houghton, *The Campaigns of the Seventeenth Maine* (Portland, Maine, 1866), 164–65; Charles H. Weygant, *History of the One Hundred and Twenty-Fourth Regiment N.Y.S.V.* (Newburgh, N.Y., 1877), 271–72; James I. Robertson, *The Civil War Letters of General Robert McAllister* (New Brunswick, N.J., 1965), 415.

roads—remained within "easy supporting distance" of Hancock and the wagons. Gregg's men were under orders to groom and resaddle their horses and sleep with weapons handy.

Steps were also taken to safeguard the army's rear. During the day, Alfred Torbert's cavalry division had patrolled in the vicinity of Culpeper, paying particular attention to the wagons. At dark, Torbert's troopers settled between Richardsville and Stevensburg, with Brigadier General George A. Custer at Stony Mountain and Colonel Thomas C. Devin's brigade near the Madden place.

The night of May 4 saw the Army of the Potomac's infantry and cavalry safely in their designated positions and supply wagons rolling into place on schedule. Grant regarded the day's work as a "great success." He had removed, he later wrote, the "most serious apprehensions I had entertained, that of crossing the river in the face of an active, large, well-appointed, and ably commanded army, and how so large a train was to be carried through a hostile country and protected." Humphreys was also delighted. There had been not a "single mishap, interruption, or delay." [32]

As darkness fell, Private Wilkeson, who had heeded admonitions to collect as much food and water as possible, strolled around Chancellorsville. In some places, polished skulls covered the ground. Leg bones, arm bones, and ribs protruded from shallow graves. Other soldiers joined him. Together they studied remains for bits of clothing to determine whether they belonged to Yankees or Confederates. They built a fire where the graves were thickest. Sitting on the long, low mounds, they talked about the previous spring's fighting. Smoke drifted through the air. Trees swayed and sighed in the wind. A veteran recounted how the year before, the wounded had helplessly burned to death in thick underbrush. Listeners shuddered and drew closer around the fire. "This region," whispered the veteran, waving his arm toward the surrounding woods, "is an awful place to fight in. The utmost extent of vision is about one hundred yards. Artillery cannot be used effectively. The wounded are liable to be burned to death. I am willing to take my chances of getting killed, but I dread to have a leg broken and then to be burned slowly; and these woods will surely be burned if we fight here. I hope we will get through this

32. Ulysses S. Grant's Report, in *OR*, Vol. XXXVI, Pt. 1, 18; Andrew A. Humphreys, *The Virginia Campaign*, 19–20.

chapparal without fighting." The speaker took off his cap and quietly smacked it clean of dust from the day's journey. The men sat silently smoking, staring into the fire. An infantry soldier, who had been stabbing a shallow grave with a bayonet, pried out a skull and rolled it across the ground. He spoke in a deep, quiet voice. "That is what you are all coming to, and some of you will start toward it tomorrow." The group broke up, most of the men scurrying back to their regimental camps. A few, including Wilkeson, remained by the dying embers and smoked. Lee, they said among themselves, was going to face Grant in the Wilderness. And all of them agreed that Lee held the advantage. After midnight, Wilkeson crept under his caisson, resting his head on a knapsack and dozing to the pops of rifle shots from cavalry pickets patrolling toward Fredericksburg. Dawn was not far off, and with it would come another march and perhaps battle. And somewhere to the west, in blackness beyond the farthest glow of Meade's dying campfires, Lee's soldiers were filing by thousands onto Orange Plank Road and the Orange Turnpike.[33]

*"The general's desire is
to bring him to battle as
soon now as possible."*

Despite efforts to keep the Union offensive secret, by May 2, Lee's men had deduced that the Federal advance was imminent. Confederates had noticed Grant's side of the river buzzing with activity. Thick smoke had been billowing up, bands had been playing, and lights had been moving at night. Accompanied by volleys of firearms, these were unmistakable signs that the Army of the Potomac was preparing to break camp. On the morning of May 2, a courier rode into the camp of the Richmond Howitzers. Congregating at their captain's tent, the soldiers heard familiar orders to pack everything they could not carry. Three years of warfare had taught these veterans to travel light. Destined for storage in Richmond, their fiddles, chessboards, and extra blankets and shirts were rolled into bundles, secured with straps, and pitched into a wagon. In two hours, the wagon was gone and the Howitzers stood in fighting trim. Each man

---

33. Wilkeson, *Recollections,* 49–54.

carried his possessions in a haversack and in a blanket rolled length-wise across his body. That evening, wind-driven rain lashed central Virginia. The next day—Tuesday, May 3—Confederate eyes strained toward Meade's camps through air washed clean by the downpour. On picket between Morton's Ford and Mine Run, McHenry Howard noticed a dust cloud stretching downriver over the Yankee side. Wagons and rifle barrels were seen parading to the right at an exposed point. Howard relayed his sightings to the Clark's Mountain lookouts, who replied that they had a full view of the movement. That evening, two Union deserters came across the river and confirmed that Grant's army was in motion.[34]

Around midnight, a guard summoned Sergeant B. L. Wynn, who was in charge of the Clark's Mountain signal station, to the observation glass. Peering through his telescope, Wynn picked out telltale flickers indicating the passage of troops in front of campfires. He immediately alerted headquarters. A question came back: Were the enemy soldiers advancing toward Germanna Ford, on the right, or toward Liberty Mills, on the left? Wynn replied that he could not determine their direction. An hour later, the signal station passed along a message from Lee: "General Ewell, have your command ready to move by daylight." Odds were that Grant was marching to the right, and that the enemy movement had already started.[35]

"So the ball is about to begin," Stuart's aide Alexander R. Boteler wrote in his diary. "We'll have stirring time here before the week is over with more than double our effective force to contend with."[36]

The direction of the enemy's march was confirmed at daybreak. Down the mountain from Wynn, guns and bayonets caught the morning sun. Roads had turned blue with Union soldiers. Canvas wagon tops traced lines of white across green fields below. The flow of troops was chiefly downriver. Clouds of dust, the sergeant in-

---

34. Dame, *From the Rapidan to Richmond*, 64–67; Howard, *Recollections*, 268. Howard expressed concern that his recollection of dust on the third might have been off by one day. Any dust on the third was probably from Federal trains rolling toward Richardsville.

35. B. L. Wynn Diary, May 4, 1864, in B. L. Wynn Papers, MDAH; B. L. Wynn, "Lee Watched Grant at Locust Grove," *Confederate Veteran*, XXI (1913), 68.

36. Alexander Boteler Diary, May 3, 1864, in William E. Brooks Collection, LC.

formed Lee, were boiling up from roads leading south and east toward Fredericksburg, with Germanna Ford the apparent object of Federal activity. Howard, at his river post, again watched a canopy of dust lazily hover over the Union line of march.

Stuart's bold troopers were busy. After briefly skirmishing with Federal cavalry at the fords, the gray scouts melted into the underbrush. Their assignment was to keep track of the Yankees, not to fight them. All day they forward reports of Grant's progress to Lee.

Patrolling just off the downriver crossings was the 1st North Carolina Cavalry, led by the intrepid Major William H. H. Cowles. At 9 A.M., Cowles discovered Union pickets at Mrs. Willis' house, on Flat Run Road, two miles below Germanna Ford. Some were on foot, although it was unclear to Cowles whether they were infantry or dismounted cavalry. Wagons could be heard clanking on Germanna Plank Road.

The main body of Fitzhugh Lee's rebel cavalry division had assembled early in the morning for a review at Hamilton's Crossing, near Fredericksburg. In attendance were General Lee's wife, Governor William ("Extra Billy") Smith, of Virginia, and other notables. The festivities were canceled, but the governor managed to make a speech to the assembled troops.[37]

At 9:30 A.M., the Clark's Mountain observation post confirmed the magnitude of Grant's advance. "From present indications," spelled out Wynn's signal flags in a message also observed by Federals across the river at Stony Mountain, "everything seems to be moving to the right on Germanna Ford and Ely's Ford roads, leaving cavalry in our front." Lee now had sufficient information for crafting his response. Grant was apparently crossing his entire force by the downriver fords, leaving behind only cavalry. That removed the danger of a second Union offensive around the other Confederate flank. Since a substantial rear guard was thus becoming unnecessary, Lee was free to maneuver with virtually his entire army.

By 10 A.M., Lee had settled on a course of action. Rather than retreating or remaining in his Rapidan trenches, he would march east

---

37. William H. H. Cowles's Report, in OR, Vol. LI, Pt. 2 Supplement, p. 888; J. D. Ferguson, "Memoranda and Itinerary of Operations of Major General Fitz Lee's Cavalry Division," in Thomas Munford Collection, DU. At 9 A.M., Sorrel informed Alexander that "many of the enemy's camps have disappeared from the front, and large wagon trains are reported moving through Stevensburg" (OR, Vol. XXXVI, Pt. 2, p. 947).

to meet Grant. Lee's reasoning cannot be reconstructed with certainty. Most Confederate reports and communications generated in 1864 were destroyed during the calamitous evacuation of Richmond the following year. Lee left few pertinent writings, and his aides' memoirs are sketchy. All that survives bearing on the Confederate general's strategic assessment early on May 4 is a telegram Longstreet sent at half past ten. "I fear the enemy is trying to draw us down to Fredericksburg," warned Lee's War Horse from his Gordonsville camp. "Can't we threaten his rear, so as to stop his move?" Concerned that Grant intended to entice the Confederates east and then to attack from the Rappahannock, Longstreet advised Lee to "keep away from there."[38]

Although incorrect, Longstreet's opinion that Grant was headed to Fredericksburg was based on a realistic appraisal. Fredericksburg was an obvious base for a Union foray against Richmond, and the Richmond, Fredericksburg and Potomac Railroad would provide an ideal conduit for Grant's supplies as his army moved south. Fredericksburg had been Burnside's favored approach to the Confederate capital in 1862 and Meade's in 1863. By taking Fredericksburg from behind, Grant would circumvent the town's natural defensive features. With a stranglehold on the railway and a path south relatively free from obstacles, he would be hard to stop. Moreover, as Longstreet pointed out, confronting Grant below Fredericksburg would expose the Army of Northern Virginia to a second Federal attack from the east.

Fredericksburg was certainly a possible Union target, but Lee thought it equally likely that Grant would turn west toward the Army of Northern Virginia. And although his surviving dispatches do not mention it, he also undoubtedly weighed the chance of Grant's proceeding south and interposing his forces between the Army of Northern Virginia and Richmond.

Now that Grant had mobilized his entire force, Lee had to act quickly. Remaining in place meant forfeiting the initiative. Retreating only moved the defensive frontier nearer Richmond and delayed without purpose the inevitable clash. As Lee had warned President Davis a few days before, evacuating the Rapidan line would probably spell the Confederacy's doom.

38. James Longstreet to Robert E. Lee, May 4, 1864, in *OR*, Vol. XXXVI, Pt. 2, p. 947.

All things considered, then, striking east toward Grant maximized Lee's opportunities to exploit whatever the enemy might decide to do. If the Yankees made for Fredericksburg, Lee could pursue, nipping at their heels. If Grant came at Lee, the Army of Northern Virginia could assume its old Mine Run line, or a variation on it. And if the enemy advanced south through Spotsylvania Court House, Lee could lunge at its exposed flank, disrupt it on the move, and as a last resort, take up a new line on the North Anna. In sum, driving toward Grant offered Lee possible openings against the enemy. Doing nothing or retreating offered only the certainty of more desperate battles later on.

Midmorning, Lee directed Ewell to start the Confederate 2nd Corps east on the Orange Turnpike. He was to leave behind a light rear guard consisting of Brigadier General Stephen D. Ramseur's brigade and six regiments drawn from Johnson's and Early's divisions. At the same time, Lee instructed Hill's 3rd Corps veterans— except for Anderson's division, which was also to stay behind to patrol the river—to advance through Orange Court House and continue east on Orange Plank Road. Lee's plan was for Ewell's soldiers to camp a few miles past Mine Run on the turnpike and for Hill's men to bivouac at New Verdiersville, just short of Mine Run on the Orange Plank Road. The two Confederate corps would be within easy supporting distance of each other and would have but a short march the next morning before encountering the Federals.

At 11 A.M., Longstreet issued orders to his two divisions—Field's and Kershaw's, camped on either side of Gordonsville—to prepare to move at once. Their objective was Richard's Shop, a village on Catharpin Road just below the headwaters of Mine Run. The recommended route was across Brock's Bridge, on the North Anna. "The commanding general," added Sorrel, who drafted the orders, "would like you to get off this afternoon, and make five or six miles on the march."[39]

It is probable that Lee and Longstreet had settled on the Catharpin Road route during their discussions the previous week. As the day wore on, however, Lee apparently had second thoughts. According to Longstreet, at 1 P.M. the Confederate army commander di-

---

39. G. Moxley Sorrel to Charles W. Field, May 4, 1864, in OR, Vol. XXXVI, Pt. 2, pp. 947–48.

rected him to take a different route. He was to march north to Orange Court House, then take up position behind Hill on Orange Plank Road.

Distributing Lee's directive "for information of the commanders," Longstreet at the same time petitioned Lee to reinstate the cross-country route across Brock's Bridge. It would be shorter than passing through Orange Court House, he argued, and would avoid overcrowding Orange Plank Road with troops and wagons from two corps. Longstreet also sought Lee's permission to continue east, passing through Richard's Shop and out Catharpin Road to its intersection with Brock Road at Todd's Tavern. Once there, he would be across Meade's southern flank with excellent prospects for inflicting mischief on the Federals. His aim was to "intercept the enemy's march, and cause him to develop plans before he could get out of the Wilderness." Lee acquiesced in his 1st Corps commander's requests.[40]

In later years, when Longstreet's collaboration with radical Republicans sullied his war record in loyal Confederate circles, his recommendation to march cross-country was unfairly construed as intransigence akin to his behavior at Gettysburg. The general's plan sprang, however, from sound military reasoning. Although Lee's route involved better roads, it also risked congestion, which might have been fatal if speed and maneuverability became important. Longstreet's strategy permitted a Confederate advance out three roads rather than two, with Ewell in front on the turnpike, Hill a short distance behind on Orange Plank Road, and Longstreet pulling up even with them on Catharpin Road sometime the next day. Under Longstreet's plan as approved by Lee, the Army of Northern Virginia would unite on a front stretching along and below Mine Run, admirably positioned either to wage a strong defense or to strike out after the enemy. Contrary to postwar polemics against Longstreet, the War Horse's idea made sense, and Lee undoubtedly adopted it for that reason.

Meanwhile, Ewell's and Hill's soldiers completed last-minute preparations. Orders went out to cook three days' rations. At about 10 A.M., another courier galloped into the Richmond Howitzers'

---

40. James Longstreet's Report, in *OR*, Vol. XXXVI, Pt. 1, p. 1054; Longstreet, *From Manassas to Appomattox*, 556–57.

camp at Morton's Ford and disappeared into the captain's tent. The men again swarmed around to hear the news. "Boys, get ready," the captain quietly told them. "We leave here in two hours." A bugle sounded, soldiers hurriedly rolled up their tent flies and blankets, and drivers scurried to haul guns down from their positions. A South Carolina brigade received commands to "fall in" while cooking. Half-baked dough and raw meal were hastily thrust into haversacks. The "accumulated plunder of months," as one soldier described it, soon filled camp streets. "Away slid the rattling, shuffling, close-jointed column," recounted a rebel, "through camp after camp deserted, out into the high road, through Orange and beyond."[41]

By noon, Confederate units were filtering down trails and back roads to the Orange Turnpike. "It was very pleasant to us to get into the stir of the moving army again," Private William Dame, of the Howitzers, reminisced years later. "The morning is bright and pleasant," recorded a soldier in the Stonewall Brigade. "All nature seems smiling on this spring morning. What a grand sight is the [Army of Northern Virginia] in motion. The whole brigade is all life—seems as though they are never to be conquered." Hearty greetings flew back and forth. A popular topic was the disparity in size between Lee's army and the enemy's. According to Dame, the soldiers assumed that Grant had about 150,000 men; they could muster no more than 35,000 infantry until Longstreet arrived. "And yet," he wrote, "knowing all this, these lunatics were sweeping along to that appallingly unequal fight, cracking jokes, laughing, and with not the least idea in the world of anything else but victory. I did not hear a despondent word, nor see a dejected face among the thousands I saw and heard that day."[42]

Hill's soldiers faced a longer march than did Ewell's. They pushed rapidly out Orange Plank Road and sustained a blistering pace all day. Little Powell, leaving the ornate Italianate mansion below Orange Court House that had served as his winter quarters, rode at the head of his troops.

---

41. Cadmus Wilcox, "Lee and Grant in the Wilderness," in *The Annals of the War Written by Leading Participants North and South* (Philadelphia, 1879), 486–89; Dame, *From the Rapidan to Richmond*, 66–69; J. F. J. Caldwell, *The History of a Brigade of South Carolinians, First Known as Gregg's, and Subsequently as McGowan's Brigade* (Philadelphia, 1866), 126; Berry G. Benson, "Reminiscences," in Berry G. Benson Papers, SHC.

42. Dame, *From the Rapidan to Richmond*, 71–72; William G. Bean, *The Liberty Hall Volunteers: Stonewall's College Boys* (Charlottesville, Va., 1964), 185.

"Enemy has struck his tents," Lee's telegraph clicked over the line. "Infantry, artillery, and cavalry are moving toward Germanna and Ely's fords. This army in motion toward Mine Run." Lee closed with his usual request for aid: "Can Pickett's division move toward Spotsylvania Court House?" After alerting Richmond that the campaign had opened, Lee bade farewell to his camp on the Bloomsbury estate east of town, and joined Hill at the head of the 3rd Corps column.[43]

As shadows engulfed Mine Run, Ewell's and Hill's columns reached their assigned positions. They were joined during the evening by units from remote Rapidan outposts. Ewell's corps camped near Robertson's Tavern—or Locust Grove, as Confederates called the place—with Early's division spread around the tavern and east out the Orange Turnpike. Johnson's division bivouacked below Early's, and Rodes's division closed up behind Johnson's. The 2nd Corps' artillery collected on the turnpike immediately behind Early. Guns continued to roll in from distant grazing lands well into the next day.

The head of Ewell's column was camped perhaps two miles from Griffin's Federal division. The turnpike between the two forces lay empty under the moonlight.

Meanwhile Hill's soldiers, some of whom had covered twenty miles since noon, pitched their tents beside Orange Plank Road near Verdiersville. Heth's division camped beyond town toward Mine Run. Wilcox' stayed at Verdiersville itself. Stuart's cavalry remained along Orange Plank Road in front of Hill, scouts advanced well toward the Yankees.[44]

Miles away to the southwest, lead elements of Longstreet's corps were hurriedly washing road dust from their faces in the North Anna River. Bivouacked near Brock's Bridge, Longstreet was confident that he could overtake the rest of the army. In an optimistic frame of mind, he notified Lee by dispatch of his "hope to reach Richard's Shop by 12 tomorrow." The War Horse had set his men an impossible task. Leaving Mechanicsville at 4 P.M., Kershaw's division had

---

43. Robert E. Lee to Braxton Bragg, May 4, 1864, in *OR,* Vol. LI, Pt. 2 Supplement, p. 887.

44. Richard S. Ewell's Report, in *OR,* Vol. XXXVI, Pt. 1, p. 1070; William Pendleton's Report, *ibid.,* 1036–38; Jubal A. Early, *Lieutenant-General Jubal A. Early, C.S.A.: Autobiographical Sketch and Narrative of the War Between the States* (Philadelphia, 1912), 344–45, hereinafter cited as *War Memoirs;* Charles S. Venable, "The Campaign from the Wilderness to Petersburg," in *SHSP,* XIV, 523; Hotchkiss, *Confederate Military History,* III, 433–35.

consumed the afternoon marching ten miles to Brock's Bridge. Field's division, which had started from over six miles above Mechanicsville, needed several more hours just to catch up. While Kershaw's men ate their dinners, Field's troops labored to join them. And once the corps was reunited, it faced another sixteen hot and dusty miles to Richard's Shop. All told, for Longstreet to keep his commitment to Lee, Field's men were going to have cover thirty-two miles between 4 P.M. on the fourth and noon on the fifth, many of them in the dark. It was more than flesh and blood could do.

Unfamiliar with the winding country roads, Longstreet asked his chief quartermaster, Erasmus Taylor, to secure a competent guide. While the rest of the 1st Corps was struggling up, Taylor appeared with James Robinson, the county sheriff and a lifelong resident of the Wilderness. Longstreet had his guide.[45]

Lee erected his tent in a stand of woods near Mrs. Rhodes's house in New Verdiersville. This had been his headquarters five months before, during the Mine Run campaign. Lee had bided his time then, waiting for Meade to attack, but the Yankees had slipped away. The general's admonitions to young Blackford, delivered to emphatic whacks from his hair brush, had gone for naught. But this time he did not intend to wait. He would push out until he found Grant and force him to battle.

Much to Lee's disappointment, no new information had turned up to shed light on Grant's plans. At 11 A.M., shortly before Lee rode to join Hill in front of the 3rd Corps' column, the cavalryman Cowles had reported a strong body of Federal horsemen near Robertson's Tavern. Their presence lent plausibility to the idea that the enemy

---

45. Longstreet, *From Manassas to Appomattox*, 557; James Longstreet to Robert E. Lee, May 4, 1864, in *OR*, Vol. LI, Pt. 2 Supplement, p. 887; G. Moxley Sorrel Diary, May 4, 1864, in MC. Fitzhugh Lee later alleged that Lee sent a guide to direct Longstreet from Gordonsville to the Wilderness but that Longstreet rejected the guide, claiming he knew the route. According to the story, Longstreet "lost his way and reached the Wilderness twenty-four hours behind time" (Fitzhugh Lee, "A Review of the First Two Days' Operations at Gettysburg and a Reply to General Longstreet," in *SHSP*, V, 184–85). Longstreet denied ever having seen Lee's guide, and Taylor and Venable refuted the claim that Longstreet had lost his way. See Walter H. Taylor to James Longstreet, August 15, 1879, Charles S. Venable to James Longstreet, July 25, 1879, both in James Longstreet Papers, DU.

sought to move west toward the Confederates. But there were equally strong indications that it planned to advance in the opposite direction. Fitzhugh Lee had spied a "heavy cavalry force" making its way toward Fredericksburg on Orange Plank Road. It was impossible to tell if the blue-clad horsemen were feeling Grant's advance or were screening the enemy's flank and rear. The evidence was ambiguous. Grant could be going either way.[46]

Waiting in idleness while Grant planned his destruction was not Lee's style. A fight was inevitable, and Lee preferred to throw the first punch. Pushing ahead without knowing Grant's location or intentions was risky, but doing nothing meant losing whatever advantage had been gained by the day's hard march.

Weighing these factors, Lee concluded that thrusting Ewell and Hill east on Orange Plank Road and the turnpike until they struck the enemy was the only way to preserve the initiative. It was premature, of course, to jump into a full-scale fray. Longstreet's corps was not yet up, Hill was still missing Anderson's division, and Ewell was short Ramseur's brigade and several regiments. All told, Lee had about thirty thousand infantry in hand and about fifteen thousand more on the way. But surely Longstreet, who "hoped" to be up by noon, would arrive before the fighting got too far advanced. If anything went wrong, reasoned Lee, Ewell and Hill could always retreat to Mine Run.

Lee's adjutant Taylor notified Ewell at 8 P.M. of the commander's decision. "He wishes you to be ready to move early in the morning," wrote Taylor. "If the enemy moves down the river, he wishes to push after him. If he comes this way, we will take our old line." In either event, Lee's objective was firm. "The general's desire," emphasized Taylor, "is to bring [the enemy] to battle as soon now as possible." Presumably similar directions were issued to Hill. Taylor did not record whether Lee's eyes flashed as he dictated his orders, or whether he brandished his brush in anticipation of the morrow's events.[47]

With matters on the immediate front settled, Lee turned to events elsewhere in Virginia. In a telegram routed through Orange Court House, President Davis had requested Lee to "direct all operations in

---

46. William H. H. Cowles to Richard S. Ewell, May 4, 1864, in OR, Vol. LI, Pt. 2 Supplement, p. 888; Ferguson, "Memoranda," in Munford Collection, DU.

47. Walter H. Taylor to Richard S. Ewell, May 4, 1864, in OR, Vol. XXXVI, Pt. 2, p. 948.

western Virginia, regarding it as your left flank." Lee's hands were full on the Rapidan, but he sent a word of direction and encouragement to John C. Breckinridge, the past vice-president of the United States who was commanding the rebel force in the Shenandoah Valley. Sigel was reportedly advancing from Winchester, wrote Lee. Breckinridge was to "try and check this Valley movement as soon as possible." At all costs, he was to prevent the enemy from gaining a hold on Lee's left. Davis had also sent disquieting news about Butler's armada. "The latest reliable intelligence," reported the president, "is that the enemy from fifteen transports were landing at Bermuda Hundred [on the James] this afternoon. Another is that thirty transports and four gun-boats have been seen at City Point." Not only was Richmond imperiled but Lee would have to forgo hope of early reinforcements. Bushrod Johnson's brigade, which had started its march to join Lee, had been recalled, and Hoke's would be delayed "an interval of some days" until the crisis was under control. "With these facts and your previous knowledge," suggested Davis, "you can estimate the condition of things here, and decide how far your own movements should be influenced thereby."[48]

Some time that evening, Lee sat in his headquarters tent beside the Rhodes house and wrote frankly to the president. The long-threatened effort to take Richmond had clearly begun, he asserted. Meade had crossed the Rapidan on Lee's right, "whether with an intention of attacking, or moving toward Fredericksburg, I am not able to say." Butler's column would "doubtless now cooperate with Genl Meade, and we may assume is as strong as the enemy can make it." Lee minced no words. "Under these circumstances," he wrote, venting frustration held in check during the winter and spring, "I regret that there is to be any further delay in concentrating our own troops." The president, he counseled, should forget about peripheral fronts and accumulate his limited resources where they were most needed. "I recommend," Lee stressed, that "the troops in N.C. belonging to this army be at once returned to it, and that Genl [Pierre G. T.] Beauregard with all the force available for the purpose, be brought without delay to Richmond." The lessons of the previous twenty-four hours were clear. "It seems to me," advised Lee, "that

48. Jefferson Davis to Robert E. Lee, May 4, 1864, in *OR*, Vol. LI, Pt. 2 Supplement, 886–87.

the great efforts of the enemy here and in Georgia have begun, and that the necessity of our concentration at both points is immediate and imperative." Having had his say, he closed in his accustomed courtly vein. "I submit my views with great deference to the better judgment of Your Excellency, and am satisfied that you will do what the best interests of the country require."[49]

As the evening progressed, information about Federal dispositions continued pouring in from Stuart's scouts. Fitzhugh Lee, whose cavalry division had retired before Hancock's advance, had unearthed particularly important intelligence. After securing Chancellorsville, some of Gregg's Federal horsemen had continued east out Orange Plank Road toward Fredericksburg. Hoping to determine the enemy's intentions, Lee had dispatched a brigade of three mounted Virginia regiments under Brigadier General Lunsford L. Lomax. "Scouts adroitly made their way to Chancellorsville," Lee later reported, "and soon returned with the information that the heads of the enemy's columns were turning west from that place, marching toward Orange Court House, and that it was a general offensive move of Grant's army, their cavalry having merely moved out the Fredericksburg road to mask or protect such a movement."[50]

An exciting dispatch from Stuart stamped 11:15 P.M. supplemented Lomax' observations. Before dark, reported Lee's cavalry commander, Union horsemen had been spotted riding out Orange Plank Road west of Parker's Store. Rather than continuing to Mine Run, the Federal party had suddenly withdrawn. A local resident provided the explanation for this unusual behavior. He had seen a courier gallop up to Wilson, who was leading the Union riders, and warn that they had advanced too far from the Union army, which could proceed no further than the "church" that night. "This must have been Wilderness Church," Stuart concluded in his dispatch, "and this accounts for the falling back."[51]

Stuart's intelligence had given Lee a revealing look behind the Union cavalry screen. What he saw was encouraging. Federal forces were massed in the vicinity of Wilderness Church and Chancel-

49. Freeman, ed., *Lee's Dispatches*, 169–74.
50. Fitzhugh Lee's Report, in MC.
51. James E. B. Stuart to Robert E. Lee, May 4, 1864, in *OR*, Vol. LI, Pt. 2 Supplement, pp. 887–88.

lorsville. The Union advance had ground to a halt in the Wilderness. Moreover, Grant's intended direction was now known. Grant planned to swing his forces toward Lee.

By Lee's reckoning, rushing Ewell and Hill forward first thing in the morning offered a realistic shot at pinning Grant in the deep woods. Their job would be to hold the Federals in place until Longstreet could arrive and administer a killing blow.

The plan, of course, posed serious dangers. Five thin rebel divisions—five-eighths of Lee's infantry strength, to be exact—would have to occupy the entire Army of the Potomac, ten Union divisions in all, until Longstreet made his way up. By Longstreet's own calculations, he did not expect to reach Mine Run until noon on the fifth, and his 1st Corps veterans could not possibly reach the Wilderness until several hours later. To exploit the opportunity that Grant had so generously offered would require Lee to keep the Yankees busy for a full day with a force less than a third their size.

The opportunities, however, were impressive. Here was a chance to execute a flanking maneuver against Grant that promised to be every bit as effective as Stonewall Jackson's attack against the Federals in these same woods a year before. Longstreet's projected advance up Catharpin Road to Todd's Tavern would situate him cleanly astride the Federal flank, superbly positioned for a devastating attack on the morning of May 6.

Lee was engaged in a match for high stakes, filled with danger. There was a distinct possibility that Grant would destroy Ewell and Hill before Longstreet arrived. But risks, as always, were part of Lee's program. If the fates smiled upon his efforts—if Ewell and Hill could check Grant in the Wilderness for all of May 5 without being destroyed in the process—Lee would possess the opportunity to tear apart Grant's left flank with Longstreet's advance and send the blue-coated invaders packing once again. Undoubtedly soothed by these pleasant thoughts, Lee stretched across his cot for a few hours of sleep.

*"Lee will fight
behind Mine Run."*

Dutch gables on the deserted farmhouse occupied by Grant traced shifting patterns as the sun crossed a clear May sky. After sending early-afternoon dispatches to Washington and to Burnside, Grant had settled down for a cold lunch, later moving to a tent pitched in the yard. Inside were a portable canvas cot, a tin washbasin on an iron tripod, two folding camp chairs, and a pine table. Stuffed into a small trunk were his underclothing, an extra pair of boots, a suit, and toilet articles.

Shortly before dark, the demure general sat down under a tent fly to an informal dinner with his staff. Officers came and went. Some devoured quick mouthfuls of food before rushing off on errands; others lingered to chat. Grant ate quietly, oblivious to the activity around him. He nibbled only plain, unseasoned portions.

In keeping with the day's largely cheery mood, a fire was built in front of the general's camp, from fence rails. After dinner, Meade strolled over from his nearby tent, unfolded a portable camp chair in front of the blaze, and settled down in the flickering light to talk things over with his chief. Grant offered Meade a cigar, but the wind kept blowing out the older man's match. Producing a little silver briquette, Grant genially lit Meade's cigar. Now and then couriers interrupted with encouraging news of developments on other fronts. Sherman's armies were moving into position and expected fighting in a few days. Butler was ready with his transports, and Sigel's advance was going as predicted.[52]

The two generals reviewed the day's events and their plans for the morrow. Already Meade had decided to alter the next morning's movements. One major change involved Sheridan's three cavalry divisions. Meade had originally intended for Wilson to accompany his right column, for Gregg to proceed with the left column, and for Torbert to remain behind until the wagons were safely over. Then Torbert was to cross at Germanna Ford and join Wilson. Reports, however, had reached Meade that pesky Jeb Stuart and his rebel horsemen were at Hamilton's Crossing, near Fredericksburg. If these rumors were correct, then advancing Gregg and Hancock through Todd's Tavern and out Catharpin Road on May 5 as planned stood to expose the wagons seriously. The supply train had become Meade's obsession. To protect his wagons against Stuart, the anxious general reshuffled Sheridan's cavalry assignments. Gregg was to stay near the wagons rather than advance with Hancock, and Torbert was

---

52. Horace Porter, *Campaigning with Grant*, 45–47.

to forget about joining Wilson and instead reinforce Gregg. Humphreys alerted Hancock that Torbert would be passing through and instructed Sheridan to "move with Gregg's and Torbert's divisions against the enemy's cavalry in the direction of Hamilton's Crossing." [53]

Shifting Sheridan's focus away from Lee and toward Stuart's reputed location left Wilson responsible for screening not only Warren and Sedgwick but Hancock as well. Properly executed, Wilson's assignment involved exploring between the two armies, uncovering Lee's whereabouts, and sparring with Lee's columns to slow their advance and give Meade time to respond. The inexperienced cavalry chief was commanding Sheridan's smallest division. The job was manifestly beyond the capacity of his meager numbers. By realigning his cavalry to deal with an imagined threat on his left, Meade had dangerously weakened his horsemen where they were most needed. As the next days' events were to show, the Federals had forfeited their numerical advantage in the saddle.

Huddled around their crackling campfire, Grant and Meade also undoubtedly discussed the Army of the Potomac's projected infantry movements. Rather than sending Meade's infantry below Mine Run as Humphreys had originally envisioned, the commanders now inclined toward establishing a static line within the Wilderness. Issued at 6 P.M. on May 4, Meade's general order for May 5 looked to orient the Army of the Potomac toward Lee on a convex line from the Rapidan to Shady Grove Church. Hancock was to march out Catharpin Road and extend north. Warren was to stop at Parker's Store and connect with Hancock's right, trailing a line of troops back to Wilderness Tavern. And Sedgwick was to follow Warren and take up the 5th Corps' old position, posting a division at Germanna Ford until Burnside heaved into view. The trains were routed to Todd's Tavern, at the intersection of Catharpin and Brock roads, and the reserve artillery to Corbin's Bridge, on the Pamunkey River, closely behind Hancock. "After reaching the points designated," directed Meade, "the army will be held ready to move forward." Infantry "flankers and pickets" were to be thrown well out and the troops "held ready to meet the enemy at any moment." And there they were to sit, as

53. Order, in OR, Vol. XXXVI, Pt. 2, p. 371; Andrew A. Humphreys to Winfield S. Hancock, May 4, 1864, *ibid.*, 375; Charles Forsyth to David McM. Gregg, May 4, 1864, *ibid.*, 389.

Grant's aide Lieutenant Colonel Cyrus B. Comstock recorded in his diary that evening, waiting "for Burnside to get up." The decision to pull the army into line and to keep it there until Burnside arrived stemmed from a growing conviction, openly expressed by Meade, that Lee would "fight behind Mine Run." Meade believed that his opinion was justified by Wilson's dispatches and by intelligence from Stony Mountain. It was reasoned that Lee's evident decision to dig in along Mine Run had generously afforded the Federals an opportunity to tidy up their own troop dispositions. As Humphreys later emphatically explained, neither Grant nor Meade "intended or wished to fight a battle in the Wilderness." Rather, they meant to establish a line within the woods as a jumping-off point.[54]

Something about the Wilderness invariably clouded Yankee minds. Maneuvering to flank Lee from a strong position the year before, the Federals had left themselves low on horsemen and had disastrously missed one of Lee's crafty decisions. And similarly this spring, Meade left his critical front exposed. At this point, it mattered little how the Federals proceeded in the morning, whether grandly, as Humphreys had originally proposed, or circumspectly, as Meade's evening plans mandated. The Union leadership's decision to remain overnight in the Wilderness, combined with lax cavalry patrols, had erased any disadvantage to the Confederates occasioned by their failure to retard the Union advance. Unknown to the Union generals spinning their plans this balmy evening, Lee's 2nd Corps—Stonewall Jackson's men, who had once before made this underbrush ring with their deep-throated yells—were poised on the turnpike chafing to rip into Meade's column at first morning's light.

Meade retired to his headquarters. A little before midnight Grant entered his own tent and turned in. The next day, thought Grant's aide Porter, would probably bring "a fight if the armies encountered each other, a foot-race to secure good positions if the armies remained apart." Little did he suspect how soon the storm would break, or that it would rage with a fury overshadowing everything that had come before.[55]

54. Badeau, *Military History,* II, 101–103; Cyrus B. Comstock Diary, May 4, 1864, in LC; Andrew A. Humphreys, *The Virginia Campaign,* 56; Order, in OR, Vol. XXXVI, Pt. 2, p. 361. For the detailed order of march for the 2nd Corps, see *OR,* Vol. XXXVI, Pt. 2, p. 376; for the 5th Corps, *OR,* Vol. XXXVI, Pt. 2, pp. 378–79; for the 1st Division of the 6th Corps, *OR,* Vol. XXXVI, Pt. 2, p. 379.

55. Horace Porter, *Campaigning with Grant,* 47.

III

MAY 5, MORNING
Lee and Grant Find Surprise and Opportunity

*"If he is disposed to fight this side of
Mine Run at once, he shall be accommodated."*

MIXED SCENTS OF brewing coffee and pine hovered over the Federal camps. The still, hot night had been oppressive and sullen, more like deep summer than spring. Blue-clad forms were roused from their fitful sleep by bugles ringing through the woods. They rose sluggishly around stacks of rifles. Aching muscles and blisters served as painful reminders of the previous day's unfamiliar exertions.

Laughter broke the dawn's silence. Someone was cracking jokes "about hunting for the Johnnies through the forest, of the grand time we should have marching down to Richmond and entering the rebel capital." Men sat silently on the ground, lips compressed, staring vacantly into the dark forest, thinking of family and home. Some leaned against trees, writing letters.[1]

Not long after sunrise, Meade's columns renewed their march. Hancock advanced from Chancellorsville out Catharpin Road, headed for Todd's Tavern. Warren started on the wagon track from Wilderness Tavern toward Parker's Store. Sedgwick prepared to descend from Germanna Ford as soon as Warren moved on.

Heading up Meade's left wing, Hancock was in fine spirits. His Gettysburg wound—an ugly groin puncture that had yielded a twisted nail to a country doctor's probe—was doing well. Out of his ambulance and on horseback, the magnetic general cut a stirring figure. A sharpshooter marching past the general and his entourage was reminded more of a "4th of July celebration than real war." This morning he was busy untangling a ferocious traffic jam caused by

---

1. Theodore Gerrish, *Army Life: A Private's Reminiscences of the Civil War* (Portland, Maine, 1882), 158–59.

Meade's last-minute change in cavalry assignments. Gregg's horse-men, positioned the day before to lead Hancock's column, now clogged Catharpin Road waiting for Torbert. Altering his line of march to avoid congestion, Hancock took a route parallel to Cathar-pin Road and just north of it. Coincidentally, this was the same road that Stonewall Jackson had employed in his deadly flanking maneu-ver the year before. Detouring around wagons and knots of cavalry-men slowed Hancock's progress to an agonizing crawl. "Marched round more everywhere in all sorts of directions, frequent halts," a Massachusetts soldier recorded in his diary. "The sun's rays were ex-ceedingly warm," another soldier recalled of the morning's tramp, "and before eight o'clock men began to stagger from the ranks and sink down by the roadside overcome by the heat." A regiment of sharpshooters fanned through the woods. Marching toward Lee without a cavalry escort was unnerving. Wilson's horsemen were sup-posed to be somewhere nearby, but so far nothing had been heard from them.[2]

Things were also getting ticklish over at Wilderness Tavern. Warren, nervous as a cat, was at his peevish worst. Breakfasting early, the finicky New Yorker greeted the morning in a tidy uniform adorned with a major general's yellow sash. His jet black hair was neatly slicked back. At thirty-four, Warren was six years younger than Hancock and sixteen younger than Sedgwick. This was a big day for the frankly ambitious young man, which accounted in part for his snappish mood. Compulsive, meticulous, and openly brilliant, he was a favorite of Meade's. He had also impressed Grant, who considered him the "man I would suggest to succeed Meade" if a change in army commanders became necessary. Warren's soaring hopes of advancement depended on how he managed his corps in the coming days. "We are going to have a magnificent campaign," he had

---

2. Charles C. Perkis Memoir, in Civil War Times Illustrated Collection, USMHI; William C. Kent to "Evarts," May 4, 1894, in Civil War Miscellaneous Collection, USMHI; Weygant, *History of the One Hundred and Twenty-Fourth Regiment N.Y.S.V.*, 285; C. A. Stevens, *Berdan's United States Sharpshooters in the Army of the Potomac* (St. Paul, 1892), 401; William Y. W. Ripley, *Vermont Riflemen in the War for the Union: A History of Company F, First United States Sharp Shooters* (Rutland, Vt., 1883), 144; Winfield S. Hancock's Report, in OR, Vol. XXXVI, Pt. 1, p. 318; Mitchell's Daily Second Corps Memoranda, in OR, Vol. XXXVI, Pt. 1, p. 350.

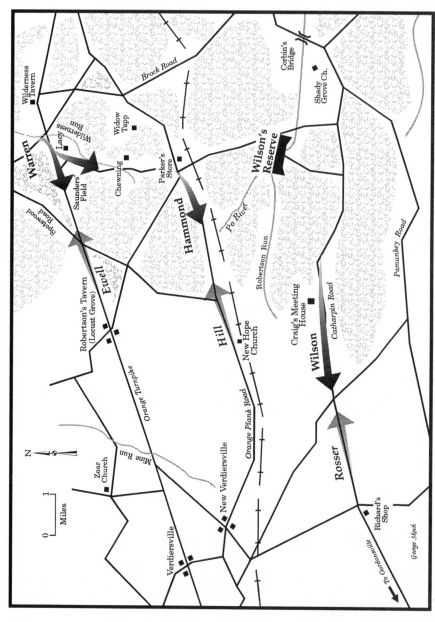

The situation during the morning of May 5

written his wife, Emily, shortly before leaving Culpeper, "and I have a situation commensurate with it." Little mistakes that on other occasions might have passed unnoticed were setting Warren boiling. For example, his ablest division commander, Charles Griffin, had neglected to follow headquarters' order to send a regiment with his wagons. Putting pen to paper at 5 A.M., Warren fired a note to Humphreys informing him of Griffin's dereliction and asking where the wayward regiment should be directed. Still stewing over an earlier incident, Warren added that he intended to make a "severe example" of an officer who had "positively failed to execute a very simple order last evening."[3]

Yet not all of Warren's concerns were petty. He was to maneuver twenty-four thousand soldiers five miles along a narrow, winding backwoods road overrun with brush while Lee's army hovered somewhere in the deep woods off to the right. Since Warren's 5th Corps was closest to the enemy, it would probably be the first Federal unit engaged.

As soon as daylight filtered through the pine boughs, Warren's engineers began laying three bridges over Wilderness Run, near the turnpike. From there they cleared a twenty-foot roadway along the trail to Parker's Store, wide enough for the corps' guns and "fighting wagons." Leaving the turnpike near the Lacy plantation, the trail wound along the steep, wooded western rim of Wilderness Run's watershed. Bothersome ravines and bogs made the going rough. A mile or so out, the track broke into an opening called Jones's Field, then plunged through another stretch of woods to the Chewning farm. There a set of bare, choppy knolls commanded Orange Plank Road and Parker's Store, an abandoned country market that formed Warren's morning objective. Strung out in a narrow file, Warren's soldiers would have to slice southwest across some of the Wilderness' worst terrain, right shoulders toward the Confederates. They would be blinded by thickets, their ranks unavoidably fractured into isolated clusters by Wilderness Run and its steep, marshy tributaries. For a few anxious hours at least, Warren's corps could anticipate an uncomfortable march.

3. Gouverneur K. Warren to wife, May 3, 1864, in Warren Collection, NYSA; Grant, *The Personal Memoirs*, II, 543; Gouverneur K. Warren to Andrew A. Humphreys, May 5, 1864, in OR, Vol. XXXVI, Pt. 2, p. 413.

Since Wilson's blue-clad horsemen had moved ahead to Parker's Store, Warren, like Hancock, was compelled to advance without a cavalry escort. He directed his soldiers to march slowly, "well closed and held well in hand, ready to meet an attack any moment." To compensate for the absence of cavalry, Warren threw out a thick cloud of infantry pickets. Foot patrols extended far to the right of the moving column and explored the paths in Lee's direction. For added safety, the corps' wagons were ordered to remain on the infantry's left, away from the rebels. Artillery batteries were dispersed among the divisions.[4]

The 5th Corps was on the move by 5 A.M. Leading off was Crawford's division of Pennsylvania Reserves, followed by Wadsworth's and Robinson's divisions. Griffin's veterans remained on the Orange Turnpike guarding the column's rear. They were to remain there until Sedgwick's 6th Corps moved down from the ford.

Griffin was an excellent choice for the critical rearguard assignment. A West Pointer and a seasoned Indian fighter, the slender, heavily moustached Ohioan was reputedly a "hard case." He was popular with his men, tough on rebels, and brazenly outspoken. Daring almost to a fault, he habitually elbowed cannoneers aside to instruct them on how to use their guns to good effect. "You are firing too high," he once chastened a battery. "Just roll the shot along the ground like a tenpin ball and knock their damned trotters from under them."[5]

Griffin had established his advanced position about a mile out the turnpike from Wilderness Tavern. Extending northward into the woods were soldiers from the 140th New York and 146th New York. On the south side were men from the 1st Michigan. Jointly they were under the command of Colonel David T. Jenkins, of the 146th. The pickets were poorly aligned, with the Michigan troops thrust several hundred yards ahead of the New Yorkers.

There seemed to be no reason for insisting that the pickets be correctly positioned. No fighting was expected for some time, least of all on the turnpike. Well behind the picket line, the main body of

---

4. Washington A. Roebling's Report, in Warren Collection, NYSA; Swan, "Battle of the Wilderness," in *PMHSM*, IV, 127. The road from the Lacy farm to Parker's Store no longer exists.

5. John J. Pullen, *The Twentieth Maine: A Volunteer Regiment in the Civil War* (Philadelphia, 1957), 179.

Griffin's division boiled coffee and sat down to "rude breakfasts," a Maine man later recalled, "with appetites such as are unknown in lives of luxury and ease." The rising sun sent "rays of light down like golden needles through the tops of the pine trees."[6]

About an hour after daybreak, with the rest of Warren's corps safely under way and no untoward developments occurring in their front, the pickets began packing. Soon they were to slip into place with the rest of Griffin's men at the end of the column weaving toward Parker's Store.

From the advanced outpost, the Orange Turnpike cut a swath slightly uphill, a straight, chalky line leading west through dense forest to the horizon. Almost as an afterthought, the blue-clad patrols took a last squinting look up the deserted roadway. Far in the distance, just above trees shimmering in the fresh spring sunlight, appeared a faint brush of dust. Straining harder, the curious Federals picked out small moving dots that slowly materialized into horsemen. Behind the riders were foot soldiers in tattered gray, slouch hats low over their eyes, rifles ready, striding ahead with a swinging, determined gait.[7]

Major George Hopper, of the 1st Michigan, had just finished breakfasting with the regiment's commander, Colonel William A. Throop. As he was buckling on his sword, a captain of obviously German ancestry ran in from the picket outpost. "Colonel, major," he blurted, "the enemy are coming, horse, foot, and artillery!" At the same moment an orderly arrived from brigade headquarters. Throop's orders were to join the procession toward Parker's Store. The Michigan commander directed the courier to ride back and report that he would stay put until headquarters had an opportunity to evaluate the new development. A Michigan aide accompanied the orderly to make sure that the brigade's commander, Brigadier General Joseph J. Bartlett, understood the gravity of the situation.[8]

Jenkins extended his line farther into the woods on each side of

6. Hopper, "Reminiscences," in MOLLUS Collection, BL; William A. Throop's Report, in OR, Vol. XXXVI, Pt. 1, p. 580; Gerrish, Army Life, 158.

7. Porter Farley, "The 140th New York Volunteers, Wilderness, May 5th, 1864," 19–20, in Porter Farley Papers, RL.

8. Hopper, "Reminiscences," in MOLLUS Collection, BL; Mary G. Brainard, Campaigns of the One Hundred and Forty-Sixth Regiment New York State Volunteers (New York, 1915), 179.

the road and called for reinforcements. Firearms leveled, the pickets braced for the customary bone-jarring impact of a Confederate charge. To their surprise, the rebel column unexpectedly stopped and began splaying gray-clad soldiers into the woods on both sides of the turnpike. The apparition had a decidedly unsettling quality and no discernible end. There was no telling how many had arrived, or exactly what they were planning to do.

In the meantime, Throop's breakfast companion, Hopper, devised an ingenious ruse. As Hopper later explained it, he ordered the captain in charge of the Michigan pickets "to march his reserve across the road in plain view of the enemy, and when they were hidden from the enemy's view on the opposite side of the road, to move back out of sight and to return to his old position and cross over again within their view." But since the rebels were beginning to deploy cavalry, Hopper had doubts about how long he could bluff them with his "little game."[9]

A mile to the east, at Wilderness Tavern intersection, Warren was mounting his oversize dapple-gray and gently spurring the horse onto the Orange Turnpike. From Warren's perspective, things were progressing smoothly. Crawford's division had disappeared down Parker's Store trail. Wadsworth's men were filing past the Lacy plantation, a few hundred yards on the other side of the turnpike, and falling into place behind Crawford.

As Warren rode to join the moving column, a staff officer galloped up in a cloud of dust, reigned in his lathered horse, and hurriedly saluted. Griffin had sent him, he panted, to warn that Confederates were advancing on his pickets.

Shock rippled through Warren's little group of horsemen. Lee was supposed to be miles away, on the other side of Mine Run, separated by a buffer of Union cavalry. At most, reasoned the excitable general, Griffin's jumpy pickets confronted a light force of rebels trying to slow Meade's advance while Lee perfected his Mine Run entrenchments. "Tell Griffin to get ready to attack at once," Warren barked to a youthful aide, then thought better of his selection of couriers and gave the assignment to an experienced staffer.[10]

Returning to his tent, Warren hastily drafted a note to headquarters. An unconfirmed report, he wrote, placed enemy soldiers on the

9. Hopper, "Reminiscences, in MOLLUS Collection, BL.
10. Schaff, *The Battle of the Wilderness*, 125–26.

Orange Turnpike. Concluding that Griffin probably faced an inconsequential rebel diversionary force, the general added that he had no intention of modifying his corps' movement. In closing, Warren could not resist offering his superiors a few words of advice. "Such demonstrations are to be expected," he lectured, "and show the necessity for keeping well closed and prepared to face toward Mine Run and meet an attack at a moment's notice." [11]

Before Warren had an opportunity to dispatch his note to Meade, another messenger arrived from Griffin. This time he carried something in writing, and it was a little more concrete than the breathless courier's earlier report. Rebel infantry were indeed on the turnpike, warned Griffin. They were forming a line of battle, and clouds of dust were boiling up in Lee's direction.

Warren added this latest intelligence as a postscript to his note to Meade and dispatched a staffer to deliver the news to the commanding general. Then he dashed off another order to Griffin. Hold the turnpike until Sedgwick arrives, he commanded. "Push a force out at once against the enemy and see what force he has." [12]

"I saw at once that the programme of the day would have to change," Warren later claimed, "but I continued to carry it out sending word back to General Meade as to the facts and keeping General Griffin in position. We were in fact by going on with the movement getting our line of battle facing the enemy." [13]

On receiving Warren's directive, Griffin ordered his brigadier Bartlett to probe west along the turnpike to find out exactly what was going on. Bartlett was something of a dandy. Once, when he appeared in a particularly flashy uniform, Griffin reputedly inquired of him, "Well, Bartlett, when will the circus arrive?" But despite occasional sartorial excess, Bartlett was an aggressive soldier. And for this ticklish assignment he wisely chose two seasoned regiments, the 18th Massachusetts and the 83rd Pennsylvania, and placed them under the command of the rough-and-tumble Colonel Joseph Hayes. Bartlett rode ahead to the picket line, spurs jangling. Hopper met him and explained the immediate danger. Advanced as they were, the Michigan pickets would be unable to offer resistance to an attack.

11. Gouverneur K. Warren to Andrew A. Humphreys, May 5, 1864, in *OR*, Vol. XXXVI, Pt. 2, p. 413.

12. Frederick T. Locke to Charles Griffin, May 5, 1864, in *OR*, Vol. XXXVI, Pt. 2, p. 416.

13. Gouverneur K. Warren to Charles Porter, November 21, 1875, in Warren Collection, NYSA.

Bartlett ordered them to drop back and connect with the 146th New York.[14]

Meanwhile Hayes tried to figure out what the Confederates had in mind. "With the aide of my glass," he later recorded in his journal, "I could plainly see the enemy filing off to the right and left of the road and apparently massing his forces." Determined to have a closer look, he formed his skirmishers in bushes along the turnpike, two companies of the 18th Massachusetts on the left and two from the 83rd Pennsylvania on the right. Quietly they worked up the roadway, hunched over in anticipation.[15]

Several hundred yards past the picket line, the Federal skirmishers came to the edge of Saunders' Field. This was a ragged, uneven old corn patch about four hundred yards deep and eight hundred yards wide. It was noteworthy as one of the few extensive clearings in the Wilderness. The field was destined to become the location of some of the Civil War's most brutal fighting. The turnpike ran more or less through the center of Saunders' Field. Halfway across was a deep swale that gouged its way roughly from north to south. To cross the swale, traffic had to take a short bypass over a temporary bridge. The field sloped uphill from the swale to the western edge of the clearing. Pausing in undergrowth, Hayes's soldiers got a clear view of the rebels. A substantial enemy force was visible on the clearing's far side. Their shovels could be seen flying as they gouged out a rough line of earthworks. Hayes's skirmishers retired from their completed scouting mission to the Union picket line under a blaze of enemy fire. During their withdrawal, an eighteen-year-old Massachusetts farmer, Charles Wilson, was shot. He became the campaign's first casualty.[16]

At 7:15 A.M., as Hayes's expedition was preparing to explore the thickets, Warren's messenger caught up with Meade, who was on

---

14. Theodore Gerrish and John Hutchinson, *The Blue and the Gray* (Portland, Maine, 1883), 405; Hopper, "Reminiscences," in MOLLUS Collection, BL.

15. Joseph Hayes Journal, May 5, 1864, in Joshua Chamberlain Collection, LC.

16. *Ibid.;* William White's Report, in *OR,* Vol. XXXVI, Pt. 1, p. 575. The clearing apparently took its name from the Saunders family, who lived nearby. It was also called Palmer's Field and Sanders' Field. See Noel G. Harrison, *Gazetteer of Historic Sites Related to the Fredericksburg and Spotsylvania National Military Park* (Fredericksburg and Spotsylvania National Military Park, 1986), 260.

his way down from Germanna Ford. Lee's infantry was on the turnpike "in some force," announced the aide, and less than two miles from Wilderness Tavern. Meade, accelerating his pace, reached the tavern in minutes. He held a hurried conference with Warren. According to an officer standing nearby, Meade emphatically exclaimed, "If there is to be any fighting this side of Mine Run, let us do it right off." Promptly he issued a spate of orders intended to array an irresistible Federal body against the Confederates on the Orange Turnpike. Canceling the day's plan, he directed Warren to "halt his column and attack the enemy with his whole force." A courier hurried south with instructions to stop Hancock at Todd's Tavern, several miles short of his assigned objective, "until the matter develops." If Warren needed help, Meade would see to it that plenty was available.[17]

At this juncture, Meade was still laboring under the erroneous impression that Lee's main body was ensconced along Mine Run. Immediately forwarding a message to Grant, the hawk-nosed Pennsylvanian offered the opinion that Lee was only "trying to delay our movement and will not give battle." Nonetheless, Meade explained, he was suspending the Army of the Potomac's advance until Griffin had "developed" the enemy in front of him. Paradoxically, Meade had correctly divined that Lee's purpose was to delay the Federal army, but had then obligingly halted his own troop movement, doing exactly as Lee had hoped he would. Meade's actions were playing into Lee's hands beyond anything the bold Virginian had a right to expect.[18]

Grant's response, which reached Meade about an hour later, was fashioned to nourish the Pennsylvanian's encouraging sign of belligerence. Grant emphatically approved Meade's new plan of thrusting every available Federal toward the phantom Confederate force on the turnpike. "If any opportunity presents itself of pitching into a part of Lee's army," Grant urged his subordinate, "do so without giving time for disposition."[19]

17. Andrew A. Humphreys, *The Virginia Campaign,* 23; Andrew A. Humphreys to Winfield S. Hancock, May 5, 1864, in *OR,* Vol. XXXVI, Pt. 2, p. 406; George G. Meade to Gouverneur K. Warren, May 5, 1864, in *OR,* Vol. XXXVI, Pt. 2, p. 404; George G. Meade's Report, in *OR,* Vol. XXXVI, Pt. 1, p. 189. The reporter Page noted, "General Meade rode up ten minutes ago and said to Warren, 'If the enemy comes near you, pitch right in with all you've got'" (Charles A. Page, *Letters of a War Correspondent,* 47).

18. George G. Meade to Ulysses S. Grant, May 5, 1864, in *OR,* Vol. XXXVI, Pt. 2, p. 403.

19. Ulysses S. Grant to George G. Meade, May 5, 1864, in *OR,* Vol. XXXVI, Pt. 2, p. 403.

Time for disposition, however, was precisely what Meade needed. In order to launch an attack out the Orange Turnpike, Warren's corps had first to be fashioned into a unified line. That would be no easy task. While Griffin's division was already in place, Crawford's lead units were just blinking into daylight at the Chewning farm, over two miles away. Wadsworth was still hacking his way up Wilderness Run valley, and Robinson remained at Wilderness Tavern.

Forming a united front toward Lee meant that the marching divisions had to halt, shift from column to line facing west, and link together, in a tricky maneuver on a crowded wooded trail with rebels hovering unseen nearby. Even worse, Wadsworth's rightmost units were going to have to grope toward Griffin's left wing by passing through uncharted stretches of wilderness. It was a high-stakes game of blindman's bluff in an intractable forest and a practical reminder of why Meade had wanted to avoid fighting there in the first place. With Warren struggling to rally against a yet undefined threat, Hancock sitting on his haunches down on Catharpin Road, and Sedgwick strung all the way back to Germanna Ford, the Army of the Potomac was far too scattered to pitch into anyone.

It was now 7:30 A.M. Determined to do his best despite the terrain's obstacles, Warren ordered Crawford, Wadsworth, and Griffin to hook up. Griffin was to prepare "to move forward and attack the enemy, and await further instructions, while the other troops are forming." Robinson's division was held in reserve near Wilderness Tavern. One of Robinson's brigades—Colonel Andrew W. Denison's Marylanders—was pushed forward to help cement the hoped-for connection between Wadsworth and Griffin and to add striking power near the turnpike.[20]

Shortly before 8 A.M., Warren rode out to make sure that things were moving according to plan. Flankers extended, Wadsworth had advanced about a mile out the Parker's Store trail. His men were nervously listening to occasional rifle discharges from their skirmishers and from Crawford's just ahead.

The stifling woods were having a bad effect on Warren's already precarious equanimity. The corps commander finally located Wadsworth near the crumbling chimney of an overseer's house. When an

---

20. Locke to Griffin, May 5, 1864, in *OR*, Vol. XXXVI, Pt. 2, p. 416; Frederick T. Locke to John C. Robinson, May 5, 1864, in *OR*, Vol. XXXVI, Pt. 2, p. 417.

aide suggested using a bare knoll nearby as a site for a battery, Warren snapped that when he wanted advice he would ask for it. Then the general set off to inspect Wadsworth's line himself. The Genesee aristocrat was busy trying to arrange his division facing west, batteries covering Parker's Store Road. "Find out what is in there," snarled Warren, stabbing a finger toward the thickets. After dispatching his chief personal aide, Roebling, to travel ahead and examine Crawford's dispositions, the irritable general rode off to check the situation on the Orange Turnpike.[21]

On the roadway, Griffin was preparing with characteristic thoroughness. He had straightened his picket line and had started constructing sturdy earthworks. Axes rang as Griffin's lead regiments, including the likes of the 20th Maine's hearty woodsmen, leveled trees for ten rods in front of the Federal position, stripped them of branches, and stacked the logs into breast-high embankments. His men would have a strong rallying point and a clear field of fire if things went wrong.

Up on the picket line, Union soldiers continued to watch a seemingly endless procession of rebels pour down the turnpike and disappear from view on either side of the road. It was impossible to gauge how many Confederates were out there or what they were doing. The most likely scenario involved a growing enemy formation extending perpendicular to the turnpike, perhaps overlapping both of Griffin's unprotected flanks.

The novelty of the situation was grasped by Griffin's troops. "Here were two great armies," wrote a bemused Federal soldier, "forming line of battle for a desperate struggle, within half a mile of each other, scarcely a movement of either of which could be observed by the other." Hopper thought that "it was as good as a stage play for us who watched from our new location the gentlemen in Gray with guns poised perpendicularly in front of them ready to drop to an aim, steal from tree to tree until they were at the edge of the woods and could look across the field and note all of our movements, the same as we had been doing by them."[22]

By this time it was clear that the Confederates were assembling

21. Schaff, *The Battle of the Wilderness*, 129–30; Frank Cowdrey's Report, in *OR*, Vol. XXXVI, Pt. 1, p. 614.

22. Amos M. Judson, *History of the Eighty-Third Regiment Pennsylvania Volunteers* (Erie, Pa., 1865), 192; Hopper, "Reminiscences," in MOLLUS Collection, BL.

a strong force, and Warren was told so. Enthusiastic cheers greeted the 5th Corps' commander as he rode along Griffin's freshly dug earthworks.

While Warren was laboring to mount the 5th Corps against invisible enemies on the turnpike, Meade began casting about for additional troops to funnel to the rapidly expanding front. Of particular concern was Warren's wide-open northern flank.

Sedgwick's 6th Corps, rumbling down from Germanna Ford, was ideally positioned to extend Warren's line northward toward the Rapidan. At 7:30 A.M., Sedgwick's lead division under George Getty had reached Warren's old encampments around Wilderness Tavern. A second division, Horatio Wright's, was still two miles north, near Spotswood plantation. From there, a farm road slanted southwest to the Orange Turnpike, passing by Saunders' Field and Warren's vulnerable right flank. The shortcut was little more than a cow path on the order of the Parker's Store trail, but it provided a solution to Meade's problem. Stiffening Wright's division with an extra brigade taken from Getty, he ordered the augmented force out the trail from Spotswood, expecting it to hook up with Warren. Notifying Warren that help was on the way, Meade also gave the temperamental 5th Corps commander another nudge. "Attack as soon as you can," he ordered, "and communicate, if possible, with Wright." [23]

Throughout these preparations, Meade continued under the misapprehension of Lee's whereabouts that had governed his planning for the preceding twenty-four hours. He mused out loud that the Confederates had "left a division to fool us here, while they concentrate and prepare a position toward the North Anna." He decided, "What I want is to prevent those fellows from getting back to Mine Run." [24]

Satisfied that his arrangements were moving apace, he sent a note to Grant summarizing how things stood. "Warren is making his disposition to attack, and Sedgwick to support him," read Meade's

---

23. George W. Getty's Report, in *OR*, Vol. XXXVI, Pt. 1, p. 676; George G. Meade to Gouverneur K. Warren, May 5, 1864, in *OR*, Vol. XXXVI, Pt. 2, p. 404.
24. Swinton, *Campaigns of the Army of the Potomac*, 420–21n.

9 A.M. dispatch to the commander in chief. "Nothing immediate from the front." Lee was "simply making a demonstration to gain time," emphasized Meade, who expressed the intention to make him pay dearly. "I shall, if such is the case, punish him," blustered the army commander in language hauntingly reminiscent of Federal boasts the previous year. "If he is disposed to fight this side of Mine Run at once, he shall be accommodated."[25]

The morning's surprises, however, were far from over. Temporarily thrown off balance by the unexpected appearance of rebels on the Orange Turnpike, Meade had forgotten to include Orange Plank Road in his calculations. That was the cavalryman Wilson's territory. Meade expected Wilson to warn of any dangers in his quarter. "My pickets report nothing new from the enemy this morning," Wilson had reported at 5 A.M., before leaving his encampment at Parker's Store and disappearing south into the leafy void. Nothing had been heard from him after that. In the absence of news to the contrary, headquarters assumed that all was well. At 9 A.M., the silence from Wilson's direction was broken. An hour-old dispatch arrived from Crawford, Warren's thick-whiskered division commander heading the procession out Parker's Store Trail. He had received Warren's earlier directive to halt and had taken up a "good position" on the Chewning farm's open fields about a mile short of the store. "There is brisk skirmishing at the Store between our own and the enemy's cavalry," he reported. For the first time, headquarters was alerted that rebels were materializing well down Orange Plank Road close to Warren's left flank. In Warren's absence—the 5th Corps commander was still off inspecting Griffin's preparations on the turnpike—Crawford's message was forwarded to Meade. The commanding general was not overly disturbed by the news. Vigorous rebel cavalry probes came as no surprise. The disturbing thing, however, was Wilson's blatant failure to do his job. Not a single communication had reached headquarters from the young cavalryman for four hours, leaving Meade to learn about Confederate movements from surprised infantry commanders, first on the turnpike and now on the Plank Road. "Dispatch from Crawford received," the testy Pennsylvanian scrawled across the message. No doubt he was seething over the ineptitude of the amateur cavalry commander, handpicked by

25. George G. Meade to Ulysses S. Grant, May 5, 1864, in *OR,* Vol. XXXVI, Pt. 2, p. 404.

Grant from his coterie of Western cronies. "I have sent to Wilson," Meade added, slipping into sarcasm, "who, I hope, will himself find out the movement of the enemy." Scouting was Wilson's job. It was a sorry state of affairs for Meade to find out about Lee's activities from startled Union infantry heads this late in the game.[26]

Ten o'clock passed. Still no word arrived from Wilson. Straight ahead, where the turnpike disappeared into the forest, a rising crescendo of firing filtered back through the trees. Encounters between blue and gray skirmishers were heating up. By now, if all was going as planned, Griffin should be ready for battle. Wadsworth should be coming up on Griffin's left and Wright slipping into place on Griffin's northern flank.

At 10:15, a courier arrived from the Chewning farm with the day's second bombshell, every bit as unnerving as the earlier news of rebels on the Orange Turnpike. The Confederate horsemen that Crawford had reported seeing over an hour before were not just scouts. They were apparently the vanguard of a substantial Confederate infantry force. Firing had sputtered out in his sector, reported Crawford. Rebels were working around his left flank and continuing eastward on Orange Plank Road.[27]

What had begun as a hopeful morning's march was rapidly taking an ugly, familiar turn. Once again, the Union high command had underestimated Lee's audacity. The true state of affairs was becoming painfully clear. Rather than huddling defensively behind Mine Run, as Meade had assumed, Lee's troops were descending down the turnpike and Orange Plank Road. Rebels were engulfing both of Warren's flanks and threatening to sever Hancock, still miles south on Catharpin Road, from the rest of the Union army. The horrible truth was that Meade's dispositions, undertaken on the erroneous premise that Lee was digging in miles away, had imperiled the entire Federal plan

26. James H. Wilson to Andrew A. Humphreys, May 5, 1864, in OR, Vol. XXXVI, Pt. 2, p. 429; Samuel W. Crawford to Frederick T. Locke, May 5, 1864, ibid., 418; Frederick T. Locke to Andrew A. Humphreys, May 5, 1864, ibid.

27. Crawford to Locke, May 5, 1864, in OR, Vol. XXXVI, Pt. 2, p. 418.

of campaign. By halting and concentrating to annihilate a suspected "diversionary force," Meade had unwittingly left the Army of the Potomac open to a devastating counterthrust from Lee.

Both of Meade's fronts were in shambles. Despite Warren's efforts, Griffin was still standing alone on the turnpike. His flanks were fair game for the Confederates. Reinforcements had simply failed to materialize. Wright had yet to start from Spotswood. Wadsworth, last heard from at 8:30, vaguely claimed to be massed in a clearing on Parker's Store Road with a "brigade stretched thinly through a piece of very thick woods, and one brigade near [Griffin]." Two miles south, Crawford was sprawled across the Chewning farm, separated from Wadsworth by a milewide gap. He was in no position to aid Griffin and was facing serious trouble himself. Not only was Warren manifestly unprepared to initiate an assault but he was in questionable shape to receive one should Lee take the initiative.[28]

Disaster was also a real possibility in Hancock's direction. Brock Road was a narrow wagon route that originated near Wilderness Tavern and wound south. It served as Hancock's tenuous link with the rest of Meade's army. Orange Plank Road intersected Brock Road neatly between the two Federal wings. According to Crawford's most recent intelligence, the newly discovered rebel force was closer to the intersection of Brock and Orange Plank roads than were any of Meade's soldiers. Unless Meade quickly pumped experienced combat units to the endangered road junction, the Army of the Potomac faced being split in two.

Serious decisions had to be made, and Meade did not want sole responsibility to rest on his shoulders. "Sedgwick," he called out, addressing his trusted friend and the commander of his 6th Corps, "I am short of staff officers. Would you lend me one?" Lieutenant Colonel Thomas W. Hyde, Sedgwick's chief aide, happened to be handy. "Go back to Germanna Ford," Meade directed Hyde, "and you will meet Grant coming to the front. Tell him Lee is moving down the plank road and the turnpike, and I have pushed Warren and [Sedgwick] out to meet him."[29]

28. James S. Wadsworth to Charles Griffin, May 5, 1864, in OR, Vol. XXXVI, Pt. 2, p. 420.
29. Hyde, Following the Greek Cross, 182–83.

*"We expected that the infantry would relieve
our detachments on the various roads."*

The gnarly, broken thickets had begun leaking Confederates all along Meade's front. The intruders were not just a few random gray scouts looking for information. They belonged to thick, sinewy columns stretching back as far as the eye could see, representing whole divisions and corps, openly spoiling for a fight and intent on wrecking Grant's grand offensive in its infancy.

Particularly disconcerting to the Federals was Lee's ability to sidle up to them before they had a hint that he was nearby. Taken by surprise, Meade had no choice but to abandon his carefully orchestrated advance. He was going to have to struggle to rearrange his forces and counter an enemy about whose location, numbers, and intentions he could only speculate.

Meade's uncomfortable predicament was largely the consequence of shortsighted cavalry dispositions. Elementary military prudence dictated that Meade should have saturated the country toward Lee with blue-clad horsemen to screen the Federal infantry's advance and to uncover and disrupt the enemy's plans. Had Meade learned on May 4 of Lee's simultaneous advance out the turnpike and Orange Plank Road, his actions on May 5 unquestionably would have been different. With proper intelligence, he would doubtless have thrown heavy concentrations across both of Lee's chosen routes to crush the rebel columns. Instead, lacking both an early warning of the Confederate advance and the mounted capacity to slow Lee's progress, Meade was forced to shuffle troops frantically to meet a contingency far different from what he had anticipated.

From the campaign's outset, Federal cavalry plans had been woefully inadequate. Initially, Meade had assigned only James Wilson's division to cover the army's critical front. These 3,500 troopers were as "nearly ready as volunteer cavalry ever is," Wilson later remarked. But they were hardly sufficient to police a ten-mile front. Meade's last-minute decision to detain Gregg at Chancellorsville and to reassign Torbert to join him there left Wilson with no prospect of reinforcements. And Meade's orders for Wilson to continue south on the morning of the fifth stretched Wilson's troopers far beyond their capacity. At Gettysburg, Lee had been caught off guard because of his cavalry's absence, and he had learned a valuable lesson. Meade was about to receive similar instruction in the Wilderness.

Although loath to admit it even when he penned his memoirs nearly fifty years later, Wilson also made some poor decisions himself that compounded the problems created by Meade's planning. Wilson's most significant error involved his failure to post pickets on the Orange Turnpike. His confusion apparently originated from imprecise language in Meade's initial marching orders for May 4. Those instructions directed Wilson to patrol Meade's right flank, "sending out strong reconnaissances" on the turnpike "until they feel the enemy, at least as far as Robertson's Tavern." Meade unquestionably intended Wilson to keep pickets on the turnpike. The young cavalry captain, however, read the instructions narrowly, as requiring him to watch the roadway only until Warren's foot soldiers occupied Wilderness Tavern, then to move on. Wilson later commented that "we expected that the infantry would relieve our detachments on the various roads and throw out their own in return, to cover and protect their flanks from the enemy." [30]

Official communications during the evening of May 4 added to the confusion. Meade's marching orders to Wilson for May 5 reminded Wilson to keep "out parties on the Orange Court-house pike and plank roads." In his last message of the day, Wilson gave assurances that the "Spotsylvania and Orange roads" were well patrolled, seeming to confirm that Meade's instructions were being followed. In a report filed months later, Wilson remarked that he had "received no counter instructions during the night," and thus continued to act "in compliance with my original order." So far as the young cavalryman was concerned, headquarters' silence meant that he was to follow Meade's initial instructions, as he interpreted them. That meant that he was to leave Warren to patrol his own front. [31]

Warren's understanding was precisely the opposite. "General Griffin's division held the road leading towards the enemy and picketed it," he later explained to a friend. "I was informed however that our mounted troops held Robertson's Tavern and that I apprehended

---

30. Wilson, *Under the Old Flag*, I, 378–80.
31. Order, in *OR*, Vol. XXXVI, Pt. 2, p. 371; James H. Wilson to Gouverneur K. Warren, May 5, 1864, *ibid.*, 378; James H. Wilson's Report, *ibid.*, Pt. 1, p. 876.

nothing. They had occupied that place and abandoned it without notifying me."[32]

It was a costly misunderstanding, the consequences of which first came to light with the unexpected buildup of rebel troops on the Orange Turnpike. In mitigation, it must be remembered that this was Wilson's first taste of field command. Precautions that might have seemed second nature to an experienced soldier simply never dawned on him.

At five o'clock on the morning of May 5, Wilson's cavalrymen struck camp and started south. Only Hammond's 5th New York, close to five hundred troopers in all, remained behind to watch Orange Plank Road and serve as Wilson's link with the rest of the Union army. Since Warren's lead elements were due shortly, the young cavalry commander assumed that Hammond's small detachment would be sufficient. He was blissfully unaware of the vacuum he was leaving in front of Meade.

Wilson's main column wound roughly southwest for about four miles. Coming out on Catharpin Road, the troopers turned west. Wilson sensed that trouble might lie ahead. Prudently he parked a brigade at Robertson Run, a little creek. His other brigade, under Colonel George H. Chapman, cautiously advanced west along Catharpin Road, watching for signs of Confederates.

Hemmed into the narrow roadway by a dense pine forest, Wilson's cavalrymen had little room for maneuver. Elements of the 1st Vermont Cavalry, skirmishers well out, led the advance. Just past a ramshackle structure known locally as Craig's Meeting House, the Federals encountered Confederate horsemen. It soon became apparent that a sizable mounted force was streaming in from the opposite direction.[33]

Tired and cranky after a night of broken slumber, the approaching rebels belonged to a particularly rugged unit of combat veterans,

32. Gouverneur K. Warren to Charles Porter, November 21, 1875, in Warren Collection, NYSA.

33. Charles Chapin Diary, May 5, 1864, in Civil War Miscellaneous Collection, USMHI; Wilson's Report, in OR, Vol. XXXVI, Pt. 1, pp. 876–77.

the Laurel Brigade, which had roots running back to the war's earliest days. Heading these Virginia horsemen was the dashing Brigadier General Thomas L. Rosser, a contemporary of Wilson's at West Point.[34]

Wilson, in his first experience leading troops in combat, wisely heeded Chapman's sound advice. Following usual practices, three-quarters of the cavalrymen dismounted and deployed as infantry, while the rest hurried the horses to cover. "The action was on at once," Wilson recalled, "and, as both sides were anxious to gain the first advantage, it soon became furious."[35]

Judging from reports filed after the dust settled, Wilson had the better of the fighting at first and drove Rosser back. Confederate resistance grew, however. Gray-clad prisoners hinted that Jeb Stuart himself had arrived with reinforcements.

Ammunition fast running low, Wilson retreated to a stronger position. Near the house of a Mrs. Faulkner, close to Craig's Meeting House, he prepared a hearty reception for his old classmate. Two batteries of horse artillery—twelve guns in all, commanded by two young West Pointers—were positioned on a rise near the house. Chapman's regiment was crouching in a deep ravine that sliced across the road.

As Rosser's Confederate riders bore down, shrapnel and canister belched from the Union guns. Federal cannon fire combed the ground, leaving it strewn with mangled corpses in gray.

Just when Rosser needed it most, help arrived. Confederate horse artillery under the energetic Major Robert P. Chew had left Gordonsville on the fourth. Marching all night and into the morning, the rebel guns reached Allman's house, about a mile to Rosser's rear, at 11 A.M. Hearing the sound of combat ahead, Chew hurriedly dispatched a section of Major James W. Thomson's battery to Rosser's assistance.[36]

In the nick of time, two of Thomson's artillery pieces rolled up and began banging away. The Federals answered by firing flaming

34. William N. McDonald, *A History of the Laurel Brigade, Originally the Ashby Cavalry of the Army of Northern Virginia and Chew's Battery* (Baltimore, 1907), 225.

35. Wilson, *Under the Old Flag*, I, 381.

36. Wilson's Report, in *OR*, Vol. XXXVI, Pt. 1, p. 877; Robert P. Chew's Report, in Leigh Collection, USMHI; Alexander Pennington's Report, in *OR*, Vol. XXXVI, Pt. 1, p. 903. The Federal pieces were from Pennington's and Fitzhugh's batteries.

projectiles that a rebel described as "something of the fireworks family." Dry grass blazed into flames around the Confederate artillery. A southern gunner later conceded that Wilson's hard-pressed batteries delivered some of the war's most accurate fire. "Their shrapnel shot exploded all around and over us," he recalled, "and the everlasting ping and thud of slugs, balls, and fragments of shell filled the air with horrid screams for an hour, and the death-dealing mixture tore and raked up the sod all around us like a raging storm of iron hail." As Chew later described it, "The fire of the enemy was very accurate, disabling so many of the cannoneers as to render it necessary for the officers to assist in working the guns."[37]

Rosser remained determined to dislodge Wilson's pieces and ordered his men ahead. They were joined by the rest of Chew's guns, which came clanking up from the rear.

Rebel horsemen thundered down the narrow road, four abreast, dust spraying from their horses' hooves. Wild screams pierced the forest and rose above the din of fast-firing Yankee cannon. Chapman's dismounted riders dropped back, remounted, and drove headlong into the frenzied Virginians. Sabers flashed, pistol shots cut through the air, and Catharpin Road boiled into a bloody, uncontrolled melee, horseman against horseman, all semblance of organization lost, each man for himself in a life-and-death grapple face-to-face with the foe. "Pistol and sabre were busy in slaughter," wrote a Confederate who participated in the affair, "while the shrieks of the stricken and the shouts of the victors mingled with the roar of battle."[38]

His front crumbling under Rosser's ferocious attack, Wilson found himself left with only a handful of soldiers near Mrs. Faulkner's. "The confusion occasioned by getting a large number of led horses back on one road was communicated to the men," reported Chapman, "and caused the men to break badly, of which the enemy was not slow to take advantage." To buy time, Wilson and his tiny band dashed forward under cover of another rattling fire of canister and shrapnel. The head of Rosser's charge scattered. Taking advan-

37. Chew's Report, in Leigh Collection, USMHI; James Wood Diary, May 5, 1864, in VSL; George Neese, *Three Years in the Confederate Horse Artillery* (New York, 1911), 259–60.

38. McDonald, *A History of the Laurel Brigade*, 226; Frank M. Myers, *The Comanches: A History of White's Battalion, Virginia Cavalry, Laurel Brigade, Hampton Division, A.N.V., C.S.A.* (Baltimore, 1871), 259.

tage of the brief respite, Wilson sounded the rally. His exhausted force dropped back to the reserve at Robertson Run. There they were momentarily safe from the hornet's nest they had unwittingly stirred up on Catharpin Road.[39]

Wilson was situated precariously between Catharpin and Orange Plank roads. Under the previous day's directive—Humphreys' general order for May 4, which so far as Wilson understood was still in effect—Hancock should have been advancing out Catharpin Road from Chancellorsville and Warren should have been slanting down from Wilderness Tavern. Neither, however, was in sight.

Even worse, disturbing news was filtering over from Parker's Store. While Wilson had been fighting his delaying action with Rosser, another rebel column had appeared on Orange Plank Road. Wilson's link with the Union army had been severed. Blocked by a formidable line of graycoats, Wilson's couriers were unable to get through to Meade.

What had happened was this. Earlier in the morning, as Wilson had disappeared south, Hammond's regiment of New York troopers— left by Wilson to cover the Plank Road—had advanced toward Mine Run. About two miles from Parker's Store, they had run headlong into rebel cavalry. Hammond had sent his horses rearward and had spread out a thin skirmish line. To play it safe, the Yankees sprayed the thickets with concentrated volleys from their repeating rifles.

It became obvious, however, that Confederates were approaching in substantial numbers. Rebel pickets began edging around Hammond's flanks, and pressure from superior Confederate numbers began to register.

Reeling in a handful of prisoners, the New Yorkers discovered that they had bitten off more than they were figuring on. The gaunt captives belonged to Brigadier General William W. Kirkland's North Carolina brigade of Henry Heth's division. Behind them was Hill's entire infantry corps. This was not just southern cavalry but rather the tip of a powerful rebel infantry column. Damming the gray tide

---

39. George H. Chapman's Report, in *OR*, Vol. XXXVI, Pt. 1, p. 897; Wilson, *Under the Old Flag*, I, 382–83.

was a hopeless proposition. Although the Federal troopers were armed with carbines, they were forced steadily back under what their commander accurately described as "vastly superior numbers." [40]

By 8 A.M., the situation on Meade's southern flank, which was out of sight and out of mind so far as Union headquarters was concerned, had reached critical dimensions. Hammond had retreated to Parker's Store. Wilson was isolated off to the south, struggling to hold his own against Rosser.

One bright spot remained. Not far to the north, the Chewning farm was starting to fill with Warren's lead infantry elements under Crawford. If Crawford rushed reinforcements to Hammond's beleaguered horsemen, Parker's Store might remain in Union hands.

Crawford had never been regarded as a decisive Federal commander. Fortunately for the Federal cause, Warren's aide Roebling was close at hand. This capable engineer and future builder of the Brooklyn Bridge had been sent to recall Crawford to the turnpike. As Hammond's dismounted troopers fought to stem the rebel tide on Orange Plank Road, Roebling rode onto the heights at the Chewning farm. From there he could view the fighting at Parker's Store.

Roebling instinctively understood the importance of the Chewning farm. "This field was a commanding plateau overlooking the ground to the north and west and connecting with the Plank Road by two good roads, one leading to Parker's Store, and the other to a point a mile east of the store," he later explained. "It became evident at once that it would be of the utmost importance to hold that field, as its possession would divide Lee's army in two parts if he attempted operations from the Plank Road and Pike at the same time; and if he attempted to pass us and attack the 2nd Corps further down the Plank Road we could fall upon his rear; again it was the best fighting ground in the whole neighborhood." Spurring his mount toward the firing, the aide found Hammond. A breathless conference followed. The hard-pressed cavalry colonel estimated that he could hold on at most for fifteen minutes. Scurrying furiously back to Crawford, Roebling informed the Pennsylvanian of Hammond's plight. [41]

40. Louis N. Boudrye, *Historic Records of the Fifth New York Cavalry, First Ira Harris Guard* (Albany, N.Y., 1865), 122; John McIntosh's Report, in *OR*, Vol. XXXVI, Pt. 1, pp. 885–86.

41. Roebling's Report, in Warren Collection, NYSA; Washington A. Roebling, "Memoranda," in Washington A. Roebling Collection, RU.

For a brief moment, it looked as if Crawford might commit his forces and save Orange Plank Road for the Federals. Deployed as skirmishers, Crawford's Pennsylvania Bucktails Regiment had been feeling its way along the path leading to Parker's Store. Before the Bucktails could reach Orange Plank Road, however, Hammond's cavalry line buckled. The Pennsylvanians took up position behind trees and logs. As Kirkland's Confederate flankers approached, the Bucktails rose and blistered them with volleys from newly issued repeating rifles. A Confederate officer urged his men to attack the Federals, whom he erroneously believed to be dismounted cavalry. "Cavalry, hell," cursed a gray-clad soldier familiar with the rugged Pennsylvanians, "cavalry don't carry knapsacks and wear bucktails." [42]

But Crawford failed to press his advantage. Rather than reinforcing the Bucktails and stiffening Hammond's defense, he decided first to solidify his position at the Chewning farm. He positioned one brigade facing south toward Parker's Store and his other west toward the woods, just in case Confederates showed up there as well. Valuable minutes were lost. By the time Crawford had his troops in place, Hammond was past helping. Still fighting valiantly, the outnumbered New York cavalrymen abandoned Parker's Store and retreated east on Orange Plank Road. As Roebling later described the state of affairs, "the enemy seemed to be unaware of [Crawford's] division being on their flanks, but kept steadily on; some of their flankers came down the S.E. road before mentioned, and fired into the rear of the right wing, but they were quickly dislodged." [43]

Once Hammond had surrendered Parker's Store, Wilson's division was for all practical purposes out of the campaign. His main body of horsemen remained concentrated along Robertson Run, isolated from the Army of the Potomac by Hill's intervening Confederate corps. Helplessly sandwiched between Rosser and Hill, Wilson could neither screen Federal infantry movements nor inform Meade of the enemy's whereabouts. There were serious concerns about whether he could even save himself. Meanwhile, Hammond, left to his own devices, continued a futile delaying action against Hill's lead

---

42. Josiah R. Sypher, *History of the Pennsylvania Reserve Corps* (Lancaster, Pa., 1865), 510; D. R. Howard Thompson and William Rauch, *History of the Bucktails* (Philadelphia, 1906), 292–95.

43. Roebling's Report, in Warren Collection, NYSA.

elements, which were inexorably grinding toward the huge gap that yawned between Hancock and the rest of the Union forces.

Buried in this dismal picture was a sterling opportunity for an innovative Federal commander, had one been there. Strung out on the roadway, Little Powell's unwary soldiers still offered a rare target to Crawford's bluecoats. The superb Federal position dominated the countryside for miles around and afforded the Yankees a bird's-eye view of Hill's column. Handily poised to plow into Hill's exposed flank, Crawford had a capital opportunity to wreck a substantial part of Lee's army and realize a persistent but elusive Federal dream. But the order to attack never came. The fleeting Union opening, filled with possibilities for a quick, decisive victory, evaporated as Hill's dusty gray-clad men filed past.

Crawford's hesitancy, frustrating as it later appeared, stemmed from several practical considerations. For one thing, he was perched out on Warren's far southern flank, beyond hope of support. If he started a fight with Hill's men, he was probably going to have to finish it himself. That was a tall order for a lone Federal division. In addition, Crawford's command consisted of older regiments whose three-year terms were due to expire within the month. Units like the Bucktails were proven warriors, but with their military obligations soon ending, the prospect of a scrap with Little Powell's veterans had nothing to recommend it. Crawford's soldiers would not have refused battle if it had come their way, but they were simply in no rush to seek out trouble.

It is impossible to determine whether Crawford's chance to strike a blow against Hill was real or whether it was a fleeting chimera—fleeting like those gray shadowy forms that kept emerging from the dense undergrowth. Whatever aggressive plans the Pennsylvanian might have been considering were negated by Meade's decision to hurl the 5th Corps toward the mounting threat on the turnpike. Around 8 A.M., just as Crawford was pondering whether he could perform valuable service on Orange Plank Road, he received Warren's order directing him to reverse direction, reach northward, and connect with Wadsworth. Unless headquarters rethought its priorities, the Pennsylvania Reserves would have to abandon the Chewning farm and Orange Plank Road to the rebels. Faced with unequivocal orders, Crawford drew in his skirmishers and fired off another message to headquarters describing conditions in his sector. Before irrevocably abdicating his advantageous position, he would sit tight and see if his latest intelligence changed Meade's plans.[44]

By midmorning, the Army of the Potomac was fast slipping into a defensive posture that threatened to erase its numerical advantage and to place it at risk along its entire front. Careless mistakes, spawned sometimes by overconfidence, sometimes by ill-considered caution, and nearly always by the slipshod gathering and interpreting of information, were occurring at every level of command.

Meade's generalship had been deficient in several respects. His cardinal error had been in presuming that his opponent, who boasted an unbroken record of aggressiveness virtually unparalleled in the history of warfare, would sit still behind Mine Run while the Federals maneuvered around him. Acting on this misconception, Meade had allowed his soldiers a leisurely evening's rest and had frittered away most of his cavalry.

Particularly puzzling was Meade's decision to abandon his offensive plan at the sight of a few gray-clad soldiers. The foe's unexpected appearance seemed to have dulled Meade's good judgment. Perhaps Grant's campfire chats had persuaded the long-suffering Meade, who was still treading on thin ice with the administration, that a vigorous show of aggression was important for keeping his position. But whatever concerns induced him to lash out at the first rebels to appear, the results were unfortunate. His precipitate action guaranteed a battle precisely where he could least afford to fight, and at the juncture of his army's being too scattered to make telling use of its numbers. Paralysis had seized the Federal leadership, and it was beginning to look as if Lee's bold gamble might pay off.

44. Frederick T. Locke to Samuel W. Crawford, May 5, 1864, in *OR*, Vol. XXXVI, Pt. 2, p. 417; Crawford to Locke, May 5, 1864, *ibid.*, 418. Commenting on Crawford's missed opportunity, William Swan—one of Ayres's aides—observed that "Hammond, knowing the route Crawford was to take, sent back for assistance, representing that Crawford would have time to occupy the strong position at Parker's Store; but Crawford evidently thought otherwise, and indeed it was but a short time before the enemy was passing along what might now be called his front. . . . I go into these details because the position at Chewning's was an important one, and much could have been made of it" (Swan, "Battle of the Wilderness," in *PMHSM*, IV, 128–29).

*"He preferred not to bring on
a general engagement before
General Longstreet came up."*

Lee rose well before daylight on May 5 and took breakfast with his staff at their tents in Mrs. Rhodes's woods near Verdiersville. He was in a cheerful, chatty mood and broke his usual injunction against discussing military matters at the table. The night's intelligence that Grant was still in the Wilderness was heartening news. Despite lengthening odds, Lee looked toward the Union army's total destruction. "He was, indeed, in the best of spirits," an aide at that early-morning breakfast later recalled, "and expressed much confidence in the result—a confidence which was well founded, for there was reason to believe that his antagonist would be at his mercy while entangled in these pathless and entangled thickets, in whose thickets disparity of numbers lost much of its importance."[45]

To exploit Meade's vulnerability fully, Lee decided on continuing the previous day's movement, pressing Ewell up the Orange Turnpike and Hill up Orange Plank Road until they encountered Yankees. After engaging the enemy, however, it was Lee's plan to avoid a pitched battle. He hoped instead to pin Meade in place until Longstreet arrived and made the numbers closer to equal.

The cavalry was to play an important part. Contrary to Union intelligence, Stuart's mounted troops were nowhere near Fredericksburg. Major General Wade Hampton's division, to which Rosser's brigade belonged, was extending feelers in front of Hill, securing the Confederate right flank and sweeping Longstreet's expected route clean of Yankees. Fitzhugh Lee's division of gray troopers had spent the night at Massaponax Church and was trotting through Spotsylvania Court House on its way to rejoin the rebel army.

Jeb Stuart, resplendent in cape and plumed hat, had spent a hectic twenty-four hours. Leaving his winter encampment near Orange Court House at midday on May 4, he had ridden cross-country to meet Lee, exuberantly leaping his mount over the intervening fences. After conferring with his commander, the indefatigable cavalryman had rushed ahead to ensure that his pickets were diligently scouting

45. Armistead Long, *Memoirs of Robert E. Lee* (New York, 1886), 327; Venable, "General Lee in the Wilderness Campaign," in *B&L,* IV, 240–41.

Grant's route of march. Returning to Verdiersville near sundown, he had reviewed Hampton's division. One of Stuart's aides remembered the tireless cavalier, plumed hat in hand, watching his soldiers file past his campfire. "It was really a grand spectacle," wrote the staffer, "to see these gallant horsemen coming toward us out of the gloom of night into the gleam of the fire making the welkin ring with their wild war cries and the earth to tremble beneath their horses hoofs." Stuart, bivouacking just behind his picket line, had stayed up most of the night monitoring information from the front. This morning, however, he was wide-awake and enthusiastically briefed Lee on news from his far-flung riders. Their reports confirmed that Grant was still in the Wilderness.[46]

Lee, swinging onto his horse, resumed his previous day's position at the head of Hill's column. A short distance past Verdiersville, the Confederates began the gentle descent to Mine Run. New spring grass gave an iridescent green cast to the previous November's earthworks. Hill's soldiers assumed that they had reached their destination and loosened their knapsacks, preparing to slip into the old fortifications. To their surprise, they were ordered up the other side and on toward the enemy. Realizing that Lee meant to initiate a fight rather than wait for Grant, the Confederates cheered and passed word along the gray line: "Marse Bob is going for them this time." With combat certain, the southerners tossed their playing cards into the roadway.[47]

Sharp pops of skirmish fire added a familiar staccato to the sound of marching Confederates. Hill's lead brigade had encountered Hammond's New York regiment. Soon, off to the south, more martial sounds swelled the cacophony, signaling that Rosser had struck Yankees there as well. As gunfire in Rosser's direction became more insistent, Stuart left to see if his brigadier needed support.

Pressed by Hill's lead elements, Hammond's soldiers slowly retreated, littering the turnpike with portents of what lay ahead. A soldier in the 47th North Carolina, which was deployed as skirmishers, later wrote home about the carnage. "We came to a dead Yankee in the road, lying flat on his back, his arms thrown out, his head turned

---

46. Boteler Diary, May 5, 1864, in Brooks Collection, LC.
47. William H. Palmer to William L. Royall, May 11, 1908, in *Some Reminiscences,* by William L. Royall (New York, 1909), 28.

back, showing a gray beard, his boots and pants taken off, his features and limbs rigid in death. Soon we came to another, shot through both legs below the knee, and yet alive. Then another dead, with an ugly bullet hole in his chest, then one wounded in the chest, then one shot in the forehead and about breathing his last. Then one shot in the mouth, the bullet passing out the back of his neck, then one poor fellow who had been severely wounded and burnt to death by the burning of the woods." Sprawled in one roadside apple orchard were ten Federals, three Confederates, and several horses, all variously mutilated. A Yankee trooper, his head blown apart by a ball that had simultaneously killed his horse, still straddled his mount in death. Another had a sword through his body, and two had grisly head gashes, attesting to the fighting's close quarters and violence.[48]

Hill, thickening his skirmish line, sent more soldiers into the fray. The Yankees were offering surprisingly vigorous resistance. Riding near the front, Hill's chief of staff, Colonel William H. Palmer, concluded that the rebels faced a "whole brigade" of "picked men" whose officers "behaved with the greatest gallantry, on horseback encouraging the men, and exposing themselves to hold their line."[49]

While Hill's column battered ahead, Ewell's Confederate 2nd Corps was breaking bivouac at Robertson's Tavern. Ewell had started the day in a feisty, combative mood. Alone except for an attendant who carried his crutches and helped manage his horse, the one-legged general was sitting down to morning coffee when an acquaintance, Robert Stiles, passed by. The rebel commander looked unusually pale and thin, noticed Stiles. He was rumpled and disheveled as though he had been up all night and had skipped breakfast. Rifle, Ewell's flea-bitten gray horse, was quietly nibbling grass nearby. Stiles remarked to himself that horse and master looked singularly alike. Lured by the prospect of a chat with the engaging general and a rare cup of coffee, Stiles accepted Ewell's invitation to dismount. Talk naturally turned to the campaign, and Stiles inquired whether Ewell had objections to divulging his orders. Bright-eyed and alert despite his evident lack of sleep, Ewell briskly answered, "No, sir; none at

---

48. Benjamin Justice to wife, May 4–7, 1864, in Justice Papers, EU; Dame, *From the Rapidan to Richmond*, 77–78.
49. Royall, *Some Reminiscences*, 28.

all—just the orders I like—to go right down the [turnpike] and strike the enemy wherever I find him."[50]

Stepping into a thick morning fog, Ewell's veterans were in an optimistic mood that matched their general's. Empty stomachs were the chief complaint. A soldier later remembered receiving only a few crackers and a small piece of meat on May 4, and those he ate at once. No provisions were distributed for the fifth. One rebel was so famished that he coaxed a wet, half-raw fragment of ashcake from a black child who was gazing openmouthed at the bedraggled spectacle marching by. Wild with excitement over the acquisition, the soldier ran to his messmates and waved a soggy cracker still bearing tiny tooth prints. "Here, fellows, I've got something," he gleefully cried. "It isn't much, but it will give us a bite apiece. Here! Look at this, a piece of bread! Let me give you some." Not yet reduced to their friend's desperate condition, they thanked him for his thoughtfulness, particularly moving "in a man hungry as a wolf," and left him to devour the morsel in peace.[51]

Leading Ewell's advance was Edward ("Allegheny") Johnson's division. Behind came Robert Rodes's division, with Jubal Early's closing up the rear. Cowles's 1st North Carolina Cavalry prowled the turnpike ahead.

Around 6 A.M., less than an hour's march from the previous night's bivouac, Ewell's column reached Saunders' Field. Seeing Yankees ahead, the Confederates began constructing a strong defensive line along the field's western boundary. Johnson, no doubt cursing and wielding his hickory stick in agitation, began spreading infantry on either side of the turnpike. Cowles's horsemen meanwhile scouted out a trail slanting to the left—Spotswood Road, the same road down which Sedgwick would later come in a belated effort to prop up Warren's right flank.

With a fight clearly brewing, Ewell sought an update on Lee's thinking. At eight he dispatched Campbell Brown, his controversial wife's son, to find the Confederate commander in chief. Riding cross-country, Brown located Lee on Orange Plank Road a few miles short of Parker's Store. Ewell had encountered "only a small picket of the

50. Stiles, *Four Years Under Marse Robert*, 244–45.
51. Dame, *From the Rapidan to Richmond*, 73–74.

enemy," Brown told Lee, and planned to "push on until he found them in force." Lee replied that contrary to his previous night's orders, he had decided against hazarding an engagement just yet.

Lee's caution stemmed from two sources. He hoped, of course, to delay the inevitable clash until Longstreet's dependable troops arrived. In addition, at this juncture Ewell and Hill were too far apart to support each other, and that dangerously weakened the fighting capacity of both wings. Not only was Ewell well in advance of Hill but the turnpike and Orange Plank Road diverged as the gray columns pushed east, further widening the gap between them. At Parker's Store, where a line drawn south from Ewell's position at Saunders' Field would intersect Hill's line of march, the routes were separated by nearly three miles. At least until Little Powell had advanced to within supporting distance, it was best for Ewell to avoid battle.

With these considerations in mind, Lee instructed Brown that Ewell "was not to advance too fast for fear of getting entangled with the enemy, while still in advance and out of reach of Hill." The 2nd Corps was to regulate its march by the 3rd Corps, whose progress could be easily monitored by the sound of firing in front of its column. As Brown later recalled Lee's orders, if Ewell encountered a large enemy force, "he did not want a general engagement brought on until Longstreet could come up, which would hardly be before night. If the enemy advanced and showed a willingness to fight he preferred falling back to our old position at Mine Run." On one point Lee was insistent. "Above all," Brown remembered, "General Ewell was not to get his troops entangled so as to be unable to disengage them, in case the enemy were in force. If he found them, he could feel them with skirmishers well supported, and ascertain their strength and then act as above shown." [52]

Returning to the turnpike, Brown found Ewell near Saunders' Field, hard at work constructing a defensive line. Brigadier General John M. Jones's Virginia brigade, which had led Ewell's advance, was already lined up perpendicular to the roadway on elevated ground along the field's tree-fringed western edge. It was a superb defensive

52. Campbell Brown, "Memorandum—Campaign of 1864," in Ewell-Stewart-Brown Collection, TSL; Richard S. Ewell's Report, in OR, Vol. XXXVI, Pt. 1, p. 1070.

position, with a clear range of fire across the clearing undulating below.

Ewell set to reinforcing Jones by ordering in the rest of Allegheny Johnson's division. Coming up to the sound of a "brisk skirmish"—probably racket from Hayes's Federal pickets exploring in Ewell's direction—George ("Maryland") Steuart's brigade filed a short way into the woods and dug in on Jones's left. It covered Saunders' Field north of the turnpike. Johnson's remaining units, the remnants of the roughhousing Louisiana Tigers, under Brigadier General Leroy A. Stafford, and Stonewall Jackson's old brigade, under Brigadier General James A. Walker, extended the developing rebel line north toward the Rapidan. Soon a solid front of rebel infantry ran the width of Saunders' Field and a considerable distance above it.

The emerging battle front was located in one of the worst parts of the Wilderness. Patching together a line was no easy matter, either for Ewell's soldiers or for Warren's men across the way. Jones's and Steuart's Confederate brigades, lodged in the woods on Saunders' Field's western edge, had the easiest going. Walker's and Stafford's rebels, however, had to claw their way through a "jungle of switch, twenty or thirty feet high, more impenetrable, if possible, than pine," in order to line up with the rest of the division. "A more difficult and disagreeable field of battle," concluded one of Ewell's veterans, "could not well be imagined." Nonetheless, after "some little delay," Johnson's division had jerry-rigged a formation of trenches and logs, low to the ground but affording ample protection so long as the men stayed down. Walker's brigade constituted the formation's northern flank, arrayed perpendicularly across the end of the rebel line to guard against an attack.

To backstop Johnson, Ewell placed Rodes's truncated division in a second line several hundred yards behind, its left wing anchored on the turnpike. Directly following Jones was Brigadier General Cullen A. Battle's Alabama brigade, and trailing south through the woods were Brigadier General George Doles's Georgians and Brigadier General Junius Daniel's North Carolinians.

By noon, some ten thousand rebel soldiers were dug in across from Warren. Early's division, another forty-five hundred men, waited behind in reserve. His three available brigades—those of Brigadier Generals John B. Gordon, Harry T. Hays, and John Pegram—were prepared to shift wherever needed. According to a Confederate report, thirteen guns were posted "on a commanding ridge" near Saunders' Field. Realizing that artillery was of limited use in that terrain, Ewell parked most of his remaining cannon back near Robertson's Tavern.[53]

Thus far, Ewell's front had remained relatively quiet. The Federals had been occupied halting their morning march, unscrambling their units, and reassembling to counter the growing Confederate threat on the turnpike. About 11 A.M., however, Ewell spied a Federal column crossing the turnpike and heading south. It was apparently nosing toward Orange Plank Road or, of particular concern to Ewell, into the gulf between Lee's two infantry wings. From the look of things, a fight was imminent. Ewell again sent to Lee for instructions, this time using as his courier the popular Sandie Pendleton, of his staff. According to Ewell, Pendleton brought back substantially the same instructions Brown did, repeating that Lee "preferred not to bring on a general engagement before General Longstreet came up." Preparations completed, Ewell awaited Warren's move, reassured as the din of firing off to the south indicated that Hill was making good progress. Help would soon be close at hand.[54]

Hill was indeed plowing handsomely ahead despite Hammond's pesky Yankee cavalrymen and their deadly carbines. His lead elements had reached Parker's Store around 8 A.M. and within an hour overran the place. A small body of enemy horsemen sniped at Hill's strung-out flank but disappeared into the thickets rather than risk a fight. As a precaution, the 38th North Carolina was assigned to guard the wagons bringing up Hill's rear. Flames roared out of control along the roadway from Wilson's bivouac fires of the previous night.

Clearing Parker's Store, Heth's division bore down on Brock Road, three dusty miles eastward. Wilcox' division followed close behind. Some South Carolinians, taking a short break to rest their tired feet, were startled by enemy cavalrymen galloping across an

---

53. Ewell's Report, in OR, Vol. XXXVI, Pt. 1, p. 1070; William Pendleton's Report, *ibid.*, 1038–40; Howard, *Recollections*, 270–71; Henry W. Thomas, *History of the Doles-Cook Brigade, Army of Northern Virginia, C.S.A.* (Atlanta, 1903), 76; William Seymour Journal, 1864, in James Schoff Collection, CL; Thomas S. Doyle Memoir, in Jedediah Hotchkiss Collection, LC.

54. Ewell's Report, in OR, Vol. XXXVI, Pt. 1, p. 1070.

open field. Scrambling pell-mell to their guns, the Confederates loaded and faced the unsuspecting Yankee squad. They nervously squeezed off a few rounds at the intruders, who fled south. Apparently one of Wilson's couriers and his escort had tried to break through to Meade and had become confused in the Wilderness' winding labyrinth of trails. Relieving tension by a "good deal of jest and laughter" at their comical overreaction to a handful of mounted men, the edgy Confederates resumed their march.[55]

About two miles east of Parker's Store was the cleared field of Widow Tapp's farm. It was one of the few open spaces for miles about. Lee chose the spot for his headquarters, and it was probably near there that he gave Pendleton his eleven o'clock orders reminding Ewell to avoid a "general engagement" on the turnpike. Hill's objective, Brock Road, was about a mile ahead.

Near noon, the gray column's forward element—Brigadier General John R. Cooke's brigade, which had relieved Kirkland's—began bucking up against stouter Federal resistance. Understandably anxious about what lay ahead, Heth slowed his division, massed it across Orange Plank Road, and advanced four guns in column toward the front. William Poague, a wiry, twenty-eight-year-old disciplinarian in charge of the division's lead artillery, urged Heth to send back most of the guns. Only one piece could operate in the narrow roadway, and the remainder risked capture if Yankees attacked in force. Poague prevailed. "This is but one of the many examples of infantry officers' manner of handling artillery," the self-assured gunner later indignantly wrote. Most of the division's pieces were lined up, north to south, along a rise in Widow Tapp's field. They commanded Orange Plank Road across three hundred yards of cleared ground.[56]

Waiting for Heth to carve out a hold on Brock Road, Lee and Hill sat under a shade tree on Widow Tapp's farm and discussed their

55. Benson, "Reminiscences," in Benson Papers, SHC; Wilcox, "Lee and Grant in the Wilderness," in *The Annals of the War*, 489; James L. Morrison, Jr., ed., *The Memoirs of Henry Heth* (Westport, Conn., 1974), 182; Caldwell, *The History of a Brigade of South Carolinians*, 126–27; Walter Clark, comp., *Histories of the Several Regiments and Battalions from North Carolina in the Great War, 1861–1865* (5 vols.; Goldsboro, N.C., 1901), II, 445–46.

56. H. C. Albright Diary, May 5, 1864, in H. C. Albright Collection, NCDAH; Monroe

concerns. A patch of dark woods two hundred yards away fringed the farm's northern boundary. Soon Stuart appeared, satisfied with Rosser's progress. While the cavalry commander joined the other generals, his aide Boteler lay down under a pine to take a nap.

Suddenly a line of Union skirmishers materialized from the shadows and nervously probed into the field, guns ready. Lee self-assuredly walked toward Orange Plank Road calling for his adjutant Taylor. Stuart stood up and stared straight at the Yankees. Hill remained still, his aide Palmer at his side.

Within pistol shot of the bluecoats, and for a moment breathlessly frozen in time, stood as rich a prize as a Yankee mind could imagine. Robert E. Lee, Jeb Stuart, and Powell Hill were helpless, unprotected, and ripe for plucking.

The sound of a horse galloping by woke Boteler from his slumbers. He sat up to see "all the generals in full flight from the field followed by their respective aides and couriers." By this time, Lee was on horseback and Hill was running. Keeping his horse between himself and the enemy, Boteler leaped into his saddle. "I expected every moment," he later wrote in his diary, "to hear a crashing volley ripping up things around me." But it was not to be. "Right about!" cried a Federal officer, oblivious to his prime catch and as alarmed at finding himself in the presence of Confederates as Lee and his generals were at the enemy's unexpected appearance. The Yankees evaporated into the shadows. Their arrival, however, had lent dramatic substance to Lee's fears. The gap between Ewell and Hill needed to be plugged.[57]

Despite the Confederate command's near brush with death, Lee must have viewed the morning's events as a success. Grant remained stymied in the deep woods. Partly by design but predominantly by chance, Lee had stopped the Union army exactly where he wanted it. Meade's decision to halt after Ewell's early appearance was an unexpected turn that played directly into Lee's hands, and Warren's delay in attacking gave the Confederate 2nd Corps the precious opportunity to consolidate. By any measure, Lee's objective—to fasten

Cockrell, ed., *Gunner with Stonewall: Reminiscences of William Thomas Poague, Lieutenant, Captain, Major, and Lieutenant Colonel of Artillery, Army of Northern Virginia, C.S.A.: A Memoir Written for His Children in 1903* (Jackson, Tenn., 1957), 87–88.

57. Boteler Diary, May 5, 1864, in Brooks Collection, LC; Royall, *Some Reminiscences*, 28; Venable, "General Lee in the Wilderness Campaign," in *B&L*, IV, 241.

Grant in the Wilderness and then buy time until Longstreet arrived, meanwhile avoiding a pitched battle—had succeeded beyond the Virginian's hopes and at negligible cost to his thin ranks. If Longstreet stuck to his envisioned timetable and reached Mine Run's headwaters by noon, the following morning might well see a decisive Confederate attack along Catharpin Road with sufficient power to roll the Yankees back across the Rapidan.

But Lee faced risks as well. In the process of pinioning Meade on the two prongs of Ewell and Hill, he had dangerously extended his army. With one rebel corps entrenched on the turnpike and another forming across Orange Plank Road, each with enemy before it, Lee faced the uncomfortable prospect of waging two separate but simultaneous battles against superior forces. Particularly disturbing was the three-mile gulf that separated the two Confederate wings. Hill's and Ewell's flanks were dangerously exposed, and neither rebel column could conveniently aid the other. The peril to Lee's army was more than an academic concern. In passing up Crawford's Pennsylvania Reserves, strongly posted on the Chewning heights, Lee had necessarily left the Yankees positioned to tear through his undefended middle and cleave the Army of Northern Virginia.

If Meade continued to dawdle, Lee might succeed in wedging a division into the gap, secure his line, and put up a brave front until Longstreet appeared. But if Grant massed against either rebel wing and threw his whole weight into an assault, a Confederate collapse would be unavoidable. Not since Antietam had the Army of Northern Virginia run a comparable risk of being overrun. It remained to be seen whether Lee could forestall the "general engagement" as he so desperately hoped to do.

*"Meade had just heard the
bravery of his army questioned."*

May 5 was destined to become one of the most exasperating days of Grant's military career. At daybreak, Meade and his staff had broken camp and ridden south, leaving Grant at his gabled farmhouse by Germanna Ford. True to his earlier promise not to meddle in Meade's conduct of the campaign, Grant did his best to let the irascible older man run his own show. He intended to stay by the Rapidan until

Burnside arrived and then to coordinate the 9th Corps' movements with Meade's.

Grant sat down alone after his staff had finished their morning meal, and he pensively sipped a steaming cup of coffee. Emboldened by the fresh brew's aroma, a young newspaperman approached the table's far end and piped up, "Well, I wouldn't mind taking a cup of something warm myself, if there's no objection." He poured himself a liberal portion, then began hungrily bolting food. Grant was lost in thought and never looked up. His aide Porter regarded the incident as a "fair sample of the imperturbability of his nature as to trivial matters taking place about him."[58]

Grant was accustomed to action. He chafed under the constraints imposed by his new position. Hours dragged by, and still no word filtered back from the leafy expanse that had so completely swallowed Meade and his army. Finally, shortly before 8:30 A.M., a messenger dashed in with a dispatch from Wilderness Tavern. Contrary to expectations, rebels had appeared on the Orange Turnpike, and Meade had stopped his advance and ordered Warren to attack "at once with his whole force." That was talk that Grant understood, and he responded in kind, drafting his quick note urging Meade to pitch into the rebels "without giving time for disposition." Burnside's advance was just then crossing the river, added Grant. As soon as he conferred with the 9th Corps commander, he intended to join Meade. Meade's message made it sound as if the war's decisive battle might erupt at any moment, and the combative general did not want to miss it. The time entries on Grant's dispatches suggest that his patience held for nineteen minutes. Then, rather than staying around for Burnside, whose slowness was already legend, the commander in chief left written instructions for his 9th Corps commander and hurriedly packed. At about nine he started south.[59]

Grant rode at the head of a long headquarters cavalcade, threading his way down Germanna Plank Road past Sedgwick's empty camps and the detritus from the previous day's march. Colonel J. War-

58. Horace Porter, *Campaigning with Grant*, 47–49.

59. Ulysses S. Grant to George G. Meade, 8:24 A.M., May 5, 1864, in *OR*, Vol. XXXVI, Pt. 2, p. 403; Ulysses S. Grant to Ambrose E. Burnside, 8:40 A.M., May 5, 1864, *ibid.*, 423–24. The question of when Grant left Germanna Ford and when he arrived at Wilderness Tavern is treated exhaustively by Edward Steere in *The Wilderness Campaign* (Harrisburg, Pa., 1960), 120–22.

ren Keifer, commanding a 6th Corps regiment in Ricketts' division, saw Grant riding by. "He was on a fine, though small, black horse, which he set well," Keifer later recalled, "was plainly dressed, looked the picture of health, and bore no evidence of anxiety about him. His plain hat and clothes were in marked contrast with a somewhat gaily dressed and equipped staff. He saluted and spoke pleasantly, but did not check his horse from a rather rapid gait." [60]

Meade's borrowed courier, Hyde, rapidly approached from the opposite direction. Saluting, Hyde gave Grant the latest intelligence about Lee's two-pronged advance, then fell in with the general's aides. Shortly after ten, Grant reached the Lacy house and dismounted. Meade walked over to meet him. It was now evident, Meade told Grant, that Lee intended to fight in the Wilderness. "That is all right," answered the man from Galena. [61]

Already Grant had begun nipping away at the fiction of Meade's independent authority over the Army of the Potomac. During the morning, Sedgwick had left Ricketts' division behind to guard the Rapidan crossings. Before leaving Germanna Ford, Grant had bypassed the formal chain of command and had directed Ricketts to rejoin his corps when Burnside arrived. Unknown to Grant, Meade wanted Ricketts instead to patrol the roads along the Union flank and had sent him an order to that effect, which reached him shortly after Grant's instructions. Confronted with contradictory orders, Ricketts sought advice from Meade's courier, who suggested that he obey Meade's order as the most recently issued. "You did just right, sir," Meade told his aide on learning of the confusion, "but go back as soon as possible and tell General Ricketts to obey General Grant's order." [62]

To keep a close eye on Meade's management of the campaign, Grant proposed establishing joint headquarters on a knoll near the Lacy house that had served earlier as Warren's command post. The generals climbed the rounded hill while their staffs erected tents beside the Orange Turnpike. A cleared spot on top gave them a view

60. Joseph Warren Keifer, *Slavery and Four Years of War* (2 vols.; New York, 1900), II, 78.

61. Hyde, *Following the Greek Cross*, 183.

62. George G. Meade to Ulysses S. Grant, 9:20 A.M., May 5, 1864, in *OR*, Vol. XXXVI, Pt. 2, p. 404; Cyrus B. Comstock to Ambrose E. Burnside, May 5, 1864, *ibid.*, 424. Hyde describes the episode involving the conflicting orders in *Following the Greek Cross*, 183–84.

down Wilderness Run and toward Wilderness Tavern. The tavern itself was obscured by trees, and budding foliage screened all signs of troops as soon as they left the roadway.

As Grant listened to Meade describe the military situation, he must have felt an uneasy sense of foreboding. A battle was taking shape, yet Meade was rapidly slipping into a defensive mind-set. Rather than seizing the initiative, he was preoccupied with protecting his flanks, which seemed to be in increasing peril as the morning wore on. Confederates were popping up everywhere. Warren, who had returned from his front-line reconnaissance and had joined the generals on the little knoll, was in a particularly tight spot. Ewell was constructing fortifications in front of him, Hill was scooting around his left flank, and now, according to word just arrived from Meade's chief engineer, Major Nathaniel Michler, more graybacks were slipping past his right. Exploring out Spotswood Road, Michler had discovered rebel cavalry—undoubtedly Cowles's men—advancing in his direction, shooting as they came. Unless they were stopped, this latest Confederate force might snap Meade's supply line and perhaps punch through to the wagon train.[63]

Grant's patience was beginning to fray. For three long hours, Meade had been prattling about attacking, but still nothing had happened. It was agonizing to watch this army of eastern dandies thrash blindly about, vainly struggling to mount an offensive. More to the point, the longer Meade's generals dawdled, the more serious the situation became. If that is what Meade meant by attacking "at once," as he had said he would at 7:30, no wonder Lee was running circles around him. Action, not bold talk, is what Grant wanted. If Lee wished to fight here, Grant intended to oblige him.

For the next half hour, couriers flew from headquarters carrying orders designed to prod the Army of the Potomac into battle. The record does not indicate who was responsible for the fresh burst of Union leadership, although the coincidence of Grant's arrival with the firmer sense of purpose suggests that he played an important role. Although Meade had initiated halting steps in the right direction, it was only upon Grant's appearance that a unified, aggressive Federal plan began to take shape.

63. Horace Porter, *Campaigning with Grant*, 49–50; Badeau, *Military History*, II, 105; Nathaniel Michler's Report, in *OR*, Vol. XXXVI, Pt. 1, p. 296.

Measures were immediately taken to block Hill's column before it reached Brock Road. On paper, Hancock was best situated to cover the endangered roadway, but practical considerations cast doubt on whether he could reach the intersection of Brock and Orange Plank roads in time. For some reason, messages from headquarters were taking inordinately long to reach the Federal 2nd Corps commander. With his corps stretched along six miles of road, its head well west of Todd's Tavern and its rear elements barely out of Chancellorsville, he would lose precious time turning his divisions around and starting them north. Finally, there was the matter of distance. Hancock had four twisting miles to cover from Todd's Tavern to the Orange Plank Road intersection. Aiming for the same objective, Hill's Confederates had less than a mile of fairly straight road. Their only obstacle was the obdurate Hammond and the tattered remains of his cavalry regiment.

All things considered, it made better sense to cull a division from Meade's reserve near Wilderness Tavern and to dispatch it down Brock Road to fight a holding action until Hancock could arrive. Sedgwick's lead division under George Getty was handily poised for the assignment. It had reached Wilderness Tavern at 7:30 and had been standing around since then. Accordingly, at about 10:30, Getty was ordered south. Simultaneously, Hancock was directed to reverse his march and to link up with Getty at the contested intersection. Once united, the commands were to push west toward Hill's hard-hitting veterans.[64]

Decisive steps had been taken at last to control the developing crisis on Orange Plank Road. Next, Warren and Sedgwick received unqualified instructions to press ahead in the turnpike sector. At 10:30, Warren issued his division commanders peremptory directives. "Push forward a heavy line of skirmishers," he ordered, "followed by your line of battle, and attack the enemy at once and push him." Delay would not be tolerated. "Do not wait for [Griffin]," Warren instructed Wadsworth, "but look out for your own left flank." Pressure was also successfully applied to start Sedgwick's troops hustling out Spotswood Road. By eleven the 6th Corps'

---

64. Getty's Report, in *OR*, Vol. XXXVI, Pt. 1, p. 676; Frank Wheaton's Report, *ibid.*, 681; Andrew A. Humphreys to Winfield S. Hancock, 1864, *ibid.*, Pt. 2, p. 407; Hancock's Report, *ibid.*, Pt. 1, pp. 318–19.

creaky wheels were in motion and Horatio Wright's division was at last slanting toward Warren's right flank.[65]

Oblivious to the confusion swirling around him, Grant lit a cigar and sat on a tree stump. Taking out a penknife, he picked up a stick and began whittling, absentmindedly carving his new thread gloves along with the wood. Apart from a brief excursion to the front, he remained on the knoll for the rest of the day, reducing the stick and his gloves to a heap of shavings and thread at his feet.[66]

Getty pulled his division into shape—it had been diminished by the brigade sent to augment Wright's Spotswood Road expedition—and started south for his rendezvous with Little Powell. Most likely it was Getty's column moving across the turnpike that Ewell glimpsed at 11 A.M. and reported to Lee. From the look of things, the race would be close. Hill's vanguard, retarded by waning resistance from Hammond's frazzled horsemen, was less than a mile from Getty's objective. The doughty Yankee had over two miles to cover. The victor would claim the junction of Brock and Orange Plank roads. Along with the Chewning farm, the crossroads was of paramount strategic importance on what was rapidly shaping up as Meade's southern flank. Getty was an ideal choice for the dramatic race against Hill for the dusty intersection deep in the Wilderness. "He is a cool man, is Getty, quite a wonder," wrote the ever-observant Lyman. "I always obey an order," Getty once bragged of himself. "If I was ordered to march my division across the Atlantic Ocean, I'd do it. At least," he added with a smile, "I would march them up to their necks in the sea, and then withdraw and report that it was impractical to carry out the order."[67] This latest assignment was well designed to test his boast.

Getty's men hit a rapid stride. Sweltering miles flew by. As the Federal troops neared the crossroads, a Union cavalry detachment came flying up the roadway in their direction. They were "strung out," one of Getty's officers later wrote, "like a flock of wild geese." The horsemen, who represented the battered remains of Hammond's

65. Frederick T. Locke to James S. Wadsworth, May 5, 1864, in OR, Vol. XXXVI, Pt. 2, p. 420; Emory Upton's Report, *ibid.*, Pt. 1, p. 665.

66. Horace Porter, *Campaigning with Grant*, 50.

67. Theodore Lyman to family, May 15, 1864, in *Meade's Headquarters*, ed. Agassiz, 91; Hazard Stevens [Getty's chief of staff], "The Sixth Corps in the Wilderness," in *PMSHM*, IV, 180.

command, paused briefly to call out that rebel infantry were advancing along Orange Plank Road, then disappeared in their dust. A slow patter of shots corroborated their warning. Getty, who had ridden ahead, sent an aide rushing back to his column. The men must come at a double-quick. Getty reached the crossroads just before the Confederates. The trim, sharp-eyed general and his staff formed a defiant blue knot squarely in the intersection's center. Their headquarters flag fluttered overhead. Looking west out Orange Plank Road, they could plainly distinguish gray forms advancing toward them. A bullet whistled by, then another. Fresh snippets of spring leaves, neatly clipped from their branches by deadly minié balls, filled the air. A leaden hail splattered around the little cluster of determined Yankees and seemed certain to annihilate them. True to form, Getty refused to budge. "We must hold this point at any risk," he firmly announced. "Our men will be up soon." [68]

Slow minutes ticked by as the stubborn general and his staff stood their ground. With scarcely a moment to spare, more panting blue forms dashed into the intersection. They belonged to Getty's lead brigade of Brigadier General Frank Wheaton's Pennsylvania Volunteers. The soldiers hastily patched together a line. "Halt! Front! Fire!" came the command. A volley of Yankee bullets blazed through the foliage and stopped the thin veneer of Confederate skirmishers in their tracks. Miraculously, Getty's only casualties were a severely wounded orderly, a dead horse, and his headquarters flag, pierced by two bullet holes.

The rest of Getty's winded soldiers puffed in, and the crossroads was theirs. Consolidating his hold upon this important piece of real estate, Getty ordered his division into two lines. Wheaton's brigade straddled Orange Plank Road, Brigadier General Henry L. Eustis' predominantly Massachusetts brigade filed to the north, and Colonel Lewis A. Grant's courageous Vermonters continued to the south. Rude defensive works were thrown up, and artillery was placed in command of the intersection.

Getty's timely arrival had temporarily stemmed Hill's advance. The question now was whether Getty's soldiers could hold until Hancock's 2nd Corps arrived.

---

68. Getty's Report, in *OR*, Vol. XXXVI, Pt. 1, p. 676; Hazard Stevens, "The Sixth Corps in the Wilderness," in *PMSHM*, IV, 189–90.

Union pickets picked their way curiously a short distance west on Orange Plank Road. Dead and wounded rebels lay within thirty yards of the intersection, so close had been the race. Prisoners confirmed that Heth's division was forming nearby in the woods. Wilcox' Confederate division was close behind. Attempts to ascertain Lee's numbers were unsuccessful. "I don't reckon Robert E. intends to fight here," predicted one Confederate prisoner, "but if he does, he'll whop you sure." As he was being led away, the saucy rebel called back to Getty's soldiers, "Sure enough, Robert E. hasn't many men, but what he's got are right good ones, and I reckon you'll find it out before you leave yere." [69]

Getty could proudly claim a measure of success, at least in the short run. The situation to the north on the turnpike, however, was not so heartening. Sedgwick's expedition along Spotswood Road seemed to be getting nowhere, and Warren was continuing to have an agonizing time massing his units into a coherent battle formation.

Warren's division heads seemed strangely resistant to doing anything quickly, and Warren seemed powerless to budge them. On the 5th Corps' left, Crawford had snuggled in behind earthworks and was obstinately refusing to abandon the Chewning heights. Warren's aide Roebling sided with Crawford and labored to convince his boss to shift more troops southward to help smash Hill's column. "It is of vital importance to hold the field where Crawford is," wrote Roebling in an emphatic dispatch to his superior. "Our whole line of battle is turned if the enemy get possession of it. There is a gap of half a mile between Wadsworth and Crawford. He cannot hold the line against an attack." [70]

But with his hands full on the turnpike, Warren concluded that

69. Getty's Report, in OR, Vol. XXXVI, Pt. 1, p. 676; Hazard Stevens, "The Sixth Corps in the Wilderness," in PMHSM, IV, 190–92. The 13th Pennsylvania, which led Getty's column, claimed to have six dead and five wounded "in this sharp little action" (William Schoyer, ed., The Road to Cold Harbor: The Field Diary of William Schoyer [Apollo, Pa., 1986]). Another soldier recorded some fifty Federal casualties. See Daniel A. Handy to father, May 5, 1864, in Book 119, FSMP.

70. Washington A. Roebling to Gouverneur K. Warren, May 5, 1864, in OR, Vol. XXXVI, Pt. 2, p. 418.

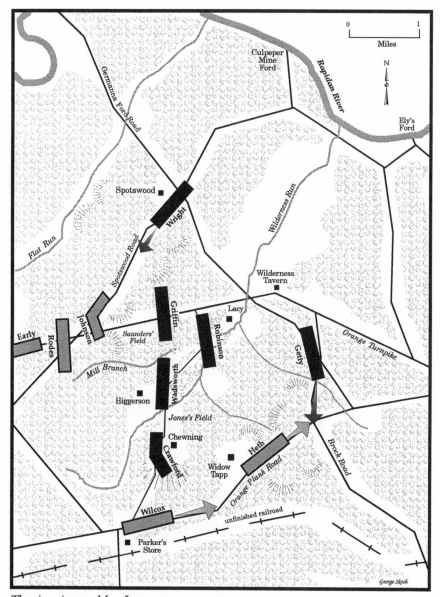

The situation on May 5 at noon

he had to leave Orange Plank Road to someone else. Messages between the Chewning farm and headquarters reflected Warren's growing frustration. At 7:30 A.M., Warren had unequivocally ordered Crawford to hook up with Wadsworth. Almost four hours later, Crawford was still asking whether he should abandon the farm and do Warren's bidding. "You will move to the right as quickly as possible," Warren curtly shot back, clearly peeved at his division head's resistance to authority. Fifteen minutes later, another note arrived at Meade's little knoll. Crawford explained that he was still investigating reports that rebels had slipped past his rear. "You must connect with General Wadsworth," Warren roared back, "and cover and protect his left as he advances." It was not until noon that Warren received confirmation that he was at last being obeyed. "The connection with Wadsworth is being made," read Crawford's dispatch, which ended with a belated attempt to justify the division commander's delay. "The enemy hold the Plank Road and are passing up."[71]

Despite assurances to Warren, Crawford's stubborn streak persisted. Instead of sending his whole division, he released only four regiments to find their way north and link up with Wadsworth. The detachment was under the command of Colonel William McCandless, a lawyer who had mastered both soldiering and the highly political world of the Pennsylvania Reserves. Unfortunately, McCandless' force was too small to form the strong left anchor that Wadsworth needed, and it was questionable whether the troops could even locate Wadsworth in the dense thickets. "McCandless was placed in such a position as to strike the left of [Wadsworth] if they went far enough in the woods" was Roebling's subsequent explanation of the plan.[72]

By late morning, Wadsworth had managed to maneuver his division's three brigades into a line extending from Saunders' Field southward. Connecting at the clearing with Griffin's division was Brigadier General Lysander Cutler's famed Iron Brigade, an outfit well suited for deep-forest fighting. It comprised regiments from Michigan, Indiana, and Wisconsin. Cutler's western woodsmen had stymied Stonewall Jackson at Second Manassas and had delayed Hill for pre-

---

71. Gouverneur K. Warren to Samuel W. Crawford, May 5, 1864, in *OR*, Vol. XXXVI, Pt. 2, p. 418; Samuel W. Crawford to Frederick T. Locke, May 5, 1864, *ibid.*, 419; Gouverneur K. Warren to Samuel W. Crawford, May 5, 1864, *ibid.*; Samuel W. Crawford to Frederick T. Locke, May 5, 1864, *ibid.*, 420.

72. Roebling's Report, in Warren Collection, NYSA.

cious hours at Gettysburg. To their left was a brigade of Pennsylvanians under bearded, craggy-faced Colonel Roy Stone, a no-nonsense lumberman from the Pennsylvania mountains whose serious demeanor belied his twenty-eight years. Brigadier General James C. Rice, closing up Wadsworth's left, had been assigned a brigade after his heroic defense of Meade's left flank at Gettysburg.

Given the opportunity, Wadsworth's troops could be expected to put up a strong fight. Wadsworth, however, was showing no inclination to hurry. On receiving Warren's pointed 10:30 A.M. order to attack, he deployed one of Stone's regiments—the 150th Pennsylvania—to sift the underbrush for Confederates. Zigzagging for half an hour through dense woods, the skirmishers finally encountered rebel pickets and slowly pushed them back. Firing grew intense, and disabled men began limping back to Wadsworth's main line. Shortly thereafter sharpshooters from the 147th New York, Rice's brigade, arrived on their left, and the woods echoed with roars from Union breechloaders. According to a participant, a deadly little battle between Yankee and Confederate skirmishers swayed back and forth in "dense undergrowth which almost completely screened the combatants on both sides from view."[73]

While skirmishers tore into each other less than a half mile away, Wadsworth's main body of soldiers, raggedly arrayed in two lines of battle, "all lay down in the woods," according to a regimental historian. Several officers gathered under an old oak tree, "chattering and chaffering in the highest spirits."[74]

Wadsworth's delay may have been inspired by the example set by Griffin, whose division was immediately to the north. Griffin stoutly objected to locking horns with Lee until Warren's entire line was in place and until Sedgwick had advanced to cover his exposed right flank. Warren sympathized with Griffin. In his view, a precipitate attack was worse than no attack at all. Meade found himself in the middle of an uncomfortable dispute. It was becoming increasingly

---

73. Thomas Chamberlin, *History of the One Hundred and Fiftieth Regiment Pennsylvania Volunteers, Second Regiment, Bucktail Brigade* (Philadelphia, 1905), 206–207; Curtis, *History of the Twenty-Fourth Michigan*, 230–31; John Kellogg, "Capture and Escape: A Narrative of Army and Prison Life," in *Wisconsin Historical Commission, Original Papers No. 2* (N.p., 1908), 7–11.

74. Rufus R. Dawes, *Service with the Sixth Wisconsin Volunteers* (Marietta, Ohio, 1890), 259.

difficult for him to justify his army's inaction to Grant, yet he was reluctant to overrule a corps commander who was not ready to fight.

While Union generals squabbled, lunchtime approached. Griffin's men boiled another round of coffee and pulled out helpings of hardtack. Sooner or later the order to charge would come, and experience had taught that fighting went a lot easier on full stomachs. "Had it not been for the bullets that tore through the branches of the trees at frequent intervals, sending showers of leaves or pine needles upon those below," wrote the chronicler of a New York regiment, "one might have supposed we were awaiting the start of some pleasure excursion rather than the beginning of a furious battle." Soldiers lay about in small groups. Some talked and loafed under the refreshing shade while others sharpened their skills at dice and mumble-the-peg. A favorite sport, invariably provoking laughter all around, was to crawl behind an unsuspecting comrade and prick him with a sword point. Ever-present, serving as a reminder of the bloody business near at hand, was the crash of falling trees. The rebels were busy strengthening their earthworks.[75]

A glimpse into the dissension dividing the Federal high command has been provided by Lieutenant Colonel William Swan, aide to Brigadier General Romeyn B. Ayres, one of Griffin's subordinates. Ayres's brigade extended north from the turnpike, then abruptly ended. There was nothing beyond but wilderness. Ewell's line stretched farther still; that meant that as soon as Ayres attacked, rebels would lap around his unprotected flank and slaughter his soldiers from front and rear. Ayres vociferously opposed moving before Sedgwick arrived to cover his dangling flank. From his perspective, going forward prior to that was little better than suicide. His officers agreed. A colonel in the 140th New York called the order to advance "nonsense."[76]

As Swan recalled it, not long after Griffin sent word that the enemy was collecting in strong force, Warren responded with orders to attack. Griffin passed the directive on to his brigade commanders. Ayres remained firm in his determination against advancing until Sedgwick's arrival and dispatched Swan with his objections. It was

75. Gerrish, *Army Life,* 159; Brainard, *Campaigns of the One Hundred and Forty-Sixth Regiment New York,* 187.

76. Elwell S. Otis to Sartell Prentice, December 26, 1888, in LC.

better to wait, urged Ayres, because in his judgment the rebels were about to assault and the Federal position was strongly entrenched. Ayres's opinion could not be dismissed lightly. A professional soldier since Mexican War times and, like Griffin, an ardent artillerist, he was noted for sound and intelligent leadership. After examining the lines with Ayres, Griffin agreed with his subordinate's assessment and sent Swan to tell Warren in no uncertain terms that he "was averse to making an attack." Apparently Warren ordered Griffin ahead anyway, and again the hardheaded general demurred. Sent on a second mission to find Warren, Swan met the 5th Corps commander on the turnpike and delivered Griffin's renewed remonstrance. Under intense pressure from Meade to mount an offensive, Warren had exhausted his patience. He responded with personal slurs against Griffin and his men. "I remember that he answered me as if fear were at the bottom of my errand," Swan later wrote. "I remember my indignation." Apparently Warren had just been chewed out by his superiors and was still smarting from embarrassment. "It was afterwards a common report in the army," added Swan, "that Warren had just had unpleasant things said to him by General Meade, and that General Meade had just heard the bravery of his army questioned."[77]

In a letter written nearly ten years later, Warren revealed the full extent of his disagreement with his superiors. Meade and Grant, he claimed, "thought it only an observing brigade of the enemy opposed to me that we might scoop and that by taking time they would get away." Warren responded that "we had no certain means of knowing" the strength of the rebel force. "It would do well to move only with matters well in hand," he urged, "as the repulse of my force would make a bad beginning." Warren reminded Meade "that the 6th Corps was coming up on my right and that if time would be given them to get in position, as soon as they announced this by attacking I could move with my whole force against their front." According to Warren, Meade sternly replied, "We are waiting for you." Against his better judgment, Warren ordered the advance to begin.[78]

Sometime around noon, Griffin's division abandoned its earth-

<hr/>

77. Swan, "The Battle of the Wilderness," in *PMHSM*, IV, 129–30; Robert Monteith, "Battle of the Wilderness, and Death of General Wadsworth," in *War Papers Read Before the Commandery of the State of Wisconsin, Military Order of the Loyal Legion of the United States* (2 vols.; Milwaukee, 1891), 411–12.

78. Warren to Porter, November 21, 1875, in Warren Collection, NYSA.

works and pressed across "woods where one thinks that not even a hare can get through."[79]

To Griffin's left, Wadsworth's men pried themselves off the ground and hacked through the forest, trying to stay apace. Immediately alignments started falling apart. Units lost sight of one another in patches of dwarf pine and matted underbrush, emerging in tangled muddles with other detachments or careering off on tangents of their own. Companies clawed single file through sharp patches of thornbush interwoven with briers and stumbled into fetid little swamps and gullies where vision was limited to a few yards. Whole regiments were swallowed up. Snapping boughs and branches and dry, crackling foliage provided some guidance, and the occasional regiment resorted to compasses. "The density of the woods prevented orders from being given by brigades," recalled a staffer. "The staff officers had difficulty in carrying the orders to regimental commanders, and I feel certain that some of the regiments went forward merely because they saw others leave the woods."[80] Overall, the advance was a discouraging preview of what lay ahead.

Shortly before 1 P.M., Griffin reached Saunders' Field. "All semblance of line of battle was gone," one of Warren's aides later wrote, "and there were gaps everywhere between regiments and brigades." The generals stopped to reform their chaotic line.[81]

Confederate earthworks traced fresh scars across the woods four hundred yards away. "The rebels were posted on the crest of the hill opposite us," recalled a soldier in the 140th New York, "just in the edge of the woods that skirted the hollow." As soon as blue uniforms emerged into the field's bright sunlight, a volley of bullets tore across from the rebel trenches. George Ryan, the 140th's colonel, dismounted as his horse began plunging uncontrollably from a leg wound. Ryan called for his men to lie down among the trees and undergrowth fringing the field.[82]

Warren was at the front again. There would be no more delays and no turning back. On the right of the turnpike was Ayres's bri-

79. Charles Seiser, ed., "August Seiser's Civil War Diary," in *Rochester Historical Society Publication*, XXII, 189.

80. Schaff, *The Battle of the Wilderness*, 151–52.

81. Swan, "The Battle of the Wilderness," in *PMHSM*, IV, 150.

82. Farley, "Reminiscences," in *Rochester Historical Society Publication*, XXII, 239.

gade; on the left, Bartlett's men, with Colonel Jacob B. Sweitzer's brigade in support. Connecting to the left was Wadsworth's division, the brigades of Cutler, Stone, and Rice spreading southward in that order. Denison's Maryland brigade was massed behind Cutler. The rest of Robinson's division anxiously waited near Wilderness Tavern, listening to distant muffled sounds of firing and watching smoke belch up along invisible picket lines and vanish in the still air. Sedgwick was nowhere in sight, and McCandless was still struggling over from the Chewning farm.

The assault up the turnpike would be made not by two corps, as Meade had earlier planned, but by two divisions forming a wavering line across nearly two miles of woodland, both flanks open to the enemy. Six hours after Meade's first order to attack, Warren was at last going forward. Confronting him was Ewell's Confederate corps, firmly entrenched with a clear field of fire across much of its front. The Federals were hobbled by disadvantages that inevitably handicapped an attacking force, particularly in this terrain. Meade, in his hurry to bring on a fight, had thrown his numerical advantage to the winds and forced Warren to attack on terms that offered little chance of success.

Sighting down rifle barrels and across Saunders' Field, the Confederates had the men of Griffin's division cleanly in range. Looking back over the abandoned corn field, blue-clad soldiers anxiously watched well-aimed rebel bullets spurt up dirt "like the big drops of a coming shower you have so often seen along a dusty road." Years later, a Union veteran recalled a "wild, wicked roar of musketry" rumbling up from the Confederate side and "reverberating through the forests with a deep and hollow sound." Rippling flashes of orange flame marked where Ewell's slouch-hatted riflemen were firing with deadly accuracy across the infernal no-man's-land.[83]

"The men who for those few minutes lay there and faced the possibilities of tragedy then inevitable can never forget it," a soldier

83. Holman S. Melcher, "An Experience in the Battle of the Wilderness," in *War Papers Read Before the Commandery of the State of Maine, Military Order of the Loyal Legion of the United States* (3 vols.; Portland, Maine, 1898), I, 77; Gerrish, *Army Life,* 161; Pullen, *The Twentieth Maine,* 184–85; Judson, *History of the Eighty-third Regiment Pennsylvania,* 192–93; Survivors' Association, *History of the Corn Exchange Regiment, 118th Pennsylvania Volunteers* (Philadelphia, 1888), 399.

in the 140th New York explained. "The suspense and dread and hope which possess men during such minutes cannot be adequately told in words." [84]

Suddenly bugles sounded. Griffin's division, two lines deep, rose from the woods and stepped into the sunlit clearing. The elaborate dance of maneuver had concluded. The time to attack had arrived. The erratic crackle of skirmish fire escalated in tempo, reaching an earsplitting roar. Ahead lay Ewell's blazing line and a quarter-mile sprint toward death.

84. Farley, "The 140th New York Volunteers, Wilderness, May 5th, 1864," 23, in Farley Papers, RL.

IV

May 5, Afternoon
The Grand Offensive Breaks Down

*"A weird, uncanny contest — a battle
of invisibles with invisibles."*

WITH A SHOUT, the Union 5th Corps lurched ahead, bowing slightly forward along the turnpike. Presented with ideal targets, Ewell's Confederate riflemen blasted away as fast as they could load. Jagged gaps appeared in the Federal formation. In some places, the Yankees made minor inroads. In others, they were decimated almost as soon as they left the cover of their earthworks. But though the details of the fighting varied, everywhere the final result was the same. For all the reasons predicted by Warren and his generals, the grand advance quickly deteriorated into an embarrassing and costly rout.

Griffin's Federal division—comprising Ayres's, Bartlett's, and Sweitzer's brigades, massed along Saunders' Field—never stood a chance of success.

Sweeping across Saunders' Field north of the roadway, Ayres's fine brigade immediately ran into trouble. Ayres's first line contained ruddy Paddy Ryan's 140th New York on the left and several United States regular battalions to the right. At Warren's signal, they sprang into a hail of bullets. A short way out, they struck the deep gully that slanted diagonally across the clearing. There, under a withering rebel fire, things began to go haywire. "Down the slope we rushed," recalled one of Ryan's soldiers, "killed and wounded men plunging to the ground."[1]

To maintain alignment in the veritable blizzard of lead, the 140th New York eased left toward the turnpike. Apparently it slanted partially over the roadbed toward the clearing's south side, like a boat adrift from its mooring. Also buffeted by a "murderous" fire, the

---

1. Farley, "The 140th New York Volunteers, Wilderness, May 5th, 1864," 23, in Farley Papers, RL.

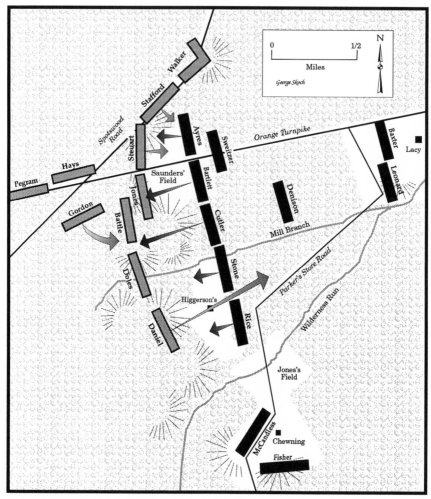

The turnpike front on May 5, 1 P.M.–3 P.M.

United States regulars bravely marched straight ahead at a steady gait, then turned slightly to the right while clambering across the swale. A fatal gap widened between Ryan's men and the regulars as they each hustled along, oblivious of their diverging lines of march. Consequently, the 140th New York approached Ewell's earthworks head on and alone, while the regulars, both flanks in the air, veered toward the rebels at a decidedly unhealthy angle.[2]

The well-disciplined Union troops reached the field's center with their formation cleanly dressed, as though on parade. According to a Federal witness, rebel fire opened from the left and swept "slowly, beautifully in its machinelike regularity, past the brigade front, and lost itself, out of sight, and by sound way off, in the woods to its right." Apparently the first volley inflicted little damage, and the Yankees accelerated to a double-quick. The sheet of fire started up again on the left. With "clockwork regularity" bullets crackled slowly across the heaving blue formation. This time men began falling. Now running, the Federals closed on the woods. Again the terrible fire started. Blue-clad bodies catapulted in all directions, falling in clumps of eight and ten. "How grim and severe it seems now," wrote a northern witness of the precise Confederate marksmanship, "in its slow, sure movement, and awful in its effect."[3]

Meanwhile, Griffin was busy sending in support for his first line. His artillerist's blood was up. The hardcase Yankee ordered two pieces from Battery D of the 1st New York Light Artillery into the fray, led by Lieutenant William H. Shelton riding a spirited chestnut horse. Guns jostled along the rutted roadway, horses galloping furiously as drivers lashed them with whips. Saunders' Field was hissing with minié balls, and Ryan's New Yorkers were pressing muzzle to muzzle against Ewell's Confederates. Perched in treetops on the field's far edge, rebel sharpshooters began picking off artillerymen and their plunging mounts one by one. The pieces rumbled over the wooden bridge across the swale and took up an exposed position that Shelton later described as "wholly unpracticable." Rapidly unlimbering, the Federal gunners aimed diagonally northwest across the field

2. *Ibid.*, 25; William H. Powell, *The Fifth Army Corps* (New York, 1896), 608–609.

3. Sartell Prentice, "The Opening Hours in the Wilderness in 1864," in *Military Essays and Recollections: Papers Read Before the Commandery of the State of Illinois, Military Order of the Loyal Legion of the United States* (4 vols.; Chicago, 1894), II, 16–17; William H. Powell, *The Fifth Army Corps* (New York, 1896), 607–608.

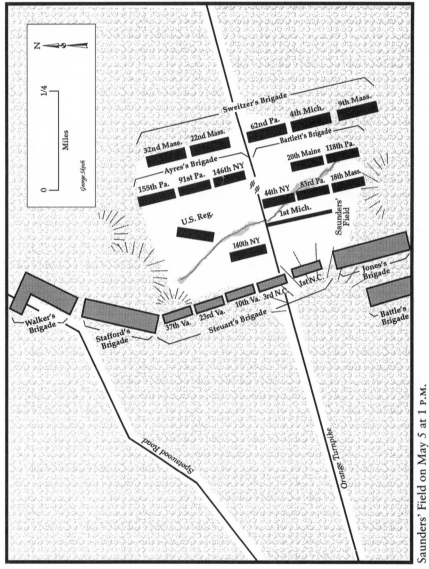

N

0   1/4

Miles

George Skoch

Sweitzer's Brigade

32nd Mass.   22nd Mass.   62nd Pa.   4th Mich.   9th Mass.

Bartlett's Brigade

20th Maine   118th Pa.

Ayres's Brigade

155th Pa.   91st Pa.   146th NY

44th NY   83rd Pa.   18th Mass.

U.S. Reg.

1st Mich.

Saunders' Field

140th NY

Jones's Brigade

1st N.C.

Walker's Brigade

37th Va.   23rd Va.   10th Va.   3rd N.C.

Battle's Brigade

Stafford's Brigade

Steuart's Brigade

Spotswood Road

Orange Turnpike

Saunders' Field on May 5 at 1 P.M.

and fired through Ryan's ranks into the opposite woods. Volleys of grape and canister scattered Yankees and rebels alike, serving only to confuse the fighting further.[4]

This stretch of Ewell's line belonged to Maryland Steuart's brigade. The Confederate brigadier had placed two tough North Carolina regiments—the 1st and 3rd—near the turnpike and had entrenched his veteran 10th, 23rd, and 37th Virginia men to the north. As the Federals approached, Steuart's superior, Allegheny Johnson, called out by way of reminder, "It is not meant to have a general engagement." A staffer responded, "But, general, it is evident that the two lines will come together in a few moments, and whether it is intended to have a general engagement or not, will it not be better for our men to have the impetus of a forward movement in the collision?" With bullets whizzing and graycoated soldiers restlessly shifting in their trenches, the suggestion made sense. "Very well," yelled Johnson above the roar, "let them go ahead a little." Raising his sword, Steuart's aide bellowed, "Forward," and another deafening volley rolled out from the rebel earthworks.[5]

While Ayres's first line was feeding into Steuart's grinding mill, the rest of his brigade was launched in a second line. This consisted of the 146th New York and two Pennsylvania regiments. At the same time, Warren shifted some of Sweitzer's brigade to the turnpike's north side. His purpose was to fill Ayres's now-vacant trenches and to provide a rallying point in case of repulse. Screened by the ragged fringe of bushes along Saunders' Field, the reserves occupied themselves succoring Ayres's wounded. Any minute they expected to hear high-pitched rebel yells signaling Ewell's countercharge.

Ayres's fresh second line strutted gamely ahead over the stubbled field. Soldiers stepped gingerly over their comrades' bodies and moved aside to let shell-shocked invalids hobble back through. The 146th New York troops, commanded by David Jenkins, presented tempting

4. Charles S. Wainwright's Report, in OR, Vol. XXXVI, Pt. 1, p. 640; Brainard, *Campaigns of the One Hundred and Forty-Sixth Regiment New York*, 189–90; Norman Leader, "The Bloodied Guns of Winslow's Battery," *Virginia Country's Civil War Quarterly*, VI, 16–17; William Shelton to father, June 5, 1864, in Rochester *Democrat and American*, July 23, 1864.

5. Howard, *Recollections*, 273; Stephen D. Thruston, "Report of the Conduct of General George H. Steuart's Brigade from the 5th to the 12th of May, 1864, Inclusive," in *SHSP*, XIV, 148; Clark, comp., *Histories of the Several Regiments and Battalions from North Carolina*, I, 200.

targets for Steuart's marksmen. They still affected the distinctive Zouave dress of white canvas leggings, flared dark blue pants, wide red sashes, and dark blue jackets trimmed in yellow. As the Zouaves hit the gully, a "withering volley" of musketry convulsed their colorful line. Another blast followed. Arms splayed wildly in the air, and bodies tumbled backward. The din was deafening. "With the rattle of the musketry was interspersed the booming of the cannon stationed on the road," remembered a Union survivor. "Their fire obliqued across the front of our line, and some of us were so close that we could feel the strong wind of the discharges."[6]

Up in front, Ryan's New Yorkers from the 140th were having an impossible time of it. After charging, the battle-wise Confederates had retired a little into the woods, drawing the Federals in after them. Underbrush interwoven with wild grapevines completely disordered the Union line. One Federal officer forced open a single-file avenue for his company by walking backward through the thickets, then re-formed his men at little clearings to try to establish connection with units on either side.

Fastening on to the 140th's exposed right flank, the rebels decimated the regiment with a blistering fire. As a New Yorker later remembered it, "The regiment melted away like snow. Men disappeared as if the earth had swallowed them."[7]

To the right of the 140th New York, the United States regulars were also finding the far woods an impossible place to fight. Their ranks had been thinned by their deadly march across Saunders' Field, but what they encountered in the thickets was even worse. It became, one of their number later recalled, "a weird, uncanny contest—a battle of invisibles with invisibles." White smoke curled from the bushes and slowly floated in fantastic designs through the sultry air. The roar of firing blotted out all other sounds. Suddenly a soldier would topple and disappear. Another would spring to his feet clutching some horrible wound. "Men's faces were sweaty black from biting cartridges," the veteran wrote, "and a sort of grim ferocity seemed to be creeping into the actions and appearance of every one

6. W. H. S. Sweet to James Grindlay, 1887, in *Campaigns of the One Hundred and Forty-Sixth Regiment New York*, by Brainard, 190–91.
7. Farley, "Reminiscences," in *Rochester Historical Society Publication*, XXII, 240; Powell, *The Fifth Army Corps*, 608n1.

within the limited range of vision." Occasionally it was possible to catch fleeting glimpses of gray, phantomlike shapes crouching under yellowing blankets of sulfurous smoke.[8]

Bayonets fixed, the survivors of the flashily attired 146th Zouave regiment charged between the 140th New York and the regulars and plugged the gap separating the two lead Union elements. Fighting deteriorated into savage matches between little clusters of soldiers. Stifling smoke obscured everything. Forms darted through thickets, firing, shouting, and wildly stabbing at anything that moved or resembled a man. "Many dashed directly into the enemy's fire in a belief that they were going to the rear," testified a Federal captain. "Officers lost control of their companies and utterly bewildered, rushed hither and thither, looking for their men." Another wrote, "Each man fought on his own resources, grimly and desperately." The 146th New York's commander disappeared in the fighting, along with nearly all of his subordinate officers. The 140th's organization was "virtually destroyed."[9]

Ayres's Pennsylvania regiments—the 91st and 155th—rushed to the aid of the regulars. They were completely overwhelmed. Rebels battered them in front and lapped around their open right flank. "It was an urgent case," related a Federal survivor. "On one side was certain death or to be taken prisoner which was as bad." Choosing flight "even at the expense of lacerated flesh and torn garments," the Pennsylvanians frantically dived through openings in a tangled mass of briers and brush. In some places, men tried to escape by wriggling away on top of the prickly foliage.[10]

Several members of the 140th New York managed to find cover in foliage near the sides of the turnpike and in the swale. Suddenly, recalled one of their number, "there were two terrific explosions in the hollow behind us, accompanied by the crash of shot through the trees and followed by a dense cloud of smoke which completely en-

8. Burgess E. Ingersoll Diary, May 5, 1864, in Civil War Miscellaneous Collection, USMHI; Powell, *The Fifth Army Corps,* 610.

9. Brainard, *Campaigns of the One Hundred and Forty-Sixth Regiment New York,* 191–92; Prentiss, "The Opening Hours in the Wilderness," in *Military Essays and Recollections,* II, 18; Farley, "The 140th New York Volunteers, Wilderness, May 5th, 1864," 27–28, in Farley Papers, RL.

10. D. P. Marshall, *History of Company K, 155th Pennsylvania Volunteer Zouaves* (N.p., 1888), 155–56.

veloped us." Union artillery pieces on the roadway were lobbing shells into their own soldiers.

More bad news was to come. Stafford's Confederate brigade, positioned on Maryland Steuart's left, looked down on Saunders' Field from a small ridge. "The enemy's ranks were as thick as blackbirds," recalled a Louisiana soldier. "Their flank was exposed to our brigade and the way we poured lead into them was a sin." [11]

Battered by numbing fire from Ewell's gray-clad riflemen and from their own troops to the rear, the wreckage of Ayres's brigade broke for the safety of the Union line. Fleeing back across the body-strewn gauntlet of Saunders' Field, they provided easy targets for Steuart's elated southerners. But not all of the Yankees retreated. Engrossed in their bloody fight for survival, the two New York regiments—what remained of the 140th and 146th—were evidently unaware that the rest of their brigade had retired. Holding on alone, they maintained a precarious Union toehold in the rebel line north of the Orange Turnpike.

South of the roadway, Bartlett's Federal brigade had stepped into Saunders' Field in tandem with Ayres's. Heading the advance there, 1st Michigan infantry fanned out across the broken, uneven field, driving rebel skirmishers toward the dark woods beyond. With "ringing cheers" and fixed bayonets, Bartlett's first line—the 83rd Pennsylvania and 18th Massachusetts, still jointly under Hayes's command, and the 44th New York—pushed into the clearing, across the swale, and on toward the Confederates. Immediately behind came a second line, the 118th Pennsylvania and the 20th Maine. "They were splendidly in line," thought a Michigan soldier, "moved rapidly, their colors all unfurled, and formed as they advanced one of the finest battle pictures that I can remember." [12]

Confederate bullets sang into Bartlett's formation, which began dropping blue forms onto the trampled corn stubble as it advanced. On came the determined Yankees, up a small rise and straight into the thickets. Michigan skirmishers hit the fringe of woods first and

11. Farley, "Reminiscences," in *Rochester Historical Society Publication*, XXII, 241; W. P. Snakenberg Memoirs, in Book 187, FSMP.

12. Hopper, "Reminiscences," in MOLLUS Collection, BL; Hayes Journal, in Chamberlain Collection, LC; William A. Throop's Report, in *OR*, Vol. XXXVI, Pt. 1, p. 580.

were immediately snapped back by a "severe fire." Gritting their teeth, soldiers in Bartlett's first line leaned into the storm of bullets as though encountering a strong wind. "A red volcano yawned before us," related a Maine man, "and vomited forth fire, and lead, and death." Bartlett's forward elements faltered but managed to hold on until the second line pulled up, stiffened with reinforcements from Sweitzer's brigade. Together they threw themselves into the Confederate guns. Fighting at point-blank range, rebel and Union lines blasted away at each other. "What a medley of sounds," a Federal veteran recalled. "The incessant roar of the rifle; the screaming bullets; the forest on fire; men cheering, groaning, yelling, swearing, and praying! All this created an experience in the minds of the survivors that we can never forget." [13]

The portion of the Confederate works along the southern half of Saunders' Field was manned by John Jones's Virginia brigade. When Bartlett's Federal attack struck, Jones was conferring a short distance back with Ewell, Early, and Rodes. "Suddenly a heavy skirmish fire opened on the front," recalled Early's aide Major John W. Daniel, "swiftly followed by volleys along the line." Jones hurriedly returned to his brigade. His aide Captain Robert D. Early—Jubal Early's nephew—mounted and hastened toward the firing, jauntily blowing a kiss back to the assembled generals. Although Jones's brigade was firmly anchored on its left to Maryland Steuart's brigade, its right was protected only by a light skirmish line of dismounted cavalry. Samuel Moore, one of Jones's aides, watched in horror as the hard-pressed Confederate formation buckled. "While hotly engaged with the enemy on our front," he later explained, "the line of skirmishers on our right was forced back, and a heavy line of infantry coming up under cover of the woods appeared on our right flank." Volleys tore into Jones's outflanked brigade. Jones and Captain Early tumbled from their horses, instantly killed. Moore fell with a bullet through his right thigh. Overpowered, Jones's leaderless Confederates dropped slowly to the rear, firing as they went. [14]

---

13. Gerrish, *Army Life*, 160; Throop's Report, in *OR*, Vol. XXXVI, Pt. 1, p. 580; DeWitt McCoy's Report, *ibid.*, 589.

14. John W. Daniel, "My Account, May 5," in John W. Daniel Collection, UV; Samuel J. Moore to John W. Daniel, June 30, 1905, *ibid.*

Aggressively pressing his advantage, Bartlett plunged forward. Soon he crashed into Cullen Battle's Confederate brigade, which had formed in Jones's support. In keeping with Lee's earlier orders to Ewell, Battle's men were under instructions "not to allow themselves to become involved, but to fall back slowly if pressed." Under the weight of Bartlett's assault, Jones's and Battle's men became intermingled. In the confusion, one of Jones's panicked officers cried out, "Fall back to Mine Run." Colonel Charles Forsyth, of the 3rd Alabama, shouted, "Is that a general order?" The response came, "Yes, the army falls back to Mine Run." Erroneously assuming that Ewell had decided against holding the line, Battle's 3rd and 5th Alabama regiments began retiring.[15]

With Confederate resistance seemingly melting before them, Bartlett's Federals kept up their momentum. "On we went," recalled a Union captain, "o'er briar, o'er brake, o'er logs and o'er bogs, through the underbrush and overhanging limbs, for about three-quarters of a mile, yelling like so many demons." Coming to a small clearing, Bartlett was finally forced to halt his exuberant dash through the broken rebel lines. His formation had disintegrated, and his units were hopelessly snarled. Time was needed to regroup.[16]

Still commanding the lead troops, Hayes received word that rebels were approaching from behind. He deployed a section of the 83rd Pennsylvania to skirmish in the rear.

Holding the right of Bartlett's second line was the 20th Maine. The regiment's bearded, frail-looking commander ordered his color-bearer into the little clearing so that his winded soldiers could rally around the regimental flag. Unexpectedly, a volley slammed into the men. The firing was coming from their right and rear, over where Ayres was supposed to be.

At first, the startled Union soldiers assumed that Ayres had mistaken them for rebels. But as the deadly volleys continued, it became apparent that they were coming from the Confederates. Unknown to Bartlett, Ayres had made little headway past Saunders' Field and was taking a nasty licking three-quarters of a mile back. Bartlett's right

15. Cullen Battle, "The Third Alabama Regiment," in Regimental Collection, ADAH; J. B. Stamp, "Ten Months in Northern Prisons," in J. B. Stamp Papers, AU.

16. Judson, *History of the Eighty-Third Regiment Pennsylvania*, 194–95.

flank and rear were wide open. His men were easy prey for the south-erners, who were rapidly re-forming, intent on teaching the Yankee contingent a lesson.

The situation went from bad to impossible. "Soon the troops on our left gave way and retired in confusion," Hayes later recorded in his journal. "We then found ourselves isolated, the enemy upon both flanks and reported to be in rear also." No option remained but to drop back in hopes of finding an opening to the main Union line. Bartlett's retreat started in good order but rapidly disintegrated into a rout. At the command "About face," the 118th Pennsylvania, popularly known as the Corn Exchange Regiment, turned and retired toward Saunders' Field. Soon realizing that they were hopelessly flanked and likely to be killed or captured, even the steadiest veterans panicked. The Federal formation crumbled into tiny knots of men. Each isolated cluster fell back a bit, then stopped to shoot nervously into the woods at rebels, real and imaginary. The 83rd Pennsylvania broke for the rear "on the double quick," with Ewell's soldiers yelling and firing into an indistinct blur of fleeing blue uniforms. "We ran almost every step of the way back," confessed a veteran of the 83rd, "and when we got there we laid down on our backs and panted like so many hounds which had just come back in from a ten hours' chase after a gang of foxes." [17]

The 20th Maine managed to find its way back, although many soldiers barely evaded capture. In a typical episode, a fifteen-man company mistakenly continued to advance, unaware that the rest of the brigade had melted away. On discovering their mistake, the sol-diers tried to cut through the rebel line that had snapped shut behind them. The brave little band lunged from the woods firing and scream-ing, "Surrender," at the top of their lungs. Thinking they were out-flanked, the rebels scattered. The relieved bluecoats darted through the opening to their earthworks, with over thirty prisoners.

In the confusion, Bartlett became separated from his staff. Unable to rally his brigade, the Union general slashed back through the

17. Hayes Journal, in Chamberlain Collection, LC; James O'Connell Memoir, in Civil War Miscellaneous Collection, USMHI; Eugene A. Nash, *A History of the Forty-Fourth Regiment New York Volunteer Infantry in the Civil War, 1861–1865* (Chicago, 1911), 184–85; Pullen, *The Twentieth Maine,* 188–89; Judson, *History of the Eighty-Third Regiment Pennsylvania,* 194; Survivors' Association, *History of the Corn Exchange Regiment,* 400.

thickets and emerged onto Saunders' Field. His uniform was torn, and blood trickled from his head and face. Wild yells rang out, and southern voices demanded Bartlett's surrender. Shaking a fist in defiance, the general proudly held himself erect and spurred his mount across the field. Volleys clipped past and plowed the ground around his horse. As the madly galloping general approached the ditch, another yell went up from the rebel side. The Confederates anticipated that he would have to slow his pace enough to present an easy target.

Gathering his reins firmly in hand, Bartlett aimed straight at the swale and stabbed his spurs into the foaming horse's sides. Nostrils dilated and ears pointed forward, his steed bunched its muscles and kicked off from the ditch's edge. A rebel bullet tore into the airborne horse and spun it in a somersault. The dead mount crashed in a heap on top of its rider on the Union side of the trench. Assuming that Bartlett had been killed, the rebels sounded another round of cheers. To everyone's surprise, a disheveled Bartlett crawled from under the dead horse. With the aid of wounded soldiers, he hobbled to safety.[18]

As refugees from the shattered Union charge began to straggle in, the magnitude of the repulse became evident. The turnpike behind Warren was clogged with ambulances and wounded men on foot asking directions to the 5th Corps' hospital. Rough tables had been erected under trees where surgeons were hacking off arms and legs in an effort to save lives. Shrieks and groans rent the air. Piles of severed limbs rose higher by the minute. Regiments were decimated. The 20th Maine, for example, had started the morning with about four hundred men. It now counted eleven killed, fifty-eight wounded, and sixteen missing, over twenty percent of its number. The commander of the 146th New York was missing—he was later learned to be dead—and the head of the 83rd Pennsylvania lay seriously wounded.

Working toward the front, Lyman saw an officer, his face covered with blood, propped in his saddle by men on either side. "Hullo, Lyman," the apparition called out, his mind obviously wandering. "Here I am; hurt a little; not much; I am going to lie down a few minutes, and then I am going back again! Oh, you ought to have seen how we drove 'em—I had the first line!" It was Hayes, of the

18. Melcher, "An Experience in the Battle of the Wilderness," in *War Papers*, I, 79-82; Gerrish, *Army Life*, 163-64, 168-69.

18th Massachusetts, Lyman's old classmate, easily mistaken for mortally wounded.[19]

Wadsworth's three brigades—Cutler's, Stone's, and Rice's, extending south from Saunders' Field in that order—had started forward at the same time as Griffin's division.

Bearing along the southern edge of Saunders' Field was Wadsworth's premier outfit, Cutler's Iron Brigade. Cutler's rightmost regiments—the 7th Wisconsin and 7th Indiana—drove into the graybacks side by side with Bartlett's soldiers and materially contributed to the collapse of Jones's section of the Confederate line. A Confederate heard them shouting as they charged, "Here's our western men!" But as the Iron Brigade bored into the thickets, the familiar story repeated itself. Cutler's units became increasingly disoriented and drifted left. In the process they separated from Bartlett and approached the second tier of rebels with their northern flank wide open.[20]

Directly ahead were Georgians under earnest-looking George Doles, a small-town businessman turned soldier who through staunch fighting had earned a reputation as one of Lee's steadiest brigadiers. Rising like specters out of a patch of dense underbrush, Doles's veterans rocked the Iron Brigade's exposed flank with a terrific volley. "Look to the right," screamed a northern officer, pointing toward a hazy Confederate line that stretched through the woods as far as the eye could see, rapidly blazing away as it advanced. In minutes, the 6th Wisconsin had lost nearly fifty men.[21]

19. Lyman to family, May 15, 1864, in *Meade's Headquarters*, ed. Agassiz, 90; Ellis Spear's Report, in *OR*, Vol. XXXVI, Pt. 1, p. 573. There were contradictory reports concerning Jenkins' fate. Some said he died on the battlefield, others that he was captured and died while trying to escape. See Brainard, *Campaigns of the One Hundred and Forty-Sixth Regiment*, 196–97n.

20. J. M. Thompson, "Reminiscences of the Autauga Rifles," in Regimental Collection, ADAH; Philip Cheek and Mair Pointon, *History of the Sauk County Riflemen, Known as Company "A," Sixth Wisconsin Veteran Volunteer Infantry, 1861–1865* (Madison, Wis., 1909), 90–91; Lysander Cutler's Report, in *OR*, Vol. XXXVI, Pt. 1, pp. 610–11; Curtis, *History of the Twenty-Fourth Michigan*, 230–34; Dawes, *Service with the Sixth Wisconsin*, 259–61.

21. Thomas, *History of the Doles-Cook Brigade*, 14, 76, 477–78; Dawes, *Service with the Sixth Wisconsin*, 260.

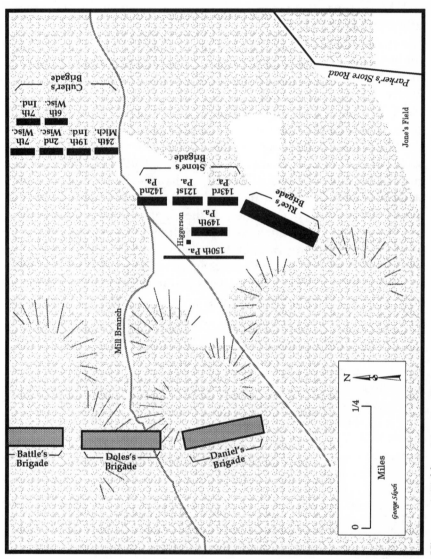

Higgerson's Field on May 5 at 1 P.M.

The true storm, however, had yet to break. Monitoring his lines with growing concern, Ewell had witnessed the Yankees punch through Jones's brigade. Although Doles and Battle appeared to be holding their own against the latest onslaught, there was no telling when they too would give way.

Firmly planting a Confederate flag in the roadway, Ewell, Early, and their staff officers labored to rally stragglers drifting back from the front. Reinforcements were imperative. Early turned to his aide Daniel. "Major," he ordered, "you will find Gordon a short distance up the pike. Ride to him as fast as you can and tell him to bring up his brigade as quick as possible." Spurring his horse "Old Whitey" around, Daniel dashed out the turnpike toward Robertson's Tavern. A short way back, he spied John Gordon, the lanky commander of Early's Georgia brigade, on the highway's south side. Riding full tilt up to Gordon, Daniel breathlessly delivered Early's message. "Major," answered Gordon, "do me a favor. Give the instructions yourself to each of my regimental commanders while I ride to the front and see the situation and prepare for the charge." Daniel replied, "Certainly, General," and as Gordon disappeared toward the sound of battle, the major rode alongside Gordon's regiments alerting them to what lay ahead. The Georgians "alternately trotted and quickstepped forward." After conferring with Early, Gordon ordered his men to file to the right. Then they were to face forward, forming a line in the woods toward the enemy.[22]

Straight and thin as a ramrod, Gordon towered high and majestic on horseback. To one of his men, he looked like a war god of old. "He's most the prettiest thing you ever did see on a field of fight," a soldier once bragged. "It'ud put fight into a whipped chicken just to look at him." A born orator, Gordon had a knack for inspiring men to a fever pitch, and his bravery was legend. This steamy May afternoon, he was in top form. The aide Daniel recalled him as he sat on his horse, "erect, his countenance intense, and his sword drawn." Yankees were so close that bullets were zinging through the Georgian ranks. "The murmur and tumult of the advancing Federal infantry

22. Daniel, "My Account, May 5," in Daniel Collection, UV. Gordon gave a more colorful description in *Reminiscences*, 237–42. He asserted that Ewell rushed to him for help, nearly hitting him with his wooden leg. According to Daniel's manuscript, Gordon overdramatized events and underplayed Ewell's and Early's involvement. I have largely followed Daniel's account.

could be heard through the woods," recalled Daniel, "and they were not more than 100 or at least more than 200 yards distant." Gordon rode to the center of his line, rose to full height in his stirrups, and in his finest voice belted out, "Forward!" With a deafening yell, the Georgians dashed for the front.[23]

"We could see nothing in front for the thick woods and smoke," one of Gordon's soldiers later recounted, "and must have gone three hundred yards before we encountered the advanced line of the enemy." Coming up alongside Battle's Confederate brigade, Gordon's troops dived into the fray.[24]

Wadsworth's tangled line was as perfectly set up for a Confederate countercharge as Gordon could have wished. Cutler was stymied in front of Doles's tenacious brigade with his right flank wide open, and Bartlett was too busy trying to save himself to care about anyone else. Even more enticingly, Stone's brigade, slated to cover Cutler's left, had bogged down in marshy ground and was nowhere in sight. Denison's Maryland brigade, assigned to advance behind Cutler, had not budged from its jump-off point, nearly a mile back. In short, the Iron Brigade had to fend for itself, not only against Doles's and Battle's men but now against Gordon's as well.

Lunging ahead, Gordon smashed into Cutler's hard-pressed units. Near the front of the Confederate charge was James Ervin Spivey, of the 26th Georgia, famed in both armies for his battle cry. "It was a kind of scream or low, like a terrible bull, with a kind of a neigh mixed along with it," recalled one of his fellow Georgians, "and it was nearly as loud as a steam whistle." Gordon's men called Spivey the Twenty-sixth Georgia's Bull and understood that the Federals referred to him as Gordon's Bull. "He would always halloo this way when we charged the enemy," recounted a Confederate, "and we were informed that the Yankees understood it as a signal to move back."[25]

23. Nichols, *A Soldier's Story of His Regiment*, 141–42; Daniel, "My Account, May 5," in Daniel Collection, UV.

24. F. L. Hudgins, "With the 38th Georgia Regiment," *Confederate Veteran*, XXVI (1918), 163.

25. Nichols, *A Soldier's Story of His Regiment*, 142; Alton J. Murray, *South Georgia Rebels: The True Wartime Experiences of the 26th Regiment Georgia Volunteer Infantry, Lawton-Gordon-Evans Brigade* (St. Mary's, Ga., 1976), 149.

Whether owing to Spivey's lung power or to the unexpected ferocity of the Georgia brigade's attack, a window opened in the Federal line. But as the Yankees gave way, the Georgians found themselves in a predicament. Having slashed open a pocket in the Union formation, they were surrounded by bluecoats. If they continued farther, the opening might close behind them and cut them off. If they did nothing or retreated, they were sure to be slaughtered.

Acting quickly—the lanky rebel brigadier later claimed he was galvanized into more thinking in a second than he normally did in a day—Gordon split his brigade down the middle and swung left and right, like a barn door hinged on both Federal flanks. The unorthodox maneuver was completed in minutes, leaving three Georgia regiments facing south, one facing north, and a thin line of men stringing the two together. "This done," Gordon later explained, "both wings were ordered forward, and, with another piercing yell, they rushed in opposite directions upon the right and left flanks of the astounded Federals, shattering them as any troops that were ever marshalled would have been shattered, capturing large numbers, and checking any further effort by General Grant on that portion of the field."[26]

For the first time in the Iron Brigade's history, it broke and tumbled rearward in confusion, setting off a chain reaction that jumbled the Federal units behind. Still waiting in reserve near Cutler's original position, Denison's Maryland brigade was trampled by retreating fugitives. Riding back and forth, his white locks streaming, Wadsworth tried to restore order. "Where is my second line?" he shouted. "Bring up my second line!" The Marylanders, hastily repairing their formation, managed to brace themselves before rebel pursuers broke through. Fighting like demons, the Confederates pounded Denison's troops. "We suffered severely," a Federal officer admitted in his report. Soon the Marylanders were flanked on both sides and in im-

---

26. John B. Gordon's Report, in OR, Vol. XXXVI, Pt. 1, pp. 1076–77. The exact point of Gordon's attack is open to debate. Several secondary sources, including superb maps prepared by the National Park Service, show Gordon striking in the vicinity of Stone or Rice. In all likelihood, Gordon's attack landed nearer to the Orange Turnpike. Gordon's men had bivouacked adjacent to the turnpike, and enemy shells were falling within their formation before they charged. Little time was consumed in maneuver. Gordon's brigade probably charged nearly straight ahead, careering into Cutler. These matters are carefully reviewed in William Cutshaw to John W. Daniel, May 30, 1905, in Daniel Collection, UV.

minent danger of capture. To make matters worse, Union fugitives had rallied in their rear and were blasting away toward the rebels, in the process pelting Denison's troops with a galling fire from behind. Retreat was in order, and Denison's crippled brigade rolled back to open ground around the Lacy house, where the rest of Wadsworth's shattered units were assembling.[27]

Flushed with triumph, Confederates carried their pursuit to the edge of the Lacy fields, scooping up prisoners and weapons. One fortunate Georgian found a full set of silver bugles, abandoned by Union musicians. "These were taken and used until the close of the war by our regimental band," he later recalled fondly.[28]

To Cutler's and Denison's left, Roy Stone's Pennsylvania brigade had wound up in a nightmare of unusually hellish proportions, even for this day. Pushing forward, the Pennsylvanians had crossed a clearing about a quarter mile below Saunders' Field. Known as Spring Hill, the clearing was the site of the Higgerson home. On its far side, it dropped down to a little creek, one of Wilderness Run's tributaries.

The brigade lined up facing the woods. The 143rd and 149th Pennsylvania regiments were in the lead, the 150th was assigned as skirmishers, and the remaining three regiments were massed behind.

Peering into dense foliage just beyond the field, a Pennsylvanian called to his companions, "That's a hell of a looking hole to send white men into." Another shouted, "Boys, label yourselves, if we must go down in there, as you will never come out again." No one's confidence was helped by the fact that the brigade's officers could be seen "swilling whiskey as they would water."[29]

Chopping through tangled bushes, Stone's troops stumbled into a swamp. Soon they were floundering in mud and water to their

---

27. L. Allison Wilmer *et al.*, *History and Roster of Maryland Volunteers* (2 vols.; Baltimore, 1898), I, 264–66; Samuel Graham's Report, in *OR*, Vol. XXXVI, Pt. 1, p. 601; Richard Bowerman's Report, *ibid.*, 604. A Federal gunner recalled seeing the "old general rushing about with sword drawn rallying his men around a flag that he had placed in position" (*History of the Fifth Massachusetts Battery* [Boston, 1902], 806).

28. Isaac G. Bradwell, "Battle of the Wilderness," *Confederate Veteran*, XVI (1908), 448.

29. Avery Harris Memoir, in Avery Harris Collection, USMHI.

waists. Alignments disintegrated. The 149th became separated from the 143rd, slipping to the rear and a little behind its sister regiment. Suddenly sheets of flame burst in the faces of Stone's men. Bullets spattered all around. Bewildered soldiers frantically struggled in slow motion to extricate themselves from the mire. Shooting toward the sound of rebel muskets, the 149th Pennsylvania poured destructive fire into the back of the 143rd Pennsylvania. "The men scattered in every direction," recalled a survivor, "most of them going down the swamp toward the right." Stone did what he could to rally his panicked brigade. "Hat off, and his coat thrown back on his shoulders," remembered one of Stone's troops, "he rode down behind [the 149th Pennsylvania,] which a line of Western troops [the Iron Brigade] had stopped, cursing them as though that were a part of his education. Swinging his sword, he drove them back to the line again." The rally, however, was short-lived. Crawling out of what one Pennsylvanian later described as "that champion mud hole of mud holes," Stone's soldiers sloshed off in all directions, uncertain of where to turn. Another soldier recalled how they "went to the rear, pell mell, like a flock of scared sheep." Large numbers were captured. Survivors filtered back to the Lacy fields, by then teeming with Federals stunned by the unexpected reverse. Blustering with rage, Stone blamed the rout on the 143rd Pennsylvania. A member of that unit seethed as he listened to Stone's contemptuous language. "I would have liked to have seen a rebel shell come and took the drunken head clean from his shoulders after he got through with his abuse," the soldier later reminisced. "Could I photograph this hell hole that we were put in, I would then ask, what in the name of justice and cause and effect, had we to do with the outflanking and envelopment of the famous old Iron Brigade." The real culprit, concluded the soldier, was the gap between Stone's and Cutler's forces. "Tell to the world if you can why then two fighting brigades (Iron Brigade and Stone's) were thus advanced to this position in this hell hole, without correction on either flank, and officers drunk."[30]

On Wadsworth's far left, Rice's Union brigade was also receiving

30. Harris Memoir, in Harris Collection, USMHI; Survivors' Association, *121st Regiment Pennsylvania Volunteers* (Philadelphia, 1906), 76–77; Chamberlin, *History of the One Hundred and Fiftieth Regiment Pennsylvania*, 207–209.

a sound thrashing. As Rice's troops moved forward, the southern end of their line—previously covered by Crawford's division—became vulnerable. The problem was exacerbated by the terrain, which caused Rice's men to drift northward. When they finally encountered rebels, they did so at an angle rather than straight on. This meant that Rice's unprotected left received the brunt of the Confederate fire.

As the rattle of musketry swelled, skirmishers brought Rice the fatal news that Confederates were circling all the way around his left. Almost simultaneously, the other end of Rice's formation became exposed as Stone's brigade collapsed. A "very destructive fire," according to one of Rice's officers, came tearing through the trees "from an unseen enemy." The Confederates responsible for Rice's distress belonged to Junius Daniel's North Carolina brigade, posted on Ewell's southern flank. A West Point graduate and Louisiana planter before the war, Daniel was a talented organizer and a strict disciplinarian. This day his rigorous training paid off. On learning that Jones had been overrun on the turnpike, Daniel had immediately tunneled into the budding underbrush a mile or so south of the roadway, where he encountered Rice's lead units in a heavily wooded depression. The Yankees squeezed off the first shots, but their bullets went high. Without breaking stride, Daniel's battle-hardened veterans leveled their guns, discharged a devastating volley, then jumped in swinging their muskets like clubs. A quick count of fleeing Yankees and of bodies piled in the hollow convinced one rebel that half the Union line had died in the blast. "On the brigade went in a full run," recorded one of Daniel's soldiers. Forming their troops about a half mile back, Union officers tried to stem the rout. Suddenly one of Wadsworth's aides rushed up with instructions to retire, and the retreat resumed. Daniel's men, exploiting their advantage, exultantly sprinted almost to the Lacy house. The 5th Corps artillery, placed there earlier to protect the Wilderness Tavern intersection, opened on the brazen rebels, who responded with a last burst of adrenaline by storming the guns. Their impetuous advance was finally halted by Federals stationed across a piece of cleared ground. Daniel's men dropped to their knees and blazed away. Both sides suffered heavily and by tacit agreement withdrew to their respective sides of the Lacy field. "Owing to General Daniel's skill and promptness in throwing in his brigade at the right moment," wrote a proud Confederate years later, "he saved the day when others were falling back, and still history gives this credit to higher officers when the move was made by him alone, and higher officers knew nothing of it until it was over."[31]

Rice's losses were severe. Two of his five regimental commanders lay wounded, along with several lesser-grade officers. The brigade's skirmish line, consisting of three companies from the 76th New York, was cut off from the main body of troops and wandered for hours in trackless forest. Most of the soldiers were either shot or captured, along with their leader. Casualties in Wadsworth's other brigades were of comparable magnitude. Cutler reported he had suffered "very heavily in killed and wounded." Particularly embarrassing was the large number of Union prisoners. Riding into the Lacy fields, Warren's aide Roebling met a disconcerting scene. Parker's Store Road was "crowded with stragglers and large crowds of soldiers pouring out of the woods in great confusion and almost panic stricken. Some said they were flanked, others that they had suddenly come upon rebs lying concealed in two lines of battle in the thick underbrush." Most of the stragglers, noted Roebling, felt secure enough to stop by the time they reached the meadow bottoms around the Lacy house.[32]

Stabilizing their line, Wadsworth's troops waged a determined holding action. The Confederates had pushed as far as they were capable of going. Things settled into a dirty little fight, unrelieved by pageantry. "As a grand, inspiring spectacle," wrote a disappointed Union volunteer, "it was highly unsatisfactory, owing to the powder smoke obscuring the vision. At times we could not see the Confederate line, but that made no difference; we kept on firing just as though they were in full view. We gained ground at times, and then dead Confederates lay on the ground as thickly as dead

31. William Hoffman's Report, in OR, Vol. XXXVI, Pt. 1, p. 623; A. P. Smith, *History of the Seventy-Sixth Regiment New York Volunteers* (Cortland, N.Y., 1867), 284; William Holland to Augustus Buell, n.d., in *The Cannoneer*, by Augustus Buell (Washington, D.C., 1890), 160–61; William L. London, "The Daniel-Grimes Brigade," in *Histories of the Several Regiments and Battalions from North Carolina*, comp. Clark, IV, 513–14; Clark, comp., *Histories of the Several Regiments and Battalions from North Carolina*, III, 44.

32. A. P. Smith, *History of the Seventy-Sixth Regiment New York*, 285–86; Cutler's Report, in OR, Vol. XXXVI, Pt. 1, pp. 610–11; Washington A. Roebling's Report, in Warren Collection, NYSA.

Union soldiers did behind us. Then we would fall back, fighting stubbornly, but steadily giving ground, until the dead were all clad in blue." [33]

Arriving from the Chewning farm, McCandless' Union brigade reached the fighting too late to be of any assistance. "We seem to have been thrown in advance of our corps," a Pennsylvanian recorded in his diary, "in such a position that we are liable to be cut off from the command." As Wadsworth's front dissolved under Ewell's counteroffensive, McCandless' men were "fired into from all sides." Surrounded by Confederates, they were compelled to cut their way to the rear or to surrender. One of McCandless' soldiers recalled passing "down the ravine of Wilderness Run, with the enemy on both sides of us." McCandless himself scarcely made it back alive. "He had lost his hat," recounted a witness, "and when we saw him riding for his life, and his gray hair flying in the air, we gave him a hearty cheer." [34]

The 7th Pennsylvania met a particularly humiliating fate. After Gordon's attack, a portion of the 61st Georgia had drifted southward. Learning from prisoners that a Union regiment was nearby, Major James Van Valkenburgh, of the 61st, took a party in search of the Federals. Unexpectedly, they stumbled into the 7th Pennsylvania. Seizing the initiative, Van Valkenburgh called back in bluff for the 60th and 61st Georgia regiments, then rode up to the northerners. "I asked for the commanding officer, and was told he was down the line," recalled Van Valkenburgh. "I rode down their line to the colonel and asked him if he commanded that regiment. He said he did. In the meantime the ten or twenty men with me advanced up also. I told the colonel he was my prisoner and demanded the surrender of his officers and men." According to one account, the senior Union officer refused and called upon the rebels to surrender. Not to be outdone, Van Valkenburgh shouted for Gordon to send up the bri-

33. Wilkeson, *Recollections*, 63.

34. Jacob Heflinger Diary, in Civil War Times Illustrated Collection, USMHI; Holland to Buell, n.d., in *The Cannoneer*, by Buell, 160–61.

gade and ordered his men forward. Finally convinced that they were heavily outnumbered, the Pennsylvanians stacked their weapons. Virtually the entire Union regiment was captured by two rebel companies. On learning that they had surrendered to a vastly inferior force, the Pennsylvanians, according to one of Gordon's soldiers, "were the worst set of mortified officers and men I have ever seen." [35]

The rest of Crawford's division, still ensconced at the Chewning farm, was in imminent danger of being isolated. Warren had no choice but to order the Pennsylvanians to withdraw up Parker's Store Road. As Crawford's men began leaving the Chewning fields, Confederates poured in from the clearing's opposite side. Fighting a heated rearguard action, Crawford's troops finally managed to establish a position near the Lacy house, facing back toward Parker's Store.

With the collapse of the Federal offensive, Maryland Steuart was free to concentrate on expelling Ayres's two New York regiments that were still precariously lodged on the rebel side of Saunders' Field. Confederates pinched around both ends of the Yankee position and encapsulated it. "We were not only flanked," discovered the New Yorkers, "but doubly flanked. Rebel troops covered the open field. We were in a bag and the string was tied." A few Yankees attempted to run back across Saunders' Field, canteens clasped tightly against the backs of their heads in reflexive attempts to ward off bullets. Some darted into the gully for protection. Others crouched behind dead artillery horses along the turnpike. "The bright red of our Zouave uniforms mingled with the sober gray and butternut of the Confederates," wrote the 146th New York's historian, "creating a fantastic spectacle as the wearers ran to and fro over the field, firing and shouting." A member of the 146th's color guard had just crossed the gully when Confederates bore down on him, anxious to cap their victory with a Yankee flag. A volley roared, and three bullets brought the color-bearer down. Another member of the color guard seized the

35. James Van Valkenburgh, "A Gallant Achievement," Macon *Telegraph*, June 1, 1864; Nichols, *A Soldier's Story of His Regiment*, 143–44.

fallen flag and was quickly killed. The guard's corporal plucked the colors from the stricken soldier's hand, darted rearward, and stumbled headlong into the gully, where he fell wounded. A passing sergeant raked up the flag and continued the flight. Ignoring rebel demands to stop and surrender, he dodged bullets by bounding side to side like a rabbit. Finally he collapsed safely behind the Union earthworks. "The flag," wrote the 146th's historian, "torn and soiled, was preserved to the regiment." Only 254 of the 556 enlisted men of the 146th New York who had marched out an hour before returned. Ten commissioned officers out of the regiment's original twenty-four responded to the evening roll call.[36]

The 146th's companion regiment, the 140th New York, sustained comparable losses. Stumbling into the Federal formation, Ryan was heard to exclaim, "My God, I'm the first colonel I ever knew who couldn't tell where his regiment was." Weeping uncontrollably, the colonel threw his arms around the neck of one of his officers. The command suffered some 268 casualties out of the 529 men who had charged into the field. Its leadership was virtually annihilated. "The gloom which settled over us was unspeakable," remembered a survivor.[37]

A whirlwind of hand-to-hand combat swirled around the Federal guns that were still blazing away from the middle of Saunders' Field. Steuart's 1st and 3rd North Carolina regiments pitched in with clubbed muskets and bayonets. "'Twas claw for claw, and the devil for us all," one of the southern combatants remembered. Abandoned by Ayres's infantry, the stubborn gunners managed to get off a few final shots, fighting alone until they were overrun by graycoats. Jamming two pistols in Shelton's face, an officer from the 61st Alabama demanded that the lieutenant surrender. As he was being led away, Shelton saw an Alabama regiment in "butternut suits and slouch hats, shooting straggling and wounded Zouaves." Only after nearly all the artillery horses were killed and the officers wounded did the cannon fall into rebel hands. "The guns were fought to the last," the

---

36. Sweet to Grindlay, 1887, in *Campaigns of the One Hundred and Forty-Sixth Regiment New York*, by Brainard, 192.

37. Farley, "Reminiscences," in *Rochester Historical Society Publication*, XXII, 242–43; Otis to Prentice, December 26, 1888, in LC; Brian A. Bennett, *Sons of Old Monroe: A Regimental History of Patrick O'Rorke's 140th New York Volunteer Infantry* (Dayton, 1992), 373–74.

5th Corps artillery chief Wainwright noted in his report, "and lost as honorably as guns could be lost." [38]

No sooner had Steuart's jubilant Confederates secured their prize than a wave of wild-eyed fugitives from Bartlett's and Cutler's Federal brigades poured onto the field, streaming from the Confederate side back toward the main Union line. Doles's and Gordon's Georgians were pounding behind in hot pursuit. Diving into the gully for shelter from the stampede, Steuart's rebels lay low "while this vast herd of fleeing Federals came rushing through and over us without firing a gun or speaking a word." Battle's Confederates jumped into the melee, thoroughly enjoying the turn of events. Proudly mounting the Union guns, flag in hand, an officer of Battle's 6th Alabama claimed the capture as his. In a hot fury, the North Carolinians clambered from the gully and demanded the guns as theirs. For a brief time Yankees were forgotten and war threatened to erupt between Battle's and Steuart's commands. Loath to see their comrades cheated out of their just due, Steuart's entire brigade appeared in support of the brave North Carolina regiments. Persuaded by numbers if not by logic, the Alabamians backed down.

As it turned out, no one was yet to have the guns. Hustling Robinson's two reserve Union brigades from Wilderness Tavern and shifting additional soldiers north of the turnpike, Warren toughened Ayres's shaky line and scraped together enough troops for a countercharge. "A scattering of men was running in, some of them crying disaster," a newly arrived soldier related, "and ahead of us there was an uproar of yelling and firing." The fresh Federals raked Saunders' Field with a destructive volley that drove the rebels back to their woods. [39]

A few hardy southerners managed to decorate the captured Union pieces with small Confederate flags and bunting. Their purpose was "to tantalize us on," surmised a Union officer. The tactic worked. With a yell, the 9th Massachusetts, of Sweitzer's brigade,

---

38. Wainwright's Report, in OR, Vol. XXXVI, Pt. 1, p. 640; Nevins, ed., Diary of Battle, 350–52; Clark, comp., Histories of the Several Regiments and Battalions from North Carolina, I, 150–51, 200–201; William H. Shelton, "Memorandum," in "The 140th New York Volunteers, Wilderness, May 5th, 1864," by Farley, 38, in Farley Papers, RL.

39. Harold Small, ed., The Road to Richmond: The Civil War Memoirs of Major Abner R. Small of the Sixteenth Maine Volunteers (Berkeley, Calif., 1939), 132; Thruston, "Report of the Conduct of General George H. Steuart's Brigade," in SHSP, XIV, 148–49.

charged onto Saunders' Field. A terrific fire of musketry exploded from ahead, driving the Federals back. In a few short minutes, the regiment lost 12 officers and 138 soldiers. Sweitzer, who had been behind the lines and had missed the slaughter, rushed up and demanded that the regiment renew its attack. "We have been in, and just come out!" explained the colonel in charge. "Well," barked Sweitzer in a loud and insolent tone, "take 'em in again." The colonel called, "Fall in, 9th." As he was preparing to give orders to advance, a staff officer appeared. "General Griffin's orders are not to take the 9th in again," he announced to the relief of the Massachusetts soldiers. According to one account, Sweitzer learned of the regiment's losses the next morning and apologized. "If Colonel Sweitzer's irrational orders had not been countermanded by General Griffin, but few, if any, of the Ninth would have come out of 'that hole' fit for duty," concluded the regiment's historian.[40]

Packed into the gully, wounded men from both armies huddled low, fearing to lift their heads in the blistering crossfire. The few who attempted to dash back to their lines simply added to the dead already lying thick in the old cornfield. Injured soldiers cried out in vain for water. Beyond either side's reach, the shiny Union guns stood as monuments in a sea of fallen blue and gray.

Saunders' Field and the woods immediately below it had been convulsed for over an hour by intense small-arms fire. "The crackle of the rifles resounding through the gloom," remarked one soldier, "resembled the noise made by swiftly rasping a stick along a paling fence, or by packs of shooting-crackers exploding in a barrel." Another described the din simply as "terrific." Back at Union headquarters, it seemed to Humphreys that the racket "approached the sublime." The close-quarters firing was murderous. "The Confederates are shooting to kill this time," a wounded Yankee muttered as he staggered to the rear. "Few of their balls strike the trees higher than ten feet from the ground. Small trees are already falling, cut down by rifle balls."[41]

Kindled by discharges from muskets, Ewell's earthworks caught

40. Daniel G. McNamara, *The History of the Ninth Regiment Massachusetts Volunteer Infantry* (Boston, 1899), 372–73.

41. John D. Vautier, *History of the 88th Pennsylvania Volunteers in the War for the Union, 1861–1865* (Philadelphia, 1894), 174; Andrew A. Humphreys, *The Virginia Campaign,* 55–56; Wilkeson, *Recollections,* 57–58.

fire. Acrid black smoke spewed across Saunders' Field, hindering rescue efforts and threatening to smother many of the wounded. Soon
the worst fears were realized and the entire clearing south of the turnpike erupted in flame. Hobbling and crawling as best they could,
injured soldiers tried to make their way to the safety of their lines or
to the roadway, which acted as a firebreak. Cartridges carried at
the waist exploded with ominous popping sounds whenever flames
reached a soldier, inflicting grisly wounds. Many preferred death at
their own hands to slowly roasting in the insidious flames. "I saw one
man," a volunteer recalled, "both of whose legs were broken, lying
on the ground with his cocked rifle by his side and his ramrod in his
hand, and his eyes set on the front." Shortly the clearing lay blackened between the armies. Heaps the size of men were charred beyond
recognition.[42]

One of Warren's aides came upon Bartlett trying to bring order
into the remains of his brigade. Blood trickled from a cheek wound
onto the general's breast. "His complexion was fair and his hair very
black," the aide later recalled, "his hat was off, and I can see his
bleeding face, as well as Griffin's deeply glum one, across all the
years." Angrily snooping around to discover what had happened to
his guns, Wainwright found Bartlett with "his mouth firmly glued
shut from excessive thirst and hallooing." Ayres manfully accepted
the blame, admitting that the guns had been lost through his brigade's "bad behavior." Wainwright, however, faulted Griffin, whom
he criticized for trying to shift responsibility to subordinates. Later,
Warren wrote across the bottom of Roebling's battle report, "The
responsibility of sending this section of artillery with the advance
rests upon me."[43]

Unaccustomed to suffering in silence, Griffin rode to the headquarters knoll at 2:45 P.M. with his mustering officer to speak his
mind. Grant and Meade were both there. Griffin, his face visibly

42. Farley, "The 140th New York Volunteers, Wilderness, May 5th, 1864," 38, in Farley
Papers, RL; Brainard, *Campaigns of the One Hundred and Forty-Sixth Regiment New York*,
195; Wilkeson, *Recollections*, 66–67.

43. Schaff, *The Battle of the Wilderness*, 159; Nevins, ed., *Diary of Battle*, 352; Roebling's
Report, with Warren's handwritten comment, in Warren Collection, NYSA. Shelton later confirmed that his captain had received orders to advance the section "in person from General
Warren" (Shelton, "Memorandum," in "The 140th New York Volunteers, Wilderness, May 5,
1864," by Farley, 37, in Farley Papers, RL).

flushed with anger, announced in a loud voice that he had driven Ewell three-quarters of a mile, but that Wright had failed to join him and Wadsworth had been forced back, leaving both his flanks exposed and compelling him to retreat to his former position. "He implied censure on General Wright," wrote Lyman, who witnessed the tantrum, "and apparently on his corps commander, General Warren." Stunned by Griffin's outburst, Grant's aide Rawlins felt his blood boiling at the open display of insubordination. Griffin's language was mutinous, piped the staffer, and warranted his censure. Grant agreed and asked Meade, "Who is this General Gregg? You ought to arrest him." Meade's temper was notorious. He was "always going bang at someone," an aide wrote home. The frustrations of military life—from tardy mule drivers to uncomprehending subordinates—invariably aroused the general's ire. Reputedly his staff was always in a "semi-terrified state." Yet something about the incident with Griffin struck an unusual chord in Meade. Noticing that the general-in-chief's coat was unbuttoned, he reached over and began fastening it, as though Grant were a little boy. "It's Griffin, not Gregg," Meade answered in a good-natured voice, "and it's only his way of talking."[44]

Meade's turnpike offensive was over by 2:30, an hour and a half after it had begun. It had failed for the reasons predicted by Warren's frontline officers. As they had foreseen, launching the attack before Sedgwick moved into place left Griffin's flank wide open. Ayres, unsupported on his right, never had a chance; his collapse imperiled Bartlett's flank, and when Bartlett fell, Cutler was left dangling. With the process mirrored from Rice's end of the line, Warren's formation had tumbled like a house of cards. As Warren concluded in his report of the affair, "The attack failed because Wright's division, of the Sixth Corps, was unable on account of the woods to get up on our right flank and meet the division (Johnson's) that flanked us." Ten years

44. Lyman to family, May 15, 1864, in *Meade's Headquarter's,* ed. Agassiz, 91; Theodore Lyman Journal, May 5, 1864, in Theodore Lyman Papers, MHS. Excerpts from the journal are reproduced in Lyman's "Addenda to the Paper by Brevet Lieutenant-Colonel W. W. Swan, U.S.A., on the Battle of the Wilderness," in *PMHSM,* IV, 167–68.

later, Warren was still stewing over having been forced to attack before he was ready and without proper support on his flanks. "If we had waited until the 6th Corps or two divisions of it got up with the enemy on the road the 6th Corps was taking, we should have begun the attack on Ewell's flank," he wrote his friend Charles Porter. "I should have had Robinson's division in supporting line, and we should have utterly crushed Ewell's corps." Instead, much of his command had been needlessly sacrificed in a charge doomed from the outset. The precipitate attack, concluded Warren, was the "most fatal blunder of the campaign."[45]

A second mistake involved the small size of the attacking force and the failure to use reserves. Even where Union troops managed to penetrate Ewell's line, as in Bartlett's and Cutler's sectors, they quickly ran out of steam. Since reserves were not put into play, it was impossible to exploit gains, and temporary successes evaporated as Ewell rallied his broken elements and sent fresh units to endangered sites. To some extent, responsibility rested on Warren's shoulders. While Griffin's and Wadsworth's divisions were brutally savaged, the cautious 5th Corps commander had kept Robinson's division in reserve and had never managed to get Crawford's engaged. The ultimate fault, of course, lay with Meade. There was no excuse for his forcing Warren forward until he was ready and until Wright's full weight could be brought to bear. By 1 P.M., Ewell had already dug in on the turnpike and Lee had no additional troops to send him. Delaying an hour or two would have made no appreciable difference in Ewell's strength but could have materially increased Warren's chance of success.

As expected, the Wilderness' choppy, densely wooded terrain had proved as formidable a foe to the Federals as had Ewell's Confederates. Meade's impressive edge in artillery was meaningless. Most of Warren's cannon had engaged in futile practice against distant rebel targets and had inflicted no discernible damage. Not a single Federal unit had escaped the disorienting effect of the wooded terrain, and for some, such as Stone's mud-caked Pennsylvanians, the natural obstacles proved fatal. Most tellingly, the attacking line had lost coherence and was robbed of the advantages of a unified, sweeping charge.

45. Gouverneur K. Warren's Report, in OR, Vol. XXXVI, Pt. 1, p. 540; Gouverneur K. Warren to Charles Porter, November 21, 1875, in Warren Collection, NYSA.

In Roebling's view, Wadsworth's men had been utterly bewildered by the twists and turns of Parker's Store Road. Instead of facing west, many units had mistakenly drifted northward, leaving their flanks vulnerable. "The thick woods prevented any change of the line on the spot," observed Roebling, "and by running back, the men did about the best thing they could."[46]

In addition, Ewell and his brigadiers had delivered a sterling performance. This had been the irascible old soldier's proudest day so far. All could agree that Ewell had been a whirlwind on the battlefield, placing men with a practiced eye and decisively shuttling troops around as necessary. He had fully justified Lee's confidence and carried out his instructions to the letter, fending off Warren's attacks while refusing to get sucked into a "general engagement."

Earlier, when the skirmishing had begun, Ewell had sent Campbell Brown once again to Lee for instructions. Brown had informed Lee that Ewell intended to fall back to Mine Run if "pushed," understanding that such was Lee's wish. As Brown later recalled, Lee replied that Pendleton "and myself had misinterpreted him, that he only meant us to fall back in case we could not hold our position." Although Lee's earlier oral instruction had caused confusion, Ewell had adopted the proper course of standing his ground.[47]

Ewell's 2nd Corps brigade commanders—particularly Gordon, Daniel, Doles, and Steuart—had performed at their aggressive best, and the resilient southern foot soldiers had done everything expected of them. In retrospect, the Federals had made several mistakes, and Ewell and his generals had skillfully exploited nearly every one of them.

*"He that a short time ago
jested is now grave."*

So far as Grant was concerned, Warren's bloody repulse along Saunders' Field and in the convoluted thickets below the clearing marked the beginning rather than the end of the day's fighting. A two-front

46. Roebling's Report, in Warren Collection, NYSA.

47. Campbell Brown, "Memorandum—Campaign of 1864," in the Ewell-Stewart-Brown Collection, TSL.

battle was laboriously taking shape, one centered around the turn-pike and another on Orange Plank Road. The tenacious little man's instincts told him to grab hold at both places and pound away. Lee might successfully fend off piecemeal attacks, but a concerted Federal push against the entire Confederate line was bound to uncover weak spots. Grant had hoped to avoid fighting in the Wilderness, but fight there he had to. In characteristic fashion, his reflexive response was to try to turn a bad situation his way by lashing back with everything at his disposal.

Grant's problem was how to concentrate the scattered blue host against Lee's cagey veterans. A cursory glance at the map offered the tantalizing possibility of forging Warren, Sedgwick, and Burnside into a steel-fisted assault against Ewell. But uniting the three Federal corps any time soon faced serious practical difficulties. Warren's stunned soldiers were enjoying a hard-earned breather after their recent mauling in the thickets. They were in no condition to start another brawl with Ewell. Spearheading Sedgwick's advance out Spotswood Road toward Warren's northern flank, Wright's division had mired down in a frustrating fire fight with rebel cavalry and skirmishers. In any event, Sedgwick lacked sufficient troops to wreak much havoc by himself. And though Burnside's large corps was theoretically capable of providing the mass necessary for a breakthrough, its footsore soldiers were just inching across the Rapidan, completely exhausted after a grueling twenty-four-hour march from their camps above the Rappahannock. Prospects for quick action were no better down on Orange Plank Road. Getty's three brigades were holding the Brock Road intersection, but they could scarcely be expected to occupy Hill's two divisions for long. Hancock's veteran 2nd Corps had been ordered to Getty's support, but getting messages to that quarter was proving exceedingly difficult. It was unclear how much more time was required for Hancock's troops to reach Getty, shuffle into place, and be ready to fight.

After Saunders' Field quieted down to sporadic potshots from nervous pickets firing across the clearing, Grant and Warren rode together to the front. The Orange Turnpike and the surrounding woods were blue with soldiers falling back to new positions. Wounded men crowded the roadway. A smoky pall hung low in the stifling air, forming a gray canopy that obscured treetops and imparted a hazy, filtered quality to the entire scene. After a sobering look at the terrain, Grant rode back to his knoll and his whittling.[48]

What the stone-faced man learned was not encouraging. Wadsworth's division was completely out of the picture and was licking its wounds near the Lacy house. Crawford's division had drawn in from the Chewning plateau and was huddled up next to Wadsworth's main body, keeping a wary eye on the trail toward Parker's Store. Griffin's division was in horrible shape. Hoping to nurse some life back into his mangled units, the outspoken general had withdrawn to his morning's trenches slightly in advance of the Parker's Store trail. There his soldiers were helping to screen Wadsworth's elements and were trying to snatch a little rest themselves. Out of Warren's entire corps, only two brigades—Colonel Samuel H. Leonard's and Brigadier General Henry Baxter's, both of Robinson's division and both of which, having arrived near the fighting's conclusion, were relatively unscathed—remained forward. They were performing valuable guard service along Saunders' Field but posed no real threat to the rebels.

The first break in what was fast threatening to become a stagnant front appeared toward three o'clock. Sedgwick's overdue 6th Corps elements, commanded by Horatio Wright, at long last emerged above Saunders' Field.

Typical of the Army of the Potomac's performance during this slow-motion day, Wright's progress had been hampered in equal part by Wilderness, Confederates, and the Federal high command. The 6th Corps' tardy start was apparently Meade's fault. Although headquarters had made up its mind by nine that morning to dispatch Wright's division to help prop up Warren, the expedition had been delayed until eleven o'clock waiting for promised reinforcements. Strengthened by a brigade from Getty's division, Wright was able to begin his advance.

Studying the world from behind a heavy moustache and goatee, Wright conveyed the impression of an earnest and sincere soldier. He was an "unassuming, sturdy solid kind," sometimes thin on imagination but fully competent to move his division with reasonable dispatch. Wright had recently transferred east from a quiet Ohio post. His brigade commanders, however, were for the most part veterans, fully versed in fighting rebels Virginia style. Particularly noteworthy

---

48. Horace Porter, *Campaigning with Grant*, 51.

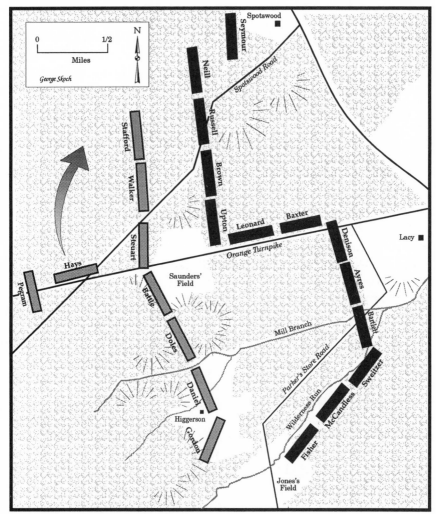

Sedgwick's assault on May 5, 3 P.M.–5 P.M.

was twenty-four-year-old Colonel Emory Upton, leading Wright's advance. Upton was by everyone's reckoning a rare military talent, humorless but blessed with the facility both to formulate brilliant moves and to bring them to fruition. Although lacking Upton's driving force, Wright's remaining brigade commanders—Colonel Henry W. Brown, at the head of a brigade of New Jersey regiments; Brigadier General David A. Russell, recognized as having excelled during maneuvers immediately preceding the Mine Run events; and Brigadier General Thomas H. Neill, temporarily detached from Getty's division—were all proven and capable combat soldiers.

Impossible terrain and superb Confederate delaying tactics, however, had slowed Wright's expedition to a harrowing crawl. Advancing up the woods road from Spotswood Plantation, Wright's Federals had wound along a narrow ridge. Wilderness Run lay to their south and tiny Flat Run to their north. Countless tributaries fed each of these creeks and cut steep-banked gullies that knifed off to all points of the compass. Hills popped up unexpectedly, separated by dark little swamps and streams. Obscure depressions and ridges, clogged with choking second growth, offered irresistible opportunities for ambush. A Union soldier described the countryside as the "awfullest brush, briars, grapevine, etc., I was ever in." [49]

Stitching a formation of troops together for any distance was out of the question. If any single guiding principle emerged from the chaotic warfare waged in this wasteland, it was that all advantages lay with the side defending its position. Wright's Federal troops had about a mile and a half to cover, which in ordinary circumstances should have taken less than an hour. This day they required nearly four. Forced to proceed Indian style in columns rather than sweeping lines, the northerners were unusually vulnerable to Confederate skirmishers. "As our line advanced," a 6th Corps doctor later explained, "it would suddenly come upon a line of graycoated rebels, lying upon the ground, covered with dried leaves, and concealed by the chaparral, when the rebels would rise, deliver a murderous fire, and retire." As a last-ditch expedient, Confederate snipers set the woods afire. Parched Yankees stumbled through a nightmarish landscape. "The ground had previously been fought over and was strewn with

---

49. Henry Keiser Diary, May 5, 1864, in Harrisburg Civil War Round Table Collection, USMHI.

wounded of both sides," reported Upton, "many of whom must have perished in the flames, as corpses were found partly consumed."[50]

Pressing forward, every inch contested, Upton finally managed to reach Saunders' Field. There he hooked up with Robinsons' two 5th Corps brigades. The long-awaited Federal connection had been achieved. Consideration was given to charging across the clearing. "It was madness," in Upton's opinion, and his judgment prevailed.[51]

While Upon lay stymied, the remainder of Wright's units attempted to form in the woods to the north. Brown's New Jersey brigade took position next to Upton, Neill's brigade moved in next to Brown, and Russell's elements fell in behind to form a reserve.[52]

Whether Wright could accomplish anything, however, remained to be seen. Ewell had used the respite following Warren's repulse to good advantage, reshuffling his troops with a practiced hand. Jones's shattered brigade was sent rearward to recuperate. Rodes's division was extended to cover its earlier position below the turnpike and Jones's former position as well. Gordon's brigade meanwhile shifted to the extreme right Confederate flank. Early's two remaining brigades—Harry Hays's and John Pegram's units—hung back as reserves, ready to fill in wherever needed.

The segment of Ewell's line responsible for repelling Wright was held by Allegheny Johnson's division, which had been rearranged after Warren's assault. Maryland Steuart's brigade was still behind formidable earthworks on the western edge of Saunders' Field. To Steuart's left was the famed Stonewall Brigade, Jackson's old Virginia command, now led by James Walker, a gregarious general whose outgoing manner had won him the nickname Stonewall Jim. To Walker's left, anchoring the far Confederate northern flank toward the Rapidan, was Leroy Stafford's rough-and-tumble outfit. Originally considered wharf rats, hotheads, and ne'er-do-wells, the colorful Louisiana brigade acquired a reputation for drinking, pillaging, and hard fighting. "Those damned Louisiana fellows may steal as

50. Henry Dalton's Report, in OR, Vol. XXXVI, Pt. 1, pp. 659–60; George T. Stevens, *Three Years in the Sixth Corps* (Albany, N.Y., 1866), 305; Emory Upton's Report, in OR, Vol. XXXVI, Pt. 1, pp. 665–66.

51. Upton's Report, in OR, Vol. XXXVI, Pt. 1, p. 665; George W. Bicknell, *History of the Fifth Regiment Maine Volunteers* (Portland, Maine, 1871), 303–304; Hazard Stevens, "The Sixth Corps in the Wilderness," in PMHSM, IV, 189.

52. Dalton's Report, in OR, Vol. XXXVI, Pt. 1, pp. 659–60.

much as they please now!" Early had once exclaimed after one of their battlefield exploits.[53]

Tension mounted as Wright's troops got into position for assault. There was an "awful silence," recalled a Confederate in the Stonewall Brigade. "He that a short time ago jested is now grave. Many are seen during this quiet to take out their Bibles and read and silently ask God to spare and shield them in the hour of battle."[54]

Almost spontaneously, fighting erupted anew. Blue and gray battle formations seesawed back and forth in a frenzied death grip, clawing for advantage in the thickets. But as before, neither side was able to achieve the upper hand. Casualties were frightful, and experienced field commanders committed blunders explainable only by their inability to see their own battle formations, much less the enemy's.

Around 3:30, Sedgwick arrived in person to supervise Wright's effort. By then, rebel artillery posted on a ridge above the turnpike had begun firing into the Union line. Stooping to adjust his horse's bit, Sedgwick's aide Hyde was smacked flat by a severed head flying through the air. The disheveled staffer lay splattered with brains and blood. Slowly struggling to his feet, Hyde was at first uncertain whether the gore dripping from his face belonged to him or someone else. "I looked up and saw the general give me a sorrowful glance," he recalled. "Two or three friends dismounted to pick me up, when I found I could get up myself, but I was not much use as a staff officer for fully fifteen minutes."[55]

The hottest fighting took place a quarter mile or so above Saunders' Field, where rebel and Yankee units blindly groped through dense undergrowth, searching for each other's northern flank. Stafford's Louisiana brigade, in venturing about a quarter mile past its

53. Richard S. Ewell's Report, in *OR*, Vol. XXXVI, Pt. 1, 1070–71; Early, *War Memoirs*, 346–47; Terry L. Jones, *Lee's Tigers: The Louisiana Infantry in the Army of Northern Virginia* (Baton Rouge, 1987), xi, 196–97. Initially, Walker advanced up Spotswood Road while Stafford formed on Steuart's left flank. After the fight against Griffin's division, Walker apparently pulled back and formed on Steuart's left flank, while Stafford worked northward and formed on Walker's left flank.

54. James McCowan Diary, May 5, 1864, quoted by Bean in *The Liberty Hall Volunteers*, 186.

55. Hyde, *Following the Greek Cross*, 184–85; Oliver Wendell Holmes, Jr., *Touched with Fire: Civil War Letters and Diary of Oliver Wendell Holmes, Jr., 1861–1864* (Cambridge, Mass., 1946), 104–105.

earthworks, ran into a line of Federals holding a low ridge. Caught up in the excitement, Stafford leaped his horse over a gully and confidently waved his Confederates forward. The Louisianians came charging behind him.

Suddenly a wild-eyed rebel courier ran up. "They are coming," he screamed, and pointed to a gap that had opened over where Walker's Stonewall Brigade was supposed to be. The Virginians had failed to keep apace with Stafford's men, and the vacant space was filling with Brown's New Jersey troops coming from the opposite direction. Walker's men had been caught in a horrible jam. Intending to connect with Stafford, Stonewall Jim had ordered his brigade to shift toward the Louisianians. As the brigade started to execute the maneuver, its skirmishers tumbled back, closely followed by a line of Federal infantry. The Virginians were slammed by a "staggering volley" from forty yards away. The 4th, 5th, and 27th Virginia regiments, which made up the rightward portion of Walker's line, received the brunt of the assault. At almost the same time, the Federal line hit Walker's left. According to a soldier in the 33rd Virginia, fighting "raged with inconceivable violence along the whole front of brigade." To relieve the pressure, Walker retired to a stronger position seventy-five yards back. "This movement was executed in perfect order under a most galling fire from the enemy who were pressing the line heavily at all points," a participant later recalled. Stafford, dangerously exposed in his advanced position, reacted decisively. Bending back his flank to contain the Yankees, he tried to slide toward Walker. This time, however, the thickets worked against the Confederates, and Stafford's brigade degenerated into a frightened and bewildered mob. Stafford had no choice but to order a retreat to his original line. As the general turned to join his disoriented soldiers, a minié ball came winging out of the greenery and sliced through his body, armpit to shoulder blade, severing his spine. Paralyzed and in excruciating pain, Stafford was carried to the rebel entrenchments and laid out under a tree. Suffering horribly, the single-minded southerner nonetheless summoned sufficient strength to exhort fresh rebel troops hurrying to the front to fight to the last man.[56]

56. Seymour Journal, May 5, 1864, in Schoff Collection, CL; Jones, *Lee's Tigers*, 195–97; Doyle Memoir, in Hotchkiss Collection, LC; Joseph Durkin, ed., *Confederate Chaplain: A War Journal of Rev. James B. Sheeran, C.S.S.R., 14th Louisiana, C.S.A.* (Milwaukee, 1960),

The reinforcements were more Louisiana soldiers under Harry Hays; they had been held in reserve for just such a moment as this. Swinging around the back of Ewell's line, Hays's brigade moved into position on the far rebel left flank, next to Walker's Virginians.

Hays, like Stafford before him, understood that he was to charge in tandem with Walker. To make sure that nothing went wrong this time, Hays sent his aide William Seymour to coordinate movements with Walker. The Virginian, however, apparently thought that Hays's men had come to relieve him. Before the misunderstanding could be corrected, Hays had pushed into the thickets just vacated by Stafford. About a half mile out, the Louisianians ran into two Federal brigades, Neill's men and Russell's fresh reserves. As the fighting heated, it became apparent that Walker again had failed to keep apace. "We could see that the Federals outflanked us by the breadth of an entire brigade," Seymour later recalled. Concluding that it was safer to advance than to retreat, Hays ordered his men ahead. Unsupported and severely outnumbered, they took a horrible beating. Seymour estimated that the Louisiana brigade lost a third of its number. The 25th Virginia, which had tagged along, was bagged nearly to a man. The 5th Wisconsin, of Russell's Union brigade, proudly claimed the capture.[57]

Hays's rebels scampered back to their original position. There they dug with tin cups and bayonets to strengthen their earthworks. Anxious to preserve the Confederate line, Walker stood high in his saddle, head up and hand raised. "Remember your name!" he shouted to his Stonewall Brigade. Jubal Early, who had come up with Hays's men, helped to rally the troops. Spying an able-bodied soldier slinking rearward, Early ordered him to the front. The man protested that he was a chaplain. "Chaplain! Chaplain, eh?" Early reportedly barked. "You have been praying these many years to get to heaven, and now when you have a chance to get there in fifteen minutes you are running away!" Confederate colors advanced in the face of a "deadly fire," and the rebel line held. "Dead and dying lay all around

---

86–87; G. M. G. Stafford, comp., *General Leroy Augustus Stafford: His Forebears and Descendants* (New Orleans, 1943), 44–45, 50–51.

57. Seymour Journal, May 5, 1864, in Schoff Collection, CL; "Extracts from a Private Letter in Hays' Louisiana Brigade, 6th Regiment," Montgomery (Ala.) *Daily Advertiser,* May 28, 1864; Doyle Memoir, in Hotchkiss Collection, LC; E. B. Quiner, *The Military History of Wisconsin* (Chicago, 1866), 519; Oliver Edwards' Report, in *OR,* Vol. XXXVI, Pt. 1, p. 672.

us," one of Walker's soldiers recorded in his diary that evening.[58]

Although he had successfully fended off the two Louisiana brigades and Walker's Virginians, Wright was making no headway of his own. Neill's brigade, which held an exposed position on the northern end of Wright's line, was particularly hard pressed and finally tumbled back to a ridge overlooking a swampy ravine. On a rise across the way, Confederates were felling trees and covering them with dirt. "The woods resounded with the strokes of their axes," related one of Wright's soldiers, "as the busy workmen plied their labor within three hundred yards, and in some places less than one hundred yards of our line, yet so dense was the thicket that they were entirely concealed from our view." Upton's front had also been fought to an impasse. "It was impossible to see the enemy," wrote a New Jersey soldier, "and though we peered into the thick woods, we were fighting invisible foemen." Unable to penetrate the Confederate line, Upton's soldiers deepened their burrows in the hard earth as best they could, huddling low to avoid the "leaden storm" raging overhead. By four, after an hour of bruising combat, both sides gave up their suicidal charges. Exhausted soldiers crouched in their trenches. Occasionally they leaped up to discharge volleys against unseen targets, then ducked down again. Men could do no more. Trying to describe the tempo of the afternoon's fighting, a 6th Corps surgeon mentioned how the "rattle of musketry would swell into a full continuous roar as the simultaneous discharge of ten thousand guns mingled in one grand concert, and then after a few minutes, became more interrupted." Next came "wild yells which always told of a rebel charge, and again the volleys would become more terrible and the broken, crashing tones would swell into one continuous roll of sound, which presently would be interrupted by the vigorous manly cheers of the northern soldiers, so different from the shrill yell of the rebels, and which indicated a repulse of their enemies." Now and then artillery provided a low, ominous rumble serving as a "double bass in this concert of death."[59]

---

58. David French Boyd, *Reminiscences of the War in Virginia*, ed. T. Michael Parrish (Austin, Tex., 1989), 24; McCowen Diary, May 5, 1864, quoted by Bean in *The Liberty Hall Volunteers*, 186.

59. Camille Baquet, *History of the First Brigade New Jersey Volunteers* (Trenton, 1910), 21; Alanson A. Haines, *History of the Fifteenth Regiment New Jersey*, 145–47; George T. Stevens, *Three Years in the Sixth Corps*, 306–307.

Meade's second round of fighting in the turnpike sector had failed as completely as his first. While generating impressive carnage, none of Wright's attacks had dented Ewell's defenses, again confirming that charges by unsupported brigades could achieve nothing in these thickets. Measuring results by goals advanced, the second bout on the turnpike, like the earlier one, had ended resoundingly in the Confederates' favor. Ewell's hardened foot soldiers had again contained Grant within the Wilderness, and the feared "general engagement" had been avoided. Every minute that Ewell kept the Federals bottled in their trenches bought more time for Longstreet. Ewell was discharging his assignment to perfection.

To a considerable extent, Ewell's success stemmed from Grant's and Meade's inability to organize a concerted assault against him. Warren had faltered because he had been forced to attack before Wright arrived. Wright had got nowhere because he, too, had been compelled to fight alone, with no support from Warren. Coordinating these commanders was Meade's responsibility, and so far he was doing a sorry job. Meade worked best when he could plan and carefully arrange his troops, and sharing the headquarters knoll with Grant doubtless cramped his style. The commander in chief was anxiously insisting that Meade send units into combat without "waiting for disposition," whereas Meade's natural inclination was to lock everything in place before attacking. The two schools of fighting were incompatible, at least as practiced by these strong-willed men. Mixing their styles produced ambivalent results that satisfied neither general and failed to achieve what either, acting alone, might have accomplished.

Another casualty of the ill-defined division of Union command responsibilities was Burnside's twenty thousand 9th Corps soldiers. They fell into the cracks of the unwieldy arrangement and hence missed a prime opportunity to assist Wright.

At the campaign's outset, Grant had positioned Burnside's four divisions astride the Orange and Alexandria Railroad from Bull Run to the Rappahannock. Edward Ferrero's black recruits guarded Manassas Junction. Brigadier General Robert B. Potter's and Brigadier

General Orlando B. Willcox' men camped fifteen miles south, near Warrenton Junction, and Brigadier General Thomas G. Stevenson's soldiers held the Rappahannock railway bridge.

Burnside's stretch of tracks ran through a guerrilla-infested region popularly known as Mosby's Confederacy. Frequent rebel raids had convinced Grant that a substantial Federal presence was necessary until Meade safely crossed the Rapidan and established a new line of supply along Virginia's tidewater rivers.

At 2 P.M. on the fourth, with Meade's lead elements solidly over the river, Burnside had received Grant's expected directive to make "forced marches," beginning immediately and continuing all night. "Dispatch received," Burnside had wired back almost two hours later, "will start column at once." [60]

Burnside took Grant's urgency to heart. By the late afternoon of the fourth, the entire 9th Corps was in motion. Ferrero's division, positioned farthest from the front, set out at six o'clock, tramped south for eight hours, then started off again at daybreak. The men struggled on until nightfall, when they collapsed from exhaustion, thirty dusty miles later but still short of the Rapidan. Willcox and Potter also hit ambitious strides, camping late on the fourth near the Rappahannock and starting early the next morning for Germanna Ford. Stevenson began well before dark on the fourth from his jumping-off point at Rappahannock Station. One soldier recalled walking part way to Culpeper, halting in the sun for several hours, then trudging on until 2 A.M., when the division bivouacked to wait for stragglers. "March the hardest I have ever been on," he recorded in his diary. He calculated that he had covered twenty-seven miles, at least six of them out of the way. [61]

Under the existing command arrangement, Grant was responsible for coordinating Burnside's movements with Meade's. Accordingly, before riding south to join Meade on the morning of May 5, the general-in-chief had left explicit instructions for the 9th Corps commander and had assigned the aide Comstock to remain behind

60. Ulysses S. Grant to Ambrose E. Burnside, May 5, 1864, in OR, Vol. XXXVI, Pt. 2, p. 380; Ambrose E. Burnside to Ulysses S. Grant, May 5, 1864, ibid.

61. Ambrose E. Burnside's Report, in OR, Vol. XXXVI, Pt. 1, p. 905; Edward Ferrero's Report, ibid., 987–88; James Ledlie's Report, ibid., 917; Robert Potter's Report, ibid., 927; Massachusetts Historical Society, War Diary and Letters of Stephen Minot Weld, 284–85.

as his liaison. According to Grant's order, Burnside, once across the Rapidan, was to place a division "on the ridge south of the river and west or southwest of [Germanna Road], and leave it there until your entire command is over, then close up as rapidly as possible with the Sixth Corps." Later, Grant forwarded directions for Burnside to mass his corps a mile below the ford and to relieve Ricketts' 6th Corps division.[62]

Most of Burnside's soldiers crossed the Rapidan in ample time to help Wright. Around 10 A.M., Stevenson's 9th Corps division rattled over the pontoons and formed on a ridge south of the river. Willcox' division crossed next, passed behind Stevenson's men, relieved Ricketts' 6th Corps division at about 1:30 P.M., and shortly afterward established a line at Wright's rear reaching north. By 2 P.M., Willcox' weary men had stacked arms and stood in readiness, expecting any minute to move to Wright's support. At three, a third division, Potter's, thundered across the pontoons and started toward Spotswood.[63]

For over an hour, while Wright's soldiers grappled in vain against Ewell's, thousands of 9th Corps reinforcements stood idly by, listening to the battle's roar and awaiting instructions to pitch in. Although these new elements mustered ample soldiers to tip the balance in Wright's favor, they never received orders to advance.

Grant's failure to hurry Burnside to Wright's assistance—and a momentous failure it was, considering that the added weight of Burnside's three available divisions would have materially advanced the chances of shattering Ewell's line—remains one of the Wilderness campaign's mysteries. Surviving contemporaneous sources only deepen the puzzle, since they unequivocally confirm that Grant intended Burnside to lend Wright a hand if it was needed. In a message to Burnside stamped 3:00 P.M., coinciding with Sedgwick's linkup with Warren on Saunders' Field, Grant directed his 9th Corps com-

---

62. Ulysses S. Grant to Ambrose E. Burnside, May 5, 1864, in OR, Vol. XXXVI, Pt. 2, pp. 423–24; Cyrus B. Comstock to Ambrose E. Burnside, May 5, 1864, ibid., 424.

63. Charles D. Todd Diary, May 5, 1864, in Civil War Times Illustrated Collection, USMHI; Committee of the Regiment, History of the Thirty-Fifth Regiment Massachusetts Volunteers (Boston, 1884), 147–49; Gregory A. Coco, ed., Through Blood and Fire: The Civil War Letters of Major Charles J. Mills (Lanham, Md., 1982), 75–76; Burnside's Report, in OR, Vol. XXXVI, Pt. 1, p. 905; John Hartranft's Report, in OR, Vol. XXXVI, Pt. 1, p. 947.

mander, "If General Sedgwick calls on you, you will give him a division." Burnside replied that Stevenson and Willcox had already been positioned according to Grant's earlier instructions. "General Potter's division will soon be up," he added, "and I will hold him subject to General Sedgwick's request." A soldier in the 59th Massachusetts, of Stevenson's division, noted in his diary: "Heard a battle raging six or eight miles in front and got all ready to start front, but the order was terminated."[64]

George T. Stevens, a surgeon in the 6th Corps and its self-proclaimed historian, later asserted that at 3:30 P.M., when the fighting was hottest, Sedgwick dispatched a runner to Burnside asking for a division to support Wright. As Stevens recounted the story, Burnside agreed to Sedgwick's request, but Grant directed Burnside to shift the troops elsewhere. Whatever the reason, Sedgwick never received reinforcements.[65]

All that can be said for sure is that signals went badly awry somewhere in the Federal chain of command. Perhaps Potter, who was not over the Rapidan until 3 P.M., was too distant from Wright to arrive in time. If so, Burnside erred by not sending Stevenson or Willcox, already close to the front, in Potter's place, and Grant was derelict in failing to insist on the substitution. But whatever the lapse, the fact remains that Burnside was available to turn the tide in Wright's favor. Mistakes and oversights at higher levels, undoubtedly induced by the bifurcated command system, held the 9th Corps from combat precisely when it was most needed. The grand Union offensive lacked the single guiding hand and consistency of leadership necessary to achieve victory against a foe like Lee.

*"Death holds high carnival
in our ranks."*

Meade's efforts to assemble a striking force on Orange Plank Road were also bogging down in frustrating delays and misunderstandings.

64. Comstock to Burnside, May 5, 1864, in *OR,* Vol. XXXVI, Pt. 2, p. 424; Ambrose E. Burnside to Ulysses S. Grant, May 5, 1864, *ibid.;* Arthur Wyman Diary, May 5, 1864, in Civil War Miscellaneous Collection, USMHI.
65. George T. Stevens, *Three Years in the Sixth Corps,* 305–306.

Communication between the headquarters knoll and Hancock had started off poorly and had deteriorated through the morning as messages went astray and crossed in transit. At 7:30 A.M., fixated on events on the turnpike, Meade had ordered Hancock to halt at Todd's Tavern, five miles south of the intersection of Brock and Orange Plank roads. His instructions were for Hancock to wait there until the rebels' intentions became clear. Unaccountably, Meade's missive did not reach Hancock until nine, an hour and a half after transmittal. By that time, Hancock's lead elements had passed the tavern and had advanced two miles west along Catharpin Road. Uncertain whether he would be told to continue or to change his route, Hancock stayed put and awaited a new communication.

Around 10:30, Union headquarters finally reacted to Hill's threatening advance on Orange Plank Road. Getty had been ordered to secure the intersection at Brock Road until Hancock arrived in force, and among the flurry of orders designed to prod the Army of the Potomac into action was a dispatch commanding Hancock to reverse direction, march to Orange Plank Road, and prepare to continue toward Parker's Store. Speed was essential. But the courier, perhaps caught up in Getty's lively little skirmish at the contested intersection, did not reach Hancock until 11:40.[66]

Complying with the directive entailed additional delay. Hancock's corps was strung from Catharpin Road almost back to Chancellorsville. It was headed west, with wagons and artillery crammed into narrow backwoods roadways. Orienting the 2nd Corps to travel north on Brock Road would take some doing. Hancock personally assumed responsibility for controlling a situation that had earmarks of a monumental traffic jam, and he rode with his staff to supervise the movement.

At noon, the rattling sound of gunfire off to the south alerted headquarters that Getty's and Hill's forward elements were skirmishing for control of the intersection at Brock and Orange Plank roads. Meade dispatched Lyman to monitor the fight and to determine if the two Federal columns could form a united front. Approaching the

---

66. George G. Meade to Ulysses S. Grant, May 5, 1864, in OR, Vol. XXXVI, Pt. 2, p. 403; Andrew A. Humphreys to Winfield S. Hancock, May 5, 1864, ibid., 406; Winfield S. Hancock to Seth Williams, May 5, 1864, ibid.; Winfield S. Hancock to Andrew A. Humphreys, May 5, 1864, ibid., 407; Andrew A. Humphreys to Winfield S. Hancock, May 5, 1864, ibid.

crossroads, Lyman encountered one of Getty's brigadiers and directed him to extend his soldiers north in search of Warren's left flank. A little farther on, Lyman found Getty sitting on the ground. Lyman informed him of Meade's hope to close the gap between the two Federal wings. Pointing into the dense underbrush, Getty explained that Hill's corps was out there, with rebel skirmishers only three hundred yards away. "For all I could see," Lyman later wrote home, "they might have been in Florida, but the occasional wounded men who limped by, and the sorry spectacle of two or three dead, wrapped in their blankets, showed that some fighting had already taken place." [67]

At the same time that Meade sent Lyman in search of Getty, he dashed off another letter to Hancock. Hill was on Orange Plank Road, the noon message said, and Getty had been dispatched to drive the rebels back, although headquarters feared "he may not be able to do so." Hancock's assignment was unequivocal. "The major-general commanding directs that you move out the plank road toward Parker's Store, and, supporting Getty, drive the enemy beyond Parker's Store, and occupy that place and unite with Warren on the right of it." [68]

Clear as the order was, it relied on a wholly erroneous assumption. Hancock was nowhere near Orange Plank Road, and it would be hours before he could possibly position his corps to move toward Parker's Store.

Riding ahead, Hancock reached Getty at the crossroads shortly after Lyman had left. Uncertain what to do next—Meade's noon message ordering him to attack toward Parker's Store had not yet arrived—he sent his chief of staff, Lieutenant Colonel Charles H. Morgan, to find Meade and get new directions. On reaching the command center across from the Lacy house, Morgan obtained firm written orders. Stamped 1:30 P.M., they repeated Meade's earlier directions for an immediate offensive. "Attack them; Getty will aid you," read the document. "Push out on the plank road and connect with Warren." [69]

---

67. Lyman to family, May 15, 1864, in *Meade's Headquarters*, ed. Agassiz, 89.

68. Andrew A. Humphreys to Winfield S. Hancock, May 5, 1864, in *OR*, Vol. XXXVI, Pt. 2, p. 407.

69. Winfield S. Hancock's Report, in *OR*, Vol. XXXVI, Pt. 1, p. 318; Andrew A. Humphreys to Winfield S. Hancock, May 5, 1864, *ibid.*, Pt. 2, p. 409.

Another hour passed. While Warren's attacks raged around the turnpike, Meade kept an anxious ear cocked for firing toward Orange Plank Road signaling Hancock's offensive. The woods in that direction remained silent.

Unknown to headquarters, its noon directive had gone astray, and Morgan with the 1:30 P.M. version had been mysteriously delayed as well. Not until 2:40 did Meade's orders to attack reach Hancock, and apparently both versions showed up simultaneously. "Your dispatches of 12 M. and 1:30 P.M. just received," Hancock wrote back, advising that his corps was finally beginning to come into view on Getty's left and would advance when prepared. "The ground over which I must pass is very bad," added the 2nd Corps commander, "a perfect thicket."[70]

But with the afternoon ticking by—lead elements of Wright's corps were just now reaching Saunders' Field—Hancock was still in no position to attack. Of his four divisions, only David Birney's had arrived. Its soldiers were immediately put to pitching up earthworks two lines deep on Brock Road to Getty's left. Coming up in a cloud of dust, Gershom Mott's division was beginning to file into place next to Birney's. Miles southward, the rest of the Federal 2nd Corps was toiling along, sweltering in oppressive heat and retarded by artillery and supply trains that clogged the narrow, tree-lined artery.

At three o'clock, Hancock received new information from headquarters. The message was stamped 2:15. Warren's attack had failed, stated the message, Wadsworth had been driven in, and Crawford had abandoned the Chewning heights, all of which complicated a convergence of the two Federal infantry wings. Crawford's "exact position is not reported yet," added headquarters in a message that reflected the confusion following Warren's unsuccessful assault. "Will send you word as soon as it is known."[71]

Meade, however, still insisted on an immediate attack out Orange Plank Road, and Hancock set about doing his best to accommodate him. Less than half of the 2nd Corps had arrived, so Hancock prepared a three-division advance. Getty was to charge straight

---

70. Winfield S. Hancock to Andrew A. Humphreys, May 5, 1864, in OR, Vol. XXXVI, Pt. 2, pp. 409–10.

71. W. G. Mitchell, 2nd Corps Daily Memoranda, in OR, Vol. XXXVI, Pt. 1, p. 350; Andrew A. Humphreys to Winfield S. Hancock, May 5, 1864, ibid., Pt. 2, p. 409.

out the roadway, supported by a 2nd Corps division on his left and another to his rear. A message was sent to Meade informing him of the arrangements.

Crossed signals, however, continued to plague the Orange Plank Road operations. For some reason, Meade still labored under the impression that Hancock's entire corps was assembled on Orange Plank Road. Perhaps he underestimated the distances involved or rashly assumed that his earlier orders directing Hancock northward had reached the general quicker than they did.

At 3:15 P.M.—Wright was slugging it out with Ewell north of Saunders' Field—Meade issued a strong directive to spur Hancock into action. This time he also recommended specific troop assignments. "The commanding general directs that Getty attack at once," read Meade's pointed missive, "and that you support him with your whole corps, one division on his right and one division on his left, the others in reserve; or such other dispositions as you may think proper, but the attack up the plank road must be made at once."[72]

To make sure that he got action, Meade had Lyman spur his mount back to the intersection of Brock and Orange Plank roads for delivery of the orders in person.

Arriving around 3:45, the headquarters staffer directed Getty to assault immediately and assured him that Hancock would join in. According to Lyman, Getty was cool to the idea and thought it "poor strategy to attack before more of the 2nd Corps was up." Nonetheless, Getty instructed his brigadiers to "prepare to advance at once." At the same time, Hancock received Meade's latest order suggesting that he advance a division on each side of Getty's assault column.[73]

Since Hancock's troops were all south of Orange Plank Road, complying with Meade's recommendation that they cover both of Getty's flanks incurred additional delay. Getty, however, would not wait. Orders were orders, and he had just received peremptory instructions from Meade to advance, with or without Hancock. Determined to waste no more time, at 4:15 he hurled his three brigades west into the dark woods on both sides of Orange Plank Road.

72. Hancock's Report, in OR, Vol. XXXVI, Pt. 1, pp. 319–20; Winfield S. Hancock to Andrew A. Humphreys, May 5, 1864, ibid., Pt. 2, p. 410; Andrew A. Humphreys to Winfield S. Hancock, May 5, 1864, ibid., 410.
73. Lyman Journal, May 5, 1864, in Lyman Papers, MHS.

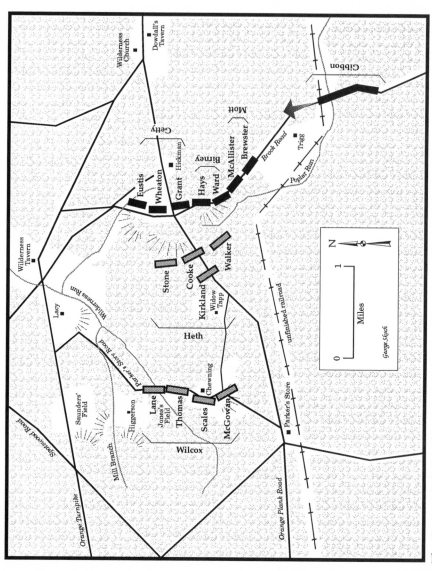

The Orange Plank Road front on May 5 at 4:30 P.M.

Behind them, Hancock's soldiers hurriedly tried to construct the formation suggested by Meade.[74]

Once again, the Confederates had made masterly use of the terrain. Orange Plank Road hugged the backbone of a shallow ridge. North was Wilderness Run, whose tributaries drained toward the Rapidan. Off to the south were gullies and streams forming the Po River's headwaters. Dense thickets carpeted a wasteland of hillocks that were generally arranged in rows like ripples on a washboard, running north to south. Festering little swamps lay in between. As a Yankee who fought there later observed, these "low ridges and hollows succeed each other, without a single feature to serve as a landmark, and no one but an experienced woodsman with a compass could keep his bearing and position and preserve his course." Confederate riflemen snuggled into well-concealed niches, ready for the Yankee assault.[75]

Holding the roadway on the rebel side was Henry Heth's division. This combat-hardened crew had been assembled from other Confederate units after Chancellorsville to provide a third division for Hill's new corps. Two North Carolina brigades, Kirkland's and Cooke's, formed the division's heart. They were strategically placed where the hottest fighting was expected, squarely across Orange Plank Road, with Cooke's men in front and Kirkland's immediately behind. North of the road was Brigadier General Joseph R. Davis' mixed Mississippi and North Carolina brigade. Davis, a lawyer and the Confederate president's nephew, had been plagued by recurrent charges of nepotism and had never met the demands of his position. He was absent, and his brigade was commanded by Colonel John M. Stone, of the 2nd Mississippi, a capable soldier and later governor of Mississippi. South of the road was an all-Virginian brigade. Its head, Brigadier General Henry H. ("Mud") Walker, had just returned after a lengthy convalescence.[76]

---

74. Hancock's Report, in *OR*, Vol. XXXVI, p. 320; Mitchell, 2nd Corps Daily Memoranda, *ibid.*, 350; George W. Getty's Report, *ibid.*, 676–77.

75. Hazard Stevens, "The Sixth Corps in the Wilderness," in *PMHSM*, IV, 191.

76. In Cooke's brigade, the 15th and 46th North Carolina were to the right of the road, the 27th and 48th to the left. See Clark, comp., *Histories of the Several Regiments and Battalions from North Carolina*, II, 446. According to Heth, Walker's brigade was held in reserve

Numbering some 6,500 soldiers, Heth's division faced an initial Federal attacking force—Getty's, Birney's, and Mott's divisions—of 17,000 men. The chance of reinforcements was slim. Lee had become increasingly concerned about the gap separating his two wings, particularly after his close brush with capture. Accordingly, the Confederate commander had ordered Cadmus Wilcox, who was heading Hill's other available division, to reach north and connect with Ewell. Hill would simply have to do the best he could with his other division—Heth's—to hold off the Yankees massing on Orange Plank Road.

Around 3 P.M., Wilcox started from Widow Tapp's farm to the Chewning pastures. Only a few Federals remained at the clearing, Crawford's division having abandoned the heights. The Chewning farmhouse proved to be a particularly useful prize. From its roof, Wilcox had an unobstructed view to Wilderness Tavern, where Federal troops were milling about.

After stationing two brigades at the Chewning farm, Wilcox continued with his remaining units in quest of Ewell, following the ridge above Wilderness Run until he caught sight of soldiers ahead. They were Gordon's men, anchoring Ewell's flank. Wilcox rushed up and began explaining his mission to Gordon. No sooner had the two generals exchanged greetings, however, than volleys of musket fire rumbled through the woods from the direction of Orange Plank Road.[77]

In Wilcox' absence, Lee had remained determined to keep the initiative. Hopeful that the Brock Road intersection was lightly defended, he had dispatched a staff officer to Heth with instructions to occupy the crossroads "without bringing on a general engagement." Heth's skirmishers reported a considerable Federal troop buildup. "Say to the general that the enemy are holding the Brock Road with a strong

---

with Kirkland's until the fighting started. Then Walker was shifted to the right of Cooke. Walker commanded his own brigade as well as Brigadier General James J. Archer's. See Henry Heth's Report, in MC; and Joe B. McBrien, *The Tennessee Brigade* (Chattanooga, 1977), 85–86, 89–91.

77. Wilcox, "Lee and Grant in the Wilderness," in *The Annals of the War*, 492.

force," Heth told the staffer. "Whether I can drive them from the Brock Road or not can only be determined by my attacking with my entire division, but I cannot tell if my attack will bring on a general engagement or not. I am ready to try if he says attack."[78]

As the aide disappeared toward Widow Tapp's farm, gunfire began crackling in front of Heth. Confederate skirmishers—a specially trained unit of sharpshooters—withdrew to Heth's main rebel line, which hugged the crest of a low ridge slicing across Orange Plank Road.

Getty's lone Federal division constituted the first wave of the Union assault. Unsupported except for two cannon borrowed from the 2nd Corps, Getty's blue-clad regiments struggled through the dense thickets. A Federal officer recalled that the ranks became "more and more crooked and disordered" as the division advanced.[79]

South of Orange Plank Road, the lead brigade of Vermonters slashed ragged swaths through switchlike saplings and creepers. These soldiers were the pride of Getty's division, Green Mountain men who had served as the Federal rear guard at Chancellorsville a year before. The brigade's head, Lewis Grant, had a balding forehead neatly balanced by a bushy beard that made him look like the successful Yankee lawyer he was. He adequately compensated for his scant military training with unabashed bravery. For his present assignment, he formed dual lines, two regiments in front and three behind. He threw two companies forward as skirmishers to test the underbrush ahead. Impossibly thick foliage limited visibility in some places to twenty yards and got the Vermonters off to a shaky start. Their advance became even more confused when the colonel in charge of pickets, who was stationed on the line's right, failed to notify the far end to move out. Skirmishers near the roadway stabbed ahead while those on the left stayed put. Troops building up behind were forced to grope forward unprotected. Apparently the mix-up also caused Grant's leftmost regiment to veer southward from the rest of the formation.[80]

About three hundred yards out, a "tremendous volley" exploded

---

78. Morrison, ed., *The Memoirs of Henry Heth*, 182–83.
79. Hazard Stevens, "The Sixth Corps in the Wilderness," in *PMHSM*, IV, 192.
80. Lewis Grant's Report, in *OR*, Vol. XXXVI, Pt. 1, pp. 696–97.

from point-blank range. The Federals had stumbled into Cooke's and Walker's Confederates, who were emptying their rifles with practiced eyes from behind their natural earthworks. Once again, the impatience of Union headquarters had turned out a recipe for disaster.

Returning fire, Lewis Grant's men slumped to the ground. "Advance!" sounded the order, and the northerners rose instinctively, only to be torn to pieces by Confederate veterans shooting to kill. "So many were at once shot down that it became plain that to advance was simply destruction," reported the Union brigade's historian. Blue forms hugged the earth, unable to move. Sheets of lead howled and whistled above. "The rebels had the advantage of position," Grant later reported, "inasmuch as the line was partially protected by a slight swell of ground, while ours was on nearly level ground." The Confederates kept up a "rapid and constant fire of musketry," wrote the Federal brigade commander. Rebel bullets cut his men down "with such slaughter that it was found impractical to do more than maintain our then present position." Grant ordered his second line to join the first, to prevent the enemy from enveloping him. Standing erect spelled certain death, so men crawled into place. "The musketry silenced all other sounds," recalled a Union soldier, "and the air in the woods was hot and heavy with sulphurous vapor. The tops of the bushes were cut away by the leaden showers which swept through them; and when the smoke lifted occasional glimpses could be got of gray forms crouching under the battle-cloud which hung low upon the slope in front." Another Vermont soldier who survived the carnage wrote home that "the woods was a dense thicket of small trees about the size of hop poles, and they stood three times as numerous as they are usually set in a hop yard; but along the whole length of the line I doubt if a single tree could have been found that had not been pierced several times by bullets, and all were hit about breast high. Had the rebels fired a little lower, they would have annihilated the whole line; they nearly did it as it was." Attrition in commanders threatened to paralyze the Vermont brigade. Colonel Newton Stone, leading the 2nd Vermont, fell with a ball through his thigh, had the wound dressed, then returned only to receive a fatal head wound. His replacement was soon killed, leaving the regiment with no field officer. Colonel George P. Foster, of the 4th Vermont, was shot through the leg, Lieutenant Colonel John L. Lewis, of the 5th Vermont, was knocked out of service with a shattered arm, and Colonel Elisha L. Barney, of the 6th Vermont, was bowled over with a mortal wound in his temple.[81]

Grant, with ammunition failing and his command fast turning into bullet-riddled corpses, called for support. Three 2nd Corps regiments—the 20th Indiana, the 141st Pennsylvania, and the 40th New York, all from Birney's division, of Brigadier General J. H. Hobart Ward's brigade—were rushed to the Vermonters' aid. Grant meanwhile located an apparent thin spot in the enemy line and proposed that the 5th Vermont, supported by two of the fresh regiments, attack there to relieve the Confederate pressure. Major Charles P. Dudley, in charge of the 5th Vermont, listened to Grant's proposal and gamely answered, "I think we can." Grant then queried the 40th New York and 20th Indiana. "We will," the soldiers replied with enthusiasm. At Grant's command, the newly arrived Federals stood and sprinted for the Confederate ridge. The front rebel line buckled, but a galling enemy fire soon had the Union troops flat on their bellies. Dudley, finding his regiment riddled from front and side, also ordered his men down. The Union advance was stymied, although not without some small rewards. Captured by the 20th Indiana were the 55th Virginia's flag and several prisoners.[82]

Things were getting desperate for the Vermonters and their reinforcements. Rebel minié balls whistled down from the little ridge, pinning them to the ground and exacting a fearful toll. It was an impossible situation. Moving meant immediate death. Lying still guaranteed slow annihilation.

Help came in the form of Mott's Federal 2nd Corps division. Mott's northernmost brigade was a mixed body of New Jersey, Massachusetts, and Pennsylvania regiments, nine in all. Their commander was the soft-spoken, puritanical, and abstinent Colonel Robert McAllister, a middle-aged family man and railroad construction engineer turned soldier who had been three times pro-

---

81. George C. Benedict, *Vermont in the Civil War* (2 vols.; Burlington, Vt., 1886), I, 424–25; Emil Rosenblatt and Ruth Rosenblatt, eds., *Hard Marching: The Civil War Letters of Private Wilbur Fisk, 1861–1865* (Lawrence, Kans., 1992), 215–16; Lewis Grant's Report, in OR, Vol. XXXVI, Pt. 1, p. 697; Thomas Seaver's Report, OR, Vol. XXXVI, Pt. 1, pp. 709–10; Stephen Pingree's Report, OR, Vol. XXXVI, Pt. 1, p. 711; Eugene Hamilton's Report, in OR, Vol. XXXVI, Pt. 1, p. 714.

82. Benedict, *Vermont in the Civil War*, I, 425–26; Lewis Grant's Report, in OR, Vol. XXXVI, Pt. 1, p. 697; P. Regis de Trobriand's Report, in OR, Vol. XXXVI, Pt. 1, p. 469; Madison Cannon's Report, in OR, Vol. XXXVI, Pt. 1, p. 473.

moted for heroism. Arriving next to Birney's division on Brock Road around 4 P.M., McAllister had set his men to constructing rough earthworks. "Old trees were rolled up and cleared of their branches," recalled one of his soldiers, "new ones cut down as fast as the few axes procurable could be made to do service; dirt, stones and rocks thrown up in rear; and in an hour's time a passable line of earthworks completed."[83]

No sooner were the works finished than the command to advance rang through the woods. A soldier recorded the time in his diary as 4:30. "Over the breastworks we went," recounted McAllister, "but the dense thicket of underbrush made it impossible for the troops to keep their proper distance." As one of his soldiers put it, the forest was "absolutely impenetrable." They had to proceed "in very irregular lines, going round the trees, creeping under the branches, and keeping as closely together as they were able." To make matters worse, Mott's other brigade—Colonel William R. Brewster's so-called Excelsior Brigade, which was advancing in tandem with McAllister's brigade on its left—began drifting to the right. McAllister's men were crowded against the Vermonters. Riding in front of his battle line under a heavy skirmish fire, McAllister herded his soldiers into the steadily diminishing open space. Slanting northward, a portion of McAllister's line slipped behind the Vermonters. This put his rightmost regiment, the 8th New Jersey, to the 5th Vermont's rear. Bullets were flying thickly, forcing the New Jersey men to lie down. The Vermonters assumed that their desperately awaited help had arrived, and they retired, leaving the prostrate New Jersey troops alone. Because of crowding at the front, the confusion was severe. Regiments overlapped, and officers frantically struggled to untangle their commands.[84]

Compressed into a closely packed mass, Mott's Federal troops were subjected to scathing fire. According to a Massachusetts soldier stationed near the formation's left, unseen Confederates opened with a "double volley" directly in front—"so sudden, so unexpected, and so deadly," he wrote. The Yankees, separated from their officers and

83. Robert McAllister's Report, in OR, Vol. XXXVI, Pt. 1, p. 487; Warren Cudworth, *History of the First Regiment Massachusetts Infantry* (Boston, 1886), 459.

84. Perkis Memoir, in Civil War Times Illustrated Collection, USMHI; McAllister's Report, in OR, Vol. XXXVI, Pt. 1, p. 487; Cudworth, *History of the First Regiment Massachusetts*, 459.

"perplexed in forcing their way through the tangled forest," responded with a few ineffectual shots. "The enemy answered with another terrific volley," recounted the soldier, "which told with deadly effect upon the foremost groups struggling along to get into some sort of fighting array, killing and wounding a large number and straightway forcing the rest to fall back." Unable to withstand the murderous fire from Mud Walker's slouch-hatted Confederates on their shallow ridge, Mott's entire division broke. As McAllister later reported, first the Excelsior Brigade folded, and then his leftmost regiment. In the end, his whole command gave way. "Regiment after regiment, like a rolling wave, fell back," recounted the Union general, "and all efforts to rally them short of the breast-works were in vain." In McAllister's estimation, accurate Confederate fire precipitated the stampede, which was fed by the fact that a large number of troops were about to leave the service. Mott's division tumbled in confusion toward Brock Road. "Our division did not do well," McAllister sheepishly acknowledged when he described the rout to his wife in a letter a few days later.[85]

The collapse of Mott's Union division severely undermined Getty's ability to hold on to the woods south of Orange Plank Road. Fortunately, help was available. Several regiments from Ward's brigade, of Birney's division, were stationed in reserve. One of those, the 124th New York, or the Orange Blossoms Regiment, had been dozing next to stacked rifles. Exhausted from the day's marching and countermarching, they remained oblivious to occasional bullets splattering overhead. Rudely roused from their slumbers when Mott's men came streaming back in disarray, the Orange Blossoms rushed down Brock Road, then leaped over Mott's old rifle pits and poured into the woods.

"We were none too soon," recorded a New Yorker from the 124th. Mott's soldiers were falling back in droves, and a "wild storm of bullets hissed and whistled through the air." Screaming Confederates pressed close behind. The Orange Blossoms resolutely advanced after halting momentarily to straighten their line and pick up

85. McAllister's Report, in OR, Vol. XXXVI, Pt. 1, p. 488; John Shoonover's Report, *ibid.*, 492–93; Thomas C. Thompson's Report, *ibid.*, 498–99; Cudworth, *History of the First Regiment Massachusetts*, 459–60; Thomas D. Marbaker, *History of the Eleventh New Jersey Volunteers from Its Organization to Appomattox* (Trenton, 1898), 161–65; James I. Robertson, ed., *The Civil War Letters of General Robert McAllister* (New Brunswick, N.J., 1965), 416.

Mott's strays. Hotly contesting every inch, the rebels retreated, leaving the ground strewn with dead and wounded. "We could seldom see the enemy's battle line because of the denseness of the foliage," wrote an Orange Blossom, "but powder flashes from the opposing lines often told that they were but a few yards apart." On reaching the "hop-pole forest" of tightly packed saplings that had given the Vermont men so much trouble, the New Yorkers caught sight of the main rebel position. Further progress was impossible, and they settled down to trading potshots with the enemy.[86]

North of Orange Plank Road, Getty's remaining two brigades were faring no better than were the Vermonters and their hard-pressed reinforcements. Tracking along the roadway in tandem with the Green Mountain men was the left of a smoothly functioning brigade, predominantly Pennsylvanian, ably led by Frank Wheaton. Wheaton's family had been torn apart by the Civil War. His father-in-law served as adjutant general of the Union armies, but another close relative sat in the Confederate Senate. Wheaton himself was a steady and dependable defender of the Union cause.

Wheaton's skirmishers slogged through a swamp under "destructive fire." Finally they crashed into rebels—mostly Cooke's North Carolinians—about an eighth of a mile out. The Confederates were posted on a northward extension of the same ridge that was causing Lewis Grant so much trouble to the south. Wheaton settled down to a grinding firefight. "For nearly an hour the fighting was incessant," the Union general reported, "and the loss proportionately great, but the enemy was too strongly posted, and could not be dislodged." After Wheaton's first line had exhausted its ammunition, fifty rounds to the man, it was replaced by a second line. Still the obstinate graybacks refused to budge.[87]

On Getty's northern flank was a mixed Massachusetts and Rhode

---

86. David Herman Diary, May 5, 1864, in Civil War Miscellaneous Collection, USMHI; Weygant, *History of the One Hundred and Twenty-Fourth Regiment, N.Y.S.V.*, 287–88.

87. Frank Wheaton's Report, in *OR*, Vol. XXXVI, Pt. 1, pp. 681–82; Thomas McLaughlin's Report, *ibid.*, 691.

Island brigade under Henry Eustis. He had graduated first in a West Point class that included such luminaries as James Longstreet—who had finished third from the bottom. Eustis had taught engineering at Harvard for a decade before the war, then had achieved a solid record in the Army of the Potomac's major battles. Although in poor health and reputedly an opium addict, Eustis generally exercised intelligent command of his brigade.

Today, however, Eustis' Federals were having a miserable time of it. Into the woods they advanced, the 2nd Rhode Island and 10th Massachusetts leading, the 7th and 37th Massachusetts forming the rear. In front of them and lapping around their flanks were John Stone's Mississippians, spearheaded by a line of sharpshooters about sixty yards in front of the rebel formation. "We were in a forest thick with undergrowth," one of Stone's Confederates said of the terrain, "and the extent of vision was not more than eighty yards in any direction, and in places not thirty." As Union troops came into view, concentrated fire erupted along the Confederate front. "An army of drummers beating the long roll could not have made a more continuous sound," recounted a rebel marksman. A Confederate hiding behind a sapling counted six bullet holes in the young tree and three through his own clothing. Lying flat, Eustis' men fired back at the flash of rebel muskets. "Men who had been in all the battles of the war up to this time, say they never saw anything like it," claimed a soldier in the 10th Massachusetts. "It seemed to come from two or three lines of battle, one above the other—a perfect hail of bullets." The 2nd Rhode Island folded, subjecting the 10th Massachusetts to a "most destructive fire." Eustis' second line wriggled into place, barely holding its own.[88]

Birney's division, stationed nearby at the intersection of Brock and Orange Plank roads, was the only remaining source of Federal

---

88. William S. Dunlop, *Lee's Sharpshooters; or, The Forefront of Battle: A Story of Southern Valor That Never Has Been Told* (Little Rock, Ark., 1899), 368–71; Dunbar Rowland, *Military History of Mississippi, 1803–1888* (Jackson, Miss., 1908), 49; Clark, comp., *Histories of the Several Regiments and Battalions from North Carolina*, III, 304; James Bowen, *History of the Thirty-Seventh Regiment Massachusetts*, 275–76; Robert Hunt Rhodes, ed., *All for the Union: The Civil War Diary and Letters of Elisha Hunt Rhodes* (New York, 1991), 144; Joseph K. Newell, *Ours: Annals of the Tenth Regiment, Massachusetts Volunteers, in the Rebellion* (Springfield, Mass., 1875), 258–59.

reinforcements. Its commander was a man to be reckoned with. Son of a prominent Alabama abolitionist and politically well connected, he was a successful Philadelphia lawyer and business entrepreneur in his own right. Only thirty-nine years old, Birney had amassed a combat record rivaling any in the army. Like Griffin, he spoke his mind fearlessly and had already won notoriety as Meade's vociferous critic by testifying against his commander during the spring Gettysburg hearings. Spindly, fond of checkered flannel shirts, and in Lyman's words, possessed of a "thin, pale, Puritanic face," Birney did not always look like a general, but he usually knew how to act like one, and this day was no exception.[89]

Assigned by Hancock to ensure that Getty received the support he needed, Birney had already committed Ward's brigade and all of Mott's division to shore up Lewis Grant's advance south of Orange Plank Road. To stabilize the fighting up Wheaton's and Eustis' way, he decided to play his trump card. Fiery Alexander Hays, the red-bearded friend of Hancock's and Grant's, would be sent in with his whole brigade.

Hays was a natural combat soldier. Handsome and indisputably brave, he had all the right credentials, including a West Point diploma, a wound from Second Manassas, and a record of gallantry at Gettysburg. "As dashing and daring an officer as ever drew a sword in his country's defense," one soldier remarked. There were intimations of drunkenness, but no one in authority seemed to pay much mind.[90]

Hays's large brigade, with a regiment of sharpshooters thrown in for good measure, was handily poised to relieve Getty's hard-pressed soldiers above Orange Plank Road. Birney ordered them to advance.

Crack marksmen from the 17th Maine headed for the far end of the Confederate formation. Stone's Mississippians greeted them with a "terrific fire," inflicting serious casualties and capturing their commander. Stumbling behind, Hays's main line faltered in the deep woods. Heavy vegetation blotted out the late afternoon's waning sunlight. "Only by the flash of the volleys of the forming lines can we know where is posted the enemy with which we are engaged,"

89. Theodore Lyman to family, May 20, 1864, in *Meade's Headquarters,* ed. Agassiz, 107.
90. Charles D. Page, *History of the Fourteenth Regiment, Connecticut,* 225.

wrote a soldier in the 93rd New York. "The woods light up with the flashes of musketry as if with lightning, while the incessant roar of the volleys sound like the crashing of thunderbolts." Some Union regiments hugged the roadway. Others went obliquely to the right, passing toward Eustis' exposed flank. Intervals opened in the Federal formation, and hand-to-hand fighting convulsed the entire battle line.[91]

Reports concerning Hays's advance are fragmentary. Next to Orange Plank Road, the 93rd New York relieved the 139th Pennsylvania, of Wheaton's brigade, which had been pinned in a thick swamp by Cooke's North Carolinians. Falling back about thirty paces, the Pennsylvanians lay down to avoid the fire. According to one account, the 93rd New York held for about twenty minutes before tumbling back over the 139th. "The rebels continued firing," a Pennsylvanian recalled, "and our regiment rose with a cheer and gave them another volley. If they had advanced then, they could have driven our line, for we had but one round of ammunition left." After retiring to let Hays's men through, a soldier in the 2nd Rhode Island, of Eustis' brigade, recorded the intensity of the fighting swirling around him. "I believe we are a few yards in rear of line under a knoll," he wrote. "The balls go over us while here. Oh, it is terrible. Now the cheers arise far above the groans of the wounded and they go so much the faster. It is an awful battle."[92]

The slaughter in Hays's ranks was severe. "Brave men are falling like autumn leaves," wrote a survivor, "and death holds high carnival in our ranks." A Maine veteran reported, "Our losses were heavy." The most deeply felt loss, however, occurred early in the advance. Characteristically riding in front of his soldiers, Hays paused near the 63rd Pennsylvania, his former regiment, and began to address the soldiers. With a sickening thwack, a stray bullet tore through the general's skull and toppled him from his saddle. Rumor had it that Hays had been tipping his canteen of whiskey and became entangled

91. Ripley, *Vermont Riflemen,* 145–47; Robert Stoddart Robertson, *Personal Recollections of the War* (Milwaukee, 1895), 91–92; Rudolph Aschmann, *Memoirs of a Swiss Officer in the American Civil War,* ed. Heintz K. Meier (Bern, 1972), 147–48.

92. Lieutenant Colonel Moody's dispatch, in *The Road to Cold Harbor,* ed. William Schoyer, 56–57; Harold G. George Memoir, in LC; Handy to father, May 5, 1864, in Book 119, FSMP.

in the strap. Straining to reach the mouth of the canteen, his head moved directly into the path of the fateful bullet.[93]

At 4:45 P.M., as Birney's and Mott's divisions were feeding into the inferno along Orange Plank Road in support of Getty, Lyman returned to the Brock Road junction. Violent musketry sounded through the woods, and an occasional ball whipped through the trees and across the roadbed. In the intersection's center, oblivious to danger, sat Hancock. He was erect on his handsome steed and rattling out orders. "It's all very well for novels," Lyman later wrote home, "but I don't like such places and go there only when ordered." The situation was starting to look desperate. "Report to General Meade," Hancock told Lyman, "that it is very hard to bring up troops in this wood, and that only a part of my corps is up, but I will do as well as I can." Out of the smoke and haze emerged one of Getty's officers. "Sir! General Getty is hard pressed and nearly out of ammunition," blurted the staffer. "Tell him to hold on," responded Hancock, "and General Gibbon will be up to help him." Hancock was referring to another Federal 2nd Corps division due to arrive at any moment. Then another officer galloped in from the left, over where the Vermonters and Mott's closely packed soldiers were frantically trying to stave off disaster. "General Mott's division has broken, sir, and is coming back," he announced. "Tell him to stop them, sir!" roared Hancock in his best battlefield voice. As the Union corps commander spoke, a mob of dispirited Federal fugitives tumbled out of the woods and crowded into the trenches lining Brock Road. Hancock dashed among them, spitting out orders and reforming shattered units. "Halt here! Halt here!" he belted. "Form behind this rifle pit." Turning to

93. Houghton, *The Campaigns of the Seventeenth Maine*, 167–68; William H. Green, "From the Wilderness to Spotsylvania," in *Papers Read Before the Commandery of the State of Maine, Military Order of the Loyal Legion of the United States* (3 vols.; Portland, Maine, 1902), II, 92–93; Charles W. Cowtan, *Services of the Tenth New York Volunteers in the War of the Rebellion* (New York, 1882), 245; George T. Fleming, ed., *Life and Letters of Alexander Hays* (Pittsburgh, 1919), 596–605; Ruth L. Silliker, ed., *The Rebel Yell and the Yankee Hurrah: The Civil War Journal of a Maine Volunteer, Private John W. Haley, 17th Maine Regiment* (Camden, Maine, 1985), 146. For an excellent attempt to make sense of the fighting on Hays's front, see D. Reid Ross, "Brigadier General Alexander Hays' Brigade at the Battle of the Wilderness, May 5, 1864," in Civil War Times Illustrated Collection, USMHI.

his chief of staff, he barked, "Major Mitchell, go to Gibbon and tell him to come up on the double-quick." No sooner had Hancock dispatched his staffer southward than Gibbon's lead unit, Colonel Samuel S. Carroll's brigade, arrived in a cloud of dust. His head held high and "calm as a May morning," according to Lyman's account, Carroll was "full of the gaudium certaminis as usual." Dashing into place at the double quick, Carroll's breathless soldiers evaporated into the thickets. "Now, I don't want any hollering," a colonel reminded his men as they glided into the wilderness. "That's childish. Prime! Forward!"[94]

Gibbon was one of Meade's favorites. A West Pointer and author of a popular military manual, he was as tough as nails and all business. "Steel-cold General Gibbon," Lyman called him, "the most American of Americans, with his sharp nose and up-and-down manner of telling the truth, no matter whom it hurts."[95]

Two of Gibbon's brigades—Carroll's and a predominantly Pennsylvania outfit under Brigadier General Joshua T. Owen—were placed under Birney, who had as good a grasp of the confused situation as anyone. Birney immediately fed the new units into the woods below Orange Plank Road to shore up the wavering Union position.

Meanwhile, Confederates had almost reached Brock Road. They were so close, Gibbon later reported, that his troops "had scarcely time to form line before they became engaged." Snatching up his remaining element—Brigadier General Alexander S. Webb's Philadelphia brigade, which had earned its spot in history by battering back the head of Lee's final assault at Gettysburg ten months earlier—Gibbon plunged into the woods. He was just in time, he later explained, "to prevent the enemy from breaking through our line on the Brock Road near the Plank Road." Disaster had barely been averted.[96]

Lyman stood watching fresh troops stream into battle. A body was carried past, covered with blood. It was Hays. "A braver man never went into action," Lyman wrote home, "and the wonder only

94. Lyman to family, May 15, 1864, in *Meade's Headquarters,* ed. Agassiz, 91–92; Lyman Journal, May 5, 1864, in Lyman Papers, MHS.

95. Lyman to family, May 20, 1864, in *Meade's Headquarters,* ed. Agassiz, 107.

96. John Gibbon's Report, in *OR,* Vol. XXXVI, Pt. 1, 429–30; Alexander S. Webb's Report, *ibid.,* 437; Charles H. Banes, *History of the Philadelphia Brigade* (Philadelphia, 1876), 227.

is that he was not killed before, as he always rode at the head of his men, shouting to them and waving his sword." Grant expressed similar sentiment on learning of Hays's death. "I am not surprised that he met his death at the head of his troops; it was just like him," remarked the commander in chief. "He was a man who would never follow, but would always lead in battle."[97]

All along the line, Gibbon's division pushed the Confederates back. To the north, Carroll's brigade catapulted over the Brock Road earthworks and charged down a slight slope and up the other side, driving the thin rebel line. Wheaton's men finally had breathing room. Confronted with an overwhelming Federal force—Heth's single Confederate division was now battling four Federal divisions—the rebels slowly retreated through dense growth. Stepping over bodies of those killed during the earlier fighting, they slipped back into their well-placed trenches.

From their position along the little ridge, the Confederates poured steady fire into anything that moved.

At 5:05 P.M., as Gibbon's soldiers were hastily forming to beat off the latest Confederate counteroffensive in the wake of Mott's collapse, Lyman fired a hurried message to Meade. Hancock had launched a "general attack," he explained, which "holds in some place, but is forced back to the Brock Road on the left," where Mott's shattered division was trying to regroup. "Gibbon is just coming up to go in," added Lyman, who also reported that Hancock's final division commander, Francis Barlow, was expected soon. The plan was for Barlow to "try a diversion on the left."[98]

About that time, Lyman received word that more rebels might be on the way. A southern prisoner, scooped up in the vicious close-quarters fighting, asserted that Longstreet was approaching from the right side of the Confederate formation. The rumor was unsubstantiated, but it made sense. Federal intelligence had last placed Long-

97. Lyman to family, May 15, 1864, in *Meade's Headquarters*, ed. Agassiz, 92; Grant, *The Personal Memoirs*, II, 528.

98. John Day Smith, *History of the Nineteenth Regiment of Maine Volunteer Infantry* (Minneapolis, 1909), 136–37; Charles D. Page, *History of the Fourteenth Regiment, Connecticut*, 234–35; Joseph R. C. Ward, *History of the One Hundred and Sixth Regiment Pennsylvania Volunteers* (Philadelphia, 1883), 240–41; Edward G. Longacre, *To Gettysburg and Beyond: The Twelfth New Jersey Volunteer Infantry, II Corps, Army of the Potomac, 1862–1865* (Hightstown, N.J., 1988), 186–88; Theodore Lyman to George G. Meade, May 5, 1864, in *OR*, Vol. XXXVI, Pt. 2, pp. 410–11.

street's corps near Gordonsville, below the rest of Lee's army and well positioned to slam into Meade's southern flank. Todd's Tavern, at the intersection of Catharpin and Brock roads, was the key to the Federal left wing. By evacuating the tavern and rushing to Getty's aid, Hancock had left the road junction vulnerable. At this point, the only Federals near Todd's Tavern included cavalry and a single infantry brigade. Although sufficient to sound the alarm if Longstreet drew near, they could hardly hold their own against the Confederate 1st Corps. For the rest of the day and much of the next, Federal planning was haunted by the specter of Longstreet's veterans materializing off their southern flank.

The unsettling possibility suggested by the talkative rebel prisoner was of course precisely what Lee had in mind. Longstreet, however, had fallen behind his projected schedule and was still nowhere in sight. It was now clear that he could not arrive before dark, which meant that Ewell and Hill would have to continue holding off Meade's entire army alone. So far they had done a superb job. But as Union commanders concentrated scattered units and fed them into battle, the sheer weight of Yankee numbers made a Federal breakthrough increasingly likely. The southern mood was one of desperation. "The officers and men of the regiment realized that the safety of the army depended upon our holding the enemy in check until the forces left behind could come up," wrote one of Heth's rebels, "and there was a fixed determination to do it, or to die." [99]

For the previous hour, darkening thickets around Orange Plank Road had witnessed some of the war's most intense, unrelieved slaughter. "There seemed to be as many dead men in our front as we had men engaged," recalled a southerner. Aiming uphill, Federal riflemen tended to overshoot their targets, while Confederates benefited from an ideal firing position. As a rebel remembered it, in one area saplings had been skinned by bullets "like a young apple tree is in the spring of the year by the rabbits." The roadway itself, related a North Carolina veteran, was a "storm center." He doubted whether "any more violent or sanguinary contest occurred during the entire Civil War than just here. The road was swept by an incessant hurricane of fire, and to attempt to cross it meant almost certain

---

99. Lyman to Meade, May 5, 1864, in OR, Vol. XXXVI, Pt. 2, p. 411; Clark, comp., *Histories of the Several Regiments and Battalions from North Carolina*, III, 304.

death." Another Confederate starkly summed up the fighting. "A butchery pure and simple it was," he recalled, "unrelieved by any of the arts of war in which the exercise of military skill and tact robs the hour of some of its horrors. It was a mere slugging match in a dense thicket of small growth, where men but a few yards apart fired through the brushwood for hours, ceasing only when exhaustion and night commanded a rest." [100]

But at this juncture—a little after 5 P.M.—night had not yet come, and rest was impossible. A few hundred yards across the stunted forest, on Brock Road, Hancock was feeding Gibbon's division into the fray. And moving up from the south was Barlow's division, whose weight would soon be added to Hancock's juggernaut. Hancock's full corps, twenty-seven thousand strong, swelled by Getty's six thousand—thirty-three thousand men in all—would soon be focused against Heth's lone Confederate division, skewing the odds to around five to one in Hancock's favor. Would Lee's audacious gamble succeed, or would it destroy the Confederate army? The answer was to turn on what happened during the next two hours in this obscure patch of Virginia woodland.

100. Clark, comp., *Histories of the Several Regiments and Battalions from North Carolina*, III, 27, 75, 118.

Federal signal officers on Pony Mountain keeping watch on Lee's position at Clark's Mountain, across the Rapidan.

Drawing by Edwin Forbes, in Library of Congress

Federal 6th Corps wagons crossing the Rapidan on pontoon bridges at Germanna Ford on May 4.
MOLLUS Collection, USMHI

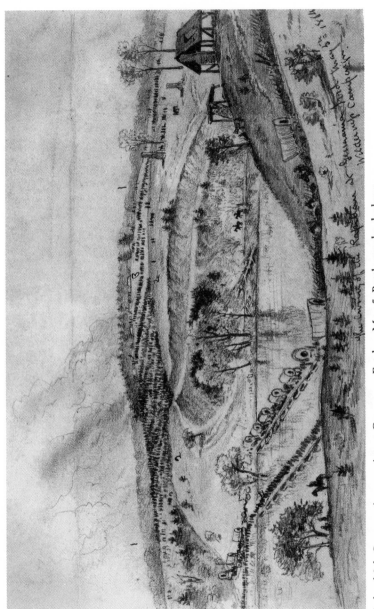

Federal 9th Corps trains crossing at Germanna Ford on May 5. Battle smoke darkens the horizon, where Ewell and Warren have begun fighting.
Drawing by Edwin Forbes, in Library of Congress

Saunders' Field, photographed in 1865 or 1866, looking from Warren's position across to Ewell's line. The Orange Turnpike appears in the foreground. The clearing rises from a swale toward Confederate earthworks.
MOLLUS Collection, USMHI

Ewell's earthworks along Saunders' Field, in a postwar photograph
MOLLUS Collection, USMHI

Federal 6th Corps units bushwhacking above the Orange Turnpike on the afternoon of May 5.

Drawing by Edwin Forbes, in Library of Congress

Ulysses S. Grant whittling and thinking
Drawing by Charles W. Reed, in Library of Congress

Federal 2nd Corps troops erecting log-and-dirt barricades on Brock Road and clearing a swath toward the Confederates.

Drawing by Edwin Forbes, in Library of Congress

Todd's Tavern, at the junction of Brock and Catharpin roads, after the war
MOLLUS Collection, USMHI

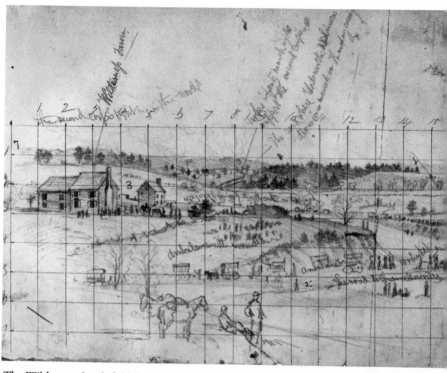

The Wilderness battlefield from north of Wilderness Tavern, looking toward Parker's Store, drawn by Edwin Forbes on May 7. Forbes's key designates the numbered landmarks: (1) the road to Ely's Ford, (2) the Orange Turnpike, (3) Wilderness Tavern, (4) the Lacy House, (5) the 5th Corps' position, (6) the 6th Corps' position, (7) the 2nd Corps' position, (8) the 9th Corps' position.
Library of Congress

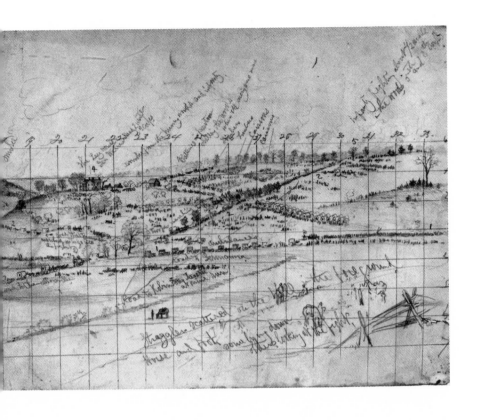

Soldiers rescuing wounded comrades from the flames
Drawing by Alfred R. Waugh, in Library of Congress

Skeletons haunting the battleground above Orange Plank Road about a year after the battle.
MOLLUS Collection, USMHI

V

May 5, Evening
Grant Strives for a Coordinated Assault

"The whole Wilderness roared
like fire in a canebrake."

AT UNION HEADQUARTERS, near Wilderness Tavern, Grant and Meade must have shared a sense of frustration. Despite determined efforts, they had failed to launch coordinated assaults against Lee's entire line. On the Orange Turnpike, first Warren and then Sedgwick had attacked. Each had suffered a costly reverse. Next, Meade's left wing—Getty's division and Hancock's corps—had pounded Hill's thin position on Orange Plank Road. But because Federal units had advanced piecemeal and without proper support, they had made scant headway. It remained to be seen whether a unified attack could be achieved before nightfall.

The Confederate army commander could monitor the fighting on both battle fronts from his headquarters at Widow Tapp's farmyard, on Orange Plank Road. Patches of smoke drifted from Ewell's direction, signaling Warren's and Sedgwick's persistent attempts to shake the hawk-nosed Virginian from his earthworks. The distinctive clatter of multiple small-arms fire, slightly muffled by intervening woods, rumbled along at a constant pitch, indicating that Ewell was holding his own.

More smoke was billowing straight ahead, where Heth's division of Hill's corps was furiously slugging it out against Getty and Hancock. The sounds there were decidedly more disturbing. The pace of combat on Orange Plank Road was escalating into a frenzy of slaughter. Wave after wave of Federal assaults was crashing against Heth's fragile Confederate line with mounting violence, threatening to swamp the rebels in a sea of blue uniforms.

Heth's lone division had reached its limit. Its last reserve, Kirkland's brigade, had already been committed, the various North Carolina regiments being sent independently to different parts of the line.

One North Carolina man remembered seeking cover behind "dead Federals so thick as to form partial breastworks."[1]

Unless Heth received reinforcements, the southern sector of Lee's front was certain to collapse. With Longstreet still nowhere in sight, the available gray-clad reserves were few. Risky as it was, Lee's practical option was to recall Wilcox' division. Only a short time before, Lee had ordered these troops northward to link Hill's and Ewell's Confederate wings. The southerner was acutely aware that bringing Wilcox back would crack open that worrisome gap between his two infantry columns. But Heth was in serious trouble. Lee would simply have to deal with the problems caused by Wilcox' recall if and when they occurred.

Wilcox' division contained four brigades, battlewise survivors of Hill's old Light Division. Decimated at Gettysburg, the command was now pitifully shy of its former strength. It was also scattered from the Chewning farm, three-quarters of a mile northwest from Heth's battle line, all the way over to Ewell's right flank, more than two miles north through the thickets. Lee ordered Wilcox' two nearest brigades to start immediately for the front. An aide continued northward with instructions for Wilcox to hurry back with the remainder of his soldiers.[2]

At the Chewning farm, Brigadier General Samuel McGowan's South Carolina brigade and a brigade of North Carolinians under Brigadier General Alfred M. Scales had just settled down for a well-earned rest. One of McGowan's chaplains led the men in prayer. "It was one of the most impressive scenes I ever witnessed," a soldier wrote afterward. "On the left thundered the dull battle; on the right the sharp crack of rifles gradually swelled to equal importance; above was the blue, placid heavens; around us a varied landscape of forest and fields, green with the earliest foliage of spring; and here knelt hirsute and browned veterans shriving for another struggle with death."[3]

A courier from headquarters pounded up in a cloud of dust. The cleric's makeshift prayer service was rudely interrupted by shouts to

1. Henry Heth's Report, in MC; Albright Diary, in Albright Collection, NCDAH; Clark, comp., *Histories of the Several Regiments and Battalions from North Carolina*, I, 596.
2. Wilcox, "Lee and Grant in the Wilderness," in *The Annals of the War*, 491–92.
3. Caldwell, *The History of a Brigade of South Carolinians*, 127–28.

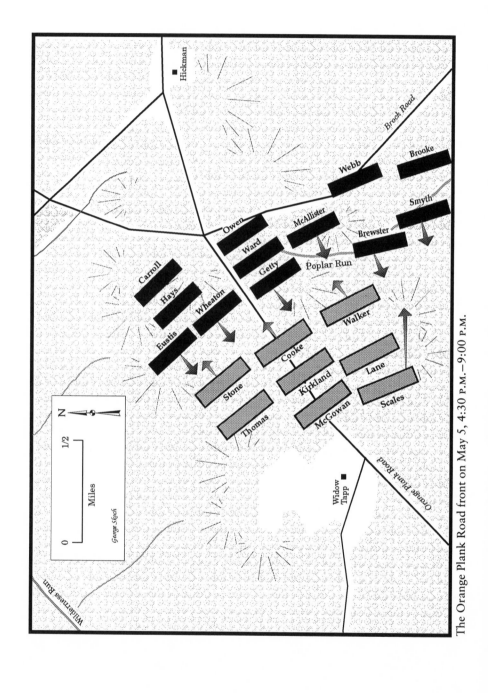

The Orange Plank Road front on May 5, 4:30 P.M.–9:00 P.M.

George Skoch

face forward and advance. Shouldering rifles and haversacks, the two Confederate brigades filed down the hillside. Across Widow Tapp's farm they went, past the 3rd Corps' artillery fringing the field's edge, then east on Orange Plank Road, pressing up the roadway under Lee's and Hill's anxious eyes. "The roar of muskets became continuous," remembered one of McGowan's soldiers, "augmented occasionally by the report of cannon, and always by the ringing rebel cheer." Artillery and ordnance wagons packed the road. Bodies sprawled here and there, and a steady procession of wounded men straggled back from the front, some walking, some crawling, others carried on stretchers. Shells whined along the rutted dirt track, plowing deadly little furrows toward the advancing troops and showering them with shrapnel.[4]

Several hundred yards east of the open field stood Hill's Confederate battle line. It was a crude affair. A thin formation of grim-faced rebels extended perhaps a quarter of a mile north of Orange Plank Road and an equal distance south of it. In some places, troops squatted close to the ground, taking advantage of whatever natural protection the land offered. In others, they hid behind crude breastworks of logs and dirt. But the situation everywhere was critical as Heth's stubborn Confederate division reeled under a relentless barrage of brutal Federal attacks. They had fended off Getty's division, only to be hit by Birney's, then Mott's, and now Gibbon's. More Yankees—Barlow's thousands, were massing on their right.

Heth and Wilcox hurriedly conferred. "I gave him my views," Heth later reported, "which were briefly that, having successfully resisted all of the enemy's attacks up to the present time, I thought that we should now, in our turn, attack."[5] Wilcox agreed.

Into this whirling kaleidoscope of battle poured McGowan's and Scales's two fresh southern brigades. Fully shrived by the chaplain's absolutions, McGowan's unit charged into the woods, three regiments above Orange Plank Road and two below. On McGowan's right, Scales's brigade crashed through matted undergrowth in relief of Mud Walker's exhausted Virginians. Vaulting over the Confederate works with a loud cheer, they dashed into the Yankees. Watches read 5:30 P.M.

4. *Ibid.*, 128.
5. Heth's Report, in MC; Morrison, ed., *The Memoirs of Henry Heth*, 183.

The rescuers slammed into the eye of a man-made hurricane. Lead and bits of trees whistled through the air.

McGowan's brigade immediately bucked up against stout Federal resistance. A section of Federal artillery had jangled up with Getty's second line of troops and was angrily lobbing shells at anything in gray that moved. The terrain was the "worst conceivable" for marching, a rebel recalled. Heth's men were also inadvertently adding to the confusion. They had remained behind when Wilcox' troops passed over their earthworks. Now they were firing through Wilcox' ranks in a misguided effort to help them against the Yankees. Because of the dense woods, their bullets were as likely to hit friends as enemies.[6]

To cap things off, the two brigades promptly became separated. Because McGowan's soldiers outdistanced Scales's, the flanks of each unit were open to attack.

To help divert Federal artillery fire, McGowans' inventive South Carolinians contrived a ruse. Squads of Confederates began darting from side to side across Orange Plank Road about a hundred yards from the Federal guns. Union artillery blasted away with canister, trying to snag the nimble-footed rebels, who always managed to leap aside in the nick of time. "At length," wrote a Federal staffer who witnessed this unusual tactic, "the object of the performance was seen; namely, to draw the fire of our guns, when the enemy charged in force on both sides of the road."[7]

McGowan's men were in trouble. A snarled tangle of saplings and bushes thoroughly disoriented their charge and prevented the brigade from striking with its full weight. The South Carolinians progressing below the road rounded a high ridge and stepped blindly into a fearsome barrage of concentrated rifle fire. A survivor later surmised that he and his more fortunate companions owed their lives to closely packed trees that helped deflect bullets. Further movement was impossible.

McGowan's units north of Orange Plank Road fared somewhat better. A witness recalled McGowan spurring his horse forward, his sword swinging overhead. His men followed with a cheer. According

6. Cadmus M. Wilcox' Report, in LC; Caldwell, *The History of a Brigade of South Carolinians*, 129.
7. Hazard Stevens, "The Sixth Corps in the Wilderness," in *PMHSM*, IV, 192–93.

226

to the brigade historian, they broke through one line of Federals, "killing large numbers and capturing more." Emboldened by success, a brazen southern standard-bearer planted his colors next to a Union cannon. But holding this forward position was out of the question. McGowan's northernmost units projected dangerously into Federal-held territory. A hasty retreat was in order. The isolated South Carolina troops drew tightly together along Orange Plank Road, well ahead of the southern army. They formed a finger surrounded on three sides by Federals. "I do not judge anyone," one of McGowan's officers later commented on the affair, "but I think it was the shortest, most huddled, most ineffective line-of-battle I ever saw." As McGowan's assault lost momentum, the Union formation snapped forward—"as the seasoned bow strongly bent springs back with redoubled force," recalled a northern officer years later. Federals crowded toward the beleaguered Confederate brigade, firing into it from straight ahead and from both sides. McGowan struggled to hold on, but the brigade's forward placement had created a death-trap. "The balls of the enemy at one point crossed the road from each side," recounted a southerner.[8]

McGowan had to tighten his formation and relinquish the captured Federal gun. Precisely which northern units recovered the cannon later became a subject of controversy. Hancock asserted in his official report that detachments from the 14th Indiana and 8th Ohio, of Carroll's brigade, rescued the piece. Years later, one of Getty's staffers disputed Hancock's claim. "As an eye witness," he wrote, "I know that the brave Vermonters and men of [Wheaton's] brigade next the Plank surged forward at the crisis without orders and drove the enemy from the guns, and that the presence of the Second Corps made no difference in the result. I know, too, that Hancock in the evening claimed that his troops recaptured the guns, and that Getty was indignant thereat, and earnestly protested that his division retook them unaided." The debate enlivened later gatherings of veterans and appears to have consumed nearly as much energy as did the precipitating incident itself.[9]

8. Correspondence of the London *Herald*, May 18, 1864, in *Lee's Sharpshooters*, by Dunlop, 398; Caldwell, *The History of a Brigade of South Carolinians*, 129–30; Stevens, "The Sixth Corps in the Wilderness," *PMHSM*, IV, 193.

9. Winfield S. Hancock's Report, in *OR*, Vol. XXXVI, Pt. 1, p. 320; Stevens, "The Sixth Corps in the Wilderness," in *PMHSM*, IV, 193.

At least one regiment from Kirkland's brigade managed to join McGowan's troops, and four Confederate artillery pieces were advanced to counter the Federal cannon. Blue and gray infantry lines seesawed across the wasteland, firing blindly into each other at close range. According to an aide, slaughter around one artillery piece was "sickening." The Confederate artillery horses were killed, immobilizing the gun. Forty soldiers from Kirkland's 44th North Carolina, led by two staff officers, volunteered to drag the gun to safety. Dodging through "incessant and murderous fire," the squad somehow managed to haul the cannon out. Only three rebels returned unhurt.[10]

While McGowan was doing his best to relieve Cooke's and Kirkland's battle-weary soldiers, Scales's North Carolinians were performing similar service for Mud Walker's fought-out Virginians on the far southern end of the rebel formation. "Charge after charge we made," reported one of Scales's men, who asserted that his brigade drove deeply into the Federals. But as on Orange Plank Road, Confederate gains were fleeting. "It was like fighting fire in the woods," recounted a southerner.[11]

As six o'clock approached, it was fast becoming evident that McGowan and Scales lacked sufficient manpower to shore up Heth's tattered line. Their spirited counterattacks, delivered in the Light Division's best tradition, had temporarily averted disaster. Union numbers, however, were stacked too heavily against them.

At this critical juncture, Hill's brigades were all hard put. On the right, Scales and Walker were girding to deflect the added weight of Barlow's entire division, massing off to their south. In the center, McGowan's bullet-riddled command, holding Orange Plank Road with the support of Cooke's and Kirkland's brigades, was frantically battling Getty's persistent soldiers and Gibbon's entire division. And

10. Obituary of Murray Taylor, *Confederate Veteran*, XVIII (1910), 82; Clark, comp., *Histories of the Several Regiments and Battalions from North Carolina*, III, 27–28. C. R. Dudley offered a different account in "What I Know about the Wilderness," in DU. Dudley, a sergeant in Company A of Poague's Artillery, asserted that the Confederate piece involved was from Ward's Battery A. According to Dudley, the gun was recovered by a detachment of Poague's men, none of whom were injured. For a vivid description of the artillery duel on Orange Plank Road from the Union perspective, see Charles A. Brockway, "Rattle of Musketry and Roar of Artillery," in *Campfire Sketches and Battle-Field Echoes*, ed. C. W. King and W. R. Derby (Springfield, Mass., 1889), 304–306.

11. Clark, comp., *Histories of the Several Regiments and Battalions from North Carolina*, I, 675.

over on Hill's left, Stone's brigade—three Mississippi regiments and one from North Carolina—was near its breaking point.

Stone's men were in a particularly bad fix, even for this bloody day. They had been battered by waves of Federal assaults—seven, according to a regimental historian—and had received no assistance at all. "The enemy was pressing us so heavily with their successive lines of fresh troops it was thought that they would annihilate us before nightfall," recounted one of Stone's troops. Another later wrote, "I shall never forget the scene. . . . Some dead, some lying flat on the ground, still others squatting had been firing at close range on level ground until they had nearly exhausted their ammunition." A third conceded, "The situation had developed a crisis." As a last-ditch effort, Stone's field officers recommended a "vigorous and impetuous charge" to repulse the attackers. Word was sent for the troops to make ready. The order to advance "was given in cold blood," recalled a Confederate sharpshooter, "and made me chilly." The prospects for survival were dim. "Thinned almost to a skirmish line, with empty guns and bayonets fixed, we were to rush on a Federal line from four to six men deep," one of Stone's veterans later explained. Another participant proudly noted that the men "expressed hope that it might not be necessary to make the charge, but there was no disposition to shirk the duty if it had been imposed." [12]

Thus far, densely wooded terrain had generally aided the Confederates by concealing their positions and disordering attacking Union forces. It was just as Federal planners had feared. The Wilderness was neutralizing Grant's massive edge in infantry and artillery and enabling a smaller force to engage him on nearly equal terms.

Another aspect of the Wilderness began to work to the southerners' advantage. Although the Federals were on the verge of overwhelming Heth's line, Hancock's command center at the intersection of Plank and Brock roads appears to have been unaware of that. The

12. W. M. Graham, "Twenty-Sixth Mississippi Regiment," *Confederate Veteran*, XV (1907), 169; Dunlop, *Lee's Sharpshooters*, 373–74; Rowland, *Military History of Mississippi*, 49; Clark, comp., *Histories of the Several Regiments and Battalions from North Carolina*, III, 304–305.

woods seemed to be hemorrhaging panicked blue-clad soldiers, which gave a wildly distorted impression of conditions at the battle-front. "The wounded stream out," recorded a newsman watching the scene, "and fresh troops pour in. Stretchers pass out with ghastly burdens, and go back reeking with blood for more. Word is brought that the ammunition is failing. Sixty rounds fired in one steady, stand-up fight, and that fight not fought out. Boxes of cartridges are placed on the returning stretchers, and the struggle shall not cease for want of ball and powder. Do the volleys grow nearer, or do our fears make them seem so?" Lyman wrote in a dispatch stamped 5:50 P.M., "We barely hold our own." Near-panic prevailed in Hancock's headquarters. "On the right the pressure is heavy," Lyman wrote, referring to Stone's portion of the rebel line, which in truth was exceedingly weak and near breaking. "General Hancock thinks he can hold the plank and Brock roads, in front of which he is, but he can't advance." After signing the message, Lyman had another thought and added a postscript: "Fresh troops would be most advisable."[13]

It so happened that fresh troops were what Grant had in mind. He did not, however, intend for them simply to shore up Hancock's seemingly hard-pressed battle line. Rather, during the course of the afternoon, the Union commander in chief had formulated a plan. If quickly executed, it promised finally to concentrate sufficient pressure against Powell Hill to crack the Confederate formation wide open.

The catalyst for Grant's plan was apparently the movement of Wilcox' Confederate division toward Orange Plank Road, which occurred around 5 P.M. The southward march of these Confederate brigades was spotted by Warren's signal officers. By 5:45, Union headquarters had been apprised that a "heavy column of the enemy's infantry [is] moving in a field this side of the plank road and going toward General Hancock."[14]

Unaware of Wilcox' earlier movement northward, Grant assumed that the Confederates in motion belonged to Ewell's corps. That meant, reasoned the Federal commander, that Ewell had weakened his line to aid Hill. Accordingly, Grant ordered two Federal re-

---

13. Charles A. Page, *Letters of a War Correspondent*, 50; Theodore Lyman to George G. Meade, May 5, 1864, in *OR*, Vol. XXXVI, Pt. 2, p. 411.
14. Frederick T. Locke to Andrew A. Humphreys, May 5, 1864, in *OR*, Vol. XXXVI, Pt. 2, p. 414.

sponses. First, he directed Warren and Sedgwick to renew their attacks on the Orange Turnpike, hoping that they might now be able to overwhelm Ewell. The results of that facet of Grant's plan will soon be apparent. Second, and of immediate importance to the fighting on Orange Plank Road, Grant decided to mobilize his reserves stationed around the Lacy House in a maneuver against Hill's exposed left flank. This second component of Grant's plan—an attack against the northern end of Hill's line—was to give Lee some very uneasy moments in the remaining daylight.

The task of assembling a force to swoop down on Hill went to Warren, who had no difficulty finding volunteers. According to the aide Roebling, Warren's subordinate Wadsworth had been "terribly chagrined" over his division's lackluster conduct during the early afternoon's offensive against Ewell. Anxious to retrieve his reputation, he asked to lead the assaulting force, and Warren assented. Robinson, another of Warren's division heads, pleaded to accompany Wadsworth. His troops were fresh, he argued, and he had seen virtually no fighting that day. It was finally decided that Robinson could go as well, taking with him Henry Baxter's brigade.

Already handily located near the Lacy House, Wadsworth's force was to work its way south along Wilderness Run, then burrow cross-country through a mile or so of thickets toward the sound of firing. "By following this direction," Roebling later explained, "he was expected to strike the enemy attacking Hancock on their left flank and rear." Around six, Wadsworth set out with Roebling serving as his guide.[15]

A few miles away at Widow Tapp's farm, Lee too had been sifting through scattered bits of intelligence for a window into his opponent's thinking. Tantalizing information had just arrived from Wilcox, who, crossing the broad Chewning pastures on his way to the Orange Plank Road front, had seen Federal soldiers around the Lacy House. These were doubtless the assembling members of Wadsworth's expeditionary force, and Wilcox noticed that they were preparing to move in Hill's direction. For Lee, the implications were

---

15. Andrew A. Humphreys to Gouverneur K. Warren, May 5, 1864, in OR, Vol. XXXVI, Pt. 2, p. 415; Washington A. Roebling's Report, in Warren Collection, NYSA; Frank Cowdrey's Report, in OR, Vol. XXXVI, Pt. 1, p. 615; Dawes, *Service with the Sixth Wisconsin*, 261.

twofold. First, Hill would have to pay close attention to his left, toward that troublesome gap. And second, perhaps of even greater interest to a fighter with Lee's aggressive instincts, Grant appeared to be weakening his turnpike forces in order to increase pressure against Hill. As Lee saw it, that might afford Ewell an opportunity to initiate an offensive on his front.

At six, Lee informed Ewell of his latest thinking. Despite repeated assaults, the enemy had made "no headway" against Hill. Longstreet's corps and Hill's remaining division under Anderson were expected by morning, which would bring the Confederate army up to full strength. He told Ewell to "send back and care for all your wounded, fill up your ammunition, and be ready to act early in the morning." Lee also related to Ewell Wilcox' report that "the enemy, who was drawn up on Wilderness Tavern ridge, is all moving up to our right," toward Hill. If Ewell's reconnaissance confirmed this intelligence, he was to explore "moving over and taking that ridge, thus severing the enemy from his base." In the event that Ewell could find "no chance to operate on their right," he was instructed to "be prepared to reenforce our right and make your arrangements accordingly." [16]

While Grant and Lee studied for chinks in each other's armor, the inferno around Orange Plank Road flared to a new intensity. Rarely before—those desperate hours on Antietam Creek jumped to mind—had the Army of Northern Virginia encountered such sustained and determined assaults. Hill's only hope was that his last reserves, Wilcox' two remaining brigades hurrying down from the direction of Ewell, would arrive before his line collapsed.

Wilcox pondered the dark undergrowth. Where should he shuttle his men when they arrived? "The troops engaged could not be seen," he later wrote of those tense moments, "the rattle of musketry alone indicating where the struggle was severest, and the points to which

16. Charles Marshall to Richard S. Ewell, May 5, 1864, in OR, Vol. XXXVI, Pt. 2, p. 952; Schaff, *The Battle of the Wilderness*, 189–92.

the reinforcing brigades should be sent." Hill himself rode forward "to encourage the men," his chief of staff, Palmer, recollected.[17]

Around 6:30, the final Confederate reinforcements, Brigadier General Edward L. Thomas' Georgia brigade and Brigadier General James H. Lane's North Carolinians, tramped up in a cloud of dust. Wilcox dispatched Thomas to the left of Orange Plank Road, where John Stone's soldiers were preparing to sacrifice themselves to preserve their position until nightfall.

Relief rolled along Stone's line as the Georgians slipped into the blood-soaked trenches. A counterattack was no longer necessary. Finished for the day, Stone's survivors collapsed in exhaustion. "Not one yard of our line had given one foot during the three hours the fearful onslaughts had been made upon us," boasted a member of Stone's 55th North Carolina, "but of the 340 of the regiment, 34 lay dead on the line where we fought and 167 were wounded. The sergeant of the ambulance corps counted the next day 157 dead Federal soldiers in front of our regiment." Another of Stone's men wrote home, "I sat in one place and shot my rifle 61 times. My company went in with 30 men and came out with 8 only."[18]

Lane's North Carolina brigade meanwhile gingerly felt its way up the south side of the roadway, preceded by a body of sharpshooters. A Virginia Military Institute graduate, Lane had held a chair in philosophy at the beginning of the war. Known as the Little General, he was described by a fellow soldier as "small of stature—a little over medium height—erect and soldierly in bearing, alert of movement, an excellent swordsman, of quiet disposition and a firm disciplinarian."[19]

Taking advantage of a lull, Lane's men managed to scoop up a respectable haul of Yankee prisoners. Just then, Barlow's long-feared assault on Heth's right flank—down Mud Walker's and Scales's way—exploded through the woods. In order to underscore the ur-

17. Wilcox, "Lee and Grant in the Wilderness," in *The Annals of the War*, 492–93; Royall, *Some Reminiscences*, 29.

18. Clark, comp., *Histories of the Several Regiments and Battalions from North Carolina*, III, 305; George W. Pearsall to wife, May 7, 1864, in George W. Pearsall Collection, NCDAH.

19. William Cox, "A Sketch of General James H. Lane," in the James H. Lane Collection, AU.

gency of Lane's assignment, Hill spoke with the brigadier himself. "I was soon after informed by General Hill in person," Lane recalled, "that a part of Scales's brigade had given way, and I was ordered to move forward and re-establish the line, letting my left rest on McGowan's right."[20]

After receiving cautions against accidentally firing into McGowan's troops, who still extended precariously toward the enemy along Orange Plank Road, Lane's soldiers moved out. Their left was about a hundred yards south of the roadway. In order to prevent enemy sharpshooters from enfilading his flank, Lane ordered the 37th North Carolina to face north and to deploy itself parallel to the road. The rest of the brigade—the 7th, 33rd, 28th, and 18th North Carolina regiments, arrayed southward in that order—stepped warily into the forest. Soon they were slogging through a swamp cluttered with dense undergrowth and decaying leaves.

As soon as Lane disappeared into the woods, Palmer turned his horse toward headquarters, at Widow Tapp's farm. In short order he met Jeb Stuart and Lee's aide Charles Venable. The men were studying with practiced ears the deafening roar caused by the latest Union onslaught. "If only night would come!" one of the riders exclaimed, voicing a sentiment shared by all. Hill's staffer stopped to explain that the renewed firing came from Lane's brigade entering the fray. Venable breathed a sigh of relief. "Thank God, I will go back and tell General Lee that Lane has just gone in and will hold his ground until other troops arrive tonight."[21]

The Yankees, however, were attacking in earnest, and there were plenty of them. Heading the latest assault was Francis Barlow, a twenty-nine-year-old eccentric who had abandoned his New York law practice at the war's outbreak, enrolled as a private, and worked his way up to head a division. Habitually sporting checkered flannel shirts and threadbare blue trousers, Barlow looked more like a "highly independent newsboy" than a general, except for the oversized cavalry saber for swatting stragglers that invariably dangled

20. James H. Lane, "History of Lane's North Carolina Brigade: Battle of the Wilderness—Report of General Lane," in *SHSP, IX,* 125–26.
21. Royall, *Some Reminiscences,* 29–30. On the order of Lane's advance, see James H. Lane's Report, Report of 7th North Carolina, Report of 18th North Carolina, Report of 28th North Carolina, Report of 37th North Carolina, all in Lane Collection, AU.

from his side. He was a firm disciplinarian, leading one of his soldiers to write home that "Barlow is so strict that there is quite a dislike created toward him in the division already." [22]

Barlow's men were the last of Hancock's troops to reach the battlefront. They swept toward the lower end of Hill's line, down where Mud Walker, Scales, and now Lane were girding to stave off the expected Federal offensive. It was nearly dark, and not all of Barlow's troops had come up, but those who were available slashed toward the sound of firing. Portions of three Federal brigades—under Colonels Nelson A. Miles, Thomas A. Smyth, and John B. Brooke— swung into the southern end of Hill's formation. According to a Union sharpshooter, the fighting "became simply terrific. The musketry was continuous and deadly along the whole line." [23]

The brunt of Barlow's attack fell on Lane's relatively fresh North Carolina men, who were still mired in a swamp below Orange Plank Road. Bolstered by a regiment from Scales's brigade, Lane's veterans at first managed to repel the northerners. As the Confederates began emerging onto dry ground, however, they encountered a strong Union formation looking down on them from a hill. Additional enemy units appeared on Lane's exposed right flank, forcing him to face the 18th North Carolina southward.

More misfortune was to come. Unknown to Lane, Wilcox had ordered McGowan to pull back. Thus, Lane's northern flank was uncovered as well. Amid the confusion, Lane's regiment on the left, the 7th North Carolina, cleared the bog. "At the time," explained a member of the regiment, "owing to the darkness, smoke, and density of the swamp it was impossible to distinguish friend from foe." When an armed column emerged on the North Carolinians' left, they as-

---

22. Lyman to family, May 20, 1864, in *Meade's Headquarters*, ed. Agassiz, 107; Charles Hamlin to sister, May 2, 1864, in Charles Hamlin Papers, NYSA. John Gordon asserted that he rescued Barlow at Gettysburg and permitted Barlow's wife to nurse him back to health. See John B. Gordon, *Reminiscences*, 151–53. Mrs. Barlow, however, said that she had been denied permission to enter the Confederate lines and had to sneak over during the night. See William M. Pegram, "Credit to Whom Credit Is Due," *Confederate Veteran*, XXIII (1915), 153.

23. John Brooke's Report, in *OR*, Vol. XXXVI, Pt. 1, p. 407; Simon Pincus' Report, *ibid.*, 420; Charles Walker and Rosemary Walker, eds., "Diary of the War by Robt. S. Robertson," *Old Fort News*, XXVIII (1965), 162–63; W. Springer Menge and J. August Shimrak, eds., *The Civil War Notebook of Daniel Chisholm* (New York, 1989), 12–13; Ripley, *Vermont Riflemen*, 146.

sumed it belonged to McGowan's brigade. It was Barlow's men. "Here a terrible fire was opened," explained Lane. Shooting into graycoats at close range, the Federals—soldiers from the 66th New York, of Barlow's division, and the 20th Indiana, of Birney's division—demanded that the Confederates surrender. Lane's ranks broke. The 7th North Carolina's commander, along with much of his regiment, fell prisoner. Lane had no choice but to retreat. This proved exceedingly difficult in a dark swamp. Federal bullets came from both flanks and from what had suddenly become Lane's rear. Berry Benson, a Confederate sharpshooter, later recalled how Orange Plank Road became "jammed with a disorderly, flying mass of Confederates." Benson passed Lane, who was on horseback immediately behind his broken troops. "Are you bringing in cartridges?" shouted Lane, assuming that Benson was part of a detail that had been sent for ammunition. "Yes, in our cartridge boxes," Benson and his companions answered, holding up their ammunition pouches and shaking them at the general. "That's right," Lane hollered back, impressed with the pluck of Benson's party. Most of Lane's soldiers managed to work their way back through the morass to the Confederate earthworks. In the confusion, however, the 28th North Carolina failed to receive Lane's order to withdraw. Continuing to press eastward, the wayward regiment captured a Federal stronghold on the swamp's far side. By taking bullets from dead and wounded Yankees, they managed to hold on until dark, when they slipped back to the main rebel line. With the brigade finally united, Lane reported to his division commander, Wilcox. He was directed to remain in place until relieved by Anderson's division, which was expected in the morning.[24]

As long as fading daylight permitted, the carnage continued. "The fight was spirited and well sustained," a Yankee reported. Blasted through the lungs with a minié ball, one of Barlow's sergeants complained when no one offered to help him from the field. "Why,

24. Lane's Report, Report of 7th North Carolina, Report of 18th North Carolina, Report of 28th North Carolina, Report of 37th North Carolina, all in Lane papers, AU; Benson, "Reminiscences," in Benson Papers, SHC; Pincus' Report, in *OR*, Vol. XXXVI, Pt. 1, p. 421; David Craft, *History of the One Hundred Forty-First Regiment, Pennsylvania Volunteers, 1862–1865* (Towanda, Pa., 1885), 178. The fighting on Lane's front is analyzed by William K. McDaid in "Four Years of Arduous Service: The History of the Branch-Lane Brigade in the Civil War" (Ph.D. dissertation, Michigan State University, 1987), 258–61.

Cassidy," called out a nearby soldier, "there's a man with all of his head blown off and he is not making half as much fuss as you are!"[25]

At seven o'clock, Lee sent another letter to Ewell reflecting his confidence. "The enemy persist in their attack on General Hill's right," began the missive. "Several efforts have been repulsed, and we hold our own as yet." Again Lee urged Ewell to see if he could "get Wilderness Tavern ridge and cut the enemy off from the river." Noting that the enemy was pressing hard against Hill, Lee emphasized the need for Ewell to hurry. "The attack on General Hill is still raging. Be ready to act as early as possible in the morning."[26]

A welcome evening's breeze began to stir. The sun's last rays filtered hazily through spiraling gunsmoke and tattered leaves. But the day's crisis was not over. Confederate scouts reported a fresh mass of Federal troops approaching Hill's northern flank near where Thomas' Georgians had slipped into Stone's former trenches. It was Wadsworth's detachment, just arriving from the Lacy fields. This was precisely what Lee had feared. Grant was exploiting the unprotected gap between the two Confederate infantry columns, pumping soldiers into the void to overrun Hill's vulnerable flank.

Hill had exhausted his reserves. Every Confederate combat soldier had been committed. The only available body of troops was the ragtag 5th Alabama battalion, attached to Walker's brigade. This force of about 150 men had been assigned to guard the cache of Federal prisoners growing behind Hill's front. There was no choice but to send the Alabamians in. And in they went, screaming at the top of their lungs.

Miraculously, the ruse worked. Wadsworth's troops had no stomach for more deep-woods combat. Their advance had been marred by a series of disasters. Shortly after leaving the safety of the Lacy fields, Wadsworth's lead units—Baxter's brigade in front, with Roy Stone's close behind—had encountered rebel pickets. As usual, the Confederates were invisible, and the Yankees responded by firing blindly into the dark forest. The pressure was too much for Stone's Pennsylvania brigade, still shaken by its encounter with Ewell's men at the mudhole near the Higgerson place. According to Wadsworth's

25. St. Claire A. Mulholland, *The Story of the 116th Regiment Pennsylvania Volunteers in the War of the Rebellion: The Record of a Gallant Command* (Philadelphia, 1899), 176.

26. Charles Marshall to Richard S. Ewell, May 5, 1864, in OR, Vol. XXXVI, Pt. 2, p. 953.

adjutant, the soldiers broke "in a disgraceful manner on seeing the fire of Baxter's skirmishers in front of them." Stone's horse reared in panic at the ruckus, pitching Stone and then falling on him. One postwar account surmised that Stone had been drunk. Whatever caused the accident, the Union general was disabled for the rest of the campaign. By the time things were straightened out, it was almost night. The final blow was the swarm of screaming Alabamians. Wadsworth's ill-fated maneuver ground to an abrupt halt about a quarter mile short of Orange Plank Road. "The resistance of the enemy had not been very severe," Roebling later observed. "The line had gradually swung around so as to be facing more nearly south, between the Widow Tapp's field and the Brock Road." [27]

For hours the forest had vibrated with a deafening roar. Abruptly, the shooting stopped. Confederates simply dropped where they stood, trenches tangled and askew, with little semblance of organized battle lines. Hill's aide-de-camp thought the southern formations "were like a worm fence, at every angle." Conditions on the Federal side were no better. Getty's soldiers, completely fought out, retired to Brock Road. Hancock's troops, fresher by degrees only, remained at the front. Less than a hundred feet separated Wadsworth's units from the end of Hill's line. In many places, hostile works were so intertwined that soldiers could hear their enemies digging and talking less than a stone's throw away. The Confederate sharpshooter Benson later recalled that "the enemy lay a biscuit's toss in front." He recorded one incident in which a Yankee accused a rebel in the neighboring trench of having canine ancestry. "The reply to this was a shot, and the reply to that was a volley, which we answered in turn, and for a while we had a little battle all to ourselves. But finally everything grew quiet, and we half-slept until dawn." A Confederate in Kirkland's brigade wrote home that "the cries of the sufferers, the rumble of wagons and artillery ambulances, the hurrying to and fro of men and animals, the neighing of horses and mules, the glare of the ruddy camp fires, all made a scene difficult to describe, but never to be forgotten." A Wisconsin officer recalled, "We lay upon the ground surrounded by dead and dying rebel soldiers."

---

27. Royall, *Some Reminiscences*, 30; Cowdrey's Report, in *OR*, Vol. XXXVI, Pt. 1, p. 615; Henry Greenleaf Pearson, *James S. Wadsworth of Genesco, Brevet Major General of United States Volunteers* (New York, 1913), 270; Roebling's Report, in Warren Collection, NYSA.

He went on, "The sufferings of these poor men, and their moans and cries were harrowing. We gave them water from our canteens and all aid that was within our power."[28]

From Getty's opening charge at 4:15 P.M. until darkness drew a curtain on the slaughter, Union and Confederate lines had slugged away at each other without letup. "The musketry was terrific and continuous," recalled one of Getty's officers. "Usually when infantry meets infantry the clash of arms is brief," he explained. "One side or the other speedily gives way. Here neither side would give way, and the steady firing rolled and crackled from end to end of the contending lines, as if it would never cease. But little could be seen of the enemy. Whenever any troops rose to their feet and attempted to press forward, they became a target for the half-hidden foe, and lost severely." Another Federal commented on how battle sounds "struck the ear with a peculiar effect from the almost total absence of artillery, usually so noisy an accompaniment of modern battle." He continued, "The men who noted this fact were men accustomed to warfare, and who knew that the fire of infantry was much more deadly than that of artillery, and never before had they heard such continuous thunder or confronted such a storm of lead as on this occasion." An officer from McGowan's command described the fighting from the Confederate perspective. "Such woods," he wrote, "if you have one line which is to remain stationary and on the defence, are an advantage; but if you attack, or if you must relieve one line with another, it is the worst place in the world. It is impossible to keep even a regiment well dressed. Then the enemy open fire on you. Some men will invariably return the fire. Gradually all join in it; and once the whole roar of battle opens, there is an end of unison of action."[29]

Hunching over his dispatch book at 9 P.M., the war correspondent Charles Page tried to capture a sense of what had happened in the little patch of woodland around Orange Plank Road. "The battle

---

28. Royall, *Some Reminiscences*, 30; George W. Getty's Report, in *OR*, Vol. XXXVI, Pt. 1, p. 677; Curtis, *History of the Twenty-Fourth Michigan*, 234; Benson, "Reminiscences," in Benson Papers, SHC; Justice to wife, May 7, 1863, in Justice Papers, EU; Dawes, *Service with the Sixth Wisconsin*, 261.

29. Hazard Stevens, "The Sixth Corps in the Wilderness," in *PMHSM*, IV, 192–93; Ripley, *Vermont Riflemen*, 146; Caldwell, *The History of a Brigade of South Carolinians*, 131.

raged for three hours precisely where it began," he wrote, "along a line of not more than half a mile. Fast as our men came up they were sent in—still no ground gained, none lost." The combat's tempo had been awesome. "The work was at close range," he wrote. "No room in that jungle for maneuvering; no possibility of a bayonet charge; no help from artillery; no help from cavalry; nothing but close, square, severe, face-to-face volleys of fatal musketry." According to an officer of the 6th Corps, "General Getty always regarded this as the hardest fought battle he ever knew. He always insisted and dwelt upon the superiority of the enemy in numbers, and when after the surrender at Appomattox he met Heth and Wilcox, whom he knew well before the war, his first questions were as to their force in this fight, and he was not surprised to find his estimate fully confirmed."[30]

The day's contest on Orange Plank Road had ended in stalemate. Forced to attack before they were ready—a fault, by the way, attributable to Meade's and Grant's impatience—Union field commanders never succeeded in effectively massing their men. Getty's troops had charged alone with no chance against Heth's well-positioned gray defenders. And as Hancock's divisions arrived—Birney, Mott, Gibbon, and Barlow, in that order—they were necessarily fed in one at a time, with varying results. North of Orange Plank Road, Hancock never achieved a sufficient concentration to penetrate the Confederate line. Below the roadway, where Union soldiers ultimately reached substantial numbers, everything went wrong. Mott's men packed themselves into too constricted a space and were decimated by deadly Confederate fire that continued until they stampeded back to their Brock Road earthworks. Birney's and Gibbon's reinforcements had flailed away in futile attempts to restore order in the confused front. Toward evening, the Federal leadership had finally injected a semblance of tactics into the formless battle. The result was a pincer movement, with Barlow slicing in from the south and Wadsworth from the north, aiming to crush Hill's rebels between the jaws of a powerful Union vice. The idea was sound, but the maneuver started too late. Before either Barlow or Wadsworth could exert sufficient pressure against Hill's line, darkness ended the fighting. "An hour or

---

30. Charles A. Page, *Letters of a War Correspondent,* 50; Hazard Stevens, "The Sixth Corps in the Wilderness," in *PMHSM,* IV, 194.

more of daylight," concluded Humphreys in his review of the battle, "and [Hill] would have been driven from the field." [31]

Looking back on the day's aborted attacks, a Federal participant ascribed the afternoon's failures to the Army of the Potomac's "one weakness, the lack of springy formation, and audacious, self-reliant initiative." He concluded, "This organic weakness was entirely due to not having had in its youth skillfully aggressive leadership. Its early commanders had dissipated war's best elixir by training it into a life of caution, and the evil of that schooling it had shown on more than one occasion, and unmistakably that day, and it had to suffer for it." The hesitant hands of earlier commanders were still slowing the Union army's reflexes. [32]

Meade's inability to overpower Hill's Orange Plank Road line also owed to the resilience of the hungry gray-clad troops. It had been Hill's finest hour as a corps commander. He had skillfully waged a defense reminiscent of the heady days in August, 1862, when the Light Division beat off Federal attacks with bayonets, rocks, and whatever came readily to hand. The only regrets about the day's performance on the Confederate side came from Heth, who had urged Wilcox to counterattack rather than simply to hold the rebel line. "This proved to be a mistake on my part," he later confessed. "I should have left well enough alone." [33]

Lee had played an energetic part in the day's fighting. Once before, at Antietam, he had assumed an active role in a battle's progress, shuttling troops from one endangered spot to the other. He had shown an outstanding genius for the craft. Similarly today, Lee had intervened on Orange Plank Road and had ordered Wilcox to the front when Heth had reached his breaking point. As Venable described it, "this battle on the plank road was fought immediately under the eye of the Commanding General." [34]

But the Army of Northern Virginia still faced a crisis. To the north, Ewell had ordered every available man into line. He had no reserves, aside from Ramseur's brigade returning from patrol duty in the Confederate rear. To the south, Hill too had reached the bottom

---

31. Andrew A. Humphreys, *The Virginia Campaign*, 33.
32. Schaff, *The Battle of the Wilderness*, 201.
33. Morrison, ed., *The Memoirs of Henry Heth*, 183; Heth's Report, in MC.
34. Venable, "The Campaign from the Wilderness to Petersburg," in *SHSP*, XIV, 524.

of his manpower pool. Night had saved Little Powell, but he was poorly positioned to resist Hancock's inevitable attack in the morning. A vastly superior force lay in front of him, and closing in from each side—Barlow to the south and Wadsworth to the north—were additional Federal forces. Without reinforcements, Hill would collapse under waves of blue-clad troops.

Lee's hope lay in Longstreet. The general had left his encampments a day before and had disappeared into the Virginia woods. As evening shadows crept over disorganized rows of Confederate soldiers huddled in the Wilderness, questions about him were on the southerners' minds. Where was he, and would he arrive before morning summoned Meade's soldiers in numbers too plentiful to resist?

"Death was in every shot."

While combat in the Orange Plank Road sector accelerated dizzyingly, important developments were occurring on the Orange Turnpike as well.

After the failure of Warren's and then Sedgwick's offensives, the woods around the turnpike had slipped into an uneasy quiet, broken only by the steady tattoo of sharpshooters feeling for weak spots in opposing battle lines. But Meade, despite the apparent stalemate developing on his northern front, still hoped to assemble a coordinated assault against Ewell. Perhaps another attack, he reasoned, this time with Warren and Sedgwick acting in unison, would shatter the Confederate line. And even if the might of two Federal corps failed to defeat Ewell, another attack would certainly keep Ewell too busy to shift reinforcements to Hill.

Warren and Sedgwick, however, were behaving as though they had no intention of renewing battle. Warren in particular seemed almost stunned by Ewell's rough handling of his corps. He had withdrawn most of his soldiers to the relative safety of the Lacy house, under the muzzles of his 5th Corps artillery. He had not budged since.

In an attempt to goad Warren back into action, Humphreys, the chief of staff, sent a strongly worded missive to the commander of the Federal 5th Corps at 4 P.M. An assault had been ordered on Orange Plank Road, explained Meade's aide, referring to Hancock's and Getty's attack against Hill. The young corps chief was to "make dispositions" to renew the offensive against Ewell "if practicable." He was not to start fighting, however, until he received Humphreys' go-ahead, which would be issued with companion orders to Sedgwick to ensure that the two corps moved in concert.

In a blunt postscript, Humphreys reminded Warren that ample soldiers would be placed at his disposal. Two of Warren's four divisions—Crawford's and Robinson's—had hardly fired a shot all day. And more fresh soldiers were on the way. Burnside had crossed the Rapidan, freeing for combat duty Ricketts' 6th Corps division, which had been guarding Germanna Ford. One of Ricketts' brigades was now assigned to support Warren. Headquarters would brook no excuses for inaction from Warren, least of all complaints that his men were worn out from earlier combat.[35]

While Warren pondered the distasteful prospect of launching another thrust against Ewell, Sedgwick busied himself exploring a promising opportunity north of the turnpike. The reports were that Ewell's corps occupied a set of entrenchments running the full length of Warren's and Sedgwick's line. That meant the rebels were stretched thin. Perhaps by reaching north, Sedgwick could overlap the Confederate left and sweep past Ewell. By then turning south, the Yankees would have a shot at crumpling the unprotected rebel flank and rolling up Ewell's battle formation. Here was an inviting chance to catch the Confederates off guard, and Sedgwick began casting about for a way to make the most of it.

In short order, Ricketts' 6th Corps division pulled up at the front. As promised by Humphreys, one brigade was sent to Warren and posted on the turnpike. The other brigade—a mixed unit of men from Ohio, Pennsylvania, and Maryland under Truman Seymour—was assigned to Sedgwick.[36]

The fresh troops augmented Sedgwick's numbers sufficiently to let him begin his surprise maneuver around Ewell. The thought of employing Seymour for the hazardous operation, however, must have

---

35. Andrew A. Humphreys to Gouverneur K. Warren, May 5, 1864, in *OR*, Vol. XXXVI, Pt. 2, p. 414; James M. Reed Diary, May 5, 1864, in James Ricketts Collection, Manassas National Battlefield Park. Reed apparently served as an aide to Ricketts on May 5 and 6. His diary spells out the division's movements.

36. Truman Seymour's Report, in *OR*, Vol. XXXVI, Pt. 1, p. 728; Reed Diary, May 5, 1864, in Ricketts Collection.

left Sedgwick uneasy, for if Seymour's troops were well rested, they were predominantly inexperienced recruits. And Seymour's capacity to lead the brigade was questionable. The general had assumed command that very morning, he was still convalescing from a serious wound, and his most recent military endeavor had been a disastrous expedition in Florida. Raw soldiers under an invalid still smarting from a recent reverse were not ideal for flanking Ewell's battlewise veterans. Seymour, however, was available, and plucking a different brigade from the battle line posed its own dangers. Sedgwick decided to gamble and ordered Seymour over to the extreme Federal right wing.

Seymour's troops executed the first part of their assignment to perfection. "Under the guide of one of General Meade's staff officers," recalled a Maryland soldier, "we filed to the right and marched through scattered timber." Soon they had formed two lines—two regiments in front and three behind—in the woods above Sedgwick. Then Union skirmishers wormed into the darkening forest and felt gingerly ahead, trying to pinpoint the exact location of Ewell's formation. Confederate pickets, however, proved craftily adept in this heavily wooded terrain. After an hour, Federal skirmishers had made negligible headway. Exasperated, Seymour decided to force the issue by advancing his first infantry line. Orders went out to J. Warren Keifer, an Ohio politician commanding the lead troops, to "press the enemy, and, if possible, outflank him upon his left."[37]

Into the woods went the 110th Ohio and 6th Maryland, "in gallant style," according to Keifer. They inched through the forest, driving back Confederate skirmishers. A gentle rise loomed ahead. Straining to see through the dense spring foliage, Keifer's men realized that a horrible mistake had been made. The slope was clear of growth and a row of log breastworks lay along the top. Rather than rounding Ewell's flank as expected, Keifer was crashing directly into strongly fortified Confederate works. Scrutinizing the entrenchments, Keifer concluded that they were too tough to assault without substantial reinforcements. He canceled the attack and sent word to Seymour.[38]

37. Eichelberer Memoir, in Civil War Miscellaneous Collection, USMHI; Keifer, *Slavery and Four Years of War*, II, 78; J. Warren Keifer's Report, in *OR*, Vol. XXXVI, Pt. 1, pp. 730–31. The brigade was arranged with the 110th Ohio and 6th Maryland in front, and the 122nd Ohio, 138th Pennsylvania, and 126th Ohio in the rear.
38. Keifer's Report, in *OR*, Vol. XXXVI, Pt. 1, p. 731.

News of Keifer's predicament, however, did not filter back to Union headquarters. So far as the Federal leadership knew, Keifer was dashing around Ewell's line, preparing to root the rebels from their trenches and setting them up for a devastating frontal attack.

Coincidentally, it was just at this point that one of Warren's signal stations reported Confederates streaming from Ewell's southern flank in the direction of the Orange Plank Road, most likely to assist Hill. When this intelligence was relayed to Grant, he concluded that Ewell must have weakened his force. Here, decided Grant, was a prime opportunity to renew the turnpike offensive.

With a true soldier's instinct, the Union commander in chief resolved to slam Ewell with every man available. Accordingly, at 6 P.M., just as Sedgwick's projected flanking maneuver should have been prying Ewell's rebels from their trenches, Meade ordered an all-out push. "The major-general commanding directs that you renew the attack on the pike immediately," stated the message to Warren, and it added, "Sedgwick is ordered to renew Wright's attack at once."[39]

The Federal leadership, however, had predicated its decision to attack Ewell upon intelligence that was incorrect on two important scores. First, those gray-clad soldiers moving south did not belong to Ewell. They were Wilcox' men, who had been recalled by Lee to help their compatriots on Orange Plank Road. Ewell's corps remained intact and as strong as ever. Second, Ewell's line did not terminate where the Federals had concluded it did. By late afternoon, the rolling woodland off Ewell's northern flank was no longer the exclusive preserve of rabbits and squirrels. Anticipating a Union foray, Ewell had drawn upon the last of his reserves, directing John Pegram's veteran Virginia brigade to extend the Confederate left toward the Rapidan. The rebels rolled together "what dead logs lay convenient," filling in chinks "with loose stones and rails readily accessible." Because of Pegram's industry, strongly fortified rebel earthworks now hugged the wooded ridges across from Seymour. Sedgwick had moved too slowly, and his fleeting opportunity to send a force around Ewell had vanished.[40]

The result of Meade's attempt to launch a unified frontal assault

---

39. Andrew A. Humphreys to Gouverneur K. Warren, May 5, 1864, in *OR,* Vol. XXXVI, Pt. 2, p. 415.

40. William Smith, "The Wilderness and Spotsylvania," in John W. Daniel Collection, DU; Buck, *With the Old Confeds,* 103–104.

was predictable. Nothing was accomplished except the spilling of more blood. Sedgwick's troops were repulsed by Confederates ensconced behind earthworks that made ingenious use of each hillock and gully. "We made a vigorous attempt to advance our lines," explained an officer of the 6th Corps in a report similar to many others concerning the encounter, "but owing to the strength of the enemy's position failed to accomplish the object." A rebel counterattack stymied the New Jersey brigade. "The Confederates came on with great dash and spirit," recorded a Federal, "charging right up to the low breastworks that the Jerseymen had thrown up, and which were on fire in several places." The New Jersey soldiers fell back, which required Upton's brigade, already covering the portion of Saunders' Field above the turnpike, to reach farther north to occupy the newly vacated position. In the process, Upton stretched his own formation to the breaking point. He could contribute nothing to the offensive against Ewell.[41]

Safely huddled behind earthworks south of the roadway, Warren's corps apparently never attempted to budge. Humphreys' orders notwithstanding, the 5th Corps commander refused to enter the deadly thickets. Undoubtedly Sedgwick's inability to dent Confederate works to the north strengthened Warren's conviction that an attack on his part would be futile. It is likely that Warren discussed the hazards of advancing with Meade and convinced the army commander that he was correct. The New York *Tribune*'s Charles A. Page reported that Meade conferred with Warren shortly after issuing his six o'clock attack order. The inference is that Warren's decision against advancing was made with Meade's knowledge and approval. Warren's inaction, however, was later cited by his detractors as another example of his insubordination.[42]

Confederate artillery also dampened Warren's enthusiasm. Ewell's gunners concentrated impressive fire along the turnpike. The 10th Vermont, of Ricketts' division, suffered frightfully. The regiment's chaplain recalled a "perfect tornado of shell, that burst above and in the midst of the men." One projectile exploded near Ricketts, killing

---

41. Alanson A. Haines, *History of the Fifteenth Regiment New Jersey*, 145–46; Baquet, *History of the First Brigade New Jersey*, 21; Daniel Bidwell's Report, in *OR*, Vol. XXXVI, Pt. 1, p. 719.

42. Charles A. Page, *Letters of a War Correspondent*, 50.

three horses and wounding one of Griffin's staffers. Another Vermonter recorded in his diary that "the air was full of solid shot and exploding shells as far each side of the pike as could be seen." A round burst inside a soldier, "completely disemboweling and throwing him high in the air in a rapidly whirling motion above our heads with arms and legs extended until his body fell heavily to the ground with a sickening thud." Nearby troops were "covered with blood, fine pieces of flesh, entrails, etc., which makes me cringe and shutter whenever I think about it." Charging into the inferno of rebel artillery was out of the question.[43]

In sum, Grant's attempt to exploit what he perceived as a promising situation in the battle's northern front came to naught. The attack, such as it was, involved only a few brigades and lasted but a short time.

The real tragedy was the fate of Keifer's men in their impossible mission to flank Ewell. Keifer informed Seymour that his line was unsupported, that he was heavily outnumbered, and that rebels overlapped both his flanks, "rendering it impossible for the troops to attain success in a further attack." A courier returned with Seymour's reply. Keifer was to assault at once. "Feeling sure that the word I had sent had not been received," the astonished Ohioan later explained, "I delayed until a second order was received to attack." In the face of two directives from his commanding general, Keifer had no choice but to obey.[44]

As his soldiers advanced, Pegram's rebel skirmishers zigzagged back to their breastworks and vaulted to safety. The Yankees fired a volley and rushed ahead. Waiting until the Federals were a pistol shot away, the Confederates rose and emptied their rifles. "Nothing could stand that fire," wrote a captain in the 13th Virginia, "and in a few moments the blue line swayed and fell back but only to be replaced by another and another until fire had tried our mettle. Each one melted as did the first; death was in every shot and we held fast to our works." Adding to the carnage was the marksmanship of Hays's 6th Louisiana. Posted on Pegram's right, it opened

---

43. Edward M. Haynes, *A History of the Tenth Regiment Vermont Volunteers* (Rutland, Vt., 1870), 64; Lemuel A. Abbott, *Personal Recollections and Civil War Diary, 1864* (Burlington, Vt., 1908), 43–44.
44. Keifer's Report, in *OR*, Vol. XXXVI, Pt. 1, p. 731.

"oblique fire which they poured into the thick Yankee columns as they advanced."[45]

Keifer explained in his official report, "It was impossible to succeed." His troops had been buffeted by a "most terrible fire from the front and flanks." Seeking whatever shelter was available, the two isolated Federal regiments fought on. "It became so dark," wrote an Ohio soldier, "that our aim had to be guided by the flash of the enemy's guns." A ball ripped through Keifer's left forearm and shattered both bones. Badly wounded, the colonel nonetheless remained for another half hour, finally stumbling to the rear around nine. Keifer's replacement later complained that he received "no orders to fall back, although I had repeatedly reported that I had no support upon my left." Finally, near ten o'clock, Seymour granted permission to retire. Back came the front line, decimated from its pointless little battle. "We lost heavily this day," a Maryland soldier wrote in his diary. "The losses of the enemy were frightful," observed a Louisiana man who had watched the carnage, "and when day dawned next morning the ground was found to be literally covered with dead bodies."[46]

Keifer was carried to a field hospital near the turnpike, where his appearance caused a stir. His pants were gone, leaving him clad only in a pair of socks, a shirt soaked in blood, and a tightly buttoned vest. His mangled right arm hung at his side. His left hand still grasped a sword firmly. The general had earlier sworn to grow his hair and beard until Richmond fell. His blood-matted locks, thought a witness, gave him a "most weird appearance." When asked by a surgeon if he wanted his wound dressed, Keifer responded, "I should not care for myself if the rascals had not cut my poor men to pieces." The general was laid on an operating table of rough boards. Arms and legs were stacked around. One observer thought they resembled

45. Buck, *With the Old Confeds,* 104; Robert D. Funkhauser Diary, in *History of the Forty-Ninth Virginia Infantry, C.S.A.: Extra Billy Smith's Boys,* by Laura V. Hale and Stanley S. Phillips (Lanham, Md., 1981), 105–106; James Baumgardner, Jr., "The Fifty-Second Virginia," in Book 134, FSMP; "The Late Operations of Lee's Army," Richmond *Sentinel,* May 24, 1864; Louis Rosenberger Diary, May 5, 1864, Louis Rosenberger Collection, USMHI; Seymour Journal, in Schoff Collection, CL.

46. Keifer's Report, in *OR,* Vol. XXXVI, Pt. 1, p. 731; David Herman Diary, May 5, 1864, in Civil War Miscellaneous Collection, USMHI; Otho Binkley's Report, in *OR,* Vol. XXXVI, Pt. 1, p. 741; John Horn's Report, in *OR,* Vol. XXXVI, Pt. 1, p. 736; Seymour Journal, in Schoff Collection, CL.

"piles of stove wood, the blood only excepted." After administering chloroform, the surgeons exposed the fractured ends of Keifer's bones, dressed them using saws and knives, and bound the bloody mass in bandages. "Next," called a surgeon, and Keifer was lifted onto a pallet on the floor. Keifer's official report reflected the Ohio colonel's bitterness. "The troops were required to maintain this unequal contest," he wrote, "under the belief that other troops were to attack the enemy upon his flank." Mention of the incident nearly four decades later still galled him. "The presence of a general officer in authority, or an intelligent staff officer representing him, would have averted the useless slaughter," he fumed in his memoirs.[47]

At sunset, while Keifer's soldiers were still battling for survival, Warren ordered another charge across Saunders' Field to try to recover the cannon that had been abandoned there during the afternoon's fighting. Colonel Peter Lyle's 90th Pennsylvania led the attack, joined on its right by the 39th Massachusetts. On clearing the bushes that lined the field, Lyle's men found themselves under a hammering barrage from artillery. "The noise was terrific," recorded a Federal. "The forest walls around the field echoed and magnified every sound." Another northerner recalled that "quite a number of the brigade were killed and wounded crossing the road; the missiles would come with a swi-s-s-s-h, filling the air full." Lacking proper support, Lyle ordered his men back. In the safety of the Federal trenches, one of Upton's men noted how "musket balls and grape flew over us like hail, but we laid very low, and none of our regiment were injured."[48]

Several Federals ducked into the gully midway across Saunders' Field for protection and were captured by pockets of rebels who had been marooned between the armies since early afternoon. It devel-

47. Haynes, *A History of the Tenth Regiment Vermont*, 64–65; Keifer, *Slavery and Four Years of War*, II, 83–86; Keifer's Report, in OR, Vol. XXXVI, Pt. 1, p. 731.

48. Andrew R. Linscott to parents, May 19, 1864, in Andrew R. Linscott Papers, MHS; Keiser Diary, in Harrisburg Civil War Round Table Collection, USMHI; Arthur A. Kent, ed., *Three Years with Company K: Sergeant Austin C. Stearns, Company K, 13th Massachusetts Infantry* (Rutherford, N.J., 1976), 258–60; Alfred S. Roe, *The Thirty-Ninth Regiment Massachusetts Volunteers, 1862–1865* (Worcester, Mass., 1914), 167–77; Harold Small, ed., *The Road to Richmond*, 132–33.

oped that this latest batch of Yankees were carrying canteens filled with whiskey, a scarce but popular commodity in Confederate ranks. Captors and prisoners made themselves "as sociable and comfortable as the situation would permit," wrote a rebel. After dark, the Confederates, well fortified with their unexpected plunder, braved skirmish fire and dodged back to their lines, Yankee prisoners in tow. According to a witness, the senior rebel officer leaned against a tree to deliver a "voluble and unsteady report," waxing eloquently about what he euphemistically termed his day's "separate operations." Under cover of darkness, soldiers from Maryland Steuart's two North Carolina regiments managed to haul the prized Union artillery pieces behind rebel lines.[49]

Darkness brought an end to the day's organized fighting, but the killing continued. In many places, opposing earthworks stood less than a hundred yards apart. Quick flashes of light from skirmish fire periodically stabbed into the darkness. "Shall that terrible night ever be erased from my memory," one of Pegram's soldiers asked years later, "the terrible groans of the wounded, the mournful sound of the owl and the awful shrill shrieks of the whippoorwill?" Ordered to establish a Confederate picket line in front of Pegram, Captain Samuel Buck collected a small force and crept into the inky night, "stumbling over the dead and dying [that] lay thicker than I ever saw them and [that were] hard to keep off . . . in the darkness." Sneaking to within speaking distance of enemy pickets, Buck ordered his soldiers to hold their fire. Across the way, he heard a Yankee captain giving similar orders. Of all the war's assignments, this was among the worst. A few jittery shots and both armies could open on each other again, blasting away madly in the darkness with their pickets in between, no one knowing when to stop. "I have seen whole lines of battle open fire," Buck recalled, "and keep it up for fifteen minutes

---

49. Howard, *Recollections*, 277–78. Howard, in *Recollections*, 280n15, observes that Confederate sources place the capture of the guns variously on May 5, 6, and 7. Union sources are similarly discrepant. The weight of authority supports May 5. See, for example, Richard S. Ewell's Report, in *OR*, Vol. XXXVI, Pt. 1, pp. 1070–71. See also Clark, comp., *Histories of the Several Regiments and Battalions from North Carolina*, I, 201: "After dark the two howitzers were brought in by details from the 1st and 3d North Carolina Regiments." According to Howard, "Whenever they were brought in, I remember the indignation of men at someone's having chalked on the guns, 'captured by Battle's brigade,' or to that effect. The guns were certainly fairly taken by Steuart's brigade."

when no enemy was in half mile of them and the only party suffering being their own skirmishers." [50]

This was a particularly risky time for picket duty. "All night," recounted a New Jersey chaplain, "we lay with arms in our hands, drawing a volley every few moments from the rebel skirmishers a few yards off." No one could sleep. Bodies were heaped on the far sides of trenches. Cries by wounded men for water went unheeded. Rescue parties shrank from the dark woods for fear of rekindling the holocaust that had abated temporarily with the setting sun. Inured as the soldiers had become to suffering, something about this Wilderness night touched the men in both the armies. "Usually there is not much groaning or outcry from wounded men on a battlefield," a rebel related in the matter-of-fact way of one knowledgeable about such things. "They do not feel acute pain, or else bear their sufferings in silence. But on this occasion circumstances seemed to make their situation peculiarly distressing, and their moans and cries were painful to listen to." On the field's far side, one of Robinson's Federals recorded his impressions. "There was no moon to light the clearing," he wrote, "only dim stars, and the air was hazy and pungent with the smoke and smell of fires yet smoldering. We couldn't see the wounded and dying, whose cries we heard all too clearly; nor could our stretcher bearers go out to find them and bring them in; the opposing lines were near, and the rebels were fidgety, and quick to shoot." A veteran from the Corn Exchange Regiment considered the unseen horrors of darkness almost as bad as Confederate guns. "Throughout the night," he penned years later, "as the fires, which had blazed since the early afternoon, drew nearer and nearer to the poor unfortunates who lay between the lines, their shrieks, cries and groans, loud, piercing, penetrating, rent the air, until death relieved the sufferer, or the rattle of musketry, that followed the advent of the breaking morn, drowned all the other sounds in its dominating roar." [51]

After the day's commotion had subsided, Warren met with Lieu-

---

50. Buck, *With the Old Confeds*, 104–105.

51. Alanson A. Haines, *History of the Fifteenth Regiment New Jersey*, 146; Howard, *Recollections*, 238; Harold Small, ed., *The Road to Richmond*, 134; Survivors' Association, *History of the Corn Exchange Regiment*, 403.

tenant Colonel Frederick T. Locke, his adjutant, and John J. Milhau, his chief surgeon, at the Lacy house to tally the day's losses. To the left of the grand entry hall was a high-ceilinged room that Warren had appropriated for his headquarters. The three men sat at a small table, illuminated by two tallow candles and a globe lantern high overhead on a mantel. Warren was still wearing his yellow sash but had laid his hat to the side.

Walking past, an aide caught sight of the general's pale face, which he noted was gloomy as usual. Milhau was calling out the aggregate casualty figures for the 5th Corps gleaned from data gathered at field hospitals. "It will never do, Locke, to make a showing of such heavy losses," Warren was saying. The aide, recently graduated from the military academy, stopped in his tracks. "It was the first time I had ever been present when an official report of this kind was being made," he later recounted, "and in my unsophisticated state of West Point truthfulness it drew my eyes to Warren's face with wonder, and I can see its earnest, mournfully solemn lines yet."[52]

For Warren, a day that had opened with rich promises of opportunity was closing on bitter notes of indecision and defeat. His corps' lackluster performance had been partially his fault and partially the result of events beyond his control. But responsibility remained his, and the general's reputation headed Meade's casualty list. The sight of the pale, self-important figure, apparently doctoring his casualty returns by candlelight, was a sad commentary on Warren's performance on the Orange Turnpike. Never again would the compulsive New Yorker command Grant's and Meade's unquestioning respect.

The real hero on this part of the battlefield was Ewell. Separated by miles of dense woodland from Lee, the excitable, balding corps commander had executed his discretionary assignment to perfection. He had displayed a fine sense of terrain, had selected a faultless battle line, and had risen to a masterly management of his reserves. Gordon and Daniel had gone in at precisely the right time and place to repel Wadsworth; Hays had deftly plugged the gap left by Stafford's repulse; and Pegram had extended Ewell's forces at the left at exactly the right moment to thwart Sedgwick's attempted turning movement. The attrition among 2nd Corps brigade commanders had been high, however. Jones was dead, and Stafford was fatally wounded. Pe-

---

52. Schaff, *The Battle of the Wilderness*, 209–10.

gram, during his repulse of Keifer, had received a nasty wound that knocked him out of action. But severe combat losses were nothing new to Stonewall Jackson's old command. With a little rest, Ewell's soldiers expected to be ready for the next day's fighting.

"A sort of duel between a Confederate brigade and a Federal division."

During the long afternoon of May 5, the Army of the Potomac's cavalry continued to flounder in their maneuvers. Philip Sheridan, Grant's protégé, was still chafing under Meade's conception of cavalry as guards for supply trains. A man of action, the energetic general wanted his cavalry in the thick of the fighting. "Smash 'em up, smash 'em up," he was always advising, and he desperately craved an opportunity to do just that. When it came to using cavalry, Meade was a Neanderthal in Sheridan's book, and Sheridan was not one to keep his feelings to himself.

The days' abortive Fredericksburg expedition fueled growing discontent between the temperamental army commander and Grant's equally testy favorite. Who first thought of the maneuver is not clear. As Humphreys later explained, Sheridan learned on May 4 that Stuart's main body of Confederate cavalry was camped below Fredericksburg at Hamilton's Crossing and "suggested that he should proceed against them." By Humphreys' account, Meade acquiesced.

Characteristically, the two men had different objectives in mind. Apparently Sheridan viewed the maneuver as an offensive operation to destroy Stuart's cavalry. Meade regarded the move as a preemptive strike to safeguard his supply trains. But whatever its purpose, a joint expedition of Gregg's and Torbert's divisions was slated to start for Fredericksburg first thing on May 5, as soon as Torbert could make his way across the Rapidan.[53]

The concerted strike, however, came to naught. Torbert spent the night on the Rapidan's north bank, just in case rebels tried to ambush the army from the rear. He started over at daylight, aiming to catch

---

53. Andrew A. Humphreys, *The Virginia Campaign,* 21, 36; Philip H. Sheridan's Report, in *OR,* Vol. XXXVI, Pt. 1, pp. 787–88. For an excellent summary of Federal cavalry movements, see "With the First New York Dragoons: From the Letters of Jared L. Ainsworth," ed. Richard Del Vechio, in Harrisburg Civil War Round Table Collection, USMHI.

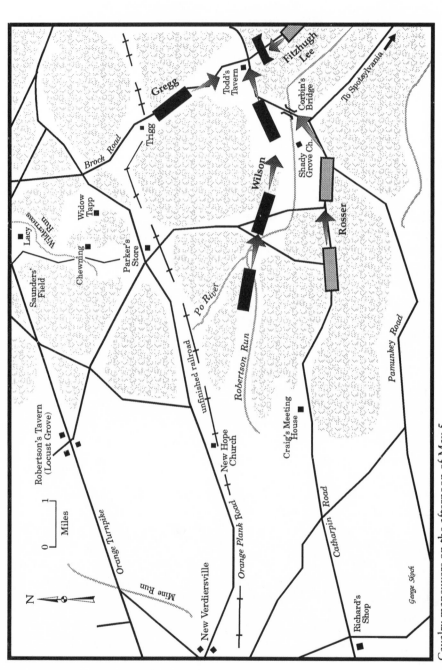

Cavalry maneuvers on the afternoon of May 5

up with Gregg at Chancellorsville. Roads below Ely's Ford, however, were clogged with supply wagons, and hours passed as Torbert's cavalrymen laboriously threaded through the trains. Torbert, who had only recently transferred from an infantry command, jostled along in excruciating pain because of an abscess near the tip of his spine. Bolts of pain racked his body with his horse's every step. It was noon before the tortured general finally reached Sheridan's headquarters near Piney Branch Church, approximately halfway between Chancellorsville and Todd's Tavern. By then, he had to relinquish command to Brigadier General Wesley Merritt, his senior brigadier. Making his way to a hospital tent, the debilitated general submitted to an operation under chloroform.[54]

Not only was Sheridan's proposed expedition by then half a day behind schedule but word arrived from Federal scouts that the quarry had escaped. While waiting for Torbert, Gregg had sent the 1st Maine and 2nd Pennsylvania toward Fredericksburg. "We struck the pike," recalled a Maine horseman, "and had a pleasant march." Only one small party of rebels was seen, and it melted into the underbrush. On reaching town, the Federals learned that Fitzhugh Lee's rebel division had started west and was circling below the armies to join Lee. A northerner summarized the situation in his diary: "Stuart reviewed the cavalry at Fredericksburg and we thought he was coming up to review us but he decided not to do so."[55]

With the object of his expedition gone, Sheridan had no choice but to cancel the planned advance. In retrospect, it was just as well that Torbert had been delayed. Had Sheridan started at first light as intended, most of his cavalry would have been squandered on a wild-goose chase, leaving Meade's wagons with no mounted escort at all.

Sometime around noon, Meade became concerned about the whereabouts of Wilson's cavalry division, which had left Parker's Store at daylight. Fearing that Wilson might be in trouble, Meade requested Sheridan to investigate.

With the Fredericksburg venture canceled, Sheridan had cavalry to spare and ordered Gregg to go in search of his missing division. Gregg was a sound choice. He was respected for "good judgment," according to a cavalryman. A reporter agreed that he was the "cool-

54. Alfred Torbert's Report, in OR, Vol. XXXVI, Pt. 1, p. 803.
55. Webb Diary, May 5, 1864, in Webb Papers, CL.

est man under trying circumstances I ever saw on the field." Todd's Tavern, at the intersection of Catharpin and Brock roads, was Gregg's initial objective. The move made sense on independent grounds. Hancock's shift northward had left a vacuum below the Union army. If the Confederates launched a sortie by way of Catharpin Road, they would have ready access to Hancock's vulnerable flank. As Sheridan saw it, Stuart's cavalry—and perhaps even Longstreet's infantry corps—could be advancing along Catharpin Road toward Todd's Tavern at that very moment. Sheridan wanted to have mounted troopers on hand to intercept them.[56]

To help Gregg plug the hole below Hancock, Sheridan advanced one of Torbert's brigades under George Custer toward Todd's Tavern. The Federal cavalry chief then dashed off a note informing Gregg that reinforcements were coming and sketched out his plans. "I will order General Wilson's division back to this place [Piney Branch Church] very early in the morning so that it may get ammunition, subsistence, and forage," he explained. "I will then relieve the other brigades of [Torbert's] Division and make them available should you be attacked."[57]

As it turned out, Wilson needed all the help he could get. The novice cavalryman had been trapped between Rosser's horsemen, to the south, and Hill's quick-stepping veterans, to the north. "I had had no word from Sheridan that day," Wilson later said in describing his predicament, "and knew absolutely nothing as to his whereabouts or even as to the position of any part of the army except my own." But there was a possible route to safety. Leading away from Wilson's position was an obscure forest track that ran parallel to Catharpin Road, now filled with Rosser's Confederates. Several miles east, the overgrown wagon trail hooked down to Catharpin Road. From there, Todd's Tavern was only two miles away. If Wilson hurried, he stood a fair chance of getting ahead of the Confederates. Urging their steeds forward with as much speed as the wooded path would permit, Wilson's horsemen—Chapman's brigade in front, then

---

56. Theodore F. Rodenbough, "Sheridan's Richmond Raid," in *B&L*, IV, 188; Tobie, *History of the First Maine Cavalry*, 252.

57. Sheridan, *Personal Memoirs*, I, 361; Sheridan's Report, in OR, Vol. XXXVI, Pt. 1, pp. 787–88; Philip H. Sheridan to Andrew A. Humphreys, May 5, 1864, in OR, Vol. XXXVI, Pt. 2, p. 427; Charles Forsyth to David McM. Gregg, May 5, 1864, in OR, Vol. XXXVI, Pt. 2, p. 429.

artillery, then Colonel John B. McIntosh's brigade bringing up the rear—raced eastward. It was a close call, particularly when Confederate scouts began harassing the rear of the Federal column. Wilson's horse Waif, a veteran of Vicksburg and Chattanooga, became spooked by the firing. Tugging violently at the reins, Wilson managed to bring Waif under control before he could bolt into the rebels.[58]

A homestead wishfully named Greenfield lay along Wilson's route. An inhabitant later recalled Yankees streaming past. "You have no idea what our feelings were when we first saw them, but they were too much frightened to do much then," she wrote. "However, they took William and sent down for Papa. Mama went up just as General Wilson ordered him on a horse. She begged him not to take Papa, and after a considerable time they concluded to leave him."[59]

Hot, sweaty, and winded, Wilson's lead brigade crossed the tiny Po River and turned onto Catharpin Road. Wilson's artillery and his remaining brigade followed closely behind. They had beaten Rosser to the junction, and the way lay clear to Todd's Tavern. But as Wilson, who was riding near the end of the Federal column, approached the intersection, rebel cavalry popped into sight. Madly spurring Waif, Wilson again barely avoided capture. His rear guard—the 18th Pennsylvania Cavalry under Lieutenant Colonel William P. Brinton—was not so fortunate. By the time Brinton arrived, the trail's junction with Catharpin Road was in rebel hands. Determined to force a way through, the Federals slammed into Rosser's troopers at full gallop, only to be driven back. Twice more the Yankees charged, and twice more they were repulsed. More Confederate horsemen appeared, convincing Brinton that it was impossible to break Rosser's hold on Catharpin Road. Melting into the woods, Brinton's cavalrymen blindly picked their way east. Late in the evening, they emerged safely onto Brock Road.[60]

Sometime after two in the afternoon, Gregg's lead elements reached the motley collection of dilapidated shacks that went by the name of Todd's Tavern. Wilson's breathless riders were just starting

---

58. James H. Wilson's Report, in *OR,* Vol. XXXVI, Pt. 1, p. 877; Wilson, *Under the Old Flag,* I, 383–84.

59. Maria Dobyns to ———, June 17, 1864, in "Greenfield," Book 50, FSMP.

60. Wilson's Report, in *OR,* Vol. XXXVI, Pt. 1, p. 877; Wilson, *Under the Old Flag,* I, 384; James H. Wilson to Andrew A. Humphreys, May 5, 1864, in *OR,* Vol. XXXVI, Pt. 2, p. 871.

to stream in. At 2:45, Gregg informed Sheridan of developments. "General Wilson is falling back to this point, followed by the enemy," he explained. "Colonel Chapman reports the enemy that attacked very superior to his [force] and compelled him to retire." Wilson himself had not yet arrived, added Gregg, "and I can't say what I will do." But the bearded Pennsylvanian, Sheridan's only experienced division head, closed on a fittingly bellicose note. "I have my command here and will receive the enemy."[61]

Actually, Gregg did more than he promised. Rather than merely waiting for Wilson, he dispatched two regiments out Catharpin Road to help detain the Confederates. Commanding was Brigadier General Henry E. Davies, Jr., a New York lawyer who had ripened into a superb cavalryman. Fresh Federals elbowed forward through Wilson's division, which was streaming toward Todd's Tavern in what one of Davies' colonels later termed a "very disordered state." About two miles from the tavern, near where Catharpin Road began sloping gently toward the Po, Davies' horsemen found the enemy. Rosser's Confederates, sabers flashing and pistols drawn, were ruthlessly flailing Wilson's rear guard. Davies ordered the 1st New Jersey's lead squad to charge. Unprepared, the southern cavaliers broke. Exuberant Jersey men pressed their advantage. In a flash, however, the rebels rallied, and soon it was Federals who were beating a retreat. To make matters worse for the northerners, a battery of rebel horse artillery appeared on the hills across the Po. Shells began screaming into the Union ranks. Advanced elements of the 1st Massachusetts, which had joined the New Jersey men at the front, bolted as rebels began shifting around their left flank. Darting back through a freshly plowed field, many of the dismounted troopers left their boots in the mud.[62]

Davies stood his ground, ordering John Kester, commanding the New Jersey regiment, to form his three remaining squadrons north of the roadway. The 1st Massachusetts was rallied into a line extending southward, and the 10th New York came up through the woods on the north side of the road. Advancing as a unit, the Union for-

61. David McM. Gregg to Charles Forsyth, May 5, 1864, in OR, Vol. XXXVI, Pt. 2, p. 429.

62. John Kester's Report, in OR, Vol. XXXVI, Pt. 1, p. 860; Thompson A. Snyder, "Recollections of Four Years with the Union Cavalry," in FSMP; William R. Lloyd, History of the First Regiment Pennsylvania Reserve Cavalry from Its Organization, August, 1861, to September, 1864 (Philadelphia, 1864), 90–91; Stanton P. Allen, Down in Dixie, 224–28.

mation loosed a deadly volley into the charging Confederates, then began firing rapidly at will. Rosser's impetus was broken. "Forward we moved," reported Kester, "as steadily as on parade, the rebels endeavoring to check us by showers of canister, but with no avail; and they hastily limbered their guns and fell back, just in time to prevent their capture." Kester's chaplain thrilled at the recollection of that "wild and resistless charge." The Federals swept on "without a halt or a check," he later explained, "over the dead and wounded rebels, crushing before them every attempt at a rally." Battling across the Po, the Yankees mounted the river's far bank. According to Davies, he drove Rosser back two miles. The Confederates conceded that the southern horsemen gave way, but termed Rosser's retreat a tactical withdrawal. Davies' troops had accomplished their objective. They had held the Confederates in check until Wilson's rear guard reached the safety of Todd's Tavern.[63]

Darkness ended the cavalry melee. Exhausted horsemen faced each other on Catharpin Road a few miles west of Todd's Tavern, probably from opposite sides of the Po. "Late this evening we had a spirited little fight on the banks of the Po, a sluggish little stream and one of the headwaters of the Mattapony," one rebel artilleryman wrote in his diary. "At first we repulsed the enemy and drove them across the Po and back on their infantry. Then and there they made a bold stand and successfully resisted our assault and further advance. We recrossed the little rivulet and camped for the night."[64]

While Rosser's Confederates were busy on Catharpin Road, Fitzhugh Lee's rebel cavalry division had worked over from Massaponax Church, where it had spent the night of the fourth. Passing through Spotsylvania Court House, Lee's division turned north on Brock Road toward the sound of fighting. About two miles below Todd's Tavern, the head of the rebel column encountered a finger of Federal cavalry that Gregg had thrust southward to protect his flank. According to Lee's adjutant, a "sharp skirmish" ensued, leaving two Confederates dead and twenty wounded. It was a minor affair, but it

---

63. Kester's Report, in OR, Vol. XXXVI, Pt. 1, p. 860; Preston, *History of the Tenth Regiment of Cavalry, New York State Volunteers*, 170–71; Pyne, *The History of the First New Jersey Cavalry*, 224–29. For the Confederate perspective, see Robert P. Chew's Report, in Leigh Collection, USMHI; McDonald, *A History of the Laurel Brigade*, 228–34; and Myers, *The Comanches*, 260–62.

64. Neese, *Three Years in the Confederate Horse Artillery*, 260–61.

defined the southern boundary of the Federal advance. That evening, Fitzhugh Lee's division linked up with Rosser, completing the containment of the Union cavalry.[65]

With Hancock's corps engaged on Orange Plank Road, the security of Meade's left flank was entirely in the hands of Sheridan's bluecoated horsemen. Gregg's weary riders planted themselves firmly across Catharpin Road, duly impressed with their assignment. Wilson's soldiers meanwhile snatched some badly needed rest in the rear. "Both men and horses were getting hungry," Wilson later wrote, "the country was equally bare of provisions and forage, and as we knew nothing yet of how it fared with the infantry, our third night was necessarily one of intense anxiety."[66]

At 6 P.M.—when Wilson was safely back in the Federal fold and Gregg was hotly dueling Rosser's fieldpieces on Catharpin Road—Meade sent Sheridan a message that reflected the commanding general's innate caution. The Union's left flank, stated Meade, rested at the intersection of Plank and Brock roads. He wanted Wilson and Gregg to keep close watch over the neighboring countryside and to protect the trains. "The infantry has been heavily pressed today along the whole line," added headquarters. "If you gain any information that leads you to conclude that you can take the offensive and harass the enemy without endangering the trains, you are at liberty to do so." But that was hardly the assignment that Sheridan wanted. Meade was again relegating his cavalry to baby-sit supply wagons and perform picket duty. Shortly after eleven, Sheridan let Meade know what he thought about his new orders. "I cannot do anything with the cavalry," he complained, "except to act on the defensive, on account of the immense amount of material and trains here and on the road to Ely's Ford. Had I moved to Hamilton's Crossing early this morning the enemy would have ruined everything." In closing, Sheridan repeated his constant refrain. "Why cannot infantry be sent to guard the trains and let me take the offensive?" But Meade had nothing more to say on the subject. For the morrow, Sheridan was to remain where he was, scouting off the lower Federal flank and keep-

---

65. Fitzhugh Lee's Report, in MC; William R. Carter Diary, May 5, 1864, in Hampden-Sydney College Library; Ferguson, "Memoranda," in Munford Collection, DU; Noble John Brooke Diary, May 5, 1864, in Noble John Brooke Collection, EU.

66. James H. Wilson to David McM. Gregg, May 5, 1864, in OR, Vol. XXXVI, Pt. 2, p. 468; Wilson's Report, *ibid.*, Pt. 1, p. 877.

ing a close eye for signs of rebel cavalry and Longstreet's worrisome veterans.[67]

With respect to the day's cavalry skirmish, both Wilson and Rosser claimed victory. According to a southern participant, the rolling fight had represented a "sort of duel between a Confederate brigade and a Federal division, in which the former had come out victorious." As the Confederates saw it, they had foiled Wilson's scouting mission and had cleared Catharpin Road of Yankees. They had stopped only when the enemy unsportingly threw in a second division. Wilson retailed a different and far less accurate version. In his official report, he erroneously claimed that "the Rebel force was considerably superior to ours." Later, when he penned his memoirs, he came up with an exceedingly self-serving account of the events. "We had been marching and fighting most of the time for two days and three nights," he explained, "swinging entirely around from the extreme right to the fartherest advanced post through field and forest in the midst of which the great battles of the Wilderness were fought. We had perfectly screened Grant's advance, engaging the enemy wherever we encountered him and making good our hold on the important points of the field."[68]

In point of fact, Wilson's expedition had been a fiasco. Not only had he neglected his single most important assignment—posting the roads toward Lee to warn if Confederates were approaching—but he had failed to keep Catharpin Road from the enemy, which left the Federal flank highly vulnerable. An impenetrable Confederate cavalry screen had been drawn over the countryside off Meade's left wing, affording the southerners wide latitude of maneuver. Longstreet's powerful 1st Corps, rumored to be advancing from that direction, could get a solid start at Meade before the Yankees had time to discover its location and to brace for the attack.

Rosser's horsemen had by all accounts given a superb performance, although some critics later asked whether they might not have been more aggressively employed. Lee had been almost as ticklish about his lines of communication as Meade had been about his.

67. Seth Williams to Philip H. Sheridan, May 5, 1864, in OR, Vol. XXXVI, Pt. 2, p. 428; Philip H. Sheridan to Andrew A. Humphreys, May 5, 1864, in OR, Vol. XXXVI, Pt. 2, p. 428.

68. McDonald, *A History of the Laurel Brigade*, 229; Wilson's Report, in OR, Vol. XXXVI, Pt. 1, p. 877; Wilson, *Under the Old Flag*, I, 384–85.

He was well aware that if the Federals severed the Army of Northern Virginia's connection with the Virginia Central Railroad, he stood to lose both his supplies and his escape route. Much as Meade had bound Sheridan to the Federal trains, Lee had tied Stuart to the Army of Northern Virginia's vulnerable underbelly to preserve the rebel army's communication with its base.

Lee's fixation on his lower flank might have unwittingly cost the Confederates a golden opportunity. A vigorous Confederate cavalry offensive in front of Hill's 3rd Corps column might have cleared Orange Plank Road of Federals and gained the Brock Road intersection before Getty or Hancock arrived. With the intersection in southern hands, Hancock would have been clipped from the rest of the Union army and unable to unite with Getty. Meade's entire left wing would have been jeopardized.

But missed possibilities aside, Stuart had every reason to be satisfied. Sheridan's cavalry had been neutralized and Catharpin Road was now clear for Longstreet to administer his long-awaited coup de grace.

One thing was certain. "The whole country between here and the Rapidan seems to be full of Yankees," wrote one of Rosser's Confederates as he stretched out on the hard ground for some rest, "and I expect that there will be some hot work in the fighting business tomorrow."[69]

"Everything in the army is to be put in."

A black, moonless night settled over Meade's camp. In places, patches of fire leapfrogged dangling vines and dead trees to erupt into blazing canopies of flame—"pulsing beacons over the dark woods," as one Federal recalled them.[70] Ambulances rumbled back from the front carrying loads that writhed under flickering torchlight. It was a lurid scene, the inevitable aftermath of the day's remorseless combat.

The Union armies formed a huge arc beginning near Germanna Ford and sweeping south across the turnpike and Orange Plank Road to a firm cavalry anchor near Todd's Tavern. Grant's tent was pitched

---

69. Neese, *Three Years in the Confederate Horse Artillery*, 260.
70. Schaff, *The Battle of the Wilderness*, 214.

in a hollow behind his command-post knoll, now littered with cigar butts and slivers of wood and gold-braided cloth. Two hundred yards away stood Meade's commodious tents. Flaps were thrown back, and colored lanterns hung on roadside poles to alert bustling couriers where to find the army's headquarters. Sedgwick's camp was on Spotswood Road, near the main track to Germanna Ford, and Warren occupied the Lacy house, plainly visible from Meade's and Grant's tents. A broad yard overflowed with orderlies, clerks, teamsters, servants, cooks, and sundry staff functionaries. The mildewed, dirty white canvas tops of some of the baggage and supply wagons of the 5th Corps cast bowed shadows on sleeping blue forms sprawled over the ground. Two miles south, Hancock had bivouacked on Orange Plank Road within a hundred yards of the fateful Brock Road junction. A mile or so farther on, massed on cleared high ground, was the 2nd Corps' artillery. Sheridan's cavalry prowled Brock Road as far as Todd's Tavern and encircled the army's supply trains at Chancellorsville.[71]

After the fighting quieted, Grant and his aides gathered at their mess table. When all the staffers completed relating what had happened on their portions of the field, the weary men walked outside and drew their chairs around a campfire. Congressman Washburne joined them, and soon Meade strolled over from his nearby bivouac and sat next to Grant.

As Grant's aide Porter recalled the conversation, the commander in chief began by expressing deep concern over the plight of the wounded soldiers. Difficult as it had been in daylight to penetrate the thickets and carry injured men to safety, at night it was virtually impossible. Bodies were invisible in the dark forest, and holding a lantern aloft spelled certain death. The slightest light or sound between battle lines was guaranteed to initiate an avalanche of firing.

Talk around the campfire turned to the day's events, which Grant viewed as a prelude to the real fighting that was to occur the following morning. "As Burnside's corps, on our side, and Longstreet's, on the other side, have not been engaged," he remarked, "and the troops of both armies have been occupied principally in struggling through thickets and fighting for position, today's work has not been much of a test of strength." Grant had no complaints about the Army of the

71. *Ibid.*, 211–14.

Potomac's performance, or at least none that he cared to voice. "I feel pretty well satisfied with the result of the engagement," he added, "for it is evident that Lee attempted by a bold movement to strike this army in flank before it could be put into line of battle and be prepared to fight to advantage; but in this he has failed." [72]

Discussion also drifted to the next day's plans. Grant had definite ideas. This time, there would be no sending of brigades, divisions, and corps into battle piecemeal. Lee had selected this spot to fight, and soon he would learn what fighting really meant. All four Union corps—Hancock's, Sedgwick's, Warren's, and Burnside's—were slated to heave forward in unison. The secessionists would be flattened like dough under a rolling pin.

Actually, as Grant's plan matured, the next morning's agenda for Lee's destruction acquired more sophistication than that of a simple all-out push. In its broader sweep, the idea was to continue the dual-front maneuver that had been halted by nightfall. Sedgwick and Warren were to renew their attack against Ewell as a diversion to occupy the Confederate 2nd Corps. The real action would meanwhile occur on Hancock's front. At 4:30 A.M., the Pennsylvanian was to attack with Getty's troops and his own corps, holding one division in reserve to watch his southern flank. Simultaneously, Wadsworth would continue his pincer movement against Hill's northern flank and close the vice that had been put in place late in the afternoon. To ensure success, Burnside's two strongest divisions were to plunge between the rebel wings, then shift southward and bludgeon Hill's flank, adding weight to Wadsworth's attack. It was an excellent plan, one that capitalized on the Federal army's impressive edge in numbers. On the face of it, there seemed to be no room for failure. [73]

During the evening, Meade issued the orders necessary to implement his portion of the attack. At eight o'clock, a circular went out directing every man "capable of bearing arms" to report "at the front before daylight tomorrow morning." Troops temporarily assigned to supply trains were to return to their commands. "For the present," emphasized the circular, "the trains must be protected by the cavalry, and every man who can shoulder a musket must be in the ranks." Since most of the army's artillery was useless, cannoneers were temporarily pressed into infantry service. Meade directed his artillery

---

72. Horace Porter, *Campaigning with Grant*, 53–54.
73. Comstock Diary, May 5, 1864, in LC; Horace Porter, *Campaigning with Grant*, 54.

chief, Brigadier General Henry J. Hunt, to "order all the regiments and detachments of heavy artillery, as well as train guards of your command, to report at these headquarters to yourself before daylight." Meade also instructed his corp commanders in their roles. Hancock was to continue over his own corps and Getty's division. "You are required to renew the attack at 4:30 tomorrow morning, keeping a sharp lookout on your left," Meade directed his 2nd Corps head. "Your right will be relieved by an attack made at the same time by General Wadsworth's division and two divisions of General Burnside's corps." At the same time, instructions were sent to Warren. As soon as Burnside arrived, Warren was to assemble his augmented corps—without, of course, Wadsworth's division and Baxter's brigade, which would continue their flanking operation against Hill—and at 4:30 A.M., he was to "renew the attack on Orange Court-House pike, where you attacked today." Sedgwick also undoubtedly received orders to advance in tandem with Warren. Later that evening, one of Sedgwick's division commanders notified his brigadiers to see that their troops had a "full supply of ammunition" for the morning. The attack was to be announced by a blast from a bugle.[74]

Grant meanwhile made certain that Burnside knew exactly what to do. "Lieutenant-General Grant desires that you start your two divisions (Stevenson and Potter) at 2:00 A.M. tomorrow punctually for this place," wrote Grant's aide Comstock from the command tent near Wilderness Tavern. The directive left nothing to debate. "You will put them in position between the Germanna Plank Road and the road leading from [Wilderness Tavern] to Parker's Store, so as to close the gap between Warren and Hancock, connecting both. You will move from this position on the enemy beyond at 4:30 A.M., the time at which the Army of the Potomac moves." In only one particular was Burnside granted discretion. "If you think there is no enemy in Willcox's front," continued Comstock, referring to Burnside's other available division, "bring him also."[75]

Around 10 P.M., Meade met with his corps heads and Burnside.

74. Seth Williams' Circular, in *OR*, Vol. XXXVI, Pt. 2, p. 406; Seth Williams to Henry J. Hunt, May 5, 1864, *ibid.*; George G. Meade to Winfield S. Hancock, 1864, *ibid.*, 412; George G. Meade to Gouverneur K. Warren, May 5, 1864, *ibid.*, 415; Henry Dalton's Orders, *ibid.*, 421.

75. Cyrus B. Comstock to Ambrose E. Burnside, May 5, 1864, in *OR*, Vol. XXXVI, Pt. 2, p. 425.

The overall attack plan was discussed, as well as each corps' role. According to an aide, after Meade's review of the projected offensive, Burnside rose grandly to his feet. The commander of the 9th Corps cut an impressive figure. His oversized moustache tumbled past his mouth to his chops, then swept dramatically up to his ears. He represented, thought the aide, "the California peach-class of men, handsome, ingratiating manners, and noted for a soldierly bearing." Burnside, throwing his shoulders back, assumed a thoughtful look. He declared resoundingly, "Well, then, my troops shall break camp by half-past two!" The assembled generals did not miss the fact that Burnside had added a half hour to the starting time assigned by Grant. The deviation, however, did not seem of consequence to the 9th Corps commander. With measured step, he threw open Meade's tent flap and strode into the night. As soon as he disappeared, knowing looks passed around the table. Meade's chief of engineers, Major James C. Duane, leaned forward and stroked his rusty beard. "He won't be up—I know him well," Duane reportedly whispered. Although Burnside had handled his troops with dispatch so far in the campaign, his "genius for slowness," to use Lyman's turn of phrase, was part of the army's lore, and Meade's generals were inclined to think the worst of him.[76]

Burnside's participation was critical. Without the weight of his fresh divisions, there was no guarantee that Hill would collapse, particularly if the Confederates continued to fight as they did on the fifth. In addition, there was the chance that Longstreet might arrive. In that event, Burnside's corps would certainly be necessary to ensure a Union victory.

A solution occurred to the somber corps heads, and they recommended it to Meade. If Burnside could not be hurried, then perhaps the attack could be delayed to give him more leisure to maneuver into place.

Meade took his generals' suggestion to heart. At 10:30 P.M., he sent Grant a short, diplomatic note asking that the morning's attack be postponed. He tactfully danced around the reason for the request.

---

76. Schaff, *The Battle of the Wilderness*, 225–27. William Marvel questions the veracity of Schaff's reporting and argues that the Army of the Potomac's commanders were unfairly predisposed to view Burnside in an unfavorable light. See William Marvel, *Burnside* (Chapel Hill, N.C., 1991), 351–52.

"After conversing with my corps commanders," wrote Meade, "I am led to believe that it will be difficult, owing to the dense thicket in which their commands are located, the fatigued condition of the men rendering it difficult to rouse them early enough, and the necessity of some daylight, to properly put in reinforcements." Assuring Grant that he had ordered the attack for 4:30 A.M., he added that he was "of the opinion it will be more likely to be simultaneous if made at 6," and he sought permission to shift the hour. Meade also expressed concern over Longstreet's expected arrival and asked for additional assistance from the 9th Corps. "I have notified Hancock to look out for his left," Meade informed his boss, "but think it will be well to have Willcox up as soon as possible." Grant's reply, penned by his secretary, William Rowley, was delivered to Meade before midnight. Meade could have an extra thirty minutes to prepare, but no more. Otherwise, wrote Rowley, Grant feared "that if delayed until 6 o'clock the enemy will take the initiative, which he desires specially to avoid." The additional troops Meade had requested from the 9th Corps would most likely be forthcoming. "General Burnside is directed to bring up General Willcox's division with his other troops if they can possibly be spared, and will probably bring them," was the aide's statement.[77]

Meanwhile Warren, whose 5th Corps was designated to partici-pate in both the turnpike and the Orange Plank Road attacks, sent his aide Roebling to Grant's headquarters to find out how he should coordinate movements with Burnside. Roebling located Comstock, the tall, sedate former West Point engineering instructor handling 9th Corps matters for Grant, and discovered that headquarters had not fully planned Burnside's role. As the two aides examined how best to employ Burnside, two options emerged: the 9th Corps could join Wadsworth and bolster his flank attack against Hill, or it could push straight ahead, capture the Chewning farm, and swoop down on Hill's rear. The latter course promised to inflict the greater dam-age if successful. But if Burnside failed to carry the heights, his corps would be wasted and Wadsworth would be deprived of crucial rein-

---

77. George G. Meade to Ulysses S. Grant, May 5, 1864, in OR, Vol. XXXVI, Pt. 2, pp. 404–405; William Rowley to George G. Meade, May 5, 1864, ibid., 405. "The attack for the morrow [May 6] was put off until 5:30, to give Burnside time to be in position to go in on Hill's left flank" (Lyman Journal, May 5, 1864, in Lyman Papers, MHS).

forcements. According to Roebling's account, Grant elected the alternative with the larger potential gain. While the Army of the Potomac attacked Ewell and Hill, Burnside was to plow between the enemy wings, take the Chewning farm, and then burrow into Hill's rear, completing the destruction of the Confederate 3rd Corps. To help Burnside find his way, Roebling agreed to accompany the 9th Corps to the Chewning farm in the morning.[78]

Although it was after midnight, the tireless Warren continued sending instructions to his division heads. "Everything in the army is to be put in," he ordered. Wadsworth was to pursue his present course, placing his division "on a line northeast and southwest" and advancing "directly southeast on the flank of the enemy in front of General Hancock." The rest of the corps was to form a tight line across the Orange Turnpike, with Crawford's division on the left and Griffin's on the right. "When you march forward," Warren reminded Crawford, "let your line of march be due west and your line of battle perpendicular [to the turnpike]. Keep closed in toward General Griffin on your right, and double back your left, so as to prevent a flank fire from any force you may drive back." A companion directive ordered Griffin, soon to be reinforced by Colonel Ira Spaulding's 50th New York Engineers, to advance in tandem with Crawford. "Don't fail to move out, all prepared, at 5:00 A.M.," reminded Warren. "I am at the Lacy house and can be seen at any time." In reserve, just in case things went wrong, were Robinson's two remaining units—the Maryland brigade and Lyle's troops—augmented by four heavy-artillery batteries brought over from Chancellorsville and containing some 2,400 effectives.[79]

Sedgwick's 6th Corps also spent the remainder of the night preparing for battle. Wright, whose division was to advance simultaneously with Warren, connected his leftmost regiment with the northern end of Warren's line just above the Orange Turnpike. Ricketts' entire division was reunited with the 6th Corps, as was Brigadier General Alexander Shaler's small brigade, which had been detached

78. Roebling's Report, in Warren Collection, NYSA.

79. Gouverneur K. Warren to Charles Griffin, May 6, 1864, in OR, Vol. XXXVI, Pt. 2, pp. 455–56; Gouverneur K. Warren to James S. Wadsworth, May 6, 1864, ibid., 458; Gouverneur K. Warren to Samuel W. Crawford, May 6, 1864, ibid., 457.

earlier to help guard supply trains. For the morning's fight, Sedgwick would have his entire corps, with the exception of Getty's three brigades, which were to remain at Orange Plank Road with Hancock.[80]

Throughout the night, Hancock remained busy reorganizing his large command for the main attack against Hill. Alert to the possibility of a surprise by Longstreet, he stoutly anchored his left flank with a contingent under the tough John Gibbon, who was given Barlow's division and most of the 2nd Corps' artillery. Gibbon placed the 2nd Corps' pieces on a cleared rise near the Trigg farm on Brock Road, from where they could easily cover possible Confederate approaches. Nelson Miles's brigade was concentrated to form a barrier across Brock Road facing south to protect against a Confederate attack from that direction. Plenty of advance warning, of course, could be expected from Gregg's augmented cavalry patrols. Gibbon then positioned the remaining infantry brigades of Colonel Paul Frank, Brooke, and Smyth behind earthworks that formed a continuous line along the western side of Brock Road, extending north from the Trigg farm to Orange Plank Road. These defensive positions were virtually impregnable.

The 2nd Corps commander, satisfied that his flank was secure, then assembled an impressive offensive array. Four divisions—Mott's, Birney's, Gibbon's, and Getty's—were massed along Orange Plank Road. Birney was placed in immediate command of the offensive force. He had handled Mott's division as well as his own during the fighting of May 5; for the sixth, he was to have Gibbon's and Getty's as well.

To give the attack depth, Birney organized his force into three lines. The brigades of McAllister, Ward, and Hays—Birney's old division with a unit thrown in from Mott's—made up the first line. They were positioned below Orange Plank Road in anticipation that Wadsworth's men would swing in from the north when the battle opened. The second line was constituted by Getty's men and Mott's remaining brigade, with Eustis and Wheaton placed north of the roadway and Lewis Grant and Brewster extending below it. Gibbon's division formed the assault column's third line and its reserve. Owen's

---

80. Reed Diary, May 5, 1864, in Ricketts Collection, Manassas National Battlefield Park; Henry R. Dalton's Report, in OR, Vol. XXXVI, Pt. 1, p. 660.

and Carroll's brigades were stationed on each side of the road, while Webb remained in the rear, ready to shift wherever he was needed.[81]

For Wadsworth's command, poised above Hill's northern flank, it was a sleepless night. After dark, the gray-haired New Yorker discovered that he was nearly out of ammunition and had ordered an aide, Robert Monteith, to procure a supply. Monteith, guiding himself by the North Star, had successfully reached the Lacy house and the army's supply wagons. His return trip was another matter. Leading a train of servants and pack mules carrying twenty thousand rounds, Monteith had worked south through the woods. Ahead were fires and moving troops. Sensing trouble, he crept forward. A rebel camp lay before him. Monteith had drifted to the right and nearly delivered Wadsworth's ammunition into Hill's hands. Stealthily retracing his steps, he found his way back to the Lacy fields, then reentered the woods farther east. In the meantime, Wadsworth had posted a string of sentinels to link his division with headquarters. It was 3 A.M. when Monteith got back, barely leaving time to distribute the ammunition. "This was the most anxious night spent during my service," Monteith acknowledged after the war.[82]

By the sun's first glow, preparations had been completed to realize Grant's grand formula for ending the war. Closely coordinate maneuvers were scheduled to click into place simultaneously at five o'clock, sending the combined Federal force forward in a sheet of flame. Wagons had been left entirely in Sheridan's hands, freeing every possible combat soldier. Troops whose primary service was no longer needed—engineers and artillerymen, for example—had been pressed into frontline duty. While over five Federal divisions neutralized Ewell's three, seven more were poised to crush Hill's two. If the movement was properly executed, Hill's destruction should be accomplished before Longstreet could arrive. And just in case Lee's War Horse showed up unexpectedly, another Federal division was waiting in reserve. It was a fine, meaty plan that went for the big stakes, and Grant was rightfully proud of it.

---

81. Hancock's Report, in *OR*, Vol. XXXVI, Pt. 1, p. 321; John Gibbon's Report, *ibid.*, 430; Francis A. Walker, *History of the Second Army Corps*, 420; Albert N. Ames Diary, May 5, 1864, in NYSA.
82. Robert Monteith, "Battle of the Wilderness," in *War Papers . . . Wisconsin*, I, 412–13.

Some factors, of course, were not to the commander in chief's liking—the battlefield in particular, which was as awkward place for fighting as one could imagine—but Grant could not change those things, and they were unlikely to affect the battle's outcome in any event. What was important was that Grant had finally arranged for every available Union soldier to fight in combinations that promised to confront the enemy with irresistible numbers. Never before had a Union general in the east concentrated his entire force against Lee. The details of Grant's plan might be criticized, but in the main his scheme represented an innovative attempt to turn the circumstances to his advantage.

How had Grant's war machine fared on its first day of combat? On balance, the Army of the Potomac had faltered, largely as a result of ill-considered command decisions at the higher levels. The fighting of May 5 had been disjointed, with no carefully reasoned purpose. Burnside had been neglected, Warren's offensive had involved only two Federal divisions, Sedgwick had assaulted alone, and Getty had initiated his attack without support. Hancock, try as he might, had never been able to bring his whole command into play. The fact that Hancock, considered one of the finest soldiers in either army, had been unable to defeat Hill's smaller force was largely a consequence of awkward timing imposed on him from above.

But even allowing for Grant's sloppy coordination, there was still something about the quiet man's style that promised a new era of warfare in Virginia. The untried Federal command structure had faltered, and the general-in-chief had impatiently pushed the reconstituted Army of the Potomac to its limits. But a distinctive mode of combat was emerging. The grinding, relentless waves of attacks that had rocked Orange Plank Road hour after hour had no precedent, unless it lay in the same single-minded determination that had starved Vicksburg into submission. Grant would keep trying until he got it right.

"The 5th, then, must be adjudged a day of lost opportunities, lost chiefly by the impatience of the Union commander," concluded a British student of Grant's 1864 campaign. "But this first day of battle had certainly impressed every officer with the fact that the command was in strong hands. There was something remorseless even in Grant's mistakes." Morning would show whether Grant had devised a plan that could defeat Lee.[83]

At 11 P.M., still sitting around the crackling campfire, Grant remarked to his staff, "We shall have a busy day tomorrow, and I think we had better get all the sleep we can tonight. I am a confirmed believer in the restorative qualities of sleep, and always like to get at least seven hours of it, though I have often been compelled to put up with much less." Congressman Washburne responded, "It is said that Napoleon often indulged in only four hours of sleep, and still preserved all the vigor of his mental faculties." Grant had an answer for him. "If the truth were known," he replied, "I have no doubt it would be found that he made up for his short sleep at night by taking naps during the day." And with that, the Federal commander in chief retired to his tent.[84]

*"I supposed somebody
knew how things stood."*

For Lee even more than for Grant, May 5 had been a harrowing day. But Lee's strong point was flexibility. Some time toward 5 P.M., as waves of Federals battered Hill's thin line, Lee decided to revise his overall strategy. Initially, he had hoped to channel Longstreet out Catharpin Road to execute one of those spectacular flank attacks that the Army of Northern Virginia habitually served up with flair. Rosser's cavalry had paved the way for Longstreet, but it was starting to look as if Hill might not be able to hold. If his line collapsed, the Confederate army would be jeopardized. Lee was ready to take chances, but considering Grant's unusual pugnacity, leaving Hill unsupported invited disaster. Accordingly, the southern strategist redefined Longstreet's role. Rather than sending him against Meade's left flank, Lee decided to shift his War Horse to Orange Plank Road and to bring him up directly in Hill's support.

83. Atkinson, *Grant's Campaigns of 1864 and 1865,* 164.
84. Horace Porter, *Campaigning with Grant,* 54–55.

Lee dispatched his trusted aide Charles Venable to find Longstreet. Trotting back to Parker's Store, Venable cut south on a side road—probably the same track Wilson had followed early that morning at the start of his ill-fated expedition. He found Catharpin Road and then turned west. Continuing past Craig's Meeting House and debris left by the day's cavalry battles, he reached the crossroads hamlet of Richard's Shop. There he found Longstreet.[85]

Longstreet's 1st Corps veterans had logged some impressive marching since leaving Gordonsville. Most of the units had started around 4 P.M. on the fourth and had trudged between ten and sixteen miles to Brock's Bridge, on the North Anna. Resuming early the next morning, they had covered another sixteen miles to Richard's Shop. "All day we marched along unused roads," recalled a soldier, "through field and thickets, taking every near cut possible." Longstreet's men had tramped thirty-two miles in twenty-four hours, but they were still almost ten miles short of the battlefield. On reaching Richard's Shop, the exhausted Confederates collapsed. Few bothered to pitch tents.[86]

The sight of winded soldiers settling into bivouac greeted Venable as he rushed up with Lee's change of marching orders. The 1st Corps was to cut through the woods, Venable explained to Longstreet, and hook up with Hill's 3rd Corps on Orange Plank Road. "My message to you," Venable reminded Longstreet in a postwar letter, "was to reach General Lee's position as soon as practicable on the morning of the 6th. 'By daylight,' was the order as I remember it." Although faithfully conveying Lee's message, Venable apparently neglected to impress on Longstreet the need for haste. As a consequence, Longstreet continued to wait while the remainder of his troops straggled

85. Charles S. Venable to James Longstreet, July 25, 1879, in Longstreet Collection, DU. Longstreet, *From Manassas to Appomattox*, 557.

86. On the timing of Longstreet's march from Mechanicsville to Richard's Shop, see Robert F. Davis Diary, May 4–5, 1864, in EU; J. B. Clifton Diary, May 4–5, 1864, in NCDAH; and Robert T. Coles, "History of the Fourth Alabama Regiment," in Regimental Collection, ADAH. Coles noted that the 4th Alabama "moved out at 4:00 P.M. on the 4th, marched twelve miles by dark, rested and fed and resumed the march, which extended without intermission through the night and all of the 5th until sundown, having marched 36 miles." G. Moxley Sorrel and Porter Alexander recalled that the head of the 1st Corps column reached Richard's Shop around 3 P.M. on the fifth. See G. Moxley Sorrel Diary, May 5, 1864, in MC; and Edward P. Alexander to father, May 29, 1864, in Edward P. Alexander Collection, SHC.

in. Most of them had arrived by dark. Then he decided to rest his soldiers a bit longer so they would be fresh for the next day's fighting. He issued orders to resume the march at 1 A.M. "The accounts we had of the day's work were favorable to the Confederates," Longstreet later explained, "but the change of direction of our march was not reassuring."[87]

Venable returned to the battlefield before dark. Lee, as the aide recalled it, was increasingly "anxious." The general expressed concern to Stuart, who promised to inform Longstreet "about the condition of things and the importance of getting up to us at the earliest possible hour in the morning." At the least, Field's division of Longstreet's Corps had to be told "to move immediately to reinforce Heth and Wilcox." But rather than going himself the cavalry commander directed his chief of staff, Major Henry B. McClellan, to convey the order to Field as quickly as possible. Tearing back along Venable's earlier route, McClellan found Field's camp. The general was sitting in front of a table. He was a "tall, portly looking man, of fine military bearing," thought a soldier, "and with a face that would be deemed remarkably handsome, but that the chin is somewhat too receding, a defect which is exaggerated in appearance by a heavy black moustache." The remains of his dinner had just been removed. Field politely listened as McClellan explained that Lee wanted him to start at once to relieve Hill. A stickler for military etiquette, the one-armed general was reluctant to act solely on McClellan's say-so. Grumbling that his troops needed rest after a hard day's march and that he had intended to start at 1 A.M., Field nonetheless began preparations for an earlier start. Offended by Field's "cold and formal" reception, McClellan withdrew and waited for his horse to catch its breath for the return journey. Half an hour later, Field summoned McClellan. He had just received another order from Longstreet directing him to begin at 1:00 A.M., he explained, and he was not about to override Longstreet's orders on oral directions from a roving cavalryman. McClellan was incensed. Longstreet's headquarters were three miles farther back, the cavalryman pointed out. The War Horse had no

---

87. Charles S. Venable to James Longstreet, July 25, 1879, in Longstreet Papers, DU; Longstreet, *From Manassas to Appomattox*, 557. Venable added, "On looking at it at this distance, I cannot [distinguish] satisfactorily between the words 'daybreak' and 'sunrise,' though I think 'daybreak' is right."

idea of the urgency for haste. "General Field's reply has never escaped my memory," wrote McClellan more than ten years later. "It was, 'I prefer to obey General Longstreet's order.'" Instead of seeking out Longstreet, McClellan angrily rode back to report Field's insubordination to Lee.[88]

In the meantime, Lee had been pondering how best to employ Ewell's corps. "General Longstreet and General Anderson are expected up early," Lee's aide Lieutenant Colonel Charles Marshall informed Ewell, "and unless you see some means of operating against their right"—referring to an assault on Meade's northern flank, which Sedgwick's evening attacks had made highly unlikely—"the General wishes you to support our right." Ewell's answer came back an hour later. His men had battled off Warren and Sedgwick. They had repulsed every Federal attack "handsomely," and Ramseur's brigade, on assignment in the rear, had now arrived. Ewell properly considered his day a success. "We have a large number of prisoners and our loss is not large, I am thankful to say, though we have to regret General Jones' death. I am entrenched along my whole line and can hold it. Special praise is due Brigadier-Generals Gordon and Daniel for their brilliant services today." Ewell was still uncertain, however, about what to do in the morning and solicited Lee's advice. "If I attack at daylight," wrote the Confederate 2nd Corps commander, "I will attack Sedgwick with Johnson supported by Ramseur."[89]

Armed with concrete intelligence about Ewell's situation, along with Venable's report placing Longstreet at Richard's Shop, Lee had sufficient information to complete the coming day's plans. Presumably Longstreet and Anderson would arrive before dawn and relieve Hill's fought-out divisions. That would enable Hill to shift northward and plug the bothersome gap between the two rebel wings. Rather than focusing Ewell southward, concluded Lee, it would be better for him to attack out the turnpike at morning's first light. Ideally, Ewell would rout Sedgwick and snap Grant's supply line. But

88. Venable to Longstreet, July 25, 1879, in Longstreet Papers, DU; Henry B. McClellan, "The Wilderness Fight: Why General Lee's Expectations of Longstreet Were Not Realized," Philadelphia *Weekly Times*, January 26, 1878; "Our Army Correspondence," *Daily South Carolinian*, May 10, 1864.

89. Charles Marshall to Richard S. Ewell, May 5, 1864, in OR, Vol. XXXVI, Pt. 2, p. 953; Richard S. Ewell to Robert E. Lee, May 5, 1864, *ibid.*, Vol. LI, Pt. 2 Supplement, pp. 889–90.

even if the Federals held, Ewell would fulfill the important secondary objective of keeping Sedgwick and Warren occupied, which would simplify Longstreet's and Hill's work on Orange Plank Road.

Lee's orders to Ewell do not appear in the official record. Judging from what happened the next day, however, he undoubtedly instructed Ewell to resume his offensive at 4:30 A.M. Ewell, exhibiting the same initiative that had characterized his actions thus far, rearranged his brigades to deliver a hard push. Gordon was shifted to the far north of Ewell's line, by Flat Run, and was aligned with the rest of Early's troops. Artillery was stationed in Gordon's support. Jones's men, still stunned by the day's events and by their commander's death, were put back into formation on the turnpike. Rodes's division remained below the roadway, while Johnson's and Early's extended above it. Throughout the night, Ewell's troops chopped trees to strengthen their earthworks.[90]

A very different situation prevailed in Hill's sector. Unlike Ewell, Hill lacked the advantage of a continuous fortified line. Battered for hours by powerful Federal attacks, Little Powell's troops had been fragmented into clusters. They huddled behind logs, rocks, and jerry-rigged earthworks facing in every direction. In this confused tangle of trenches, blue-coated and gray-coated soldiers constantly blundered into each other's works. There was no definable Confederate battle formation. As Heth put it, "Wilcox's troops and my own were terribly mixed up." Wilcox said his line was "very irregular and much broken and required to be rearranged." A rebel sharpshooter accurately summed up the situation. Hill's divisions, he recalled, "lay in the shape of a semicircle, exhausted and bleeding, with but little order or distinctive organization." The Confederate formation, such as it was, could never withstand a concerted attack.[91]

Heth and Wilcox made their way together to Hill's tent. The ailing Confederate 3rd Corps commander was camped in Widow Tapp's field, just off Orange Plank Road and next to the hub of

90. Ewell to Lee, May 5, 1864, in *OR*, Vol. LI, Pt. 2 Supplement, pp. 889–90.
91. Morrison, ed., *The Memoirs of Henry Heth*, 184; Wilcox, "Lee and Grant in the Wilderness," in *The Annals of the War*, 494; Dunlop, *Lee's Sharpshooters*, 32.

Poague's rightmost gun. As Hill's chief of staff, Palmer, remembered the conversation, Heth and Wilcox reported that their lines sprawled "at every angle" and would be difficult to straighten. Hill instructed his two division commanders to leave their troops alone, emphasizing that "General Lee's orders were to let the men rest as they were." By way of explanation, Hill added that "General Longstreet would be up by, or soon after, midnight, and would form in the rear of the line before daylight." The plan was "to let the men of the 3rd Corps fall back after Longstreet's troops were in position—Longstreet's troops in the first line for the next day, Anderson's division of the 3rd Corps and the other divisions forming a second line."[92]

Heth's memory of the conversation differed somewhat from Palmer's, but not substantially. As Heth recalled it, Hill was sick and remained on his campstool by the fire. When Heth approached, the frail corps commander extended a friendly hand and said, "Your division has done splendidly today; its magnificent fighting is the theme of the entire army." Nonplussed, Heth replied, "Yes, the division has done splendid fighting, but we have other matters to attend to just now." After describing the intermingling of his and Wilcox' troops, Heth suggested, "Let me take one side of the road and form a line of battle, and Wilcox the other side and do the same; we are so mixed, and lying at every conceivable angle, that we cannot fire a shot without firing into each other. A skirmish line could drive both my divisions and Wilcox's, situated as we are now. We shall certainly be attacked early in the morning." According to Heth, Hill responded, "Longstreet will be up in a few hours. He will form in your front. I don't propose that your division shall do any fighting tomorrow, the men have been marching and fighting all day and are tired. I do not wish them disturbed."[93]

Wilcox, after another close look at his disordered lines, decided to press the matter farther. Around 9 P.M., he went to Lee's tent, which was pitched nearby in Widow Tapp's field. He intended to recommend that Hill leave only a skirmish line, and that his own troops retire to a more defensible position. As Wilcox stepped inside, Lee stated that he had just finished a complimentary report on Wilcox' and Heth's divisions. A note had also come in from Anderson,

92. Royall, *Some Reminiscences*, 30.
93. Morrison, ed., *The Memoirs of Henry Heth*, 184.

added Lee, and he exuberantly held the message aloft for Wilcox to see. Anderson intended to bivouac at Verdiersville that night, explained the army commander, "but he had been instructed to move forward; he and Longstreet will be up, and the two divisions that have been so actively engaged will be relieved before day." Hearing this welcome news—essentially confirming what Hill had said earlier—Wilcox broached nothing about the condition of his lines and made no effort to rectify them.[94]

Shortly after Wilcox left, McClellan returned from his frustrating encounter with Field. Lee had just sat down to a late supper. Still in a huff, the cavalryman described his rude reception. Rather than arriving at 1 A.M., Longstreet would only then be setting out. That meant he would barely be in place before sunrise. Impressed with the situation's gravity, McClellan volunteered to ride back with written orders from Lee. The imperturbable general-in-chief demurred. "No, major," he said, "it is now past ten, and by the time you could return to General Field and he could put his division in motion, it would be one o'clock, and at that hour he will move."[95]

Apparently Lee changed his mind, however, and sent a third courier—Catlett C. Taliaferro—with instructions to find Longstreet "and urge him to use the utmost diligence in coming to his assistance." On receiving Lee's latest directive, Longstreet instructed Taliaferro, "Go back to General Lee and tell him that I shall be with him at daylight and do anything he wants done." In parting, Taliaferro cautioned, "The Yankees are on this road and you had better be careful." Longstreet responded, "You be off, sir, and give my message to General Lee. I will take care of any Yankees on this road."[96]

As the night wore on with no sign of Longstreet, concern over Hill's fractured lines continued to haunt the 3rd Corps leadership. Around 11 P.M., an incident dramatized Hill's vulnerability. Soldiers from one of Lane's regiments, the 18th North Carolina, were still trying to slip back into the rebel position. An officer of the regiment worked his way over to Orange Plank Road, then walked straight up the roadway into the Confederate lines. Recognizing Wilcox, he ran up to the general. He had just broken through Hancock's corps, he

94. Wilcox, "Lee and Grant in the Wilderness," in *The Annals of the War,* 494–95.
95. McClellan, "The Wilderness Fight," Philadelphia *Weekly Times,* January 26, 1878.
96. Catlett C. Taliaferro to John W. Daniel, January 7, 1907, in Daniel Collection, UV.

expostulated, without meeting a single Confederate soldier. "He evidently did not believe a word of it," the indignant officer later reported of Wilcox, "and was not over polite in letting me know it." Determined to impress his superiors with the situation's gravity, the officer told his story to his regimental commander and to Lane, who urged Wilcox to establish a picket line. "He assured them that there was a [Confederate] division in his front," the officer reported in disgust, "and told them not to disturb the men [but] let them rest till morning." [97]

Wilcox and Heth, however, were uneasy. Despite Lee's assurance of timely reinforcements, they continued to pester Hill about their disjointed lines. According to Heth, he visited Hill twice more, and Wilcox backed up his efforts. On Heth's last visit, Hill exploded. "Damn it, Heth," he bellowed, "I don't want to hear any more about it; the men shall not be disturbed." Heth later wrote, "The only excuse I make for Hill is that he was sick." Upset, Heth went in search of Lee. He could not find the commander in chief's tent, he later maintained.[98]

In point of fact, Hill, too, was growing increasingly worried, and after midnight he rode out to visit Lee. According to Palmer, "General Lee repeated his orders"—Longstreet would soon arrive and relieve Hill's men—and Hill returned to his camp. "We could not sleep," recalled Palmer, "but waited for news of Longstreet; for we knew that at the first blush of the morning the turning attack on our right would open with overwhelming numbers, and, unsupported, the men must give way." Hill's division commanders were distraught. "I walked the road all night," remembered Heth. "Twelve, two, three o'clock came, and half-past three, and no reinforcements," Wilcox recalled regarding his anxious vigil.[99]

97. Clark, comp., *Histories of the Several Regiments and Battalions from North Carolina*, II, 47–48. The 27th North Carolina, of Cooke's brigade, had the unusual experience of marching in tandem with a body of unidentified troops. Noticing that the strangers were well equipped and carried uniform knapsacks, a rebel who looked closer found to his "utter astonishment" that he was among Yankees. See John A. Sloan, *Reminiscences of the Guilford Grays, Co. B, 27th North Carolina Regiment* (Washington, D.C., 1883), 82.

98. Morrison, ed., *The Memoirs of Henry Heth*, 184. Since Lee's tent was nearby, in Widow Tapp's field, and since Wilcox and Palmer had no difficulty finding Lee that evening, Heth's statement that he could not locate the Confederate commander does not ring true.

99. Royall, *Some Reminiscences*, 30–31; Morrison, ed., *The Memoirs of Henry Heth*, 184; Wilcox, "Lee and Grant in the Wilderness," in *The Annals of the War*, 495.

Temporarily suppressing concern over Longstreet, Lee penned a report to Richmond summarizing the day's success. A strong attack had been made on Ewell, he wrote, who had repulsed it, capturing prisoners and four artillery pieces. The enemy had then concentrated on Hill, but Heth and Wilcox had "successfully resisted repeated and desperate assaults." Rosser, too, had done well and defeated a hostile cavalry force on the army's right flank. "By the blessing of God we maintained our position against every effort until night, when the contest closed," reported the rebel commander. "We have to mourn the loss of many brave officers and men." Conspicuously absent from the report was any prediction about the next morning.[100]

Far to the southwest, Longstreet's 1st Corps started from Richard's Shop as 1 A.M. arrived. Kershaw's division was in the lead, with Field's following and Alexander's artillery bringing up the rear. "Such a march, and under such conditions, was never before experienced by the troops," recalled one of Kershaw's men. The Confederate column groped along, attempting to save time by taking shortcuts through the dense forest. "Along blind roads, overgrown by underbrush, through fields that had lain fallow for years, now studded with bushes and briars," pressed Longstreet's men. Soldiers stumbled and fell in the inky darkness. "Sometimes the head of the column would lose its way," recalled a Confederate, "and during the time it was hunting its way back to the lost bridle path, was about the only rest we got." Longstreet was frustrated by the slow going. "The road was overgrown by the rough bushes," he later explained, "except the side-tracks made by the draft animals and the ruts of wheels which marked occasional lines in its course." Where the unused path crossed fields, even the guides lost their way. Longstreet ordered his divisions to double up into tighter and more efficient marching bodies. Onward clawed the 1st Corps through the Wilderness' dense growth in a desperate race against the rising sun.[101]

In the meantime, the aide Taliaferro had informed Lee of Longstreet's assurances. Lee was becoming increasingly concerned and sent Taliaferro back with a "more urgent request that he must strain every nerve to reach our lines before day." Taliaferro rode off into

---

100. Robert E. Lee to secretary of war, May 5, 1864, in OR, Vol. XXXVI, Pt. 2, p. 951.
101. Sorrel Diary, May 6, 1864, in MC; Dickert, History of Kershaw's Brigade, 344; Longstreet, From Manassas to Appomattox, 559.

the blackness. A few miles along, he intercepted Longstreet's column on the march. The War Horse seemed impatient. "Return to General Lee and tell him to rest easy," he instructed the aide. He "would be with him before day and prepared to execute any order he desired." [102]

Four o'clock and daylight approached. The tension at Widow Tapp's field became unbearable. At the first glow in the east, Hill painfully climbed onto his horse and rode off to inspect the interval between his and Ewell's troops. His sickness was now fully upon him. Palmer remained in the clearing, staring into the campfire by Poague's guns. Wilcox, who could stand the waiting no more, had ordered works constructed where Longstreet's new arrivals—assuming they ever came—were to form. As light spread over the forest, Confederate soldiers edged up to the designated line with shovels, but the enemy was too close for them safely to begin digging. In Hill's trenches, recalled a Mississippi soldier, "all were praying for the arrival of Longstreet." Heth, too, found the waiting intolerable. When he finally glimpsed what he took as daylight's first streak, he mounted his horse and trotted at half speed up Orange Plank Road to look for Longstreet. "I rode two or three miles in the direction of Mine Run," Heth recounted. "No Longstreet." Dejected, he returned to his division. [103]

At about the same time, Poague, whose cannon lined Widow Tapp's farm and commanded Orange Plank Road in case the Federals managed to break through, approached the front to retrieve the artillery piece of his that had been rescued during the previous evening's action. "As I went along the Plank Road to get the gun," Poague recounted, "I was surprised to see the unusual condition of things." Dawn had arrived, but nearly all the soldiers were asleep and their rifles were stacked, some in rows along the roadside. "I asked an officer the meaning of the apparent confusion and unreadiness of our lines," recalled Poague, "and was told that Hill's men had been informed that they were to be relieved by fresh troops before daylight, and were expecting the relieving forces any minute. I asked where

---

102. Taliaferro to Daniel, January 7, 1907, in Daniel Collection, UV.

103. Royall, *Some Reminiscences*, 31; Wilcox, "Lee and Grant in the Wilderness," in *The Annals of the War*, 495; Rowland, *Military History of Mississippi*, 49; Morrison, ed., *The Memoirs of Henry Heth*, 184.

the Yankees were. He didn't know certainly, but supposed they were in the woods in front. He struck me as being very indifferent and not at all concerned about the situation. I could not help feeling troubled, although I supposed somebody knew how things stood." [104]

Sunlight was sifting through the trees, casting long shadows on tiny pockets of the tattered gray-clad soldiers who made up Hill's formation. Across the way, Hancock's, Getty's, and Wadsworth's troops shouldered their rifles and took position for the grand charge to end the war. Off to the left toward the turnpike, an explosion of artillery and small-arms fire signaled that Ewell had launched his offensive. The din blotted out all other sounds. Then slowly, almost imperceptibly at first, rifle shots began to ring through the Wilderness nearby. Hancock's skirmishers were starting their advance along Orange Plank Road. Faster came the discharges, followed by the unmistakable sound of men moving through the forest.

Hill's scattered veterans glanced back. Orange Plank Road lay straight and empty behind them in the morning light. Inexplicably, Lee had elected to stake all on Longstreet, and Longstreet had not arrived. This time, it seemed, Lee had pushed his luck too far.

104. Cockrell, ed., *Gunner with Stonewall*, 88–89.

VI

MAY 6, MORNING
The Tide Shifts

*"Tell General Meade we are
driving them most beautifully."*

SHORTLY BEFORE 5 A.M., a signal gun sounded. Two massive Federal assault columns began converging on Hill's disordered Orange Plank Road defenses. Straight along the road from the east came Hancock's corps, strengthened by Getty's division. Slanting through the woods from the north came Wadsworth's augmented division. The jaws of the powerful Union vice were closing precisely as Grant had hoped.

Cartridge boxes filled, Wadsworth's troops surged toward Hill's flank and a junction with Hancock. Rice's brigade constituted the right flank of the attacking column, Baxter's the center, and Cutler's the left flank. Roy Stone's troops—now led by Edmund Dana, of the 143rd Pennsylvania—brought up the rear. "It was a bright May morning," noticed one of Baxter's soldiers, "and as the troops marched through the thick growth of hazel, the rays of the sun, that here and there penetrated the deep shade of the Wilderness, were reflected as well from the unsheathed swords of the officers as from the muskets of the men." [1]

Hancock's force advanced simultaneously with Wadsworth's and immediately encountered Confederates. "The enemy could see us no better than we could see them," recounted a Union soldier, "but they could hear us as the brake crackled around us, and they could very well guess at what course to direct their fire." Well-aimed rebel minié balls sliced into the head of Hancock's formation. "There is a feeling of uneasiness in the stoutest heart in facing danger that one cannot

1. William H. Locke, *The Story of the Regiment* [11th Pennsylvania] (Philadelphia, 1868), 325–26; Dawes, *Service with the Sixth Wisconsin*, 261–62; Chamberlin, *History of the One Hundred and Fiftieth Regiment Pennsylvania*, 215; Richard Coulter's Report, in *OR*, Vol. XXXVI, Pt. 1, p. 596; Frank Cowdrey's Report, in *OR*, Vol. XXXVI, Pt. 1, p. 615.

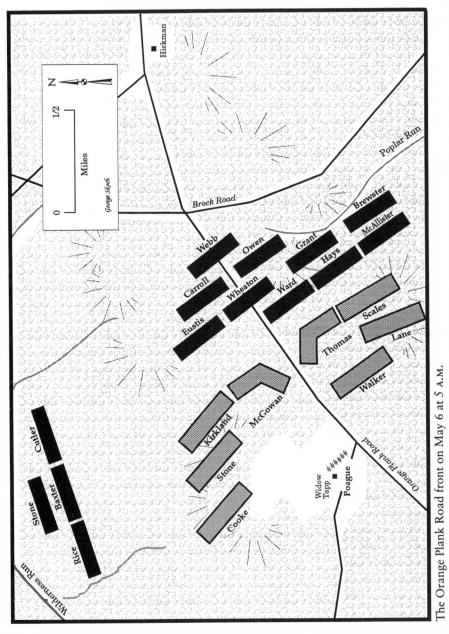

The Orange Plank Road front on May 6 at 5 A.M.

see and know," a northerner reflected. "The mystery is double intensified by the sudden, silent dropping dead, or fatally wounded, of men on either hand that somehow does not seem to connect itself with the constant roar of musketry that is going on."[2]

In Widow Tapp's field, Palmer was staring pensively into a campfire next to Poague's guns. Glancing up, he saw a burly, bearded figure on horseback. It was Longstreet. Palmer jumped to his feet and seized Longstreet's hand. "Ah, General," exclaimed the staffer, who had formerly served under Longstreet. "We have been looking for you since twelve o'clock last night. We expect to be attacked at any moment, and are not in any shape to resist." Longstreet began to answer, "My troops are not up, I have ridden ahead." The rest of what the general said was lost in a deafening roar of musketry. The Federal assault had started. Turning his horse with deliberation, Longstreet started back to meet his soldiers. As he disappeared, Hill returned from his early morning reconnaissance to the north. Together, the ailing 3rd Corps commander and his aide rode onto Orange Plank Road in the direction of the firing.[3]

Developments were not favorable to the Confederates. The full weight of Hancock's and Wadsworth's Federal columns had smashed into the unprepared southern lines, hitting first on the Confederate right and then lapping across the entire rebel formation. "The musketry increased rapidly in volume and soon was of the heaviest kind," observed Wilcox, whose division was closest to the enemy.[4]

Some rebel brigades put up a stiff fight before dropping back. Others fired a few random shots and retreated. But across Hill's entire battle line, the picture was generally the same. The Confederate 3rd Corps crumpled under the Union onslaught.

The anatomy of the Confederate collapse can be reconstructed with some precision. South of the Orange Plank Road, the Federals caught Scales's brigade completely by surprise. In growing daylight, soldiers from the 141st Pennsylvania could see the 13th North Carolina's flag hanging lazily from a staff. "I'll have that flag," announced

---

2. Galwey, *The Valiant Hours*, 197–98; Charles D. Page, *History of the Fourteenth Regiment, Connecticut*, 241–42; Weygant wrote that "Hancock started a few minutes ahead of the prescribed time" (*History of the One Hundred and Twenty-Fourth Regiment N.Y.S.V.*, 290).

3. Royall, *Some Reminiscences*, 31.

4. Wilcox, "Lee and Grant in the Wilderness," in *The Annals of the War*, 496.

a Federal captain, and the chase was on. Sergeant Stephen Rought sprinted for the flag, splitting open a Confederate color-bearer's head with the stock of his musket. "I've got it! I've got it!" he screamed as blue-clad troops overran the rebel line.[5]

Erroneously assuming that sufficient pickets separated the brigade from the Yankees, only a few of Scales's men had prepared earthworks. Not long after daylight, a North Carolina colonel heard the cry "Look out in front." He later explained, "I looked, and the woods were blue with the enemy." He called to Scales, but it was too late to organize a defense. The brigade was nearly surrounded. Waving his sword overhead, Scales shouted, "Follow me," and hurriedly improvised a withdrawal. But his order to retreat was lost in the din. Oblivious to danger, several members of the 38th North Carolina fought on. One rebel recalled how the line seemed to evaporate, leaving his companions and him in the Federal ranks. "The boys in blue passed right along beside us and yelled at us, 'get back to the rear, Johnnies, to the rear,'" he explained.[6]

Lane's brigade was positioned directly behind Scales's. Expecting relief before morning, Lane had not bothered to entrench. "None of the brigades seemed to be in line," remembered one of Lane's soldiers. Many regiments were lying "just as they had fought." Another soldier observed that the brigade was "out of ammunition and the arms so badly fouled from the firing in the engagement of the 5th that but few of them would fire." As dawn blossomed and reinforcements failed to arrive, Lane attempted to re-form his brigade perpendicular to Orange Plank Road. Before he could finish, Federals erupted "in large force" through an opening in Scales's rapidly dissolving formation. The 33rd North Carolina, which had just begun a hasty breakfast of captured Yankee rations, scrambled to patch together breastworks of dirt and branches. Strutting back and forth, one of Lane's colonels was hit five times by enemy bullets. The 33rd "fought like heroes," Lane reported, but "could not long stand the terrible fire on our front and flank." The 37th North Carolina's

---

5. Craft, *History of the One Hundred Forty-First Regiment, Pennsylvania*, 180; Casper Tyler's Report, in *OR*, Vol. XXXVI, Pt. 1, p. 477.

6. Clark, comp., *Histories of the Several Regiments and Battalions from North Carolina*, I, 676; Thomas Alfred Martin, "Autobiography," FSMP.

historian reported that the assault created "confusion worse confounded." His regiment was "borne gradually back by other disorganized troops without firing a gun."[7]

Tumbling rearward, Scales's and Lane's troops thoroughly disorganized Mud Walker's brigade, which was drawn up behind them. One of Lane's regiments—the 18th North Carolina—managed to make a brief stand with elements from Walker's brigade, but the resistance was short-lived. Federals began swarming from the right "in such numbers," a soldier in the regiment later reported, "it was deemed expedient to withdraw." Thomas' Georgia brigade, which had shifted below Orange Plank Road during the night, met a like fate. "Our lines extended into the enemy's nearly in the shape of a 'V' or horse shoe," a Georgia man recorded. The enemy "advanced in three columns cross firing on our brigade from three directions from the front, right flank, and rear." The Georgians had "nearly exhausted our ammunition when our right flank was nearly all captured and killed and we were ordered to fall back."[8]

The Confederate formation south of Orange Plank Road lost all coherence. "We were forced back in disorder," Lane candidly admitted, although he did not blame his soldiers. "Brave men are sometimes forced to turn their back to the foe," he later explained. In Lane's view, responsibility lay with superiors who had discounted the need to prepare a defensive line. "If a mistake was made either on the night of the 5th or morning of the 6th," concluded the brigadier, "the fault was elsewhere than with my command."[9]

Immediately north of Orange Plank Road, McGowan's South Carolina brigade also found itself in a deadly predicament. Not only were his skirmishers driven in so as to uncover the men toward the brigade's front, but the collapse of the Confederate line below the

7. James H. Lane's Report, Report of 18th North Carolina, Report of 28th North Carolina, all in Lane Collection, AU.

8. Report of 18th North Carolina, Report of 37th North Carolina, both in Lane Collection, AU; George W. Hall Diary, May 6, 1864, in UG. According to Caldwell, "Thomas' brigade was immediately on the right of the road," connecting on its left with McGowan. "The line of our brigade struck the road at an acute angle, making a salient with Thomas' brigade" (Caldwell, *The History of a Brigade of South Carolinians*, 131–32). Caldwell's description is supported by the Hall Diary. Thomas was either in front of Lane's brigade or immediately to the left of it, between Lane and McGowan.

9. Lane's Report, in Lane Collection, AU.

roadway left McGowan's southern flank bare. Federals swarmed from "in front as well as on the right flank," recounted a South Carolina officer. "The pressure was irresistible," and the brigade ceased to exist as a fighting unit. "There was no panic and no great haste," an officer later explained. "The men seemed to fall back [out of] a deliberate conviction that it was impossible to hold the ground, and, of course, foolish to attempt it. It was mortifying, but it was only what every veteran has experienced." [10]

In reserve behind McGowan, Kirkland's brigade hurriedly tried to construct a battle line. A rebel soldier, Lewis Young, was sent by Kirkland to ascertain the exact whereabouts of the Federals. Working forward to where McGowan's line had been a few minutes before, he came upon a large body of Yankees. Young whirled his horse; a ball tore through his elbow, and another burned a line across the pit of his stomach. His horse careered into a tree, pitching him to the ground. Still dodging bullets, he managed to sprint back to Kirkland and report "our truly embarrassing position." But before Kirkland could gird his men, Wadsworth struck from the north. "A furious attack was made on our left flank," recorded another of Kirkland's soldiers, "and the unformed line was rolled up as a sheet of paper would be rolled without the power of effective resistance." As with other Confederate units, Kirkland's brigade was willing to fight; it simply had no place to form. "If even a single brigade had changed front to the left before the enemy struck their flank they might have stemmed the tide and have stopped the rout," concluded a soldier from the 11th North Carolina. "But no brigadier seems to have thought of it, and the situation was desperate. All the advantage of yesterday's hard fighting was about to be lost." [11]

A member of the 26th North Carolina appraised the situation candidly. "We did not take proper precaution and were surprised by the enemy, and our brigade came very near being stampeded." According to a sharpshooter, the brigade fled "without scarcely firing a shot." Calling the rout "perfectly disgraceful," he added, "I am ashamed to say it, but I don't think I ever saw troops behave so

---

10. Caldwell, *The History of a Brigade of South Carolinians*, 132–33.

11. Lewis Young to family, May 7, 1864, in Robert Newman Gourdin Collection, EU; Clark, comp., *Histories of the Several Regiments and Battalions from North Carolina*, I, 595.

badly. . . . The men were still, doubtless, under the influence of the panic of the evening previous, and they ran like deer through the woods, leaving the enemy far behind. And the further they went, the greater seemed to grow their fright." [12]

Only two Confederate brigades managed to hold their ground, and they only temporarily. Stone's troops were at first swamped by an "irresistible tidal wave of retreating Confederates." According to a Mississippi sharpshooter, the soldiers were "borne backward amidst the struggling mass, some of whom were firing toward the enemy through their own ranks." Another Confederate called it "one of the worst stampedes I ever saw." Stone labored to rally his soldiers. "Steady men! Steady! Form on your colors," he shouted. "The appearance of Colonel Stone on his battle horse," a witness later wrote, "as he rode from color bearer to color bearer, locating them on a line and calling on the men to form on their respective regimental colors, has never been effaced from my memory." Seizing the initiative, Stone advanced a unit of sharpshooters. The situation called for extreme measures, and the rebels took the unusual step of propping wounded Yankees against trees in front of their position. "They plead against the experiment as inhuman," related a Confederate, "but we replied that their own men would certainly not fire on them, and that the object in view was to stop the firing." The tactic worked, and Stone's line held while the fighting raged off to his right and rear.[13]

Cooke's North Carolinians were bivouacked in a straw field north of Orange Plank Road, directly behind Stone. Contrary to orders, they had prepared earthworks and positioned an artillery battery on a nearby knoll. As the wave of blue troops came into view, Confederate guns opened fire. Bloody swaths appeared in Wadsworth's advancing Federal line. Rice's Federal brigade, located closest to the Confederates, suffered heavily. In an attempt to silence the troublesome pieces, Rice ordered the 56th Pennsylvania and the 76th New York toward the guns. The Federals managed to capture a few pickets, but Cooke's rebels pulled the guns to safety. From their

12. Albright Diary, May 6, 1864, in Albright Collection, NCDAH; Samuel Finley Harper to father, May 6, 1864, in Samuel Finley Harper Collection, NCDAH.

13. Rowland, *Military History of Mississippi*, 49; Dunlop, *Lee's Sharpshooters*, 376–79; Graham, "Twenty-Sixth Mississippi Regiment," 169; Clark, comp., *Histories of the Several Regiments and Battalions from North Carolina*, III, 305.

new vantage point, they continued to bombard Rice with deadly accuracy.[14]

But the Confederates lacked the firepower to delay the Federal advance for long. Inexorably, Hancock's column pressed toward Widow Tapp's field, where a careworn Lee watched remnants of Hill's division spilling to the rear. Swinging down from the north, Wadsworth's troops sliced through the rebel lines and broke onto Orange Plank Road. Grant's plan was working. The Federal concentration had been achieved. One more push, and Hill would be crushed.

As viewed by Federal frontline troops, the fighting had been "close and savage." One Union soldier recalled that "sometimes our advance was very slow and every inch hotly contested, and then again we progressed some distance in a short time, but all the while and continuously fighting an almost if not quite unseen enemy in thick woods." Another wrote of "the roar of musketry, the dying groans of the wounded, the hellish yells of the rebels, and the shouts and cheers of the Union men, mingled together, all making a noise and confusion that is hard to describe." It was, recalled a Pennsylvania officer, "bushwhacking with the enemy on a grand scale." Demoralized rebels came running into Hancock's line, hands raised high, entreating the Federals not to shoot. "They were evidently badly frightened," thought a Union soldier, "as well they might be." The bluecoats chanted, "Come on in, Johnny, come on in, Johnny," and held their fire when it appeared that doing so might encourage the rebels to surrender. A northerner later remarked that "to an onlooker, I think the advance that morning was the grandest display of military strength that was ever seen on this continent. We press on in six parallel lines of battle, and as the mighty host advances along the plank road, it seemed as if nothing could check its progress."[15]

Back at the intersection of Brock and Orange Plank roads, Han-

14. John A. Sloan, *Reminiscences of the Guilford Grays*, 83–84; Clark, comp., *Histories of the Several Regiments and Battalions from North Carolina*, III, 118; A. P. Smith, *History of the Seventy-Sixth Regiment New York*, 291; William Hoffman's Report, in *OR*, Vol. XXXVI, Pt. 1, p. 623.

15. Francis A. Walker, *History of the Second Army Corps*, 421; Charles D. Page, *History of the Fourteenth Regiment, Connecticut*, 242; Banes, *History of the Philadelphia Brigade*, 229; D. G. Crotty, *Four Years' Campaigning in the Army of the Potomac* (Grand Rapids, 1874), 127–28; Chamberlin, *History of the One Hundred and Fiftieth Regiment Pennsylvania*, 215.

cock could not conceal his excitement. The mood there was far different from what it had been the previous afternoon. Arriving at the 2nd Corps command center around 5:30 A.M., Lyman was greeted by a jubilant Hancock. "We are driving them beautifully," exclaimed the corps commander, his face wreathed in smiles. "Tell Meade we are driving them most beautifully. Birney has gone in, and he is clearing them out be-au-ti-fully." The sound of musketry receding to the west lent objective confirmation to Hancock's optimism. At 5:40, Lyman dashed off a note to Meade. "General Hancock went in punctually, and is driving the enemy handsomely," he began, mimicking Hancock's turn of phrase. There was still no sign of Longstreet, he reported, but Hancock had prepared rifle pits on his left in case the Confederate 1st Corps showed up there, and scouts were ranging well afield. "Birney has joined with Wadsworth," the message ended. At the same time, Hancock penned a note to Meade repeating the good news. "We have driven the enemy from their position, and are keeping up the Plank Road, connecting with Wadsworth, taking quite a number of prisoners." Lyman had brought a report from Meade, however, that temporarily dampened Hancock's optimism. "I am ordered to tell you, sir," he explained, "that only one division of General Burnside is up, but that he will go in as soon as he can be put in position." Hancock's smile faded. "I knew it," he exclaimed vehemently. "Just what I expected. If he could attack now, we would smash A. P. Hill all to pieces!" [16]

Burnside's fresh troops would indeed have been welcome. An hour of intense fighting in the tangled thickets had sapped Hancock's momentum. Units had drifted apart and others had become intermingled. Pockets of Confederate resistance had disordered the blue lines even more. "In some cases [the troops] were heaped up in unnecessary strength," wrote Hancock's assistant adjutant general Walker. "Elsewhere great gaps appeared; men, and even officers, had lost their regiments in the jungle; the advance had not been, could not have been, made uniformly right to left, and the line of battle ran here forward, and there backward, through the forest; thousands had

---

16. Theodore Lyman to family, May 16, 1864, in *Meade's Headquarters,* ed. Agassiz, 93–94; Theodore Lyman to George G. Meade, May 6, 1864, in *OR,* Vol. XXXVI, Pt. 2, p. 439; Winfield S. Hancock to Andrew A. Humphreys, May 6, 1864, in *OR,* Vol. XXXVI, Pt. 2, p. 439.

fallen in the furious struggle; the men in front were largely out of ammunition." Another Federal reported that "when the men were ordered forward, the difficulty of penetrating the brush in line compelled them to break up into squads and march by the flank; regiments would thus become separated from brigades, and brigades from divisions, and, when the attempt was made to reestablish a line, numerous gaps existed."[17]

Wadsworth's appearance further jumbled the Federal ranks. His men careered onto Orange Plank Road from the north, driving a pack of fleeing rebels before them. Slamming into the side of Hancock's column, they forced the soldiers of the 2nd Corps to the left. According to a Wisconsin officer, "The men became jammed and crowded, and there was much confusion." In charge of Hancock's assault column, Birney slowed his advance to give the division commanders a chance to rectify their lines. Some units were shifted into new positions. Getty, who had started off astride Orange Plank Road, moved below the roadway. Wadsworth meanwhile worked to disentangle his troops from those of the 2nd Corps and to form them north of the road, closely massed. After issuing directions intended to bring order out of the prevailing chaos, Birney rode back to report the state of affairs to Hancock.[18]

While the Federals girded for their decisive lunge into Hill's broken formation, the wreckage of the Confederate 3rd Corps streamed west from the front. The extent of the rout was variously perceived. Palmer later affirmed that the Confederates retired slowly and in order, holding together on the roadway. But Porter Alexander asserted

17. Francis A. Walker, *History of the Second Army Corps,* 422; George A. Hussey and William Todd, *History of the Ninth Regiment N.Y.S.M.—N.G.S.Y.N (Eighty-Third N.Y. Volunteers), 1845–1888* (New York, 1889), 325. McAllister's experience was typical of that of other Union field commanders. His brigade was assigned to move beside Ward's brigade on the Federal left flank. Unfortunately, the commander of McAllister's skirmish line was captured. Ordering the skirmishers out himself, McAllister started blindly through the thickets in search of Ward. Mott, commanding the division, directed McAllister to place three regiments under William Sewell, of the 5th New Jersey. Thereafter, "a colonel that I did not know asked me to relieve him. . . . I did so, and he retired, and I saw him no more." McAllister tried to guide his men by the troops to his right. "We advanced with the line as it advanced, and halted when it halted, skirmishing as we moved along, driving the enemy back" (Robert McAllister's Report, in *OR,* Vol. XXXVI, Pt. 1, p. 488).

18. Tyler, *Recollections of the Civil War,* 151; Dawes, *Service with the Sixth Wisconsin,* 262; Francis A. Walker, *History of the Second Army Corps,* 422–23; Lysander Cutler's Report, in *OR,* Vol. XXXVI, Pt. 1, p. 611; George W. Getty's Report, *ibid.,* 677.

that once Hill's flanks collapsed, the rebel line rapidly rolled up toward the center: "The men, appreciating that their position was no longer tenable, fell back from both flanks into the Plank Road, and came pouring down the road past the open field near the Tapp House, where Lee stood among the tall and scattered pines." The road, confirmed a Confederate soldier, was a "scene of utter, and apparently, irremediable confusion, such as we had never witnessed before in Lee's army." Everywhere were "standing and moving wagons, horses and mules, and threading their way through the tangled mass, each with his face to the rear, were hundreds of the men of Wilcox's and Heth's divisions, which were being driven from their lines." A Confederate staff officer, who remembered the scene as "appalling," was to write, "Fugitives from the broken line of the 3rd Corps were pouring back in disorder and it looked as if things were past mending."[19]

Lee and Hill were furiously attempting to restore order. The commander in chief's composure was shattered. He was "excited and chagrined," recalled an onlooker, and he spoke "rather roughly" to unheeding soldiers. Spotting McGowan bobbing along in a sea of gray uniforms, Lee rushed to the brigadier and shouted, "My God! General McGowan, is this splendid brigade of yours running like a flock of geese?" McGowan answered, "General, the men are not whipped. They only want a place to form, and they will fight as well as ever they did." Wilcox materialized out of the vortex of troops and reported on his division's perilous condition. Lee had no time to listen. It was obvious what had happened. Without reinforcements, all was lost. "Longstreet must be here," Lee exclaimed in exasperation. "Go bring him up." Relegated to the role of messenger, Wilcox rode off, swept along by soldiers hurrying to escape the Federal onslaught. In anticipation of the worst, Lee directed his aide Taylor to ride to Parker's Store and prepare the army's supply train for immediate retreat. Venable was dispatched to help find Longstreet.[20]

Leading the Union drive was Hays's brigade, now commanded

19. Royall, *Some Reminiscences*, 31; Alexander, *Military Memoirs*, 503; Joseph B. Polley, *Hood's Texas Brigade: Its Marches, Its Battles, Its Achievements* (New York, 1910), 230; Sorrel, *Recollections*, 240.

20. Caldwell, *The History of a Brigade of South Carolinians*, 133; Alexander, *Military Memoirs*, 503; Wilcox, "Lee and Grant in the Wilderness," in *The Annals of the War*, 496; Venable, "The Campaign from the Wilderness to Petersburg," in *SHSP*, XIV, 525.

by Elijah Walker, of the 4th Maine. His regiment and the 17th Maine punched ahead of the main Federal body. Well behind them were Wadsworth's forces, slowed by confusion in their ranks. Suddenly the Maine soldiers emerged from the forest into daylight. They had reached Widow Tapp's field.[21]

Blue uniforms began to appear on the eastern edge of the clearing. More lapped around to the south. Here was the last line of Confederate resistance. Across the clearing's center, ranged north to south, stood Poague's cannon. Sited on a slight rise, rebel artillerymen had a clear field of fire covering Orange Plank Road and the woods from where the enemy was approaching. A hasty barricade of rails and logs provided the gunners some protection from the bullets that had begun whistling across the clearing.

Grasping at a last opportunity to buy time, Hill ordered Poague to shoot obliquely across the road. Palmer protested. The retreating Confederates had not yet finished crossing in front of the guns. Hill was insistent. There must be no delay. The guns must open, and they must begin immediately.

Assuming that a full battle line followed closely behind the enemy skirmishers, Poague initiated a slow fire with short-range shells. Flames spit from the rebel guns. Smoke filled the air, and projectiles whined into the approaching Federals, doing "great execution." One piece maintained steady fire down Orange Plank Road, effectively keeping the way cleared of Yankees.

Encountering unexpected resistance, the Union advance slowed. But twelve guns, however bravely manned, could not stop an army. Federals began edging around the field, threatening to envelop the gunners. Still Poague's pieces roared, swinging more to the north and south to still the relentless blue tide. Pandemonium reigned. "The cannon thundered, musketry rolled, stragglers were fleeing, couriers riding here and there in post-haste," wrote a Confederate who witnessed the scene. "Minie balls began to sing, the dying and wounded were jolted by the flying ambulances, and filling the road-side, adding to the excitement, the terror of death." Years later, Jennings C. Wise, in his study of Lee's artillery, judged Poague's stand one of the bravest

---

21. George W. Verrill, "The Seventeenth Maine at Gettysburg and in the Wilderness," in *War Papers Read Before the Commandery of the State of Maine, Military Order of the Loyal Legion of the United States* (3 vols.; Portland, Maine, 1898), I, 277–79.

of the war. "The gunners worked with almost superhuman energy," wrote Wise, "the muzzles belched their withering blast." And nearby sat Lee on his horse, acutely aware that each minute bought by Poague brought Longstreet's soldiers closer. "What glory for a soldier!" concluded Wise. "This single incident brought more of honor to the little colonel of artillery than most soldiers attain in a life of service."[22]

Hill, a former artilleryman, had dismounted and was helping to fire one of the guns. "Why does not Longstreet come?" an aide heard Lee ask. "This was one of the most anxious times I felt during the war," recalled Samuel Harper, of Hill's staff. "The minutes seemed like hours, and the musketry was getting uncomfortably near and everything looked like disaster."[23]

In the midst of smoke and chaos and hurrying soldiers, Lee caught sight of a tightly massed body of troops. They were swinging confidently up Orange Plank Road into Widow Tapp's field, marching toward the enemy, not away from them. They were clad in gray, but they were not Hill's men. Longstreet's corps had come at last.

"Keep cool, men,
we will straighten this
out in a short time."

"Like a fine lady at a party, Longstreet was often late in his arrival at the ball," opined Private William Dame, of the Richmond Howitzers. "But he always made a sensation and that of delight, when he got in, with the grand old First Corps sweeping behind him as his train." And so it was this bright spring morning, as the armies buckled down to the serious business of attempting to annihilate each other. The Longstreet of Gettysburg and East Tennessee was a ghost of the past.

22. Cockrell, ed., *Gunner with Stonewall*, 88–89; William Pendleton's Report, in *OR*, Vol. XXXVI, Pt. 1, pp. 1036–38; Royall, *Some Reminiscences*, 31; R.C., "Texans Always Move Them," *The Land We Love*, V, 482; C. R. Dudley, "What I Know About the Wilderness," in DU; Jennings C. Wise, *The Long Arm of Lee; or, The History of the Artillery of the Army of Northern Virginia* (2 vols.; Lynchburg, Va., 1915), 767. I am grateful to George Skoch for identifying R.C. as Robert Campbell, who served in Company A of the 5th Texas and after the war became a prominent newspaperman.

23. Clark, comp., *Histories of the Several Regiments and Battalions from North Carolina*, I, 547–48; Samuel Finley Harper, "Reminiscences," in Harper Collection, NCDAH.

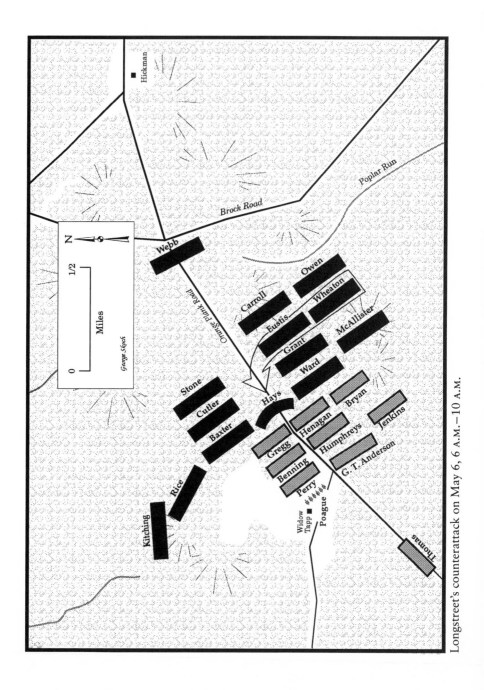

Longstreet's counterattack on May 6, 6 A.M.–10 A.M.

On May 6, Lee's War Horse of old, the hero of Antietam and Chickamauga, rode at the head of the Army of Northern Virginia's 1st Corps.[24]

At the earliest blush of light, Longstreet's column hurried through Parker's Store and turned right, onto Orange Plank Road. Kershaw's Division, headed by Colonel John W. Henagan's South Carolina brigade, led the way. Crammed into the roadway beside Kershaw was Longstreet's other division, under Field. "Thinking the emergency might be great," Field later explained, "instead of halting until the rear of Kershaw's column passed, I moved parallel with him, the head of his column being maybe a hundred yards or so in advance of mine." A Mississippi soldier described it as a "race and a run" between the two divisions. "We could hear in the faint distance growing louder and rumbling deeper, the burst of shells, the jarring growl, and the roll of musketry." A South Carolinian later wrote, "Every man stripped himself for the fight and I have never seen so much yellow corn meal thrown away in my life." An Alabama man remarked how "the sun, blood red from the effect of the smoke of battle, was just appearing above the Wilderness."[25]

Longstreet's powerful column clipped through Parker's Store and the site of Hill's infirmary. High stacks of arms and legs were unintended monuments to the previous day's fighting. Ahead was Lee's artillery reserve. The men of the Richmond Howitzers made no attempt to contain their excitement. They had fought under Longstreet during the war's earlier years and still considered themselves part of his corps. The cry was raised, "Look out down the road. Here they come!" Dame remembered the moment years later. "The instant the head of his column was seen," he recounted, "the cries resounded on every side, 'Here's Longstreet. The old War Horse is up at last. It's all right now.'"[26]

The 1st Corps pressed on, increasing its speed. Troops packed

24. Dame, *From the Rapidan to Richmond*, 85.

25. Dickert, *History of Kershaw's Brigade*, 345; Charles W. Field, "Campaign of 1864 and 1865," in *SHSP*, XIV, 543; W. M. Abernathy, "Our Mess: Southern Army Gallantry and Privations, 1861–1865," in W. M. Abernathy Collection, MDAH; John Daniel McDonell, "Recollections of the War," FSMP; Coles, "History of the Fourth Alabama Regiment," in Regimental Collection, ADAH.

26. William F. Perry, "Reminiscences of the Campaign of 1864 in Virginia," in *SHSP*, VII, 50–51. Dame, *From the Rapidan to Richmond*, 84–85.

the road, eight abreast, Kershaw's division on the right and Field's on the left. Musketry filled the air. "Double-quick," shouted Brigadier General John Gregg, heading the brigade of regiments from Texas and Arkansas that was near the front of Field's division. Signs of the morning's battle mounted. A few soldiers filtered to the rear, then more, then streams of men, some in litters, some supported by comrades, some making their way alone. These were the remnants of Hill's broken divisions. As one of Longstreet's brigadiers recalled, Hill's fugitives came "swarming through the woods, heedless of their officers, who were riding in every direction shouting to gain their attention." The soldiers of the 1st Corps gleefully chided the retreating Confederates. "Do you belong to General Lee's army?" they asked. "You don't look like the men we left here. You are worse than Bragg's men." One of Longstreet's incredulous artillerymen called to an excited officer on horseback, "Major, what's the matter? Are not those men being marched back?" The major swore, "No! God damn 'em. They are running!"[27]

Striding through a swirl of gray uniforms, Longstreet's soldiers never slowed their pace. "In perfect order, ranks well closed, and no stragglers, those splendid troops came on," wrote an onlooker, "regardless of the confusion on every side, pushing their steady movement onward like a river in the sea of confused and troubled human waves around them." A week later, Alexander described the stirring sight to his father: "We met Heth's and Wilcox's divisions pouring down the road in a perfect rout through which we marched until the minie balls were thick and fast and the men began to fall." Venable, who met Longstreet about a half mile before Widow Tapp's farm, recorded his impression fifteen years later. "It was superb, and my heart beats quicker to think about it even at this distance of time."[28]

Longstreet was in a decisive frame of mind. Venable remembered his "imperturbable coolness which always characterized him in times of perilous action." John C. Haskell, one of Longstreet's artillerymen,

27. J. B. Clifton Diary, May 6, 1864, in J. B. Clifton Papers, SHC; Perry, "Reminiscences of the Campaign of 1864 in Virginia," in *SHSP*, VII, 51; Field, "Campaign of 1864 and 1865," in *SHSP*, XIV, 543; Dickert, *History of Kershaw's Brigade*, 346; Gallagher, ed., *Fighting for the Confederacy*, 357.

28. Evander M. Law, "From the Wilderness to Cold Harbor," in *B&L*, IV, 124; Alexander to father, May 19, 1864, in Alexander Collection, SHC; Charles S. Venable to James Longstreet, July 25, 1879, in Longstreet Collection, DU.

recalled how "Longstreet, always grand in battle, never shone as he did here." The general "rode up and down the lines, encouraging, exhorting, and steadying the men, with an effect on them that no other leader I ever saw had on his troops."[29]

Kershaw's lead elements stamped up first and were directed south of Orange Plank Road. Coming up within minutes, Field's men also began to form below the road. But no sooner had Field managed to shunt a brigade into position—Brigadier General George T. ("Tige") Anderson's force of Georgians—than orders came from Longstreet to shift his division to the left, above the roadway. The enemy was pressing hard. A counterattack had to be made at once. As Field later explained, the order was to "charge with any front I could make."

Field acted with dispatch. Near at hand was Gregg's brigade from Texas and Arkansas, one of the army's finest fighting units. Field ordered Gregg to execute a right wheel into line above the road and perpendicular to it, directly behind Poague's guns. Next in order was Brigadier General Henry L. Benning's Georgia brigade, followed by Brigadier General Evander McIver Law's Alabamians, now commanded by Colonel William F. Perry, from the 44th Alabama. Brigadier General Micah Jenkins' South Carolina brigade closed in reserve. Hidden behind the slight rise crowned by Poague's artillery, the massing Confederates were invisible to the enemy.[30]

Gregg's troops swept past the batteries where Lee was standing. Gregg was a stranger to Lee, having served in the Confederacy's west-

29. Venable, "The Campaign from the Wilderness to Petersburg," in *SHSP*, XIV, 525; John Haskell, "Memoirs of Lieut. Col. John Haskell,"in DU; Gilbert E. Govan and James W. Livingood, eds., *The Haskell Memoirs: John Cheves Haskell* (New York, 1960), 63.

30. Joseph B. Kershaw's Report, in *OR*, Vol. XXXVI, Pt. 1, p. 1061; Field, "Campaign of 1864 and 1865," in *SHSP*, XIV, 543. An article in the London *Herald* of May 18, 1864 (reproduced in *Lee's Sharpshooters*, by Dunlop, 401–403), reported that Kershaw reached the front first, with Field forming in reserve. "The truth is," Field later responded, "that my division was just formed in column by brigades; that the exultant, jubilant enemy was met and driven back by three of the brigades, Gregg's Texans, Benning's Georgians, and Perry's Alabamans; and that the fate of the day and the army's is due, I firmly believe, to those three brigades; that I did not form upon Kershaw, and had no connection with him until late in the day." As Field analyzed it, the mistaken belief that he had supported Kershaw "was natural, because a few minutes before Kershaw was leading, but I formed and charged first—the ground was open in my front and impassable in his, and the enemy was just in my track" (Field, "Campaign of 1864 and 1865," in *SHSP*, XIV, 546–47). One of Poague's gunners had a contrary view: "My judgment is that the Mississippians, South Carolinians, and other troops across the Plank Road were 'in it' about three minutes before the Texas Brigade fired a shot" (Dudley, "What I Know About the Wilderness," in DU).

ern armies before joining the 1st Corps during the Tennessee campaign. Flushed with excitement, Lee eased his horse next to Gregg
and shouted above the din, "General, what brigade is this?"

"The Texas brigade," came the answer.

"I am glad to see it," cried Lee. "When you go in there, I wish
you to give those men the cold steel—they will stand and fight all
day, and never move unless you charge them." Pausing to study the
approaching blue line, Lee added by way of encouragement, "The
Texas brigade always has driven the enemy, and I want them to do it
now. And tell them, General, that they will fight today under my
eye—I will watch their conduct. I want every man of them to know
I am here with them."

"Attention Texas Brigade," Gregg boomed for all to hear. "The
eyes of General Lee are upon you. Forward. March."

Lee could not contain his excitement. He raised high in his stirrups. Emotion transformed his face. Tearing off his hat and waving it
high, he shouted, "Texans always move them!"[31]

"A yell rent the air that must have been heard for miles around,"
recalled a Texan near Gregg's front ranks, "and but few eyes in that
old brigade of veterans and heroes of many a bloody field was un-
dimmed by honest, heartfelt tears." Leonard Gee, one of Gregg's
couriers, summed up the feeling. "I would charge hell itself for that
old man," he swore in a voice choked with emotion.[32]

The Texans continued on, eight hundred strong, straight at the
Federals. Still agitated, Lee spurred his horse through the cannon and
advanced with Gregg's soldiers. At first the Texans did not notice that
Lee was with them. Part way across the field, however, it became
apparent that he intended to lead the charge himself. That would
never do. Ahead was death, especially for a man on horseback.

"Go back, General Lee. Go back!" came the cry, spreading across
the entire column. But Lee would not stop. The Texans slowed their

---

31. R.C., "Texans Always Move Them," 481–82; Polley, *Hood's Texas Brigade*, 231. In
reconstructing this incident, I have relied primarily on Charles S. Venable to James Longstreet,
October 26, 1877, in James Longstreet Papers, SHC, and on Venable's "The Campaign from
the Wilderness to Petersburg," in *SHSP*, XIV, esp. 525–26. Venable was the only aide of Lee's
present. For additional versions of the events, see Douglas Southall Freeman, *R. E. Lee: A
Biography* (4 vols.; New York, 1935), III, 288n5; and Harold B. Simpson, *Hood's Texas Brigade: Lee's Grenadier Guard* (Dallas, 1983), 396–98.

32. R.C., "Texans Always Move Them," 482.

pace, looking over at the bareheaded man. Lee's gray hair splayed in the breeze. His eyes were fixed on the front. "We won't go on unless you come back," the troops shouted, but he ignored their pleas. Several soldiers attempted to lead the general's horse to the rear, and a particularly tall Texan seized his rein. It appeared to one onlooker that "five and six of his staff would gather around him, seize him, his arms, his horse's reins, but he shook them off and moved forward."[33]

According to Venable, who was the only aide present, Gregg remonstrated with Lee. "Well then, I will go back," replied the rebel commander, and began turning his horse around. "Yonder is General Longstreet," cried Venable, pointing out the commander of the 1st Corps to Lee. Lee and Longstreet conferred briefly on troop dispositions; then Lee moved a little way off. Taking advantage of the opportunity, Venable informed Longstreet of Lee's attempt to lead the Texas brigade's charge. Something had to be done to prevent him from risking his life again.[34]

Longstreet handled the assignment with "affectionate bluntness," the staffer later recounted. Riding over to Lee, Longstreet assured the gray-haired general that he could restore the Confederate line if given a free hand. But if not needed, he would like to leave, "as it was not quite comfortable where we were." As Longstreet recalled it, Lee was "off his balance." Reluctantly, the Virginian rode to the rear, leaving the immediate details of the fighting to his trusted subordinate. Taking firm control, Longstreet ordered Hill's soldiers to re-form while he prepared his 1st Corps to counterattack. Up and down, Longstreet rode, his horse at a walk, addressing each regiment as it slipped into line. "Keep cool, men, we will straighten this out in a short time— keep cool," Palmer heard him repeating.[35]

Gregg's Texans, part of McGowan's outfit, and much of Stone's

33. *Ibid.*, 482–83; Polley, *Hood's Texas Brigade*, 231.

34. Venable to Longstreet, October 26, 1877, in Longstreet Papers, SHC; Venable, "The Campaign from the Wilderness to Petersburg," in *SHSP*, XIV, 525. Poague later recalled that Lee "was perfectly composed, but his face expressed a kind of grim determination I had not observed either at Sharpsburg or Gettysburg. Traveller was quiet but evidently interested in the situation, as indicated by his raised head with ears pointing to the front. But there was no rearing or plunging on the part of the horse and no waving of sword by General Lee as is represented in a painting of the scene I saw some years ago" (Cockrell, ed., *Gunner with Stonewall*, 90–91).

35. Venable to Longstreet, October 26, 1877, in Longstreet Papers, SHC; Longstreet, *From Manassas to Appomattox*, 560–61; Royall, *Some Reminiscences*, 32.

Mississippi brigade held the ground around Poague's guns. The area south of Orange Plank Road was rapidly filling with Kershaw's division. "I have always thought that in its entire splendid history the simple act of forming line in that dense undergrowth, under heavy fire and with the Third Corps men pushing to the rear through the ranks, was perhaps [the 1st Corps'] greatest performance for steadiness and inflexible courage and discipline," wrote Longstreet's aide Sorrel.[36]

Longstreet's plan of attack was characteristic of his military style. The general massed his corps in column on each side of Orange Plank Road, facing the enemy along a narrow front. Taking advantage of his tightly packed formation, Longstreet planned to send his men forward almost simultaneously. Brigade after brigade would pound into the Union line with the objective of repelling the enemy and cleaving their formation in half.

"Load and cap your pieces, men. Hold them well up," sounded the command. "The jingle of the hundreds of iron ramrods up and down the line denoted that something horrible was soon to take place," a Texan recalled. Moving almost as one body, Longstreet's two divisions welled toward the approaching Federals.[37]

North of Orange Plank Road, Gregg's brigade sprinted ahead. Yankee sharpshooters began picking off the men in the fore. Brushing aside a cloud of blue-clad skirmishers, Gregg's soldiers plunged toward the far woods. A galling fire thinned their ranks. But onward they charged, into the first line of Federals. That line broke; another waited just ahead. "The storm of battle became terrific," a Confederate survivor wrote home. "The Texas Brigade was alone; no support on our right, and not only none on our left, but a terrible enfilading fire poured on us from that direction." Straight into the main Federal battle line streamed the Texans. "There was a terrible crash, mingled with wild yells," recalled a rebel participant, "which settled down into a tremendous roar of musketry." Severely outnumbered,

36. Sorrel, *Recollections*, 240.
37. O. T. Hanks, *History of Captain B. F. Benton's Company, Hood's Texas Brigade, 1861–1865* (Austin, Tex., 1984), 28–29.

Gregg's brigade exchanged a brutal, stand-up fire with an enemy no more than twenty yards away. "Death seemed to be our portion," thought one of Gregg's soldiers.[38]

Gregg's Confederates charged again. This time the Union line bowed back. But the Federals were too numerous for the lone rebel brigade. Face-to-face fighting continued, with neither side willing to retreat. "For 25 minutes we held them steady," boasted a Confederate who lived through the carnage, "and at the expiration of that time more than half of our brave fellows lay around us dead, dying and wounded, and the few survivors could stand it no longer." So severe was the combat that many Federals fired without finishing loading. Later, a rebel recalled ramrods driven into trees so deeply that he could not pull them out. Gregg was nearly killed, and blood flowed from several bullet wounds in his horse. His seasoned troops could not withstand such punishment. At his command, they grudgingly gave ground. The brigade had been diminished to a skirmish line. Of 800 men who went into action, fewer than 250 returned unharmed. The 5th Texas lost its commander, its officers, and nearly two-thirds of its troops. The 3rd Arkansas lost its colonel and all but two officers. Some companies were almost obliterated. In one, a single soldier survived to answer the next day's roll call. The price had been high, but Gregg had accomplished his goal. He had rocked the Union assault column back on its heels.[39]

And a few paces behind came Rock Benning's brigade. With characteristic ferocity, the Georgians flew into the Federals, who were still reeling from their fight with the Texans. "There were no commands given after the deadly contest began," recalled a rebel. "They could not have been heard." The division commander Field at first viewed the results as "signally cheering." Benning's impetuous advance, however, exposed his right flank to "deadly fire" from Federals positioned below Orange Plank Road, and additional enemy units threatened his left. In short order, the Georgia brigade, accord-

38. Joseph B. Polley, *Soldier's Letters to Charming Nellie* (New York, 1908), 232; Hanks, *History of Captain B. F. Benton's Company*, 28; R.C., "Texans Always Move Them," 485.

39. B. L. Aycock, "A Sketch: The Lone Star Guards," in FSMP; Hanks, *History of Captain B. F. Benton's Company*, 29; R.C., "Texans Always Move Them," 485; Polley, *Hood's Texas Brigade*, 232; Calvin L. Collier, *They'll Do to Tie To: The Story of the Third Regiment, Arkansas Infantry, C.S.A.* (Little Rock, Ark., 1988), 178–79; Field, "Campaign of 1864 and 1865," in *SHSP*, XIV, 544.

ing to Field, was "badly cut up." Benning rode up on his huge iron gray horse, "spurs rattling like as many trace irons." A bullet tore through his left shoulder, fracturing the bones. "Severely but not dangerously wounded," the doctor decided.[40]

Longstreet continued his hammering blows. As Benning was carted away on a litter, Law's Alabama brigade moved into place. Nearby stood Lee, his face flushed and his black coat draping his shoulders. Staff officers gathered close behind him. The commander in chief's eyes were fixed below Orange Plank Road, where Kershaw's division was also locked in combat. "Send an active young officer down there," Lee barked. A Confederate colonel thought that the general "looked as though he ought to have been and was the monarch of the world." A soldier in the ranks had a different impression. Lee "appeared to be very much perturbed over his misfortune, and the only time I ever saw him excited." Taking notice of the Alabamians, Lee asked, "What troops are these?" A private in the 15th Alabama called back, "Law's Alabama brigade." Lee shouted, "God bless the Alabamans. Alabama soldiers, all I ask of you is to keep up with the Texans." To William Perry, who was commanding Law's brigade, the effect was electrifying. "It was impossible not to feel that every man that passed him was, for the time being, a hero," he later wrote.[41]

Under Lee's approving eye, the Alabamians completed their battle formation "at a double-quick step." Along the northern shoulder of Orange Plank Road they swept, toward where Gregg and Benning had fought and slightly to the north. The route of attack that Perry chose required him to divide his brigade into two wings. His leftmost unit—consisting of the 15th, 44th, and 48th Alabama—was to cross Widow Tapp's farm well above Orange Plank Road. Its projected path led across a narrow swamp, then up a hill from which Wadsworth's Federal division, arrayed four lines deep, had just

40. George McRae, "With Benning's Brigade in the Wilderness," Atlanta *Journal*, August 17, 1901; J. H. Gresham, "Benning's Brigade in the Wilderness Again," Atlanta *Journal*, September 7, 1901; Field, "Campaign of 1864 and 1865," in *SHSP*, XIV, 543–44; John Rozier, ed., *The Granite Farm Letters: The Civil War Correspondence of Edgeworth and Sallie Bird* (Athens, Ga., 1988), 164.

41. Perry, "Reminiscences of the Campaign," in *SHSP*, VII, 52; Coles, "History of the Fourth Alabama Regiment, in Regimental Collection, ADAH; George Reese, "Sketch for His Family by General George Reese," *Confederate Veteran*, XIV, 111; William C. Oates, *The War Between the Union and the Confederacy and Its Lost Opportunities* (New York, 1905), 343–44.

moved forward. While Perry's left column attacked Wadsworth, the remainder of the brigade—the 4th and 47th Alabama—was to proceed directly up Orange Plank Road. Perry's left wing slugged into the "dense masses" of enemy holding the morass and the hill behind it. "My front rank fired a volley without halting," Perry recounted, "and the whole line bounded forward with the characteristic yell." Taken by surprise, the enemy returned sporadic shots and gave way.[42]

The Alabamians plunged through the swamp in hot pursuit. Unexpectedly, bullets began slanting in from their left. More Federals occupied a patch of woods two hundred yards to the north. Unless the southerners acted quickly, they risked being enfiladed and cut off from the Confederate army.

Perry's response was to order the 15th Alabama's outspoken and flamboyant commander, Colonel William C. Oates, to wheel his regiment leftward and to "attack furiously." Without missing a step, the 15th Alabama spun through a sixty-degree arc and sprinted ahead. Perry watched approvingly as Oates's men drove the Federals—who Perry estimated outnumbered the Alabamians more than two to one—in the "wildest confusion before them." Perry later described Oates's maneuver as "one of the most brilliant movements I have ever seen on a battlefield." From prisoners, Oates learned that he had routed the 15th New York Heavy Artillery. He took little pride in the feat. The defeated Federals had had a sheltered experience guarding Washington. This had been their first exposure to combat, and they had been no match for the veteran Alabamians. Oates had only two men killed and eleven wounded. "I always attributed it to two things," he later explained. "First, that the troops of the enemy were not veterans—they were unused to battle; and, secondly, the rapidity and boldness of my movement, and the accuracy of the fire of my men."[43]

Perry's left wing was still too weak to drive Wadsworth's division from its low hill. Crouching in the swamp, the Confederates were blistered by intense fire. Soldiers in the 48th Alabama broke and sought protection behind trees. The 44th Alabama's commander gamely rode up and down, a flag in his left hand and a sword in his right. Perry himself jumped into the fray. A Union bullet winged into his horse, tumbling the brigade commander to the ground.

At this critical moment, Oates again came to Perry's rescue. After

42. Perry, "Reminiscences of the Campaign," in *SHSP*, VII, 52.
43. *Ibid.*, 53; Oates, *The War Between the Union and the Confederacy*, 347.

scattering the New Yorkers who had been harassing Perry's left, Oates had crossed the swamp and advanced to the rise. That put him just above the Federals. He was apparently joined by elements of Gregg's Texas brigade, which had regrouped after their costly charge across Widow Tapp's field. From his position, he could see Wadsworth's line as it poured "well-directed volleys" into Perry's ranks below. Oates responded by swinging his regiment squarely across Wadsworth's flank. As Oates related it, a single volley from his soldiers "stopped their racket." The enemy bolted, and Perry's beleaguered left wing pressed its momentary advantage. The high ground east of Widow Tapp's field was regained by the Confederates.[44]

Perry, after consolidating his hold, dispatched a staff officer to alert Lee that a Union counterattack might "outflank and envelop" his Alabama brigade. "I was guilty of the irregularity of reporting directly to the commander-in-chief," Perry confessed, "because I did not know where General Field was to be found, and was communicating knowledge that I thought General Lee ought to have at once." Lee replied that the Alabamians would soon be relieved. Concerned that Lee might unnecessarily weaken some other portion of his line, Perry sent an aide to inform the southern commander "that the men had supplied themselves with ammunition from the boxes of the enemy, that they were still able to do good fighting, and that I only needed to have my flanks protected."[45]

Meanwhile Perry's right wing, reinforced from Field's division and perhaps with units from Hill's corps, seesawed in a protracted battle along Orange Plank Road. At first the Confederates made impressive headway, badly shredding Baxter's Union brigade. "The whole front was lighted up with deadly volleys," reported a northerner, who thought that Perry's attack hit "with the force of an avalanche." Baxter was wounded, and his lead regiments folded, carrying the rest of the brigade with them. In order to stiffen Wadsworth's collapsing Federal formation, Eustis' and Wheaton's brigades were transferred from below Orange Plank Road to Wadsworth's sector.

44. Perry, "Reminiscences of the Campaign," in *SHSP*, VII, 54; Oates, *The War Between the Union and the Confederacy*, 347. The involvement of the Texas brigade is mentioned by Polley in *Hood's Texas Brigade*, 232–33. The 11th Pennsylvania, which received Oates's attack, later reported a "most galling fire on our right flank." See Coulter's Report, in *OR*, Vol. XXXVI, Pt. 1, p. 596.

45. Perry, "Reminiscences of the Campaign," in SHSP, VII, 55–56.

Eustis' brigade came first in a column of regiments, the 37th Massachusetts leading. As soon as the fresh troops arrived, Wadsworth directed them into the fight. Eustis refused to comply and halted his brigade. Unaware of the disagreement between Wadsworth and Eustis, the 37th Massachusetts proceeded alone. "It was like a charge through the wildest regions of Dante's Inferno," recorded the regiment's historian. "Over the swamps, between the saplings, through the bushes and briers the men forced themselves, firing as they went, clearing the human opposition away with the bayonet." But the job was too much. Squeezed on both sides by Longstreet's Confederates, the Massachusetts men dropped back to their brigade.[46]

Still, the timely arrival of Eustis' and Wheaton's reinforcements momentarily shifted the advantage to the Federals. Not only was Perry's right wing heavily outnumbered, it had outpaced the Confederate forces below Orange Plank Road.

Perry had no choice but to withdraw under "severe fire." Protective cover was available behind captured enemy works. There the southerners re-formed and charged again, this time with better success. Eustis' right flank was "in the air," and rebels began enveloping it. By this time, however, the Alabama ranks had been "terribly thinned," and more Federal units were gathering in their front and to their right. The Alabamians had to sound another retreat. As they retired, they were joined by remnants of Benning's 20th Georgia. Before Perry could launch a new charge, General Field arrived. The three brigades that he had fed into battle—Gregg's, Benning's, and Perry's—were in shambles. "This is all of my command that I can find," he remarked in dismay. Vetoing another attack, the Confederate commander set about reorganizing the scattered remnants of his division.[47]

"Major General Field endeared himself to every man of his command by his cool daring and efficiency," observed a Georgia soldier.

---

46. Coles, "History of the Fourth Alabama Regiment," in Regimental Collection, ADAH; Locke, *The Story of the Regiment*, 326–27; Bowen, *History of the Thirty-Seventh Regiment Massachusetts*, 277–78; Oliver Edwards, "Memorandum," in Illinois State Historical Library, Springfield; Getty's Report, in *OR*, Vol. XXXVI, Pt. 1, p. 677; Frank Wheaton's Report, in *OR*, Vol. XXXVI, Pt. 1, p. 682.

47. Perry, "Reminiscences of the Campaign," in *SHSP*, VII, 57; Coles, "History of the Fourth Alabama Regiment," in Regimental Collection, ADAH; Field, "Campaign of 1864 and 1865," in *SHSP*, XIV, 544.

Hitting in quick succession, the determined Texans, Georgians, and Alabamians had all but obliterated the northern half of the Federal assault column. Wadsworth's division was no longer a functioning combat force. According to a Union witness, Wadsworth's troops were "driven back, and badly scattered, a large portion of them taking the route over which they had marched the night before." Masses of demoralized Yankees fled toward the Lacy house. Among them were survivors of Cutler's famed Iron Brigade. Baxter's brigade also sustained "severe losses" and was temporarily integrated into Hancock's corps. Wadsworth and his brigadier Rice remained near the front, trying to restore order.[48]

At the same time that Field's Confederates were pounding Wadsworth north of Orange Plank Road, Kershaw's division was flexing its muscles below the roadway.

Kershaw, like Field, had reached Widow Tapp's field just as Hill's men came cascading from the far woods. Kershaw immediately ordered Henagan's South Carolina brigade to form below the road in an area of scrubby pine. "Before the movement could be completely executed," Kershaw reported, "the retreating masses of Heth's and Wilcox's divisions broke through my ranks." Yankees followed closely behind. "A perfect hail of bullets came flying overhead and through our ranks," recalled a South Carolina officer, "but not a man moved, only to allow the stampeded troops of Heth's and Wilcox's to pass to the rear." Kershaw dashed to the head of the brigade. He knew these soldiers well, for he had commanded them until his recent promotion to division head. An observer recalled Kershaw's "eyes flashing fire," and remarked on how the general was "sitting his horse like a centaur—that superb style as Joe Kershaw only could." Kershaw's words were few but to the point: "Now, my old brigade. I expect you to do your duty." [49]

Down a gentle slope ran Henagan's men, dressing their lines as

48. Joseph P. Fuller Diary, May 6, 1864, in Joseph P. Fuller Collection, GDAH; Cutler's Report, in OR, Vol. XXXVI, Pt. 1, p. 611; Coulter's Report, in OR, Vol. XXXVI, Pt. 1, p. 596.

49. Kershaw's Report, in OR, Vol. XXXVI, Pt. 1, p. 1061; Dickert, History of Kershaw's Brigade, 346.

they advanced. From ahead came "withering fire," and gray-clad forms began dropping to the ground. "Hold your fire," cried Henagan's officers, urging their soldiers to wait until they had clear targets. A "long line of blue could be seen under the ascending smoke of thousands of rifles," recalled a Confederate. "The red flashes of their guns seemed to blaze in our very faces." Henagan's brigade crashed into the Union line, jarring the 2nd South Carolina northward and creating a gap in the rebel formation. Enemy units began slipping into the interval. Turning to Brigadier General Benjamin G. Humphreys, whose brigade of Mississippians had just arrived, Longstreet ordered, "Form your line, General." One of Humphreys' soldiers recalled that "we had just halted and were panting like lizards." The winded soldiers quickly regrouped—"wounded men and minie-balls were coming through our ranks before we got loaded"—and dashed toward the endangered spot.[50]

Two of Kershaw's brigades were by then engaged. "Men rolled and writhed in their last death struggle," recounted a South Carolina soldier. "Wounded men groped their way to the rear, being blinded by the stifling smoke. All commands were drowned in this terrible din of battle—the earth and elements shook and trembled with the deadly shock of combat." Humphreys later wrote of his brigade's charge across Widow Tapp's field, "It was a terrible ordeal." In one twenty-man company, eighteen soldiers were casualties. A Mississippi man boasted that "our brigade had done good fighting before, but I thought it reached a climax on that occasion."[51]

Kershaw's assault had caught the Federals positioned below Orange Plank Road—Hancock's 2nd Corps, reinforced by Getty's division—completely by surprise.

A crack unit of Union sharpshooters had been exploring ahead of Hancock's column. Kershaw's initial onslaught ripped through the Union marksmen and tore squarely into Birney's and Mott's Federal

50. Dickert, *History of Kershaw's Brigade*, 346–47; William Wallace, "Operations of Second South Carolina Regiment in Campaigns of 1864 and 1865," in *SHSP*, VII, 128; Abernathy, "Our Mess," in Abernathy Collection, MDAH; Benjamin Humphreys, "Sunflower Guards," in J. F. H. Claiborne Papers, SHC; W. Garth Johnson, "Barksdale-Humphreys Mississippi Brigade," *Confederate Veteran*, I (1893), 207.
51. Dickert, *History of Kershaw's Brigade*, 347; Humphreys, "Sunflower Guards," in Claiborne Papers, SHC; Johnson, "Barksdale-Humphreys Mississippi Brigade," 207; John Coxe, "Last Struggles and Successes of Lee," *Confederate Veteran*, XXII (1914), 356.

divisions. According to a northerner, the first sign that things had gone amiss was a "rattle of musketry like the boiling cauldrons of hell, as is represented to us by our good Chaplains." The Federal front was "shattered and broken" almost immediately. Disorganized clumps of blue-clad soldiers slumped to the rear. A partial explanation for Kershaw's success lies in the confused condition of Hancock's ranks. An officer in the 141st Pennsylvania later explained that "during the entire morning's operation there had been neither a general nor staff officer along this portion of the line." Ammunition had run low, and the advancing Union line had lost its formation in the swampy, heavily wooded terrain. Birney's division drifted off course. Parts of Gibbon's division—primarily from Carroll's brigade—edged into the breach, only to be overwhelmed by Kershaw's rebels.[52]

As Birney's and Mott's formations disintegrated, the job of fending off Kershaw fell to Hancock's second line. Initially, that had consisted of Getty's division. But two of Getty's three available brigades—Eustis' and Wheaton's—had just been ordered to move above Orange Plank Road to help Wadsworth. All that remained to Getty was Lewis Grant's Vermont brigade.

Shrill rebel yells rent the air. Sheets of lead tore into the Union ranks. A bullet struck Getty in the shoulder. Bleeding profusely, the general was led to the rear. Command of the division devolved on Frank Wheaton, Getty's senior brigadier. Wheaton, however, had his hands full fighting Field's Confederates north of Orange Plank Road. The played-out Vermonters had become responsible for defending the entire lower portion of the Union formation.

The Vermont troops had one advantage. When Kershaw sliced through the lead Federal elements, the Vermont brigade happened to occupy a low rise. It was a strong natural position, capped by earthworks constructed by Powell Hill's troops the preceding day. Crouched behind the makeshift fortification, Lewis Grant's troops repelled successive waves of attacks. Their position became precarious, however, when Wadsworth's line to their right gave ground

52. Winfield S. Hancock's Report, in *OR*, Vol. XXXVI, Pt. 1, pp. 320–21; C. A. Stevens, *Berdan's United States Sharpshooters*, 403–404; Ripley, *Vermont Riflemen*, 148–51; Galwey, *The Valiant Hours*, 198; Tyler's Report, in *OR*, Vol. XXXVI, Pt. 1, p. 477; Charles D. Page, *History of the Fourteenth Regiment, Connecticut*, 236–37; Cowtan, *Services of the Tenth New York*, 248–51; Craft, *History of the One Hundred Forty-First Regiment, Pennsylvania*, 181.

under Field's pounding. Confederate bullets then whistled in from Grant's northern flank as well as from in front. Rather than retreating, Grant chose the riskier course of facing a regiment northward to protect the exposed end of his brigade's line. "Perhaps the valor of Vermont troops and the steadiness and unbroken front of those noble regiments were never more signally displayed," the brigadier later reported. "They stood out in the very midst of the enemy, unyielding, dealing death and slaughter in front and flank." [53]

Grant's Vermonters could not hold for long. But reinforcements were on the way. Owen's and Carroll's brigades, bloodied during the initial attack, had regrouped. Rushing forward, they passed through the Green Mountain men and on toward the Confederates.

The Union troops, however, were too disorganized to make telling use of their numbers. "The struggle up to this point had been over ground so rough and through a thicket so dense," recounted a soldier in Carroll's brigade, "that when a halt was called to reform, only a small part of any one company could be assembled." An attempt to restore order was made by shouting through the woods, "Hello, Carroll's brigade!" [54]

Holding ground was difficult; advancing was out of the question. Kershaw's Confederate foot soldiers were firing from ahead while rebel artillery at Widow Tapp's farm hurled shells with disconcerting accuracy. One projectile struck a tree next to the commander of the 12th New Jersey, and its flying splinters painfully disabled him. His successor somehow persuaded the frightened soldiers to resist their instinct to flee. They dug in, hoping to hold on until more reinforcements arrived. The 14th Connecticut hunkered down behind breastworks of fallen trees stacked by Hill's men the previous night. On Carroll's right, a company of new recruits dropped back to reload. Panic ensued, and the 10th New York folded, company by company, "similar to the fall of a row of bricks." A quick-thinking color guard saved the day. Waving a flag, he ran to the front. "The effect was electrical," according to a witness. Inspired by his example, the regiment rallied and regained its position. [55]

53. Getty's Report, in OR, Vol. XXXVI, Pt. 1, p. 677; Wheaton's Report, *ibid.*, 682; Lewis Grant's Report, *ibid.*, 698–99; Benedict, *Vermont in the Civil War*, I, 429–31.

54. Galway, *The Valiant Hours*, 198.

55. Longacre, *To Gettysburg and Beyond*, 189–90; Charles D. Page, *History of the Fourteenth Regiment, Connecticut*, 237; Cowtan, *Services of the Tenth New York*, 248–51.

Kershaw meanwhile was deploying another Confederate brigade, Brigadier General Goode Bryan's Georgians, to lend muscle to his attack. Bryan's men had been delayed by the difficulties of organizing a coherent battle line in a "dense thicket under a severe fire of the enemy" while being "constantly broken through by men hurrying to the rear." As Bryan later said, his brigade's discipline was "severely tried." But despite these obstacles, he managed to overrun some of Grant's log breastworks. The Confederate brigade's ammunition was, however, swiftly depleted.[56]

Kershaw at that point had three brigades actively engaged: Henagan's, Humphreys', and Bryan's. These Confederate elements formed a connected line in the woods below Orange Plank Road. Directly across from them, protected behind makeshift earthworks, were the Federals, consisting of the divisions of Mott and Birney, in addition to Owen's, Carroll's, and Grant's brigades. The northerners had the advantage of numbers, and they were fighting "obstinately," as Kershaw later put it. "It seemed for a time as if the whole Federal army was upon us—so thick and fast came the death dealing missiles," remembered a southerner. Combat below Orange Plank Road reached a fevered pitch as the Federal left wing's full weight bore down on Kershaw's three brigades. "Both armies stood at extreme tension," a Confederate officer recalled of those moments. "The cord must soon snap one way or the other, or it seemed all would be annihilated." Kershaw refused to relinquish his hold. Casting about for more reinforcements, he considered bringing up his final brigade, Brigadier General William T. Wofford's Georgians. These troops, however, were too distant to assist in the immediate crisis. They had been assigned earlier to protect the 1st Corps' wagon trains and were still behind the army. With no other choice, Kershaw rode to the head of his three-brigade line and ordered another charge. The response was immediate, enabling him to recover enough high ground to establish a defensible position. Even more important, he was finally able to connect his division's left flank with Field's right, so that Longstreet's corps ran in an unbroken line across Orange Plank Road into the woods on each side.[57]

56. Goode Bryan's Report, in OR, Vol. XXXVI, Pt. 1, pp. 1063–64.
57. Kershaw's Report, in OR, Vol. XXXVI, Pt. 1, p. 1061; Dickert, *History of Kershaw's Brigade*, 347–48.

Kershaw's advance had been as impressive as Field's. The South Carolinian, a soldier wrote that evening, "exposed himself most daringly and showed much skill in putting his men into action and managing them under heavy fire." The division's performance was particularly impressive given that none of Kershaw's senior officers were professional military men. Kershaw and Henagan were lawyers, and Humphreys and Bryan were planters. But the casualties had been severe. "Regiments were left without commanders; companies, without officers," reported one of Henagan's men. Two of the South Carolina brigade's six regimental commanders were killed, and two were wounded.[58]

At that juncture—it was now around eight in the morning—Richard Anderson's division of Hill's corps reached Widow Tapp's field. Anderson's men, who had stayed in the rear to patrol the Rapidan, had been marching all morning from Verdiersville and had fallen in behind Longstreet's column on Orange Plank Road. Although the newly arrived troops belonged to Hill's corps, Lee placed them under the direct command of Longstreet. By that action, Lee lent formal substance to the reality of the Confederate command structure in the Orange Plank Road sector. This was Longstreet's fight, and he was doing a spectacular job of it, even by Lee's exacting standards.

Longstreet decided to hold Anderson's division in reserve. Apparently he placed most of the recent arrivals north of Orange Plank Road in support of Field's division. Abner Perrin's fresh Alabama brigade joined Perry's Alabamians behind the log works that they had so resolutely held. Together the two Alabama brigades formed an imposing line of rebel muskets.[59]

The impact of Longstreet's counteroffensive on Hancock's frame of mind was vividly described by the aide Lyman. Shortly after six o'clock that morning, wounded Union troops began dribbling back

---

58. Susan Leigh Blackford, comp., *Letters from Lee's Army; or, Memories of Life in and out of the Army in Virginia During the War Between the States* (New York, 1947), 245; Dickert, *History of Kershaw's Brigade*, 347–48.
59. Perry, "Reminiscences of the Campaign," in *SHSP*, VII, 57.

to the intersection of Orange Plank and Brock roads. One soldier approached Lyman at the Federal 2nd Corps headquarters with a gray-clad captive in tow. "I was ordered to report that this prisoner here belongs to Longstreet's corps," the man announced. "Do you belong to Longstreet?" Lyman asked. "Ya-as," drawled the dust-caked captive. Hancock ordered artillery into the roadway, and soon cannon were lobbing solid shot over retreating bluecoats toward the Confederates. "The streams of troops came faster and faster back," Lyman reported in a letter home. "Here a field officer, reeling in the saddle; and there another, hastily carried past on a stretcher." The aide remained at the crossing, helping to turn back shirkers and soldiers who were obviously exaggerating their injuries.[60]

At 6:20, Lyman sent a dispatch to Meade notifying him of the deteriorating situation. "The left of our assault has struck Longstreet," the aide wrote headquarters. Rebels were "filing to the south of the Plank Road—our left; how far not yet developed." Ten minutes later, Lyman transmitted an update to headquarters. "We about hold our own against Longstreet," the staffer informed Meade, "and many regiments are tired and shattered." He emphasized that it was important to relieve the pressure on Hancock. Perhaps Burnside, whose corps was supposed to be advancing toward Hancock's right flank, could attack "as soon as possible." Interpreting Lyman's missive as a request for reinforcements, headquarters replied that the army's only reserve was a 9th Corps division near Wilderness Tavern. The troops would be ordered to Hancock "should it become absolutely necessary," but Hancock was to call for them "only in case of the last necessity."

At seven, Hancock penned his response. Initiative was slipping from his control. "They are pressing us on the road a good deal," Hancock informed headquarters. "If more force were here now I could use it; but I don't know whether I can get it in time or not. I am filling up the [ammunition] boxes of the men who are returning, and re-establishing my lines, closing up with right."[61]

60. Lyman to family, May 16, 1864, in *Meade's Headquarters,* ed. Agassiz, 94.

61. Theodore Lyman to George G. Meade, 6:20 A.M., May 6, 1864, Theodore Lyman to George G. Meade, 6:30 A.M., May 6, 1864, Andrew A. Humphreys to Winfield S. Hancock, 7:00 A.M., May 6, 1864, all in *OR,* Vol. XXXVI, Part 2, p. 440; Winfield S. Hancock to Andrew A. Humphreys, 7:10 A.M., May 6, 1864, *ibid.,* 440–41.

By 8 A.M., Longstreet's counterattack, like Hancock's initial assault, had spent its force. Neither contestant was capable of making headway against the other, and neither was willing to retreat. Mere feet apart but virtually invisible to each other, the blue and the gray continued their slaughter with unabated violence. The musketry was "savage in its character," wrote one of Carroll's troops, "and was too severe to allow of bringing in those of the wounded who still lay on the lines of the advanced position." The 10th New York's historian recorded that "the atmosphere of the woods was now thick and heavy with sulphurous smoke. There seemed not wind enough to raise the dense shroud which clung to our lines." Soldiers were unable to discern friends from enemies. "The continuous rack of musketry—the excitement—the cheers of our own brigade— the sometimes sharp and again sullen yells of the enemy—all of this happening in our own immediate vicinity, had deadened our senses to the fact that we were not alone engaged." To the rear ran "the dusty Plank Road, along which, as far as the eye could reach, moved a procession of wounded, borne on blankets and stretchers." [62]

While Longstreet continued hammering, Hill was busy forming Heth and Wilcox into a line that stretched from Widow Tapp's clearing to the Chewning farm. Scouting ahead, Hill, his aide Palmer, and the rest of his staff rode into the Chewning yard and dismounted. They examined the ground carefully, oblivious to developments around them. The sound of a fence being dismantled drew their attention. Looking up, Hill and his aides saw Federal infantrymen preparing to advance. "Mount, walk your horses, and don't look back," Hill ordered his staffers. Steadily, the small group rode from the clearing. For the second time in two days, Hill had narrowly avoided capture. The gap was soon plugged, this time for good. Lane's brigade, which had briefly rested in the Chewning field the day before, again occupied it. Earthworks were erected to secure the brigade's position. Later, as Palmer passed an assemblage of Federal prisoners, a northerner called out, "Were you not at the house a short time ago?" Palmer answered that he had indeed been there. The soldier began expostulating with his officers, who had been captured with

---

62. Cowtan, *Services of the Tenth New York,* 251–52.

him. "I wanted to fire on you," he explained to Palmer, "but my colonel said you were farmers riding from the house."[63]

After Longstreet's arrival, Hill played no significant role in the Orange Plank Road fighting. It had become Longstreet's show, and even Lee was reluctant to interfere with his War Horse's management of the battle. When things settled down, Hill dispatched Palmer to request that one of Anderson's brigades, all of which had been temporarily assigned to Longstreet, be returned to him. Lee told the staffer to "see General Longstreet about it." Doubtless reveling in his role as the army's deliverer, Longstreet magnanimously offered, "Certainly, Colonel, which one will you take?" Palmer answered, "The lead one," and returned to Hill with the reinforcements.[64]

Longstreet had reason to be proud. Within two hours, he had dramatically reversed the battle's momentum. Through an impressive feat of arms, the 1st Corps, assisted by scattered elements of Hill's command, had seized the offensive and established a new front several hundred yards east of Widow Tapp's clearing. With two divisions—almost the same number of troops that had been available to Hill earlier in the morning—Longstreet had brought nearly five victorious Union divisions to a standstill, mauling several so badly that they had ceased to function as combat units. "In a short time he was master of the field," wrote Palmer of Longstreet, "and everybody felt that way about it." Hill's soldiers were mortified. "After putting up such a battle the day before, to have been found by Longstreet's troops retiring, and in more or less confusion was dreadful," Palmer admitted in a postwar letter to a friend. It was particularly galling that Longstreet's troops were unaware of the 3rd Corps' valiant defense the previous afternoon. "They only knew that with a conspicuous courage and steadiness they had redeemed a losing battle, and saved the Army of Northern Virginia from disaster."[65]

---

63. Royall, *Some Reminiscences*, 33–34. The Federals were apparently from the 6th New Hampshire, of Burnside's Corps. Lieutenant George W. Osgood, of Company K, later told of approaching the Chewning field with a detail of some seventy-five men. "A solitary horseman in citizen's dress was seen riding slowly away from the cabin," he recalled. The figure must have been Hill. See Lyman Jackman and Amos Hadley, *History of the Sixth New Hampshire Regiment in the War for the Union* (Concord, N.H., 1891), 226.

64. Royall, *Some Reminiscences*, 33–34.

65. *Ibid.*, 32–33.

"Things were slightly mixed."

Grant and his staff spent the night of May 5–6 in tents near Wilderness Tavern. They were awakened at four in the morning by the sound of troops filing down Germanna Plank Road. More Federal soldiers heading for the battlefront came streaming down the Orange Turnpike. Orderlies, cooks, and teamsters were bustling everywhere. "Bodies of woods, solitary trees on the ridges, and vacant sky-arched distances, were stealing into view as we hastily breakfasted," remembered a Union staffer. A low ground fog filled hollows and gullies. The general-in-chief, already notorious for unusual eating habits, surprised even his aides. Selecting a cucumber, he sliced it, poured vinegar on the pieces, and then downed the concoction. After clearing his palate with a cup of strong coffee, Grant summoned his servant Bill, who brought a fistful of cigars. Lighting one, Grant stuffed the rest—twenty-four in all—into his pockets. Thus armed, he walked over to his knoll next to the turnpike and began pacing slowly back and forth, intently listening for the battle to begin.[66]

At early light, Warren mounted his massive dapple-gray horse and began heading out the turnpike toward the battle line. His bright yellow sash and scarlet saddle blanket contrasted sharply with the fresh green spring foliage. Rising morning mist gave the scene a dreamlike quality.

Warren's 5th Corps was again responsible for the battle sector along the Orange Turnpike. Griffin's division had reoccupied its previous day's position along the eastern edge of Saunders' Field, with Bartlett's brigade north of the turnpike, Ayres's below the roadway, and Sweitzer's massed in support. On Griffin's left, where Wadsworth's men had fought the day before, was Crawford's Pennsylvania division. Two of Robinson's brigades, reinforced by a heavy artillery brigade freshly arrived from Chancellorsville, remained in reserve at the Lacy farm.

The woods on Warren's left were unoccupied, which created a gap of over a mile between Warren's and Hancock's wings. As envisioned by Grant, the vacancy would be temporary. At any moment,

---

66. Schaff, *The Battle of the Wilderness*, 227–29; Horace Porter, *Campaigning with Grant*, 56.

Burnside was supposed to be occupying Crawford's former stronghold at the Chewning farm.

Sedgwick's Sixth Corps spread north through the woods on Warren's right. Uncle John's troops were apprehensive. "The enemy throughout the night was continually strengthening his lines," reported an officer on Sedgwick's extreme northern flank. "The felling and cutting of trees was continual, and the movement of guns to [the Confederate] left was distinctly heard." Sedgwick's men regarded these sounds as unmistakable signs that the rebels intended to strike in their sector.[67]

True to form, Ewell's Confederates were indeed planning to attack. During the night, Ewell had skillfully rearranged his artillery batteries, massing pieces on his extreme left and more on each side of the turnpike. A battalion covered the gap between his corps and Hill's. Ewell's riflemen stacked trees in front of their trenches, branches sharpened and pointed toward the enemy. These abatis, as the obstacles were called, were meant to delay Union attackers while rebel guns pounded them to bits. In front of the abatis in a thin line, thirty to forty feet apart, lay Confederate sharpshooters armed with Enfield rifles. They were deadly marksmen. "From what I saw on going over the ground the next morning," recalled one of Gordon's Georgians, "very few shots fired by them were ineffectual."[68]

At daybreak, rebel batteries to the left and front of Griffin's line opened "effective" fire. Federal batteries south of the turnpike shot back at smoke from the rebel guns.

Sedgwick, like Hancock, was under orders to attack at five o'clock. Ewell, however, beat him to the punch. At 4:45, rebels poured over their earthworks toward Sedgwick's formation. It was a "fierce charge," recalled a Union witness, and it caught the northerners off guard. The roar of battle soon reached Sedgwick, who had set up headquarters close behind his lines on Spotswood Road. The 6th Corps commander made light of Ewell's attack. "Sedgwick says

67. Powell, *The Fifth Army Corps*, 616; John Lentz's Report, in OR, Vol. XXXVI, Pt. 1, p. 555; William Tilton's Report, in OR, Vol. XXXVI, Pt. 1, pp. 559–60; William White's Report, in OR, Vol. XXXVI, Pt. 1, p. 576; Henry Dalton's Report, in OR, Vol. XXXVI, Pt. 1, pp. 659–60; Truman Seymour's Report, in OR, Vol. XXXVI, Pt. 1, p. 728.

68. Richard S. Ewell's Report, in OR, Vol. XXXVI, Pt. 1, pp. 1070–71; Pendleton's Report, *ibid.*, 1040; Isaac G. Bradwell, "Second Day's Battle of the Wilderness," *Confederate Veteran*, XXVIII (1920), 20.

Ewell's watch must be fifteen minutes ahead of his," reported a war correspondent.[69]

Apparently Ewell intended first to probe the Federal defenses, then to attack in strength if circumstances warranted. His beginning assault, launched against the northern sector of Sedgwick's formation, made no significant impression. The Confederates were driven back, followed by a wave of Federals. Soon both sides were pitching in for all they were worth.

Fire belched from opposing earthworks in rolling waves of death that swept off toward the south. Before long, Sedgwick's entire front was ablaze. "The volleys of musketry echoed and reechoed through the forest like peals of thunder, and the battle surged to and fro, now one party charging, and now the other, the interval between the two armies being fought over in many places as many as five times, leaving the ground covered with dead and wounded," wrote a 6th Corps surgeon. "Those of the wounded able to crawl reached one or the other line, but the groans of others, who could not move, lent an additional horror to the terrible scene whenever there was a lull in the battle."[70]

Along much of Sedgwick's front, it was impossible for anyone to cross the fire-swept ground. Upton's brigade was pinned in place, as was Brown's. Russell's brigade "laid under a severe fire from the enemy's sharpshooters all day." The Federals suffered heavily from rebel artillery bombardments.[71]

In an effort to break the impasse, troops near the northern end of Sedgwick's formation tried to breach Ewell's defenses. These soldiers belonged to Neill's brigade, strengthened by some New Jersey regiments. Ewell, however, had arranged a devilish welcome. Surging forward, Neill's men found themselves slogging through a marsh laced with a thick growth of prickly brush. Ahead waited Confederates, posted on a ridge and firing into the northerners with deadly accuracy. As Neill's charge lost momentum, wounded Yankees started drifting to the rear. One disabled soldier hobbled past Sedgwick. "How is it at the front?" inquired the general. "There is very hard

69. Washington A. Roebling's Report, in Warren Papers, NYSA; George T. Stevens, *Three Years in the Sixth Corps*, 309; Charles A. Page, *Letters of a War Correspondent*, 52.

70. George T. Stevens, *Three Years in the Sixth Corps*, 309.

71. Baquet, *History of the First Brigade New Jersey*, 211; Emory Upton's Report, in OR, Vol. XXXVI, Pt. 1, p. 666; Daniel Bidwell's Report, in OR, Vol. XXXVI, Pt. 1, p. 719.

fighting, sir," the injured man replied, "but we will whip them sure." Sedgwick responded with a smile. "I should think by the sound that there was some fighting; of course we will whip them." Neill's brigade, however, retired under the blistering Confederate fire with heavy losses. Oliver Wendell Holmes, Jr., assigned to division headquarters, summed up the miserable affair in his diary: "A simultaneous attack was tried at 5:00 A.M. Advanced some way—not much effected however—a marsh, abatis and battery in our front—General [Wright] managed to keep himself and staff pretty well in range of shells—Lost some prisoners stuck up to waist in marsh, in their attempt to charge."[72]

As combat escalated in front of Sedgwick, Warren's troops waited for the signal to attack. Their mood, a soldier later recalled, was one of "anxious expectancy." The men of Griffin's division, ensconced along Saunders' Field, were haunted by memories of the previous afternoon's slaughter. Enemy fortifications were "plainly to be seen across the open field, a quarter of a mile ahead," noted a Pennsylvanian. Confederate artillery shells arched above Warren's line, and rebel sharpshooters fired at every movement. "Any one who assumed a perpendicular position was sure to make himself a target for the enemy," recalled a New Yorker. The only safe spot in the vicinity of Saunders' Field was a ravine just east of the clearing. As the New Yorker put it, the whole affair involved "extreme discomfort." Upon learning of Sedgwick's inability to budge Ewell's Confederates, Warren decided against throwing his corps into the fray. "The enemy was found to be entrenched," he reported by way of explaining his inactivity, "and but little impression could be made." One of Warren's officers later advanced the excuse that "the Sixth Corps on our right was to commence the assault and when it became actively engaged our corps was to advance to the attack at once." So long as the 6th Corps remained in its trenches, he maintained, the 5th Corps had no choice but to stay put.[73]

Warren's soldiers, of course, were relieved by their commander's

---

72. Oliver Edwards' Report, in *OR,* Vol. XXXVI, Pt. 1, p. 672; Theodore Gold, "Memorial Day Exercises in Memory of General John Sedgwick," quoted by Winslow in *General John Sedgwick,* 157–58; Holmes, *Touched with Fire,* 106.

73. Nash, *A History of the Forty-Fourth Regiment New York,* 185–86; Judson, *History of the Eighty-Third Regiment Pennsylvania,* 195; Gouverneur K. Warren's Report, in *OR,* Vol. XXXVI, Pt. 1, p. 540.

decision. Charging across Saunders' Field the previous day had been a bloody proposition. Now that the Confederates had used the night to perfect their earthworks, attempting to cross the field would be nothing short of suicide.

Headquarters, however, felt differently about the matter. In the woods to the south, Hancock's advance was going unexpectedly well. From all reports, it appeared that Hill's Confederate line was in shambles. To prevent Ewell from assisting Hill, it was deemed important for Warren at least to act as though he intended to attack.

Accordingly, around 6 A.M., Meade tactfully tried to rouse Warren. "The major-general commanding desires that you will throw your pickets and skirmishers well out to the front," stated a message from Meade's chief of staff Humphreys to the Union 5th Corps commander. A half hour later, Warren dutifully notified Humphreys that he was making progress. Griffin's division had driven rebel skirmishers back to their main line, Warren explained, and the corps' artillery was rumbling into position. These preliminary movements, however, only served to afford Warren another excuse for delay. "I think it best not to make the final assault until the preparations are made," the general informed headquarters.[74]

It was about at this point that things began to go awry on the Federal left wing. Warren sensed that something was wrong when Roebling reported rebels "cheering as if in considerable force" in the direction of Parker's Store. "I have informed General Burnside," Warren notified headquarters, adding that "it is too smokey to see anything." Anticipating renewed rebel efforts on his own front, Warren directed Griffin to keep firing down the turnpike with artillery to prevent "the enemy from using it in the smoke." At 7:15 A.M., headquarters alerted Warren that Longstreet had emerged on Hancock's left. And this time Meade's chief of staff did not mince words. "The major-general commanding considers it of the utmost importance that your attack should be pressed with the utmost vigor," he informed the spindly New Yorker. "Spare ammunition and use the bayonet." Still Warren hesitated. About the same time that he received Meade's strongly worded directive, he was being assured by subordinates that the Confederate works were impregnable. For ex-

---

74. Andrew A. Humphreys to Gouverneur K. Warren, May 6, 1864, in OR, Vol. XXXVI, Pt. 2, p. 449; Gouverneur K. Warren to Andrew A. Humphreys, May 6, 1864, ibid., 450.

ample, Crawford, who was located just below the turnpike, warned that "the enemy have a strong line of entrenchments in our front. My left is strongly felt by the enemy."[75]

Warren's instincts counseled caution. The general considered himself a scientific soldier and a master at the craft of maneuver. Frontal assaults against fortified works were antithetical to his nature. The previous day, he had acquiesced against his better judgment in Meade's order to attack. The result had been ruinous. This time, he would not compromise his principles. Despite headquarters' relentless carping, Warren was not going to budge.

At the same time that Warren was ordered forward, instructions to attack went to Sedgwick. That seasoned fighter gamely responded by attempting another foray against Ewell's northern flank. Seymour, whose 6th Corps brigade had failed signally in a similar attempt the evening before, was ordered in. Seymour's soldiers were understandably reluctant to move. "Every man," recalled a Pennsylvanian, "from the private soldier up to the regimental commander, knew by the experience of the previous night, and by the difficulties already met, that such an attack in such force, was next to madness." The rebels were virtually invisible in the woods. 'We opened fire on them by the sound of their muskets, that being the only way we could locate them," explained a Maryland soldier.[76]

Pegram's Confederate brigade still occupied earthworks across from Seymour. A rebel later remembered that he had just sat down to boil coffee water when the Federals struck. "Before the water got hot the pickets began firing and bullets coming over head and striking the trees assured us it was not a false alarm," he wrote. "By the time our men got up our skirmish line was in and another battle was raging."[77]

Seymour's northerners charged in five waves. "As fast as we could break one another one would come up," recounted a southerner.

---

75. Gouverneur K. Warren to Andrew A. Humphreys, 7 A.M., May 6, 1864, in 5th Corps Letterbook 7A, Warren Papers, NYSA; Andrew A. Humphreys to Gouverneur K. Warren, May 6, 1864, in OR, Vol. XXXVI, Pt. 2, p. 450; Samuel W. Crawford to Gouverneur K. Warren, May 6, 1864, in OR, Vol. XXXVI, Pt. 2, p. 457.

76. Osceola Lewis, History of the One Hundred and Thirty-Eighth Regiment Pennsylvania Volunteer Infantry (Norristown, Pa., 1866), 85–88; Eichelberer Memoir, in Civil War Miscellaneous Collection, USMHI.

77. Buck, With the Old Confeds, 106.

"Terrible," is how another rebel described the Union attack. "We were behind our breastworks," he explained, "a great advantage, but they maintained their attack and fusillade for two long hours and of course a great many of our men were killed and wounded in aiming their guns over the breastworks."[78]

But the Confederates held the advantage of position. Seymour's troops, riddled by small-arms and artillery fire, were repulsed with heavy losses. "The enemy's line still extended beyond our right," reported Seymour, "and our formation was even now thin and weak for attacking."[79]

Pegram's soldiers were elated at the novelty of fighting from behind earthworks. "Men standing in line got in paroxysms of laughter and shouted, 'Say, boys, isn't this the mos'est fun for the leastest money?'" recalled a Confederate. "Tears from laughter made lines on powder-grimed faces, and a general spirit of hilarity prevailed." One rebel, caught up in the spirit of things, stood to load his gun. A Yankee bullet ripped a gaping hole in his throat. "He fell back almost into my lap," recorded his messmate, "but nothing could be done for him, and he died without speaking a word." The killing continued even after Seymour's Federals withdrew. Enticed by fat knapsacks and haversacks on dead Yankees, hungry Confederates darted into the no-man's-land between the lines. Many were shot by Union snipers. "Our men who were not wounded or killed fired 80 rounds of cartridges that morning," one of Pegram's soldiers recorded in his diary, "and we were constantly handing them the guns of the killed and wounded so that theirs could cool off. And we also lost a great many men—more by the explosion of shells which were constantly bursting over our heads and falling behind our works, as the Yankees by this time had the range down fine."[80]

Upon the failure of Seymour's sortie, Meade abandoned his efforts in the turnpike sector. Ewell was too well entrenched, the chance of a Union breakthrough was remote, and the cost in lives did not justify continuing to hurl soldiers against Confederate earthworks. While Longstreet and Hancock continued to claw viciously

78. *Ibid.*; Robert D. Funkhauser Diary, May 6, 1864, in *History of the Forty-Ninth Virginia*, by Hale and Phillips, 107–108.

79. Seymour's Report, in *OR*, Vol. XXXVI, Pt. 1, p. 729.

80. William Smith to John W. Daniel, October 17, 1905, in Daniel Collection, DU; Funkhauser Diary, May 6, 1864, in *History of the Forty-Ninth Virginia*, by Hale and Phillips, 108.

for advantage along Orange Plank Road, the contestants around the Orange Turnpike settled into a deadly but militarily unproductive exchange of firepower. They accomplished little beyond perpetuating the stalemate that had developed during the afternoon of May 5. For the rest of the day, Warren's and Sedgwick's corps were relegated to holding Ewell in place so as to keep him from assisting Hill.

For Ewell's soldiers, the impasse represented a welcome respite from the morning's bloody work. "The balance of this dreadful day was spent in caring for the wounded and dying and perhaps burying our dead," a Confederate scrawled in his diary.[81]

"It was all blind work."

The grand offensive that was Grant's design was failing to take shape. On the northern front, Warren and Sedgwick had mired down in a grueling version of trench warfare against Ewell. To the south, Hancock's and Wadsworth's carefully orchestrated offensive was being shredded by Longstreet's counterattack. And it was becoming apparent that Burnside's projected strike between the two Confederate wings was also unraveling.

According to Grant's scheme, Burnside's 9th Corps was to serve as an independent mass of maneuver, slipping into the gap between the two Confederate wings and descending on Hill's rear at Parker's Store. But congestion on the roads and uninspired leadership had set the 9th Corps so far behind schedule that it appeared the battle might finish without Burnside's troops ever seeing Confederates.

On the face of it, there was nothing unconscionable about the schedule that Grant had arranged for his 9th Corps commander. The three divisions intended for the operation—Potter's, Wilcox', and Stevenson's—were camped well below the Rapidan, with most of the troops on Germanna Plank Road near the Spotswood Plantation. None of the soldiers were farther than five miles from Wilderness Tavern, the jumping-off point for their projected sweep between the rebel wings. For Burnside to execute his assignment, it was necessary only that he reach the tavern by 4 A.M., an hour before the general

81. Seymour's Report, in OR, Vol. XXXVI, Pt. 1, p. 728; Hale and Phillips, *History of the Forty-Ninth Virginia*, 108.

advance was meant to begin. Presumably the corps would achieve that destination after an easy two hours on a major roadway.

By most accounts, Burnside's men started south between 1 and 2 A.M. Getting to Wilderness Tavern, however, turned out to be a nightmare. Germanna Plank Road was directly behind the 6th Corps' battle line. Wagons, guns, troops, and hospital accoutrements filled the roadway.[82]

At four o'clock, Warren's staffer Roebling rode to the pike to direct Burnside's lead elements into place. The 9th Corps was not there. Growing apprehensive, Meade and Lyman left their headquarters tent and joined Roebling's anxious vigil. Finally they sent an officer to investigate the cause of the delay. He returned and explained that he had been able to locate only one of Burnside's divisions. The road was blocked by artillery, he added, and he asked whether Meade wanted him to order the guns aside. "No, sir," Meade snapped, "I have no command over General Burnside." To Lyman, the incident represented another "mishap" of the army's divided leadership.[83]

Around five, the 9th Corps' vanguard loomed into sight and weary troops assembled in the fields around Wilderness Tavern. "Presently," recalled Lieutenant Colonel Byron M. Cutcheon, commanding the 20th Michigan, "from off down the Brock Road to the south, in front of the Second Corps, came the crash of musketry, with the occasional declaration of artillery. The sound came nearer. It rolled up the line toward us like the closing of a gigantic pair of shears." Battle was raging on both fronts, and still the 9th Corps was not in place.[84]

Roebling and Lyman had already been assigned elsewhere. Another of Warren's aides, Lieutenant Morris Schaff, was selected to guide the 9th Corps to the Chewning farm and thence to the rear of Hill's troops. While the troops were busy forming, Schaff searched in vain for Burnside. Shortly after six, the long-awaited general rode

82. Ambrose E. Burnside's Report, in *OR*, Vol. XXXVI, Pt. 1, p. 906 [1 A.M.]; Robert Potter's Report, *ibid.*, 927 [1 A.M.]; William B. Reynolds' Report, *ibid.*, 934 [2 A.M.]; Charles H. Edgerly Diary, in Harrisburg Civil War Round Table Collection, USMHI.

83. Roebling's Report, in Warren Papers, NYSA; Lyman Journal, May 6, 1864, in Lyman Papers, MHS.

84. Byron M. Cutcheon, "Autobiography," in Byron M. Cutcheon Papers, BL; Schaff, *The Battle of the Wilderness*, 231–32.

into view. He was mounted on a bobtailed horse and wore a drooping army hat encircled with a gold cord. A large entourage accompanied him. Schaff rode up and identified himself. The general's response did not bode well. "Like the Sphinx," Schaff was to recall, Burnside "made no reply, halted, and began to look with a most leaden countenance in the direction he was to go." After an embarrassingly long period of silent reflection, Burnside started toward the Lacy house. He had uttered still not a word to Schaff. Concluding that he was not wanted, Schaff was about to leave when he saw Grant's aide Babcock riding rapidly in his direction. "What's the news, Babcock?" Schaff shouted. Without halting, Babcock called back, "Hancock has driven them a mile, and we are going to have a great victory."[85]

In short order, however, headquarters began receiving the disturbing series of messages from Hancock reporting Longstreet's counteroffensive. Concerned to maintain a sizable reserve, Grant ordered Burnside to leave Stevenson's 9th Corps division at Wilderness Tavern. Burnside's two remaining divisions, Potter's and Wilcox', were to continue toward the Chewning farm as originally planned.

Around 6:30 A.M., Burnside at long last started with his diminished command along the cow path to Parker's Store. In the lead was Potter's division, and Wilcox' men followed closely. Potter deployed the 6th New Hampshire as skirmishers, while the 48th Pennsylvania ranged through the thickets that pressed in on each side of the column. Although finally under way, Burnside seemed indifferent to his superiors' exhortations to hurry. No sooner had he started than he decreed a halt. His troops were exhausted from two days of hard marching. It seemed to Burnside that the moment was right to prepare coffee and breakfast. More precious time passed as Burnside's soldiers kindled fires for their morning meal. Their repast was disturbed only by sounds of fierce fighting drifting through the woods from both sides of their column.[86]

Around 7:30, Burnside's troops resumed their march. Soon they encountered enemy pickets. A rebel artillery battalion—probably

85. Schaff, *The Battle of the Wilderness*, 232.

86. Burnside's Report, in OR, Vol. XXXVI, Pt. 1, p. 906; Potter's Report, *ibid.*, 927; Cyrus B. Comstock to Ambrose E. Burnside, May 6, 1864, *ibid.*, Pt. 2, p. 460; Committee of the Regiment, *History of the Thirty-Sixth Regiment Massachusetts Volunteers*, 150.

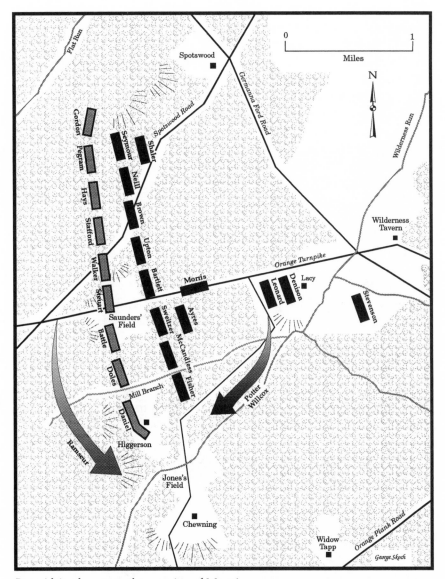

Burnside's advance on the morning of May 6

Lieutenant Colonel William J. Pegram's guns, skillfully positioned during the evening by Hill—covered the area between the Confederate 2nd Corps and 3rd Corps.

As Burnside's column lumbered up, Confederate pieces began blasting away with fire that Potter described as brisk. The Federals stopped and formed a battle line in the woods. Colonel Zenas R. Bliss, commanding one of Potter's brigades, recalled in his unpublished memoirs that as Burnside and his "numerous staff and orderlies" moved up, they were greeted by a volley of artillery shells. "The first one struck in front of us about twenty yards and rolled on the ground but did not explode," remembered Bliss. "The second passed directly over my head and struck the ground about the same distance in rear of me, doing no damage whatsoever. In a few seconds another came over the woods and striking near Burnside's staff knocked the dust and dirt on many of them." [87]

Exploring ahead, Potter discovered a sizable southern infantry force across his path. The interlopers belonged to Ramseur's North Carolina brigade. These fresh troops had formed Ewell's rear guard, picketing the Rapidan while the rest of the rebel army moved on. After patrolling north as far as Culpeper to make sure that the Federals had left, Ramseur's brigade had circled back to the Wilderness. It had rejoined Ewell, bivouacking well behind the Confederate line. Wisely, Ewell had decided to hold Ramseur in reserve.

As Burnside's foremost elements began materializing between Ewell and Hill, Ramseur was ordered into the breach. "Moving at a double-quick," reported the southern brigadier, "I arrived just in time to check a large flanking party of the enemy, and by strengthening and extending my skirmish line half a mile to the right of my line I turned the enemy's line." [88]

Deadly skirmishes rattled back and forth in the woods. At one juncture, soldiers of the 17th Vermont crawled fifty yards on their hands and knees to drive some of Ramseur's Confederates from behind a rail fence. Expecting to hold the position, the troops stacked their knapsacks on the ground. A Confederate charge drove the men away, and the knapsacks filled with clothing were joyously appropri-

---

87. Potter's Report, in OR, Vol. XXXVI, Pt. 1, p. 927; Zenas R. Bliss, "Reminiscences," in Zenas R. Bliss Collection, USMHI.

88. Stephen D. Ramseur's Report, in OR, Vol. XXXVI, Pt. 1, p. 1081; J. D. Bone, "Reminiscences," in J. D. Bone Papers, NCDAH. Ramseur's Report mistakenly refers to May 6 as May 7.

ated by Ramseur's men. At another point, the southerners routed a unit of Federal sharpshooters. The rebels found a Bible in the Ojibwa language, indicating that the marksmen were Indians.[89]

Ramseur's stout resistance threw Burnside's advance into confusion. Moreover, as time dragged on, it became apparent to Burnside that more rebels were occupying the Chewning farm. Hill's soldiers had been relieved by Longstreet and were working their way northward to connect with Ramseur. Soon two strong Confederate infantry forces, supported by artillery, would block Burnside's way.

While attempting to figure out what to do next, Burnside was joined by Grant's chief aide, Comstock. Burnside, Comstock, Roebling, and Burnside's aide Major General John G. Parke entered into a "long consultation." As Roebling recalled it, everyone agreed that progress was impossible so long as rebels held the high ground around the Chewning farm. "No one liked the idea of taking the hill by assault," Roebling later reported, "and the reluctance was increased by an occasional cannon ball coming down among the party." Someone suggested that Crawford, who formed the left flank of Warren's line across the turnpike, should advance and join the right flank of the 9th Corps. Intimately familiar with the 5th Corps' dispositions, Roebling explained that if Crawford moved forward, he would follow the turnpike at an angle leading him away from Burnside. "More than an hour was lost doing nothing," Roebling later remarked in frustration, "while the firing over by Wadsworth grew very heavy."[90]

Still the Federal high command failed to appreciate that the 9th Corps had been fought to a standstill. At 8 A.M., the army commander assured Hancock that "two of Burnside's divisions have advanced nearly to Parker's Store, and are ordered to attack to their left, which will be your front." The dispatch continued, "They ought to be engaged now and will relieve you." But Burnside was nowhere near Parker's Store. Assurances that he would relieve Hancock were wishful thoughts that bore no relation to reality.[91]

Around nine, Federal headquarters finally realized the extent of

89. Clark, comp., *Histories of the Several Regiments and Battalions from North Carolina*, I, 721; Reynolds Report, in *OR*, Vol. XXXVI, Pt. 1, p. 934; William H. Randall, "Reminiscences," in William H. Randall Papers, BL.

90. Roebling's Report, in Warren Collection, NYSA.

91. George G. Meade to Winfield S. Hancock, May 6, 1864, in *OR*, Vol. XXXVI, Pt. 2, p. 441.

Burnside's predicament. By then, the Chewning farm was firmly in Hill's hands. There remained no choice for Grant but to scrap the 9th Corps' original objective. Instead of attempting to slip Burnside behind the rebels, Grant decided to send him straight south until he reached Hancock's northern flank.

Whether the 9th Corps could have achieved its original goal if it had stuck to Grant's timetable is worth asking. If Burnside had left Wilderness Tavern by 5 A.M. and if he had forgone his stop for breakfast, he would have gained two advantages. First, he would have retained Stevenson's experienced division, and second, he would have reached the battle zone long before Hill began moving in that direction. Although he still would have confronted Ramseur's brigade and the cannon, he would have done so with the added weight of his best combat division. His chance of overcoming Ramseur would have been substantially increased, and he would have encountered no further opposition on his way across the Chewning farm and into the rear Confederate ranks. Located above and slightly behind the Confederate lines, Burnside would have been ideally situated to neutralize Longstreet and to advance the contemplated destruction of Lee.

The 9th Corps' costly failure to stay on its schedule had several causes. The delay in reaching Wilderness Tavern, which threw the entire timing out of kilter, was primarily Meade's and Grant's doing. The route should have been kept clear and Burnside's advance coordinated with units of the 6th Corps on Germanna Plank Road. Burnside's decision to halt for a leisurely breakfast compounded the delay. It has never been clear why Burnside, with two divisions, was unable to punch through Ramseur's single Confederate brigade. Burnside's actions during the rest of the day raise the question whether he devoted his full energies to the task. It is also relevant to ask what he might have accomplished if his expeditionary force had not been stripped of Stevenson's division at the outset.

In any event, a message was sent to Hancock informing him of Burnside's new route. The 9th Corps, stated the directive, was expected to attack "on or near the Plank Road." Hancock was to "attack at the same time with Burnside."[92]

92. Andrew A. Humphreys to Winfield S. Hancock, May 6, 1864, in *OR*, Vol. XXXVI, Pt. 2, p. 442. For an interpretation of events more sympathetic to the 9th Corps commander, see Marvel, *Burnside*, 355–56.

This latest pronouncement from headquarters could not have struck Hancock as answering his concerns. How could he "attack at the same time with Burnside" unless he knew when and where Burnside's troops would arrive? And how could he be expected to coordinate an attack with Burnside when the 2nd Corps had its hands full holding its own against Longstreet? Headquarters manifestly failed to comprehend the degree of confusion on Orange Plank Road.

As it developed, Burnside was not destined to reach the vicinity of Orange Plank Road for several hours. Over a mile of intractable wilderness separated Burnside's two divisions from Hancock. Leaving behind one of Willcox' brigades to detain Ramseur's Confederates, Burnside withdrew his remaining troops—Potter's division and Colonel John F. Hartranft's brigade, of Willcox' division—and started them in Hancock's direction. Potter later described the route as leading through "dense wood and an almost impenetrable undergrowth." There were no trails. Nothing provided guidance except the sound of battle, which seemed to echo from all directions.

For the rest of the morning, the 9th Corps remained lost to the Federal war effort. Occasionally messages emerged from the undergrowth, but the troops themselves seemed to have been swallowed up by the Wilderness. One note from Comstock reached headquarters at 10:50. Burnside had "gained 1 1/2 miles to his left to connect with Wadsworth, and now moves at once toward Hancock's firing," stated the message. The connection, however, must have involved only Burnside's skirmishers. The main body of his troops still had over an hour of bushwhacking before them. As noon approached, Grant lost patience with Burnside. "Push in with all vigor so as to drive the enemy from General Hancock's front," Grant's chief of staff Rawlins wrote the 9th Corps commander. "Get in on the Orange and Fredericksburg Plank Road at the earliest possible moment." Rawlins could not resist adding a comment about Burnside's lagging. "Hancock has been expecting you for the last three hours," he scolded, "and has been making his attack and dispositions with a view to your assistance." To the extent that Rawlins implied censure on Burnside, he failed to take into consideration that the commander of the 9th Corps was performing as well in the Wilderness terrain as any other Federal generals were. After five hours of effort during the morning of the fifth, Warren had scarcely managed to form two divisions into a battle line. Wright had taken hours to traverse a short segment of the Spotswood Trail, and Wadsworth had encountered unspeakable frustrations trying to cut through tangled brush to reach Hill's flank. In searching out Hancock, Burnside did not have the aid of a path, much less of a reliable map. His failure to join with Hancock during the morning seriously crippled the Federal offensive, but it would be incorrect to lay the sole responsibility on him.[93]

With the Federal offensive around the turnpike deadlocked and Burnside's expedition gone astray, Hancock was left to his own devices. And what a perplexing morning it was turning out to be. The Federal 2nd Corps commander, acting with his usual decisiveness, was trying to concentrate available units toward the battlefront. One after another, however, his attempts were frustrated by faulty intelligence and by difficulties inherent in coordinating troop movements in the Wilderness.

Hancock's continuing uncertainty about Longstreet's exact strength and position bulked large in his thinking. Longstreet was known to have three divisions. So far, Hancock could account for only two of them, Field's and Kershaw's. The whereabouts of Longstreet's third division—Major General George E. Pickett's—remained a mystery, as did the location of Hill's third division, under Anderson. Hancock's nightmare was that the two missing enemy divisions were advancing up Catharpin Road toward his left flank.

Hancock's puzzlement about Longstreet's location raised serious questions in the Union general's mind concerning how he should deploy his left wing. He had already arrayed a strong defensive line, manned by five brigades under Gibbon, extending south along Brock Road. The formation terminated at the Trigg farm, where a massive stand of artillery anchored the army's flank. Hancock's fighting instincts suggested that, rather than holding these troops idle, he should advance them below Orange Plank Road to reinforce units already actively engaged against Longstreet. But with two Confederate divisions unaccounted for, Hancock was ambivalent about or-

93. Potter's Report, in *OR,* Vol. XXXVI, Pt. 1, p. 928; Cyrus B. Comstock to Ulysses S. Grant, May 6, 1864, *ibid.,* Pt. 2, p. 460; John A. Rawlins to Ambrose E. Burnside, May 6, 1864, *ibid.,* 461.

dering Gibbon forward. Advancing Gibbon would necessarily weaken his southern flank. That would be risky. If the missing Confederates suddenly appeared on Brock Road, Hancock would need every man there he could muster.[94]

It was in this frame of mind that Hancock issued an order that later stirred heated controversy. As Hancock recalled the events, at around 7 A.M., when Longstreet's counterattack was reaching its peak, he directed Gibbon to send forward Barlow's entire division. This force constituted the larger part of Hancock's left wing. As matters turned out, however, only one of Barlow's brigades advanced, a unit commanded by Paul Frank, later described by Warren's aide Schaff as a "whiskey pickled, lately-arrived, blusterous German," long on pretension and short on talent. It soon became plain that Frank's brigade was not to be the salvation of Meade's beleaguered force. Later, Gibbon swore that he had never received orders from Hancock to advance Barlow's entire division. He had only been told to advance a brigade, which he did. Barlow agreed with Gibbon's version, asserting that "to the best of my knowledge and belief no orders were sent to [advance my division] and certainly none were ever received by me." He added that "as Gen. Hancock was close at hand all the time, I do not see how he could have failed to know that any order which he may have given to attack was not obeyed. It seems to me that it must have been impossible that he did not know that there was no movement by us. Why then, was the order not repeated? And why, if the order was given and not obeyed, w[as] not [Gibbon] called to account for [his] non-performance?" Contemporaneous records contain little that might contribute to resolving the discrepancy in recollections. There are no surviving dispatches from Hancock requesting Gibbon to advance Barlow's full division. The only pertinent entry is a message from Hancock at 7:10 A.M. notify-

94. "Looking at the action after so long a time has elapsed," Hancock wrote in February, 1865, "it seems that the expected movement of Longstreet on the left flank, on the morning of the 6th, had a very material effect upon the result of the battle. I was not only cautioned officially that the movement was being made, but many incidents . . . such as the skirmishing and artillery fire on Barlow's flank, the heavy firing in the direction of Todd's Tavern, where Sheridan was to attack Longstreet, and the report of the infantry moving on the Brock Road from the direction of Todd's Tavern, confirmed me in the belief that I would receive a formidable attack on my left. This paralyzed a large number of my best troops, who otherwise would have gone into action at a decisive point on the morning of the 6th" (Hancock's Report, in OR, Vol. XXXVI, Pt. 1, p. 325).

ing headquarters that "Barlow is putting in a brigade on the enemy's right flank, and I will follow it up, if necessary, and have so directed." Barlow claimed that the order referred to was the only command he had received.[95]

Whatever Hancock's intentions might have been, Gibbon dispatched Frank's lone brigade along the underbelly of the Federal assault column on Orange Plank Road. McAllister's brigade occupied this portion of the Union line. Approaching the staid Pennsylvanian, Frank announced his intention of passing through. McAllister, who apparently harbored an intense dislike of Frank, responded that his skirmishers were out and cautioned Frank against proceeding farther. "I have orders to find the enemy wherever I can find him, and whip him," crowed Frank. Spurring his horse with a flourish, Frank rounded McAllister's left flank and disappeared toward the rebels. Frank's soldiers hacked through the "densest underbrush" and drove back a thin line of Confederate skirmishers. Suddenly the surprised Federals stumbled onto the main Confederate formation. The woods seemed to explode. In short order, over a third of the 125th New York became casualties, including the regiment's commander. Ammunition exhausted, Frank's remaining troops retired toward McAllister's line, and Frank requested support from McAllister. The general was in no mood to cooperate. His orders, he smugly explained, were to remain with his division. Shortly the rest of Frank's troops tumbled back. Still incensed by Frank's arrogance, McAllister stopped the fugitives and refused to let them through. "I want to get ammunition," Frank pleaded. Fully enjoying Frank's distress, McAllister informed the brigadier that a mule train had just arrived. If Frank would detail a detachment, McAllister's sergeants would lead it to ammunition. Before Frank could think of a graceful way to decline, the rebels mounted another assault. McAllister had no choice

95. *Ibid.*, 321; Winfield S. Hancock to Andrew A. Humphreys, May 6, 1864, *ibid.*, Pt. 2, pp. 440–41; John Gibbon, *Personal Recollections of the Civil War* (New York, 1928), 386–411. Francis Walker, who was with Hancock all morning, later observed that "my mind has always inclined toward Gibbon's view of the occurrence" (Francis A. Walker, "General Gibbon in the Second Corps," in *Personal Recollections of the War of the Rebellion: Addresses Delivered Before the Commandery of the State of New York, Military Order of the Loyal Legion of the United States* [4 vols.; Portland, Maine, 1898], II, 315). Schaff's description of Frank is from his *The Battle of the Wilderness*, 260. Lyman described Frank as a man "who tried to make up for want of nerve with strong drink" (Lyman, "Addenda," in *PMHSM*, IV, 169).

but to let Frank's men pass through. "This is the last I saw of him or his command," related McAllister.[96]

At the same time that Hancock was attempting to strengthen the lower portion of his attack column with troops from Gibbon's wing, he was striving to pump more combat units north of Orange Plank Road. The situation there was becoming increasingly precarious. Wadsworth's collapse had made reinforcements imperative.

Just how badly things had deteriorated was vividly demonstrated to Warren's aide Schaff, who was traveling through the woods with orders for Wadsworth. "Swarms of stragglers" were everywhere. Soldiers from Cutler's Iron Brigade told him that they had been driven with "heavy losses." Continuing ahead, Schaff found Cutler, who was accompanying part of his broken command. "He was rather an oldish, thin, earnest-looking Round-head sort of a man, his light stubby beard and hair turning gray," noted the aide. "He was bleeding from a wound across his upper lip, and looked ghastly, and I have no doubt felt worse." Schaff inquired about Wadsworth. "I think he is dead," answered Cutler. "Yes, we saw him fall," confirmed an officer. In fact, only Wadsworth's horse had been shot. The indomitable New Yorker was still alive and attempting to re-form his splintered division.[97]

Schaff returned to Union headquarters near the Lacy house and reported Wadsworth's collapse to Meade. At first, the general dismissed Schaff's description of the chaotic Federal front as an exaggeration. But as Cutler's troops limped into view, Meade became impressed with the gravity of the situation. Unless help arrived at once, he decided, there was danger that rebels might exploit the breach in Wadsworth's line and overrun the Federal command center.

With the only readily available reinforcements being some of Warren's units, the heavy artillery brigade, and Stevenson's division, all posted in fields around the Lacy house and Wilderness Tavern, Meade immediately called on his 5th Corps commander for assistance. "The Major General commanding directs that you suspend your operations on the right," he wrote Warren, who so far had

---

96. Robert McAllister's Report, in *OR*, Vol. XXXVI, Pt. 1, pp. 488–89; Nelson Penfield's Report, *ibid.*, 403; Ezra D. Simons, *The One Hundred Twenty-Fifth New York State Volunteers* (New York, 1888), 198–200.

97. Schaff, *The Battle of the Wilderness*, 235–36.

achieved nothing in that direction anyway. "Send some force to prevent the enemy from pushing past your left, near your headquarters. They have driven in Cutler in disorder and are following him." [98]

As a protective tactic, 5th Corps cannon that were massed in the fields around the Lacy house began a heavy barrage over the heads of Cutler's soldiers. The intense Federal artillery activity provoked a like response from Ewell's Confederate guns posted on the far side of Saunders' Field. Soon Confederate gunners found the range, and shells began exploding near Grant's command post.

The general-in-chief was seated on a stump. For a few moments, it appeared that the fighting might reach him. Grant rose and surveyed the scene, cigar smoke mingling with smoke from Union cannon. "General, wouldn't it be prudent to move headquarters to the other side of the Germanna road till the result of the present attack is known?" suggested an edgy officer. Grant responded quietly, punctuating his remarks with puffs from his cigar. "It strikes me it would be better to order up some artillery and defend the present location." A Federal battery was obediently rolled forward. The precaution, it developed, was unnecessary. Union artillery fire deterred Confederates from entering the Lacy clearing. [99]

Hancock meanwhile did his best to try to shore up the portion of his front ranks weakened by Wadsworth's collapse. Two of Getty's brigades—Eustis' and Wheaton's—had been moved earlier to Wadsworth's side of Orange Plank Road. Hancock ordered them to extend even farther north to help fill the void. As a result, Eustis and Wheaton were stretched extremely thin. Fighting below Orange Plank Road—down where Lewis Grant's Vermonters were embroiled with Kershaw's Confederates—was still raging fiercely. Consequently, no troops could be drawn as reinforcements from that quarter. Hancock decided to commit his last reserve, Alexander Webb's brigade. These troops were to advance to Getty's line, then extend northward and fill in wherever Wheaton directed them.

Webb was one of Hancock's premier brigade commanders. Only twenty-nine years old, he had participated in most of the Army of the Potomac's campaigns and had won a medal of honor at Gettysburg.

---

98. George G. Meade to Gouverneur K. Warren, May 6, 1864, in *OR*, Vol. XXXVI, Pt. 2, p. 451.

99. Buell, *The Cannoneer*, 164–65; Horace Porter, *Campaigning with Grant*, 59.

Lyman considered him "jolly and pleasant," although the aide expressed annoyance at the general's "way of suddenly laughing in a convulsive manner, by drawing in his breath, instead of letting it out—the way which goes to my bones." But Lyman regarded Webb as a "thorough soldier, wide-awake, quick, and attentive to detail," despite this distracting quirk.[100]

Webb's usual attentiveness failed him in the Wilderness, however. His brigade proceeded along Orange Plank Road toward the battle front after leaving its reserve position near Hancock's command center. Reasonably expecting that he would reach Getty's line before encountering rebels, he neglected to take the usual precaution of screening his way with pickets.

The Wilderness had a habit of disorienting even the most seasoned troops. Somehow, as they made their way through dense foliage and heavy smoke and over uneven ground, Webb's soldiers passed unawares through Getty's lines and stumbled into Confederates. Rather than joining an organized battlefront as they had expected, they found themselves fighting for their lives.

Taking stock, Webb discovered rebels everywhere, including on his flanks. The bewildered general ordered his men to fall back as best they could. "I am still at a loss to determine whether or not it was my duty to attack and attempt to drive the enemy on the plank road, or to hold my position in connection with a line taken up by the rest of the army," he later explained in a tone reflective of the confusion in the Union ranks. "I tried to drive the enemy and failed to do so, and I believe because I struck him at a time when I had no reason to suppose that I would meet any but General Getty's command."[101]

Fortunately for Webb, help was on the way. After Grant ordered Burnside to leave Stevenson's division near Wilderness Tavern, continuing pessimism in Hancock's reports persuaded Union headquarters to release this division and send it to Hancock's assistance. Around 7 A.M., Stevenson's reinforcements started down Germanna Ford Road to Brock Road. Sometime after eight, the head of the

100. Hancock's Report, in *OR*, Vol. XXXVI, Pt. 1, pp. 321–22; Theodore Lyman to family, March 3, 1865, in *Meade's Headquarters*, ed. Agassiz, 307.

101. Alexander S. Webb's Report, in *OR*, Vol. XXXVI, Pt. 1, pp. 437–38; George A. Bruce, *The Twentieth Regiment of Massachusetts Volunteer Infantry* (Cambridge, Mass., 1906), 352.

column reached Hancock's command post. Boylston Adams, of the 56th Massachusetts, noticed as he marched past the junction "that superb soldier General Hancock sitting on his horse by the side of a brass 12-pounder pointed down the road." [102]

One of Stevenson's brigades—Colonel Daniel Leasure's three-regiment outfit—halted near Hancock. Stevenson's other unit—Colonel Sumner Carruth's mixed brigade of Massachusetts volunteers and United States regulars—was directed onto Orange Plank Road toward the battlefront. It was Hancock's hope that the added weight of Carruth's brigade would enable him to retrieve the initiative. Forming above the roadway, Carruth's men advanced into what one of them remembered as a "thick underbrush of scrub-pine, briars, etc." Another officer remarked that "it was impossible to see half a rod in front." The newly arrived brigade immediately became embroiled in a "fearful" tempo of combat that raged afresh along the interface of the two armies. Stephen M. Weld, of the 56th Massachusetts, described the musketry as "one continual roll, at long intervals broken by the loud booming of a cannon." Another Federal recalled how the "Confederate fire resembled the fury of hell in intensity, and was deadly accurate. Their bullets swished by in swarms. It seems to me that I could have caught a pot full of them if I had had a strong iron vessel rigged on a pole as a butterfly net." [103]

An already impossible situation was made even worse as Hancock and Birney issued conflicting orders. Webb, who remained at the front, valiantly pitched in to try to straighten out the mess. New arrivals were completely bewildered. Even Weld later conceded that "things were slightly mixed." Stevenson's assistant adjutant general summed up the situation, "It was all blind work, and the confusion of commanders made things worse." It took a while to sort out exactly who was in charge above Orange Plank Road. Webb, acting

---

102. According to Lyman, Webb's troops wheeled onto Orange Plank Road at 7 A.M., and Stevenson's men arrived just before eight. See Lyman to family, May 16, 1864, in *Meade's Headquarters*, ed. Agassiz, 94–95; and Theodore Lyman to George G. Meade, in *OR*, Vol. XXXVI, Pt. 2, p. 442. For a description of the events, see Z. Boylston Adams, "In the Wilderness," in *Civil War Papers* (2 vols.; Boston, 1900), II, 376.

103. Massachusetts Historical Society, *War Diary and Letters of Stephen Minot Weld*, 285–86; Coco, ed., *Through Blood and Fire*, 77–78; and Wilkeson, *Recollections*, 71–72. Warren Wilkinson presents a good modern account of the fighting on Carruth's front in *Mother, May You Never See the Sights I Have Seen: The Fifty-Seventh Massachusetts Veteran Volunteers in the Last Year of the Civil War* (New York, 1990), 72–83.

with characteristic decisiveness, ordered Carruth's soldiers to fall into line with his own. Together the two brigades began edging the rebels back. Stevenson remained in the rear and apparently acquiesced in this arrangement. Wadsworth, however, considered the sector immediately above Orange Plank Road his responsibility. Although still busy trying to reorganize his shattered division, he wanted to make the important decisions concerning what he regarded as his territory. In addition, he outranked Stevenson and Webb and insisted on exercising command over them. Ultimately, the disagreement was resolved in Wadsworth's favor.[104]

The infusion of fresh Union soldiers had the sole effect of prolonging the purposeless blood letting. To the Confederate Alexander, it seemed that the Federals were making another "supreme effort." But Union forces remained unable to achieve a coordinated assault. In an incident typical of the confusion in the northern ranks, Wadsworth dispatched one of Webb's regiments—the 20th Massachusetts—to the left of Orange Plank Road without informing Webb. Unsupported, the Massachusetts soldiers suffered heavily and gained no significant ground. North of the roadway, Webb and Carruth launched wave after wave of futile attacks in an attempt to dislodge the rebels from a low rise. Federal units were severely intermingled. "No regiment in the line," Webb later wrote, "had on its flanks regiments of its own corps." Progress was impossible. "My men had lost their dash" Webb remarked in belated explanation of the failure. "They had no feeling of confidence and had had time to discover that the enemy's line was overlapping my right."[105]

Near nine o'clock, Hancock, while trying to untangle the muddle on Webb's front, received a disconcerting message from headquarters. Sheridan had been ordered to attack Longstreet with a cavalry division "on the Brock Road." That was startling news. To Hancock, the

104. Alexander S. Webb, "Through the Wilderness," in *B&L*, IV, 159–60; Webb's Report, in *OR*, Vol. XXXVI, Pt. 1, pp. 437–38; Coco, ed., *Through Blood and Fire*, 78; Massachusetts Historical Society, *War Diary and Letters of Stephen Minot Weld*, 286.

105. Gallagher, ed., *Fighting for the Confederacy*, 359; Webb's Report, in *OR*, Vol. XXXVI, Pt. 1, pp. 437–38; Committee of the Regiment, *History of the Thirty-Fifth Regiment Massachusetts*, 225–26; Nathaniel W. Bunker, "War Record," in CL.

message could mean but one thing. Headquarters believed that Longstreet's missing division was advancing toward his lower flank. Off to Hancock's south, the roar of musketry seemed to be increasing. The noise appeared to lend objective confirmation to the message from headquarters. Hancock's presumption was that Sheridan had encountered rebels in the vicinity of Todd's Tavern. At 9:10, an aide dashed to Hancock with news that confirmed the general's worst fears. Enemy troops, the aide reported, were indeed advancing toward Brock Road. As Hancock later recounted, the report strengthened his "impression that Longstreet was executing the flank movement, concerning which I had been cautioned during the night."[106]

At this stage, Hancock had committed all his troops. In light of the threat apparently emerging off his lower flank, the beleaguered general decided to pull units from his wing on Orange Plank Road and dispatch them southward. Accordingly, at 9:15, he directed Birney to detach a brigade from his battle formation for use on the corps' lower flank. Birney selected Eustis' brigade for the assignment. Ten minutes later, Carroll, too, was ordered to send a regiment down Brock Road without delay. At 9:40, Hancock changed his mind. Rather than undertaking the ticklish task of extracting Eustis' brigade under enemy fire, he decided to order Leasure's freshly arrived 9th Corps brigade toward Todd's Tavern. Orders contradicting Hancock's earlier instructions emanated from the 2nd Corps command center. Any of Eustis' units that had managed to disengage themselves from the enemy were to return to their positions. Leasure was to continue south on Brock Road. Confusion reigned as troops marched to and fro.[107]

In the middle of attempting to reorganize to counter the reputed threat from the south, Hancock received another frantic message from headquarters, this one concerning his northern flank. Confederates, warned the dispatch, were still attempting to exploit Wadsworth's collapse. Enemy units were pressing past the lower end of Warren's line and had already managed to advance within three-

106. Hancock's Report, in OR, Vol. XXXVI, Pt. 1, p. 322; 2nd Corps Daily Memoranda, *ibid.*, 352; Andrew A. Humphreys to Winfield S. Hancock, May 6, 1864, *ibid.*, Pt. 2, p. 442.

107. Hancock's Report, in OR, Vol. XXXVI, Pt. 1, p. 322; 2nd Corps Daily Memoranda, *ibid.*, 352; Theodore Lyman to George G. Meade, May 6, 1864, *ibid.*, Pt. 2, p. 443.

eighths of a mile of the Lacy house. "The major-general commanding directs that you make immediate dispositions to check this movement of the enemy across and through General Warren's left," stated the message from headquarters. To underscore the urgency, Humphreys added a postscript. "We have no more troops to spare here." Again Hancock was compelled to improvise. At 9:50, he asked Birney to initiate additional measures to help fill the gap caused by Wadsworth's collapse. Birney pulled more troops from his thinning formation and advanced them northward across the open area, loosely connecting with Warren. The Federal line at last stretched unbroken from Orange Plank Road to the Orange Turnpike.[108]

By this time, Hancock's offensive had been robbed of momentum. Hancock had kept busy shifting his forces, first to the south and then to the north, to fend off rebel detachments that seemed to be emerging from nowhere. It was impossible for him to organize a concerted attack. Rather than controlling events, Hancock was reacting to Confederate initiatives, real and imaginary. The grand Union assault that had begun so promisingly at 5 A.M. was in shambles. The overriding concern was no longer how to defeat Lee. The question was whether Federal units could be juggled quickly enough to keep the Confederates from overpowering the Union lines.

Ironically, the latest enemy thrusts existed only in the minds of the Union generals. The firing in the direction of Todd's Tavern was real enough, but it had nothing to do with Longstreet. Rather, one of Sheridan's divisions had encountered Rosser's Confederate cavalry brigade. The racket that Hancock heard was from a hard-fought skirmish. There was no danger to his flank. And the Confederate infantry columns reported to be on Brock Road were in fact a body of several hundred Federal convalescents marching from the rear to join Hancock. Somehow, in a mistake that has never been explained, a nervous Federal scout had misidentified them as Pickett's Confederate division. Unknown to the Federals, Pickett's troops posed no threat

108. Edward R. Platt to Andrew A. Humphreys, 1864, in OR, Vol. XXXVI, Pt. 2, p. 451; Andrew A. Humphreys to Winfield S. Hancock, May 6, 1864, *ibid.*, 442; 2nd Corps Daily Memoranda, *ibid.*, Pt. 1, pp. 352–53.

at all. They were nearly a hundred miles away, manning the defenses near Richmond.[109]

Similarly, there was no real danger of a Confederate attack through the gap left by Wadsworth's collapse. The Federal leadership had overreacted at the sight of Cutler's broken brigade streaming from the woods. The rebels lacked the manpower to exploit their breakthrough. To Federal minds, however, the appearance of gray uniforms at the clearing's edge portended a full-fledged attack. The reality was described by a Federal cannoneer near the Lacy house. "We stood at a ready, pieces sighted and lanyards in hand for several minutes, expecting to see the enemy's line emerge from the brush," he recounted. "But the Johnnies, when they came to the edge of the brush and saw 18 guns looking at them from the Lacy house knoll, hesitated, and instead of charging, as we expected them to do, lay down in the edge of the brush and began sharpshooting at us and our then rallying infantry." According to the artilleryman, "there was not during the whole 6th of May any Rebel more than ten rods outside the edge of the brush that fringed the Lacy clearing, and even those didn't stay out of the brush long." [110]

Sometime around ten, the Orange Plank Road sector settled into troubled silence. Longstreet and Hancock had fought themselves to exhaustion. Neither side had reinforcements to feed into battle. Union commanders admitted that their earlier hopes for a quick victory were dashed. In the battle's northern part, Federal troops huddled ineffectively in front of Ewell's firmly entrenched battle line. The impossibility of achieving anything was openly conceded in joint dispatches to Sedgwick and Warren time-stamped 10:35 A.M. Both Federal corps, directed headquarters, were to "suspend" their attacks. "You will at once throw up defensive works to enable you to hold your position with the fewest possible number of men," continued the directive, "and report at once what number of men you will have disposable for an attack upon Hancock's right." [111]

Federal reverses along Orange Plank Road seemed to add fuel to earlier doubts about the wisdom of organizing the Union army into

109. Hancock's Report, in *OR*, Vol. XXXVI, Pt. 1, p. 322.
110. Buell, *The Cannoneer*, 164–65.
111. Andrew A. Humphreys to Gouverneur K. Warren, May 6, 1864, in *OR*, Vol. XXXVI, Pt. 2, pp. 451–52; John Sedgwick to Andrew A. Humphreys, May 6, 1864, *ibid.*, 459–60.

three large corps—or into four, if Burnside's independent force was included in the count. By midmorning, the formal Federal corps structure had been abandoned. Sedgwick's best division—Getty's—had been detached to Hancock. Four of Warren's brigades were now operating independently under Wadsworth, who was also reporting to Hancock. And the 9th Corps had been splintered into three units. One brigade remained below Saunders' Field, facing off with Ramseur's Confederates; Potter's division, augmented with one of Willcox' brigades, was searching for Hancock; and Stevenson's division had been assigned in its entirety to Hancock.

Hancock's command had grown to almost unmanageable proportions, forcing the general to divide it informally into two wings. Within the unofficial arrangement, Birney oversaw the Orange Plank Road offensive and Gibbon managed the lower wing's defense.

Humphreys later reflected that the wooded Wilderness countryside rendered large Federal corps impractical: "Five infantry corps of about 15,000 each would have been a more judicious organization, owing to the difficulty of communication between the corps commander and the subordinate commanders in a battle in such a country, and the consequential difficulty of prompt and efficient control of extensive lines of battle, especially at critical moments, or when unforeseen exigencies occurred." Humphreys also thought that it had been a mistake to assign Hancock divisions from other corps. "It is well known," Humphreys later observed, "that the personal character of a general officer in moments of difficulty has a powerful influence upon the result."[112]

More flexible organization of the Union expeditionary force seemed to be required if Lee was to be defeated. Unfortunately, the Federal leadership had been forced to experiment at a highly inopportune time. The consequence was a stalled offensive.

*"The ordeal was a terrible
one for cavalry"*

The intense firing near Hancock's southern flank that had generated concern at the Federal 2nd Corps headquarters had come from a bloody little cavalry fight.

112. Andrew A. Humphreys, *The Virginia Campaign,* 4–5.

During the previous night, Sheridan's three mounted divisions had formed a barrier to shield the Army of the Potomac's underside. Gregg's division was stationed at Todd's Tavern. Torbert's division, now under Wesley Merritt, was camped over two miles southwest of Chancellorsville at Catharine Furnace, a place named after an iron-smelting kiln that had fallen into ruins. And Wilson's division, still smarting from its skirmish with Rosser's Confederate horsemen, had rejoined its supply wagons at Chancellorsville. According to a Federal cavalryman, Wilson's exhausted riders "seemed much chagrined over their defeat."[113]

At 2 A.M. on May 6, Custer's brigade, of Torbert's division, was ordered to shift toward Brock Road to bolster the Federal cavalry presence off Hancock's left flank. The route took the troopers west along the same country road that Stonewall Jackson's men had used for their flanking maneuver the previous spring.

Years later, a soldier in the 7th Michigan retained a vivid recollection of the movement. "Fires had been lighted up by the sides of the roads," he wrote, "which revealed, by their glare, long lines of infantry, cavalry, and artillery, filing up the tortuous ways in all directions, in wavy motions, like the undulations of some vast serpent." An antique blast furnace had been coaxed to life and illuminated the countryside. It seemed to the impressionable soldier as though "the demon of destruction was floundering and belching out tongues and volumes of flames in the murky depths below." On a more mundane plane, the night march involved "falling into 'chug-holes,' stumbling over obstructions, getting caught in the snares of log bridges and rough pieces of 'corduroy,' and running foul of overhanging branches."[114]

Toward morning, Custer's Michigan horsemen, popularly known as Wolverines, reached their objective and bivouacked in a wooded patch along the eastern edge of Brock Road, near its junction with Catharine Furnace Road. Close to their right lay the southern terminus of Meade's infantry line at the Trigg farm. To their left, Brock

113. J. H. Kidd, *Personal Recollections of a Cavalryman with Custer's Michigan Cavalry Brigade in the Civil War* (Ionia, Mich., 1908), 264–65; George Custer's Report, in *OR*, Vol. XXXVI, Pt. 1, p. 816; Charles Forsyth to David McM. Gregg, May 6, 1864, in *OR*, Vol. XXXVI, Pt. 2, p. 468.

114. Asa B. Isham, "Through the Wilderness to Richmond," in *Sketches of War History, 1861–1865: Papers Read Before the Ohio Commandery of the Military Order of the Loyal Legion of the United States* (2 vols.; Cincinnati, 1888), I, 200–201.

Road continued southward for a few miles toward Gregg's division at Todd's Tavern. Across the road was a cleared field. And west of the clearing passed a country trail that slanted southwest and continued diagonally down to Catharpin Road, striking it a short distance east of the Po River.

In part, the little trail accounted for Sheridan's decision to advance Custer's brigade to this location. Longstreet's troops were reputedly about, and it was feared that the Confederates might use the obscure path to bypass the Federal forces at Todd's Tavern, slicing unexpectedly into the lower end of Hancock's battle formation.

Around eight, Union headquarters became convinced that Longstreet was executing a surprise attack in the vicinity of Todd's Tavern. Orders were accordingly sent to Sheridan to "make an attack with a division of cavalry on Longstreet's flank and rear by the Brock Road." As Custer recalled it, Sheridan subsequently instructed him to "move out the Brock pike for the purpose of harassing Longstreet's corps, which was reported to be moving on Hancock's left flank." [115]

The orders were based on the false assumption that Longstreet's missing third division was somewhere nearby. Since Custer was on Brock Road and in communication with Gregg at Todd's Tavern, he knew that no Confederates had been spotted in that sector. The instructions were puzzling in the extreme because they called upon Custer to attack a body of Confederates that he knew did not exist. But before he could do anything about his impossible assignment, real Confederates appeared. Earlier that morning, Rosser's rebel cavalry brigade had crossed the Po and had filed onto the wooded trail toward the Trigg farm. On approaching Brock Road, one of Rosser's officers inquired how far he was to advance. "Tell him," replied Rosser, "to drive [the enemy] as far as he can." Southern horsemen tightened their ranks and trotted briskly ahead.[116]

At first, Rosser met little resistance. Custer had stationed a few pickets from the 1st Michigan along the trail to alert him of approaching Confederates. Rosser's troopers easily overpowered them and pressed confidently onward, oblivious to Custer's main body waiting on the other side of Brock Road. "A picket shot was heard, then another, and another," recounted Major James H. Kidd, of the

115. Custer's Report, in *OR*, Vol. XXXVI, Pt. 1, p. 817.
116. McDonald, *A History of the Laurel Brigade*, 234.

6th Michigan. "Thicker and faster the spattering tones were borne to our ears from the woods in front. Then, it was the 'rebel yell'; at first faint, but swelling in volume as it approached." In a swirl of dust, rebel horsemen dashed into the field, driving the Michigan pickets before them.[117]

Custer had been accompanying his pickets when Rosser's gray-clad troopers appeared. He had torn back, his distinctive curly locks streaming behind him. According to a Federal participant, he came bursting from the woods barely ahead of his pursuers. On reaching his brigade, he curbed his charger and ordered the band to strike up a tune. Saber arm extended toward the Confederates in grand style, the flamboyant Federal cavalry commander shouted, "Forward, by divisions." Custer's Michigan horsemen trotted boldly to the strains of "Yankee Doodle," reaching the field just as Confederates emerged from the clearing's opposite side. The antagonists charged toward each other at "full career." A deep ravine in the middle of the field forced the horsemen to pull their mounts up short. There they aimed into each other's ranks and opened fire. A few brave souls clattered into the gully. The distinctive ring of steel on steel filled the air.[118]

Leading the Confederate charge was Colonel Elijah V. White's battalion, christened Comanches by Rosser because of its wild and reckless charges. This time the Comanches were overwhelmed, as the unit's historian later put it, by "swarming masses of Yankees." More rebels fed into the fray—the 11th, 12th, and 7th Virginia cavalry. Each was repulsed in turn. Concluding that he could never break Custer's line with frontal attacks, Rosser ordered a rebel detachment to circle around the Federal right wing. Custer, however, spotted the rebel party. He correctly surmised its intention was to "turn my right flank and gain possession of the Furnace road in my rear." Deftly Custer shifted the 6th Michigan to block Rosser's ploy.[119]

Kidd ordered his bugler to sound the "rally." Blue-clad horsemen flocked to the regimental colors and hurried north. Immediately above the ravine, they found the Confederates. Although heavily outnumbered, the Michiganers used their Spencer carbines to deadly ef-

---

117. Kidd, *Personal Recollections*, 266–67.

118. James Rowe, "Reminiscences," in MOLLUS Collection, BL; Kidd, *Personal Recollections*, 267–68.

119. Myers, *The Comanches*, 266; Custer's Report, in *OR*, Vol. XXXVI, Pt. 1, p. 816.

fect and held their ground. Dismounted gray riders, however, began edging around Kidd's line. Kidd, bending back his formation to protect his flank and rear, dispatched a courier requesting help. At this critical juncture, Torbert's other mounted Federal brigade, under Thomas Devin, arrived. Custer directed one of Devin's regiments, along with his own 5th Michigan, to Kidd's right. "The reinforcements came none too soon," a relieved Kidd admitted after the fight. The advantage once again shifted as fresh Union troops formed behind Kidd. "Steady men, forward," commanded Colonel Russell A. Alger, of the 5th Michigan. Exploiting the turn of events, Custer advanced his entire formation. Unable to resist two federal brigades, Rosser's Confederates broke for the woods. "No one who witnessed it," Kidd claimed years later, "can ever forget the superb conduct of Colonel Alger and his men when they swung into line on the right of the Sixth Michigan and turned a threatened reverse into a magnificent victory."[120]

Custer, as his horsemen exultantly drove the rebels, received a section of artillery from Gregg, who had heard musketry and concluded that more substantial firepower might be needed. Stationing eight pieces by the roadway, Custer ordered his guns "to fire as rapidly as they could be loaded and aimed." The artillery barrage, in conjunction with the fierce mounted counterattack, produced the desired result. The enemy, Custer gloated afterward, was "driven from the field in great disorder, leaving his dead and many of his wounded upon the ground. We also captured a considerable number of prisoners."[121]

But Rosser was determined to hold on. The Confederate ordered up artillery—a single piece, according to the brigade's historian—and planted it on rising ground near the clearing's edge. A few well-placed blasts halted the bluecoats. Custer's battery, however, renewed its efforts with impressive effect. "The ground was strewn with the dead and dying," wrote one of Rosser's soldiers. Rosser's rebels dropped farther back, re-forming behind their gun. A deadly and unequal artillery duel raged across the fire-swept field. The lonely rebel piece blazed away, enveloped in smoke and bursting Federal

---

120. Russell Alger's Report, in *OR*, Vol. XXXVI, Pt. 1, p. 827; Kidd, *Personal Recollections*, 269–71.
121. Custer's Report, in *OR*, Vol. XXXVI, Pt. 1, p. 816.

shells. Most of the Union projectiles passed overhead and exploded among Confederate cavalrymen. "The care of the dead and dying, and the plunging of the wounded and frightened horses, created unavoidable confusion," conceded a southerner. "The ordeal was a terrible one for cavalry, and though apparently deaf to orders amidst the thunder of bursting shells, yet most of the men held firm. The number of killed and wounded was considerable." [122]

Rosser positioned himself expectantly near the Confederate gun, fearing that Federal horsemen might hurtle across the field at any moment. Jeb Stuart was there also. Prancing among exploding shells, he exhorted the gray-clad soldiers to remain steady.

Help arrived in the form of two Confederate batteries—James Thomson's and John J. Shoemaker's, shifted over from Catharpin Road by Chew. Returning heavy fire, the rebel guns repelled the Federal pieces. Chew ordered Thomson's guns leftward to engage a particularly troublesome Federal battery that was enfilading Rosser. The move proved to be a mistake. The rebel cannoneers came under the "harassing" fire of sharpshooters, and a column of dismounted Yankees slipped between Shoemaker and Thomson. Chew had no choice but to pull his guns back.

The Federal guns were arrayed in a semicircle, their right end thrust forward. "There are two expressions in the military vocabulary that describe situations usually fatal to the party occupying them," one of Rosser's officers later explained. "The first of which is that terrible word, 'flanked,' and the second, 'artillery cross-fire.' This second is what tried the mettle of the boys of Chew and Thomson that day." [123]

One of Rosser's troopers later described the encounter as the brigade's "bloodiest day of the war." Another Confederate manning Chew's artillery agreed, writing that night of the "hissing flames, the sharp, rattling, crashing roar of musketry, the deep bellowing of the artillery mingled with the yells of charging, struggling, fighting war machines, the wailing moans of the wounded and the fainter groans

---

122. McDonald, *A History of the Laurel Brigade,* 235–37; James Wood Diary, May 6, 1864, in James Wood Papers, VSL.

123. McDonald, *A History of the Laurel Brigade,* 237; Robert P. Chew's Report, in Leigh Collection, USMHI; John J. Shoemaker, *Shoemaker's Battery: Stuart Horse Artillery, Pelham's Battalion, Army of Northern Virginia* (Gaithersburg, Md., n.d.), 70–71; Myers, *The Comanches,* 267.

of the dying." Smoke, he recounted, had been "so thick and dense sometimes during the day that it was impossible to discern anything fifty paces away, and at midday the smoke was so thick overhead that I could just make out to see the sun, and it looked like a vast ball of red fire hanging in a smoke-veiled sky." The very elements, it seemed to him, regarded the carnage with displeasure. "Even the midday sun refused to look with anything but a faint red glimmer on the tragical scene that was being enacted in the tangled underbrush where the lords of creation were struggling and slaughtering each other like wild beasts in a jungle." [124]

By noon, the cavalry engagement was over. Neither side had budged. Custer hailed the fight as a victory, based upon severe Confederate casualties and the fact that the field remained in Union hands. But the southerners also regarded the skirmish as a job well done. Although suffering heavily, they had immobilized two-thirds of Sheridan's cavalry, Gregg at Todd's Tavern and Custer at the junction of Furnace and Brock roads.

Fitzhugh Lee kept his cavalry division largely out of the fray, since he was mindful that his primary task was to protect Confederate supply lines. Early in the morning, Brigadier General Williams C. Wickham's brigade had dismounted and advanced on foot, driving Gregg's pickets to near Todd's Tavern. Gregg's main force, however, was too firmly positioned for the brigade to dislodge. According to Lee's adjutant, Wickham's men did little more than spar lightly with Gregg along Brock Road. But as Lee viewed it, his presence below Todd's Tavern served an important purpose. "I was so located" the rebel cavalry commander stated in his report, "as to retard any prolongation of Grant's left toward points on the Central Railroad." [125]

In point of fact, Confederate cavalry had indirectly accomplished more than anyone realized at the time. The din from Rosser's fight, exacerbated by the intense artillery bombardment, had helped persuade Hancock that Longstreet's missing division was bursting through the woods near the Trigg farm. That illusion had induced the Federal 2nd Corps commander to concentrate a substantial body

124. McDonald, *A History of the Laurel Brigade,* 234; Neese, *Three Years in the Confederate Horse Artillery,* 261–62.

125. Fitzhugh Lee's Report, in MC; Ferguson, "Memoranda," in Munford Collection, DU; Carter Diary, May 6, 1864, in Hampden-Sydney College Library; Ressler Diary, May 6, 1864, in Civil War Times Illustrated Collection, USMHI.

of troops on Brock Road to guard against the expected onslaught. Thus occupied, much-needed Union soldiers had been withheld from Hancock's battle line on Orange Plank Road. As events were shortly to demonstrate, Hancock's failure to buttress his attack column's southern flank was to have important consequences for the rest of the day's fighting.

VII

MAY 6, MIDDAY
Lee Struggles to Retain the Initiative

*"No greater opportunity could
be given to an aspiring
young staff officer."*

BEFORE THE WAR, construction had begun on a rail link between Fredericksburg and Orange Court House. Work crews had cleared a right-of-way. Low spots had been filled and elevations leveled to produce an even roadbed. The outbreak of hostilities, however, had stopped progress. No crossties or rails had been laid.

Proceeding west from Fredericksburg, the graded right-of-way ran about two miles below Chancellorsville. It passed near Catharine Furnace, crossed Brock Road at the Trigg farm, then bent slightly northwest and paralleled Brock Road for a short distance. As it neared Orange Plank Road, the unfinished railroad curved broadly to the left until it again pointed west. From there, the grade continued more or less even with Orange Plank Road and less than a quarter of a mile below it.[1]

The railbed offered an excellent route, as yet unexploited, for moving troops through the Wilderness. The right-of-way sliced through the leafy expanse immediately below Longstreet's southern flank. A powerful force drawn from Gibbon's idle Federal left wing might easily advance unnoticed past the Confederates. Emerging in the rebel rear, such an expedition would have an unprecedented opportunity to restore the initiative to Grant. But the route might also provide Lee an ideal path for executing one of his famous flanking maneuvers. By marching east along the roadbed, a Confederate force

---

1. The railway was completed in 1877. A narrow-gauge line owned by the Potomac, Fredericksburg and Piedmont Company and known locally as Poor Folk and Preachers, it was sold in 1925 to the Virginia Central Railroad and the next year was converted to standard gauge. The right-of-way can still be traced through fields and woods. See the *Orange County Historical Society Newsletter*, October, 1989.

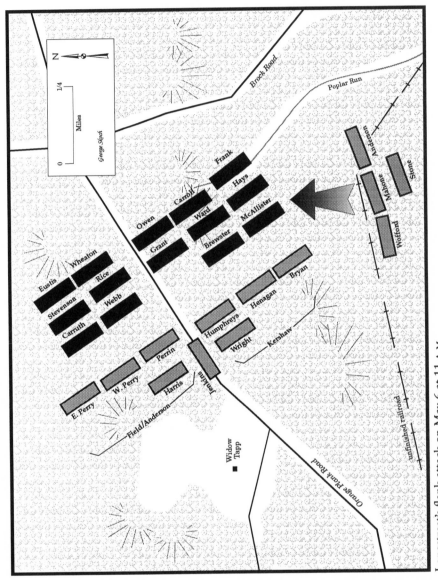

Longstreet's flank attack on May 6 at 11 A.M.

could glide unseen beneath the Union army and emerge at will anywhere along Hancock's southern flank.

Despite the unfinished rail line's obvious advantages, neither army had yet availed itself of the route. There can be no doubt, however, that each side was aware of its existence. Although Federal maps printed in bulk just before the campaign did not show the railway, Hancock's entire corps had crossed the railroad grade the previous day. Later, some of Gibbon's troops had recrossed the roadbed on their way back to the Trigg farm. Part of Gibbon's defensive line incorporated cuts and fills near Brock Road. One of Nelson Miles's staffers made mention in his diary on May 5 of the "rail road embankment which had never been completed." But apparently the Federals did not consider exploring the grade to see if it might serve as a route for moving troops.[2]

The rebels were also familiar with the right-of-way. They had thoroughly canvassed the ground during the Chancellorsville and Mine Run campaigns, and some of Lee's soldiers were native to the region. Lee's campaign map did not originally designate the rail line, but the army commander and his staff could not have been ignorant of its existence. Instead, no opportunity had arisen for exploiting it. On May 5, Hill had been fighting for survival. And during the early hours of the sixth, the southerners had been fully occupied trying to bludgeon back Hancock's assault column.[3]

By eight in the morning, however, Hill's Confederate front along Orange Plank Road had been restored. Longstreet and Anderson had arrived, which added three fresh Confederate divisions to Hill's two. With the immediate crisis resolved, Lee once again could contemplate offensive action. Continuing to batter against Hancock was obviously hopeless. What was needed was a way to swing a column around the Federals. A surprise attack against Hancock's flank or

---

2. A copy of the Federal campaign map is in Letterbook 7A, Warren Collection, NYSA. After the war, Humphreys remarked that if Barlow's division had advanced during the morning as Hancock intended, "whether by the unfinished railroad, which was much the best route, . . . its line would have extended across the railroad bed west of the bend, and none of the enemy's troops could have entered or crossed the bed without its being known to our troops, and Longstreet's flanking attack could not have been made without due preparation to meet it" (Andrew A. Humphreys, *The Virginia Campaign*, 45n1).

3. A copy of Lee's campaign map is in MC.

rear posed the best opportunity for crumpling the Union line and stampeding the enemy back across the Rapidan.

Skirmishers from Wofford's Georgia brigade, positioned on the Confederate right end, explored through the woods. The Confederate flank, they learned, was directly opposite the Federal flank, which could be turned by a force operating out the uncompleted railway grade. According to one report, Wofford forwarded that information to Longstreet and asked for permission to execute the attack.[4]

Any flanking maneuver was going to have to be conducted under Longstreet's direction. The commander of the Confederate 1st Corps, however, had a limited understanding of the terrain. Absent from both the Chancellorsville and Mine Run campaigns, he had no first-hand familiarity with the area. To compensate for that, Lee assigned to Longstreet the Army of Northern Virginia's chief engineer, Major General Martin L. Smith.

Smith's background was unusual for a Confederate general. A native of New York and a graduate of West Point, he had married a Georgia belle, moved to the South, and embraced the region as his homeland. Upon the South's secession, he had allied himself with the Confederacy. Smith was an accomplished engineer and had helped design the works around Vicksburg. Captured when the city fell to Grant, he had only a short while before returned to active service. Although new to the Army of Northern Virginia, he was an old acquaintance of Longstreet, who regarded him highly. Smith, Longstreet later wrote, was a "splendid tactician as well as skilful engineer, and gallant withal."

While fighting raged on Orange Plank Road, Smith was ordered—whether by Lee or Longstreet is not clear—to search for a way to turn Hancock's left flank. Working below Widow Tapp's farm, Smith and his party emerged onto the railroad cut. Cautiously they walked east along it through the leafy greenery. Soon the sound of battle came from their left. They were astride Hancock's flank, and not a Federal was in sight. Studying the lay of the land, the astute engineer caught another favorable feature. A series of ridges extended northward from the railroad bed to Orange Plank Road. Be-

---

4. "Wofford's Georgia Brigade," Atlanta *Southern Confederacy*, June 15, 1864; James Goggin to James Longstreet, August 10, 1887, in Longstreet Collection, SHC.

tween the ridges were troughs. To Smith's practiced eye, the natural depressions were handy avenues leading directly to Hancock's unprotected flank. Here was the route that Lee was seeking.

Around 10 A.M., Smith returned from his reconnaissance. Reporting to Longstreet, he could give assurances that the Federal line extended but a short distance beyond Orange Plank Road. The enemy position was exposed, he explained, and invited an attack from the railroad cut.[5]

That was precisely Longstreet's type of maneuver. Unlike at Gettysburg, there would be no frontal assault. Instead, the decisive blow would be delivered by a column slipping into place and then descending upon the surprised Federals. In the meantime, the main rebel force on Orange Plank Road would keep the enemy occupied. Once the flanking column began rolling up the opposing line, the contingent on Orange Plank Road would plow into the enemy's disordered ranks. Here was a plan calculated to ensure the enemy's destruction, and Longstreet energetically threw himself into it.

But first, several practical problems had to be addressed. Paramount was the question of which units should constitute the flanking force. Three fresh brigades were immediately available. From Field's division was Tige Anderson's brigade, which had been held in reserve below Orange Plank Road while Gregg, Benning, and Perry battered Wadsworth's Federals into a mass of disorganized fugitives. From Kershaw's division were Wofford's Georgians, who had recently arrived with the 1st Corps supply trains, and whose pickets had discovered the opportunity in the first place. And finally, from Anderson's division was Brigadier General William Mahone's Virginia brigade.

Senior of the three brigade commanders, Mahone was a wiry, fidgety man who appeared perpetually on the verge of starvation. Mahone's wife, on hearing that her emaciated husband was recovering from a flesh wound, was said to have quipped, "Now I know it is serious, for William has no flesh at all." He was an eccentric of the first order. Sorrel recalled one sweltering summer day when Mahone strode from his tent wearing a pleated brown linen jacket buttoned to his trousers like a little boy's outfit. A huge panama hat topped off

---

5. Sorrel, *Recollections*, 241; Longstreet, *From Manassas to Appomattox*, 561–62; James Longstreet's Report, in *OR*, Vol. XXXVI, Pt. 1, p. 1055.

his unusual uniform. "A cow was always by his quarters," recalled Sorrel, "and laying hens cackled loud, besides many luxuries. Delicate in physique, he had to nourish himself carefully." But the little man was a scrapper. Dangerous is how another of Longstreet's brigadiers described him. Son of a Virginia tavern keeper, he had reputedly won a substantial sum gambling with one of his father's wealthy guests. He had used the money to attend the Virginia Military Institute and had served as a construction engineer for various Virginia railroads. At the war's outbreak, he was president of the Norfolk and Petersburg line. He kept that position during the hostilities and conducted railroad business from his tent. Until the campaign in progress, Mahone's performance had been adequate but unremarkable.[6]

Sorrel, who had accompanied Smith on his explorations, was selected to lead the flanking party. Calling Sorrel aside, Longstreet offered his popular aide the opportunity of a lifetime. "Colonel, there is a fine chance of a great attack by our right," Longstreet said to his twenty-six-year-old staffer, a former bank clerk with no experience leading troops. "If you will quickly get into those woods, some brigades will be found much scattered from the fight. Collect them and take charge. Form a good line and then move, your right pushed forward and turning as much as possible to the left." Longstreet added, "Hit hard when you start," but then tempered his command with his accustomed caution: "Don't start until you have everything ready. I shall be waiting for your gunfire, and be on hand with fresh troops for further advance." Sorrel later reminisced, "No greater opportunity could be given to an aspiring young staff officer, and I was quickly at work." Without delay, he assembled the three brigades and led them south. Along the way, he came upon John Stone's brigade drawn from Mississippi and North Carolina. Though these veterans' numbers had been considerably reduced by their earlier stand against Hancock's assaults, they were eager to continue fighting. Shouldering their rifles, they fell into step with Sorrel's flanking column.[7]

6. Alexander, *Military Memoirs*, 504–505; "Biographical Information on Mahone," in Leigh Collection, USMHI; Perry, "Reminiscences of the Campaign," in *SHSP*, VII, 59; Sorrel, *Recollections*, 276–77.

7. Sorrel, *Recollections*, 241–42; Longstreet's Report, in *OR*, Vol. XXXVI, Pt. 1, p. 1055; Venable, "The Campaign from the Wilderness to Petersburg," in *SHSP*, XIV, 526. Heth noted that Stone's brigade had been cut off from the rest of the division by Longstreet's advance and

On reaching the unfinished railroad, the Confederate force, by now four brigades strong, swung east. The soldiers followed the railroad bed for about a half mile, to where it began its sharp bend south. Musketry echoed from the left. Sorrel's men had passed the battle front and were positioned immediately below Hancock's left flank. The energetic young staffer called his party to a halt. One by one, the Confederate brigades faced north. On the right, closest to the sharp bend, was Anderson's. Mahone's was in the center, and Wofford's on the left. Most likely, Stone's troops remained in reserve. Arranged to attack up one of the ravines that Smith had discovered, the Confederates were packed tightly together, forming a mass of troops several lines deep.[8]

Time was short. Sorrel's Confederates had scarcely assembled when the order to advance rang through the woods. After about 10 A.M., quiet had settled over the Wilderness. Even picket firing seemed to be gradually sputtering out. The Federal troops who made up the left wing of Hancock's column—predominantly Birney's, Mott's, and Getty's divisions—were taking advantage of the tempo-

---

hence was fortuitously situated to join the flank attack. See Henry Heth's Report, in MC. Who was in charge of the flanking movement is a matter of controversy. Mahone reported that "as the senior brigadier, I was by Lieutenant-General Longstreet charged with the immediate direction of this movement" (William Mahone's Report, in OR, Vol. XXXVI, Pt. 1, p. 1090). Some fourteen years later, Mahone wrote that the movement "was made by my own with two other brigades—Wofford's and Tige Anderson's—all under my immediate command" (William Mahone to Edward B. Robins, May 9, 1879, in Military Historical Society of Massachusetts Collection, BU). Sorrel insisted that Longstreet had given him "full authority to control the movement" (G. Moxley Sorrel to John R. Turner, January 19, 1892, in Recollections, by Sorrel, 300). Sorrel's assertion is supported by Lee's aide Walter Taylor in General Lee, 234, and by James Longstreet to Robert E. Lee, May 19, 1864, in Recollections, by Sorrel, 247; Longstreet's letter recommended Sorrel's appointment to brigadier general. The War Horse stated in his report, written in March, 1865, "Special directions were given to Lieutenant-Colonel Sorrel to conduct the brigades of Generals Mahone, G. T. Anderson, and Wofford beyond the enemy's left." He added, "Much of the success of the movement on the enemy's flank is due to the very skillful manner in which the move was conducted by Lieutenant Colonel Sorrel" (Longstreet's Report, in OR, Vol. XXXVI, Pt. 1, p. 1055).

8. Mahone's Report, in OR, Vol. XXXVI, Pt. 1, pp. 1090–91. Several years after the war, Mahone asserted that his brigade alone struck the Federal flank, while Wofford's and Anderson's brigades traversed the woods between Hancock's advanced line and Brock Road. See Mahone to Robins, May 9, 1879, in Military Historical Society of Massachusetts Collection, BU. For a fascinating collection of reminiscences by Confederate foot soldiers concerning the flank attack, see SHSP, XX, 68–95; the reminiscences are in War Talks of Confederate Veterans, comp. George Bernard (Petersburg, Va., 1892), 87–106. Many of the original letters are in George Bernard Collection, SHC.

rary lull. Weary soldiers stretched on the ground to snatch a few minutes' rest. Some kindled little fires to brew coffee.

Robert McAllister's brigade, of Mott's division, held the extreme left end of the Union line. Curious about what the rebels were up to, McAllister and an orderly passed through the Federal pickets and edged their way from tree to tree. Cautiously peering through the dense growth, the Federal general spied Confederates in a ravine ahead. A short distance farther on, he could make out the railroad cut, where more rebels were gathering in large numbers. Working his way back, he dispatched an aide to his division commander to alert his superiors concerning what he had discovered.[9]

The flinty Union brigadier's warning came too late. Positioning himself beside the 12th Virginia, of Mahone's brigade, Sorrel grasped his reins tightly in one hand and waved his hat high overhead with the other. "Follow me, Virginians!" he exclaimed. "Let me lead you." Striding forward in a compact body, the four Confederate brigades funneled up the ravine directly into Hancock's unprotected flank. At the same time, elements of Kershaw's rebel division resumed their attack, pounding Hancock from straight ahead along Orange Plank Road.[10]

The result was precisely as Longstreet had hoped. Sorrel's blow landed squarely on the end of McAllister's unsuspecting formation. McAllister attempted to bring his soldiers around to face Sorrel's flanking force, but completing the maneuver in the dense woods was painfully slow.

Alarmed by the firing, Mott rode to investigate. Just as McAllister began describing the situation to him, more Confederates ex-

9. Robert McAllister's Report, in OR, Vol. XXXVI, Pt. 1, p. 489. Precisely which unit formed the Union left flank is not clear. According to Hancock, Frank's brigade, detached shortly before from Barlow's division, received the attack. See Winfield S. Hancock's Report, in OR, Vol. XXXVI, Pt. 1, p. 323. Hancock's account is consistent with that of his aide-de-camp William Mitchell, who recorded Frank as first hit. See William Mitchell, Daily Memorandum, May 6, 1864, in OR, Vol. XXXVI, Pt. 1, p. 353. McAllister, however, reported that Frank had disappeared rearward some two hours before the assault. That McAllister explored the woods to his left and found Confederates there substantiates that Frank was not between McAllister and the rebels. See McAllister's Report, in OR, Vol. XXXVI, Pt. 1, p. 489. Frank filed no report that survives. The only report from his regimental commanders is the submission of Nelson Penfield, of the 125th New York, in OR, Vol. XXXVI, Pt. 1, p. 403, which tends to support Hancock's and Mitchell's understanding. McAllister's account can be squared with the others by assuming that Frank was posted below and somewhat behind McAllister.

10. William C. Smith to John R. Turner, February 26, 1892, in SHSP, XX, 81.

ploded from the woods to the west, where McAllister's front had been minutes before. These were Kershaw's lead elements. Caught between two ferocious rebel attacks, McAllister's brigade broke. McAllister himself barely escaped alive. Suffering from a camp ailment, he was too ill to walk, and his horse was soon riddled with bullet holes. The wounded mount stumbled through the thickets, scarcely able to bear its rider. Somehow the general managed to reach the safety of Brock Road before his horse collapsed and died.[11]

After overcoming McAllister's initial resistance, Sorrel's southerners clawed north through the Federal formation. Successive Union brigades toppled like dominoes. To one Federal officer, the Confederates seemed "like an army of ghosts rising out of the earth." He added, "Such an apparition will unsettle the stoutest nerves." A rebel recalled how "the crackle of the small arms, the bomb of the artillery, the hussah of the Yanks, the rebel yell sounding in the air, made pandemonium worse confounded."[12]

McAllister's experience was repeated as Sorrel's Confederates progressed northward toward Orange Plank Road. The 40th New York tried to turn toward the Confederate column, but bullets snapping from all around persuaded the soldiers to withdraw "in order to escape being captured." The 141st Pennsylvania's historian reported that his regiment retired toward Brock Road "without supports, without ammunition, with lines badly broken." While attempting to swing around and face Sorrel, Carroll's brigade discovered that it had been flanked, and began to give way. "One by one" Carroll's troops broke, recalled a northerner, "then in twos and threes, until at last they went in such numbers as to give the appearance of a general skedaddle." Armed with Spencer repeating rifles, a few of Carroll's soldiers fired back at the elusive gray forms, aiming close to the ground and inflicting severe casualties. But the rebels kept coming. "There was nothing left of us now but broken little squads," recorded a soldier in the 8th Ohio. "All that remained for us to do was to get back to our lines, running if possible." The experience was a nightmare. "A man would come against some elastic

---

11. McAllister's Report, in *OR*, Vol. XXXVI, Pt. 1, pp. 489–90.

12. Francis A. Walker, *History of the Second Army Corps*, 427–28; Hancock's Report, in *OR*, Vol. XXXVI, Pt. 1, p. 323; Mason Whiting Tyler, *Recollections of the Civil War* (New York, 1912), 154; W. M. Abernathy, "Our Mess: Southern Army Gallantry and Privations, 1861–1865," in W. M. Abernathy Collection, MDAH.

chinkapin tree," recounted the soldier, "bending it down before him, when it would suddenly spring back with a vicious blow in the face of the man behind. Our clothes were literally torn to shreds." One blue-clad fugitive recollected how a sharp stick tore out the seat of his pantaloons and exposed him "unmercifully to the enemy." [13]

Farther north, Lieutenant Colonel Charles Weygant attempted to save his 124th New York from Sorrel's advance. "I might as well have tried to stop the flight of a cannon ball by interposing the lid of a cracker box," he later conceded. "Caught up as by a whirlwind," explained Weygant, his regiment was "broken to fragments; and the terrible tempest of disaster swept on down the Union line, beating back brigade after brigade, and tearing to pieces regiment after regiment, until upwards of twenty thousand veterans were fleeing, every man for himself, through the disorganizing and already blood-stained woods, toward the Union rear." As the rout gained momentum, blue-clad officers darted through the melee. "Rally men, rally, for God and your country's sake, rally," they shrieked, waving swords overhead. Their efforts were wasted. "The colors were no sooner planted by those in front," complained a Union commander, "than they were swept away, and in some instances trampled under foot by those from the rear, who, while doing their best to get out of range of the enemy's bullets, continually echoed and re-echoed the 'Rally men, rally.'" To one Federal, the woods seemed to have become a "vast, weird, horrible slaughter pen." Enshrouded in smoke, the Confederate line sparked with rifle flashes. The effect, thought the Federal, was "like heat lightning from a cloudy horizon." [14]

Riding out Orange Plank Road to try to stem the disaster, Birney approached a cluster of fugitives from the 124th New York. The Union general drew rein at the roadside, his staff gathering behind him. Just then a Confederate cannon ball hissed along the roadway. Flying over the New Yorkers, the shell exploded almost directly under Birney's horse. Expecting the worst, the soldiers anxiously waited for the smoke to clear. Birney's staff had disappeared. The general, recalled an onlooker, was still gripping his horse, which had become

13. Madison M. Cannon's Report, in OR, Vol. XXXVI, Pt. 1, pp. 473–74; Craft, *History of the One Hundred Forty-First Regiment, Pennsylvania,* 181; Charles D. Page, *History of the Fourteenth Regiment, Connecticut,* 242–43; Galwey, *The Valiant Hours,* 199–200.

14. Weygant, *History of the One Hundred and Twenty-Fourth Regiment N.Y.S.V.,* 293–94.

"wholly unmanageable, and could be seen bounding from one side of the road to the other."[15]

Sorrel's flanking force appeared irresistible. Prancing near the head of the Confederate column, Mahone remained in the thick of the fighting. The little man darted everywhere, shouting orders and driving his gray-clad soldiers relentlessly forward. At one juncture, the 6th Virginia encountered a pocket of Union resistance and began stacking up twenty-five or thirty ranks deep. Mahone was immediately on the spot. "What regiment is this in this confusion?" he shouted in his clear, shrill whine. "The 6th Virginia," came the answer. "The 6th Virginia regiment of my brigade?" he asked, sarcasm thick in his voice. "That splendidly drilled regiment—in this condition?" Fearing their general's wrath more than Yankee bullets, the regiment resumed its advance.[16]

Sorrel, too, was vindicating Longstreet's confidence in him. As the Confederate column neared Orange Plank Road, the 12th Virginia's color-bearer got mired knee-deep in a swamp. Concerned that the attack would stall, Sorrel spurred into the morass. "Give me the colors," he demanded, "and I will lead the charge." The soldier proudly refused to relinquish the flag. "We will follow you," he called back, still gripping the staff. Braving a veritable storm of bullets, Sorrel emerged onto firm ground. Behind him came the colors. "I do not remember to have seen during the whole period of the war a finer exhibition of prowess than I witnessed that day in Colonel Sorrel," a Virginia soldier wrote after the war. "The move through the woods in pursuit of the retreating Federals was highly exciting," recalled a southerner. "The men seem[ed] to have lost all sense of danger, although hostile bullets were doing some deadly work." Another Confederate remembered "the woods echoing with the heavy discharge of musketry and the 'rebel yell' sounding from more than a thousand Confederate throats, the men in the finest spirits as they pressed on." Abandoned Union cooking fires set portions of the woods ablaze, adding to the confusion.[17]

Sorrel's venture had succeeded beyond expectation. In less than

15. *Ibid.*, 295.

16. E. M. Field to John Turner, n.d., in *SHSP*, XX, 84–86.

17. John Turner to G. Moxley Sorrel, January 13, 1892, in *SHSP*, XX, 69–70; G. Moxley Sorrel to John Turner, January 19, 1892, in *SHSP*, XX, 71–74; George Bernard to John Turner, n.d., in *SHSP*, XX, 75–76.

an hour, his Confederates had chewed their way through Hancock's formation to Orange Plank Road. Organized Union resistance below the roadway was nonexistent. As Hancock ruefully conceded to Longstreet after the war, "You rolled me up like a wet blanket."[18]

The picture was much the same north of Orange Plank Road. Federal reinforcements that had been pumped in during the morning—Owen's and Webb's 2nd Corps brigades and Carruth's 9th Corps brigade—were grouped near the roadway. The remnants of Wadsworth's division, stiffened by Wheaton's and Eustis' 6th Corps brigades, extended northward. Wadsworth, now in charge of all the troops in his sector, was busy trying to figure out the location of each of his units.

Apparently Wadsworth was feeling the weight of his years. He was "exhausted and worn out," he confided to his aide Monteith, and he expressed concern that he had become "unfit to command." In justice to his men, ventured the general, he ought to turn over his division to someone else. Thoughtfully chewing a cracker, Wadsworth mused that Cutler, head of the famed Iron Brigade, would make a worthy successor.[19]

While Wadsworth was engaging in soul-searching, his soldiers noticed that Federals below the road were fading back, though the cause of the retreat was not immediately evident. The retiring soldiers "did not seem to be demoralized in any manner," recalled an officer in Owen's Philadelphia brigade, "nor did they present the appearance of soldiers moving under orders, but rather of a throng of armed men who were returning dissatisfied from a muster. Occasionally some fellow, terror-stricken, would rush past as if his life depended on speed, but by far the larger number acted with the utmost deliberation in their movements." Wadsworth and his staff were powerless to stop the collapse. One officer grabbed a frightened soldier who tried to pull free. "I am surely wounded," cried the man. Unconvinced, the officer whacked the soldier across his back with the flat of his sword. Certain that he had been shot, the man screamed, "Now I know I am

18. Longstreet, *From Manassas to Appomattox*, 568.
19. Monteith, "Battle of the Wilderness," in *War Papers . . . Wisconsin*, 414–15.

wounded." The cowering soldier presented such a pathetic spectacle that he was permitted to continue rearward.[20]

The cause of the retrograde movement soon came out. Sorrel's flanking force was approaching Orange Plank Road, driving Hancock's corps before it. Unless the Confederates were stopped, they would cross the roadway and continue into Wadsworth's ranks.

To complete Wadsworth's difficulties, Longstreet launched another assault directly against the front of the silver-haired New Yorker's line. The attacking Confederates belonged to Field's division, reinforced by at least two brigades from Anderson's division. Now Wadsworth faced much the same combination that had rolled up the Federals below him. Sorrel was working onto Wadsworth's left flank while more Confederates were harassing him from straight ahead.

Decisive action was imperative. Wadsworth, snapping out of his reverie, began barking orders. Webb was standing nearby. "Go to the left," commanded Wadsworth, "and stop the retreat of those troops to our left who are flying to the Brock Road." As Webb disappeared southward, Wadsworth attempted to reorient a portion of his line toward Orange Plank Road. "I will throw these two regiments on their flank," he shouted to Monteith over the roar of musketry, referring to Rice's 56th Pennsylvania and 76th New York. "You hurry forward with [Cutler's] brigade." While Monteith turned back toward the Lacy farm to retrieve Cutler, Wadsworth ordered his brigadier Rice to change front and re-form parallel to Orange Plank Road. The objective, Wadsworth explained, was to block Sorrel's advance at the roadway. Shifting in the way directed, Rice immediately found his position untenable. Rebel batteries firing from Widow Tapp's farm enfiladed his line and rained a deadly hail of lead. From a nearby hill, Confederate sharpshooters kept up a killing fire. To make matters worse, Field's Confederate division chose that moment to advance. Rice's formation crumbled, attacked on what had become its right flank.[21]

In the midst of this confusion, one significant pocket of Federal resistance offered a potential rallying point. Webb's crack regiment,

20. Banes, *History of the Philadelphia Brigade*, 231.
21. Webb, "Through the Wilderness," in *B&L*, IV, 160; Monteith, "Battle of the Wilderness," in *War Papers . . . Wisconsin*, 415; A. P. Smith, *History of the Seventy-Sixth Regiment New York*, 291–92; Chamberlin, *History of the One Hundred and Fiftieth Regiment Pennsylvania*, 217; William Hoffman's Report, in *OR*, Vol. XXXVI, Pt. 1, p. 624.

the 20th Massachusetts, had formed behind log-and-earth breast-works erected near Orange Plank Road by Hill's Confederates the previous night. A deep ravine between the earthworks and the rebel attackers gave the Bay State regiment additional protection.

Wadsworth, however, seemed oblivious to the strength of this key position. Riding up to Colonel George N. Macy, the regiment's commander, he demanded, "What are you doing there? Who commands here?" Stepping forward, Macy answered, "I do. And have been placed here by General Webb to hold this position at any cost." Wadsworth grew excited. "I command these troops and order you forward," he roared. "Very well," responded Macy, "but we are 2nd Corps troops." Here was the linchpin to saving the Federal formation, argued the colonel, who had returned to the army not long before, after losing a hand at Gettysburg. Advancing from the strong-hold would compromise the entire line. In addition, urged Macy, his men would be uselessly slaughtered. Wadsworth was furious at what he viewed as Macy's insubordination. If Macy feared to attack, snorted the gray-haired general, he would lead the charge himself. Digging his spurs into his horse, Wadsworth brandished his antique Revolutionary War sword overhead and bounded over the works toward the enemy. Macy gathered his officers around him and ordered them to follow Wadsworth. "It is certain death," he added. "Great God, that man is out of his mind." [22]

Cheering, the Massachusetts soldiers leaped over the barricade and into the woods. Ahead, stretched on the ground to avoid detection, lay elements of the 8th Alabama, Perrin's brigade. Their commander had instructed them "not to fire until I should give the order, which would not be until they could see the whites of their eyes." The tactic worked to perfection. Volleys whined into Macy's ranks "from an unseen enemy only a few yards away, though invisible." Macy collapsed with a bullet in his foot. Major Henry L. Abbott, one of the army's promising young officers, assumed command of the regiment. Ordering his soldiers to fire from a prone position, he ignored his own advice and strolled erect, back and forth, as an inspiration to his men. Seeing one of his company commanders stand up, Abbott screamed, "For God's sake, Harry, lie down." The words

22. William T. Mali to Edward B. Robins, October 26, 1888, Gustave Magnitzky to Edward B. Robins, September 21, 1888, both in MOLLUS Collection, HU.

were hardly out of his mouth when a bullet tore through his abdomen. He was carried to the rear on a blanket.[23]

Reluctantly, Wadsworth conceded that it was impossible to advance. But before he could turn, his horse panicked and bolted toward the Alabamians. The old warrior struggled with his reins and managed to yank the animal around. Another crash of Confederate rifles ripped through the woods. A bullet bore through the back of Wadsworth's head, splattering brains over his aide's coat. Wadsworth slumped in his saddle. The aide caught the general as he fell and lowered him to the ground. Wadsworth stared at the treetops, brain matter oozing from a hole in his skull. Vaulting into Wadsworth's vacant saddle, the aide escaped through a torrent of flying bullets.[24]

As the 20th Massachusetts retired to its log barricade, Webb returned from his unsuccessful attempt to rally the troops below the roadway. His brigade was now in column on Orange Plank Road, positioned there by Wadsworth to stave off Sorrel's flanking party. One of Webb's regiments, the 19th Maine, had exhausted its ammunition and fallen rearward to replenish its supply. Hearing the rising musketry, the Maine men rushed back.

By this time, the entire Union line had dissolved. Lewis Grant's Vermont brigade was tumbling from the woods "in a confused mass," recorded a surprised Maine soldier. In vain, Grant struggled to rally the Vermonters. "They were crowded together in such a huddle and the pursuing enemy was so close upon them that it was hardly possible for them to re-form," reported the onlooker. Eustis, whose brigade was located nearby, was completely overwhelmed by the quickly moving Confederate offensive. "He seemed paralyzed," wrote the 37th Massachusetts' Colonel Oliver Edwards of Eustis, "and asked me to command the brigade, which I did, retiring the brigade." Webb's command fought a stubborn delaying action. As soon as the Vermont brigade had passed through their ranks, they opened fire on

23. Bruce, *The Twentieth Regiment of Massachusetts*, 353–54; Alexander S. Webb's Report, in Vol. XXXVI, Pt. 1, p. 438; Robert Scott, ed., *Fallen Leaves: The Civil War Letters of Major Henry Livermore Abbott* (Kent, Ohio, 1991), 251–53. Webb mourned after Abbott's death that "my brigade lost in him its best soldier."

24. Schaff, *The Battle of the Wilderness*, 271; Pearson, *James S. Wadsworth of Genesco*, 283–84; Bruce, *The Twentieth Regiment of Massachusetts*, 353; *In Memoriam: James Samuel Wadsworth, 1807–1864* (Albany, N.Y., 1916), 115–19. Pasted into the copy of *In Memoriam* in the library at the University of North Carolina, Chapel Hill, is a handwritten description of events in which A. A. Herbert presented the Confederate perspective.

the pursuing rebels. According to Webb, the 19th Maine "stayed with me to hold the Plank Road and to deceive the Confederates by fighting as though they had a continuous line." The 56th and 57th Massachusetts, of Carruth's 9th Corps brigade, joined Webb's desperate defense. But the small Federal rear guard was powerless to stop the onslaught. The leader of the 57th—William F. Bartlett—was struck by a ball just above his right temple. Stunned, he was carried off draped over the neck of a horse. The new commander of the 56th Massachusetts—his predecessor had been killed by a rebel ball through the neck a few minutes before—spotted a body of rebels slipping behind his regiment and asked Webb for permission to retreat. "Get out of there as damned quick as you can!" barked Webb. As Webb himself later described it, he ordered the rest of his units "to break like partridges through the woods for the Brock Road." [25]

Longstreet's success was by then virtually complete. His flanking movement had overrun the left wing of Hancock's line. When Hancock's right flank had turned to meet the threat, it had been swamped by fresh waves of rebels. By noon, Hancock's formation lay ruined and a Confederate victory seemed likely. All that remained was for Longstreet to cinch his success by sweeping eastward, gathering prisoners and herding the enemy toward the Rapidan.

As the head of Sorrel's column neared Orange Plank Road, Mahone's 12th Virginia was forced to detour around a patch of flaming woods. In the process, the regiment slipped to the right. The exuberant Virginians found themselves advancing alone, separated from the rest of Sorrel's units. Bursting across the roadway, the Virginians continued in hot pursuit of fleeing Yankees. The enemy were running "in utter confusion and rout," recorded a Confederate, and catching Federals became something of a sport. Spying a blue-clad fugitive, a rebel officer shouted, "Don't shoot! We will catch him." The Federal

---

25. John Day Smith, *History of the Nineteenth Regiment of Maine*, 137–43; Webb's Report, in *OR*, Vol. XXXVI, Pt. 1, p. 438; Webb, "Through the Wilderness," in *B&L*, IV, 160–61; Massachusetts Historical Society, *War Diary and Letters of Stephen Minot Weld*, 286; Tyler, *Recollections of the Civil War*, 150; Edwards, "Memorandum," in Illinois State Historical Library; Francis W. Palfrey, ed., *Memoir of William Francis Bartlett* (Boston, 1878), 99–101.

dodged behind a tree, then as the Confederates approached darted away again. "Let him have it," ordered the southern officer. Rifles cracked, and the soldier crumpled to the ground. Some fifty yards north of Orange Plank Road, the 12th Virginia reached a relatively flat, sunken area. Concerned that it had pushed too far ahead of the flanking column, the regiment re-formed and started back toward the roadway.[26]

Sorrel reached Orange Plank Road in the van of his troops. His first thought was to notify Longstreet of his success and to request fresh soldiers. Turning left, he trotted west toward the main Confederate line. Lee, Longstreet, and an assortment of staffers and generals were gathered in a small knot on the road. So far, everything had proceeded according to plan. Longstreet, Sorrel later recalled, was "happy at the success." The burly Confederate was busy congratulating his generals. Seeing Field nearby, Longstreet rode over and seized his division commander by the hands. "He congratulated me in warm terms on the fighting of my troops and the result of the assault," Field was to recall. Lee was making sure that logs the enemy had thrown across the road as breastworks were cleared to let Confederate cannons through. Two 12-pounder Napoleons and a 24-pounder howitzer from Colonel David G. McIntosh's battalion were being advanced to support the attack.[27]

John Haskell, who was helping advance the guns, noticed a body in a general's uniform lying on the roadside. His hat and boots were gone, and the buttons had been cut off his coat. On confirming that the man was still alive, Haskell had two orderlies stick muskets into the ground and spread a blanket over them. The inert form was dragged under the makeshift awning. It was Wadsworth, still breathing but unconscious.[28]

Questions about what the Confederates should do next were resolved with the appearance of Martin Smith, Lee's enterprising engineer. During the fighting, Smith had explored farther along the uncompleted railroad. His goal on his second reconnaissance was to determine whether another flanking movement could be successfully

26. Statement of John R. Patterson, in *SHSP*, XX, 93–94.

27. G. Moxley Sorrel to John Turner, January 19, 1892, in *SHSP*, XX, 73; Sorrel, *Recollections*, 243; Field, "Campaign of 1864 and 1865," in *SHSP*, XIV, 545; David Gregg McIntosh, "A Ride on Horseback in the Summer of 1910," in David Gregg McIntosh Papers, SHC.

28. Govan and Livingood, eds., *The Haskell Memoirs*, 65.

executed against Hancock's defenses on Brock Road. Smith's news was exactly what the War Horse had hoped to hear. As Longstreet later recalled the conversation, Smith "reported a way across the Brock Road that would turn Hancock's extreme left." Delighted with Smith's work, Longstreet invited the engineer to lead a new Confederate flanking party. Wofford's Georgians, who had finished their assignment with Sorrel, were to form the spearhead of Smith's new attack. Losing no time, Smith disappeared. Soon Wofford's brigade was slipping south toward the railroad right-of-way. If all went well, in short order the brigade would be administering another surprise to the Federals.[29]

Also riding with the distinguished party of Confederate generals was Micah Jenkins. One of Field's top brigadiers, Jenkins had played little part thus far in the day's fighting. During the morning's attacks, his South Carolina brigade had been held in reserve. Now, however, Jenkins was to assume a prominent role. With the Union line in shambles, his brigade was to lead a Confederate attack straight up Orange Plank Road, slicing through the disordered enemy ranks and taking Brock Road, less than a half mile away.

Kershaw, who was to cooperate with Jenkins in the attack, understood that his job was to assault the "position of the enemy upon the Brock Road, before he could recover from his disaster. The order to me was to break their line and push all to the right of the road towards Fredericksburg."[30]

Jenkins was in frail health. During the spring, a patch of carbuncles had erupted between his shoulder blades. A close friend attributed the problem to undernourishment, noting that "healthy, active young men cannot live on a cracker, coffee, and a handful of berries, without nature protesting." Shortly before the campaign, Longstreet had granted Jenkins a short leave to recuperate. Jenkins had returned as sick as ever and had been carried to battle in an ambulance. But despite excruciating pain, he insisted on leading his troops.

Jenkins was acutely aware of the importance of his mission. Summoning Colonel Asbury Coward, of the 5th South Carolina, he shared his thoughts with his longtime friend. "Old man," he began,

29. Longstreet, *From Manassas to Appomattox*, 563.
30. Joseph B. Kershaw's Report, in *OR*, Vol. XXXVI, Pt. 1, p. 1062.

"we are in for it today. We are to break the enemy's line where the Brock Road cuts across the pike. The point," he added, indicating the direction with his extended arm, "lies just over there, I think." Smiling a familiar broad-faced grin, the general continued. "Your regiment is the battalion of direction. Tell your men that South Carolina is looking for every man to do his duty to her this day." At about this time, Porter Alexander happened by. He was on an assignment to find Jeb Stuart, to determine whether the Confederate cavalryman knew of a favorable position from which Confederate artillery could harass Hancock's flank. Jenkins' soldiers were loading their muskets in preparation for their attack. Shaking hands with Jenkins, Alexander good-naturedly mocked his friend's style of address. "Old man, I hope you will win that next grade this morning," said the artilleryman. "Well," answered Jenkins, turning to his men, "we are going to fight for old South Carolina today, aren't we, boys?"[31]

Jenkins' troops, many of them dressed in new uniforms made of cloth "so dark a gray as to be almost black," confirmed their readiness with a shout.[32]

The preparations complete, Longstreet, Jenkins, Kershaw, and a host of orderlies and staffers started east at the head of the main Confederate troop column. Jenkins was in an expansive mood. "Sorrel, it was splendid," he gushed, and threw an arm around the staffer's shoulder. "We shall smash them now." He confided to Longstreet, "I am happy," and he continued, "I have felt despair for the cause for some months, but am relieved, and feel assured that we will put the enemy back across the Rapidan before night." Turning to his brigade, which was marching close behind, Jenkins called out, "Why do you not cheer, men?" He was greeted by a hearty round of shouts.[33]

Longstreet's aide Andrew Dunn suggested that the general was too exposed at the head of the column. "That is our business," replied the 1st Corps commander, and continued on.[34]

31. Natalie J. Bond and Osmun L. Coward, eds., *The South Carolinians: Colonel Asbury Coward's Memoirs* (New York, 1968), 130–34; Gallagher, ed., *Fighting for the Confederacy,* 359.

32. Govan and Livingood, *The Haskell Memoirs,* 65.

33. Dawson, *Reminiscences of Confederate Service,* 115; Sorrel, *Recollections,* 243; Longstreet, *From Manassas to Appomattox,* 563.

34. Andrew Dunn to George Bernard, July 1, 1892, in *SHSP,* XX, 95.

Just ahead, Mahone's 12th Virginia was returning from its brief foray to the north side of Orange Plank Road. Coming from the south, the remainder of Mahone's regiments were starting to spill onto the roadway. Through the thick forest growth, they glimpsed armed troops moving in their direction. The uniforms were dark, more like Union blue than rebel gray. Assuming that the approaching figures were Yankees, the soldiers aimed at the indistinct forms.

Shots rang out and deadly minié balls whizzed through the air. Someone cried out, "Show your colors." The 12th Virginia's color-bearer—the same man who had refused to give the flag to Sorrel a few minutes before—kept his wits. Boldly striding into the roadway, he waved the flag overhead. The headquarters cavalcade was caught in cross fire. Jenkins' soldiers fell to their knees and aimed blindly into the brush. Realizing that the shooting came from Confederates, Kershaw dashed into Jenkins' troops in an attempt to prevent an even greater tragedy. "They are friends," he screamed. Immediately understanding what had happened, Jenkins' men held their fire. Bullets ricocheted through the woodland. In these thickets, where figures could be perceived only dimly through smoke and trees, men on horseback ran a special risk. A lead projectile tore through Jenkins' skull, tumbling the handsome South Carolinian from his horse. "F-r-i-e-n-d-s!" screamed Kershaw. Longstreet rode forward to try to stop the firing. He was a heavy man and maintained a firm seat in his saddle. Looking over, Sorrel saw Longstreet lift straight up, then drop down hard. A confused look clouded Longstreet's face. Blood spurted from a gaping hole in his neck. More gushed from an exit wound behind his right shoulder. Not yet fully comprehending what had happened, the War Horse tried to turn and ride back. Slowly he slumped in his saddle. His body began to flop from side to side. Seeing that Longstreet was about to fall, his aides jumped to the ground. They quieted his horse, then lifted Longstreet and laid him under a tree.[35]

35. Kershaw's Report, in *OR*, Vol. XXXVI, Pt. 1, p. 1062; Sorrel, *Recollections*, 243; Longstreet, *From Manassas to Appomattox*, 563–64; William McWillie Notebook and Diary, in McWillie Family Papers, MDAH. Rumors abounded concerning the shooting. Conner, who did not witness the events, wrote that Longstreet "could have saved himself by jumping from his horse, but he rode forward to endeavor to stop the fire" (Conner to mother, May 15, 1864, in *Letters of General James Conner*, ed. Moffett, 128). A soldier in Jenkins' brigade later said that when a staff member, upon Longstreet's orders, picked up and unfurled a Union flag that the general had spotted in the roadway, approaching Virginians fired on it. See Mixson, *Remi-*

*"They had fought all they meant
to fight for the present."*

Longstreet was bleeding profusely from where a bullet had entered his neck and passed out his right shoulder. His staff conducted a hurried examination and concluded that the wound was fatal. Francis Dawson, a British volunteer, mounted and darted rearward to find a doctor. "Giving the sad news to the first surgeon I could find," he later wrote, "I made him jump on my horse, and bade him, for Heaven's sake, ride as rapidly as he could to the front where Longstreet was." It just so happened that Dawson had given his mount to Dr. J. S. D. ("Dorsey") Cullen, the 1st Corps' medical director. Cullen reached the prostrate Longstreet without delay. The general was choking on his own blood. Laboring feverishly, the doctor tried to stanch the hemorrhage.[36]

Longstreet, despite his condition, remained preoccupied with the battle. Propped against a tree, a bloody froth bubbling at his mouth, he called orders to a passing colonel. "Tell General Field to take command," he rasped, "and move forward with the whole force and gain the Brock Road." Field was quickly summoned to Longstreet's side. Realizing that his injury might be fatal, Longstreet conducted a whispered conversation with his division commander. "Assume command of the corps," Longstreet told him. "Press the enemy." Longstreet's instructions to his aide-de-camp were in the same spirit. "He urged me to hasten to General Lee," Sorrel later recorded, "report what had been accomplished, and urge him to continue the movement he was engaged on; the troops being all ready, success would surely follow, and Grant, he firmly believed, be driven back across the Rapidan."[37]

Dr. Cullen meanwhile managed to check the flow of blood. The general was lifted onto a litter and a hat placed over his face to shield him from the sun. Word traveled quickly, and gray-clad soldiers crowded the road to verify reports of Longstreet's injury for themselves. The inert form, face covered, seemed to confirm their worst fears. "He is dead, and they are telling us he is only wounded," sol-

---

niscences of a Private, 70–71. The letters from members of the 12th Virginia collected in *SHSP*, XX, beginning on p. 95, do not, however, mention a Federal flag's being involved.

36. Dawson, *Reminiscences of Confederate Service*, 115.

37. Sorrel, *Recollections*, 243–44; Field, "Campaign of 1864 and 1865," in *SHSP*, XIV, 545.

diers murmured. Concerned about the morale of his corps, Longstreet drew on his seemingly inexhaustible reserve of energy and lifted his hat with his left hand. The response was immediate. "The burst of voices and the flying of hats in the air," Longstreet later reminisced, "eased my pains somewhat." Longstreet was lifted into an ambulance, and a somber procession jostled toward the Confederate hospital tents at Parker's Store. The general's staff rode silently with the wagon, one distraught officer standing on the conveyance's rear step to be nearer the injured Longstreet. "I never on any occasion during the four years of the war saw a group of officers and gentlemen more deeply disturbed," recorded a passing artillery major. "They were literally bowed down with grief. All of them were in tears. One, by whose side I rode for some distance, was himself severely hurt, but he made no allusion to his wound, and I do not believe he felt it." The artilleryman looked inside. Longstreet's hat, coat, and boots had been removed and the blood had drained from his face. "I noticed how white and dome-like his great forehead looked and, with scarcely less reverent admiration, how spotless white his socks and his fine gauze undervest, save where the black red gore from his breast and shoulder had stained it. While I gazed at his massive frame, lying so still, except when it rocked inertly with the lurch of the vehicle, his eyelids frayed apart till I could see a delicate line of blue between them, and then he very quietly moved his unwounded arm and, with his thumb and two fingers, carefully lifted the saturated undergarment from his chest, holding it up for a moment, and heaved a deep sigh." Within the hour, Longstreet's ambulance had reached the Confederate field hospital. There Dr. Cullen and three other surgeons probed the wound. It was, they concurred, "not necessarily fatal." [38]

The same could not be said for Jenkins. A bullet had smashed through his temple and entered his brain. For a while he had babbled incoherently, cheering and imploring his men to sweep the enemy into the river. Soon he became too weak to talk.

On hearing the fatal blast of musketry, Jenkins' friend Coward had hurried back. When he arrived, Longstreet was being lifted into an ambulance. Jenkins lay delirious on a litter. Kershaw had re-

---

38. Longstreet, *From Manassas to Appomattox*, 566; Stiles, *Four Years Under Marse Robert*, 247; Dunn to Robert E. Lee, May 6, 1864, in *OR*, Vol. LI, Pt. 2 Supplement, p. 893.

mounted and was urging haste. Enemy cannon balls crashed among the trees, howling over the wounded men.

Coward knelt by Jenkins' side. "Jenkins . . . Mike, do you know me?" he whispered. There was no answer. First Jenkins' hand convulsed, then his whole body shook with a spasm. Coward stood in shock as his friend's body was lifted into an ambulance. John Bratton, of the 6th South Carolina, assumed command of Jenkins' brigade.[39]

Lee had been riding on Orange Plank Road not far behind Longstreet's cavalcade and received word of the tragedy shortly after it occurred. The Englishman Dawson was with Longstreet's ambulance when Lee rode up and looked inside. "I shall not soon forget the sadness in his face, and the almost despairing movement of his hands, when he was told that Longstreet had fallen," Dawson later wrote.[40]

The Confederate commander in chief's situation was perplexing. Longstreet's plan had succeeded brilliantly. The mastermind of the maneuver, however, was in no condition to carry it through. Lee understood the broad outline of the operation, but the details were known only to Longstreet.

Lee's and Longstreet's aggressiveness had created a favorable opportunity to wreck Grant's advance. All that remained to cinch victory was for Longstreet's corps to capture Brock Road. Speed was of the essence. But the Southern troops were unable to advance as an organized fighting force in their existing configuration. And it would never do to hurl an unruly mob against Hancock's defenses on Brock Road. With Longstreet out of the picture, time was needed to locate the 1st Corps units, untangle them, and orient them toward a common objective.

Bringing order into the victorious Confederate units would be no easy task. Longstreet's corps had become thoroughly tangled during its advance. It was now in fragments, each facing a different direction. Sorrel's flanking force was poised to continue north, Smith's contingent was starting south toward the unfinished railroad, and the remainder of Field's and Kershaw's divisions was plowing east. In Field's words, the 1st Corps was "somewhat mixed up." As he

---

39. Bond and Coward, eds., *The South Carolinians*, 135; Govan and Livingood, eds., *The Haskell Memoirs*, 66.
40. Dawson, *Reminiscences of Confederate Service*, 116.

viewed the situation, "no advance could be possibly made until the troops parallel to the road were placed perpendicular to it. Otherwise, as the enemy had fallen back down the road, our right flank would have been exposed to him, besides our two bodies being on the road at the same point, one perpendicular and the other about parallel to it, neither could move without interfering with the other." The confusion was compounded with the arrival of Richard Anderson. The 3rd Corps division commander had played little part in the day's events, but he ranked above Field and Kershaw. Military convention dictated that he lead Longstreet's forces. Field dutifully relinquished command, which placed responsibility for renewing Longstreet's assault in someone who knew nothing about the battleground or the location and condition of the troops. As Field later remarked, straightening things out necessarily "consumed some precious time."[41]

Sorrel's force had punched into the flank of Hancock's attack column at about 11 A.M. After perhaps half an hour, Birney, who was responsible for the management of the Federal column, concluded that resistance was futile. He was still rattled by the Confederate shell that had exploded under his horse. Returning to Hancock's command center, he conducted a hurried conference with his chief. The troops, he said, could not adjust their formation in the woods. The only course was to order them back to Brock Road to re-form them on

41. Field, "Campaign of 1864 and 1865," in *SHSP*, XIV, 545–46. Field leaves the impression that he commanded the 1st Corps for the rest of the day, remarking that "only after the battle had been fought and won" was Anderson placed over the corps. Sorrel makes it clear that Anderson was not formally appointed to corps command until May 7. See Sorrel, *Reminiscences*, 248–50. Longstreet, however, states that though Field initially assumed command of the corps, Anderson "came into command as senior" before Field had an opportunity to untangle the Confederate lines. See Longstreet, *From Manassas to Appomattox*, 564–65. *The Haskell Memoirs* assert that Lee, upon learning of Longstreet's wounds, immediately sent for Anderson "to take command of the corps" (Govan and Livingood, eds., *The Haskell Memoirs*, 65–66). In a postwar letter, Anderson further confounded the record by noting that "Longstreet was severely wounded about mid-day on the 7th and soon afterwards, General Lee placed me in command of his corps" (C. Irvin Walker, *The Life of Lieutenant General Richard Heron Anderson of the Confederate States Army* [Charleston, S.C., 1917], 159). It seems probable that Anderson was placed over Field during the afternoon but did not receive his formal appointment until the next day.

their original line of battle behind the breastworks. In effect, urged the distraught Federal commander, Hancock should place his imprimatur on the retreat already under way. Yielding to his subordinate, Hancock officially ordered his wing to retire to Brock Road.

While Confederates toiled to renew their offensive, Hancock's forces withdrew in disarray. "Our lines broke and ran like sheep," one of Carruth's soldiers recorded in his diary. "It was a regular skedaddle," confirmed one of Wheaton's men. Hancock's aide Walker observed that "on the right of the Plank Road, where the troops came back under orders, the regiments are generally entire, though greatly depleted by losses and by straggling; but on the left of the Plank Road, many regiments are to be found in companies or squads." Log-and-dirt earthworks erected the previous evening along Brock Road's western edge offered the northerners sanctuary. One of Carroll's soldiers declared, "It was our one hope—shattered, fatigued, and out of ammunition as we were by this time—to get across the parapet and, after a short rest in the hollow ground to the rear, to re-form and be again ready for action."[42]

Happily for the Federals, disorder in the southern ranks had completely stalled the Confederate attack. Only occasional clusters of rebels were able to make it as far as Brock Road. A handful of brave southerners charged the Federal works "yelling like devils," an Ohio man remembered. After a few Federal volleys, however, the Confederates melted into the woods. Taking advantage of the reprieve, Hancock's soldiers labored feverishly to strengthen their defenses. A steady sprinkling of Union fugitives clambered in from the forest. "Every minute some men who had not been seen since the break in the morning would appear with woebegone expressions," recalled a soldier, "and would at once begin to relate their adventures and hairbreadth escapes."[43]

Lyman watched the collapse of Hancock's offensive from the intersection. As the sound of musketry drew nearer, stragglers began to appear, followed by a crowd of blue-clad soldiers in full retreat. "They were not running, nor pale, nor scared, nor had they thrown

---

42. Wyman Diary, May 6, 1864, in Civil War Miscellaneous Collection, USMHI; Henry T. Waltz Diary, May 6, 1864, in Ralph G. Poriss Collection, USMHI; Francis A. Walker, *History of the Second Army Corps*, 429–30; Hancock's Report, in OR, Vol. XXXVI, Pt. 1, p. 323; Galwey, *The Valiant Hours*, 200.

43. Galwey, *The Valiant Hours*, 200.

away their guns," remarked Lyman. "They had fought all they meant to fight for the present, and there was an end of it! If there is anything that will make your heart sink and take all the backbone out of you, it is to see men in this condition!" Drawing his sword, Lyman rode among the retreating soldiers, trying to persuade them to rally at the rifle pits. "I would get one squad to stop," he explained, "but, as I turned to another, the first would quietly walk off." Determined to stem the rout, Lyman ran to a German carrying a flag from Stevenson's division. "Jeneral Stavenzon, he tell me for to carry ze colors up ze road," was the soldier's explanation for his hasty progress eastward. "I will run you through the body," threatened Lyman, sword still in hand, "if you don't plant those colors on the rifle pit!" The frightened soldier complied, although Lyman later observed, "I guess he didn't stick."[44]

The Brock Road earthworks were soon jammed with milling blue forms. Color sergeants stabbed flags into the embankment to provide rallying points for units as they arrived. Staff officers directed exhausted soldiers to their divisions and brigades. The troops, "faces begrimed with powder, but showing no anxiety for the result of the coming attack," fell into place toward the enemy. According to the 124th New York's commander, there was soon a "wall of refuge in the Wilderness" representing "one of the strongest lines of temporary works it had ever been my fortune to stand behind." Considering the confusion, thought the New Yorker, the soldiers had rallied "in an incredibly short space of time."[45]

Around 11:30 A.M., Lyman informed Meade of the latest development. "The rebels have broken through Barlow's right," ran his message to headquarters, "and are now pushing us back along the plank road. General Gibbon has been sent for to close the gap. Sharp firing along the plank road." Hancock also dispatched an aide with his account of the affair. "Owing to a heavy attack by Longstreet on my left," reported Hancock, "my troops have been forced to retire to the Brock road, where the line of battle has been re-established."[46]

44. Lyman to family, May 16, 1864, in *Meade's Headquarters*, ed. Agassiz, 95–96.

45. Banes, *History of the Philadelphia Brigade*, 232; Weygant, *History of the One Hundred and Twenty-Fourth Regiment N.Y.S.V.*, 295–96; Henry Harrison Stone Pocket Diary, May 6, 1864, in Harrisburg Civil War Round Table Collection, USMHI.

46. Theodore Lyman to George G. Meade, May 6, 1864, in *OR*, Vol. XXXVI, Pt. 2, p. 444; Hancock's Report, *ibid.*, Pt. 1, 323.

Meade's reaction was predictable. He considered it essential to shift more infantry from the turnpike southward to reinforce Hancock, and to concentrate cavalry to protect the supply trains.

Attempts to pry troops loose from Warren and Sedgwick met with little success. At noon, the army commander informed Warren than Hancock was "very heavily pressed" and had been forced to retire. "It may perhaps be necessary either to make an advance from your left, or send troops to him from your command. Have some in readiness." Warren's reserves, however, were already depleted. Wadsworth's division and a portion of Robinson's had been badly chewed up on Orange Plank Road. The only encouraging news involved Cutler, who had managed to rally a respectable portion of his command. Warren had just received sad intelligence, however, concerning Wadsworth. "An aide of Wadsworth has just come in," stated a dispatch to headquarters at 12:45 P.M. "He reports that the general is killed; that he was with him when he was struck in the head about half an hour ago. The body was left on the ground." Under these circumstances, concluded Warren, he could spare no more than a brigade.[47]

Sedgwick was also solicited to help satisfy Hancock's need for troops. The forthright old warrior responded that "not a regiment should be withdrawn" from his formation. "General Wright is strongly of that opinion" he added. "If absolutely necessary," however, he could send Russell's brigade, which had suffered little during the previous two days' fighting. Sedgwick's caution gave Meade second thoughts about weakening his northern front. Ewell's Confederates had been quiet for a while, which probably meant they were contemplating another attack. Prudence suggested retaining a respectable force there. Accordingly, at 1:30, Meade instructed Warren to dispatch only one of Robinson's remaining brigades to Hancock. A half hour later these reinforcements, along with two regiments of heavy artillery, pulled into place behind Hancock's line on Brock Road. Later, after improving earthworks, Sedgwick volunteered Upton's and Morris' brigades. By that time, however, Hancock had concluded that he had sufficient soldiers to hold his position.[48]

47. George G. Meade to Gouverneur K. Warren, May 6, 1864, in OR, Vol. XXXVI, Pt. 2, p. 452; Lysander Cutler to Frederick T. Locke, May 6, 1864, ibid., 459; Edward R. Platt to Andrew A. Humphreys, 1864, ibid., 452.

48. John Sedgwick to Andrew A. Humphreys, May 6, 1864, in OR, Vol. XXXVI, Pt. 2,

As for the Union cavalry, it was far too scattered for Meade's preference, particularly with a Confederate breakthrough threatening. Gregg's division confronted Fitzhugh Lee's cavalry force at Todd's Tavern, Torbert's division was occupied with Rosser farther north, and Wilson's division was recuperating in the Federal rear at the Alrich farm, near Chancellorsville. Even the normally daring Sheridan was advising caution. "I think it best not to follow up any advantage gained, as the cavalry is now very far out," he wrote Meade at 11:40 A.M. "I do not wish to give [the Confederates] any chance of getting at our trains."[49]

Sheridan's intimation that the army's supplies might be in jeopardy provoked an immediate response from Meade. "General Hancock has been heavily pressed and his left turned," headquarters informed Sheridan. "The major-general commanding thinks that you had better draw in your cavalry so as to secure the protection of the trains." Sheridan later claimed that he had never meant to suggest that Meade withdraw the Union cavalry. He explained in his memoirs that his troopers had been "most successful" up to this juncture. He considered it unwise for Meade to extend the Federal cavalry forces any farther, but he never had the intention of recommending the drastic step of recalling the mounted Federal divisions from their forward positions.[50]

Sheridan's later protestations notwithstanding, the contemporaneous record discloses that he complied with Meade's orders without objection. Doubtless, reports that Hancock's left had been turned gave Sheridan cause for alarm. If the report was true, a rebel column

pp. 459–60; Andrew A. Humphreys to Gouverneur K. Warren, May 6, 1864, ibid., 453; John Sedgwick to Andrew A. Humphreys, May 6, 1864, ibid., 460.

49. Philip H. Sheridan to Andrew A. Humphreys, May 6, 1864, in OR, Vol. XXXVI, Pt. 2, p. 466.

50. Andrew A. Humphreys to Philip H. Sheridan, May 6, 1864, ibid., 467; Sheridan, Personal Memoirs, I, 363. Sheridan, in his report written in May, 1866, characteristically blamed Meade for his own abandonment of the forward positions his troopers held. Referring to Meade's suggestion that he withdraw closer to the wagons in light of Longstreet's assault, Sheridan wrote, "I obeyed this order, and the enemy took possession of the Furnaces, Todd's Tavern, and Piney Branch Church, the regaining which cost much fighting on the 6th and 7th, and very many gallant officers and men" (Philip H. Sheridan's Report, in OR, Vol. XXXVI, Pt. 1, p. 788). Sheridan took a similar position in Personal Memoirs, 362–63. The decision to abandon Todd's Tavern and Brock Road was a bad one, fostered by excessive panic over Longstreet's appearance. But contemporaneous dispatches imply that Sheridan was a more willing participant than he admitted in his later writings.

might be able to come between the Union cavalry corps and the Federal infantry.

Sheridan thus summoned his mounted units toward the army's wagon train. Gregg was directed to relinquish Todd's Tavern and to pull back to the Alrich farm. Custer was to leave his stronghold on Brock Road, retrace his morning's route, and resume his earlier position at Catharine Furnace. And Wilson was to report to Sheridan at his Chancellorsville headquarters. The withdrawal was accomplished, but not without difficulty. As Gregg's troops left Todd's Tavern, Rosser's irrepressible horsemen pounded their rear guard.[51]

Brock Road below the Trigg farm was abandoned to the rebels. Meade had surrendered his hold on the direct highway south without a fight. The general's increasingly defensive mind-set was also apparent in his attempts to move his supply wagons to safety. Sheridan dispatched a regiment to "scour" the countryside toward United States Ford, a major Rapidan crossing east of Ely's Ford. The 2nd Corps trains, the cavalry chief advised headquarters at 2:30 P.M., were already heading to Ely's Ford. He had sent along a body of 1,300 dismounted cavalrymen to help ensure their safety.[52]

To all appearances, Grant's spring offensive had collapsed. With the rout of Hancock and Wadsworth, the chief concern in Union minds became how to preserve the Army of the Potomac, not how to attack Lee. Sorrel's dramatic sweep into Hancock's unsuspecting flank had conclusively demonstrated that the Army of Northern Virginia was anything but beaten. The Confederates seemed fully capable of executing their deadly tricks at will.

Even the stoutest Union hearts were demoralized. "This had been an awful day," one of Mott's soldiers wrote in his diary. "All our boys are tired." Returning from a conference with Meade, Lyman found Hancock sitting alone behind the Brock Road earthworks. His staff was still busy attempting to organize a defensive line. The 2nd Corps

51. Charles Forsyth to David McM. Gregg, May 6, 1864, in OR, Vol. XXXVI, Pt. 2, p. 470; Webb Diary, May 6, 1864, in Webb Papers, CL.

52. Joseph P. Elliott Diary, May 6, 1864, in Civil War Miscellaneous Collection, USMHI; Philip H. Sheridan to Andrew A. Humphreys, May 6, 1864, in OR, Vol. XXXVI, Pt. 2, p. 467.

commander looked exhausted and invited Lyman to join him. His troops, he told the aide, had rallied but were "very tired and mixed up, and not in a condition to advance." He had urged his generals to put the "utmost exertion" into reordering their units, but he predicted that severe losses in field officers would make the task difficult. Although the dispirited general was confident he could hold the road against an attack, he had concluded that offensive action was manifestly impossible.[53]

"It would be to
hazard too much."

As 2 P.M. approached, the opposing armies remained separated by several hundred yards of woodland. Hancock's soldiers huddled wearily behind their Brock Road earthworks, waiting for the sound of high-pitched rebel yells that would signal the renewal of the carnage. To the west, Lee was still toiling to arrange his tangled units for an assault. The country between the Federal defensive works and the Confederates was a no-man's-land of snipers and death.

Suddenly the sound of heavy firing began rattling through the woods. Surprisingly, the shooting did not herald the beginning of the expected Confederate assault but announced the launching of Burnside's long-awaited attack against Longstreet's northern flank. Burnside's wayward 9th Corps—or to be more exact, three brigades of the corps—had finally reached its objective. The Union commander's timing, however, was horribly off. Slated to attack at around 5:30 that morning, Burnside had arrived some eight hours late. His corps, however, was in the right spot. For a few hopeful minutes, it looked as though the rotund, genial commander might at last play a meaningful part in the battle.

What had happened was this. Around midmorning, after Burnside had been ordered to abandon his position on Parker's Store Trail and to cut his way south, his objective became the northern flank of Longstreet's battle line. Leaving a brigade to hold off Ramseur's Confederates, Burnside had peeled off his remaining three brigades and dispatched them toward Orange Plank Road.

---

53. Lyman Journal, May 6, 1864, in Lyman Papers, MHS; Stone Pocket Diary, May 6, 1864, in Harrisburg Civil War Round Table Collection, USMHI.

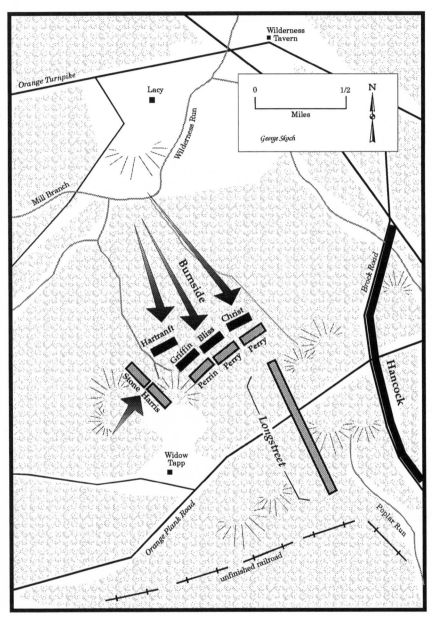

Burnside's assault on the afternoon of May 6

Dense forest retarded Burnside's expedition appreciably. As the hours passed, Grant become increasingly exasperated. Finally, the commander in chief delegated his trusted aide Porter to instruct the 9th Corps commander to "move on without a moment's delay, and connect with Hancock's right at all hazards." Porter caught up with Burnside taking his ease. Burnside's troops, observed Porter, were "endeavoring to obey orders as best they could, but, in struggling through underbrush and swamp, all efforts to keep up their alignment were futile." Characteristically, Burnside refused to let his soldiers' agonizingly slow progress dampen his spirits. A champagne basket brimming with lunch had been arranged for the corps commander's early afternoon repast. Always a genial host, Burnside invited Porter to join him and his staff in sampling the "attractive contents of the hamper." Unable to resist the feast, Porter decided that his urgent orders could wait a while longer, and he joined the general for lunch. His decision, Porter later explained, was based on the "recognized principle of experienced campaigners, who always eat a meal wherever they can get it, not knowing where the next one is to come from. It was called 'eating for the future.'"[54]

Leading Burnside's press toward Orange Plank Road was Potter's division. A lawyer and the son of an Episcopalian bishop, Potter had skyrocketed up the chain of command. According to the ever-quotable Lyman, he was a "grave, pleasant-looking man, known for his coolness and courage."[55] Inclined to excessive formality and a fastidious dresser, he habitually wore an overly neat brigadier general's uniform. But Potter was no martinet. He had fought in the war's bloodiest engagements and had proved to be a keen combat officer. His two brigades were under Zenas Bliss and Colonel Simon G. Griffin, a stalwart New Hampshire lawyer and politician who, like Potter, had won advancement on merit.

Augmenting Potter's division was John Hartranft's brigade, from Willcox' division. Hartranft had been haunted by an embarrassing debacle early in the war, when his soldiers abandoned the field because their terms of service had expired. His subsequent career, how-

54. Ambrose E. Burnside's Report, in OR, Vol. XXXVI, Pt. 1, p. 906; Horace Porter, *Campaigning with Grant*, 60–61.
55. Theodore Lyman to family, June 17, 1864, in *Meade's Headquarters*, ed. Agassiz, 166–67.

ever, had revealed talent. Although his star was to rise later in the war—and even more afterward, when he served two terms as Pennsylvania's governor—he was already achieving recognition as one of the Union army's ablest brigadiers.

Not until about 1:30 P.M. was Burnside's procession able to reach the exposed northern end of the Confederate line. Gingerly exploring toward the unprotected terminus of Longstreet's formation, Potter arranged his division parallel to Orange Plank Road, facing south. Hartranft's brigade was posted on Potter's right wing and somewhat back. A short distance across a swampy ravine, rebels could be seen milling about. The Confederate line's exact configuration was difficult to ascertain. As Potter later remarked, he was "entirely unable to see anything from the thickness of the wood." A Massachusetts soldier recalled that "the heat was intense" and "the men were almost exhausted from their long march of the previous day." It was impossible for Federal troops to see down their own battle line farther than a few men in either direction. Any conclusion about what the rest of the corps was doing required guesswork. Potter issued the only feasible instructions. At his signal, the troops were to advance, trying to stay as closely connected as possible.[56]

Grant's aide Comstock, still with Burnside's column, was not satisfied. Noting that Bliss's brigade was positioned to attack by the flank, Comstock told Bliss to wait and sought out Burnside. "General, the rebels are right in front of us in the woods," Grant's aide suggested to Burnside. "Don't you think it would be better for Bliss to move in a line of battle?" Burnside replied, "If you order it, it is." Comstock answered in his short, quick way: "I order it." And so Bliss rearranged his troops into two lines, three regiments in front and two behind.[57]

While Burnside was busy arranging his troops, Longstreet's corps had been struggling to orient its tangled lines to the east in preparation for an assault toward Brock Road. The northern end of Longstreet's formation—the sector Burnside was preparing to attack— was held by Perry's Alabama brigade, of Field's division. These troops

---

56. Robert Potter's Report, in *OR*, Vol. XXXVI, Pt. 1, p. 928; Charles E. Wood Diary, May 6, 1864, in Civil War Miscellaneous Collection, USMHI; Henry S. Burrage, *History of the Thirty-Sixth Regiment Massachusetts Volunteers* (Boston, 1884), 152.

57. Bliss, "Reminiscences," in Bliss Collection, USMHI.

had been badly worn from the morning's severe fighting. Perry was worried and ordered his trusted lieutenant Oates to find out whether the nearby woods contained Yankees. Exploring northward with two regiments, Oates discovered Burnside's force massing in the woods off Perry's left and sent word back that a "formidable attack" was brewing. Perry dispatched a courier to Lee with the news and began shifting the remainder of his brigade toward the endangered area.

Just then a staff officer galloped up to Perry. Lee intended to begin the general advance toward Brock Road at any moment, the rider announced. Perry was to move forward with the rest of the rebel line. Perry was in a quandary. "This order," he later wrote, "caused me to hesitate in considerable perplexity as to what I ought to do." But the imminent prospect of Burnside's attack resolved the matter. If he advanced as Lee wished, the brigadier feared that his left flank would be decimated by the Federal 9th Corps. Under the circumstances, Perry decided to ignore Lee's order and to concentrate instead on securing his flank. Riding to the far left of his line, he found Oates's force ensconced behind a pile of logs. Nearby was a small Florida brigade under Brigadier General Edward A. Perry. The Floridians, however, had neglected to conform with Oates. Instead, they had formed at right angles to the Alabamians. Their line projected a hundred yards past Oates's defenses toward Burnside. The two Confederate brigadiers—William Perry and Edward Perry—jointly decided that the Floridians and Oates's two Alabama regiments should advance eastward together to "feel for the enemy." Oates protested. As soon as he advanced, he argued, he would emerge from behind a small hill, exposing his men to Burnside. William Perry rejected Oates's apprehension, and Edward Perry yielded to the Alabama officer's judgment. Oates was "probably mistaken," they concurred, and ordered him to prepare.[58]

Shortly after settling on the move, William Perry stopped to chat with a group of Alabama troops. Turning to an acquaintance resting against a tree, he remarked with satisfaction, "I propose this evening to make a spoon or spoil a horn." The men, puzzled as to what Perry meant, remained silent.[59]

---

58. Perry, "Reminiscences of the Campaign," in *SHSP,* VII, 60–61; Oates, *The War Between the Union and the Confederacy,* 349–50.

59. Coles, "History of the Fourth Alabama Regiment," in Regimental Collection, ADAH.

With well-founded trepidation, the small Confederate force began snaking through the foliage. The Florida brigade led, with Oates' men following close behind. At that moment, Burnside's troops attacked. A gun sounded, and Potter's division tumbled into the swampy ravine that separated his men from the Confederate flank. The Federals pressed on, firing into Perry's ranks. "When we turned the hill, we got it," Oates later wrote in describing the unexpected Union assault. Oates did his best, ordering his troops to change front and begin tossing up log works. Within minutes, Oates's skirmishers had been driven in and Burnside's Federals had struck his main line. The Floridians caught the brunt of the attack. Burnside's troops, wrote Oates, hit the Florida brigade "squarely in the flank and decimated it at once." The Alabamians fought back fiercely. As a Federal later conceded, "the foeman was worthy of our steel." In a desperate attempt to reverse the tide, Oates ordered his two Alabama regiments to charge. With a piercing shout, gray-clad soldiers rushed into the swamp that was swarming with northerners.[60]

Once fully aware of the contours of the Confederate position, the Federals adjusted their skirmish line and drove the southerners across the morass into their makeshift entrenchments. One Union observer thought the Confederate breastworks were made of felled trees, brush, and bodies of dead rebels. But whatever their composition, it had become clear that the rebel works slashed diagonally through the woods to the northeast. In order to adjust to the enemy's line, Bliss halted his soldiers and shifted them to the right.

While the Federals dressed their lines, the rebels unleashed a nasty blaze of fire from their wooded slope. Potter, protecting his exposed flank, threw back his leftmost regiment, then steadied his brigade to charge. "Forward, double-quick!" sounded Potter's command, and the blue line heaved ahead. "The enemy poured in terrific volleys," recalled a northerner. "Their bullets whistled around us and thinned our ranks, but the advance was not checked."[61]

The left of Burnside's blue line struck first. Scaling the rebel breastworks with a rush, the 36th and 45th Massachusetts captured

60. Potter's Report, in *OR*, Vol. XXXVI, Pt. 1, p. 928; Burrage, *History of the Thirty-Sixth Regiment Massachusetts*, 153; Oates, *The War Between the Union and the Confederacy*, 350.

61. Burrage, *History of the Thirty-Sixth Regiment Massachusetts*, 153; Potter's Report, in *OR*, Vol. XXXVI, Pt. 1, p. 928.

fortifications directly in their front. A bloody fight raged along the jerry-rigged Confederate breastworks. On Bliss's front, the 51st New York was unable to hold, creating an opening that Oates quickly moved to exploit. "In a brief time, though to us it seemed an age," wrote one of Bliss's soldiers, "the enemy rallied, moved upon our left flank, swept round toward our rear, and we were subjected to a fearful fire of musketry at short range." Several Federal units retired in confusion. Others struggled to retain their hard-won gains. In an effort to direct reinforcements to the endangered Federal left wing, Major William F. Draper, of the 36th Massachusetts, leaped onto the log breastworks. Immediately he became a target for Confederate sharpshooters. An alert northerner saved the major's life by whacking aside a rebel musket aimed at the erect blue form. The deflected ball passed through Draper's hat and was followed shortly by another that tore through his shoulder and left him lying senseless on the ground. The slaughter continued—"terrible and bloody," according to a Massachusetts man.[62]

The rebel foray around the Union left flank also caught the 11th New Hampshire by surprise. The regiment had punched through the first line of Confederates and exuberantly pressed ahead. When the regiment's colonel, Walter Harrison, found his men alone in the eerie underbrush, he called for reinforcements. But before help could arrive, rebels appeared on his left. Attempts to form a new line under fire were futile. The regiment dissolved into a "promiscuous crowd of fugitives running as fast as their legs could carry them." Harrison, who had outdistanced his regiment, found himself surrounded by a dozen rebels, guns leveled at his chest.[63]

During the delay bought by the blood of Oates's two hard-pressed regiments, the Floridians and the remainder of Perry's Alabamians managed to rally. Together they hurled their weight against the Federals, who "fought gallantly," recorded a Yankee, "but the force upon our left was too strong, and our line was compelled to retire." At the height of battle, Bliss was surprised to see a Federal brigadier general and some two hundred men making their way

---

62. Jackman and Hadley, *History of the Sixth New Hampshire,* 221–23; Burrage, *History of the Thirty-Sixth Regiment Massachusetts,* 153–54; William B. Reynolds' Report, in *OR,* Vol. XXXVI, Pt. 1, p. 934.

63. Leander W. Cogswell, *A History of the Eleventh New Hampshire Regiment Volunteer Infantry in the Rebellion War, 1861–1865* (Concord, N.H., 1871), 341–59.

toward him. It was General Stevenson, also of the 9th Corps, who was still trying to collect the remains of his division. Noticing that Stevenson's men were cheering, Bliss asked if they could pitch in. "As soon as the men heard this request," Bliss recorded in his memoirs, "they marched off, and the general said, he could do nothing with them, and I did not see them afterwards." The Federal reverse, however, was temporary. Until this juncture, Burnside had held Hartranft in reserve. As Bliss retired in confusion, Hartranft threw the 2nd, 8th, and 17th Michigan into the fray. These fresh units formed a firm point around which retreating blue-clad soldiers could rally.[64]

Soon the contending blue and gray lines reached uneasy equilibrium, neither able to gain the upper hand. Burnside's attack had generated impressive casualties, but it yielded no tangible military gains, chiefly because Hancock refused to send support. On hearing the firing, Lyman urged Hancock to join in, but the Federal 2nd Corps commander declined. Hancock's aggressive spirit had been broken. "He said with much regret that it would be to hazard too much," Lyman recorded in his journal, "though there was nothing in his immediate front." According to the staffer, "we were obliged to listen to Burnside's fighting without any advance on our part." At 2:00 P.M., Lyman informed headquarters of the situation in Hancock's sector. "All the enemy seem to have gone to fight Burnside," wrote Meade's aide. "There is no enemy in Hancock's front south of the Orange Plank Road." Hancock's line, he added, was "not organized enough to advance."[65]

Back at their knoll near the Lacy house, Grant and Meade discussed the best way to renew the Orange Plank Road initiative. The fight had manifestly gone out of Hancock, and Burnside was unable to achieve any "important results," as Porter termed it, by himself. The obvious solution was for Hancock and Burnside to attack simultaneously, a feat the army commanders had been attempting in vain to achieve all day. They determined to try once again. At 3 P.M., Hancock received a communication describing the new plan. It was headquarters' recommendation that as long as Burnside required no

64. Bliss, "Reminiscences," in Bliss Collection, USMHI; John Hartranft's Report, in OR, Vol. XXXVI, Pt. 1, p. 948; Constance Luce's Report, *ibid.*, 957.

65. Lyman Journal, May 6, 1864, in Lyman Papers, MHS; Theodore Lyman to George G. Meade, May 6, 1864, in OR, Vol. XXXVI, Pt. 2, p. 444.

assistance and the enemy remained quiescent, Hancock's soldiers were to rest. At 6 P.M., the dispatch continued, Hancock was to make a "vigorous attack" in conjunction with Burnside. A joint charge, Meade predicted, would "overthrow the enemy." Hancock dashed off a reply. The tone of it reflected his continuing shock over the morning's reversal. "The present partially disorganized condition of the command renders it extremely difficult to obtain a sufficiently reliable body to make a really powerful attack," he complained. "I will, however, do my best and make an attack at that hour in conjunction with General Burnside." [66]

To plumb Lee's intentions, Hancock ordered Leasure's brigade to determine if any rebels were forming within striking distance of the defenses on Brock Road. Starting from Hancock's southern flank, Leasure's soldiers were to advance a few hundred yards into the woods, then sweep north along the entire front of the Union 2nd Corps. It was a hazardous assignment. "Everyone seemed to think that it was the intention to risk the loss of the brigade to find out the position of the enemy," one of Leasure's soldiers later recalled. The men clambered over the breastworks and into a nightmarish landscape. Picking through patches of smoldering underbrush, they worked north between the two armies. Dead and wounded soldiers lay strewn over the ground. Dust and smoke made the air almost unfit to breathe. Only a few gray-clad sharpshooters ventured into the no-man's-land. The main Confederate line had drawn back. Reaching Orange Plank Road, Leasure's soldiers crossed into the woods beyond. Suddenly General Mott rode up. "Colonel, for God's sake, get your men out of here," ordered the division commander. To their intense relief, Leasure's troops returned to the Federal fold, taking position behind the main line, just below Orange Plank Road. [67]

While gunfire from Burnside's inconclusive fight continued to crackle through the woods, Hancock's troops relaxed behind their

66. Horace Porter, *Campaigning with Grant*, 61–62; George G. Meade to Winfield S. Hancock, May 6, 1864, in *OR*, Vol. XXXVI, Pt. 2, 444–45; Winfield S. Hancock to George G. Meade, *ibid.*, 445.

67. Silas Stevenson and W. H. Hoffman, quoted by William G. Gavin in *Campaigning with the Roundheads: The History of the Hundredth Pennsylvania Veteran Volunteer Infantry Regiment in the American Civil War, 1861–1865* (Dayton, 1989), 387–89; Hancock's Report, in *OR*, Vol. XXXVI, Pt. 1, p. 323; Charles F. Walcott, *History of the Twenty-First Regiment Massachusetts Volunteers, in the War for the Preservation of the Union, 1861–1865* (Boston, 1882), 316.

earthworks. Convinced that the rebels were at last finished for the day, Lyman went in search of his friend Abbott. The 2nd Corps hospital occupied a field about two miles behind the lines. Lyman, picking his way among the dead and dying, found Abbott on a stretcher, with mortal wounds received during Longstreet's flank attack. Macy lay nearby with a wound in his foot. Lyman helped Macy to Abbott's side. The two men stood quietly over Abbott's motionless form as he breathed his last. "It was a pitiful spectacle," Lyman wrote his family, "but a common one that day." [68]

Contrary to Hancock's expectations, Lee had no intention of forfeiting the next move. While Hancock waited behind his Brock Road works and Burnside continued to spar with Perry's Alabamians, Lee persisted in trying to organize his jumbled forces for yet another assault. The difficulties in aligning the tangled Confederate ranks, however, were considerable. As a private in Jenkins' brigade noted, the woods were "remarkably thicker than any we had yet encountered." Worse still, it seemed as if every tree "had a bullet through it from the hard fighting that had just gone on there, causing these white oak runners to bend down from being top heavy. These bullets all seemed to go through about the height of a man's waist. In tumbling down they made an almost impassable barrier. Together with this obstacle the dead and dying were so thick that we could not help stepping on them." But by 4 P.M., Lee's battle line was in order. Gray-clad ranks crouched in the woods in a formation stretching from north to south, intersecting Orange Plank Road. Longstreet's corps constituted the first line. On the northernmost flank was Perry's brigade, still holding off Burnside's troops. Field's division carried the line to Orange Plank Road, and Kershaw's men continued it southward to the unused railway cut. Elements of Hill's corps were packed behind to increase the striking power. In front, spearheading the assault, was Jenkins' brigade, anxious to avenge its leader's death. [69]

This time, there were to be no elaborate flanking maneuvers. In-

---

68. Lyman to family, May 16, 1864, in *Meade's Headquarters*, ed. Agassiz, 97.
69. Mixson, *Reminiscences of a Private*, 70; Field, "Campaign of 1864 and 1865," in *SHSP*, XIV, 546.

stead, Lee planned to advance straight up Orange Plank Road at the enemy, recapturing the offensive through a ruthless frontal assault. Less than a year before at Gettysburg, he had tried to redeem a battle by charging the center of the enemy formation and overwhelming it by sheer force. So on this day in the Wilderness, Lee girded for a desperate, almost foolhardy assault against Hancock's Brock Road works. The impetus, he hoped, would finally achieve the breakthrough that had eluded him.

"Nothing was left us but an inglorious retreat."

The Army of Northern Virginia was accustomed to attacking strongly held positions. Hancock's defenses on Brock Road, however, posed a challenge of the highest order. The western edge of the roadway was stacked with log and dirt earthworks reaching chest high. A brush-free corridor had been slashed in front of this imposing barricade to ensure an unobstructed field of fire. Felled timber had been piled against the works, branches honed to sharp points facing the Confederates.

The battle order of Hancock's units can be reconstructed with a fair degree of precision. The wing north of Orange Plank Road consisted primarily of units lent to Hancock during the day's fighting. Anchoring the line's uppermost flank near the junction of Brock and Germanna Ford roads were Colonel J. Howard Kitching's two heavy-artillery regiments. These raw troops had joined Wadsworth during the early morning hours and had received a fearful mauling at the hands of Oates's Alabamians. Ranging south from Kitching were Eustis' 6th Corps brigade, two brigades from Robinson's 5th Corps division, then Owen's 2nd Corps brigade. Abutting Orange Plank Road itself and guarding the critical intersection were Grant's and Wheaton's 6th Corps brigades. Carroll's, Rice's, and Leasure's brigades stood in reserve to ensure the safety of the crossroads.

Hancock's 2nd Corps extended the Union formation below Orange Plank Road. Birney's division was arrayed in three lines of battle, then Mott's in two. Smyth's and Webb's brigades came next, each in single lines. Barlow's division, still under Gibbon's overall command, closed off the Union southern flank.

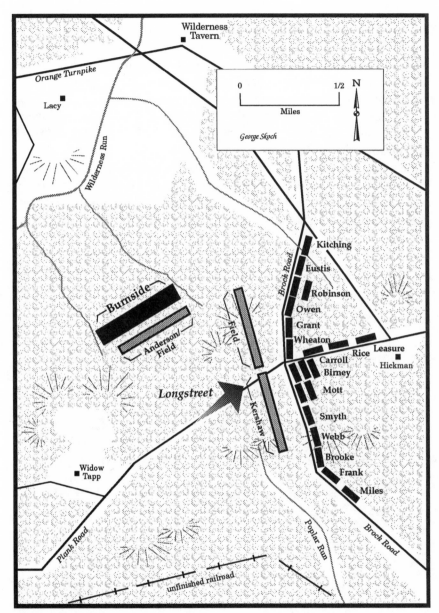

The Brock Road front on May 6 at 5 P.M.

Hancock's line was buttressed by judiciously placed artillery. The previous evening, Captain Edwin B. Dow's 6th Maine battery, temporarily attached to Mott's division, had occupied a clearing three hundred yards below Orange Plank Road. Captain Frederick M. Edgell's 1st New Hampshire battery had filled an open spot to Dow's left. Around midmorning on the sixth, a section of Dow's guns had advanced to the crossroads under the personal supervision of Birney. All told, twelve Federal pieces commanded the intersection of Brock and Orange Plank Roads.[70]

At 4:15 P.M., an advancing Confederate battle line pounded back Hancock's pickets. Gray-clad soldiers burst from the far woods, screaming their battle cry. Lee had launched the attack that he hoped would finally pierce the Federal formation. The rebels—"unquenchable fellows," as Lyman described the determined assailants—came on with unprecedented ferocity. One Federal veteran remembered the southerners arranged "in a line of battle on a charge, bugles sounding, seeming confident that they would carry everything before them." A Massachusetts soldier described the attack as the "most desperate assault of the day." A member of the Orange Blossoms Regiment recalled the "terrific crash of riflery all along the lines" and the "impetuous and persistent" advance of Longstreet's men. The newspaperman Page captured the spirit of the charge. This was the "most wicked assault thus far encountered—brief in duration, but terrific in power and superhuman momentum."[71]

Bent on success, the Confederates rushed into the cleared area in front of the Federal works. A concentrated barrage of Union firepower—"heavy fire that made the bark fly from the saplings"—rocked them back. Unwilling to retreat, the southerners dropped to their knees thirty yards from the earthworks and fired into the Federal defenders. Smoke and bullets and death filled the air. Hancock's troops, protected by their abatis and barricade, held the upper hand. "Our men were but little exposed," recalled a soldier in the Philadel-

70. Hancock's Report, in OR, Vol. XXXVI, Pt. 1, p. 354; Schaff, The Battle of the Wilderness, 290; Edwin Dow's Report, in OR, Vol. XXXVI, Pt. 1, p. 514; Frederick Edgell's Report, in OR, Vol. XXXVI, Pt. 1, p. 519.

71. Lyman to family, May 16, 1864, in Meade's Headquarters, ed. Agassiz, 97; John Day Smith, History of the Nineteenth Regiment of Maine, 138; Cudworth, History of the First Regiment Massachusetts, 462–63; Weygant, History of the One Hundred and Twenty-Fourth Regiment, N.Y.S.V., 296; Charles A. Page, Letters of a War Correspondent, 55.

phia brigade, "and [the Confederate] position gave [the Federals] an opportunity to repay the severe handling they had received in the early morning." Occasionally a Union soldier toppled over, shot through the head, hand, or shoulder. Otherwise, recalled the historian of the 124th New York, "the rapid fire of the foe had but slight effect on our line, behind its bullet proof cover; over the top of which we, with deliberate aim, hurled into their exposed but unwavering line an incessant and most deadly fire. Again and yet again did their shattered regiments in our front close on their colors, while fresh troops from the rear moved up and filled the gaps." [72]

Lee's afternoon attack, initiated with high hopes of cleaving the Union line, had stalled in front of Hancock's works. In part, Lee's failure stemmed from the strength of the Federal position. But also important was Lee's inability to bring his available troops to bear. Fragmentary Confederate reports suggest that the Wilderness checked Lee much as it had earlier thwarted the Federals. Kershaw, whose division constituted the southern wing of Lee's attacking force, was able to maneuver only Wofford's Georgia brigade into action. Field, whose division was located above Orange Plank Road, had only slightly better luck.

In Jenkins' brigade—then commanded by John Bratton—Coward's 5th South Carolina held the left. As Coward understood it, Colonel Robert E. Bowen's 2nd South Carolina was on his right and the 6th South Carolina was in reserve.

Just before the attack began, Bratton instructed Coward to keep in contact with Tige Anderson's Georgia brigade on his left and to "move when it moved." The Georgians, however, began their advance without notice. In order to keep up, Coward was forced to shift to the left. In the ensuing confusion, Colonel James R. Hagood's 1st South Carolina regiment ended up on Coward's right. Also moving forward and leftward to preserve contact with Coward, Hagood's men met a "heavy volley from the enemy." Moreover, the regiment assigned to Hagood's right flank seemingly disappeared. "In the density of the forest [I] concluded it had temporarily gotten lost and I gave no more thought to it," Hagood later explained. Edging ahead,

72. McDonell, "Recollections of the War," in FSMP; Banes, *History of the Philadelphia Brigade*, 233; Weygant, *History of the One Hundred and Twenty-Fourth Regiment, N.Y.S.V.*, 296.

Jenkins' men received the brunt of the enemy fire. Confederate regiments became entangled in a repeat of the confusion that had plagued Federal forces for the previous two days. On learning that Hagood, not Bowen, was on his right, Coward asked him to aim for the Federal cannoneers, then rushed back to his own regiment. "My legs were nearly given out, my voice entirely so," Coward later wrote, from the "shuttlecock business." [73]

For a half hour, the unequal contest continued. Just when Lee's offensive seemed doomed, fortuity gave the Confederates an opening. Brush below Orange Plank Road caught fire, and a rising afternoon breeze drove the conflagration toward the Federals. "Presently huge clouds of strong black pine smoke, such as almost eats one's eyes out, rolled over and completely enveloped our regiment," recalled a northerner. Crackling through dry undergrowth, the fire reached the log barricade and took hold "with wonderful rapidity." Heat and smoke thereby accomplished what the southerners had been unable to achieve. Some of Mott's division, joined by soldiers from Ward's brigade, abandoned their works and broke. According to Hancock's aide Walker, Ward himself jumped onto a caisson and departed for the rear. A gap yawned in the Federal defenses. [74]

Jenkins' old brigade seized its opportunity. With a fearsome yell, the South Carolinians dashed for the breach. One Federal thought they looked like "so many devils through the flames, charging over the burning works upon our retreating lines." Jenkins' friend Coward

73. Kershaw's Report, in *OR*, Vol. XXXVI, Pt. 1, p. 1062; Bond and Coward, eds., *The South Carolinians*, 136; James Hagood's Report, in *OR*, Vol. XXXVI, Pt. 1, p. 1068. According to a reporter traveling with Lee's army, the rebel formation "moved forward in the form of the letter V, with the sharp point toward the enemy. G. T. Anderson, known in the corps as 'Tiger Anderson,' formed the apex of the line" (Peter Wellington Alexander, "From General Lee's Army," *Daily South Carolinian*, May 8, 1864).

74. Cudworth, *History of the First Regiment Massachusetts*, 463; Francis A. Walker, *History of the Second Army Corps*, 432. When Ward's line collapsed, Hancock's aide Charles Morgan hurried rearward to help rally stragglers. He later reported that "on one of the caissons, when they were brought to a stop further to the rear, I saw, afterwards, General Ward riding through his troops but making no exertions to rally them." Only at Morgan's direction did Ward get off the caisson to collect his men. Ward later said that his horse had bolted and that he had hopped onto a caisson as the quickest way to reach his troops. Ward's service with the Army of the Potomac was terminated on May 12, 1864, when Birney discovered him drunk and had him arrested. See Charles Noble to David Birney, May 7, 1864, in FSMP; Charles Morgan's Report of May 26, 1864, in FSMP; and J. H. Hobart Ward's Report of May 11, 1864, in FSMP.

was in the vanguard. Leaping onto the blazing breastworks, he stabbed his regimental colors into the timber as a rallying point. One Yankee recalled little red Confederate flags all along the parapet. "It was a critical moment," recalled a Federal 2nd Corps aide, "rather from the generally strained and tired condition of our troops, than from the actual number of the Confederates who had thus gained entrance." Page chronicled the impact of Longstreet's men as they stormed the works. "The first few minutes we were staggered," he reported. "Stragglers for the first time in this fighting streamed to the rear in large numbers, choking the roads and causing a panic by their stampede and incoherent tales of frightful disaster."[75]

The breach lay squarely before massed Federal artillery, and never did Union guns perform more vigorous service. Dow's Napoleons opened with shell and case shot. Deadly projectiles exploded directly over the parapet swarming with Confederates. At this close range, the slaughter was fearful. Five times Dow's gunners knocked to the ground the Confederate flag by which they were guiding their fire. Waves of rebels materialized through a fiery curtain to replant the tattered cloth on the captured works.

As the opening widened in the Federal earthworks, Confederates began edging around Dow's right end. In desperation, Dow ordered his gunners to fire double-shotted canister. Pellets erupted point-blank into the charging Confederates. Edgell's artillery chimed in. Lieutenant William H. Rogers' section on Orange Plank Road crossed fire with Dow, adding more hissing bolts of iron to the din.[76]

While Union pieces held the Confederates in check, Federal infantry rushed to the endangered spot. From the south came Brooke's brigade, of Barlow's division. Forming a wedge perpendicular to Brock Road, Brooke's men charged toward the gap created by Mott's collapse. From just below Orange Plank Road came Leasure's three regiments, and dashing from above the road at a clip came Carroll's fine brigade. Carroll had been wounded in the arm earlier but had stubbornly refused to step down. Now he enjoined his men with a

75. Ward, *History of the One Hundred and Sixth Regiment Pennsylvania*, 242; Bond and Coward, eds., *The South Carolinians*, 136; Galwey, *The Valiant Hours*, 201; Francis A. Walker, *History of the Second Army Corps*, 432–33; Charles A. Page, *Letters of a War Correspondent*, 55. Confusion in one portion of the Federal ranks is well documented in *History and Roster of Maryland Volunteers*, by Wilmer et al., 267–69.

76. Dow's Report, in *OR*, Vol. XXXVI, Pt. 1, p. 514; Edgell's Report, *ibid.*, 519.

"fiery speech" and led them onto the "blackened and smoking works." There, according to a New York soldier, they "opened a most deadly fire into the very faces of the bleeding foe on the opposite side." [77]

In an unusual twist, Roy Stone's ill-fated Pennsylvania brigade finally got a chance to shine. Totally disorganized by Longstreet's morning offensive, members from various Pennsylvania regiments had managed to form a skeleton brigade. Attaching themselves to Owen, and then to Webb, the troops had ended up behind the intersection of Orange Plank and Brock roads. According to a series of postwar letters, these troops were ordered into the fray by Hancock.[78]

Dow's cannon fell silent as Federal infantrymen mounted the breach. "With a tremendous shout," recalled a participant, "over the works rushed the Union line with clubbed muskets, swords, and bayonets, right at the now totally demoralized Confederates, who broke for the rear, and fled in the wildest disorder across the slashing and down through the woods again." [79]

Disorganization in Confederate ranks helped doom the rebel attack. When Coward initially penetrated the Federal works, he had jubilantly informed his superior Bratton that he had captured the Brock Road defenses. An additional regiment, he thought, would enable him to seize the Union artillery or to "continue forward and drive the enemy out of the wood beyond." Just then Tige Anderson, whose Georgians were fighting on Coward's left, discovered Federals pouring into his undefended left flank. Anderson sent word that he was retreating. "There was nothing to do," recorded a frustrated Coward, "but to order my men back to where the advance had started." Hagood had to retire in turn. "My men and ammunition almost exhausted," he later related, "I deemed it inexpedient to attempt anything further. I abandoned this position only when the

77. John Brooke's Report, in OR, Vol. XXXVI, Pt. 1, p. 408; John Gibbon's Report, ibid., 430; Samuel Carroll's Report, ibid., 447; Galwey, The Valiant Hours, 201; Cowtan, Services of the Tenth New York, 255; Weygant, History of the One Hundred and Twenty-Fourth Regiment N.Y.S.V., 298; Gavin, Campaigning with the Roundheads, 391–96.

78. The involvement of Roy Stone's troops is described in Henry Elder to J. W. Hoffman, September 22, 1872, and John A. Black to J. W. Hoffman, October 23, 1872, both in Winfield Scott Hancock Collection, DU.

79. Weygant, History of the One Hundred and Twenty-Fourth Regiment, N.Y.S.V., 298.

troops on my left gave way (there was none on my right during any part of the advance) and the enemy threatened to cut me off."[80]

A soldier in the 1st Massachusetts afterward recalled that the parapet was littered with Confederates "writhing in the agonies of death." The fighting had been brief but intense. "I never saw such firing in my life," recounted a New Jersey man. "There wasn't a tree . . . but what was all cut to pieces with balls, and the dead and wounded was lying thick. It was an awful sight." One of Stevenson's men thought the musketry the "most terrible ever heard." A Maine soldier summarized the melee: "While in some places Longstreet's men planted their colors on our works, in about fifteen minutes those not killed went back howling."[81]

The response of the Federal leadership to the rebel onslaught had been predictably confused. On hearing the firing, Lyman had ridden to Meade and urged renewing Burnside's attack. Hurriedly returning to Orange Plank Road, Lyman was told that rebels had cut Hancock's line in half. "This turned out an exaggeration," he later observed. At the time, however, the Confederate charge had assumed serious proportions in the minds of Union leaders. "I cannot get to Hancock and am on the crossroad," Lyman wrote Meade. "I hear musketry as if Burnside were attacking, but not heavy." On the heels of Lyman's report came a missive from Birney. Rebels had broken through Mott's division at Orange Plank Road, reported Hancock's wing commander, and had separated Hancock's two southernmost divisions from the army. Grant and Meade were seated against a tree when this latest intelligence arrived. They quietly consulted, then studied each other in silence. Grant was the first to speak. "I don't believe it," he said.[82]

Neither general, however, was inclined to take risks, particularly

---

80. Bond and Coward, eds., *The South Carolinians*, 136; John G. Webb to family, May 7, 1864, in Leigh Collection, USMHI; Hagood's Report, in *OR*, Vol. XXXVI, Pt. 1, pp. 1068–69.

81. Cudworth, *History of the First Regiment Massachusetts*, 464; John Mitchell Diary, quoted by Longacre, in *To Gettysburg and Beyond*, 192; Frederick Petit to family, May 20, 1864, in Civil War Times Illustrated Collection, USMHI; John Day Smith, *History of the Nineteenth Regiment of Maine*, 138. Hancock credited Carroll with the repulse. See Winfield S. Hancock to J. W. Hoffman, September 7, 1872, in Hancock Collection, DU.

82. Lyman to family, May 16, 1864, in *Meade's Headquarters*, ed. Agassiz, 97; Theodore Lyman to George G. Meade, May 6, 1864, in *OR*, Vol. XXXVI, Pt. 2, p. 445; Charles A. Page, *Letters of a War Correspondent*, 55.

in the face of Lee's unremitting belligerence. At 5:30, a pointed order reached Warren at the Lacy house. "Send what men you can spare to General Hancock's assistance," it stated. "The enemy has broken through his line, and communication between the two parts is cut off. Get Sedgwick's two brigades to supply the place of yours." A companion message went to Lyman. "Tell General Stevenson, from General Meade, to report at once to General Hancock and if he cannot find him to report at once to General Birney with his troops." The ink on Meade's plea for reinforcements had scarcely dried when reassuring news arrived from Hancock. The enemy had been "finally and completely repulsed," Hancock reported, after an "exceedingly vigorous" attack. Hancock's ammunition, however, was exhausted, and the general was uncertain about his next move. In view of developments, he was reluctant to launch the attack scheduled for six o'clock. "I find some slight prospect of attacking farther up the Brock Road," he advised, "but I do not like to leave my position to make an advance with this uncertainty." [83]

Five minutes later, Hancock repeated his doubts to Meade. His ammunition was depleted and his wagons were too distant to resupply the front-line troops. Moreover, the rebels were unusually active on his right side, where his line was weakest. "Therefore," he concluded with regard to Meade's proposed offensive, "my opinion is adverse, but I await your order." Hancock's reluctance left Meade no choice but to cancel the offensive. "The Major General commanding directs that you do not attack today," stated a message that headquarters issued at 5:45. [84]

A set of orders, however, had apparently already gone out directing Burnside to renew his assault. It was too late to call off the 9th Corps. As the rattle of musketry died out before Hancock's slashings, Burnside once again threw his troops against the northern flank of Longstreet's battle line.

This time, Burnside had better hope for success. Earlier he had

---

83. Andrew A. Humphreys to Gouverneur K. Warren, May 6, 1864, in *OR*, Vol. XXXVI, Pt. 2, p. 454; Andrew A. Humphreys to Theodore Lyman, May 6, 1864, *ibid.*, 446; Winfield S. Hancock to George G. Meade, May 6, 1864, *ibid.*, 445–46.

84. Winfield S. Hancock to George G. Meade, May 6, 1864, in *OR*, Vol. XXXVI, Pt. 2, p. 446; Andrew A. Humphreys to Winfield S. Hancock, May 6, 1864, *ibid.*, 447.

left one of Willcox' brigades—Colonel Benjamin C. Christ's unit—to keep Ramseur's Confederates in check. Willcox, who was "extremely" fatigued and fretful, had remained with Christ's command. Between 2 and 3 A.M., the force had received orders to join Burnside. Rather than clawing through the woods as Potter had done earlier, Willcox brought his men back to the Lacy house, then followed a more direct path toward the left of Potter's line. "For half a mile it seemed to me we walked through the ranks of the dead and the dying," remarked Cutcheon, commanding the 20th Michigan. "The woods were full of them. It was a ghastly spectacle, and a poor preparation for valiant deeds." Christ's brigade formed on Potter's left, overlapping a portion of the rebel line. Christ rode along the formation, shouting, "Throw off your knapsacks and go in and give them hell."[85]

Burnside's two divisions charged in concert. Advancing on the double-quick, Christ's brigade ran down a hill and up another. The 50th Pennsylvania, which formed the center of Christ's formation, slammed directly into Confederates. "The rebels were surprised by this gallant charge and tried to fall back," related a New Hampshire man, "but we were too quick for them."[86]

Alarmed by swelling sounds of firing, William Perry ordered his 47th Alabama into action. He arrived in time to witness the 47th doubling back, enemy pouring around its flank. "I endeavored to steady and re-form it with its front so changed as to face them," Perry explained, "but they were too near at hand and their momentum was too great. Nothing was left us but an inglorious retreat, executed in the shortest possible time and without regard to order."[87]

With the collapse of the 47th, Perry's position became untenable. Oates, who was at the site of Burnside's attack, was in a particularly dangerous spot. His ammunition was nearly exhausted, and Federals seemed to be popping up everywhere. "To have remained longer would have subjected us to capture," Oates explained. "I therefore ordered a retreat, and we had a lively run for three or four hundred yards."[88]

85. Orlando B. Willcox's Report, in OR, Vol. XXXVI, Pt. 1, p. 941; Byron M. Cutcheon's Report, ibid., 966; Cutcheon, "Autobiography," in Cutcheon Papers, BL.

86. Cutcheon, "Autobiography," in Cutcheon Papers, BL; Jackman and Hadley, History of the Sixth New Hampshire, 222–24.

87. Perry, "Reminiscences of the Campaign," in SHSP, VII, 61.

88. Oates, The War Between the Union and the Confederacy, 350.

Fortunately for Perry, Confederate reinforcements came streaming into the fight. During the afternoon, elements from Richard Anderson's 3rd Corps division had formed north of Orange Plank Road in support of the main Confederate line. Slated to participate in the attack against the Brock Road defenses, Brigadier General Nathaniel H. Harris' Mississippi brigade had received orders to "move forward through the woods east of the Plank Road, and drive the enemy." As the Mississippians began working ahead, they discovered Burnside's soldiers in the process of renewing their attack against Perry. Harris comprehended the danger immediately. As he saw it, the Federals intended to cut off the Alabama and Florida units. Harris sent his brigade forward in an "impetuous and unexpected charge." Abner Perrin's Alabama brigade, from Anderson's division, and Stone's ever-present brigade, from Heth's division, apparently pitched in as well. The Federals, Harris later reported, were "driven in handsome style some distance, into a strongly entrenched position." The Confederate brigades of Stone, Harris, and the two Perrys joined to form a barrier facing northward in Burnside's direction. "Desperate and repeated efforts were made by the enemy to dislodge us," reported Harris, "but they were repulsed with heavy loss." The threat to Longstreet's flank had been averted once again.[89]

Thoroughly exhausted, Oates's troops collapsed in a field to rest. An Alabama man recalled that "as soon as we could take in the situation through which we had so suddenly passed, we laughed most heartedly, giving Colonel Perry full credit for his miscarried little coup-de-main." Perry rode slowly by. He had been shot and was bleeding freely. Worse still, his pride had been sorely injured. Years later, Perry still regarded with chagrin Burnside's rout of his command. "It was the first time since its organization and until it folded its colors forever at Appomattox, it was the last—that the brigade ever was broken on the battle field."[90]

89. Nathaniel Harris' Report, in William Mahone Collection, VSL; Nathaniel Harris to Charles J. Lewis, March 22, 1899, in Nathaniel Harris Papers, SHC; Eugene Ott, Jr., "The Civil War Diary of James J. Kirkpatrick, 16th Mississippi, C.S.A." (M.A. thesis, Texas A & M University, 1984); Austin C. Dobbins, ed., *Grandfather's Journal: Company B, Sixteenth Mississippi Infantry Volunteers, Harris' Brigade, Mahone's Division, Hill's Corps, A.N.V.* (Dayton, 1988), 191.

90. Coles, "History of the Fourth Alabama Regiment," in Regimental Collection, ADAH; Oates, *The War Between the Union and the Confederacy*, 350; Perry, "Reminiscences of the

Perry was not the only general in distress. Across the way, Bliss was bathing his head in a spring. He had not eaten for three days and, according to the 9th Corps' casualty returns, was "sunstruck." Wrapping a handkerchief around his head to stop the pain, Bliss looked up and saw a colonel from the 51st New York. "He had been shot in the head, knocking out his left eye, and taking away the bridge of his nose," Bliss later wrote. Another soldier staggered by with the end of his lower jaw shot away. "He motioned for a drink from my canteen," recalled Bliss. "I had two, one of which contained whiskey, and I held them both up and told him what was in them. He took the whiskey, but when he attempted to drink it, it ran into the wound, causing him to cry out with pain. He passed to the rear, and I saw him no more." Musketry on Burnside's front had been intense. "Although we could not see thirty yards in any direction when we commenced the fight on account of the thick foliage of the young pines," recalled Bliss, "by night they had all been cut down by rifle balls, and we could see as far almost as one could in ordinary timber. The bushes were mowed to the ground." One of Hartranft's Michigan soldiers recorded in his diary, "Harder fighting I never saw before and never wish to see again. Went about a mile to the rear and lay down for the night, nearly exhausted from exertion."[91]

By six o'clock, fighting on Burnside's and Hancock's fronts had subsided. The woods around Orange Plank Road lay silent. As if to punctuate the end of the day's carnage in this sector, a message from Grant arrived at 9th Corps headquarters. Hancock's attack had been canceled, explained the commander in chief. Burnside was directed to "hold your own and be governed entirely by circumstances." If the rebels attacked Hancock, Burnside was told, he should "give such aid as you can. After dark, and all is quiet, put your men in a good position for defense and for holding our line, and give your men all the rest they can get."[92]

Campaign," in *SHSP*, VII, 62. The Florida brigade, small to begin with, suffered "very heavily"; among its injured was General Perry. See Francis P. Fleming, ed., *Memoir of Captain C. Seton Fleming, of the Second Florida Infantry, C.S.A.* (Jacksonville, Fla., 1884), 94.

91. Bliss, "Reminiscences," in Bliss Collection, USMHI; Todd Diary, May 6, 1864, in Civil War Times Illustrated Collection, USMHI.

92. Ulysses S. Grant to Ambrose E. Burnside, May 6, 1864, in *OR*, Vol. XXXVI, Pt. 2, p. 462. Lyman explained in a letter home that when the rebels assaulted Hancock's works, he rode to Meade to ask that Burnside renew his attack. "This [Burnside] did, without further orders and with excellent effect" (Agassiz, ed., *Meade's Headquarters*, 97). Lyman noted in his

Elated at their spectacular rescue of the Confederate army, Long-street's battle-weary veterans nonetheless shared a common belief that their commander's fateful wounding had robbed them of victory. "I have always thought that had General Longstreet not been wounded," wrote Lee's aide Taylor, "he would have rolled back that wing of General Grant's army in such a manner as to have forced the Federals to re-cross the Rapidan." Alexander similarly concluded that "but for Longstreet's fall, the panic which was fairly under way in Hancock's corps would have been extended and have resulted in Grant's being forced to retreat across the Rapidan."[93]

In all likelihood, however, the opportunity presented by Sorrel's brilliant flank attack amounted to less than was later imagined. For a brief period, Hancock's forces were indeed routed and ripe for plucking. Within a half hour, however, they had rallied on the Brock Road works, and Lee's window of opportunity had slammed forever shut. Field, who assumed command upon Longstreet's disability, testified that during the fleeting opportunity, his forces were in no condition to attack. Had Longstreet eluded the fateful bullet, it is improbable that he could have corrected his confused ranks before Hancock fortified his Brock Road works.[94]

Most intriguing of the afternoon's puzzles is why Lee, after four hours' delay, still ventured to assault Hancock's firmly entrenched line. Alexander considered the charge a flagrant lapse of judgment. "The attack ought never, never to have been made," he bitterly wrote. "It was sending a boy on a man's errand. It was wasting good soldiers whom we could not spare. It was discouraging pluck and spirit by setting it an impossible task."[95]

In retrospect, the final spasm of Confederate aggressiveness on Orange Plank Road was a predictable consequence of Lee's military philosophy. From the Virginian's perspective, the entire two days of fighting served as a prelude to assaulting the Federal left wing. Long-street's drive, so brilliantly initiated in the morning and materially advanced by Sorrel's maneuver, could not be left unexploited. Risks

---

journal, "Of his own accord General Burnside immediately put in a division to relieve the pressure. 'The best thing old Burn did during the day,' as General Meade remarked." See Lyman Journal, May 6, 1864, in Lyman Papers, MHS.

93. Walter H. Taylor, *General Lee*, 236; Gallagher, ed., *Fighting For the Confederacy*, 360.

94. Field, "Campaign of 1864 and 1865," in *SHSP*, XIV, 545.

95. Gallagher, ed., *Fighting for the Confederacy*, 363.

had been too great and losses too severe to forgo the offensive. Unless Lee took a final shot at the Federal line, it was difficult to justify all that had come before.

Lee, his friend Heth once remarked, was the most "belligerent" man in the Confederate army. So long as a desperate charge held a glimmer of succeeding, Lee felt compelled to try. The alternative was to concede stalemate, which at this juncture was tantamount to accepting defeat. That he could not do.

VIII

MAY 6, EVENING
The Armies Reach Stalemate

*"The greatest opportunity ever
presented to Lee's army."*

JOHN GORDON WAS a born fighter. The lanky commander of Ewell's
Georgia brigade needed only a quick survey of the ground to intuit
his best move. He was thirty-two years old and one of the finest combat officers in either army.

An hour or so after midnight on May 5, after the firing had died
out, Gordon's Georgians shifted to Ewell's far-left flank, next to Pegram's brigade. Gordon dispatched scouts eastward to feel out the
Union line while his soldiers enjoyed a few hours' sleep. At early
dawn, the scouts reported back. The Federal line ended in a thick
patch of woods across from Pegram. Gordon's brigade was unop-
posed and stretched past the end of Sedgwick's formation. The Georgians, it seemed, were splendidly poised to enfilade the Federals with
little resistance.

Gordon also received encouraging intelligence from Confederate
patrols. Cowles's 1st North Carolina cavalry had been watching the
countryside below the Rapidan, from Germanna Ford westward.
From time to time, Cowles's riders came in with information. Gordon had been instructed to note the communications and to forward
them to Ewell.

As the sun burned off the early-morning mist, Gordon sensed the
opportunity of a lifetime. If his scouts were correct, his brigade was
positioned to slice across the Federal supply line and to roll up
Grant's northern flank. The news seemed too good to be true. To
ensure that there had been no mistake, Gordon ordered more gray-
clad scouts into the woods. Their job was to verify the initial reports,
then to work around the Federal rear and determine whether enemy
troops were waiting in reserve.

The results of the second foray were all that Gordon could have wished. "The former report was not only confirmed as to the exposed position of that flank," Gordon later explained, "but the astounding information was brought that there was not a supporting force within several miles of it." Only a handful of northern vedettes were in the woods. A determined assault would brush them aside with ease. Gordon later acknowledged that his mind was "throbbing with the tremendous possibilities to which such a situation invited us, provided the conditions were really as reported."[1]

By then, the sun had risen. The rest of Ewell's line was engaged in battering back Sedgwick's morning attacks. Around six, during a lull in the fighting, a few of Cowles's Confederate cavalrymen arrived. "I am going to scout with a cavalryman in the woods," Gordon informed his staff. "We will have to run for it, if discovered, and the fewer, the better in the crowd. You all wait here." Thomas Jones, one of Gordon's aides, watched as Gordon and the cavalryman slipped from the Confederate line, worked their way down to Flat Run, and then turned right into a thick patch of woods about a half mile past the enemy line. "I recall watching them with our glasses as long as they were in sight, expecting every minute to see them fired upon and run in," Thomas later wrote. Apprehensive about the general's safety, a squad of Confederate skirmishers slinked over to where Gordon had turned into the woods. Jones joined them, then crept behind the Federal line, working south parallel to Sedgwick's formation. Seeing no sign of Gordon, he returned to the waiting squad.[2]

About an hour later, Gordon and his escort appeared. He was ebullient. Earlier reports had been correct "in every particular." In addition, the terrain afforded the Confederates an ideal place to form for attack. A few hundred yards above the Union flank was a small field, concealed from the Federals by some woods. Gordon could use the clearing to organize his troops before sending them forward. Circling back, Gordon had insisted on examining the end of the Union line. "Dismounting and creeping slowly and cautiously through the dense woods," he later recounted, "we were soon in ear-shot of an unsuppressed and merry clatter of voices. A few feet nearer and through a narrow vista, I was shown the end of General Grant's tem-

---

1. Gordon, *Reminiscences*, 243–44; John B. Gordon's Report, in *OR*, Vol. XXXVI, Pt. 1, p. 1077.
2. Thomas Jones to John Daniel, December 29, 1904, in Daniel Collection, DU.

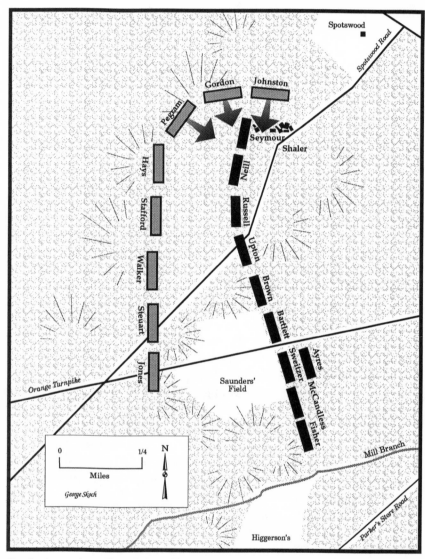

Gordon's attack on the evening of May 6

porary breastworks. As far as the eye could reach, the Union soldiers were seated on the margin of the rifle-pits, taking their breakfast. Small fires were burning over which they were boiling their coffee, while their guns leaned against the works in their immediate front."[3]

He was satisfied. "The revelation," he wrote, "amazed me and filled me with confident anticipation of unprecedented victory." As he saw it, his own men were to descend on the coffee-drinking Yankees while the rest of Ewell's corps launched a simultaneous attack against the Federal front. "As each of Sedgwick's brigades gave way in confusion," planned Gordon, "the corresponding Confederate brigade, whose front was thus cleared on the general line, was to swing into the column of attack on the flank, thus swelling at each step of our advance the numbers, power, and momentum of the Confederate forces as they swept down the line of works and extended another brigade's length to the unprotected Union rear." Grant's offensive capacity would be destroyed, and as Gordon envisioned the results, the Army of the Potomac's very existence would be jeopardized.[4]

Gordon explained what he had seen to Jones and dispatched the staffer to find Early, his immediate superior. Early, it developed, was on business near the turnpike, so Jones started in that direction. Ahead, in a small clearing, he saw Ewell. A field officer was emphatically ordering the general out of the open space, which had become a target for a Yankee sharpshooter hidden in a tree.

Jones explained Gordon's plan to the corps commander, adding that Gordon wanted to attack the enemy's left flank with his brigade and one or two others. During the conversation, Early rode up. He was unimpressed and spoke "rather sharply" to Jones. Federal troops, argued Early, must be hovering off the Confederate left, and Burnside's corps was probably in reserve. If Gordon attempted his proposed attack, the Confederate flankers would be flanked in turn by the Federal 9th Corps. "I remember General Early saying in the conversation that a repulse of three brigades would be very disastrous at this time," Jones later wrote. He dutifully relayed Early's objections to Gordon. The brigadier bridled at Early's summary dismissal of his proposal. He had personally reconnoitered and was certain that Early was wrong about Burnside's location. There were no Yan-

3. Gordon, *Reminiscences*, 244.
4. *Ibid.*, 244–47.

kees supporting the Union flank. Early's reaction was based on faulty assumptions.[5]

Gordon, certain of his own grasp of the situation, rode with Jones to the command center of the Confederate 2nd Corps. It was between eight and nine o'clock, and Ewell and Early were both there. Jones could not hear what the men were saying but took them "to be in very earnest conversation." Gordon later claimed that he urged the "prompt adoption and vigorous execution" of his plan. Early reflexively opposed the suggestion. "He was so firmly fixed in his belief that Burnside's corps was where he declared it to be," Gordon complained, "that he was not perceptibly affected by the repeated reports of scouts, nor by my own statement that I myself had ridden for miles in rear of Sedgwick's right, and that neither Burnside's corps nor any other troops were there." Ewell hesitated. The decision rested on his shoulders. He had no personal knowledge of the ground and was reluctant to oppose Early, his self-appointed military conscience and Gordon's superior. "In view of General Early's protest," Gordon claimed, Ewell "was unwilling to order the attack or to grant me permission to make it, even upon my proposing to assume all responsibility of disaster, should any occur." Ewell's aide Campbell Brown later confirmed that Ewell had initially favored Gordon's proposal "but begged out of it by Early's strong personal appeals until he could go to examine the ground himself." Gordon left the conference angry. "General Early evidently didn't believe a word of what I told him of what I had seen myself," he told Jones.[6]

Ewell's recollection of the meeting coincided essentially with Gordon's. The impetuous brigadier, wrote Ewell, had reported that the Federal left was exposed and had urged turning it, "but his views were opposed by General Early, who thought the attempt unsafe." Ewell felt that the difference of opinion between Early and Gordon required his personal examination of the terrain. "Pressing business," Ewell later claimed, prevented him from conducting a reconnaissance until late in the afternoon.[7]

Shortly after the meeting, Gordon received another message from

5. Jones to Daniel, December 29, 1904, in Daniel Collection, DU.

6. Ibid.; Brown, "Memorandum—Campaign of 1864," in Ewell-Stewart-Brown Collection, TSL; Gordon, Reminiscences, 255–56.

7. Richard S. Ewell's Report, in OR, Vol. XXXVI, Pt. 1, p. 1071.

Cowles. It seemed to support Early's objections. Enemy infantry were pressing Cowles's scouts near Mrs. Willis' house, north of Gordon's brigade and immediately west of the road from Germanna Ford. "A force should be sent in this direction at once," urged Cowles, "a regiment for skirmishing until more could be brought up if necessary." Moreover, thought Cowles, the Federals that he had discovered probably presaged a strong Union movement around the Confederate flank. "This move," wrote Cowles, "if continued, flanks you about two miles to your left." Gordon forwarded the missive to Early, but not without comment. "This must be a feint," he wrote across the bottom of Cowles's report. "This cavalry could keep us informed til the movement here could be made. I still think it best to make the move I spoke of, and it will check any move to our left. If made I should like the order at once. I could feel of them very soon, and then if necessary look after this flanking party."[8]

Early was unimpressed. Although he was considered a difficult and opinionated man, his staunch resistance to Gordon's plan stemmed from more than obstinacy. He had received intelligence that Burnside's large Union corps, as yet unengaged, was still in reserve behind Sedgwick. Moreover, as Early recorded in his memoirs, "our cavalry scouts [communicated] that a column of the enemy's infantry was moving between our left and the river, with the apparent purpose of turning our left flank." And according to Early, Ewell concurred with his assessment. "The impolity of an attack at this time was obvious," Early observed, "as we had no reserves, and, if it failed, and the enemy showed any enterprise, a serious disaster would befall, not only our corps, but General Lee's whole army."[9]

Gordon, it is now plain, was correct. Sedgwick had neglected to anchor his northern flank on a strong natural formation. Moreover, the bulk of Burnside's corps, which provided the only meaningful support for this glaring weak spot in the Union line, had moved away during the early morning hours. By ten o'clock, most of Burnside's

---

8. William H. H. Cowles to John B. Gordon, with endorsement from Gordon, May 6, 1864, in OR, Vol. XXXVI, Pt. 2, p. 962. John Daniel later questioned whether Cowles's message was addressed to John B. Gordon or to the Confederate cavalryman of the same initials, James B. Gordon, who happened to be Cowles's brigade commander. In a careful analysis, Jones concluded that the message had been sent to John Gordon. See Jones to Daniel, December 29, 1904, in Daniel Collection, DU.

9. Early, *War Memoirs*, 348.

combat troops lay stymied along Parker's Store Trail several miles south of Sedgwick's endangered flank. The 9th Corps' only other experienced division—Stevenson's—had been dispatched to Orange Plank Road to help Hancock. The only Federal reserve anywhere near Sedgwick during most of May 6 was Ferrero's division, assigned to guard the Germanna Ford crossing. Untried in combat, Ferrero's men posed no serious impediment to Gordon's proposal. Undoubtedly it had been Ferrero's exploration out country roads to the west of Germanna Ford that had caught Cowles's attention. The Confederate 2nd Corps leadership had mistakenly assumed that Ferrero's defensive dispositions were offensive in character.

As the day advanced, the situation increasingly favored Gordon's proposal. For weeks, Lee had been pleading with Richmond for his missing units, in particular for Brigadier General Robert D. Johnston's North Carolina brigade. Stationed near Taylorsville, twenty miles above Richmond, the brigade was finally released late on the morning of May 5. Its ranks were full, "its field officers all present, and the spirits of the veteran soldiers good," a brigade member later recalled. By forced marches, the Confederates pressed toward the Wilderness. "Army mules fell dead in their traces under the severe strain," recounted a soldier in the 23rd North Carolina, "but without stopping for bivouac, or hardly for rest, we held out and reached the Plank Road." When the road-weary southerners arrived—it was about 1 P.M. on the sixth—they were shunted into the woods above Gordon, extending the Confederate flank even farther past Sedgwick's Federals.[10]

With the arrival of Johnston's reinforcements, Gordon again appealed to his superiors for permission to attack. Again he returned disappointed, complaining to his aide Jones that "he could not get them to let him attack."[11]

While Ewell's northern flank was becoming stronger, Sedgwick's was becoming weaker. The 6th Corps was stretched thin. The fighting of May 5 had exacted a fearsome toll, the attacks of the following morning had depleted Sedgwick's numbers even more, and as the day

10. Robert D. Johnston's Report, in Daniel Collection, UV; Clark, *Histories of the Several Regiments and Battalions from North Carolina,* I, 288, 640, II, 241.
11. Jones to Daniel, December 29, 1904, in Daniel Collection, DU.

advanced, incessant Confederate sniper and artillery fire continued to reduce the 6th Corps' rolls. Seymour, whose brigade occupied the flank, termed his losses "very heavy," including the "choicest and best of officers." Attempts were made to strengthen the Federal works with logs, but Confederate sharpshooters rendered the task difficult. "Contact was so close and exposure so great," Seymour recounted, "as to forbid this work by day." The problem was compounded when Neill's brigade, posted to Seymour's left, shifted south to help fill growing gaps in the 6th Corps' line. Stretching to occupy a longer front, Seymour's brigade was thinned even further.[12]

Belatedly, Sedgwick did what he could to shore up his flank. Around 2 P.M., he moved Alexander Shaler's brigade of three New York regiments to the Federal right wing and placed the troops under Seymour's command. Initially Shaler occupied a line perpendicular to the Union front, facing north and closing the Federal flank. During the afternoon, however, as Neill's brigade edged southward, Shaler was forced to deploy one regiment as skirmishers and to detach another to assist Neill. An exploratory charge against Ewell's line further depleted Seymour's force and resulted, as the disgusted Shaler later reported, "in no earthly good." By this time, Seymour's formation had become so attenuated that Shaler's last regiment was called into the front ranks. No protecting force remained on the Federal flank. "The most extraordinary fact was seen that an army of 100,000 men had its right flank in the air with a single line of battle without entrenchments," Shaler later wrote of the situation. "I lost no time in informing Genl. Seymour that I would not be held responsible for any disaster that might befall the troops at this point, calling on him for at least 4,000 or 5,000 more men to properly defend that point." Seymour later confirmed that the situation was as Shaler described it. "The two brigades were now virtually in a single line," he stated in his report. Only two regiments—the 138th Pennsylvania and the 110th Ohio, which had been bled dry during Keifer's fight the previous evening—formed any kind of rear guard.[13]

12. George T. Stevens, *Three Years in the Sixth Corps*, 310–11; Truman Seymour's Report, in OR, Vol. XXXVI, Pt. 1, pp. 728–29.

13. Alexander Shaler Diary, May 6, 1864, in NYHS. Seymour's Report, in OR, Vol. XXXVI, Pt. 1, p. 729.

In the meantime, Ewell had reconsidered Gordon's plan and had decided to give it a try. Gordon, supported by Johnston's fresh brigade and Pegram's men, was to advance against Sedgwick's flank.

The reason for Ewell's change of heart has been the subject of considerable discussion. Ewell asserted that he postponed Gordon's attack until he had an opportunity to reconnoiter the area personally, then ordered the assault on his own authority. "After examination," he wrote in his report, "I ordered the attack, and placed Robert D. Johnston's brigade . . . to support Gordon."[14]

Ewell's aide Brown, writing after the war, supported Ewell's version and offered an explanation for his delay: "Now I know of my personal knowledge that General Ewell was in favor of this but begged out of it by Early's strong personal appeals until he could go to examine the ground himself, when he at once ordered an attack. But the delay thus occasioned was considerable, as General Early found General Ewell just summoned to General Lee and had to delay the investigation until his return."[15]

Early, however, claimed that the decision to attack had been his. "When the column threatening our left had been withdrawn," he asserted in his memoirs, "and it had been ascertained that Burnside had gone to Grant's left, on account of the heavy fighting on that flank, at my suggestion, General Ewell ordered the movement which Gordon had proposed."[16]

Gordon, in his official report, was silent concerning why his plan had been approved. "Late in the afternoon of May 6 I received orders from Major-General Early to form my brigade" was all that he mentioned of the subject. When he penned his memoirs forty years later, however, he had a dramatic story to tell.[17]

According to him, at around 5:30 P.M. he, Early, and Ewell were

14. Ewell's Report, in *OR*, Vol. XXXVI, Pt. 1, p. 1071.
15. Ewell Letterbook, in Ewell-Stewart-Brown Collection, TSL.
16. Early, *War Memoirs*, 348–49.
17. Gordon's Report, in *OR*, Vol. XXXVI, Pt. 1, p. 1077.

at the Confederate 2nd Corps headquarters. Lee rode up, frustrated by his failure to break through Hancock's defenses on Brock Road. "Cannot something be done on this flank to relieve the pressure upon our right?" the Confederate commander in chief inquired. Gordon glumly listened while his superiors discussed the possibilities. Finally he could restrain himself no longer. "I felt it my duty," he explained, "to acquaint General Lee with the facts as to Sedgwick's exposed flank, and with the plan of battle which had been submitted and urged in the early hours of the morning and during the day." Early reiterated his objection that because Burnside was behind Sedgwick's right, Gordon's proposal was too hazardous. "With as much earnestness as was consistent with the position of junior officer," recalled Gordon, "I recounted the facts to General Lee, and assured him that General Early was mistaken; that I had ridden several miles in Sedgwick's rear, and that neither Burnside's corps nor any other Union troops were concealed in the woods." Lee immediately grasped the potential of Gordon's plan. Having just come from Orange Plank Road, he knew that Burnside was located to the south. "His words were few," related Gordon, "but his silence and grim looks while the reasons for that long delay were being given, revealed his thoughts almost as plainly as words could have done." The attack would wreak havoc on the Union line, concluded Lee. The charge had to be made forthwith.[18]

Gordon's account of Lee's intervention was published after Lee, Ewell, and Early had died. As soon as Gordon's version appeared, Early's aide John Daniel denounced it as a fabrication. Several other aides agreed with Daniel's contention. Lee, they maintained, had not visited the turnpike until May 7. Daniel suggested that Gordon's aging memory had caused the general to conflate a meeting with Lee on the seventh with events of the sixth.[19]

18. Gordon, *Reminiscences,* 258.
19. Daniel prepared a manuscript aimed at refuting Gordon's claim that Lee had visited the turnpike front and had overruled Ewell and Early in favor of Gordon. The manuscript is in Daniel Collection, UV. "This is incorrect according to my personal knowledge and also according to Gordon's previous official testimony," wrote Daniel, the previous testimony referring to Gordon's battle report. Denying that Lee visited the Confederate left flank at any time on May 6, Daniel observed, "I would probably have seen him as I was on the pike with Early

Daniel declared that he had been present when the decision was made to assault Sedgwick's right. At about 5:30 P.M., he asserted, Gordon rode up to Early and asked for permission to attack. Daniel recalled that Gordon added, "If it fails it is my fault and if it succeeds it is your victory." Early replied, "Very well, General Gordon, go and do it." Lee, Daniel reiterated, was not present. If that is right, the Georgian's placement of Lee at his meeting with Ewell and Early must have been generated by the old warrior's failing memory, as Daniel charitably suggested, if not by darker causes, such as his professed dislike of Early.[20]

Evidence whether Lee visited Ewell's flank on the afternoon of May 6 may lie in a postwar exchange of letters between Gordon and Lee that has hitherto been overlooked by chroniclers of the campaign. On February 6, 1868, Gordon sent Lee copies of some battle reports. In his cover letter, the Georgian told Lee that he did "not remember having seen you [on] that flank" before May 7, and that he "was not aware of your desire to make a movement on that flank prior to that time. I am glad to know that such was your wish."[21]

Lee replied to Gordon on February 22, 1868. He expressed himself as "not certain whether I saw you before your attack on the 6th. I visited your flank, but you might have been then engaged in your reconnaissances. I may have confounded our conversation subsequent to your attack with my visit to General Ewell before it took place."[22]

A few days later after this exchange of letters—March 3, 1868, to be exact—Lee chatted with a close friend, William Allen, and the subject of Ewell's performance in the Wilderness arose. According to

near Ewell that afternoon almost continuously. So would Lieut. Thomas Jones, A.D.C. of Gordon's staff, and Major R. W. Hunter of Edward Johnson's staff and Col. J. P. Smith of Ewell's staff. So could J. R. Taff and John G. Williams of Ewell's staff. So would Col. T. H. Carter of the artillery. They all tell me they did not see General Lee. The story of the battle makes it plain that Lee was fully engaged on the right. Both Gordon's report and the orders given to Gordon by Early, in my presence, conclude the question." At least one witness took up the cudgel for Gordon. In 1920, Isaac G. Bradwell, of the 31st Georgia, wrote that just before sundown on the sixth, he saw Gordon explaining to Lee "what he had been begging to do all day." See Bradwell, "Second Day's Battle," 20.

20. John Daniel, Manuscript on May 6, 1864, in Daniel Collection, UV.

21. John B. Gordon to Robert E. Lee, February 6, 1868, provided by W. E. Cutshaw to John Daniel, in Daniel Collection, UV.

22. Robert E. Lee to John B. Gordon, February 22, 1868, in Gordon Family Papers, UG.

notes Allen made shortly after the conversation, Lee spoke of repeatedly urging Ewell to launch a "full attack in flank" supported with "all of Ewell's corps and others if necessary, and to rout the enemy." It was Lee's impression that Early had influenced Ewell to delay.[23]

Considering all the evidence, the most that can be said with certainty is that Lee and Ewell conferred some time on the afternoon of the sixth. Where their meeting took place is unclear. Campbell Brown implied that Ewell, "summoned," went to Lee; Lee in his letter to Gordon in 1868 asserted that he went to Ewell. Lee's statement to Allen that he had urged Ewell to make a flank attack rings true. During the afternoon, Lee was attempting to assemble a force to attack Hancock's line. Certainly he would have spoken with Ewell about the possibility of a simultaneous attack.

Whether Gordon was present at the meeting between Ewell and Lee also remains unclear. If Lee visited Ewell as he states in his letter, Gordon would have been nearby and capable of attending the meeting. The import of Lee's letter to Gordon is that he was unsure whether Gordon had been present. And Gordon's testimony is inconsistent. In 1868 he said that he had not discussed the flank attack with Lee, but in 1903 he not only insisted that he had discussed it but provided details of the conversation.

Three aspects of Gordon's final account are troubling. First, he alleges that Lee overruled Ewell and Early in Gordon's favor. Such behavior would have been inconsistent with Lee's style of command. Second, the timing of the meeting as described by Gordon is all wrong. At 5:30, when he places the conference, the Confederate attack against Hancock's works was in its final stages. Lee had assumed responsibility for the assault. It is improbable that he would have been absent during the attack. Finally, there is the question how Gordon could in 1903 recall details of a meeting that in 1868 he could not even remember took place.

What really happened? There is no version that satisfactorily reconciles all the evidence. The most probable scenario is that Lee talked with Ewell before the assault against Hancock, his purpose being to find out if Ewell could initiate an attack of his own. The subject of

23. William Allen's Notes of a Conversation with Lee on March 3, 1868, in Allen Papers, SHC.

Gordon's proposed flank attack was probably discussed, with Lee giving his approval. In all likelihood, Gordon was not present. In later years, the Georgian presumably embellished the story, inflating his own involvement and taking a slap at his professed antagonist, Early, by having Lee dramatically overrule Early's objections. Elsewhere in his *Reminiscences,* Gordon performed similar manipulations, building around a kernel of truth a dramatic story featuring himself as the hero.[24]

Confederate preparations for the attack were speedily completed. Just beyond the end of the Union line was an open field, cut by a deep ravine that formed a T across the Union formation. Gordon's brigade moved into the clearing. On Gordon's left, poised to slice behind the Federals, was Johnston's brigade. Facing squarely against the Federal front on Gordon's right were Pegram's men. The three Confederate brigades were to advance simultaneously, crushing the Union flank and initiating Sedgwick's collapse. Daniel was to coordinate Gordon's and Johnston's flank assault with Pegram's frontal attack.

One of Gordon's Confederates later described the brigade's preparations. "We were told to move to the left with our heads low and not to make the least noise," recalled the soldier. "When we reached the ravine we moved up into the field and formed the entire brigade, with the sharpshooters deployed a few feet in front. All orders were given in a whisper."[25]

Near the extreme end of the Union line, the 1st battalion of the 4th New York Heavy Artillery Regiment was finishing its day's work. During the afternoon, the New Yorkers had erected shallow fortifications for artillery. "Another squad of men was digging a trench in which to bury the dead," recorded the regiment's historian, "and still another detail were carrying the fallen ones and laying them in their last homes." Toward sunset, the New York battalion retired behind its works. A spring was located nearby, and two men at a time were

---

24. Porter Alexander later wrote that on returning to Orange Plank Road after the wounding of Longstreet he learned that the attack Longstreet had intended to make was going to be followed up. "I don't recall seeing General Lee about," wrote the artilleryman. "I think he must have been on a visit to Ewell" (Gallagher, ed., *Fighting for the Confederacy,* 362).

25. Gordon, *Reminiscences,* 249; Bradwell, "Second Day's Battle," 20.

permitted to fetch water. Federal soldiers on the front stacked their arms, and some veterans hung their belts on their rifle stocks. Cooking fires sprang up, and the woods filled with comforting scents of pork and coffee. Wounded Federals, however, continued filtering back from the skirmish line. Some of them voiced premonitions of an impending attack. "You fellows had better dig out of this; you'll get hell in a minute," a hollow-eyed soldier warned. A Union officer sensed the growing panic. "Steady boys; don't fire till you get the order," he called out.[26]

"The fact was that the lines in front had been stretched out very thin; the front line had either been gobbled or fallen back to the second, and that now was giving way," wrote a New York soldier. A 6th Corps surgeon summarized the situation: "For thirty-six hours the Sixth Corps, stripped of three brigades of its veteran troops [Getty's], weary from fighting and fasting, its right unprotected, had been patiently waiting the relief promised it long ago, and steadily holding its ground until the corps was almost destroyed."[27]

The first sign that things had gone irretrievably wrong was an "unearthly screeching and yelling," followed by a "swarm of gray-coats sweeping onto us from the right rear." Blue-clad figures bolted rearward "at an astonishing gait." As a doctor in the 4th New York remembered it, "Suddenly out of the dusk in front, and to the rear of us, burst the Ki-yi Ki-yi close to us, and with it the rebels were seen crossing the breastwork we had just put up. The men in front of us were so much surprised that they immediately ran, leaving the pork in the pan and the coffee on the fire and their arms. Some of our boys raised up to run, but under command lay down again until the front line men ran in among us, when we joined them on the stampede."[28]

Shaler's formation disintegrated under the unexpected attack. Plunging into the fractured Federal flank, Gordon's men began tearing through Seymour's brigade. Portions of Seymour's command shifted rearward. They held briefly, but the Confederate onslaught seemed irresistible. The 110th Ohio, on Shaler's left, watched as troops to their right retreated in "wild confusion," then joined the

---

26. Hyland C. Kirk, *Heavy Guns and Light: A History of the 4th New York Heavy Artillery* (New York, 1890), 158–59.
27. George T. Stevens, *Three Years in the Sixth Corps,* 310–11.
28. Kirk, *Heavy Guns and Light,* 159–60.

stampede themselves. The commander of the 122nd Ohio had a terrifying tale to tell. "So quick were the movements of the enemy that when I first discovered them in our rear, they were in rear of the center of my regiment, scattering the second line with all speed." The rebel breakthrough, he later judged, was the result of "gross negligence." As Seymour reported the debacle, his line "rolled up with great rapidity." A Federal engineer wrote home, "We had a run for it." He went on, "Staff officers yelling and calling on the men to rally and support the artillery and the men throwing away their guns and running like mad men and them Rebs a yelling as they came up on the charge with that peculiar yell they have. It sounds like a lot of school boys just let loose. I thought Hell had broke loose." [29]

From the perspective of Gordon's troops, the attack was proceeding like clockwork. A soldier from the 61st Georgia recalled how he and his compatriots "marched around on a circuit-flank movement," coming upon the Federals "all resting, cooking and eating; with their guns stacked, their blankets spread down and some of their little tents stretched. . . . We fired one volley at them, raised a yell, and charged them. They fled at once, leaving their guns, blankets, knapsacks, haversacks, tents, canteens, some hats and, in fact, everything they had." The rout seemed to the pleased Confederate "like scaring up a bunch of partridges or crows, for the Yankees left us almost as partridges could. It was like shooting birds on the wing." [30]

Shortly, however, the southerners encountered stiffer opposition. Positioned below Seymour, Neill's brigade fought back with determination. Although attacked in front by Pegram's rebels, Neill's troops managed to form a double line, rear units facing toward Gordon's flankers. Neill was also bedeviled by the panicked refuse of Shaler's and Seymour's brigades. "This, with a heavy attack of the enemy on our front," recounted the unit's official report of the affair, "came near sweeping away the brigade." Wave after wave of gray figures emerged from the evening's darkness. "Shoot them, bayonet them, stop them any way you can," a Union officer screamed above

29. Seymour's Report, in *OR*, Vol. XXXVI, Pt. 1, p. 729; J. Warren Keifer's Report, *ibid.*, 732; John Horn's Report, *ibid.*, 736–37; Otho Binkley's Report, *ibid.*, 742; William Ball's Report, *ibid.*, 745–46; Aaron Ebright's Report, *ibid.*, 748; Matthew McClennan's Report, *ibid.*, 751–52; Samuel Bradbury to family, May 19, 1864, in Samuel Bradbury Collection, DU.

30. Nichols, *A Soldier's Story of His Regiment,* 148–49.

the din. Bullets whined, and Federal soldiers fired back at muzzle blasts that sparkled like the light of a thousand fireflies.[31]

When Gordon's attack hit, Shaler and Seymour were at Sedgwick's headquarters on Spotswood Road. "Well, general, we have repulsed two attacks today," Seymour was warning, "but my men are pretty shaky, and I should be very fearful in case of another attack." The sound of gunfire indicated that the general's worst fear had been realized. The three men rushed toward the endangered front to try to rally the panicked troops.[32]

Sedgwick arrived just as Seymour's last line of breastworks gave way. Rebels pounded through the breach, led by an officer mounted on a black horse. The rider leveled his pistol at Sedgwick and shouted, "Surrender, you Yankee S.O.B." Before the apparition could fire, a New Yorker shot him down. Sedgwick, along with the remains of the New York regiment, bolted for a nearby wagon track on which Neill's men had formed. Ewell's cannoneers, however, had the road clearly in range, and the Federals lacked supporting artillery. Shells whistled into the Union ranks. One shot, recalled a northerner, "cleaned the road for twenty rods, scattering the men in a mangled mass to the right and left." Sedgwick struggled to organize the fugitives. "Halt! For God's sake, boys, rally!" he cried, hatless and swinging a sword. "Don't disgrace yourselves and your general in this way!" Spying a color-bearer, Sedgwick boomed out, "Come here, my boy!" The man gingerly advanced as ordered, inspiring several brave souls to join him. Another rebel volley tore from the woods, bringing down the color-bearer and injuring Sedgwick's horse. "Damned devils," the general muttered and rode off "at a terrible pace" looking for reinforcements.[33]

Shaler madly tried to re-form his brigade along the wagon track. "For God's sake, men, make a stand on this road, if you think anything of the Army of the Potomac, make a stand on this road!" he

31. Daniel Bidwell's Report, in OR, Vol. XXXVI, Pt. 1, p. 719; Alanson A. Haines, History of the Fifteenth Regiment New Jersey, 148–50.

32. Charles Whittier, "Reminiscences," in Boston Public Library.

33. Kirk, Heavy Guns and Light, 162–64.

was heard to exclaim. Quickly he was surrounded by a dozen or more Confederates, "each having his gun pointed in the direction of my innocent carcass," he later confided to his diary. "To my extreme disgust and mortification," he wrote, "I found myself a prisoner of war and captured by a dozen or more straggling vagabonds." A "nasty nosed ruffian" jerked away Shaler's sword and handed it to a Confederate officer. Stripped of his "splendid stallion," Shaler was led to the rear and turned over to one of Gordon's subordinates, who treated him kindly after relieving him of his gold belt.[34]

Seymour met a like fate. Riding toward the enemy to ascertain their position, he too fell into rebel hands. He and Shaler were later reunited at Robertson's Tavern, behind Ewell's line. They were "kindly treated," Shaler admitted, "and furnished with a comfortable bed and breakfast." A Confederate later recalled that Seymour's tall, thin frame made "quite a contrast" to the short, rotund Shaler as the two captured generals were marched away.[35]

When the Confederate attack began, several 6th Corps officers rushed to Meade's command center, near the Lacy house. Meade was away at Grant's headquarters, but Humphreys took their breathless message. Sedgwick's line, they reported, had rolled up, enemy troops now occupied the position, and "part of them were advancing down the Germanna Plank Road on our right and rear, following the fugitives from Shaler's and Seymour's brigades." Rumor had it that both Sedgwick and his division commander Wright had been captured. Humphreys snapped out orders to meet the crisis. Members of the provost guard, along with reinforcements that Warren had earlier provided and some nearby reserve artillerists, were directed toward the breach. Humphreys then notified Meade, who returned at once with Grant.[36]

More bad news arrived from the front. Two aides on Sedgwick's staff darted up, as Lyman recalled it, in a "great flurry." The 6th

34. Shaler Diary, May 6, 1864, in NYHS.
35. Seymour's Report, in OR, Vol. XXXVI, Pt. 1, p. 729; Nichols, A Soldier's Story of His Regiment, 149. According to the Richmond Examiner of May 18, 1864, Seymour and Shaler were marched to Orange Court House. Seymour had the good sense to keep his mouth shut. Shaler, however, attracted a crowd by standing stiffly erect, thrusting a thumb into his belt, and glowering up and down the street. He used a whistle-stop at Charlottesville to deliver a vituperative speech and was ultimately deposited in Libby Prison.
36. Andrew A. Humphreys, The Virginia Campaign, 50–51n2.

Corps had been broken and driven back. Enemy troops were advancing on Germanna Plank Road. Headquarters was in danger. Coolly Meade inquired of the excited aides, "And where are Upton's and Shaler's brigades, that Sedgwick said he could spare me this morning?" When they answered, "I don't know," Meade at his sarcastic best asked, "Do you mean to tell me that the 6th Corps is not to do any more fighting this campaign?" The reply was, "I am fearful not." As Lyman recalled it, Grant seemed a little worried, but Meade kept his composure. "Nonsense!" he said, "If they have broken our lines, they can do no more tonight!"[37]

Couriers continued to stream in with tales of disaster. Grant carefully attempted to sift fact from rumor. Send reinforcements to the endangered points, he directed. Getting down to business, the commander in chief strolled over to his own camp, pulled up a stool in front of his tent, and lit a fresh cigar. In the panic gripping headquarters in the darkening woods, Grant remained a reassuring point of calm.

Soldiers poured back from the shattered front into the fields around Wilderness Tavern. "Everything was panic stricken, and a general stampede ensued," observed an Alabama soldier being held in a prison compound near Grant's command center. "Ambulances, head quarters, commissary and quarter master's wagons, in the confusion and hurry to get to the rear, made numerous collisions and were upset and broken down." The captives, believing they were about to be liberated, "rent the air with repeated wild rebel yells."[38]

At the height of the excitement, an officer rushed to Grant and urgently volunteered advice. "General Grant, this is a crisis that cannot be looked upon too seriously," he warned. "I know Lee's methods well by past experience; he will throw his own army between us and the Rapidan, and cut us off completely from our communications." Grant stood, pulled the cigar from his mouth, and spoke his mind. "Oh, I am heartily tired of hearing about what Lee is going to do," he roared back with unaccustomed heat at the startled officer. "Some of you seem to think he is suddenly going to turn a double

37. Theodore Lyman to family, May 17, 1864, in *Meade's Headquarters*, ed. Agassiz, 98; Lyman Journal, May 6, 1864, in Lyman Papers, MHS; Theodore Lyman to John Ropes, in *Recollections*, by Howard, 283*n*19; Charles A. Page, *Letters of a War Correspondent*, 57.

38. Stamp, "Ten Months," in Stamp Papers, AU.

somersault, and land in our rear and on both of our flanks at the same time. Go back to your command, and try to think what we are going to do ourselves, instead of what Lee is going to do." [39]

As Grant supposed, the danger had been exaggerated. The crisis soon passed. Neill's formation bent back, but somehow it held. One of Neill's officers later credited the successful resistance to "the unflinching bravery of the officers and men." [40]

The rebel attack had run out of steam. Coordinating three assaulting brigades proved impossible in the deep woods. According to Early, masses of Gordon's soldiers retired in confusion. Colonel C. A. Evans, of the 31st Georgia, informed Early that his regiment had struck impenetrable enemy breastworks. "I immediately ordered Pegram's brigade forward and directed Colonel Evans to guide it," Early recorded in his memoirs. Pegram's soldiers groped in neardarkness through dense thickets. Through a "misconception of orders," three of Pegram's regiments moved to the right and two to the left, dividing the command. Colonel John S. Hoffman, who had assumed brigade leadership after Pegram's injury the previous evening, had two horses shot from under him and lost contact with his troops. There was "much confusion produced by the difficulties of advance," recorded Early. A soldier confirmed the disarray. "Conflicting orders," he wrote, were issued in such profusion that "on reaching the immediate front of the Federal works the men were in scattered groups." No company remained "under effective control of its captain." One regiment—the 13th Virginia—overran the Union line, but nightfall curtailed progress. [41]

Johnston's Confederate brigade also lost its bearings. The tired North Carolinians had formed behind Gordon with little idea of what was expected of them. As Johnston later remarked, "I was entirely uninformed as to the position of the enemy and plans for the attack and I knew nothing of the character of the ground." Flailing through the woods, he found that "it was impossible to see anything in front of the line fifty feet and I had to be guided by the noise and firing, which commenced in a few moments and soon became very

39. Horace Porter, *Campaigning with Grant*, 68–70.
40. Bidwell's Report, in *OR*, Vol. XXXVI, Pt. 1, p. 719.
41. Early, *War Memoirs*, 349; "The Late Operations of Lee's Army," in Richmond *Sentinel*, May 24, 1864; Isaac G. Bradwell, "One Hour Saved the Union," *Confederate Veteran*, XXXIV (1926), 252–53.

warm." In the general confusion, Johnston's brigade slipped eastward. Some of his troops contributed to the panic in Seymour's brigade, while others continued to Germanna Plank Road. It was doubtless these stray bands of Johnston's Confederates who inspired the rumor that rebels had severed the road and were descending on Meade's command center. Johnston was soon persuaded that he had strayed dangerously far from the main body of Confederates. Hearing officers shouting commands in the woods, he called out, "What command is this?" The reply came back, "The 137th Pennsylvania regiment." Realizing that Yankees were re-forming in force nearby, Johnston ordered his men back to their starting point.[42]

In the gathering darkness, Early's aide Daniel, whose assignment was to coordinate the rebel units, lost touch with Gordon. Discovering that the attack was stalling, Daniel tried to lead one of Pegram's regiments to Gordon's assistance. A bullet smashed through his leg and disabled him. All semblance of coordination evaporated. Ewell decided against involving the rest of his line. Hays's brigade, positioned to Pegram's right, stayed in its trenches. "We stood under arms, expecting orders to carry on the movement," recounted one of Maryland Steuart's men, "but it was deemed too hazardous."[43]

Meanwhile, Federal reinforcements stiffened Sedgwick's northern flank. Morris' brigade, which was stationed in reserve below Seymour, shifted toward the fighting. Two of Morris' regiments—the 10th Vermont and the 106th New York—faced north and formed a line to help Seymour's stragglers rally. According to the 10th Vermont's historian, Morris' men gave three rousing cheers, "as only soldiers can give them." Gambling that the Confederates would remain dormant around Saunders' Field, Sedgwick drew also on Upton for aid. At about 7 P.M., Upton dispatched the 121st New York and 95th Pennsylvania northward at a double-quick. Marching the length of Sedgwick's line, the column came under a galling Confederate barrage. Tangled vegetation threw the Federal reinforcements into further confusion. But by the time they reached the rifle pits near Sedgwick's headquarters, the danger had passed. Neill's brigade, but-

---

42. Johnston's Report, in Daniel Collection, UV.
43. Daniel, Manuscript on May 6, 1864, in Daniel Collection, UV. Walker's brigade, which was positioned next to Hays's, also never left its earthworks during Gordon's attack. See Thomas S. Doyle, "Memoir," in Hotchkiss Collection, LC.

tressed by Morris' and some of Seymour's units, had saved the day. Crawford's Pennsylvania Reserves were roused from dinner near the Lacy farm when the ruckus started. Roebling, who guided the division onto Germanna Plank Road, found the way "filled with an excited crowd of soldiers apparently scared to death; they amounted in number to almost a division, and not a single one could tell me why he was running." On learning that Sedgwick's flanks were secure, Roebling led the Pennsylvanians back to their dinners.[44]

Gordon's foray had bagged several hundred Federal infantrymen and two brigadier generals. The Federal leadership had been panicked. But his attack had failed in its larger purpose. Sedgwick had swung back his flank and anchored it tightly against Germanna Plank Road. The Yankees had wavered, but they had preserved their line's integrity. Neill's brigade, which once again had proved its steadiness, now held Sedgwick's reinforced flank.

Gordon, miffed over his repulse, personally appealed to some of Pegram's troops to try again. "He came to us with hat off and the tears streaming down his face and begged us to go with him and capture the Yankee breastworks," a Virginian recorded in his diary. Several of Pegram's men agreed and followed Gordon into the night. There ensued an eerie march "through a perfect jungle standing in water which we had to wade through in pitch darkness over entirely strange ground."[45]

Regrouped Federals were waiting behind their new line, anxiously anticipating another Confederate assault. A soldier in the 4th New York remembered the "tired and hungry body of troops who, with bayonets fixed, lay as quiet as death awaiting the onslaught of the enemy." Years later, a Union surgeon still vividly recalled that night. "The stars shone through the openings among the trees upon a long line of dusky forms lying close behind the sheltering breastworks," he wrote, "as silent as death but ready at an instant to pour out a storm of destruction." Around ten, Gordon's makeshift force approached the Union works, hoping to gain the advantage of surprise. Snapping twigs, however, gave them away. Immediately "every

44. Haynes, A History of the Tenth Regiment Vermont, 66–67; William H. Morris' Report, in OR, Vol. XXXVI, Pt. 1, p. 723; Emory Upton's Report, ibid., 666; Washington A. Roebling's Report, in Warren Collection, NYSA.

45. George Q. Peyton, A Civil War Record for 1864–1865, ed. Robert A. Hodge (Fredericksburg, Va., 1981), 22; Hale and Phillips, History of the Forty-Ninth Virginia, 109.

man was aroused and alert" on the Union line. A Federal officer cried, "Fire," and the parapets erupted in flame. As a Confederate recalled the incident, "We thought we saw men lying on the ground in our front, and supposing them to be our skirmishers, we marched up to them when they raised up and put their guns almost against our heads and fired." Another rebel remembered, "We got within fifteen feet of the Yankees before we saw them. They poured a shower of balls at us." Heavily outgunned, Gordon was forced to abandon his unofficial foray. "Scarcely a man of the Union force was injured by this charge," claimed a Federal, "but the dead and wounded from the rebel ranks literally covered the ground."[46]

Although Grant tried to communicate his accustomed aplomb, his aides recognized signs of strain. The commander strolled restlessly up and down, stopping occasionally to sit on a stump or on the ground or to lean against a tree. He whittled incessantly, snatching up small twigs and sharpening them like lead pencils. As he finished a stick, he sliced a band around it, snapped it in two, discarded the pieces, then selected another twig and resumed the operation. His thread gloves—a gift from Mrs. Grant, surmised the staff, that the general had donned either from a sense of obligation to his wife or out of a mistaken notion that such gear was requisite in the East—were in shambles. By nightfall his fingernails protruded through holes worn in the cloth fingers.

Around eight o'clock, as Gordon's attack was trailing off, Hancock visited Grant's headquarters. The Federal Second Corps commander was fatigued but in a cheery mood. Grant reached into his pocket, intending to offer Hancock a cigar. Only one remained. During the day, Grant had smoked twenty cigars, "all very strong and formidable in size," recollected Porter. "But it must be remembered that it was a particularly long day. He never afterward equaled that record in the use of tobacco."[47]

The near-collapse of Sedgwick's corps was the last straw. Accord-

46. Kirk, *Heavy Guns and Light,* 166–67; Hale and Phillips, *History of the Forty-Ninth Virginia,* 109; Peyton, *A Civil War Record,* 22.
47. Horace Porter, *Campaigning with Grant,* 70.

ing to chief of staff Rawlins, Grant met the crisis "outwardly with calmness and self-possession." When the danger had passed, however, Grant dropped his guard. "He withdrew to his tent," Rawlins later told the cavalryman Wilson, "and, throwing himself face downward on his cot, instead of going to sleep, gave vent to his feelings in a way which left no room to doubt that he was deeply moved." His staff was disturbed by the display. "They had been with him in every battle from the beginning of his career," wrote Wilson, "and had never before seen him show the slightest apprehension or sense of danger; but on that memorable night in the Wilderness it was much more than personal danger which confronted him. No one knew better than he that he was face to face with destiny, and there was no doubt that he realized it fully and understood perfectly that retreat from that field meant a great calamity to his country as well as to himself." [48]

A few minutes after Grant entered his tent, Gordon launched his second attack. Porter looked in and saw the general sleeping "as peacefully as an infant." He awakened Grant and informed him of the assault, along with more dire predictions of a Confederate breakthrough. Aware that his flank had been soundly reinforced, Grant concluded that the report was a "gross exaggeration." He turned over in his bed and went back to sleep. [49]

After the headquarters staff had retired, the journalist Cadwallader pulled up a seat by the fire in front of Grant's tent. Despite the late hour, Cadwallader was wide-awake. "Unpleasant thoughts," he recalled, "ran riot through my mind." As he saw it, the Army of the Potomac had waged two days of murderous battle with little to show for its efforts. Lee had compelled Grant to fight on a field of the rebel's choosing, and the Federals had suffered fearful losses. "We had scarcely achieved a rod of the battlefield at the close of a two days' contest," mused Cadwallader, "and now had come the crowning stroke of rebel audacity in furiously storming the center of our line, and achieving temporary success." Cadwallader had accompanied Grant on most of his earlier campaigns. He had suffered through the Tallahatchie expedition, he had shared Grant's elation at Vicksburg's fall, and he had witnessed the unexpectedly

48. Wilson, *A Life of John A. Rawlins*, 215–17.
49. Horace Porter, *Campaigning with Grant*, 71.

easy Federal victory at Chattanooga. Could it be, wondered Cadwallader, that he had followed Grant "to the dark and tangled thickets of the Wilderness, to record his defeat and overthrow, as had been recorded of every commander of the Army of the Potomac?" Glancing across the embers, Cadwallader saw a figure slumped in an army chair. It was Grant. The general's hat drooped over his face, and the high collar of an old blue army overcoat covered his ears. There he sat, legs crossed, eyes on the smoldering ashes. At first Cadwallader thought that the general was dozing. Then he noticed him nervously shift his legs. He was not asleep. Rather, he was deep in thought. Grant noticed the correspondent, straightened, and began chatting about indifferent subjects unrelated to the war. After a half hour of idle conversation, Cadwallader remarked that if they were to get any sleep, they should retire to their tents. Grant smiled. Lee had been giving them "sharp work," he commented, and entered his tent.[50]

After the war, debate raged over how close Gordon had come to succeeding and whether his plan might have changed the battle if it had been implemented earlier. Early, in his memoirs, belittled Gordon's accomplishments. "It was fortunate," he wrote, "that darkness came to close this affair, as the enemy, if he had been able to discover the disorder on our side, might have brought up fresh troops and availed himself of our condition. As it was, doubtless, the lateness of the hour caused him to be surprised, and the approaching darkness increased the confusion in his ranks, as he could not see the strength of the attacking force, and probably imagined it to be much more formidable than it really was."[51]

Johnston blamed poor preparation for the Confederates' failure to achieve all that Gordon expected. "If proper information had been given me," he later wrote, "I would have accomplished a great deal more and believe that the results of the action would have been far greater and more disastrous to the enemy." An officer in Pegram's brigade agreed. "The extent of the success of Gordon's movement,

---

50. Cadwallader, *Three Years with Grant,* 180–82.
51. Early, *War Memoirs,* 350.

brilliant as it was, was checked and restricted in its results by the failure of combined and concentrated cooperation on the part of Pegram's or Early's old brigade. And that failure resulted from the separation of the brigade under conflicting orders."[52]

Gordon was convinced that he would have inflicted severe harm had darkness not intervened. His chief complaint was that Early and Ewell had restrained him until it became "too late to reap more than a pittance of the harvest which had so long been inviting the Confederate sickle." Two months after the battle, Gordon asserted that "an hour more of daylight now would have insured the capture of a considerable portion of the Sixth Army Corps." He was openly contemptuous of Early and Ewell. "I must be permitted in this connection to express the opinion that had the movement been made at an early hour and properly supported," he wrote, "each brigade being brought into action as its front was cleared, it would have resulted in a decided disaster to the whole right wing of General Grant's army, if not in its entire disorganization." The disappointed brigadier was still fuming nearly forty years later when he set down his recollections. While his superiors dawdled through the daylight hours of May 6, claimed Gordon, "the greatest opportunity ever presented to Lee's army was permitted to pass."[53]

The relative merits of the conflicting claims are difficult to judge. Both Early and Gordon had strong motives to justify their actions after the fact, and the friction that developed between the two strong-willed men during the following months sparked a lifetime feud that throws into question anything that either later said about the other. One of Warren's aides, however, felt that if Gordon's attack had been coordinated with Longstreet's assault on the lower Federal flank, "nothing . . . could have saved the Army of the Potomac." Lee's adjutant shared that sentiment. "It must ever be a source of regret," he wrote, "that the opportunity to inflict a serious blow upon this flank of General Grant's army was not sooner availed of." Although Lee never officially criticized Ewell's actions, he expressed disappointment after the war at the "missed opportunity." Lee was reported as saying, "When Gordon did go, it was too late in the day, and he

52. Johnston's Report, in Daniel Collection, UV; Baumgardner, "The Fifty-Second Virginia," in Book 134, FSMP.

53. Gordon's Report, in OR, Vol. XXXVI, Pt. 1, p. 1078; Gordon, Reminiscences, 261.

was not supported with sufficient force to accomplish anything decisive."[54]

Grant's battle report praised Sedgwick's valor and said nothing of the general's neglect in permitting Gordon's surprise. Some critics were less charitable. "This stampede was the most disgraceful thing that happened to the celebrated 6th corps during my experience of it," complained Lyman. "The handling of [Wright's and Ricketts'] divisions on the 5th and 6th of May was slow and feeble." Humphreys scored Sedgwick for failing to post his flank and for missing a marvelous opportunity of his own. According to Humphreys, Sedgwick's division commander Wright had discovered early on the sixth that Ewell's flank was unprotected. Sedgwick had inclined toward attacking, but Meade had directed him to hold his reserves ready to reinforce Hancock. Accordingly, Sedgwick took no offensive action of his own. "Had general Sedgwick suggested this flank attack for those brigades or the support of his own flank by them, it would have been acceded to," Humphreys later suggested. "There must have been some neglect in the videttes or skirmish line in keeping a look-out on that ground," he added, "otherwise timely notice would have been given of the presence of Gordon."[55]

Seymour came in for especially harsh criticism. A diarist from the 10th Vermont recorded that the general "seemed to be dazed" during the afternoon of the sixth. Writing Halleck on May 7, Grant blamed Seymour's troops for the collapse of Sedgwick's flank. "Milroy's old brigade was attacked and gave way in the greatest confusion," he explained, "almost without resistance, carrying good troops with them." A Pennsylvanian who took part in Seymour's fiasco of the sixth put it more bluntly: "Those who participated in that desperate charge in the morning and were carried away in the confusion of the evening's retreat, well know that the disastrous failure of the former and the disgrace of the latter were attributable only to the imbecility of commanding officers."[56]

54. Schaff, *The Battle of the Wilderness*, 326; Walter H. Taylor, *General Lee*, 237; William Allen, Notes of a Postwar Conversation with Lee, March 3, 1868, in Allen Papers, SHC.

55. Lyman Journal, May 6, 1864, in Lyman Papers, MHS; Andrew A. Humphreys, *The Virginia Campaign*, 50.

56. Abbott, *Personal Recollections and Civil War Diary*, 45; Ulysses S. Grant to Henry W. Halleck, May 6, 1864, in *OR*, Vol. XXXVI, Pt. 2, p. 480; Lewis, *History of the One Hundred and Thirty-Eighth Regiment*, 90.

Later, Seymour's subordinate Keifer attempted to set the record straight, arguing that Seymour's troops had been made into "scapegoats" by Grant, who needed someone to blame for the bungle. Seymour's brigade, Keifer pointed out, had not even occupied the Federal flank. It was Shaler's brigade that had folded, permitting rebels to enfilade Seymour's rear lines. Seymour, Keifer conceded, might have handled the situation better, but his men fought bravely.[57]

In the end, Gordon's plan accomplished little more than to add names to casualty lists. Through the remainder of the night, parties from both sides tried to recover injured soldiers. "Our men were unable even to take care of their own wounded, which lay scattered through the woods in the rear," wrote a Union surgeon. "So the rebel wounded lay between the two armies, making the night hideous with their groans."[58]

"Make all preparations during the day for a night march to take position at Spotsylvania Court House."

A surgeon's diary entry caught the prevailing mood in Federal camps. "We were driven back over much of the ground that was gained yesterday," he wrote. "This war is horrid. . . . Everything looks dark." A soldier in the 76th New York was similarly disheartened. "The result of the battle very doubtful," he penned. "The rebels are evidently in great force and determined to win."[59]

Judging from remarks by Confederate prisoners, more bitter fighting lay ahead. Captured rebels insisted that they had won a great victory. But they also expressed grudging admiration for Grant. A Massachusetts officer heard a southerner voice "great surprise that our army had not fallen back as usual, and commented almost with enthusiasm, upon the cool and determined manner in which their most furious charges had been repulsed. They were evidently at a loss to understand what such invincible resolution might portend, and seemed depressed and chagrined at its results." A Rhode Islander

57. Keifer, *Slavery and Four Years of War*, II, 84.
58. George T. Stevens, *Three Years in the Sixth Corps*, 319.
59. Horatio Soule Diary, May 6, 1864, in Civil War Miscellaneous Collection, USMHI; Uberto A. Burnham Diary, May 6, 1864, in Uberto A. Burnham Papers, NYSA.

stopped to study one "strangely assorted assemblage of warriors" whose "attire was a medley of all the dry goods store of the Confederacy." Jackets and trousers with black facings and slouch hats predominated, as did homemade knapsacks cut from carpets and quilts. "The men themselves were lank, yellow, long-limbed, weather-beaten, rough-haired fellows, but they were terrible soldiers, possessing the hardihood of wild animals. They were as tireless on the march as wolves." An aged rebel from the 5th Texas provoked considerable interest. He had been captured at Gregg's farthest advance on the sixth, after being crippled by a bullet. His guards belonged to an artillery regiment in which he had served during the Mexican War. They were particularly solicitous and engaged him in animated conversation. When asked his opinion of the battle, he gave a heated response. "Battle be damned. It ain't no battle. It's a worse riot than Chickamauga was! You Yanks don't call this a battle, do you? At Chickamauga, there was at least a rear. It's all a damned mess. And our two armies ain't anything but howlin' mobs." His captors agreed. The affair resembled "more a gigantic piece of Indian fighting or bushwhacking of pioneer days than a battle." [60]

Grant's difficulties, from his own point of view, had two origins. One, to be sure, involved the "unquenchable" aggressiveness of Lee's veterans, to use Lyman's turn of phrase. Lee had risen considerably in Grant's estimation. Comparing Lee with the ranking Confederate general in the west, Grant remarked that "Joe Johnston would have retreated after two days of such punishment." But equally responsible for the Union failure was the seeming ineptness of Meade and his generals. They had failed to justify the confidence placed in them at the campaign's outset. The predicament was starkly described by the aide Schaff, who wondered with the rest of the Federal army what the morrow might bring. "Two days of deadly encounter," he wrote, "every man who could bear a musket had been put in; Hancock and Warren repulsed, Sedgwick routed, and now on the defensive behind breastworks; the cavalry drawn back; the trains seeking safety behind the Rapidan; thousands and thousands of killed and wounded, . . . and the air pervaded with a lurking feeling of being

60. Cudworth, *History of the First Regiment Massachusetts*, 465; William P. Hopkins, *The Seventh Regiment Rhode Island Volunteers in the Civil War, 1862–1865* (Providence, 1903), 167; Buell, *The Cannoneer*, 168.

face-to-face with disaster. What, what is the matter with the Army of the Potomac?"[61]

The Union army's overwhelming size should by itself have guaranteed success, but careless generalship had forfeited the golden opportunity. One of Meade's brigadiers later recalled how the soldiers "felt deep mortification" at their failure to beat Lee. "From personal contact with the regiments who did the hardest fighting," the officer later remarked, "I declare that the individual men had no longer the confidence in their commanders which had been their best and strongest trait during the past year."[62]

Grant's attempts to coordinate Burnside and Meade had been a failure. On May 5, Burnside stood idle while the nearby 6th Corps sustained fearful losses. Designated on the sixth to slice between Ewell and Hill, Burnside had accomplished little more than pecking ineffectually at Hill and Longstreet's combined line. No one had expected much from Burnside, and his failure to meet Grant's timetable was viewed as but another example of his inveterate slowness. The judgment of his contemporaries may have been overly harsh, however; his delays in the Wilderness were caused in significant part by difficult terrain and road conditions beyond his control. Also responsible was the unwieldy command structure that treated Burnside as head of a separate army. The battle of the Wilderness was a textbook example of the pitfalls of a divided top command.

All of Meade's corps heads had fallen short. Warren displayed a disconcerting mix of caution and stubbornness. Often overlooked, however, is that his initial instincts had been correct. Confronted with an unknown number of rebels on the turnpike, he had cautioned against attacking until his own corps was unified and Sedgwick had arrived. Had Warren's advice been followed, it is likely that Ewell would have been crushed. "Hill would have stood alone and nothing except retreat could save him," Warren later explained to a friend. "Longstreet was not up, and if General Lee had made any attempt to hold on at the Wilderness, we should have finished him there. This is not an afterthought of mine," insisted Warren. "I saw it at once at

61. Theodore Lyman to family, May 18, 1864, in *Meade's Headquarters*, ed. Agassiz, 102; Schaff, *The Battle of the Wilderness*, 326.
62. Webb, "Through the Wilderness," in *B&L*, IV, 163.

the time." Meade's and Grant's impatience, concluded Warren, had squandered the opportunity for decisive victory.[63]

The sacrifice at Saunders' Field seemed to have broken Warren's spirit. The previous November, he had canceled an assault against seemingly impregnable Confederate works at Mine Run. His instincts were the same in the Wilderness, and the massacre that occurred when Meade forced his hand only served to harden Warren's resolve. Thereafter, he did everything within his power to avoid frontal assaults. The result was an erosion of Warren's standing within the army.

Although Sedgwick had shown an avidity to fight, he had accomplished no more than Warren had. On May 5, he waged disjointed skirmishes against Ewell's northernmost brigades. The next day, he failed to attack Ewell's flank or to safeguard his own. Gordon's success was a direct consequence of Sedgwick's neglect. Grant's faith in the old warrior must have been shaken.

Touted as the Army of the Potomac's steadiest general, Hancock, too, had failed to live up to his reputation. On the fifth, he had been unable to achieve a unified push capable of breaking Hill's resilient line even though he outnumbered his adversary substantially. After a promising start the next morning, he had suffered a reverse every bit as humiliating as Sedgwick's. He had overlooked the significance of the unfinished railroad, neglected to safeguard his flank, and permitted Longstreet to move four brigades off his left wing without detection. But despite his bumbling, he retained the confidence of his superiors. Lyman termed Hancock's performance "brilliant," praising "the vigor with which he brought up his men on the 5th through a difficult country, and the skill and rapidity with which he pushed them into action, [and] his cheerful courage under reverse." Meade is said to have remarked, "Bully Hancock is the only one of my corps commanders who will always go right in when I order him."[64]

Meade's and Sheridan's conflicting views over the proper use of cavalry remained unresolved. Thus far, Sheridan's horsemen had served as scouts and as guards for supply trains. They had failed

63. Gouverneur K. Warren to Charles Porter, November 21, 1875, in Warren Collection, NYSA.
64. Lyman Journal, May 6, 1864, in Lyman Papers, MHS.

miserably in the first function, permitting Lee's entire army to approach undetected. And in the second function, which required the cavalrymen to remain close to the army's wagons, they had kept Sheridan from concentrating his riders into the powerful striking force he envisioned.

The Army of the Potomac's foot soldiers were judiciously undecided about Grant. Before the campaign, most had been inclined to give him the benefit of the doubt. Charles Francis Adams, writing his father on May 1, reported that "the feeling about Grant is peculiar—a little jealousy, a little dislike, a little envy, a little want of confidence—all in many minds and now latent; but it is ready to crystalize at any moment and only brilliant success will dissipate the elements. All, however, are willing to give him a full chance and his own time to do it."[65]

Now Grant had tested his mettle against Lee and had been frustrated. Grumbling in the ranks suggested that the new commander in chief's grace period was over. Brigadier General Marsena R. Patrick, the Army of the Potomac's provost marshal, had scrutinized Grant. "I do not see that Grant does anything but sit quietly about, whittle, smoke, and let [his aide John Rawlins] talk big," he wrote in his diary.[66]

Grant never publicly commented on his own performance during his opening round against Lee. He must, however, have regretted his failure to take the Army of the Potomac more firmly in hand. Redefining the working relationship between himself and Meade would be a priority in the succeeding days.

Over the years, Grant's overland campaign has been depicted as a series of frontal assaults against fortified Confederate positions with little pretense at generalship. Grant's performance in the Wilderness does not support that view. The campaign began with maneuvers intended to pry Lee from behind his Rapidan earthworks. The fifth of May was consumed chiefly in reacting to Lee's unexpected appearance and in jockeying for position. With the Union forces well in hand by nightfall, Grant laid plans for the sixth that were calculated to avoid the strongest rebel fortifications and to bring

65. Charles Francis Adams, Jr., to father, May 1, 1864, in *A Cycle of Adams Letters, 1861–1865,* ed. Worthington Chauncey Ford (2 vols.; Boston, 1920), II, 128.

66. Sparks, *Inside Lincoln's Army,* 369.

irresistible pressure against the weaker rebel right wing. Key to the plan was Burnside's cleaving between the Confederate wings and striking in Hill's rear lines.

Grant's agenda for the sixth represented a prudent use of his forces. In his maneuvers around Vicksburg, he had proved that he could wield an army with considerable agility. His attempts to repeat that performance in the Wilderness met with frustration. The expeditionary force's awkward command structure and newly reorganized units thwarted any concerted action. But to characterize as blind attacks Grant's attempts to patch together a coordinated push does not do justice to his performance in the Wilderness. As for the battle, Grant considered it a draw. "At present we can claim no victory over the enemy, neither have they gained a single advantage," he wrote Washington on the seventh. "The enemy pushed out of his fortifications to prevent their position being turned, and have been sooner or later driven back in every instance." [67]

In a letter home, Lyman concluded that "the result of this great Battle of the Wilderness was a drawn fight, but strategically it was a success, because Lee marched out to stop our advance on Richmond, which, at this point, he did not succeed in doing." By way of explanation, Lyman added that "the Rebels had a very superior knowledge of the country and had marched shorter distances. Also I consider them more daring and sudden in their movement; and I fancy their discipline on essential points is more severe than our own—that is, I fancy they shoot a man when he ought to be shot, and we do not. As to fighting, when two people fight without cessation for the best part of two days, and then come out about even, it is hard to determine." [68]

Grant's hammering had taken an onerous toll on his own forces. According to Federal returns, Grant had had 2,246 soldiers killed, 12,037 wounded, and 3,383 captured. The total loss was officially reckoned at 17,666 officers and men. But as Schaff had learned while watching Warren falsify his returns, those responsible for reporting losses had every reason to minimize the figures, and some did so. It is fair to estimate that the Battle of the Wilderness cost Grant's

---

67. Grant to Halleck, May 7, 1864, in OR, Vol. XXXVI, Pt. 2, p. 480; Grant, *The Personal Memoirs,* II, 534.
68. Lyman to family, May 17, 1864, in *Meade's Headquarters,* ed. Agassiz, 98–99.

expeditionary force some 17 percent of its number. As might be expected, casualties were heaviest among veteran units. Hancock's 2nd Corps, for example, reported 5,092 losses out of 28, 854 soldiers present for duty. The corps' fighting brigadier, Alexander Hays, lay dead, along with at least eight regimental commanders. Warren's 5th Corps' tally showed 5,132 losses; 2,000 of the casualties were in Wadsworth's division, which had been heavily engaged on Orange Plank Road, and 1,748 were attributed to Griffin's division, which had borne the brunt of the initial foray against Ewell. Wadsworth was dead, and two of Warren's brigadiers—Baxter and Stone—lay disabled. Sedgwick's 6th Corps' losses were reported at slightly over 5,000. Not surprisingly, 3,000 were in Getty's division, which had fought alongside Hancock's veterans. Lewis Grant's Vermonters held the dubious honor of losing more men—1,269, by the official count—than did any other Union brigade. Getty himself was wounded, and two of Sedgwick's brigadiers—Seymour and Shaler—were prisoners. Burnside's 9th Corps emerged relatively intact, counting only 1,640 members killed, wounded, or captured. In all, 209 Federal officers had been mortally wounded.[69]

Humphreys later tried to make Grant's casualties more understandable by explaining that the Federals generally initiated attacks against entrenched rebel positions. One of Hancock's aides noticed that, despite the loss of many valuable officers, the ratio of wounded officers to foot soldiers was lower than usual. Hidden by vegetation, the Federal brass made less conspicuous targets than in the past.[70]

Before dark, Grant studied a military map with Porter, sitting with his legs tucked under him like a tailor. "I do not hope to gain any decided advantage from the fighting in this forest," Porter recalled Grant's saying. "I did expect excellent results from Hancock's movement early this morning, when he started the enemy on the run; but

---

69. "Return of Casualties in the Union Forces," in *OR*, Vol. XXXVI, Pt. 1, pp. 119–37; Powell, *The Fifth Army Corps*, 629–31; Francis A. Walker, *History of the Second Army Corps*, 435–40.

70. Andrew A. Humphreys, *The Virginia Campaign*, 53–55.

it was impossible for him to see his own troops, or the true position of the enemy, and the success gained could not be followed up in such a country. I can certainly drive Lee back into his works, but I shall not assault him there; he would have all the advantage in such a fight. If he falls back and entrenches, my notion is to move promptly toward the left. This will, in all probability, compel him to try and throw himself between us and Richmond, and in such a movement I hope to be able to attack him in a more open country, and outside of his breastworks."[71]

Grant had firmed his decision to leave the Wilderness. The place presented little opportunity for victory. To the north, Ewell's Confederates occupied high country across from Sedgwick. In the Saunders' Field sector, Warren stared glumly across a charred wasteland at more Confederate fortifications bristling with firepower. Stretching southward along the high ridge dominating Wilderness Run were Hill's infantrymen, craning for a glint of blue uniforms. Now entirely in Confederate hands, the Chewning farm had been incorporated into Lee's line. And below Orange Plank Road, Longstreet's veterans continued the rebel defenses to the unfinished railroad. During the night, Kershaw's division labored to construct earthworks below the railbed to provide a firm anchor for the southern Confederate flank.

As Humphreys observed, "To attack a position of such character situated as this was and covered by a tangled forest that inevitably disordered the attacking force as they advanced, was not judicious; it promised no success." If Grant stayed where he was, Lee was certain to attempt more surprises modeled after Gordon's evening attack. Next time, the outcome might be disastrous. Supplying the Union army also posed problems. Provisioning troops from the Brandy Station railhead was impossible. While Fredericksburg was a prospective supply depot, Federal wagon trains would be vulnerable to attacks from rebel cavalry. And most important, Grant's goal was to batter the rebels southward, aiming for a junction with Butler near Richmond. Continuing to slug it out in the Wilderness meant abandoning the master plan and leaving Butler to his own devices.[72]

What route should the Army of the Potomac take? One possibil-

---

71. Horace Porter, *Campaigning with Grant*, 65–66.
72. Andrew A. Humphreys, *The Virginia Campaign*, 52.

ity involved withdrawing across the Rapidan or east toward Fredericksburg. But retreat, or even the appearance of it, was not an option that Grant was temperamentally prepared to accept. Not only would a pullback undermine the Union army's morale but it would spell political disaster for the Lincoln administration. In addition, disengaging from Lee would endanger the smaller Federal armies cooperating with Grant.

Some ten miles below the Wilderness lay the crossroads town of Spotsylvania Court House. Advancing there would keep Meade between Lee and Richmond, shielding Butler and most likely drawing Lee out of his stronghold. The country was fairly open, at least in comparison with the dismal forest where the armies were camped. Roads fanned from the courthouse, affording considerable flexibility. Provisioning would be simple. Supplies could be shipped up the Rappahannock to Fredericksburg, then transported by road. Perhaps above all else, shifting to Spotsylvania would break the existing deadlock while avoiding any semblance of retreat.

The trickiest part involved disengaging from the Confederates. It was possible, of course, simply to face south and march down Brock Road. The dangers in that, however, were obvious. The moving army would be defenseless.

Grant's solution, embodied in a directive issued at 6:30 A.M. on May 7, was to thrust the army south on two roads, each column within supporting distance of the other. Sedgwick's 6th Corps was to drop east to Chancellorsville, then work generally south toward Spotsylvania by country roads. Reinforced by Burnside's 9th Corps, Sedgwick's troops would amount to a solid reserve, protecting the army's supply wagons and supporting the front line closest to the enemy.

Once Sedgwick began to move, Federal troops next in order—Warren's 5th Corps—were to begin south on Brock Road, passing behind Hancock. Then Hancock's troops would file into place, following Warren. By sunup on the eighth, the entire Federal mass was expected to reunite around Spotsylvania, athwart Lee's direct route to Richmond.

In order to steal a march on Lee, secrecy was critical. "All vehicles should be got out of hearing of the enemy before the troops move," Grant emphasized in his directive, "and then move off quietly." Since battle could erupt at any moment, the Union forces would maintain a compact body while they maneuvered.[73]

The plan was an astute one, making optimal use of the terrain and the road networks. It also had the advantage of placing the Wilderness stalemate in a light that was not discreditable to the Federals. The recent carnage could be viewed as the opening salvo of a protracted battle to end the war in Virginia.

Grant's directive represented the maturation of his thinking. Lee, Grant was conceding, could not be beaten here. But the campaign was not over. Grant would fight again, next time on fields that offered him the upper hand. Lincoln's new commander in chief had been checked, but not defeated.

The directive also revealed much about the evolving relationship between Grant and Meade. Grant was no longer satisfied with merely articulating general objectives and then quietly leaving details to Meade. The previous two days had painfully demonstrated Meade's inability to concentrate his forces with decision. Henceforth, Grant was telling Meade precisely which units to move and where to move them. Grant intended to assume an active role in the Army of the Potomac's daily affairs.

*"The old deacon would say
that God willed it thus."*

"Early this morning," began Lee's evening dispatch to Richmond, "as the divisions of Genl Hill engaged on yesterday were being relieved, the enemy advanced and created some confusion. The ground lost was recovered as soon as the fresh troops got into position, and the enemy driven back to his original line. Afterwards we turned the left of his front line and drove it from the field, leaving a large number of his dead and wounded in our hands, among them Genl Wadsworth. A subsequent attack forced the enemy into his entrenched lines on the Brock Road, extending from Wilderness Tavern on the right to Trigg's Mill." The battle's result, concluded Lee, had been mixed. "Every advance on [Grant's] part," he wrote, "thanks to a merciful

73. Ulysses S. Grant to George G. Meade, May 7, 1864, in *OR*, Vol. XXXVI, Pt. 2, p. 481.

God, has been repulsed. Our loss in killed is not large, but we have many wounded, most of them slightly, artillery being little used on either side." But there was also reason for sorrow. "I grieve to announce that Lieut Gen Longstreet was severely wounded, and Genl Jenkins killed. Genl Pegram was badly wounded yesterday. Genl Stafford, it is hoped, will recover." He did not.[74]

Lee's losses, though fewer than Grant's, were grievously felt. Fallen men could not be replaced. After the war, Alexander attempted a computation of Confederate casualties but found returns for only 112 of 183 Confederate regiments engaged. Assuming that Confederates were shot and captured in the same proportion as Federals, Alexander estimated Lee's casualties at around 7,750 men. Union sources reckoned that Lee lost closer to 11,000 soldiers. Independent Confederate reports lend some support to the estimate. Hill's returns for April 20 placed the 3rd Corps' enrollment at slightly over 20,000 soldiers. Early, who replaced Hill on the morning of the eighth, affirmed that the 3rd Corps numbered about 13,000 "muskets for duty." If Early's figures were correct, Hill's command—which was probably the Confederate unit that saw heaviest action during the battle—lost 7,000 men. Ewell, in his battle report issued almost a year later, claimed that his killed and wounded numbered about 1,250. On the assumption of the accuracy of these figures, as well as of the overall 11,000 total for the Confederate army, Longstreet's casualties would come to around 3,000 soldiers, a number that seems accurate. Longstreet's corps was involved in only one day's fighting, but it was a very bloody one.[75]

At this juncture, Lee did not feel satisfied that he could predict Grant's next move. Perhaps Grant would renew his attacks, perhaps he would attempt to maneuver past the Confederates on one of the several routes toward Richmond, or perhaps, like his predecessors, he would retreat across the Rapidan. Until Lee understood the enemy's plans, he had little choice. The Army of Northern Virginia was safely ensconced in an eminently defensible position. Judging by Grant's actions during the previous two days, there was an excellent chance that the Federals would renew their attacks. Lee could hope

74. Robert E. Lee to James A. Seddon, May 6, 1864, in *OR*, Vol. XXXVI, Pt. 2, p. 960.

75. Walter H. Taylor, *Four Years with General Lee*, 176; Alexander, *Military Memoirs*, 508–509; Andrew A. Humphreys, *The Virginia Campaign*, 54; Early, *War Memoirs*, 352.

for no better place for waging his defense. For the time being, he decided to leave his army where it was, girded to fend off anticipated waves of bluecoats. As Taylor described Lee's thinking, the Confederate commander "hesitated to assail the enemy in his intrenched position, and hopefully awaited attack."[76]

In a narrow sense, Lee had won a victory. He had stopped the latest Union drive on Richmond and had fought Grant to a standoff. The letters and diary entries of Lee's soldiers show that his men considered the battle a success. "The Yankees have been seriously beaten," Lee's stoic artillery chief Brigadier General William Pendleton wrote home. A soldier from North Carolina informed his wife, "The enemy are evidently much worsted and their plans frustrated. Our army is in splendid condition, confident of success and victory, trusting in God and Genl. Lee."[77]

But in a broader perspective, the battle manifested a Confederate failure. The southerners had been unable to maintain the initiative. Now the Army of Northern Virginia's offensive capacity was spent. The armies faced each other across a few hundred yards of shattered brush. The grand maneuvers that had served Lee so well in the past were no longer possible. The only reasonable course of action remaining to the Confederates was to stay in their strong defensive line and wait for Grant to make a mistake.

Grant's hammering was working. If attrition continued at the same rate, Grant had to win. Mathematics dictated that Confederate numbers would soon become so small that inevitably Lee's veterans were going to be overwhelmed.

Confederates came to view the Battle of the Wilderness as their "lost" chance to stem a near-irresistible tide. Fate, they claimed, intervened and robbed them of success just when victory lay within their grasp. In 1877, a prominent southerner—Leigh Robinson, formerly of the Richmond Howitzers—addressed the Virginia Division of the Army of Northern Virginia in Richmond. Speaking of the Wilderness, he

76. Walter H. Taylor, *Four Years with General Lee*, 129.

77. William Pendleton to wife, May 7, 1864, in William Pendleton Collection, SHC; Benjamin Justice to family, May 7, 1864, in Justice Papers, EU.

voiced a widely held sentiment. "Twice that day another Chancellorsville was in our hands," he asserted, "and twice it was dropped," referring to Longstreet's and Gordon's aborted offensives. "Had Longstreet been a few minutes later," claimed Robinson, "Lee's army would, or, at least, should have been defeated. Had he been a few minutes earlier, or not been wounded, Grant would have been driven across the river, in the ignominious defeat of his predecessors."[78]

Southerners also came to credit Lee with nearly faultless generalship. He had divined Grant's plan of campaign, went the accolade, and had craftily trapped the Federals in the deep woods. Unfortunately, Ewell had been indecisive, Hill careless, and Longstreet slow. But if it had not been for subordinates' failings, Lee would have defeated Grant and driven the Union army across the Rapidan.

In point of fact, Lee made several decisions during the battle which put his army and his cause in serious jeopardy. Outnumbered two to one by an enemy with a virtually boundless capacity to replace losses, Lee chose offense as his best defense. He was willing to gamble everything on a decisive blow. The decision was consistent with his temperament, but its wisdom was open to debate. In the Civil War era, the attacking forces necessarily sustained high losses, generally greater than those of the defender. The South, with its dwindling resources, could ill afford extensive casualties.

In northern Georgia, Lee's counterpart faced a superior force and studiously avoided battle. It was Johnston's hope to husband his resources until he could induce Sherman to attack. In the end, neither Lee nor Johnston met with success, so trying to weigh the relative merits of their differing strategies by reference to results yields no clearcut verdict. Later in 1864, Lee did resort to defensive tactics, receiving Grant's hammerblows from behind earthworks. And in those battles, Lee was generally able to inflict the higher proportion of casualties. If Lee had avoided the bloodbath of the Wilderness and instead had swung across Grant's path and fought defensively from a prepared position, he might more effectively have preserved his army's fighting capacity.

Lee is also open to criticism for failing to take measures ensuring that he would encounter Grant in the Wilderness. He gambled in-

---

78. Leigh Robinson, *The South Before and at the Battle of the Wilderness* (Richmond, 1878), 88.

stead that his army would be able to shift quickly from its earthworks to intercept Grant. In the event, Lee's response was anything but rapid. Even though the Clark's Mountain lookouts identified the main Federal thrust at daylight on May 4, the Confederates frittered away much of the morning. Lead contingents of Hill's and Ewell's corps were not under way until noon, and Longstreet's did not get started until around four in the afternoon. At that juncture, Union troops already occupied Wilderness Tavern and Chancellorsville. Had Grant wished, he could have passed on unhindered.

There is no basis for the popular perception that Lee, through astute planning, trapped Grant in the Wilderness. He was merely the fortunate beneficiary of sloppy Federal planning and reconnaissance. Lee's inaction—his failure to take affirmative steps to impede Grant's progress or to accelerate his own army's response—exposed the Confederates to peril. Had the Federals proceeded according to Humphreys' original timetable, there would have been no Battle of the Wilderness. And had Wilson's troopers been vigilant, Lee instead of Grant would have received an ugly surprise on the morning of May 5.

On neither day of the battle was Lee able to coordinate his forces effectively. The battle was fought piecemeal, one front on the Orange Turnpike and another on Orange Plank Road, with little concerted action between the two wings. Preoccupied with developments in Hill's sector, Lee left Ewell largely alone. Consequently, the advantages of unified Confederate assaults—for example, simultaneous flanking attacks by Gordon and Longstreet—were never realized.

In fairness, it must be recognized that Lee's headquarters were located on Orange Plank Road, which became the focus of Grant's offensive. Lee's personal involvement was sorely needed there. According to his aides, he actively supervised Hill's deployments on May 5. The collapse of Hill's line on the sixth appears to have upset Lee's equilibrium temporarily, but by early afternoon the general had recovered his composure. The wounding of Longstreet and the advancing sickness of Hill, however, required Lee to undertake duties normally left to corps commanders. According to Field, "General Lee was near me giving verbal directions" during maneuvers leading up to the Brock Road assault.[79]

The failure to rectify Hill's lines during the night of May 5–6

79. Field, "Campaign of 1864 and 1865," in *SHSP*, XIV, 547.

was a blunder that nearly destroyed the Confederate army. Who was responsible? Wilcox and Palmer asserted that Hill had acted on orders from Lee, who believed that Longstreet would arrive in time to relieve the exhausted 3rd Corps. Heth insinuated that Hill had become too ill to make rational judgments. Heth recounted a later conversation in which Lee, having listened patiently to his account of how he attempted to rouse Hill on the night of May 5, responded that "a division commander should always have his division prepared to receive an attack." Heth answered, "That is certainly so, but he must also obey the positive orders of his superior." According to Heth, Lee remained silent. "He knew a splendid opportunity had been lost, one that never occurred again," Heth concluded. "I think General Lee never forgave Wilcox or me for this awful blunder." [80]

Despite Heth's loyal attempt to exonerate Lee, responsibility rests squarely on the rebel commander's shoulders. Palmer's and Wilcox' accounts leave no doubt that Lee knew the state of affairs and did nothing about it because he trusted in Longstreet's imminent arrival. Lee should have instructed Hill to prepare for the worst. His failure to do so was perhaps the greatest lapse of his military career.

The doomed Confederate charge against Hancock's Brock Road defenses ranks with Lee's controversial decisions to hold firm at Antietam and to assault Meade on the third day's fighting at Gettysburg. Temperamentally inclined toward aggressive warfare, Lee's solution to impasse was attack. In light of the disorganized condition of his line and the strength of his opponent, the odds of success were negligible. Lee, however, was a gambler. As he often expressed it, the outcome would be decided by providence. When the odds were stacked against success, Lee seemed to abandon logical thought. The result was severe casualties when the South could least afford them.

Before the campaign, Lee had harbored doubts about his corps commanders' abilities to meet the demands of a rigorous campaign. The two days of the Battle of the Wilderness added new reasons for concern.

Ewell performed well defensively, deftly repelling Warren's and Sedgwick's assaults and keeping five enemy divisions at bay. But he continued to exhibit the lack of initiative in offensive operations that earlier had marred his generalship. Ewell's orders for the sixth had

---

80. Morrison, ed., *The Memoirs of Henry Heth*, 185.

been discretionary; he was to sever the Army of the Potomac from its base or support Hill. He failed to do either, and he deferred Gordon's proposed flanking movement until too late. Ewell lacked the aggressive spirit that Lee considered essential to success.

Hill too started off well. Throughout May 5, he mounted one of the Army of Northern Virginia's most impressive defenses. But at nightfall, when fighting ceased, he left his line in shambles. To the extent that Hill acted with Lee's concurrence, the fault is not solely his. But a nagging suspicion remains that Lee did not fully comprehend the disarray on Hill's front. Impressing Lee with the fact that the 3rd Corps could not fight unless reorganized was Hill's job. By failing to make that point clear to Lee, he must share the blame for the near-destruction of the Confederate army. On the sixth, Hill's sickness almost incapacitated him. Within a few days he became so ill that he had to relinquish active management of his corps.

Jeb Stuart's cavalry corps also lacked its usual vigilance. Although Stuart was responsible for ascertaining the location of Grant's army, he failed to do so with precision. Ewell, who camped a mere two miles from Warren's lead troops, did not learn of Warren's whereabouts until encountering him on the morning of the fifth. Confederate reconnaissance on Orange Plank Road was also lax. Lee's communications with Heth make it clear that the Confederate army commander did not know the strength of the force in front of him. Getty's three brigades were thus able to stall Hill's two divisions for several precious hours until Hancock's reinforcements arrived and secured the intersection at Brock Road.

For the Confederates, one of the Wilderness' greatest tragedies was the loss of Longstreet. Comparisons with Stonewall Jackson's earlier death were inevitable. Like Jackson, Longstreet had been shot accidentally during a brilliant flanking maneuver. The incidents had occurred almost a year apart and within a few miles of each other. As Taylor later observed, "A strange fatality attended us! Jackson killed in the zenith of his successful career; Longstreet wounded when in the act of striking a blow that would have rivalled Jackson's at Chancellorsville in its results; and in each case the fire was from our own men. A blunder! Call it so; the old deacon would say that God willed it thus."[81]

81. Walter H. Taylor, *General Lee*, 236–37.

After the war, Longstreet was taxed with having moved too slowly. Had he reached the battleground earlier, went the argument, Hill's line would have held and the Federals would have been defeated. Longstreet's progress, however, was not as bad as critics claimed. His failure to start from Gordonsville until 4 P.M. on May 4 was attributable to discussions with Lee concerning the best route. Once under way, the 1st Corps made passable time to Richard's Shop, the rear division covering some thirty-two miles in approximately twenty-four hours.

Less easily extenuated is Longstreet's decision to rest his corps at Richard's Shop from 5 P.M. on the fifth until 1 A.M. on the sixth, eight precious hours during which the army's fate hung in the balance. Longstreet's men certainly needed rest, but the general was conscious of the necessity of reaching the battlefield before sunrise. Here he miscalculated. Setting the departure for one o'clock allowed for no possible hindrances, and a proposed shortcut turned into a costly delay. In retrospect, the wiser course would have been to break camp earlier, or to have pushed through to the Wilderness and rested the men there.

But it must not be ignored that, had Longstreet reached the battlefield before sunup on the sixth, he would have occupied Hill's old line. Subjected to the full weight of Hancock's assaults, it is likely that he would have crumpled as Hill did. Longstreet's arrival after the Federal assault lost its momentum worked to the Confederates' advantage. The element of surprise was his, and he was able to overcome Hancock's forces in part because their cohesion had dissolved during their pursuit of Hill. The explosion of Longstreet's corps into Widow Tapp's farm after Hancock's troops had stalled was the battle's turning point. Longstreet's tardiness saved the day for the Confederates.

The Battle of the Wilderness left the Army of Northern Virginia's leadership in disorder. Longstreet was severely wounded, Hill was too ill to manage troops, and Ewell, after a promising start, seemed to lack the aggressive spark so critical to Lee's mode of warfare. At the brigade level, Jenkins, Jones, and Stafford were dead, and Pegram and Benning were wounded. The army commander would have to remain deeply involved in details that in better days he could have delegated to subordinates.

It was also becoming clear that Grant had a degree of dogged persistence unknown in his predecessors. For the first time, Lee was facing an opponent with determination that matched his own. The Wilderness appeared to confirm Longstreet's ominous prediction. Grant, Lee's War Horse had warned, would fight "every day and every hour till the end of the war." And so it would be.

"Hell itself had usurped
the place of earth."

During the afternoon of May 6, Spencer Welch, a Confederate surgeon, made his rounds. One stop was Kershaw's field hospital on Orange Plank Road. Sorrowfully, he walked among the wounded of the 3rd South Carolina. Colonel James D. Nance, a friend and the regiment's commander, lay dead. A lawyer before the war, Nance had been considered the "best all round soldier in Kershaw's brigade, none excepted." Next to Nance lay another of Welch's friends, Colonel Franklin Gaillard, a fiery southern editor who had commanded the 2nd South Carolina. Wounded Yankees sprawled everywhere.[82]

In a large fly tent near the roadside lay General Wadsworth. One of Kershaw's officers, Colonel D. Augustus Dickert, visited the tent out of curiosity. The gray-haired northerner, he understood, commanded more ready gold than the Confederacy held in its treasury. A hat covered the general's face. Dickert lifted it and looked underneath. Wadsworth's labored breathing, his closed eyes, and his cold, clammy face indicated that the end was near. "There lay dying the multi-millionaire in an enemy's country," mused Dickert, "nor a friend near to hear his last farewell or sooth[e] his last moments by a friendly touch on the pallid brow."[83]

Most of Wadsworth's possessions had been taken. Bob Archer, of Mahone's brigade, got his pocketbook containing ninety dollars in greenbacks. John Bolote, later of the Norfolk police force, got his gold watch. The general's silver spurs went to another soldier, as did his elegant field glasses. Sorrel ended up with Wadsworth's map. "It was a good map of Virginia," he remarked, "and of use afterwards."[84]

The next morning, Major Z. Boylston Adams was roused from

82. Spencer G. Welch, *A Confederate Surgeon's Letters to His Wife* (New York, 1911), 94.

83. Dickert, *History of Kershaw's Brigade*, 352.

84. Westwood A. Todd, "Reminiscences," in Westwood A. Todd Papers, SHC; Sorrel, *Recollections*, 243.

his sleep by something dripping from above. A soldier in the 56th Massachusetts, Adams had been wounded during the fighting on Orange Plank Road. Carried off by Confederates, he had spent the night in Kershaw's field hospital. Adams wiped his face. His hands were covered with blood. Looking around, he discovered that he was lying under a low canopy constructed from a poncho. All around stood men in white aprons. Next to his head was a severed leg. Hearing Adams' cries, one of the aproned figures stepped back and looked under the poncho. "Hulloa! How did you come there?" he asked. Several white-sheeted men helped pull Adams out, laughing at what had happened. Apparently Adams had been stuffed under an operating table the evening before and then forgotten. Several hours later, two surgeons arrived, smelling strongly of whiskey. After examining Adams' wounds, they determined that an operation was necessary. During the afternoon, he was placed on the table and chloroformed. A five-inch section was removed from his fibula. When Adams regained consciousness, he was lying under a tent fly. Next to him was a Federal officer. Adams lifted the man's eyelids; the stare was vacant. The man's pulse was regular, his breathing was a little labored, and occasionally he heaved a deep sigh. His mouth was drawn down at the left side, and his right arm was paralyzed, indicating to Adams an injury to the left side of the brain. Looking closely, Adams determined that a musket ball had entered the top of the man's head a little to the left of the median line. His left hand lay quietly on the breast of his buttoned coat. It clutched a scrap of paper on which was written, "Gen. James S. Wadsworth."[85]

During the afternoon, rebel officers crowded into the tent to see Wadsworth. The general remained unconscious. For a while he toyed with the trigger on a musket that had been placed nearby. Whenever anyone tried to read the paper grasped in his fingers, he would frown and become restless. His hand moved to and fro as if searching for something. When the paper was returned, he clutched it tightly and lay his hand across his breast. "Do you mean to say this is James S. Wadsworth of New York, the proprietor of vast estates in the Genesee valley, the candidate for governor in 1862?" visitors would ask Adams. "I'd never believe that they had such men as that in their army," some of the onlookers remarked. Later, a rebel outfitted in

85. Adams, "In the Wilderness," in *Civil War Papers*, II, 388–89.

stars and gold buttons and lace visited the tent. He was obviously intoxicated. An ugly scene developed. The drunken Confederate swore at Adams for vouching that the unconscious man was Wadsworth. Union officers were crazy abolitionists, mercenaries, low politicians, and hirelings from foreign armies, swore the rebel, who demanded of Adams who he was. Adams replied that he came from Massachusetts. The answer excited the man's rage. He cursed Massachusetts, cursed Boston, and swore that he would one day read the roll of his slaves from Bunker Hill. Adams took umbrage, which made matters worse. The Confederate drew a revolver from his belt, cocked it, and was about to shoot the invalid when his friends caught hold of the weapon and pushed him from the tent. Adams heard one of them exclaim, "Look here, you can't shoot that man." [86]

On Saturday night, Confederate surgeons examined Wadsworth's wound. They confirmed that a ball had entered near the top of his head and had proceeded forward. The projectile was lodged in the anterior lobe of the left side of his brain. Adams conjectured that the general's horse had pitched forward. The bullet had struck as the general bent down, either from his horse's fall or in anticipation of a volley. By this time, Wadsworth was unable to swallow. His captors tried to feed him with a spoon, but food dribbled from the corners of his mouth and onto his beard. Except for occasional sighs, he lay in a calm slumber. Surgeons removed a piece of Wadsworth's skull. The bullet was not evident, so they probed in his brain for the ball. Adams considered the procedure "bad surgery." [87]

After dark, a civilian slipped into Adams' tent through a rear entrance. "My name is Patrick McCracken, and I have a little farm a few miles out," he explained. "I have heard that General Wadsworth is here wounded, and I want to do something for him." It developed that years before, McCracken had been arrested as a spy. His family had appealed to Wadsworth for leniency, promising that if Wadsworth permitted him to return home, McCracken would not assist the Confederate cause. Wadsworth had granted their request. McCracken assured Adams that he had kept his promise, and consequently was distrusted by the Confederates. He wanted to help

86. Gallagher, ed., *Fighting for the Confederacy,* 364; Adams, "In the Wilderness," in *Civil War Papers,* II, 390–91.

87. Adams, "In the Wilderness," in *Civil War Papers,* II, 391.

Wadsworth and offered to bring the general food and milk. Adams replied that Wadsworth could not swallow. McCracken insisted on leaving provisions anyway and invited Adams to consume them if Wadsworth could not. The next day—Sunday, May 8—Wadsworth died. McCracken took the general's body to his farm at Oak Woods, about seven miles west on Orange Plank Road. Before the body was removed, Adams cut a lock of Wadsworth's hair. Later, after he was released from prison, he gave it to Mrs. Wadsworth in Boston.[88]

Throughout the evening of May 6 and into the next day, the Wilderness hemorrhaged wounded men and prisoners. Orange Plank Road was packed with wagons jostling blood-soaked soldiers toward Orange Court House. The wounded were transported in springless wagons. "We were tossed about often," recalled a Confederate, "and sometimes violently." At Orange Court House, the "suffering humanity" was laid out on the train platform. Hundreds of boxcars waited at the siding to carry the wounded to the hospital at Lynchburg.[89]

On the morning of the seventh, Longstreet was placed in an ambulance bound for Orange Court House. Accompanying him were Dr. Dunn and the staffers Lieutenant Colonel Osmun Latrobe and Thomas J. Goree, who had also been wounded. Erasmus Taylor, Longstreet's quartermaster, came to see the men off. Holding Taylor's hand, Longstreet pleaded, "Don't leave me until you see me safe on the cars at Orange." At noon, the ambulance stopped at a home on Orange Plank Road. Taylor had thoughtfully brought along whiskey, sugar, and ice, and occupied himself during the halt making juleps. The wounded men as well as their escorts shared the refreshment, and the remainder of the journey was a lively affair. Dunn, who was a large man, became so intoxicated that he caused his horse to trip and fell off the mount. Latrobe shouted out some good-natured jibes. "Dunn cursed him for all the damned fools that had ever been," Taylor later recalled, "Latrobe and I being convulsed with laughter." The night was spent at Meadow Farm, the Taylor estate near Orange. The next day, Taylor saw his charges safely onto a train. Longstreet was nursed back to health at a relative's home in Lynchburg. He returned

88. *Ibid.*, 391–92.
89. William E. Trahern, "Biography," in William Trahern Papers, VHS.

to active command in time to participate in the Confederacy's final struggles.[90]

Grant's field hospitals were also busy. Thousands of men "stretched upon every available spot of ground for many rods around," observed a Federal doctor on visiting one of the 6th Corps' hospitals. He remarked on how the soldiers seemed to have been wounded "in every conceivable way, men with mutilated bodies, with shattered limbs and broken heads, men enduring their injuries with heroic patience, and men giving way to violent grief, men stoically indifferent, and men bravely rejoicing that it is only a leg." Around midnight, Union surgeons were ordered to halt their grisly work. The Federal army was preparing to move, and hospitals had to shift as well. The wounded were loaded onto wagons and transported along the turnpike to Chancellorsville. They arrived near morning. New tents were erected, and piles of severed arms and legs began to rise at the new site. The next day, wagons began to roll toward Fredericksburg, where injured men hoped to receive more consistent treatment.[91]

While hospital wagons rumbled through the darkness and Lee and Grant pondered their strategies, the exhausted combatants slumped in their trenches. Fires had caught in the undergrowth, and large tracts were wrapped in flame. "The blaze ran sparkling and crackling up the trunks of the pines, till they stood a pillar of fire from base to topmost spray," recalled a soldier from Maine. "Then they wavered and fell, throwing up showers of gleaming sparks, while over all hung the thick clouds of dark smoke, reddened beneath by the glare of flames."[92]

Porter also remembered the night as a scene of "unutterable" terror. "Forest fires raged; ammunition trains exploded; the dead were roasted in the conflagration; the wounded, roused by its hot breath, dragged themselves along, with their torn and mangled limbs, in the mad energy of despair, to escape the ravages of the flames; and every

90. Osmun Latrobe Manuscript, in Osmun Latrobe Papers, VHS; Erasmus Taylor Memoir, in Erasmus Taylor Papers, VHS.
91. George T. Stevens, *Three Years in the Sixth Corps*, 314–19; Randall, "Reminiscences," in Randall Papers, BL.
92. Henry C. Houston, *The Thirty-Second Maine Regiment of Infantry Volunteers* (Portland, Maine, 1903), 101.

bush seemed hung with shreds of blood-stained clothing," he recorded years later. "It seemed as though Christian men had turned to fiends, and hell itself had usurped the place of earth."[93]

"It was awful," scrawled a Vermont soldier in his diary. "This is the real thing."[94]

Burial parties were busy all night and the following day. A Texan recalled how corpses from Gregg's brigade were laid side by side in a shallow trench next to Orange Plank Road. A rude headboard was placed over the remains of each soldier with his name carved on it. On a tall, stately oak next to the roadway hung a sign identifying the graveyard. Texas Dead—May 6, 1864, it read.[95]

The armies began moving toward Spotsylvania the night of May 7 and were for the most part gone from the Wilderness by the eighth. Gravediggers had no opportunity to complete their work. Bodies remained exposed between former battle lines and in obscure thickets and hollows. One southerner estimated that fewer than 10 percent of the Federal dead had been interred. A week later, a Confederate hurrying through the Wilderness remarked on the overpowering stench. Putrefying corpses and carcasses, he complained, "lay in every conceivable shape and position." Over a year after that, an expedition from Washington assigned to bury the soldiers reported that "it was no unusual occurrence to observe the bones of our men close to the abatis of the enemy; and in one case several skeletons of our soldiers were found in their trenches."[96]

The flag of each army was embossed with the names of the battles in which it fought. Fingers were now busy stitching a new name: The Wilderness. Little did the troops suspect how soon another name would be added. Less than ten miles down the road stood the little town of Spotsylvania Court House.

93. Horace Porter, *Campaigning with Grant*, 72–73.
94. Abbott, *Personal Recollections and Civil War Diary*, 49.
95. Polley, *Soldier's Letters*, 233.
96. Polley, *Hood's Texas Brigade*, 233–34; *Names of Officers and Soldiers Found on the Battle-Fields of the Wilderness and of Spottsylvania Court House, Va.* (Washington, D.C., 1864), v.

APPENDIX
The Order of Battle

ARMY OF THE POTOMAC
Major General George G. Meade

PROVOST GUARD
Brigadier General Marsena R. Patrick
1st Massachusetts Cavalry, Companies C and D
80th New York
3rd Pennsylvania Cavalry
68th Pennsylvania
114th Pennsylvania

ARTILLERY
Brigadier General Henry J. Hunt

RESERVE ARTILLERY
Colonel Henry S. Burton

1st Brigade
Colonel J. Howard Kitching
6th New York Heavy Artillery
15th New York Heavy Artillery

2nd Brigade
Major John A. Tompkins
5th Maine, Battery E
1st New Jersey, Battery A
1st New Jersey, Battery B
5th New York Battery
12th New York Battery
1st New York, Battery B

3rd Brigade
Major Robert H. Fitzhugh
9th Massachusetts Battery

1st Brigade Horse
Artillery
Captain James M. Robertson
6th New York Battery
2nd U.S., Batteries B and L
2nd U.S., Battery D
2nd U.S., Battery M
4th U.S., Battery A
4th U.S., Batteries C and E

2nd Brigade Horse
Artillery
Captain Dunbar R. Ransom
1st U.S., Batteries E and G
1st U.S., Batteries H and I
1st U.S., Battery K
2nd U.S., Battery A

15th New York Battery
1st New York, Battery C
11th New York Battery
1st Ohio, Battery H
5th U.S., Battery E

2nd U.S., Battery G
3rd U.S., Batteries C, F, and K

VOLUNTEER ENGINEER BRIGADE
Brigadier General Henry W. Benham

50TH NEW YORK ENGINEERS
Lieutenant Colonel Ira Spaulding

BATTALION U.S. ENGINEERS
Captain George H. Mendell

2ND ARMY CORPS
Major General Winfield S. Hancock
1st Vermont Cavalry, Company M

1ST DIVISION
Brigadier General Francis C. Barlow

1st Brigade
Colonel Nelson A. Miles
26th Michigan
61st New York
81st Pennsylvania
140th Pennsylvania
183rd Pennsylvania

2nd Brigade
Colonel Thomas A. Smyth
28th Massachusetts
63rd New York
69th New York
88th New York
116th Pennsylvania

3rd Brigade
Colonel Paul Frank
39th New York
52nd New York
57th New York
111th New York
125th New York
126th New York

2ND DIVISION
Brigadier General John Gibbon
2nd Company Minnesota
Sharpshooters

1st Brigade
Brigadier General Alexander S. Webb
19th Maine
1st Company Sharpshooters
15th Massachusetts
19th Massachusetts
20th Massachusetts
7th Michigan
42nd New York
59th New York
82nd New York (2nd Militia)

2nd Brigade
Brigadier General Joshua T. Owen
152nd New York
69th Pennsylvania
71st Pennsylvania
72nd Pennsylvania
106th Pennsylvania

3RD DIVISION
Major General David B. Birney

1st Brigade
Brigadier General J. H. Hobart Ward
20th Indiana
3rd Maine
40th New York
86th New York
124th New York
99th Pennsylvania
110th Pennsylvania
141st Pennsylvania
2nd U.S. Sharpshooters

2nd Brigade
Brigadier General Alexander Hays
4th Maine
17th Maine
3rd Michigan
5th Michigan
93rd New York
57th Pennsylvania
63rd Pennsylvania
105th Pennsylvania
1st U.S. Sharpshooters

4TH DIVISION
Brigadier General Gershom Mott

1st Brigade
Colonel Robert McAllister
1st Massachusetts
16th Massachusetts
5th New Jersey
6th New Jersey
7th New Jersey
8th New Jersey
11th New Jersey
26th Pennsylvania
115th Pennsylvania

2nd Brigade
Colonel William R. Brewster
11th Massachusetts
70th New York
71st New York
72nd New York
73rd New York
74th New York
120th New York
84th Pennsylvania

4th Brigade
Colonel John R. Brooke
2nd Delaware
64th New York
66th New York
53rd Pennsylvania
145th Pennsylvania
148th Pennsylvania

3rd Brigade
Colonel Samuel S. Carroll
14th Connecticut
1st Delaware
14th Indiana
12th New Jersey
10th New York battalion
108th New York
4th Ohio
8th Ohio
7th West Virginia

Artillery Brigade
Colonel John C. Tidball
6th Maine, Battery F
10th Massachusetts Battery
1st New Hampshire Battery
1st New York, Battery G
4th New York Heavy, 3rd battalion
1st Pennsylvania, Battery F
1st Rhode Island, Battery A
1st Rhode Island, Battery B
4th U.S., Battery K
5th U.S., Batteries C and I

5TH ARMY CORPS
Major General *Gouverneur K. Warren*
12th New York battalion

1ST DIVISION
Brigadier General *Charles Griffin*

1st Brigade
Brigadier General *Romeyn B. Ayres*
140th New York
146th New York
91st Pennsylvania
155th Pennsylvania
2nd U.S., Companies B, C, F, H, I, and K
11th U.S., Companies B, C, D, E, F, and G, 1st battalion
12th U.S., Companies A, B, C, D, and G, 1st battalion
12th U.S., Companies A, C, D, F, and H, 2nd battalion
14th U.S., 1st battalion
17th U.S., Companies A, C, D, G, and H, 1st battalion
17th U.S., Companies A, B, and C, 2nd battalion

2nd Brigade
Colonel *Jacob B. Sweitzer*
9th Massachusetts
22nd Massachusetts
32nd Massachusetts
4th Michigan
62nd Pennsylvania

2ND DIVISION
Brigadier General *John C. Robinson*

1st Brigade
Colonel *Samuel H. Leonard*
16th Maine
13th Massachusetts
39th Massachusetts
104th New York

2nd Brigade
Brigadier General *Henry Baxter*
12th Massachusetts
83rd New York
97th New York
11th Pennsylvania
88th Pennsylvania
90th Pennsylvania

3rd Brigade
Colonel *Andrew W. Denison*
1st Maryland
4th Maryland
7th Maryland
8th Maryland

3RD DIVISION
Brigadier General *Samuel W. Crawford*

1st Brigade
Colonel *William McCandless*
1st Pennsylvania Reserves
2nd Pennsylvania Reserves
6th Pennsylvania Reserves
7th Pennsylvania Reserves
11th Pennsylvania Reserves
13th Pennsylvania Reserves

3rd Brigade
Colonel *Joseph W. Fisher*
5th Pennsylvania Reserves
8th Pennsylvania Reserves
10th Pennsylvania Reserves
12th Pennsylvania Reserves

4TH DIVISION
Brigadier General *James S. Wadsworth*

1st Brigade
Brigadier General *Lysander Cutler*
7th Indiana
19th Indiana
24th Michigan
1st New York Battalion Sharpshooters
2nd Wisconsin
6th Wisconsin
7th Wisconsin

2nd Brigade
Brigadier General *James C. Rice*
76th New York
84th New York
95th New York
147th New York
56th Pennsylvania

3rd Brigade
Colonel *Roy Stone*
121st Pennsylvania
142nd Pennsylvania
143rd Pennsylvania
149th Pennsylvania
150th Pennsylvania

3rd Brigade
Brigadier General Joseph J. Bartlett
20th Maine
18th Massachusetts
1st Michigan
16th Michigan
44th New York
83rd Pennsylvania
118th Pennsylvania

Artillery Brigade
Colonel Charles S. Wainwright
Massachusetts, Light Battery C
Massachusetts, Light Battery E
1st New York, Battery D
1st New York, Batteries E and L
1st New York, Battery H
4th New York Heavy, 2nd battalion
1st Pennsylvania, Battery B
4th U.S., Battery B
5th U.S., Battery D

6TH ARMY CORPS
Major General John Sedgwick
8th Pennsylvania Cavalry

1ST DIVISION
Brigadier General Horatio G. Wright

1st Brigade
Colonel Henry W. Brown
1st New Jersey
2nd New Jersey
3rd New Jersey
4th New Jersey
10th New Jersey
15th New Jersey

2nd Brigade
Colonel Emory Upton
5th Maine
121st New York
95th Pennsylvania
96th Pennsylvania

3rd Brigade
Brigadier General David A. Russell
6th Maine
49th Pennsylvania
119th Pennsylvania
5th Wisconsin

2ND DIVISION
Brigadier General George W. Getty

1st Brigade
Brigadier General Frank Wheaton
62nd New York
93rd Pennsylvania
98th Pennsylvania
102nd Pennsylvania
139th Pennsylvania

2nd Brigade
Colonel Lewis A. Grant
2nd Vermont
3rd Vermont
4th Vermont
5th Vermont
6th Vermont

3rd Brigade
Brigadier General Thomas H. Neill
7th Maine
43rd New York
49th New York
77th New York
61st Pennsylvania

3RD DIVISION
Brigadier General James B. Ricketts

1st Brigade
Brigadier General William H. Morris
14th New Jersey
106th New York
151st New York
87th Pennsylvania
10th Vermont

2nd Brigade
Brigadier General Truman Seymour
6th Maryland
110th Ohio
122nd Ohio
126th Ohio
67th Pennsylvania
138th Pennsylvania

Artillery Brigade
Colonel Charles H. Tompkins
4th Maine, Battery D
1st Massachusetts, Battery A
1st New York, Independent Battery
3rd New York, Independent Battery
4th New York Heavy, 1st battalion
1st Rhode Island, Battery C
1st Rhode Island, Battery E
1st Rhode Island, Battery G
5th U.S., Battery M

4th Brigade
Brigadier General Alexander Shaler
65th New York
67th New York
122nd New York
82nd Pennsylvania

4th Brigade
Brigadier General Henry L. Eustis
7th Massachusetts
10th Massachusetts
37th Massachusetts
2nd Rhode Island

CAVALRY CORPS
Major General Philip H. Sheridan
6th U.S.

1ST DIVISION
Brigadier General Alfred T. A. Torbert

1st Brigade
Brigadier General George A. Custer
1st Michigan
5th Michigan
6th Michigan
7th Michigan

2nd Brigade
Colonel Thomas C. Devin
4th New York
6th New York
9th New York
17th Pennsylvania

Reserve Brigade
Brigadier General Wesley Merritt
19th New York
6th Pennsylvania
1st U.S.
2nd U.S.
5th U.S.

2ND DIVISION
Brigadier General David McM. Gregg

1st Brigade
Brigadier General Henry E. Davies, Jr.
1st Massachusetts
1st New Jersey
6th Ohio
1st Pennsylvania

2nd Brigade
Colonel J. Irvin Gregg
1st Maine
10th New York
2nd Pennsylvania
4th Pennsylvania
8th Pennsylvania
16th Pennsylvania

3RD DIVISION
Brigadier General James H. Wilson

1st Brigade
Colonel John B. McIntosh
1st Connecticut
2nd New York
5th New York
18th Pennsylvania

2nd Brigade
Colonel George H. Chapman
3rd Indiana
8th New York
1st Vermont

9TH ARMY CORPS
Major General Ambrose E. Burnside

1ST DIVISION
Brigadier General Thomas G. Stevenson

1st Brigade
Colonel Sumner Carruth
35th Massachusetts
56th Massachusetts
57th Massachusetts
59th Massachusetts
4th U.S.
10th U.S.

2nd Brigade
Colonel Daniel Leasure
3rd Maryland
21st Massachusetts
100th Pennsylvania

Artillery
2nd Maine Battery (B)
14th Massachusetts Battery

2ND DIVISION
Brigadier General Robert B. Potter

1st Brigade
Colonel Zenas R. Bliss
36th Massachusetts
38th Massachusetts
51st New York
45th Pennsylvania
48th Pennsylvania
7th Rhode Island

2nd Brigade
Colonel Simon G. Griffin
31st Maine
32nd Maine
6th New Hampshire
9th New Hampshire
11th New Hampshire
17th Vermont

Artillery
11th Massachusetts Battery
19th New York Battery

3RD DIVISION
Brigadier General Orlando B. Willcox

1st Brigade
Colonel John F. Hartranft
2nd Michigan
8th Michigan
17th Michigan
27th Michigan
109th New York
51st Pennsylvania

2nd Brigade
Colonel Benjamin C. Christ
1st Michigan Sharpshooters
20th Michigan
79th New York
60th Ohio
50th Pennsylvania

Artillery
7th Maine, Battery G
34th New York Battery

4TH DIVISION
Brigadier General Edward Ferrero

1st Brigade
Colonel Joshua K. Sigfried
27th U.S. Colored Troops
30th U.S. Colored Troops
39th U.S. Colored Troops
43rd U.S. Colored Troops

2nd Brigade
Colonel Henry G. Thomas
30th Connecticut (Colored)
19th U.S. Colored Troops
23rd U.S. Colored Troops

Artillery
Pennsylvania Independent Battery D
3rd Vermont Battery

Cavalry
3rd New Jersey
22nd New York
2nd Ohio

Artillery Reserve
Captain John Edwards, Jr.
27th New York Battery
1st Rhode Island, Battery D
1st Rhode Island, Battery H
2nd U.S., Battery E
3rd U.S., Battery G
3rd U.S., Batteries L and M

Provisional Brigade
Colonel Elisha G. Marshall
14th New York Heavy Artillery
24th New York Cavalry (Dismounted)
2nd Pennsylvania Provisional Heavy
  Artillery

ARMY OF NORTHERN VIRGINIA
General Robert E. Lee

1ST ARMY CORPS
Lieutenant General James Longstreet

FIELD'S DIVISION
Major General Charles W. Field

Jenkins' Brigade
Brigadier General Micah Jenkins
1st South Carolina
2d South Carolina (Rifles)
5th South Carolina
6th South Carolina
Palmetto Sharpshooters

Gregg's Brigade
Brigadier General John Gregg
3rd Arkansas
1st Texas
4th Texas
5th Texas

Law's Brigade
Colonel William F. Perry
4th Alabama
15th Alabama
44th Alabama
47th Alabama
48th Alabama

KERSHAW'S DIVISION
Brigadier General Joseph B. Kershaw

Kershaw's Brigade
Colonel John W. Henagan
2nd South Carolina
3rd South Carolina
7th South Carolina
8th South Carolina
15th South Carolina
3rd South Carolina battalion

Humphreys' Brigade
Brigadier General Benjamin G. Humphreys
13th Mississippi
17th Mississippi
18th Mississippi
21st Mississippi

Wofford's Brigade
Brigadier General William T. Wofford
16th Georgia
18th Georgia
24th Georgia
Cobb's (Georgia) Legion
Phillip's (Georgia) Legion
3rd Georgia Battalion Sharpshooters

ARTILLERY
Brigadier General E. Porter Alexander

Haskell's Battalion
Major John C. Haskell
Flanner's (North Carolina) Battery
Garden's (South Carolina) Battery
Lamkin's (Virginia) Battery
Ramsay's (North Carolina) Battery

Huger's Battalion
Lieutenant Colonel Frank Huger
Fickling's (South Carolina) Battery
Moody's (Louisiana) Battery
Parker's (Virginia) Battery
Smith's (Virginia) Battery
Taylor's (Virginia) Battery
Woolfolk's (Virginia) Battery

Cabell's Battalion
Colonel Henry C. Cabell
Callaway's (Georgia) Battery
Carlton's (Georgia) Battery
McCarthy's (Virginia) Battery
Manly's (North Carolina) Battery

Bryan's Brigade
Brigadier General Goode Bryan
10th Georgia
50th Georgia
51st Georgia
53rd Georgia

Anderson's Brigade
Brigadier General George T. Anderson
7th Georgia
8th Georgia
9th Georgia
11th Georgia
59th Georgia

Benning's Brigade
Brigadier General Henry C. Benning
2nd Georgia
15th Georgia
17th Georgia
20th Georgia

2ND ARMY CORPS
Lieutenant General Richard S. Ewell

EARLY'S DIVISION
Major General Jubal A. Early

Pegram's Brigade
Brigadier General John Pegram
13th Virginia
31st Virginia
49th Virginia
52nd Virginia
58th Virginia

Johnston's Brigade
Brigadier General Robert D. Johnston
5th North Carolina
12th North Carolina
20th North Carolina
23rd North Carolina

Gordon's Brigade
Brigadier General John B. Gordon
13th Georgia
26th Georgia
31st Georgia
38th Georgia
60th Georgia
61st Georgia

JOHNSON'S DIVISION
Major General Edward Johnson

Stonewall Brigade
Brigadier General James A. Walker
2nd Virginia
4th Virginia
5th Virginia
27th Virginia
33rd Virginia

Jones's Brigade
Brigadier General John M. Jones
21st Virginia
25th Virginia
42nd Virginia
44th Virginia
48th Virginia
50th Virginia

Steuart's Brigade
Brigadier General George H. Steuart
1st North Carolina
3rd North Carolina
10th Virginia
23rd Virginia
37th Virginia

RODES'S DIVISION
Major General Robert E. Rodes

Daniel's Brigade
Brigadier General Junius Daniel
32nd North Carolina
43rd North Carolina
45th North Carolina
53rd North Carolina
2nd North Carolina battalion

Ramseur's Brigade
Brigadier General Stephen D. Ramseur
2nd North Carolina
4th North Carolina
14th North Carolina
30th North Carolina

Battle's Brigade
Brigadier General Cullen A. Battle
3rd Alabama
5th Alabama
6th Alabama
12th Alabama
26th Alabama

ARTILLERY
Brigadier General Armistead L. Long

Braxton's Battalion
Lieutenant Colonel Carter M. Braxton
Carpenter's (Virginia) Battery
Cooper's (Virginia) Battery
Hardwicke's (Virginia) Battery

Nelson's Battalion
Lieutenant Colonel William Nelson
Kirkpatrick's (Virginia) Battery
Massie's (Virginia) Battery
Milledge's (Georgia) Battery

Page's Battalion
Major Richard C. M. Page
W. P. Carter's (Virginia) Battery
Fry's (Virginia) Battery
Page's (Virginia) Battery
Reese's (Alabama) Battery

Cutshaw's Battalion
Major Wilfred E. Cutshaw
Carrington's (Virginia) Battery
A. W. Garber's (Virginia) Battery
Tanner's (Virginia) Battery

Hays's Brigade
Brigadier General Harry T. Hays
5th Louisiana
6th Louisiana
7th Louisiana
8th Louisiana
9th Louisiana

Stafford's Brigade
Brigadier General Leroy A. Stafford
1st Louisiana
2nd Louisiana
10th Louisiana
14th Louisiana
15th Louisiana

Doles's Brigade
Brigadier General George Doles
4th Georgia
12th Georgia
44th Georgia

Hardaway's Battalion
Lieutenant Colonel Robert A. Hardaway
Dance's (Virginia) Battery
Graham's (Virginia) Battery
C. B. Griffin's (Virginia) Battery
Jones's (Virginia) Battery
B. H. Smith's (Virginia) Battery

3RD ARMY CORPS
Lieutenant General Ambrose P. Hill

ANDERSON'S DIVISION
Brigadier General Richard H. Anderson

Perrin's Brigade
Brigadier General Abner Perrin
8th Alabama
9th Alabama
10th Alabama
11th Alabama
14th Alabama

Mahone's Brigade
Brigadier General William Mahone
6th Virginia
12th Virginia
16th Virginia
41st Virginia
61st Virginia

Harris' Brigade
Brigadier General Nathaniel H. Harris
12th Mississippi
16th Mississippi
19th Mississippi
48th Mississippi

HETH'S DIVISION
Major General Henry Heth

Davis' Brigade
Colonel John M. Stone
2nd Mississippi
11th Mississippi
42nd Mississippi
55th North Carolina

Cooke's Brigade
Brigadier General John R. Cooke
15th North Carolina
27th North Carolina
46th North Carolina
48th North Carolina

Walker's Brigade[a]
Brigadier General Henry H. Walker
40th Virginia
47th Virginia
55th Virginia
22nd Virginia
13th Alabama
1st Tennessee (Provisional)
7th Tennessee
14th Tennessee

WILCOX' DIVISION
Major General Cadmus M. Wilcox

Lane's Brigade
Brigadier General James H. Lane
7th North Carolina
18th North Carolina
28th North Carolina
33rd North Carolina
37th North Carolina

McGowan's Brigade
Brigadier General Samuel McGowan
1st South Carolina (Provisional)
12th South Carolina
13th South Carolina
14th South Carolina
1st South Carolina (Orr's Rifles)

Scales's Brigade
Brigadier General Alfred M. Scales
13th North Carolina
16th North Carolina
22nd North Carolina
34th North Carolina
38th North Carolina

ARTILLERY
Colonel R. Lindsay Walker

Poague's Battalion
Lieutenant Colonel William T. Poague
Richard's (Mississippi) Battery
Utterback's (Virginia) Battery
Williams' (North Carolina) Battery
Wyatt's (Virginia) Battery

Pegram's Battalion
Lieutenant Colonel William J. Pegram
Brander's (Virginia) Battery
Cayce's (Virginia) Battery
Ellett's (Virginia) Battery
Marye's (Virginia) Battery
Zimmerman's (South Carolina) Battery

McIntosh's Battalion
Lieutenant Colonel David G. McIntosh
Clutter's (Virginia) Battery
Donald's (Virginia) Battery
Hurt's (Alabama) Battery
Price's (Virginia) Battery

Perry's Brigade
Brigadier General Edward A. Perry
2nd Florida
5th Florida
8th Florida

Wright's Brigade
Brigadier General Ambrose R. Wright
3rd Georgia
22nd Georgia
48th Georgia
2nd Georgia Battalion

Kirkland's Brigade
Brigadier General William W. Kirkland
11th North Carolina
26th North Carolina
44th North Carolina
47th North Carolina
52nd North Carolina

Thomas' Brigade
Brigadier General Edward L. Thomas
14th Georgia
35th Georgia
45th Georgia
49th Georgia

Richardson's Battalion
Lieutenant Colonel Charles Richardson
Grandy's (Virginia) Battery
Landry's (Louisiana) Battery
Moore's (Virginia) Battery
Penick's (Virginia) Battery

Cutts's Battalion
Colonel Allen S. Cutts
Patterson's (Georgia) Battery
Ross's (Georgia) Battery
Wingfield's (Georgia) Battery

CAVALRY CORPS
Major General James E. B. Stuart

HAMPTON'S DIVISION
Major General Wade Hampton

Young's Brigade
Brigadier General Pierce M. B. Young
7th Georgia
Cobb's (Georgia) Legion
Phillips' (Georgia) Legion
20th Georgia Battalion
Jeff Davis (Mississippi) Legion

Butler's Brigade
Brigadier General Matthew C. Butler
4th South Carolina
5th South Carolina
6th South Carolina

Rosser's Brigade
Brigadier General Thomas L. Rosser
7th Virginia
11th Virginia
12th Virginia
35th Virginia Battalion

FITZHUGH LEE'S DIVISION
Major General Fitzhugh Lee

Lomax' Brigade
Brigadier General Lunsford L. Lomax
5th Virginia
6th Virginia
15th Virginia

Wickham's Brigade
Brigadier General Williams C. Wickham
1st Virginia
2nd Virginia
3rd Virginia
4th Virginia

WILLIAM H. F. LEE'S DIVISION
Major General William H. F. Lee

Chambliss' Brigade
Brigadier General John R. Chambliss
9th Virginia
10th Virginia
13th Virginia

Gordon's Brigade
Brigadier General James B. Gordon
1st North Carolina
2nd North Carolina
5th North Carolina

HORSE ARTILLERY
Major R. Preston Chew

Breathed's Battalion
Major James Breathed
Hart's (South Carolina) Battery
Johnston's (Virginia) Battery
McGregor's (Virginia) Battery
Shoemaker's (Virginia) Battery
Thomson's (Virginia) Battery

Bibliography

MANUSCRIPTS

Alabama Department of Archives and History, Montgomery

John B. Crawford Collection.
Regimental Collection.
    Battle, Cullen. "The Third Alabama Regiment."
    Burton, J. Q. "Forty Seven Regiment Alabama Volunteers, C.S.A."
    Coles, Robert T. "History of the Fourth Alabama Regiment."
    Thompson, J. M. "Reminiscences of the Autauga Rifles."

Alderman Library, University of Virginia

Eugene N. Cox Diary.
John W. Daniel Collection.
    Robert D. Johnston's Report.
    Moore, Samuel J. Letter.
    Stribling, John. Letter.
    Taliaferro, Catlett C. Letter.
Thomas L. Rosser Papers.

Special Collections, Auburn University Libraries

James H. Lane Collection.
    Cox, William. "A Sketch of General James H. Lane."
    James H. Lane's Report.
    Report of 7th North Carolina.
    Report of 18th North Carolina.
    Report of 28th North Carolina.
    Report of 37th North Carolina.
J. B. Stamp Papers.

Bentley Historical Library, University of Michigan

Byron M. Cutcheon Papers.
Mollus Collection.
   Hopper, George. "Reminiscences."
   Rowe, James. "Reminiscences."
   William H. Randall Papers.

Boston Public Library

Whittier, Charles A. "Reminiscences."

Eleanor S. Brockenbrough Library, Museum of the Confederacy, Richmond

Henry Heth's Report.
Fitzhugh Lee's Report.
G. Moxley Sorrel Diary.

William L. Clements Library, University of Michigan

Bunker, Nathaniel W. "War Record."
James Schoff Collection.
   William Seymour Journal.
Nathan B. Webb Papers.

Manuscript Department, Eastern Carolina University Libraries

Francis W. Knowles Diary.
Scales, Alfred. Letters.

Eggleston Library, Hamden-Sydney College

William R. Carter Diary.

Fredericksburg and Spotsylvania National Military Park Library

Aycock, B. L. "A Sketch: The Lone Star Guards."
Baumgardner, James, Jr. "The Fifty-Second Virginia."
Brewster, Sayre Daniel. Letter.
Cooper, Isaac. Letters.
Crawford, David. Letters.
"Greenfield."
Handy, Daniel A. Letters.
McDonnell, John Daniel. "Recollections of the War."
Martin, Thomas Alfred. "Autobiography."
Alexander Pattison Diary.

George H. Sheffield Diary.
W. P. Snakenberg Memoirs.
Snyder, Thompson A. "Recollections of Four Years with the Union Cavalry."
S. W. Winfield Diary.

University of Georgia Libraries

Gordon Family Papers.
George W. Hall Diary.

Georgia Department of Archives and History, Atlanta

Charles Baldwin Diary.
Joseph P. Fuller Diary.
George Hopkins Reminiscences.
Wilder, Benjamin F. Letter.

Historical Society of Pennsylvania, Philadelphia

E. C. Gardiner Collection.
  Henry Carey Baird Papers.
Andrew A. Humphreys Papers.
George G. Meade Collection.
  Biddle, James C. Letters.
John L. Smith Papers.

Houghton Library, Harvard University

MOLLUS Collection.
  J. G. Wiggin Diary.
  Robins, Edward B. Letters.

Illinois State Historical Library, Springfield

Edwards, Oliver. "Memorandum."

Manuscript Division, Library of Congress

William E. Brooks Collection.
  Alexander Boteler Diary.
Joshua Chamberlain Collection.
  Joseph Hayes Journal.
Cyrus B. Comstock Diary.
Harold G. George Memoir.
Jedediah Hotchkiss Collection.
  Thomas S. Doyle Memoir.

Henry J. Hunt Journal.
Otis, Elwell S. Letter.
Cadmus M. Wilcox Papers.

Manassas National Battlefield Park Library

James Ricketts Collection.
  James M. Reed Diary.

Massachusetts Historical Society, Boston

Andrew R. Linscott Papers.
Theodore Lyman Papers.

Mississippi Department of Archives and History, Jackson

W. M. Abernathy Collection.
Crawford, John Berryman. Letters.
McWillie Family Papers.
  William McWillie Notebook and Diary.
B. L. Wynn Papers.

Mugar Library, Boston University

Military Historical Society of Massachusetts Collection.
  Mahone, William. Letter.

New York Historical Society, New York.

Alexander Shaler Diary.

New York State Archives, Albany

Albert N. Ames Diary.
Braman, Charles W. Letters.
Uberto A. Burnham Papers.
Charles Hamlin Papers.
Gouverneur Kemble Warren Collection.
  5th Corps Letterbook.
  Washington A. Roebling's Report.

North Carolina Department of Archives and History, Raleigh

H. C. Albright Collection.
J. W. Bone Papers.
J. B. Clifton Diary.

Samuel Finley Harper Collection.
George W. Pearsall Collection.

William R. Perkins Library, Duke University

Samuel Bradbury Collection.
John W. Daniel Collection.
   Smith, William. Letter.
   Jones, Thomas. Letters.
Dudley, C. R. "What I Know About the Wilderness."
Winfield Scott Hancock Collection.
Haskell, John. "Memoirs of Lieut. Col. John Haskell."
James Longstreet Papers.
Thomas Munford Collection.
   Ferguson, J. D. "Memoranda and Itinerary of Operations of Major General Fitz
   Lee's Cavalry Division."

Rundel Library, Rochester, N.Y.

Porter Farley Papers.

Special Collections and Archives, Rutgers University Libraries

Washington A. Roebling Collection.

Southern Historical Collection, University of North Carolina

Edward P. Alexander Collection.
William Allen Papers.
George Bernard Collection.
Berry G. Benson Papers.
J. F. H. Claiborne Papers.
   Humphreys, Benjamin. "Sunflower Guards."
J. B. Clifton Papers.
Nathaniel Harris Papers.
James Longstreet Papers.
David Gregg McIntosh Papers.
William Pendleton Collection.
Anne Linebarger Snuggs Papers.
Westwood A. Todd Papers.
Samuel H. Walkup Papers.
Joseph F. Waring Papers.

Tennessee State Library and Archives, Nashville

Brown-Ewell Papers.
   Order Book.

Ewell-Stewert-Brown Collection.
  Brown, Campbell. "Memorandum—Campaign of 1864."
  Ewell Letterbook.

United States Army Military History Institute, Carlisle, Pa.

Zenas R. Bliss Collection.
Civil War Miscellaneous Collection.
  Alfred Apted Diary.
  Timothy Bateman Diary.
  Henry C. Campbell Memoir.
  Charles Chapin Diary.
  Grayson Eichelberer Memoir.
  Joseph P. Elliott Diary.
  Luther C. Furst Diary.
  David Herman Diary.
  Burgess E. Ingersoll Diary.
  Kent, William C. Letter.
  Oberlin, William Penn. Letter.
  James O'Connell Memoir.
  Sawtelle, Levander. Letter.
  Horatio Soule Diary.
  Charles E. Wood Diary.
  Arthur Wyman Diary.
Civil War Times Illustrated Collection.
  Gardner, Charles. "My Experience in the First Maine Cavalry."
  Harshberger, A. Notes.
  Jacob Heflinger Diary.
  Kent, William C. Letter.
  Charles C. Perkis Memoir.
  Petit, Frederick. Letters.
  Isaac H. Ressler Diary.
  Ross, D. Reid. "Brigadier General Alexander Hays' Brigade at the Battle of the
    Wilderness, May 5, 1864."
  Charles D. Todd Diary.
Avery Harris Collection.
Harrisburg Civil War Round Table Collection.
  Charles H. Edgerly Diary.
  Henry Keiser Diary.
  Henry Harrison Stone Pocket Diary.
Lewis Leigh Collection.
  "Biographical Information on Mahone."
  Robert P. Chew's Report.
  Howard, Francis Marion. Letters.
  Pollard, Charles E. Letters.
  Runzer, John L. Letter.

Webb, John G. Letters.
Ralph G. Poriss Collection.
Henry T. Waltz Diary.
Louis Rosenberger Collection.
Justin Turner Collection.

Virginia Historical Society, Richmond

C. Thomas Davis Diary.
Scott, Alfred L. "Memoirs of Service in the Confederate Army."
James E. Phillips Journal.
Osmun Latrobe Papers.
Buckner M. Randolph Diary.
Erasmus Taylor Papers.
William E. Trahern Papers.

Virginia State Library, Richmond

Joseph McMurran Diary.
William Mahone Collection.
    Nathaniel Harris' Report.
John F. Sale Diary.
Byrd C. Willis Diary.
James Wood Papers.

Robert W. Woodruff Library, Emory University

John Bratton Collection.
Noble John Brooke Collection.
Robert F. Davis Diary.
Robert Newman Gourdin Collection.
    Young, Lewis. Letters.
Benjamin W. Justice Papers.

Newspapers

Atlanta *Journal,* August 17, September 7, 1901.
Atlanta *Southern Confederacy,* June 15, 1864.
Daily South Carolinian, May 8, 10, 1864.
Macon (Ga.) *Telegraph,* June 1, 1864.
Montgomery (Ala.) *Daily Advertiser,* May 28, 1864.
Philadelphia *Weekly Times,* January 26, 1878.
Richmond *Examiner,* May 18, 1864.
Richmond *Sentinel,* May 24, 1864.
Rochester (N.Y.) *Democrat and American,* July 23, 1864.

OFFICIAL COMPILATIONS

Harrison, Noel G. *Gazetteer of Historic Sites Related to the Fredericksburg and Spotsylvania National Military Park*. 2 vols. Fredericksburg and Spotsylvania National Military Park, 1986.

Names of Officers and Soldiers Found on the Battle-Fields of the Wilderness and of Spottsylvania Court House, Va. Washington, D.C., 1865.

War of the Rebellion: A Compilation of the Official Records of the Union and Confederate Armies. 130 vols. Washington, D.C., 1880–1901.

BIOGRAPHIES, MEMOIRS, AND PERSONAL NARRATIVES

Abbott, Lemuel A. *Personal Recollections and Civil War Diary, 1864*. Burlington, Vt., 1908.

Adams, Z. Boylston. "In the Wilderness." In *Civil War Papers*, II, 373–99. 2 vols. Boston, 1900.

Agassiz, George R., ed. *Meade's Headquarters, 1863–1865: Letters of Colonel Theodore Lyman from the Wilderness to Appomattox*. Boston, 1922.

Alexander, Edward P. *Military Memoirs of a Confederate*. New York, 1907.

Allen, Stanton P. *Down in Dixie: Life in a Cavalry Regiment in the War Days, from the Wilderness to Appomattox*. Boston, 1888.

Aschmann, Rudolph. *Memoirs of a Swiss Officer in the American Civil War*. Edited by Heintz K. Meir. Bern, 1972.

Bean, William G. *Stonewall's Man: Sandie Pendleton*. Chapel Hill, N.C., 1959.

Bernard, George, comp. *War Talks of Confederate Veterans*. Petersburg, Va., 1892.

Blackford, Susan Leigh, comp. *Letters from Lee's Army; or, Memoirs of Life in and out of the Army in Virginia During the War Between the States*. New York, 1947.

Blackford, William W. *War Years with Jeb Stuart*. New York, 1945.

Bond, Natalie J., and Osmun L. Coward, eds. *The South Carolinians: Colonel Asbury Coward's Memoirs*. New York, 1968.

Boyd, David French. *Reminiscences of the War in Virginia*. Edited by T. Michael Parrish. Austin, Tex., 1989.

Bradwell, Isaac G. "Battle of the Wilderness." *Confederate Veteran*, XVI (1908), 447–48.

———. "One Hour Saved the Union." *Confederate Veteran*, XXXIV (1926), 252–53.

———. "Second Day's Battle of the Wilderness." *Confederate Veteran*, XXVIII (1920), 20–22.

Brooks, Noah. *Mr. Lincoln's Washington*. New York, 1896.

Buck, Samuel D. *With the Old Confeds: Actual Experiences of a Captain in the Line*. Baltimore, 1925.

Buel, Clarence C., and Robert U. Johnson, eds. *Battles and Leaders of the Civil War*. 4 vols. New York, 1884–88.

Buell, Augustus. *The Cannoneer*. Washington, D. C., 1890.

Cadwallader, Sylvanus. *Three Years with Grant*. New York, 1961.

"Captain Murray F. Taylor." *Confederate Veteran*, XVIII (1910), 82–83.

Carter, Robert G. *Four Brothers in Blue; or, Sunshine and Shadows of War of the Rebellion: A Story of the Great Civil War from Bull Run to Appomattox*. Washington, D.C., 1913.

Chesnut, Mary B. *A Diary from Dixie*. New York, 1905.

Cockrell, Monroe, ed. *Gunner with Stonewall: Reminiscences of William Thomas Poague, Lieutenant, Captain, Major, and Lieutenant Colonel of Artillery, Army of Northern Virginia, C.S.A.: A Memoir Written for His Children in 1903*. Jackson, Tenn., 1957.

Coco, Gregory A., ed. *Through Blood and Fire: The Civil War Letters of Major Charles J. Mills*. Lanham, Md., 1982.

Coxe, John. "Last Struggles and Successes of Lee." *Confederate Veteran*, XXII (1914), 356–59.

Crotty, D. G. *Four Years' Campaigning in the Army of the Potomac*. Grand Rapids, 1874.

Culpeper Historical Society. *Historic Culpeper*. Culpeper, Va., 1974.

Dame, William M. *From the Rapidan to Richmond and the Spottsylvania Campaign*. Baltimore, 1920.

Dana, Charles A. *Recollections of the Civil War*. New York, 1899.

Dawson, Francis W. *Reminiscences of Confederate Service*. Edited by Bell Wiley. Baton Rouge, 1980.

Dobbins, Austin C., ed. *Grandfather's Journal: Company B, Sixteenth Mississippi Infantry Volunteers, Harris' Brigade, Mahone's Division, Hill's Corps, A.N.V.* Dayton, 1988.

Douglas, Henry K. *I Rode with Stonewall*. Chapel Hill, N.C., 1940.

Dowdey, Clifford, and Louis H. Manarin, eds. *The Wartime Papers of R. E. Lee*. New York, 1961.

Durkin, Joseph, ed. *Confederate Chaplin: A War Journal of Rev. James B. Sheeran, C.S.S.R., 14th Louisiana, C.S.A.* Milwaukee, 1960.

Early, Jubal A. *Lieutenant-General Jubal A. Early, C.S.A.: Autobiographical Sketch and Narrative of the War Between the States*. Philadelphia, 1912.

Farley, Porter. "Reminiscences of the 140th Regiment New York Volunteer Infantry." In *Rochester Historical Society Publication*, XXII, 199–263.

Field, Charles W. "Campaign of 1864 and 1865." In *SHSP*, XIV, 542–63.

Fleming, Francis P., ed. *Memoir of Captain C. Seton Fleming, of the Second Florida Infantry, C.S.A.* Jacksonville, Fla., 1884.

Fleming, George T., ed. *Life and Letters of Alexander Hays*. Pittsburgh, 1919.

Ford, Worthington Chauncey, ed. *A Cycle of Adams Letters, 1861–1865*. 2 vols. Boston, 1920.

Freeman, Douglas Southall. *R. E. Lee: A Biography*. 4 vols. New York, 1935.

———, ed. *Lee's Dispatches to Jefferson Davis*. New York, 1957.

Fulton, William Frierson, II. *The War Reminiscences of William Frierson Fulton II*. Gaithersburg, Md., 1986.

Gallagher, Gary W., ed. *Fighting for the Confederacy: The Personal Recollections of General Edward Porter Alexander*. Chapel Hill, N.C., 1989.

Galwey, Thomas F. *The Valiant Hours: An Irishman in the Civil War.* Harrisburg, Pa., 1961.

Garber, A. W. "Artillery Work at Wilderness." In *SHSP,* XXXIII, 341–43.

Gardner, Alexander. *Gardner's Photographic Sketchbook of the Civil War.* 2 vols. Washington, D.C., 1866.

Gerrish, Theodore. *Army Life: A Private's Reminiscences of the Civil War.* Portland, Maine, 1882.

Gerrish, Theodore, and John Hutchinson. *The Blue and the Gray.* Portland, Maine, 1883.

Gibbon, John. *Personal Recollections of the Civil War.* New York, 1928.

Gordon, John B. *Reminiscences of the Civil War.* New York, 1903.

Goss, Warren Lee. *Recollections of a Private: A Story of the Army of the Potomac.* New York, 1890.

Govan, Gilbert E., and James W. Livingood, eds. *The Haskell Memoirs: John Cheves Haskell.* New York, 1960.

Grant, Ulysses S. *The Personal Memoirs of U. S. Grant.* 2 vols. New York, 1885.

———. "Preparing for the Campaigns of '64." In *B&L,* IV, 97–117.

Green, William H. "From the Wilderness to Spotsylvania." *Papers Read Before the Commandery of the State of Maine, Military Order of the Loyal Legion of the United States.* Vol. II of 3 vols. Portland, Maine, 1902.

Hamlin, Percy G. *The Making of a Soldier: Letters of R. S. Ewell.* Richmond, 1935.

———. *Old Bald Head.* Strasburg, Va., 1940.

Hancock, Almira R. *Reminiscences of Winfield Scott Hancock.* New York, 1887.

Harris, James S. *Historical Sketches: 7th North Carolina Regiment.* Ann Arbor, Mich., 1978.

Harris, W. H. "Report of General Harris Concerning an Incident of the Wilderness." In *SHSP,* VII, 131.

Heater, Jacob. "Battle of the Wilderness." *Confederate Veteran,* XIV (1906), 262–64.

Holmes, Oliver Wendell, Jr. *Touched with Fire: Civil War Letters and Diary of Oliver Wendell Holmes, Jr., 1861–1864.* Cambridge, Mass., 1946.

Hood, John B. *Advance and Retreat: Personal Experiences in the United States and Confederate States Armies.* New Orleans, 1880.

Hotchkiss, Jedediah. "Virginia." In *Confederate Military History,* ed. Clement Evans. Atlanta, 1899.

Howard, McHenry. *Recollections of a Maryland Confederate Soldier and Staff Officer Under Johnston, Jackson, and Lee.* Baltimore, 1914.

Huffman, James. *Ups and Downs of a Confederate Soldier.* New York, 1940.

Hughes, Nathaniel, ed. *Liddell's Record.* Dayton, 1985.

Humphreys, Henry H. *Andrew Atkinson Humphreys: A Biography.* Philadelphia, 1924.

Hyde, Thomas W. *Following the Greek Cross; or, Memories of the Sixth Army Corps.* Boston, 1894.

In Memoriam: James Samuel Wadsworth, 1807–1864. Albany, N.Y., 1916.

Isham, Asa. "Through the Wilderness to Richmond." In *Sketches of War History, 1861–1865: Papers Read Before the Ohio Commandery of the Military Order of the Loyal Legion of the United States,* I, 199–217. 2 vols. Cincinnati, 1888.

Jordan, David M. *Winfield Scott Hancock: A Soldier's Life.* Bloomington, Ind., 1988.

Keifer, Joseph Warren. *Slavery and Four Years of War.* 2 vols. New York, 1900.

Kellogg, John. "Capture and Escape: A Narrative of Army and Prison Life." In *Wisconsin Historical Commission, Original Papers No. 2.* N.p., 1908.

Kent, Arthur A., ed. *Three Years with Company K: Sergeant Austin C. Stearns, Company K, 13th Massachusetts Infantry.* Rutherford, N.J., 1976.

Kidd, James H. *Personal Recollections of a Cavalryman with Custer's Michigan Cavalry Brigade in the Civil War.* Ionia, Mich., 1908.

King, C. W., and W. R. Derby, eds. *Campfire Sketches and Battle-Field Echoes,* Springfield, Mass., 1899.

King, Horatio C. "Brevet Major-General James S. Wadsworth." In *In Memoriam: James Samuel Wadsworth, 1807–1864.* Albany, N.Y., 1916.

Law, Evander M. "From the Wilderness to Cold Harbor." In *B&L,* IV, 118–44.

Lee, Fitzhugh. "A Review of the First Two Days' Operations at Gettysburg and a Reply to General Longstreet." In *SHSP,* V, 162–94.

Long, Armistead. *Memoirs of Robert E. Lee.* New York, 1886.

Longstreet, James. *From Manassas to Appomattox: Memoirs of the Civil War in America.* Philadelphia, 1896.

Lyman, Theodore. "Addenda to the Paper by Brevet Lieutenant-Colonel W. W. Swan, U.S.A., on the Battle of the Wilderness." In *PMHSM,* IV, 165–73.

———. "Uselessness of the Maps Furnished to Staff of the Army of the Potomac Previous to the Campaign of May, 1864." In *PMHSM,* IV, 77–80.

McClellan, Henry B. "The Wilderness Fight: Why General Lee's Expectations of Longstreet Were Not Realized." Philadelphia *Weekly Times,* January 26, 1878.

McDonald, Archie P., ed. *Make Me a Map of the Valley: The Civil War Journal of Stonewall Jackson's Topographer.* Dallas, 1973.

McKim, Randolph H. *A Soldier's Recollections.* New York, 1910.

McMahon, Martin T. "From Gettysburg to the Coming of Grant." In *B&L,* IV, 81–94.

Marvel, William. *Burnside.* Chapel Hill, N.C., 1991.

Mason, Edwin C. "Through the Wilderness to the Bloody Angle at Spottsylvania Court House." In *Glimpse of the Nation's Struggle: Papers Read Before the Commandery of the State of Minnesota, Military Order of the Loyal Legion of the United States,* 291–312. St. Paul, 1898.

Massachusetts Historical Society. *War Diary and Letters of Stephen Minot Weld.* Boston, 1979.

Meade, George, ed. *The Life and Letters of George Gordon Meade, Major General, United States Army.* 2 vols. New York, 1913.

Melcher, Holman S. "An Experience in the Battle of the Wilderness." In *War Papers Read Before the Commandery of the State of Maine, Military Order of the Loyal Legion of the United States,* I, 73–84. 3 vols. Portland, Maine, 1898.

Menge, W. Springer, and J. August Shimrak, eds. *The Civil War Notebook of Daniel Chisolm.* New York, 1989.

Mixson, Frank M. *Reminiscences of a Private.* Columbia, S.C., 1910.

Moffett, Mary C., ed. *Letters of General James Conner, C.S.A.* Columbia, S.C., 1933.

Monteith, Robert. "Battle of the Wilderness, and Death of General Wadsworth." In *War Papers Read Before The Commandery of the State of Wisconsin, Military Order of the Loyal Legion of the United States*, I, 410–15. 2 vols. Milwaukee, 1891.

Morrison, James L., Jr., ed. *The Memoirs of Henry Heth*. Westport, Conn., 1974.

Morse, F. W. *Personal Experiences in the War of the Great Rebellion, from December, 1862, to July, 1865*. Albany, N.Y., 1866.

Neese, George. *Three Years in the Confederate Horse Artillery*. New York, 1911.

Nevins, Allan, ed. *Diary of Battle: The Personal Journals of Colonel Charles S. Wainwright*. New York, 1962.

Nicolay, John G., and John Hay. *Abraham Lincoln: A History*. 10 vols. New York, 1890.

Oates, William C. *The War Between the Union and the Confederacy and Its Lost Opportunities*. New York, 1905.

Page, Charles A. *Letters of a War Correspondent*. Boston, 1899.

Palfrey, Francis W., ed. *Memoir of William Francis Bartlett*. Boston, 1878.

Pearson, Henry Greenleaf. *James S. Wadsworth of Genesco: Brevet Major General of United States Volunteers*. New York, 1913.

Pegram, William W. "Credit to Whom Credit Is Due." *Confederate Veteran*, XXIII (1915), 153.

Perry, William F. "Reminiscences of the Campaign of 1864 in Virginia." In *SHSP*, VII, 49–63.

Peyton, George Q. *A Civil War Record for 1864–1865*. Edited by Robert A. Hodge. Fredericksburg, Va., 1981.

Polley, Joseph B. *Soldier's Letters to Charming Nellie*. New York, 1908.

Pond, George E. "Kilpatrick's and Dahlgren's Raid to Richmond." In *B&L*, IV, 95–96.

Porter, Charles H. "Opening of the Campaign of 1864." In *PMHSM*, IV, 1–24.

Porter, Horace. *Campaigning with Grant*. New York, 1897.

Prentice, Sartell. "The Opening Hours in the Wilderness in 1864." In *Military Essays and Recollections: Papers Read Before the Commandery of the State of Illinois, Military Order of the Loyal Legion of the United States*, II, 99–119. 2 vols. Chicago, 1894.

R.C. "Texans Always Move Them." *The Land We Love*, V, 481–86.

Reese, George. "Sketch for His Family by General George Reese." *Confederate Veteran*, XIV (1906), 110–12.

Rhodes, Robert Hunt, ed. *All for the Union: The Civil War Diary and Letters of Elisha Hunt Rhodes*. New York, 1991.

Robertson, James I. *General A. P. Hill: The Story of a Confederate Warrior*. New York, 1987.

———, ed. *The Civil War Letters of General Robert McAllister*. New Brunswick, N.J., 1965.

Robertson, Robert Stoddart. "From the Wilderness to Spottsylvania." In *Sketches of War History, 1861–1865: Papers Read Before the Ohio Commandery of the Military Order of the Loyal Legion of the United States*, I, 252–92. 2 vols. Cincinnati, 1888.

————. *Personal Recollections of the War.* Milwaukee, 1895.

Rodenbaugh, Theodore F. "Sheridan's Richmond Raid." In *B&L*, IV, 188–94.

Ropes, John C. "Campaign in Virginia in 1864." In *PMHSM*, IV, 363–405.

Rosenblatt, Emil, and Ruth Rosenblatt, eds. *Hard Marching: The Civil War Letters of Private Wilbur Fisk, 1861–1865.* Lawrence, Kans., 1992.

Royall, William L. *Some Reminiscences.* New York, 1909.

Rozier, John, ed. *The Granite Farm Letters: The Civil War Correspondence of Edgeworth and Sallie Bird.* Athens, Ga., 1988.

Schoyer, William, ed. *The Road to Cold Harbor: The Field Diary of William Schoyer.* Apollo, Pa., 1986.

Scott, Robert, ed. *Fallen Leaves: The Civil War Letters of Major Henry Livermore Abbott.* Kent, Ohio, 1991.

Seiser, Charles, ed. "August Seiser's Civil War Diary." In *Rochester Historical Society Publication,* XXII, 174–98.

Sheridan, Philip H. *Personal Memoirs of P. H. Sheridan.* 2 vols. New York, 1888.

Silliker, Ruth L., ed. *The Rebel Yell and Yankee Hurrah: The Civil War Journal of a Maine Volunteer, Private John W. Haley, 17th Maine Regiment.* Camden, Maine, 1985.

Small, Harold, ed. *The Road to Richmond: The Civil War Memoirs of Major Abner R. Small of the Sixteenth Maine Volunteers.* Berkeley, Calif., 1939.

Sorrel, G. Moxley. *Recollections of a Confederate Staff Officer.* New York, 1917.

Sparks, David S., ed. *Inside Lincoln's Army: The Diary of Marsena Rudolph Patrick, Provost Marshal General, Army of the Potomac.* New York, 1964.

Stafford, G. M. G., comp. *General Leroy Augustus Stafford: His Forebears and Descendants.* New Orleans, 1943.

Stevens, George T. *Three Years in the Sixth Corps.* Albany, N.Y., 1866.

Stiles, Robert. *Four Years Under Marse Robert.* New York, 1903.

Swan, William W. "Battle of the Wilderness." In *PMHSM*, IV, 117–63.

Taylor, Richard. *Destruction and Reconstruction: Personal Experiences of the Late War.* New York, 1879.

Taylor, Walter H. *Four Years with General Lee.* Norfolk, Va., 1877.

————. *General Lee: His Campaigns in Virginia, 1861–1865, with Personal Reminiscences.* Norfolk, Va., 1906.

Taylor, Emerson. *Gouverneur Kemble Warren: Life and Letters of an American Soldier.* New York, 1932.

Tyler, Mason Whiting. *Recollections of the Civil War.* New York, 1912.

Venable, Charles S. "The Campaign from the Wilderness to Petersburg." In *SHSP*, XIV, 522–42.

————. "General Lee in the Wilderness Campaign." In *B&L*, IV, 240–46.

von Borcke, Heros. *Memoirs of the Confederate War for Independence.* Philadelphia, 1867.

Walker, C. Irvin. *The Life of Lieutenant General Richard Heron Anderson of the Confederate States Army.* Charleston, S.C., 1917.

Walker, Charles, and Rosemary Walker, eds. "Diary of the War by Robt. S. Robertson." *Old Fort New,* XXVIII (1965), 162.

Walker, Francis A. "General Gibbon in the Second Corps." In *Personal Recollec-*

tions of the War of the Rebellion: Addresses Delivered Before the Commandery of the State of New York, Military Order of the Loyal Legion of the United States, II, 290–315. 4 vols. Portland, Maine, 1898.

———. *General Hancock.* New York, 1895.

Webb, Alexander S. "Through the Wilderness." In *B&L,* IV, 152–69.

Welch, Spencer G. *A Confederate Surgeon's Letters to His Wife.* New York, 1911.

Wilcox, Cadmus. "Lee and Grant in the Wilderness." In *The Annals of the War Written by Leading Participants North and South.* Philadelphia, 1879. Issued by Philadelphia *Weekly Times.*

Wilkeson, Frank. *Recollections of a Private Soldier in the Army of the Potomac.* New York, 1887.

Wilson, James H. *A Life of John A. Rawlins.* New York, 1916.

———. *Under the Old Flag.* 2 vols. New York, 1912.

Winslow, Richard Elliott, III. *General John Sedgwick: The Story of a Union Corps Commander.* Novato, Calif., 1982.

Wynn, B. L. "Lee Watched Grant at Locust Grove." *Confederate Veteran,* XXI (1913), 68.

Unit Histories

Banes, Charles H. *History of the Philadelphia Brigade.* Philadelphia, 1876.

Baquet, Camille. *History of the First Brigade New Jersey Volunteers.* Trenton, 1910.

Beale, R. L. T. *History of the Ninth Virginia Cavalry in the War Between the States.* Richmond, 1899.

Bean, William G. *The Liberty Hall Volunteers: Stonewall's College Boys.* Charlottesville, Va., 1964.

Benedict, George C. *Vermont in the Civil War.* 2 vols. Burlington, Vt., 1886.

Bennett, Brian A. *Sons of Old Monroe: A Regimental History of Patrick O'Rorke's 140th New York Volunteer Infantry.* Dayton, 1992.

Bicknell, George W. *History of the Fifth Regiment Maine Volunteers.* Portland, Maine, 1871.

Boudrye, Louis N. *Historic Records of the Fifth New York Cavalry, First Ira Harris Guard.* Albany, N.Y., 1865.

Bowen, James L. *History of the Thirty-Seventh Regiment Massachusetts Volunteers in the Civil War of 1861–1865.* Holyoke, Mass., 1884.

Brainard, Mary G. *Campaigns of the One Hundred and Forty-Sixth Regiment New York State Volunteers.* New York, 1915.

Bruce, George A. *The Twentieth Regiment of Massachusetts Volunteer Infantry.* Cambridge, Mass., 1906.

Burrage, Henry S. *History of the Thirty-Sixth Regiment Massachusetts Volunteers.* Boston, 1884.

Caldwell, J. F. J. *The History of a Brigade of South Carolinians, First Known as Gregg's, and Subsequently as McGowan's Brigade.* Philadelphia, 1866.

Chamberlin, Thomas. *History of the One Hundred and Fiftieth Regiment Pennsylvania Volunteers, Second Regiment, Bucktail Brigade.* Philadelphia, 1905.

Chambers, C. C. "The Coahoma Invincibles." *Confederate Veteran*, XXXI (1923), 461–63.

Cheek, Philip, and Mair Pointon. *History of the Sauk County Riflemen, Known as Company "A," Sixth Wisconsin Veteran Volunteer Infantry, 1861–1865.* Madison, Wis., 1909.

Clark, Walter, comp. *Histories of the Several Regiments and Battalions from North Carolina in the Great War, 1861–1865.* 5 vols. Goldsboro, N.C., 1901.

Cogswell, Leander W. *A History of the Eleventh New Hampshire Regiment Volunteer Infantry in the Rebellion War, 1861–1865.* Concord, N.H., 1891.

Collier, Calvin L. *They'll Do to Tie To: The Story of the Third Regiment, Arkansas Infantry, C.S.A.* Little Rock, Ark., 1988.

Committee of the Regiment. *History of the Thirty-Fifth Regiment Massachusetts Volunteers.* Boston, 1884.

Committee of the Regiment. *History of the Thirty-Sixth Regiment Massachusetts Volunteers.* Boston, 1884.

Cowtan, Charles W. *Services of the Tenth New York Volunteers in the War of the Rebellion.* New York, 1882.

Craft, David. *History of the One Hundred Forty-First Regiment, Pennsylvania Volunteers, 1862–1865.* Towanda, Pa., 1885.

Cudworth, Warren. *History of the First Regiment Massachusetts Infantry.* Boston, 1886.

Curtis, O. B. *History of the Twenty-Fourth Michigan of the Iron Brigade.* Detroit, 1891.

Davis, Charles E., Jr. *Three Years in the Army: The Story of the Thirteenth Massachusetts Volunteers from July 16, 1861, to August 1, 1864.* Boston, 1894.

Dawes, Rufus R. *Service with the Sixth Wisconsin Volunteers.* Marietta, Ohio, 1890.

Dickert, D. Augustus. *History of Kershaw's Brigade.* Newberry, S.C., 1899.

Dunlop, William S. *Lee's Sharpshooters; or, The Forefront of Battle: A Story of Southern Valor That Never Has Been Told.* Little Rock, Ark., 1899.

Gavin, William G. *Campaigning with the Roundheads: The History of the Hundredth Pennsylvania Veteran Volunteer Infantry Regiment in the American Civil War, 1861–1865.* Dayton, 1989.

Glover, Edwin A. *Bucktailed Wildcats: A Regiment of Civil War Volunteers.* New York, 1960.

Graham, W. M. "Twenty-Sixth Mississippi Regiment." *Confederate Veteran*, XV (1907), 169.

Haines, Alanson A. *History of the Fifteenth Regiment New Jersey Volunteers.* New York, 1883.

Haines, William P. *History of the Men of Company F, with Description of the Marches and Battles of the 12th New Jersey Volunteers.* Mickleton, N.J., 1897.

Hale, Laura V., and Stanley S. Phillips. *History of the Forty-Ninth Virginia Infantry, C.S.A.: Extra Billy Smith's Boys.* Lanham, Md., 1981.

Hanks, O. T. *History of Captain B. F. Benton's Company, Hood's Texas Brigade, 1861–1865.* Austin, Tex., 1984.

Haynes, Edward M. *A History of the Tenth Regiment Vermont Volunteers.* Rutland, Vt., 1870.

Hays, Gilbert A. *Under the Red Patch: Story of the Sixty-Third Regiment, Pennsylvania Volunteers, 1861–1864.* Pittsburgh, 1908.

History of the Fifth Massachusetts Battery. Boston, 1902.

History of the Nineteenth Regiment Massachusetts Volunteer Infantry, 1861–1865. Salem, Mass., 1906.

Hopkins, William P. *The Seventh Regiment Rhode Island Volunteers in the Civil War, 1862–1865.* Providence, 1903.

Houghton, Edwin B. *The Campaigns of the Seventeenth Maine.* Portland, Maine, 1866.

Houston, Henry C. *The Thirty-Second Maine Regiment of Infantry Volunteers.* Portland, Maine, 1903.

Hudgins, F. L. "With the 38th Georgia Regiment." *Confederate Veteran,* XXVI (1918), 161–63.

Hussey, George A., and William Todd. *History of the Ninth Regiment N.Y.S.M.—N.G.S.N.Y. (Eighty-Third N.Y. Volunteers), 1845–1888.* New York, 1889.

Hutchinson, Nelson V. *History of the Seventh Massachusetts Volunteer Infantry in the War of the Rebellion of the Southern States Against Constitutional Authority, 1861–1865.* Taunton, Mass., 1890.

Jackman, Lyman, and Amos Hadley. *History of the Sixth New Hampshire Regiment in the War for the Union.* Concord, N.H., 1891.

Johnson, W. Gart. "Barksdale-Humphreys Mississippi Brigade." *Confederate Veteran,* I (1893), 206–207.

Jones, Terry L. *Lee's Tigers: The Louisiana Infantry in the Army of Northern Virginia.* Baton Rouge, 1987.

Judson, Amos M. *History of the Eighty-Third Regiment Pennsylvania Volunteers.* Erie, Pa., 1865.

Kirk, Hyland C. *Heavy Guns and Light: A History of the 4th New York Heavy Artillery.* New York, 1890.

Krick, Robert K. *Parker's Virginia Battery.* Berryville, Va., 1975.

Lane, James H. "History of Lane's North Carolina Brigade: Battle of the Wilderness—Report of General Lane." In *SHSP,* IX, 124–29.

Leader, Norman. "The Bloodied Guns of Winslow's Battery." *Virginia Country's Civil War Quarterly,* VI, 15–20.

Lewis, Osceola. *History of the One Hundred and Thirty-Eighth Regiment Pennsylvania Volunteer Infantry.* Norristown, Pa., 1866.

Lloyd, William R. *History of the First Regiment Pennsylvania Reserve Cavalry from Its Organization, August, 1861, to September, 1864.* Philadelphia, 1864.

Locke, William H. *The Story of the Regiment* [11th Pennsylvania]. Philadelphia, 1868.

Longacre, Edward G. *To Gettysburg and Beyond: The Twelfth New Jersey Volunteer Infantry, II Corps, Army of the Potomac, 1862–1865.* Hightstown, N.J., 1988.

McBrien, Joe B. *The Tennessee Brigade.* Chattanooga, 1977.

McDonald, William N. *A History of the Laurel Brigade, Originally the Ashby Cavalry of the Army of Northern Virginia and Chew's Battery.* Baltimore, 1907.

McNamara, Daniel G. *The History of the Ninth Regiment Massachusetts Volunteer Infantry.* Boston, 1899.

Marbaker, Thomas D. *History of the Eleventh New Jersey Volunteers from Its Organization to Appomattox.* Trenton, 1898.

Marshall, D. P. *History of Company K, 155th Pennsylvania Volunteer Zouaves.* N.p., 1888.

Mulholland, St. Claire A. *The Story of the 116th Regiment Pennsylvania Volunteers in the War of the Rebellion: The Record of a Gallant Command.* Philadelphia, 1899.

Murray, Alton J. *South Georgia Rebels: The True Wartime Experiences of the 26th Regiment Georgia Volunteer Infantry, Lawton-Gordon-Evans Brigade.* St. Mary's, Ga., 1976.

Myers, Frank M. *The Comanches: A History of White's Battalion Virginia Cavalry, Laurel Brigade, Hampton Division, A.N.V., C.S.A.* Baltimore, 1871.

Nash, Eugene A. *A History of the Forty-Fourth Regiment New York Volunteer Infantry in the Civil War, 1861–1865.* Chicago, 1911.

Newell, Joseph K. *Ours: Annals of the Tenth Regiment, Massachusetts Volunteers, in the Rebellion.* Springfield, Mass., 1875.

Nichols, George W. *A Soldier's Story of His Regiment and Incidentally of the Lawton, Gordon, Evans Brigade.* Jesup, Ga., 1898.

Page, Charles D. *History of the Fourteenth Regiment, Connecticut Volunteer Infantry.* Meriden, Conn., 1906.

Polley, Joseph B. *Hood's Texas Brigade: Its Marches, Its Battles, Its Achievements.* New York, 1910.

Powell, William H. *The Fifth Army Corps.* New York, 1896.

Preston, N. D. *History of the Tenth Regiment of Cavalry, New York State Volunteers.* New York, 1892.

Pullen, John J. *The Twentieth Maine: A Volunteer Regiment in the Civil War.* Philadelphia, 1957.

Pyne, Henry R. *The History of the First New Jersey Cavalry.* Trenton, 1871.

Quiner, E. B. *The Military History of Wisconsin.* Chicago, 1866.

Rhodes, John H. *The History of Battery B, First Regiment Rhode Island Light Artillery.* Providence, 1894.

Ripley, William Y. W. *Vermont Riflemen in the War for the Union: A History of Company F, First United States Sharp Shooters.* Rutland, Vt., 1883.

Roe, Alfred S. *The Thirty-Ninth Regiment Massachusetts Volunteers, 1862–1865.* Worcester, Mass., 1914.

Rowland, Dunbar. *Military History of Mississippi, 1803–1888.* Jackson, Miss., 1908.

Shoemaker, John J. *Shoemaker's Battery: Stuart Horse Artillery, Pelham's Battalion, Army of Northern Virginia.* Gaithersburg, Md., n.d.

Simons, Ezra D. *The One Hundred Twenty-Fifth New York State Volunteers.* New York, 1888.

Simpson, Harold B. *Hood's Texas Brigade: Lee's Grenadier Guard.* Dallas, 1983.

Sloan, John A. *Reminiscences of the Guilford Grays, Co. B, 27th North Carolina Regiment.* Washington, D.C., 1883.

Small, A. R. *The Sixteenth Maine Regiment in the War of the Rebellion, 1861–1865.* Portland, Maine, 1886.

Smith, A. P. *History of the Seventy-Sixth Regiment New York Volunteers.* Cortland, N.Y., 1867.

Smith, J. L. *History of the Corn Exchange Regiment 118th Pennsylvania Volunteers, from Their First Engagement at Antietam to Appomattox, to Which Is Added a Record of Its Organization and a Complete Roster.* Philadelphia, 1888.

Smith, John Day. *History of the Nineteenth Regiment of Maine Volunteer Infantry.* Minneapolis, 1909.

Stevens, C. A. *Berdan's United States Sharpshooters in the Army of the Potomac.* St. Paul, 1892.

Stevens, Hazard. "The Sixth Corps in the Wilderness." In *PMHSM,* IV, 176–203.

Survivors' Association. *121st Regiment Pennsylvania Volunteers.* Philadelphia, 1906.

Sypher, Josiah R. *History of the Pennsylvania Reserve Corps.* Lancaster, Pa., 1865.

Terrill, J. Newton. *Campaign of the Fourteenth Regiment New Jersey Volunteers.* New Brunswick, N.J., 1884.

Thomas, Henry W. *History of the Doles-Cook Brigade, Army of Northern Virginia, C.S.A.* Atlanta, 1903.

Thomson, D. R. Howard, and William Rauch. *History of the Bucktails.* Philadelphia, 1906.

Thruston, Stephen D. "Report of the Conduct of General George H. Steuart's Brigade from the 5th to the 12th of May, 1864, Inclusive." In *SHSP,* XIV, 146–53.

Tobie, Edward P. *History of the First Maine Cavalry.* Boston, 1887.

Vautier, John D. *History of the 88th Pennsylvania Volunteers in the War for the Union, 1861–1865.* Philadelphia, 1894.

Verrill, George W. "The Seventeenth Maine at Gettysburg and in the Wilderness." In *War Papers Read Before the Commandery of the State of Maine, Military Order of the Loyal Legion of the United States,* I, 261–82. 3 vols. Portland, Maine, 1898.

Waite, Otis F. R. *New Hampshire in the Great Rebellion.* Concord, N.H., 1873.

Walcott, Charles F. *History of the Twenty-First Regiment Massachusetts Volunteers, in the War for the Preservation of the Union, 1861–1865.* Boston, 1882.

Walker, Francis A. *History of the Second Army Corps in the Army of the Potomac.* New York, 1887.

Wallace, William. "Operations of Second South Carolina Regiment in Campaigns of 1864 and 1865." In *SHSP,* VII, 128–31.

Ward, Joseph R. C. *History of the One Hundred and Sixth Regiment Pennsylvania Volunteers.* Philadelphia, 1883.

Weygant, Charles H. *History of the One Hundred and Twenty-Fourth Regiment N.Y.S.V.* Newburgh, N.Y., 1877.

Wilkinson, Warren. *Mother, May You Never See the Sights I Have Seen: The Fifty-Seventh Massachusetts Veteran Volunteers in the Last Year of the Civil War.* New York, 1990.

Wilmer, L. Allison, *et al. History and Roster of Maryland Volunteers.* 2 vols. Baltimore, 1898.

Wise, Jennings C. *The Long Arm of Lee; or, The History of the Artillery of the Army of Northern Virginia.* 2 vols. Lynchburg, Va., 1915.

CAMPAIGN STUDIES

Atkinson, C. F. *Grant's Campaigns of 1864 and 1865: The Wilderness and Cold Harbor*. London, 1908.

Badeau, Adam. *Military History of Ulysses S. Grant from April, 1861, to April, 1865*. 3 vols. New York, 1881.

Dowdey, Clifford. *Lee's Last Campaign*. Boston, 1960.

Frassanito, William A. *Grant and Lee: The Virginia Campaign, 1864–1865*. New York, 1983.

Hotchkiss, Jedediah. *Confederate Military History*. Vol. III of 12 vols. Atlanta, 1899.

Humphreys, Andrew A. *The Virginia Campaign of '64 and '65*. New York, 1883.

Robinson, Leigh. *The South Before and at the Battle of the Wilderness*. Richmond, 1878.

Schaff, Morris. *The Battle of the Wilderness*. Boston, 1910.

Scott, Robert Garth. *Into the Wilderness with the Army of the Potomac*. Bloomington, Ind., 1985.

Steere, Edward. *The Wilderness Campaign*. Harrisburg, Pa., 1960.

Stribling, Robert M. *Gettysburg Campaign and Campaigns of 1864 and 1865 in Virginia*. Petersburg, Va., 1905.

Swinton, William. *Campaigns of the Army of the Potomac*. New York, 1866.

Trudeau, Noah André. *Bloody Roads South: The Wilderness to Cold Harbor, May–June, 1864*. Boston, 1989.

THESES AND DISSERTATIONS

Flanagan, Vincent. "The Life of General Gouverneur Kemble Warren." Ph.D. dissertation, City University of New York, 1969.

McDaid, William K. "Four Years of Arduous Service: The History of the Branch-Lane Brigade in the Civil War." Ph.D. dissertation, Michigan State University, 1987.

Ott, Eugene, Jr. "The Civil War Diary of James J. Kirkpatrick, 16th Mississippi, C.S.A." M.A. thesis, Texas A & M University, 1984.

Index

Abbott, Maj. Henry L., 364–65, 389
Adams, Charles Francis, 434
Adams, Maj. Z. Boylston, 338, 447–50
Alabama units: *3rd,* 154; *4th,* 273n,
    305; *5th,* 154, 237; *8th,* 364;
    15th, 304, 305; *44th,* 299, 304;
    47th, 305, 399; *48th,* 304; *61st,*
    168, 169
Alexander, Brig. Gen. E. Porter: on
    Lee's strategy, 11; on Ewell, 15; on
    Grant's plans, 28, 80n; on May 5,
    273n; on May 6, pp. 280,
    292–93, 339, 369, 402, 416n; on
    Confederate casualties, 440
Alexandria, 20, 48
Alger, Col. Russell A., 347
Allen, William, 414–15
Alrich farm, 378, 379
Anderson, Brig. Gen. George T.
    ("Tige"), 299, 355, 357, 363, 393,
    394n, 396
Anderson, Maj. Gen. Richard H.: as
    Hill's division commander, 17, 25;
    and maneuvering for position on
    May 4, pp. 82, 87; on May 5,
    pp. 232, 236; and plans for May 6,
    pp. 275, 277–78; on May 6,
    pp. 313, 316, 332, 353, 400; as
    commander after wounding of
    Longstreet, 374
Annapolis, 20, 48
Antietam, Battle of, 10, 21, 129, 232,
    241, 444

Archer, Bob, 447
Archer, Brig. Gen. James J., 194n
Arkansas *3rd,* 303
Army of Northern Virginia: shortages
    affecting, 8–9; enlistments in,
    9–10; characteristics of, 12; lead-
    ership of, 12–18; before Battle of
    the Wilderness, 17, 20, 21, 24, 29;
    number of soldiers in, 21; number
    of, before Battle of the Wilderness,
    34, 87; monitoring of Union army
    by, on May 4, pp. 66, 78–80,
    89–90; maneuvering of, for posi-
    tion on May 4, pp. 70–71, 73, 78–
    90; monitoring of, by Union forces,
    70–71; on May 5 morning, 99–
    102, 105–10, 115–29, 132; and
    Wilson's encounter with Rosser on
    May 5 morning, 112–15; and bat-
    tle at Saunders' Field on May 5 af-
    ternoon, 142–74; in second round
    of fighting on May 5 afternoon,
    176–84; on Orange Plank Road
    on May 5 afternoon, 187–208,
    222; on Orange Plank Road late on
    May 5 afternoon, 222–29; advan-
    tages of, in Battle of the Wilderness,
    229–30; on Orange Plank Road
    on May 5 evening, 231–42; as-
    sessment of fighting by, 241–42,
    261–62, 280, 428–29, 439–
    46; situation of, at end of May 5,
    pp. 241–42, 263–64; on Orange

Turnpike on May 5 evening, 242–49; cavalry of, on May 5 afternoon and evening, 253–62; and plans for May 6, pp. 272–82; on Orange Plank Road on May 6 morning, 283–95; and Longstreet's arrival on May 6 morning, 295–302; and Longstreet's counterattack on May 6 morning, 296, 302–16; on Orange Turnpike on May 6 morning, 317–24; Burnside's advance against, on May 6 morning, 324–32; Hancock's advance against, on May 6 morning, 332–41; and cavalry fight on May 6 morning, 343–50; and Longstreet's flank attack on May 6 at midday, 351–66; and Burnside's assault on May 6 afternoon, 380–89, 398–401; and Brock Road front on May 6 afternoon, 389–98; and Gordon's attacks on May 6 evening, 404–30; appearance of, 431; order of battle of, 464–70

Army of Tennessee, 46

Army of the James, 47

Army of the Potomac: before Battle of the Wilderness, 8, 25, 29–35; maps used by, 33–34; number of, before Battle of the Wilderness, 34; quality of soldiers in, 34–35; leadership of, 37–41; cavalry of, 40–41; Grant's general strategy for, 46–47; divided leadership of, 48, 131, 325, 432; and plans before Battle of the Wilderness, 49–58; maneuvering of, for position on May 4, pp. 60–78; monitoring of, by Confederate forces, 66, 78–80, 89–90; monitoring of Confederate forces by, on May 4, pp. 70–71; and plans on eve of Battle of the Wilderness, 91–93; on May 5 morning, 94–119, 128, 129–44; and Wilson's encounter with Ros-

ser on May 5 morning, 112–15; and battle at Saunders' Field on May 5 afternoon, 142–74; assessment of fighting by, 172–74, 240–41, 263–64, 271–72, 429–36; 6th Corps of, in second round of fighting on May 5 afternoon, 176–84; and Meade's forces on Orange Plank Road on May 5 afternoon, 187–93; on Orange Plank Road on May 5 afternoon, 187–208, 222–29; on Orange Plank Road on May 5 evening, 231–42; on Orange Turnpike on May 5 evening, 242–49; cavalry of, on May 5 afternoon and evening, 253–62; and plans for May 6, pp. 262–71; on Orange Plank Road on May 6 morning, 283–95; Longstreet's counterattack against, on May 6 morning, 296, 302–16; on Orange Turnpike on May 6 morning, 317–24; and Burnside's advance on May 6 morning, 324–32; and Hancock's offensive on May 6 morning, 332–41; and cavalry fight on May 6 morning, 343–50; Longstreet's flank attack against, on May 6 at midday, 351–66; Burnside's assault on May 6 afternoon, 380–89, 398–401; and Brock Road front on May 6 afternoon, 389–98; Gordon's attacks against, on May 6 evening, 404–30; order of battle of, 454–63

Ayres, Brig. Gen. Romeyn B.: on May 5 morning, 140–41; in battle at Saunders' Field on May 5 afternoon, 142–43, 145, 149–52, 154, 167–72; on May 6 morning, 317

Babcock, Col. Orville E., 58, 326

Badeau, Adam, 58

Barlow, Brig. Gen. Francis C.: leadership capabilities of, 38; and maneuvering for position on May 4, pp. 63, 65; on May 5 afternoon, 206, 208, 225, 240; on May 5 evening, 233–36, 240; at Gettysburg, 235n; and plans for May 6, p. 269; on May 6 morning, 333–34; and railroad grade in Wilderness, 353n; on May 6 afternoon, 390, 395

Barney, Col. Elisha L., 197

Bartlett, Brig. Gen. Joseph J.: on May 5 morning, 99, 101–102; in battle at Saunders' Field on May 5 afternoon, 143, 145, 152–56, 160, 169, 171–73; on May 6 morning, 317

Bartlett, William F., 366

Battle, Brig. Gen. Cullen A., 125, 154, 159, 169

Battle of the Wilderness: challenges facing Lee and Grant during, 7; Lee's planning before, 22–29; military advantages of setting of, 27–28; Grant's planning before, 49–58; Humphreys' plan for, 50, 52–56; and Union army's maneuvering for position on May 4, pp. 60–78; plan of attack on eve of, 91–93; on May 5 morning, 94–144; and Union forces on May 5 morning, 94–119, 128, 129–44; and Confederate troops on May 5 morning, 99–102, 105–10, 115–29; and Wilson's encounter with Rosser on May 5 morning, 112–15; Meade's errors during, 119, 240–41, 245–46, 330; and Getty's encounter with Confederates on Orange Plank Road, 133–36; and battle at Saunders' Field on May 5 afternoon, 142–74; on May 5 afternoon, 145–208, 253–62; assessment of Union fighting in, 172–74, 240–41, 263–64, 271–72, 429–36; and 6th Corps in second round of fighting on May 5 afternoon, 176–

84; and Burnside's divisions on May 4–5, pp. 184–87; Grant's errors during, 186–87, 240, 247, 271–72, 330; and Orange Plank Road on May 5 afternoon, 187–208, 222; on May 5 evening, 222–82; aspects of setting of, working to Confederate advantage, 229–30; and Orange Plank Road on May 5 evening, 231–42; assessment of Confederate fighting in, 241–42, 261–62, 280, 428–29, 439–46; and Orange Turnpike on May 5 evening, 242–49; and cavalry action on May 5, pp. 253–62; and plans for May 6, pp. 262–82; on May 6 morning, 283–350; and Orange Plank Road on May 6 morning, 283–95; Longstreet's arrival at, on May 6 morning, 295–302; and Longstreet's counterattack on May 6 morning, 296, 302–16; and Orange Turnpike on May 6 morning, 317–24; and Burnside's advance on May 6 morning, 324–32; and Hancock's offensive on May 6 morning, 332–41; and cavalry fight on May 6 morning, 343–50; and Longstreet's flank attack on May 6 at midday, 351–66; on May 6 at midday, 351–403; and Burnside's assault on May 6 afternoon, 380–89, 398–401; and Brock Road front on May 6 afternoon, 389–98; Lee's errors during, 390, 402–403, 442–44; and Gordon's attacks on May 6 evening, 404–30; on May 6 evening, 404–52; fires after, 451–52; order of battle for, 454–70

Baxter, Brig. Gen. Henry: after battle at Saunders' Field on May 5 afternoon, 176; on May 5 evening, 231, 237–38; plans for May 6, p. 265; on Orange Plank Road on May 6 morning, 283, 306; wounding of, 306, 436

Beauregard, Gen. Pierre G. T., 88

Benning, Brig. Gen. Henry L. ("Rock"), 299, 303–304, 307, 355, 446

Benson, Berry, 236, 238

Bermuda Hundred, 88

Birney, Maj. Gen. David B.: leadership capabilities of, 38; maneuvering of, for position on May 4, p. 63; on May 5 afternoon, 190, 194, 197–205, 225, 240; division of, on May 5 evening, 236; plans of, for May 6, pp. 269–70; on May 6 morning, 291, 292, 309–10, 312, 338, 341, 343; on May 6 at mid-day, 357–58, 360–61, 374–75; on May 6 afternoon, 390, 398; and Ward's arrest, 394n

Blackford, William W., 12, 86

Bliss, Col. Zenas R., 328, 383, 386–87, 401

Bolote, John, 447

Boteler, Alexander R., 79, 128

Bowen, Col. Robert E., 393

Bradwell, Isaac G., 414n

Bragg, Gen. Braxton, 14

Brandy Station, 25, 29, 30–32, 43–45, 63, 437

Bratton, Col. John, 21, 373, 393–94, 396

Breckinridge, John C., 88

Brewster, Col. William R., 198, 269

Brinton, Lt. Col. William P., 257

Bristoe Station, 39

Brock Road: on May 4, pp. 83, 92; on May 5 morning, 109, 126–27, 133, 134; on May 5 afternoon, 188, 190, 194–95, 198, 199, 204–206, 208; Todd's Tavern on, 207; on May 6 morning, 332–33, 340, 344, 350, 368; on May 6 at mid-day, 373, 376, 378n, 379, 383, 384, 402, 444; front at, on May 6 afternoon, 389–98; map of, 391

Brock's Bridge, 82, 83, 85–86, 273

Brooke, Col. John B., 235, 269, 395

Brown, Maj. Campbell, 16, 123–24, 126, 174, 415

Brown, Col. Henry W., 178, 179, 181, 319

Brown, Lizinka, 15–16

Bryan, Brig. Gen. Goode, 312, 313

Buck, Capt. Samuel, 250–51

Bull Run, 30, 49

Burial parties, 452

Burnside, Maj. Gen. Ambrose E.: and plans to capture Richmond, 19; movement of, from Annapolis to Alexandria, 20, 48–49; before Battle of the Wilderness, 30, 32; in Annapolis, 48; Grant's coordination of Meade and, 48, 325, 432; and review of 9th Corps in Washington, D.C., 48; and plan before Battle of the Wilderness, 56–57, 92, 93; in Fredericksburg, 81; Grant's wait for, on May 5 morning, 130; on May 5, pp. 130, 175, 185–87, 243, 271; position of, at outset of Battle of the Wilderness, 184–85; on May 4, p. 185; Grant's errors concerning, 186–87; and plans for May 6, pp. 264–68; slowness of, 266, 291, 330, 382; on May 6 morning, 291, 314, 318, 321, 343, 409–10; advance of, on May 6 morning, 324–32; maps concerning, 327, 381; Grant's impatience with, 331, 382; assault by, on May 6 afternoon, 380–89, 397–401, 412; casualties of, 436; and plans for leaving Wilderness, 438

Butler, Maj. Gen. Benjamin F.: and plans for attack against Richmond, 1, 3, 5; Grant's strategy for, 47, 49, 51, 57–58, 88, 437, 438; and Grant's crossing of the Rapidan, 72; at Bermuda Hundred, 88; transports of, 91

Cadwallader, Sylvanus, 32, 67, 69, 426
Carroll, Col. Samuel S.: on May 5 afternoon, 205, 206; on May 5 evening, 227, 270; on May 6 morning, 310–12, 315, 340; on May 6 at midday, 359, 366, 375; on May 6 afternoon, 390, 395–96; wounding of, 395
Carruth, Col. Sumner, 338, 339, 362
Carter, Col. T. H., 414n
Casualties: Union, 102, 121–22, 156–57, 165, 167–68, 196–97, 203–204, 223, 248–49, 251–52, 263, 334, 387, 388–89, 411, 426, 435–36, 447–52; Confederate, 136, 165–66, 182, 233, 238–39, 252–53, 303, 309, 313, 323, 387, 388, 439–40, 446, 447–52
Catharine Furnace, 344, 351, 379
Catharine Furnace Road, 344
Catharpin Road: before Battle of the Wilderness, 9, 54, 55; on May 4, pp. 69, 73, 82–83, 90–92; on May 5 morning, 94, 104, 108, 112, 114–15; Confederate attack on, 129; Hancock on, 188; Todd's Tavern on, 207; on May 5 afternoon, 256–62; on May 5 evening, 272, 273; on May 6 morning, 332, 345, 348
Cavalry. See Confederate Cavalry; Union Cavalry
Chancellorsville, 55, 65, 69, 76–78, 89, 90, 115, 188, 255, 268, 317, 344, 379, 438, 451; Battle of, 10, 21, 51, 54, 195, 353, 445
Chapman, Col. George H., 112–14, 256, 258
Charleston, 19
Charlottesville, 20
Chattanooga, Battle of, 42, 46, 427
Chew, Maj. Robert P., 113, 114, 348
Chewning farm: on May 5 morning, 97, 107, 108, 109, 116–18, 119n, 129, 136, 138, 143; on May 5 afternoon, 166, 167, 190, 194; on May 5 evening, 223, 231; plans for Union capture of, 267, 268; on May 6, pp. 315, 316n, 318, 325, 326, 329, 330, 437
Chickamauga, Battle of, 14
Christ, Col. Benjamin C., 399
City Point, 88
Clark's Mountain, 25–26, 61, 70, 73, 79, 80, 443
Cole's Hill, 30
Comanches, 346
Comstock, Lt. Col. Cyrus B., 93, 185–86, 265, 329, 331, 383
Confederate 1st Corps: leadership of, 13–14; before Battle of the Wilderness, 21–22, 26–28; and maneuvering for position on May 4, pp. 81–83, 85–87, 90; on May 5 afternoon, 206–207; casualties of, 252–53, 440; Union speculation on position of, 256, 261, 266, 267, 269, 291; and plans for May 6, pp. 272–77, 282; march of, from Mechanicsville to Richard's Shop, 273; on May 5 evening, 273–75, 280–81; arrival of, on May 6 morning, 295–302; counterattack of, on May 6 morning, 296, 302–16, 321, 323–24, 326, 329, 333, 342, 353; on May 6 morning, 297–99, 302, 304, 306–13, 332, 336; flank attack of, on May 6 at midday, 351–66; on May 6 at midday, 367–74, 383–84; commander of, after wounding of Longstreet, 371, 374; assessment of fighting of, 442, 443, 446. See also Alexander, Brig. Gen. E. Porter; Field, Maj. Gen. Charles W.; Kershaw, Brig. Gen. Joseph B.; Longstreet, Lt. Gen. James
Confederate 2nd Corps: at Morton's Ford, 4–5; leadership of, 14–16; and maneuvering for position on

May 4, pp. 70, 73, 79, 82, 83, 85, 87, 90, 93; on May 5 morning, 122–29; in battle at Saunders' Field on May 5 afternoon, 143–61, 164–74; assessment of fighting of, 252, 280, 443–45; casualties of, 252–53, 440; Unions plans against, for May 6, pp. 264, 270; and plans for May 6, pp. 275–76; on May 6 morning, 282, 318–24, 328, 336, 342; Gordon's attacks on May 6 evening, 406, 416–26. *See also* Early, Maj. Gen. Jubal A.; Ewell, Lt. Gen. Richard S.; Johnson, Maj. Gen. Edward; Long, Brig. Gen. Armistead L.; Rodes, Maj. Gen. Robert E.

Confederate 3rd Corps: leadership of, 17; and maneuvering for position on May 4, pp. 73, 82–87, 90; on May 5 morning, 115–29, 124, 132–35, 188; on May 5 after-noon, 175, 189, 194, 207, 223, 228–29, 243, 256, 316; on May 5 evening, 225, 230–38, 240–41, 281–82, 364; situation of, at end of May 5, pp. 241–42, 353; Union plans against, for May 6, pp. 264, 265, 268–70; and plans for May 6, pp. 272, 273, 275–82; on May 6 morning, 285–95, 301, 308, 310, 315–17, 321, 324, 330, 353; casualties of, 440; assessment of fighting of, 443–45. *See also* Anderson, Brig. Gen. Richard H.; Heth, Maj. Gen. Henry; Hill, Lt. Gen. Ambrose S.; Wilcox, Maj. Gen. Cadmus M.

Confederate Bureau of Conscription, 9–10

Confederate Cavalry: and maneuvering for position on May 4, pp. 80, 85, 89, 91, 92, 120–21, 253; on May 5 morning, 112–15, 120–21; on May 5 afternoon and evening, 253–62; map of maneuvers of, on May 5 afternoon, 254; Lee's use of, 261–62; on May 6 morning, 343–50; on May 6 at midday, 378–79; assessment of fighting of, 445. *See also* Chew, Maj. R. Preston; Lee, Maj. Gen. Fitzhugh; Stuart, Maj. Gen. James E. B.

Connecticut *12th*, 311

Conner, Col. James, 15, 16, 370n

Cooke, Brig. Gen. John R.: on May 5 morning, 127; on May 5 afternoon, 193, 194n, 196, 203, 228; troops of, marching with Union soldiers, 279n; on Orange Plank Road on May 6 morning, 289–90

Corbin's Bridge, 92

Corn Exchange Regiment, 155, 251

Coward, Col. Asbury, 368–69, 372–73, 393–96

Cowles, Maj. William H. H., 80, 86, 123, 132, 404, 405, 409–10

Craig's Meeting House, 112, 113

Crawford, Brig. Gen. Samuel W.: leadership qualities of, 39; maneuvering of, for position on May 4, pp. 63, 74; on May 5 morning, 98, 100, 104–109, 116–19, 129, 136, 138; in battle at Saunders' Field on May 5 afternoon, 164, 167, 173, 190; after battle at Saunders' Field, 176, 194; troops of, on May 5, p. 243; and plans for May 6, p. 268; on May 6 morning, 317, 329; on May 6 evening, 424

Cullen, Dr. J. S. D. ("Dorsey"), 371

Culpeper, 25, 29–31, 36, 45, 58, 77, 328

Culpeper Court House, 18, 29

Culpeper Mine Ford, 61, 76

Culpeper-Fredericksburg Pike, 63

Custer, Brig. Gen. George A., 39, 77, 256, 344–49, 379

Cutcheon, Lt. Col. Byron, 325, 399

Cutler, Brig. Gen. Lysander: Iron Brigade of, 138–39; in battle at Saunders' Field on May 5 afternoon, 143, 157, 160, 161*n*, 163, 165, 169, 172, 173; on May 6 morning, 283, 308, 335, 342; leadership ability of, 362; on May 6 at midday, 363, 377

Dame, Pvt. William, 84, 295, 297
Dana, Charles, 38
Dana, Edmund, 283
Daniel, Maj. John W., 153, 159–60, 409*n*, 413–14, 416, 423
Daniel, Brig. Gen. Junius, 125, 164–65, 252, 275
Davies, Brig. Gen. Henry E., Jr., 258–59
Davis, Jefferson: and army shortfalls, 10; reprimand of Longstreet by, 14; and Meade's buildup of troops, 18–19, 21; assassination plot against, 31; and Lee's battle strategy, 81, 87–89
Davis, Brig. Gen. Joseph R., 193
Dawson, Francis, 371, 373
Denison, Col. Andrew W., 104, 143, 160–62
Devin, Col. Thomas C., 77, 347
Dickert, Col. D. Augustus, 447
Doles, Brig. Gen. George, 125, 157, 159, 160, 169
Douglas, Henry Kyd, 24
Dow, Capt. Edwin B., 392, 395, 396
Draper, Maj. William F., 386
Duane, Maj. James C., 266
Dudley, Maj. Charles P., 197
Dunn, Andrew, 369
Dunn, Dr., 450

Early, Maj. Gen. Jubal A.: on Ewell, 15; leadership qualities of, 16, 17, 25; and maneuvering for position on May 4, pp. 82, 85; on May 5, pp. 123, 153, 159, 182, 276; after battle at Saunders' Field on May 5 afternoon, 179; on Louisiana

troops, 179–80; and Gordon's attack plan, 407–409, 412–16, 413*n*, 427–28; on May 6 evening, 422; casualties of, 440
Early, Capt. Robert D., 153
Eastern theater map, 2
Edgell, Capt. Frederick M., 392, 395
Edwards, Col. Oliver, 365
Ellwood home, 74
Ely's Ford, 25, 26, 28, 29, 54, 55, 60, 63, 65, 67, 68, 70, 80, 85
Eustis, Brig. Gen. Henry L.: on May 5, pp. 135, 201–203, 269; on May 6 morning, 306–307, 310, 336, 340; on May 6 at midday and in afternoon, 362, 390
Evans, Col. C. A., 422
Ewell, Lizinka Brown, 15–16
Ewell, Lt. Gen. Richard S.: at Morton's Ford, 4; leadership qualities of, 12, 14–16, 17, 41; wife of, 15–16; patrol of Rapidan by, 22; at Clark's Mountain, 25; before Battle of the Wilderness, 27, 28; defeat of Seymour's brigade by, 39; and Humphreys' plan for Battle of the Wilderness, 56; and maneuvering for position on May 4, pp. 70, 73, 79, 82, 83, 85, 87, 90; on May 5 morning, 120, 122–29, 132, 134, 140; in battle at Saunders' Field on May 5 afternoon, 143–45, 147, 149, 152–55, 159, 164, 166, 172–74, 231; after battle at Saunders' Field, 179; in second round of fighting on May 5 afternoon, 182, 184, 186, 191, 194, 207, 222, 223; on May 5 evening, 230–32, 237, 243, 245, 246, 281, 404, 405; situation of, at end of May 5, p. 241; assessment of fighting of, 252, 280, 443–46; casualties of, 252–53, 440; Union's plans against, for May 6, pp. 264, 270; and plans for May 6, pp. 275–76; on May 6 morn-

ing, 282, 318–24, 328, 336, 342; on May 6 at midday, 377, 410–12; and Gordon's attack plan, 407–408, 412–15, 428–29, 445; on May 6 evening, 423, 437

Excelsior Brigade, 198–99

Faulkner house, 113, 114

Federal army. *See* Army of the Potomac; *headings beginning with* Union

Ferrero, Brig. Gen. Edward, 48, 184, 185, 410

Field, Maj. Gen. Charles W.: as division head, 14, 25, 27; and maneuvering for position on May 4, pp. 82, 86; and plans for May 6, pp. 274–75, 278; on May 5 evening, 280; on May 6 morning, 297–99, 306–308, 332; on May 6 at midday and in afternoon, 355, 363, 367, 373–74, 383, 393, 402; as commander after wounding of Longstreet, 371, 374, 402; Lee's instructions to, 443

Flat Run, 75, 178, 276

Flat Run Road, 80

Forsyth, Col. Charles, 154

Foster, Col. George P., 196

Frank, Col. Paul, 269, 333–35, 358*n*

Fredericksburg, 25, 32, 80–82, 87–89, 253, 255, 351, 437, 438; Battle of, 10

Gee, Leonard, 300

Georgia units: *20th,* 307; *26th,* 160; *31st,* 414*n,* 422; *61st,* 166–67, 418

Germanna Ford, 20, 25, 26, 28, 29, 54, 55, 60, 63, 66–68, 70, 75, 80, 85, 92, 104, 109, 243

Germanna Plank Road, 63, 64, 68, 74, 75, 80, 130, 186, 317, 324, 325, 330, 337–39, 420–24

Getty, Brig. Gen. George W.: leadership capabilities of, 38, 134; and maneuvering for position on May 4, pp. 64, 75; on May 5 morning, 106, 133–36, 175, 188, 240; on May 5 afternoon, 176, 178, 189–91, 194–204, 207, 208, 225, 227, 228, 243; on May 5 evening, 238–39; and plans for May 6, pp. 264, 265, 269; assessment of fighting of, 271; on May 6 morning, 282, 283, 292, 309–10, 336, 337, 343, 445; wounding of, 310, 436; on May 6 at midday, 357–58; on May 6 evening, 417; casualties of, 436

Gettysburg, Battle of, 11, 13, 14, 17, 21, 35, 37, 39, 42–44, 83, 110–11, 138–39, 205, 223, 235*n,* 301*n,* 336, 355, 364, 390, 444

Gibbon, Brig. Gen. John: leadership capabilities of, 38; and maneuvering for position on May 4, p. 63; on May 5 afternoon, 204–206, 208, 225, 228, 240; and plans for May 6, p. 269; on May 6 morning, 310, 332–35, 343; and railroad grade in Wilderness, 353; on May 6 at midday and in afternoon, 376, 390

Gordon, James B., 409*n*

Gordon, Brig. Gen. John B.: critique of performance of, on May 5, pp. 252, 275; on May 5 morning, 125; in battle at Saunders' Field on May 5 afternoon, 159–61, 166–67, 169; after battle at Saunders' Field, 179, 194; at Gettysburg, 235*n;* on May 5 evening, 276; on May 6 morning, 404–409; and plan for May 6 attack on Union forces, 404–12; attacks by, on May 6 evening, 406, 416–26; Ewell's response to plan of, 407–408, 412–15, 445; assessment of attack of, on May 6 evening, 427–30

Gordonsville, 21, 22, 25, 26, 27, 56, 73, 82, 113, 207, 273, 446

Goree, Thomas J., 450

Grant, Col. Lewis A.: on May 5,

pp. 135, 195–97, 202, 269; on May 6, pp. 310–12, 336, 365, 390; casualties of, 436

Grant, Ulysses S.: and plans for May 6, pp. 262–71, 324; challenge faced by, during Battle of the Wilderness, 7; as commander of all Union armies, 18, 42–46; Confederates' hypotheses of plans of, 19, 26, 28; on sutler wagons, 24–25; and cavalry, 40; leadership qualities of, 41–42, 45, 130, 271–72, 430, 446–47; Meade on, 41–46; earlier campaigns of, 42, 57, 426–27, 435; headquarters of, 45, 58, 68, 90–93, 131–32, 212; general war strategy of, 46–47; and divided leadership of Army of the Potomac, 48, 131, 325, 432; and plan for Battle of the Wilderness, 49–58, 91–93; on May 3 evening, 58–59; and maneuvering for position on May 4, pp. 67–72, 77; on eve of Battle of the Wilderness, 91–93; on Warren, 95; on May 5 morning, 103, 106–107, 129–34; on May 5 afternoon, 171–72, 174–76, 184; and assessment of Union fighting, 172–74, 240–41, 263–64, 271–72, 429–36; on May 4, pp. 185–86; errors of, 186–87, 240, 247, 271–72, 330; on Hays's death, 206; and plans for May 5 evening, 230–31; on May 5 evening, 237, 245, 247; on restorative qualities of sleep, 272; eating habits of, 317; on May 6 morning, 317, 326, 330, 331, 336, 337; impatience of, with Burnside, 331, 382; on May 6 at midday, 379, 382, 387; on May 6 afternoon, 397–98, 401; on May 6 evening, 420–22, 425–27; cigar smoking of, 425; Meade's relationship with, after Battle of the Wilderness, 434, 439; and plans for leaving Wilderness, 436–39

Greenfield homestead, 257

Gregg, Brig. Gen. David McM.: leadership of cavalry by, 40; and maneuvering for position on May 4, pp. 60–61, 63, 65, 68–69, 76–77, 89; and plan for Battle of the Wilderness, 91, 92; on May 5, pp. 95, 110, 255–58, 260, 269; and Fredericksburg expedition on May 5, pp. 253, 255; on May 6, pp. 344, 345, 347, 349–50, 355, 378–79

Gregg, Brig. Gen. John, 298–307, 431

Griffin, Brig. Gen. Charles: leadership qualities of, 39, 98; and maneuvering for position on May 4, pp. 63, 66, 74–75, 85; on May 5 morning, 97–111, 133, 139–42; in battle at Saunders' Field on May 5 afternoon, 143–57, 170–73; after battle at Saunders' Field, 176; and plans for May 6, p. 268; on May 6 morning, 317, 318, 320, 321; casualties of, 436

Hagood, Col. James R., 393–94, 396–97

Halleck, Maj. General Henry W., 1, 6, 429

Hamilton's Crossing, 80, 91, 92, 253

Hammond, Lt. Col. John, 73, 115–17, 119*n*, 121, 126, 133, 134

Hampton, Maj. Gen. Wade, 120–21

Hancock, Maj. Gen. Winfield S.: before Battle of the Wilderness, 29–30; leadership qualities of, 36, 37, 38, 41; and maneuvering for position on May 4, pp. 60, 61, 63, 65, 67–69, 76, 89; and plan for Battle of the Wilderness, 91, 92; on May 5 morning, 94–95, 103, 104, 108, 109, 112, 133, 135, 188; on May 5 afternoon, 175, 189–91, 193, 204–207, 227, 229–30, 240, 242–43, 256, 260; on May 5 evening, 238, 278; camp of, on May 5 evening, 263; and plans for May 6, pp. 264, 265, 267, 268–69; assessment of fighting of, 271, 431, 433; on May 6 morning, 282, 283, 285, 290–92, 309–10, 317, 321, 323–24, 326, 329–45, 349–50, 353, 410, 436–37, 446; impact of Longstreet's counteroffensive on, 313–15; and railroad grade in Wilderness, 353; on May 6 at midday, 357–58, 362, 363, 366, 368, 373–80, 387–89, 402; and rest for troops on May 6 afternoon, 387–89; on May 6 afternoon, 390–93, 397–98, 401, 444; on May 6 evening, 425; casualties of, 436; and plans for leaving Wilderness, 438

Harper, Samuel, 295

Harris, Brig. Gen. Nathaniel, 400

Harrison, Walter, 386

Hartranft, Col. John F., 331, 382–83, 387, 401

Haskell, John C., 298–99, 367

Hayes, Col. Joseph, 101, 102, 125, 152, 154–57

Hays, Brig. Gen. Alexander, 5, 202–206, 293–94, 436

Hays, Brig. Gen. Harry T., 125, 179, 182, 247–48, 252, 269, 423

Henagan, Col. John W., 297, 308–309, 312, 313

Heth, Maj. Gen. Henry: leadership of, 17, 25; and maneuvering for position on May 4, p. 85; on May 5 morning, 115, 126, 127, 136, 240; on Orange Plank Road on May 5 afternoon, 193–95, 206–208, 222–23, 225, 226, 228, 229; after Appomattox, 240; assessment of fighting of, 241, 280; and plans for May 6, p. 274; on May 5 evening, 276–81; on May 6 morning, 293, 298, 308, 315; on Longstreet's flank attack on May 6 at midday, 356n; on Lee, 403, 445

Higgerson place, 237

Higgerson's Field, 158, 162

Hill, Lt. Gen. Ambrose P.: leadership qualities of, 12, 16–17, 41; patrol of Rapidan by, 22; at Clark's Mountain, 25; before Battle of the Wilderness, 27, 28; at Bristoe Station, 39; and Humphreys' plan for Battle of the Wilderness, 56; and maneuvering for position on May 4, pp. 73, 82–87, 90; on May 5 morning, 115, 117–18, 120–22, 124, 126–29, 132–35, 188; at Gettysburg, 138–39; on May 5 afternoon, 175, 189, 194, 207, 223, 228–29, 243, 256; on May 5 evening, 225, 230–38, 240–41, 281–82, 364; situation of, at end of May 5, pp. 241–42, 353; Union's plans against, for May 6, pp. 264, 265, 268–70; and plans for May 6, pp. 272, 273, 275–81; assessment of fighting of, 280, 443–45; illness of, 281, 443, 446; on May 6 morning, 285, 290, 293–95, 301, 308, 310, 315–17, 321, 324, 330, 353; on May 6 afternoon, 389; on May 6 evening, 437; casualties of, 440

Hoffman, Col. John S., 422

Holmes, Oliver Wendell, Jr., 320

Hopper, Maj. George, 99–101, 105

Hospitals, 156, 248–49, 297, 389, 447–52

Hotchkiss, Maj. Jedediah, 16

Howard, McHenry, 79–80

Humphreys, Andrew A.: as chief of staff, 31; and plan of attack before Battle of the Wilderness, 50, 52–56, 61, 71, 72, 92, 115; and maneuvering for position on May 4, p. 61; on Battle of the Wilderness, 93, 343, 437; and Griffin's dereliction before Battle of the Wilderness, 97; on battle at Saunders' Field on May 5 afternoon, 170; review by, of May 5 action, 241; on May 5, pp. 242–43; on Fredericksburg expedition, 253; on May 6, pp. 321, 341, 420; and railroad grade in Wilderness, 353n; on Sedgwick, 429; on Union casualties, 436

Humphreys, Brig. Gen. Benjamin G., 309, 312, 313

Hunt, Brig. Gen. Henry J., 265

Hunter, Maj. R. W., 414n

Hyde, Lt. Col. Thomas W., 109, 131, 180

Indiana units: 3rd Cavalry, 64; 7th, 157; 14th, 227; 20th, 197, 236

Infirmaries. See Hospitals

Ingalls, Brig. Gen. Rufus, 33, 56, 61

Iron Brigade, 138–39, 157, 160–61, 163, 308, 335–36, 362

Jackson, Thomas J. ("Stonewall"), 14, 39, 51, 90, 93, 95, 125, 138, 253, 344, 445

James River, 19, 22, 26, 47, 49, 88

Jenkins, Col. David T., 98, 99–100, 149–50, 156, 157n

Jenkins, Brig. Gen. Micah, 299, 368–70, 372–73, 389, 440, 446

Johnson, Bushrod, 88

Johnson, Maj. Gen. Edward ("Allegheny"): leadership of, 16, 17, 25; and maneuvering for position on May 4, pp. 82, 85; on May 5 morning, 123, 125; on May 5 afternoon, 149, 172, 179; Confederate plans against, for May 6, p. 275; on May 5 evening, 276

Johnston, Gen. Joseph E., 8, 46, 431

Johnston, Brig. Gen. Robert D., 410, 412, 416, 422–23

Jones, Brig. Gen. John M.: on May 5 morning, 124–25; in battle at Saunders' Field on May 5 afternoon, 153–54, 157, 159, 164; after battle at Saunders' Field, 179; death of, 252, 275, 276, 446

Jones, Thomas, 405, 407–408, 409n, 414n

Jones's Field, 97

Keifer, Col. J. Warren, 130–31, 244–45, 247–49, 253, 411, 430

Kershaw, Brig. Gen. Joseph B.: as division head, 14, 25, 27; and maneuvering for position on May 4, pp. 82, 85–86; on May 5 evening, 280; on May 6 morning, 297–99, 302, 304, 308–13, 332, 336; on May 6 at midday, 355, 358–59, 368–70, 372–74; on May 6 afternoon, 389, 393; on May 6 evening, 437

Kester, Lt. Col. John W., 65, 258–59

Kidd, Maj. James H., 345–47

Kirkland, Brig. Gen. William W.: on May 5 morning, 115, 117, 127; on May 5 afternoon, 193, 194n, 222–23, 228; on May 5 evening, 238; on Orange Plank Road on May 6 morning, 288

Kitching, Col. J. Howard, 390

Lacy plantation and house: on May 4, p. 74; on May 5 morning, 97, 100, 131; on May 5 afternoon, 162–65, 167, 176, 189; on May 5 evening, 231, 242, 252, 263, 268, 270; on May 6 morning, 326, 335–36, 342, 399; on May 6 at midday and in afternoon, 363, 398; on May 6 evening, 420, 424

Lane, Brig. Gen. James H., 233–36, 278–79, 286–87, 315

Latrobe, Lt. Col. Osmun, 450

Laurel Brigade, 113

Law, Brig. Gen. Evander McIver, 299, 304

Leasure, Col. Daniel, 338, 340, 388, 390, 395

Lee, Maj. Gen. Fitzhugh: before Battle of the Wilderness, 22, 24, 28–29; and maneuvering for position on May 4, pp. 80, 87, 89; on guide for Longstreet, 86n; on May 5, pp. 120, 255, 259–60; on May 6, pp. 349, 378

Lee, Robert E.: response of, to Morton's Ford attack, 6, 11–12; challenge faced by, during Battle of the Wilderness, 7; defensive posture of, in 1864, 8–10; and Rapidan works, 8; record of, as general before 1864, pp. 10–11; leadership qualities of, 11–12, 35–36, 403, 431; relationship of, with Longstreet, 13, 17–18; and planning during winter of 1864, pp. 18–22; soldiers' response to, 21–22, 24; and planning during spring of 1864, pp. 22–29; and Union plot to burn Richmond and assassinate Davis, 31; Mine Run campaign against, 36–37, 52, 86; Grant's planning for confrontation with, 49–58; Lincoln's advice to Meade on battling, 49, 51; and maneuvering for position on May 4, pp. 70–71, 73, 78–90; headquarters of, 86, 88, 127–28, 222, 231–32, 443; and planning before Battle of the Wilderness, 89–90; at Gettysburg, 110–11, 205, 301n, 390, 444; on May 5 morning, 120–21, 123–24, 127–29; near-brush with capture on May 5 morning, 128, 194; and battle at Saunders' Field on May 5 afternoon, 174; on May 5 afternoon, 194, 223; and plans for May 5 evening, 231–32; on May 5 evening, 237, 245, 279; assessment of Confederate fighting by, 241–42, 261–62, 280, 428–29, 439–46; and Confederate cavalry, 261–62; and plans for May 6,

pp. 272–82; on May 6 morning, 290, 293, 295, 299–301, 304, 313, 316, 353–55; and Texas Brigade, 299–301; at Sharpsburg, 301n; and railroad grade in Wilderness, 353; on May 6 at midday, 367, 373, 380, 384; and Brock Road front on May 6 afternoon, 389–98, 402–403; errors of, 390, 402–403, 442–44; on May 6 afternoon, 402; need of, for more troops on May 6, p. 410; and Gordon's attack plan, 413–16, 428–29

Lee, Mrs. Robert E., 80

Leonard, Col. Samuel H., 176

Lewis, Lt. Col. John L., 196–97

Liberty Mills, 20, 26, 27

Lincoln, Abraham, 41–43, 45, 47, 48

Locke, Lt. Col. Frederick T., 251–52

Locust Grove, 85

Lomax, Brig. Gen. Lunsford L., 89

Longstreet, Lt. Gen. James: leadership style of, 12–14, 17–18, 41, 298–99; relationship of, with Lee, 13, 17–18; and Lee's plans in winter of 1864, p. 19; in Charlottesville, 20; Lee's review of troops of, 21; at Gordonsville, 22, 207; at Clark's Mountain, 25; before Battle of the Wilderness, 26–27, 28; on Grant, 42, 447; and Grant's plan for Battle of the Wilderness, 56; and maneuvering for position on May 4, pp. 73, 81–83, 85–87, 90; guide for, 86; Lee's wait for, 120, 124, 126, 129, 242, 282; at West Point, 201; on May 5 afternoon, 206–207, 223, 232; casualties of, 252–53, 440; Union speculation about, 256, 261, 266, 267, 269, 291, 332; and plans for May 6, pp. 272–77, 282; and march from Mechanicsville to Richard's Shop, 273; on May 5 evening, 273–75, 280–

81; arrival of, on May 6 morning, p. 285; arrival of troops of, on May 6 morning, 295–302; counterattack of, on May 6 morning, 296, 302–16, 321, 323–24, 326, 329, 333, 342, 353; maps concerning, 296, 352; Sheridan's attack on, 339–40; and attack on Todd's Tavern on May 6 morning, 345; division of, near Trigg farm on May 6 morning, 349; flank attack of, on May 6 at midday, 351–66; on May 6 at midday, 367–69, 383–84; wounding of, 370–71, 374n, 402, 416n, 440, 443, 445, 446, 450–51; on May 6 afternoon, 389, 395; on May 6 evening, 437; assessment of fighting of, 442, 443, 444, 446

Louisiana 6th, 247–48

Louisiana Tigers, 125, 179–81

Lyle, Col. Peter, 249

Lyman, Lt. Col. Theodore: on Mine Run campaign, 36–37; on Hancock, 38, 433; and Meade, 43; on Grant, 45, 57; on Meade's strategy, 47; and maneuvering for position on May 4, pp. 65, 66; and battle at Saunders' Field on May 5 afternoon, 156–57, 172; on May 5 afternoon, 188–89, 191, 204–206, 230; on Burnside, 266; on May 5 evening, 268; on May 6 morning, 291, 313–15, 325; on Webb, 337; on May 6 at midday, 375–76, 379–80, 387; on Potter, 382; at hospital on May 6, p. 389; on May 6 afternoon, 392, 397, 398, 401n; on May 6 evening, 420–21; on Sedgwick, 429; on Confederates, 431; assessment of Union and Confederate fighting by, 435

McAllister, Col. Robert, 197–99, 269, 292n, 334–35, 358–59

McCandless, Col. William, 138, 143, 166–67

McClellan, Maj. Henry B., 274–75, 278

McCracken, Patrick, 449–50

McCreery, Sergeant Van, 3, 6

McGowan, Brig. Gen. Samuel, 223, 225–28, 234–36, 239, 287–88, 293

McIntosh, Bob, 3–4, 6

McIntosh, Col. David G., 367

McIntosh, Col. John B., 257

Macy, Col. George N., 364, 389

Madden, Willis, 60, 61

Madden place, 77

Mahone, Brig. Gen. William, 355–58, 361, 366–67, 370

Maine units 1st, 255; 4th, 294; 6th, 392; 17th, 202; 19th, 365, 366; 20th, 105, 152, 154, 155, 156

Manassas, Second Battle of, 138, 202

Manassas Junction, 184

Marshall, Lt. Col. Charles, 275

Marvel, William, 266n

Maryland 6th, 244

Massachusetts units: 1st, 258, 397; 7th, 201; 9th, 169–70; 10th, 201; 18th, 101, 102, 152; 20th, 339, 364, 365; 36th, 385–86; 37th, 75, 201, 307, 365; 39th, 249; 45th, 385–86; 56th, 338, 366, 448; 57th, 366

Massaponax Church, 120, 259

Meade, Gen. George G.: before Battle of the Wilderness, 8, 17–22, 25–29; and plans before Battle of the Wilderness, 29–30; headquarters of, 31–35, 45, 66–68, 131–32, 212; and Union plot to burn Richmond and assassinate Davis, 31; criticism of strategy of, 35–36, 37, 43, 45, 132, 184, 202; at Gettysburg, 35, 37, 39, 42, 43, 44, 139, 444; Mine Run campaign of, 36–37, 52, 54, 66; generals under,

37–41; and cavalry, 40–41, 253, 260, 264, 270, 433–34; on Grant, 41–42; and Grant as commander in chief, 43–46; Lyman on strategy of, 47; and divided leadership of Army of the Potomac, 48, 131, 325, 432; and reduction of army's possessions before Battle of the Wilderness, 48; Lincoln's advice to, on battling Lee, 49, 51; and Grant's plan before Battle of the Wilderness, 51–53, 56, 57; and instructions before Battle of the Wilderness, 60, 61; and maneuvering for position on May 4, pp. 65–67; and Fredericksburg, 81; on eve of Battle of the Wilderness, 91–93; on May 5 morning, 94–95, 102–103, 106–11, 119, 128–32, 139–41; errors of, during Battle of the Wilderness, 119, 240–41, 245–46, 330; on May 5 afternoon, 171–73, 176, 184; on Orange Plank Road on May 5 afternoon, 187–93, 222; on May 5 evening, 242, 245–46; Sheridan's view of, 253; and Wilson's cavalry division, 255; and plans for May 6, pp. 262–67; on May 6 morning, 291, 314, 321, 323, 325, 335–36, 429; on May 6 at midday, 376–79, 387–88; on May 6 afternoon, 397–98, 401*n;* on May 6 evening, 420–21; Grant's relationship with, after Battle of the Wilderness, 434, 439; after Battle of the Wilderness, 438
Meade, Mrs. George G., 44–45
Mechanicsville, 20, 27, 28*n,* 85–86, 273*n*
Merritt, Brig. Gen. Wesley, 255, 344
Michigan units: *1st,* 98, 99, 345; *2nd,* 387; *5th,* 347; *6th,* 346, 347; *7th,* 344; *8th,* 387; *17th,* 387; *20th,* 325, 399

Michler, Maj. Nathaniel, 132
Miles, Col. Nelson A., 235, 269, 353
Milhau, John J., 252
Mine Run, 26, 53–56, 70–73, 78, 82, 85, 87, 93, 103
Mine Run campaign, 11, 12, 36–37, 39, 52, 54, 66, 86, 353, 433
Mississippi *2nd,* 193
Mitchell, Major, 205
Mitchell, William, 358*n*
Monteith, Robert, 270, 362, 363
Moore, Samuel, 153
Morgan, Lt. Col. Charles H., 189, 190, 394*n*
Morris, Brig. Gen. William H., 377, 424
Morton, Jeremiah, 15, 70
Morton Hall, 15, 25, 70
Morton's Ford, 1, 3–6, 11, 49, 79, 84
Mosby's Confederacy, 185
Mott, Brig. Gen. Gershom: leadership capabilities of, 38; and maneuvering for position on May 4, p. 63; on May 5 afternoon, 190, 194, 197–200, 202, 204, 206, 225, 240; plans for May 6, p. 269; on May 6 morning, 292*n,* 309–10, 312; on May 6 at midday, 357–58, 388; on May 6 afternoon, 390, 392, 394, 395

Neill, Brig. Gen. Thomas H.: on May 5 afternoon, 178, 179, 182, 183; on May 6 morning, 319–20; on May 6 at midday, 411, 424; on May 6 evening, 418, 422, 423–24
New Hampshire units: *1st,* 392; *6th,* 316*n,* 326; *11th,* 386
New Jersey units: *1st,* 258; *1st Cavalry,* 65; *5th,* 292*n; 8th,* 198; *12th,* 311; *15th,* 66
New Verdiersville, 70, 82, 86
New York units: *1st Light Artillery,* 147, 149; *4th,* 417, 424; *4th Heavy Artillery,* 416–

17; *5th,* 73, 112, 115, 121; *10th,* 258–59, 311, 315; *40th,* 197, 359; *44th,* 152; *50th* Engineers, 268; *51st,* 386, 401; *66th,* 236; *76th,* 165, 289, 363, 430; *93rd,* 203; *106th,* 423; *121st,* 423; *124th,* 199–200, 360, 393; *125th,* 334, 358n; *140th,* 98, 140, 142, 144, 145, 147, 150–52, 168; *146th,* 98, 102, 149–52, 156, 167–68

North Anna River, 22, 53, 82, 85, 273

North Carolina units: *1st,* 64, 80, 123, 149, 168, 404; *3rd,* 149, 168; *7th,* 234, 235, 236; *11th,* 288; *13th,* 285–86; *18th,* 234, 235, 278, 287; *23rd,* 410; *26th,* 288–89; *27th,* 279n; *28th,* 234, 236; *33rd,* 234; *37th,* 234; *38th,* 126, 286; *44th,* 228; *47th,* 121–22; *55th,* 233

Oates, Col. William C., 305–306, 384–86, 390, 399–400

Ohio units: *8th,* 227, 359; *110th,* 244, 411, 417–18; *122nd,* 244n, 418; *126th,* 244n

Orange and Alexandria Railroad, 9, 25, 26, 31, 49, 51, 53, 184

Orange Blossoms Regiment, 199–200, 392

Orange Court House, 8, 25, 72–73, 82, 83, 84, 87, 89, 120, 351, 450

Orange Plank Road: on May 2–3, pp. 54, 56; on May 4, pp. 72, 73, 74, 78, 82, 83, 84, 85, 87, 89; on May 5 morning, 97, 107, 108, 109, 110, 115, 116, 118, 120, 129; Hammond's troops on, on May 5 morning, 112; Heth's division on, 127, 193–95; Getty's encounter with Confederate forces on, 133–36, 175; after battle at Saunders' Field on May 5 afternoon, 175; on May 5 afternoon, 187–208, 222–29; maps of, 192, 224, 284; Getty's division on, on May 5 afternoon,

195–97; on May 5 evening, 231–42; on May 6 morning, 282–95, 324, 350; on May 6 at midday, 355, 387; on May 6 afternoon, 390

Orange Turnpike: on May 2–3, p. 54; on May 4, pp. 70, 74, 78, 82, 84, 85, 87; on May 5 morning, 98, 99, 100–101, 103, 104, 107, 108, 110, 112, 120, 129, 130; Wilson's failure to post pickets on, 111; map of, 146; after battle at Saunders' Field on May 5 afternoon, 175–76; on May 5 evening, 231, 242–49; on May 6 morning, 317–24

Osgood, Lt. George W., 316n

Owen, Brig. Gen. Joshua T., 205, 269–70, 312, 362, 390, 396

Page, Charles, 67–68, 239–40, 246, 392, 395

Palmer, Col. William H.: on May 5, pp. 122, 128, 234, 277, 279, 279n, 281; on May 6, pp. 294, 315–16; on Longstreet, 316; on Hill, 444

Palmer's Field. *See* Saunders' Field

Pamunkey River, 92

Pamunkey Road, 54

Parke, Maj. Gen. John G., 329

Parker's Store: on May 4, pp. 72–74, 89; on May 5 morning, 94, 97, 98, 99, 100, 104, 107, 115–17, 119n, 126, 255; on May 5 afternoon, 167, 188, 189; on May 6 morning, 293, 297, 321, 324, 326, 329

Parker's Store Road, 105, 109, 165, 167, 174, 332, 380, 410

Patrick, Brig. Gen. Marsena R., 434

Patton, Maj. William, 64

Pegram, Brig. Gen. John: on May 5, pp. 125–26, 179, 245, 247, 250; critique of performance of, on May 5, p. 252; wounding of, 252–53, 440, 446; on May 6, pp. 322–23, 328, 412, 416, 418, 422, 423; and Gordon's troops, 404, 427–28

Pendleton, Lt. Col. Alexander S. ("Sandie"), 15, 16, 126, 127, 174
Pendleton, Brig. Gen. William, 441
Penfield, Nelson, 358n
Pennsylvania units: 2nd, 255; 7th, 166–67; 13th, 136; 18th Cavalry, 257; 48th, 326; 56th, 289, 363; 83rd, 101, 102, 154, 155, 156; 88th, 152; 90th, 249; 91st, 151; 95th, 423; 118th, 152, 155; 137th, 423; 138th, 244n, 411; 139th, 203; 141st, 197, 285–86, 359; 143rd, 162–63, 283; 149th, 162–63; 150th, 139, 162; 155th, 151
Perrin, Abner, 313, 364, 400
Perry, Brig. Gen. Edward A., 384, 400
Perry, Col. William F.: on May 6 morning, 299, 304–307, 313; on May 6 at midday, 355, 383–84, 386, 389; on May 6 afternoon, 399–400; wounding of, 400
Pickets and picket duty, 250–51, 279, 286, 326, 328, 337, 345, 355, 392
Pickett, Maj. Gen. George E., 332, 341–42
Piney Branch Church, 255, 256
Po River, 193, 257–59
Poague, William, 127, 277, 281–82, 285, 294–95, 299, 301n, 302
Pony Mountain, 70
Porter, Charles, 173
Porter, Lt. Col. Horace: on May 3 evening, 58; on May 4, pp. 69, 71, 93; on May 5, pp. 130, 263; on May 6, pp. 382, 387; on Grant's cigar smoking, 425; on fires after Battle of the Wilderness, 451–52
Potter, Brig. Gen. Robert B.: on May 5 afternoon, 184, 185, 186, 187; and plans for May 6, p. 265; on May 6 morning, 324, 326, 328, 331, 343, 399; leadership characteristics of, 382; on May 6 at midday, 382–83, 385

Prisoners of war: Union soldiers as, 233, 249–50, 275, 315–16, 420; Confederate soldiers as, 236, 290, 314, 430–31

Ramseur, Brig. Gen. Stephen D., 82, 275, 328–31, 343, 380, 399
Rapidan front, map of, 23
Rapidan River: 3, 6, 8, 19, 22, 25, 51, 54, 56, 65, 66, 71–72, 186
Rapidan works, 1, 8, 11, 20, 22, 27, 49
Rappahannock River, 29, 30, 49, 438
Rappahannock Station, 185
Rawlins, Brig. Gen. John A.: as adviser to Grant, 42, 43; at Grant's commissioning as commander in chief, 42; on evening of May 3, p. 58; and battle at Saunders' Field on May 5 afternoon, 172; on May 6, pp. 331, 426
Rhode Island 2nd, 201, 203
Rhodes house, 86, 88
Rice, Brig. Gen. James C.: leadership qualities of, 139; in battle at Saunders' Field on May 5 afternoon, 143, 157, 163–66, 172; on Orange Plank Road on May 6 morning, 283, 289–90, 308; on May 6 at midday and in afternoon, 363, 390
Richard's Shop, 82, 83, 86, 273, 275, 280, 446
Richardsville, 60, 61, 63, 65, 68, 77
Richmond, 1, 47, 53, 58, 81, 88, 437
Richmond, Fredericksburg and Potomac Railroad, 81
Richmond Howitzers, 1, 3–4, 78–79, 83–84, 297, 441
Ricketts, Brig. Gen. James B.: leadership capabilities of, 38; and maneuvering for position on May 4, pp. 64, 75; on May 5 morning, 131; relief of, by Burnside's corps on May 5 afternoon, 186; on May 5 evening, 243, 246–47; and plans for May 6,

p. 268; assessment of Sedgwick's handling of, 429

Robertson Run, 112, 115

Robertson's Tavern, 72, 74, 85, 86, 111, 122, 126, 420

Robinson, James, 86

Robinson, Brig. Gen. John C.: leadership qualities of, 39; and maneuvering for position on May 4, pp. 63, 74; on May 5, pp. 98, 104, 143, 169, 173, 179, 231, 243, 251, 268; on May 6, pp. 317, 377, 390

Robinson, Leigh, 441–42

Rodes, Maj. Gen. Robert E.: leadership of, 16, 17, 25; and maneuvering for position on May 4, pp. 73, 85; on May 5, pp. 123, 125, 153, 276; after battle at Saunders' Field on May 5 afternoon, 179

Roebling, Maj. Washington A.: on May 4, p. 66; on May 5 morning, 105, 116, 117, 136, 138; and battle at Saunders' Field on May 5 afternoon, 165, 171, 174; on Wadsworth, 231; on May 5 evening, 238, 267–68; on May 6, pp. 321, 325, 329, 424

Rogers, Lt. William H., 395

Rosser, Brig. Gen. Thomas L.: on May 5 morning, 113–17, 121, 128; on May 5 afternoon, 256–62; assessment of fighting of, 280; on May 6 morning, 341, 344–49; on May 6 at midday, 378–79

Rowley, William, 267

Russell, Brig. Gen. David A., 178, 179, 182, 319, 377

Ryan, Col. George ("Paddy"), 145, 147, 149, 150, 168

Saunders' Field: on May 5 morning, 102, 106, 123, 124–25, 126, 138; Union and Confederate positions before battle at, 142–44; beginning of battle at, on May 5 after-noon, 144, 145; Griffin's division in, 145–57; map of situation at, on May 5 afternoon, 148; casualties at, 156–57, 165, 168; Wadsworth's brigades at, 157–66; Stone's brigade at, 162–63; Rice's brigade at, 163–66; McCandless' brigade at, 166–67; final stages of battle at, 167–72; Steuart's brigade at, 167–69; Ewell's earthworks on fire at, 170–71; Griffin's anger about, 171–72; mistakes made by Union forces at, 172–74; second charge at, on May 5 evening, 249–50; on May 6 morning, 320–21, 336; on May 6 evening, 437

Scales, Brig. Gen. Alfred M., 223, 225, 226, 228, 233–35, 285–87

Schaff, Lt. Morris, 325–26, 333, 335, 431, 435

Sedgwick, Maj. Gen. John: and Morton's Ford skirmish, 1, 3, 5–6; before Battle of the Wilderness, 30; leadership capabilities of, 37, 38–39; and maneuvering for position on May 4, pp. 60, 64, 66, 69, 75–76; and plan for Battle of the Wilderness, 92; on May 5 morning, 94, 98, 101, 104, 106, 109, 131, 133, 136; empty camps of, on May 5 morning, 130; at May 5 noon, 143; on May 5 afternoon, 175, 176–87, 222; on Orange Turnpike, 222; on May 5 evening, 231, 242–46, 252; camp of, on May 5 evening, 263; and plans for May 6, pp. 264, 265, 268–69; assessment of fighting of, 271, 429, 431, 433; Confederate plans against, for May 6, pp. 275–76; on May 6 morning, 318–20, 322, 324, 342, 343, 405, 409–10; on May 6 at midday, 377, 410–12; on May 6 afternoon, 398; on May 6 evening, 416, 419–21,

423–26, 437; casualties of, 436; and plans for leaving Wilderness, 438

Seven Days, 10

Sewell, William, 292n

Seymour, Brig. Gen. Truman: leadership capabilities of, 38–39; on May 5 evening, 243–45, 248; on May 6 morning, 322–23; casualties of, 411; on May 6 evening, 417–20, 423, 424; as prisoner of war, 420, 436; assessment of fighting of, 429–30

Seymour, William, 182

Shaler, Brig. Gen. Alexander, 268–69, 411, 417–21, 436

Sharpsburg, Battle of, 301n

Shelton, Lt. William H., 147, 168, 171n

Shenandoah Valley, 19, 22, 47, 49, 53, 88

Sheridan, Maj. Gen. Philip H.: leadership of cavalry by, 40–41; and plan for Battle of the Wilderness, 91, 92; on May 5 afternoon and evening, 253–61, 263, 270; on Meade, 253; on May 6 morning, 339–41, 344–45, 349; on May 6 at midday, 378–79; assessment of fighting of, 433–34

Sherman, Maj. Gen. William T., 8, 91

Shiloh, Battle of, 57

Shoemaker, John J., 348

Sigel, Maj. Gen. Franz, 47, 49, 58, 88, 91

Sime (Englishman), 72–73

Smith, Col. J. P., 414n

Smith, Maj. Gen. Martin L., 354, 367–68, 373

Smith, William ("Extra Billy"), 80

Smyth, Col. Thomas A., 235, 269, 390

Sorrel, Lt. Col. G. Moxley: on Longstreet, 13–14; on May 4, 80n, 82; on Longstreet's march, 273n; on May 6 at midday, 355–63, 365–

67, 369–71, 373, 374, 379, 402; on commander of 1st Corps after wounding of Longstreet, 374n; and Wadsworth's map, 447

South Carolina units: 1st, 393; 2nd, 309, 393; 5th, 368–69, 393; 6th, 373

Spaulding, Col. Ira, 268

Spivey, James Ervin, 160–61

Spotswood plantation, 106, 109, 178, 186, 324

Spotswood Road, 123, 132–34, 136, 175, 263, 318, 332, 419

Spotsylvania Court House, 54, 82, 120, 259, 438, 452

Spotsylvania Road, 73, 111

Spring Hill, 162

Stafford, Brig. Gen. Leroy A.: on May 5 morning, 125; in battle at Saunders' Field on May 5 afternoon, 152; in second round of fighting on May 5 afternoon, 179–82, 252; fatal wounding of, 252, 440, 446

Stanton, Edwin M., 1, 36, 42

Steuart, Brig. Gen. George H. ("Maryland"): at Morton's Ford skirmish, 4; on May 5 morning, 125; in battle at Saunders' Field on May 5 afternoon, 149–53, 167–69; in second round of fighting on May 5 afternoon, 179, 180n; capture of Union guns by North Carolina regiments of, 250; on May 6 evening, 423

Stevens, George T., 187

Stevensburg, 25, 30, 58, 63, 64, 65, 68, 77

Stevenson, Brig. Gen. Thomas G.: on May 5 afternoon, 185–87; and plans for May 6, p. 265; on May 6 morning, 324, 326, 335, 337–39, 410; on May 6 at midday and in afternoon, 376, 387, 397, 398

Stiles, Robert, 122

Stone, Col. John M., 193, 201, 202,

229, 230, 233, 301–302, 356–57, 400

Stone, Col. Newton, 196

Stone, Col. Roy: on May 5 morning, 139; in battle at Saunders' Field on May 5 afternoon, 143, 157, 160, 162–63, 173; on May 5 evening, 237–38; on May 6 morning, 283, 289; on May 6 afternoon, 396; wounding of, 436

Stonewall Brigade, 125, 179, 180, 181, 182

Stony Mountain, 70, 71, 73, 77, 80, 93

Stuart, Maj. Gen. James E. B. ("Jeb"): on Longstreet, 13; Union troops' response to, 40; and maneuvering for position on May 4, pp. 80, 85, 89, 91, 92, 120–21, 253; on May 5, pp. 113, 120–21, 128, 234, 255, 256, 262; and Lee's concern on May 5 evening, 274; on May 6, pp. 348, 369; assessment of fighting of, 445

Supplies: for Union forces, 32–33, 47–48, 55, 58–59, 69, 263, 270, 379, 437, 438; and basic survival rules, 58–59; for Confederate forces, 78–79, 261–62

Sutlers, 24–25, 48

Swan, Lt. Col. William, 119n, 140–41

Sweitzer, Col. Jacob B., 143, 145, 149, 169–70, 317

Swinton, William, 57

Taff, J. R., 414n

Taliaferro, Catlett C., 278, 280–81

Tallahatchie expedition, 426

Tapp's farm: on May 5 morning, 127; on May 5 afternoon, 194, 195; on May 5 evening, 222, 225, 231, 234, 276, 277, 279n, 281; on May 6 morning, 285, 290, 293–95, 304, 306, 308, 309, 311, 313, 315, 316, 354, 446; on May 6 at midday, 363

Taylor, Erasmus, 86, 450

Taylor, Lt. Col. Walter H., 24, 87, 128, 293, 357n, 402, 441, 445

Taylorsville, 410

Texas 5th, 303, 431

Texas Brigade, 298–304, 306, 431

Thomas, Brig. Gen. Edward L., 233, 237, 287

Thomson, Maj. James W., 113, 348

Throop, Col. William A., 99, 100

Todd's Tavern: on May 2–3, p. 28; on May 4, pp. 83, 90–93; on May 5 morning, 94, 103, 133; on May 5 afternoon, 188, 207, 256–59; on May 6 morning, 333n, 340, 341, 344, 345, 349; on May 6 at midday, 378–79

Torbert, Brig. Gen. Alfred T. A.: leadership of cavalry by, 40; maneuvering for position on May 4, p. 77; and plan for Battle of the Wilderness, 91–92; on May 5, pp. 95, 110, 253, 255, 256; and Fredericksburg expedition, 253, 255; on May 6, pp. 344, 347, 378

Trigg farm, 269, 332, 344, 349, 351, 353

Union 2nd Corps: at Morton's Ford, 3–5; before Battle of the Wilderness, 29–30; Hancock's leadership of, 37, 38; and maneuvering for position on May 4, pp. 60, 61, 63, 65, 67–69, 76, 89; on May 5 morning, 116, 133, 135; on May 5 afternoon, 175, 189–91, 197–200, 204–207, 227; artillery of, on May 5 evening, 263, 269; and plans for May 6, pp. 264, 265, 267, 268–70; on May 6 morning, 282, 283, 285, 290–92, 309–10, 317, 321, 323–24, 326, 329–45, 349–50, 436–37; on May 6 at midday, 357–58, 362, 363, 366, 368, 373–80, 387–89; rest for, on

May 6 afternoon, 387–89; on May 6 afternoon, 390–93; assessment of fighting of, 431, 433; casualties of, 436; and plans for leaving Wilderness, 438. *See also* Barlow, Brig. Gen. Francis C.; Birney, Maj. Gen. David B.; Gibbon, Brig. Gen. John; Hancock, Maj. Gen. Winfield S.; Mott, Brig. Gen. Gershom

Union 5th Corps: before Battle of the Wilderness, 29; leadership of, 37, 39–40; and maneuvering for position on May 4, pp. 60, 63–66, 68, 69, 72–75; and plan before Battle of the Wilderness, 92; on May 5 morning, 94–112, 136, 138–43; in battle at Saunders' Field on May 5 afternoon, 145–74; and second round of fighting on May 5 afternoon, 176, 222; on May 5 evening, 230–31, 242–46; artillery of, 242; assessment of fighting of, 252, 271, 431, 432–33, 444; casualties of, 252, 436; camps of, on May 5 evening, 263; and plans for May 6, pp. 264–68; on May 6 morning, 317–18, 320–22, 324, 329, 331, 335–36, 340–43; and plans for leaving Wilderness, 438. *See also* Crawford, Brig. Gen. Samuel W.; Griffin, Brig. Gen. Charles; Robinson, Brig. Gen. John C.; Wadsworth, Brig. Gen. James S.; Warren, Maj. Gen. Gouverneur K.

Union 6th Corps: and Morton's Ford skirmish, 1, 3, 5–6; before Battle of the Wilderness, 30; leadership of, 37, 38–39; and maneuvering for position on May 4, pp. 60, 64, 66, 69, 75–76; on May 5 morning, 106, 131, 133–36, 141; on May 5 afternoon, 172–73, 176–91; on May 5 evening, 242–47, 252; and plans for May 6, pp. 264, 265, 268–69; assessment of fight-

ing of, 271, 429, 431, 433; on May 6 morning, 318–20, 330; on May 6 at midday, 410–12; on May 6 evening, 416, 417, 419–26; casualties of, 436; and plans for leaving Wilderness, 438. *See also* Getty, Brig. Gen. George W.; Ricketts, Brig. Gen. James B.; Sedgwick, Maj. Gen. John; Wright, Brig. Gen. Horatio G.

Union 9th Corps: movement of, from Annapolis to Alexandria, 20, 48–49; before Battle of the Wilderness, 30, 57; number of, before Battle of the Wilderness, 34; as separate army, 48; in Washington, D.C., 48–49; and maneuvering for position on May 4, p. 71; Grant's wait for, on May 5 morning, 130; on May 4–5, pp. 184–87; position of, at outset of Battle of the Wilderness, 184–85; and plans for May 6, pp. 264–68; advance of, on May 6 morning, 324–32, 343; assault by, on May 6 afternoon, 380–89, 397–402; assessment of fighting of, 432; casualties of, 436; and plans for leaving Wilderness, 438. *See also* Burnside, Maj. Gen. Ambrose E.; Ferrero, Brig. Gen. Edward; Potter, Brig. Gen. Robert B.; Stevenson, Brig. Gen. Thomas G.; Willcox, Brig. Gen. Orlando B.

Union Cavalry: Meade's view of, 40–41, 253, 260, 264, 270, 433–34; reorganization of, 40–41; and maneuvering for position on May 4, pp. 60, 63, 65, 68, 69, 73–74, 76–77; on May 5 morning, 110–15; on May 5 afternoon and evening, 253–63; map of, 254; on May 6 morning, 343–50; on May 6 at midday, 378–79. *See also* Gregg, Brig. Gen. David McM.;

Sheridan, Maj. Gen. Philip H.; Torbert, Brig. Gen. Alfred T. A.; Wilson, Brig. Gen. James H.

Upton, Col. Emory, 178–79, 183, 246, 319, 377, 421, 423

Van Valkenburgh, Maj. James, 166–67
Venable, Charles, 234, 241, 273–75, 293, 298, 301
Verdiersville, 73, 85, 120, 121, 278, 313
Vermont units: *1st* Cavalry, 112; *2nd,* 196; *4th,* 196; *5th,* 196, 197, 198; *6th,* 197; *10th,* 423, 429; *17th,* 328
Vicksburg, Battle of, 42, 426, 435
Virginia units: *4th,* 181; *5th,* 181; *6th,* 361; *7th* Cavalry, 346; *10th,* 149; *11th* Cavalry, 346; *12th,* 358, 361, 366–67, 370; *12th* Cavalry, 346; *23rd,* 149; *25th,* 182; *27th,* 181; *33rd,* 181; *37th,* 149; *55th,* 197
Virginia Central Railroad, 25, 262, 351*n*

Wadsworth, Brig. Gen. James S.: leadership qualities of, 39–40; and maneuvering for position on May 4, pp. 63, 74; on May 5 morning, 98, 100, 104–105, 108, 109, 118, 133, 138–40, 142; in battle at Saunders' Field on May 5 afternoon, 143, 157–66, 172–74, 190, 231, 252; after battle at Saunders' Field, 176, 231; on May 5 evening, 237, 240, 270; and plans for May 6, pp. 265, 267–68; on May 6 morning, 282, 310, 317, 324, 329, 331–32, 335–36, 339–43, 390; on Orange Plank Road on May 6 morning, 283, 285, 288–92, 308; and Longstreet's counterattack on May 6 morning, 304–306; on May 6 at midday, 355, 362–65, 379; exhaustion of, 362; wounding of,

365, 367, 377, 447–50; casualties of, 436; death of, 436, 439, 447–50
Wainwright, Col. Charles S., 32, 169, 171
Walker, Elijah, 294
Walker, Lt. Col. Francis A., 55, 375, 394
Walker, Brig. Gen. Henry H. ("Mud"): on May 5 afternoon, 193, 196, 199, 225, 228; on May 5 evening, 233, 235, 237; on Orange Plank Road on May 6 morning, 287, 291–92
Walker, Brig. Gen. James A., 125, 179, 180*n*, 181–83
Ward, Brig. Gen. J. H. Hobart, 197, 199, 202, 269, 292*n*, 394
Warren, Emily, 97
Warren, Maj. Gen. Gouverneur K.: at Morton's Ford, 4; on Butler, 5; before Battle of the Wilderness, 29; leadership qualities of, 37, 39–40, 95; and maneuvering for position on May 4, pp. 60, 63–66, 68, 69, 72–75; and plan for Battle of the Wilderness, 92; on May 5 morning, 94–112, 115, 116, 118, 126, 128, 130, 133, 136, 138–43, 322; Grant on, 95; in battle at Saunders' Field on May 5 afternoon, 142–43, 145, 149, 167, 169, 171–74, 179, 184, 186, 189, 190; after battle at Saunders' Field, 175; and second round of fighting on May 5 afternoon, 176, 222; on Orange Turnpike, 222; on May 5 evening, 230–31, 235, 242–46, 251; reaction of, to Ewell's fighting on May 5, pp. 242–43, 433; assessment of fighting of, 252, 271, 431–33; camp of, on May 5 evening, 263; and plans for May 6, pp. 264–68; Confederate plans against, for May 6, p. 276; on May 6 morning, 317–18, 320–22, 324, 329, 331,

335–36, 340–43; on May 6 at midday and in afternoon, 377, 398; on May 6 evening, 420, 436, 437; and plans for leaving Wilderness, 438

Warrenton Junction, 185

Washburne, Elihu B., 42, 67, 272

Washington, D.C., 48–49, 53, 71

Webb, Brig. Gen. Alexander S., 205, 336–39, 362–66, 390, 396

Welch, Spencer, 447

Weld, Stephen M., 338

Weygant, Col. Charles, 360

Wheaton, Brig. Gen. Frank: on May 5 morning, 135; on May 5 afternoon, 200, 202, 206; on May 5 evening, 227, 269; on May 6 morning, 306–307, 310, 336; on May 6 at midday and in afternoon, 362, 375, 390

White, Col. Elijah V., 346

Wickham, Brig. Gen. Williams C., 349

Widow Tapp's farm. *See* Tapp's farm

Wilcox, Maj. Gen. Cadmus M.: leadership of, 17, 25; and maneuvering for position on May 4, p. 85; on May 5 morning, 136; on May 5 afternoon, 194, 203, 223, 225, 226; on May 5 evening, 230–36, 245, 276–81; on Battle of the Wilderness after Appomattox, 240; assessment of fighting of, 241, 280; and plans for May 6, pp. 267, 274; on May 6 morning, 285, 293, 298, 308, 315, 324, 326, 331; on Hill, 444

Wilderness, Battle of the. *See* Battle of the Wilderness

Wilderness Church, 89

Wilderness Run, 74, 97, 162, 166, 178, 193, 231, 437

Wilderness Tavern: on May 2–3, p. 54; on May 4, pp. 68, 72, 74, 92; on May 5 morning, 94, 95, 98, 100, 104, 106, 109, 115, 132, 133, 143; on May 5 afternoon, 164, 169,

194; on May 5 evening, 222, 232, 237; on May 6 morning, 314, 324–26, 335, 337; on May 6 evening, 421

Wilkeson, Private Frank, 58–59, 77–78

Willcox, Brig. Gen. Orlando, 184–87, 343, 399

Williams, John G., 414*n*

Willis, Mrs., house of, 80, 409

Wilson, Charles, 102

Wilson, Brig. Gen. James H.: leadership of cavalry of, 40; on May 3 evening, 58; and maneuvering for position on May 4, pp. 60, 63, 64, 68, 71, 72–74, 93; and plan for Battle of the Wilderness, 91–92; on May 5 morning, 95, 98, 107–17, 127; on May 5 afternoon, 255–61; on May 6, pp. 344, 378–79, 426

Wisconsin units: *5th,* 182; *6th,* 157; *7th,* 157

Wise, Jennings C., 294–95

Wofford, Brig. Gen. William T., 312, 354–55, 357, 368, 393

Wright, Brig. Gen. Horatio G.: leadership capabilities of, 38; and maneuvering for position on May 4, pp. 64, 75; on May 5 morning, 106, 108, 109, 134, 186; and battle at Saunders' Field on May 5 afternoon, 172, 173, 190; after battle at Saunders' Field, 175; in second round of fighting on May 5 afternoon, 176–84, 186–87, 191; and Grant's error, 186–87; on May 5 evening, 245; and plans for May 6, p. 268; on May 6 morning, 320, 331–32; on May 6 at midday, 377; assessment of Sedgwick's handling of, 429

Wynn, Sgt. B. L., 79

Young, Lewis, 288